D1402747

COORDINATED ELDERLAW RESEARCH FROM WEST

Elderlaw:
Advocacy for the Aging
Joan M. Krauskopf, Robert N. Brown, Karen Tokarz and Allan D. Bogutz

Guidelines for State Court Decision Making in
Life-Sustaining Medical Treatment Cases
Coordinating Council on Life-Sustaining Medical Treatment Decision
Making by the Courts

Social Security Disability Practice
Charles T. Hall

Medical Proof of Social Security Disability
David A. Morton, III, M.D.

Social Security Claims and Procedures
Harvey L. McCormick

Medicare and Medicaid Claims and Procedures
Harvey L. McCormick

West's Legal Forms—Estate Planning
Henry J. Lischer, Jr., Donald J. Malouf and Alan D. Lieberson

Federal Social Security Laws
Selected Statutes and Regulations
Annual pamphlet

SOCIAL SECURITY REPORTING SERVICE

Cases
Code
Regulations
Rulings
Topical Index
Digest Index
Bi-weekly Pamphlet Service

WESTLAW®
Social Security Databases

FGB–CFR	Code of Federal Regulations
FGB–CS	Federal Cases
FGB–FR	Federal Register
FGB–SSR	Social Security Rulings

ELDERLAW: ADVOCACY FOR THE AGING

SECOND EDITION

By

JOAN M. KRAUSKOPF
Professor of Law, Ohio State University
College of Law

ROBERT N. BROWN
Professor of Law, University of Detroit Mercy
School of Law

KAREN L. TOKARZ
Professor of Law, Washington University
School of Law

ALLAN D. BOGUTZ
Bogutz & Gordon, P.C.
Tucson, Arizona

Volume 2

Chapters 14 to 27
Appendices
Tables—Index

ST. PAUL, MINN.
WEST PUBLISHING CO.
1993

WEST'S COMMITMENT TO THE ENVIRONMENT

In 1906, West Publishing Company began recycling materials left over from the production of books. This began a tradition of efficient and responsible use of resources. Today, more than 98% of our legal books and 75% of our college texts are printed on acid-free, recycled paper consisting of 50% new paper pulp and 50% paper that has undergone a de-inking process. We also use soy-based inks to print many of our books. West recycles nearly 22,650,000 pounds of scrap paper annually—the equivalent of 187,500 trees. Since the 1960s, West has devised ways to capture and recycle waste inks, solvents, oils, and vapors created in the printing process. We also recycle plastics of all kinds, wood, glass, corrugated cardboard, and batteries, and have eliminated the use of styrofoam book packaging. We at West are proud of the longevity and the scope of our commitment to the environment.

West pocket parts are printed on recyclable paper and can be collected and recycled with newspapers. Staples do not have to be removed because recycling companies use magnets to extract staples during the recycling process.

Elderlaw Vol. 2

 PRINTED ON 10% POST CONSUMER RECYCLED PAPER

WESTLAW® ELECTRONIC RESEARCH GUIDE

---

1. Coordinating Legal Research with WESTLAW

Elderlaw: Advocacy for the Aging is a useful guide for the practitioner dealing with legal problems of the aged. WESTLAW provides additional resources. This guide is to assist in your effective use of WESTLAW resources to supplement research using this treatise.

2. Databases

A database is an aggregation of documents with one or more features in common. A database may contain statutes, court decisions, administrative materials, or commentaries. Every database has its own identifier. Database identifiers are used to identify the database to be searched. The WESTLAW Directory is a comprehensive listing of databases, with information about each database, and the types of documents each contains.

3. Updating Statutes

WESTLAW statutory databases may be used to ascertain whether a particular section of the United States Code dealing with social security has been amended after a bound volume or pocket part of the statutes was printed. Check the WESTLAW Directory to see the coverage of USC (United States Code). Sign on to USC and using the desired title number and section number, a query is entered in the following form:

ci(42 +3 405)

4. Retrieving Cases Citing a Statute

To find cases citing a particular statute, sign on to the appropriate caselaw database. Using the desired section number a query is entered in the following form:

"42 U.S.C***" "42 U.S." "Title 42" /7 423

5. Key Number Search

WESTLAW may be used to search any topic and key number in West's Key Number System. To retrieve cases with at least one headnote classified to the topic Social Security and Public Welfare ☞143.60, sign on to a caselaw database and enter:

356Ak143.60

The topic name (Social Security and Public Welfare) is replaced by its numerical equivalent (356A) and the ☞ by the letter k. A list of topics and their numerical equivalents is in the WESTLAW Reference Manual and is also available in the WESTLAW Directory.

6. Retrieving a Regulation in the Code of Federal Regulations

To find the text of a federal regulation, sign on to CFR database. Using the desired citation, a query is entered in the following form:

ci(20 +3 416.413)

This will retrieve section 416.413 of Title 20 of the Code of Federal Regulations.

7. Retrieving a Federal Register Document

To find the text of a Federal Register document, sign on to FR database. Using the desired citation, enter a query in the following form:

ci(52 +2 14289)

This will retrieve 52 FR 14289.

8. Date Searching

A WESTLAW search may be limited to a particular time space. Such a search may be used to find materials added to WESTLAW after the closing of a publication. The query

addeddate(5/31/90) & 356ak140.30

will retrieve cases added to WESTLAW after May 31, 1990 and containing a headnote classified to Social Security and Public Welfare ☞140.30.

9. Insta–Cite® for Retrieving Case History and Parallel Citations

Insta–Cite® may be used to find parallel citations and the history of a case by entering a command in the following form:

ic 796 F.2d 151

All parallel cites will be displayed together with the history of the case reported at 796 F.2d 151.

10. Shepardizing™ a Case with WESTLAW

Sign on to the Shepard's® database and enter a case citation in the following form:

sh 433 So.2d 1230

The Shepard's information for the case reported at 433 So.2d 1230 will be displayed.

11. WIN (WESTLAW Is Natural)

WIN allows you to use natural language to retrieve cases. You can frame your query in plain English terms that describe your issue. For example:

Typical Boolean Search:

judicial "judge" "court" /s review! /s administrative /s decision hearing ruling /s "part A"

WIN Search:

when is judicial review of medicare part A hearing available

12. General Information

The information provided above illustrates some of the ways WESTLAW can complement research using *Elderlaw: Advocacy for the Aging*. However, this brief overview illustrates only some of the power of WESTLAW. The full range of WESTLAW search techniques is available to support your research from this series. Please consult the WESTLAW manual for additional information.

For information about subscribing to WESTLAW, please call 1–800–328–0109.

*

SUMMARY OF CONTENTS

Volume 1

Volume 2

SUMMARY OF CONTENTS

APPENDICES

TABLE OF CONTENTS

Volume 1

CHAPTER 1. BACKGROUND

A. WHAT IS AGING?

B. THE DEMOGRAPHICS OF AGING

C. FEDERAL PROGRAMS FOR THE AGING

XI

TABLE OF CONTENTS

CHAPTER 2. THE PRACTICE OF ELDER LAW

A. GENERAL ISSUES OF AN ELDER LAW PRACTICE

B. DEVELOPING AND MARKETING THE PRACTICE

C. SPECIFIC CONSIDERATIONS

D. CHARGING FOR SERVICES

CHAPTER 3. AGE DISCRIMINATION

A. GENERALLY

B. AGE DISCRIMINATION ACT OF 1975

TABLE OF CONTENTS

C. AGE DISCRIMINATION IN EMPLOYMENT ACT OF 1967

D. FEDERAL CONSTITUTION

TABLE OF CONTENTS

CHAPTER 4. AGE AND DISABILITY DISCRIMINATION

A. GENERALLY

B. REHABILITATION ACT OF 1973

C. SECTION 227 OF HOUSING AND URBAN–RURAL RECOVERY ACT OF 1983

D. FAIR HOUSING AMENDMENTS ACT OF 1988

E. AMERICANS WITH DISABILITIES ACT OF 1990

TABLE OF CONTENTS

CHAPTER 5. CONSUMER CREDIT PROTECTION

A. GENERALLY

B. EQUAL CREDIT OPPORTUNITY ACT

C. TRUTH–IN–LENDING ACT

D. FEDERAL TRADE COMMISSION DOOR–TO–DOOR SALES RULE

E. REAL ESTATE SETTLEMENT PROCEDURES ACT

TABLE OF CONTENTS

F. FAIR DEBT COLLECTION PRACTICES ACT

G. CONSUMER CREDIT ENFORCEMENT AGENCIES

CHAPTER 6. UNFAIR AND DECEPTIVE TRADE PRACTICES PROTECTION

A. GENERALLY

B. FEDERAL TRADE COMMISSION ACT

C. MAGNUSON–MOSS WARRANTY ACT

TABLE OF CONTENTS

D. UNFAIR AND DECEPTIVE TRADE PRACTICES: STATE LAW

CHAPTER 7. CONSUMER FRAUDS TARGETED AT OLDER CONSUMERS

A. GENERALLY

B. HEALTH FRAUD AND MEDICAL QUACKERY

TABLE OF CONTENTS

C. INSURANCE FRAUD

D. HOME REPAIR AND IMPROVEMENT FRAUD

E. COMMON CONS AND BUNCO SCHEMES

F. BUSINESS OPPORTUNITY AND INVESTMENT FRAUD

G. REAL ESTATE FRAUD

H. TELEMARKETING AND MAIL SCHEMES

I. FUNERAL FRAUD

J. NURSING HOME FRAUD

TABLE OF CONTENTS

K. AUTOMOBILE FRAUD

L. SOCIAL FRAUD

M. LIVING TRUSTS FRAUD

CHAPTER 8. PLANNING FOR INCAPACITY

A. GENERALLY

B. DURABLE POWERS OF ATTORNEY

C. LIVING WILLS

D. TRUSTS

E. JOINT TENANCY WITH RIGHT OF SURVIVORSHIP

TABLE OF CONTENTS

F. ATTORNEY FOLLOW–UP

CHAPTER 9. MANAGING INCAPACITY

CHAPTER 10. MEDICARE AND PRIVATE SUPPLEMENTAL INSURANCE

A. GENERAL INFORMATION

TABLE OF CONTENTS

B. ELIGIBILITY

C. COVERAGE—HOSPITAL INSURANCE—PART A

D. COVERAGE—SUPPLEMENTARY MEDICAL INSURANCE—PART B

TABLE OF CONTENTS

TABLE OF CONTENTS

I. PRIVATE MEDICAL INSURANCE; "MEDIGAP" INSURANCE

CHAPTER 11. MEDICAID

A. GENERALLY

B. ELIGIBILITY

TABLE OF CONTENTS

CHAPTER 12. LONG–TERM CARE

A. NURSING HOMES

TABLE OF CONTENTS

TABLE OF CONTENTS

TABLE OF CONTENTS

C. LEGISLATIVE ACTIVITY

D. ADVISING CLIENT OR CLIENT'S FAMILY

Volume 2

CHAPTER 14. ANATOMICAL DONATIONS

A. GENERALLY

B. MANNER OF EXECUTING ANATOMICAL GIFTS

C. DELIVERY, AMENDMENT, REFUSAL, AND REVOCATION OF DONATIONS

D. ACCEPTANCE AND DISPOSITION OF DONATED BODY OR PARTS

TABLE OF CONTENTS

CHAPTER 15. SOCIAL SECURITY RETIREMENT BENEFITS

A. GENERALLY

B. "RETIREMENT" OR "OLD AGE" ELIGIBILITY

C. SURVIVOR'S BENEFITS

D. COMPUTATION, REDUCTIONS, AND OVERPAYMENTS

TABLE OF CONTENTS

TABLE OF CONTENTS

CHAPTER 16. SOCIAL SECURITY DISABILITY

A. GENERAL INFORMATION

B. ELIGIBILITY

C. DISABILITY

TABLE OF CONTENTS

TABLE OF CONTENTS

TABLE OF CONTENTS

TABLE OF CONTENTS

TABLE OF CONTENTS

C. NONSERVICE–CONNECTED DISABILITY (PENSIONS)

D. MEDICAL BENEFITS

E. MISCELLANEOUS BENEFITS

F. APPLYING FOR VETERANS' ADMINISTRATION BENEFITS

G. APPEALING VETERANS' ADMINISTRATION DECISION AND VETERANS' JUDICIAL REVIEW ACT OF 1988

TABLE OF CONTENTS

TABLE OF CONTENTS

CHAPTER 23. PRIVATE EMPLOYMENT PENSIONS

CHAPTER 24. TAX BENEFITS

A. FEDERAL INCOME TAX

TABLE OF CONTENTS

TABLE OF CONTENTS

TABLE OF CONTENTS

CHAPTER 14

ANATOMICAL DONATIONS

Table of Sections

A. GENERALLY

WESTLAW Electronic Research

See WESTLAW Electronic Research Guide preceding the Summary of Contents.

––––––––––

Library References:

C.J.S. Dead Bodies §§ 2–9.
West's Key No. Digests, Dead Bodies ⚷1, 9.

A. GENERALLY

§ 14.1 Introduction

Utilization of anatomical parts after death is a relatively recent development. In the last several decades, advances in surgical techniques and the development of potent immunosuppressive drugs have

made life-saving transplants possible. With this possibility came difficult legal and moral questions and the need for legislative regulation of
efforts to supply and use organs.[1]

In 1965 the National Conference of Commissioners on Uniform
State Laws (NCCUSL) established a committee to research and prepare
a Uniform Anatomical Gift Act (UAGA). By August of 1968, at which
time the committee completed its version of the act,[2] 43 states and the
District of Columbia already had some statutory provisions[3] regulating
the donation of human body parts after death.[4] The UAGA was an
attempt to introduce more certainty and order into this rapidly expand-
ing field by dealing in as comprehensive a manner as possible with the
competing interests and legal questions posed by the utilization of
human bodies after death.[5]

Within one year after promulgation of the 1968 UAGA, almost one-
half the states had adopted it with little or no change. By 1973 all the
states and the District of Columbia were "uniform" jurisdictions.

In the mid-eighties it became apparent that the 1968 UAGA was
not producing the supply of organs its authors envisioned.[6] Problems
that continued after the enactment of the 1968 UAGA included a low
incidence of donations, a failure to recover organs despite written
directives, and a failure to approach systematically family members to
discuss organ donations.[7]

§ 14.1

1. See R. Veatch, Death, Dying and the
Biological Revolution (rev. ed. 1989);
Blumstein & Sloan, Special Issue on Organ
Transplantation, 14 J. Health Pol. Pol'y &
L. 1 (1989).

2. Uniform Anatomical Gift Act, 8A
U.L.A. 15 (1968). [hereinafter 1968
UAGA] (WESTLAW: ULA database,
**ci(anat /2 1968 /2 refs & prefa-
tory**).

3. The profusion of individual, often inconsistent regulations was seen by many
commentators as inhibiting the donation of
anatomical donations. See, e.g., Krauskopf, The Law of Dead Bodies: Impeding
Medical Progress, 19 Ohio St.L.J. 455
(1958).

4. Commissioners' Prefatory Note, 1968
UAGA, supra note 2, at 16–17 (WESTLAW:
ULA database, **ci(anat /2 1968 /2
refs & prefatory**).

5. The NCCUSL identifies five "principal competing interests" and 12 "principal
legal questions" in relation to the donation
of dead bodies for use after death. 1968
UAGA, supra note 2, at 16–17 (WESTLAW:
ULA database, **ci(anat /2 1968 /2
refs) & prefatory & principal**).

6. A 1985 report by the Hastings Center stated: "[i]t has become apparent that
the public policy instituted in 1969 [by
promulgation of the Uniform Anatomical
Gift Act in 1968] is not producing a sufficient supply of organs to meet the current
or projected demand for them." Unif. Anatomical Gift Act, 8A U.L.A. 2 (1987) [here-
inafter 1987 UAGA].

7. Id. Several problems highlighted by
the Hastings Center were noted in the
1987 UAGA prefatory notes (WESTLAW:
ULA database, **ci(anat /2 1987 /2
refs) & prefatory**).

In 1985 the NCCUSL appointed a committee to draft amendments to the 1968 UAGA.[8] The committee's efforts led to the adoption of a New Uniform Anatomical Gift Act, the major features of which included a simplified structure for the act, a simplified procedure for making an anatomical gift, and measures to increase the likelihood that donor intentions are followed.[9]

The 1987 UAGA has not been embraced as swiftly as its 1968 counterpart was upon its conception. As of 1991, fourteen states have adopted the 1987 UAGA.[10] Because thirty-six jurisdictions have as yet to adopt the 1987 UAGA, the following sections discuss both the 1968 and 1987 acts and highlight the differences between the two acts. Also discussed are provisions of other state and federal laws bearing on anatomical donations.

§§ 14.2–14.10 are reserved for supplementary material.

B. MANNER OF EXECUTING ANATOMICAL GIFTS

§ **14.11** Persons Who May Execute Anatomical Gifts

An anatomical gift can be made by the person whose organ, tissue, or body is being donated as long as the donor is an adult (usually 18 years of age) and of sound mind when making the donation.[1] In addition, both versions of the UAGA allow a decedent's spouse, adult children, certain other family members, and guardian to make an anatomical donation under specified circumstances.[2] Also authorized to make such donations, under certain circumstances, are public health officials such as coroners and medical examiners.[3]

§ **14.12** Inter Vivos Document or Card

A gift of all or part of one's body may be made by the execution of a document (or card) of gift to that effect.[1] Although no specific words are required, forms are suggested by the NCCUSL, and the document

8. Begleiter, The Uniform Anatomical Gift Act, 3 Probate & Property 51 (1989) [hereinafter Begleiter].

9. Id.

10. The adopting states are Arkansas, California, Connecticut, Hawaii, Idaho, Minnesota, Montana, Nevada, North Dakota, Rhode Island, Utah, Vermont, Virginia, and Wisconsin. See 1987 UAGA, supra note 6, Table of Adopting Jurisdictions.

§ 14.11

1. 1968 UAGA, supra § 14.1, note 2, at § 2(a); 1987 UAGA, supra § 14.1, note 6, at § 2(a).

2. See discussion in § 14.16 infra.

3. Id.

§ 14.12

1. 1968 UAGA, supra § 14.1, note 2, at § 4(b); 1987 UAGA, supra § 14.1, note 6, at § 2(b).

should be clear about the scope and use of the donation.[2] The document or card can be designed so that it can be carried easily on the person of the donor.

Under the 1968 UAGA, the card or document must be signed by the donor in the presence of at least two witnesses, who also must sign the document or card in the presence of the donor. If the donor is unable to sign, the card or document may be signed for the donor at the donor's direction in his or her presence and in the presence of two witnesses who must sign in the presence of the donor.[3] To simplify the making of anatomical gifts, the 1987 UAGA deleted the requirement of witnesses to a document of gift except where the donor is unable to sign.[4]

This method of donation offers the advantage of speedy execution of the gift, although it does not encourage the client to draft an entire will which he or she may need. To enhance the effectiveness of anatomical donations by documents of gift, the 1987 UAGA instructs public safety personnel "to make a reasonable search for a document of gift."[5] Similarly, hospital personnel are to inquire at or near admission whether a patient is an organ or tissue donor and, if so, to obtain a copy of the document of gift.[6]

§ 14.13   Operator or Chauffeur License

Although not specifically authorized by the 1968 UAGA, many states permit the execution of an anatomical gift by completion of a statement found on the reverse of an operator's or chauffeur's license.[1] The 1987 UAGA specifically allows consent to anatomical gifts to be attached or imprinted on a donor's motor vehicle operator's or chauffeur's license, if such attachment or imprintment meets the requirements for executing a document of gift.[2]

This method of donation is simple to execute, and the license is likely to be carried by the donor on admission to a hospital, thus

---

2. 1968 UAGA, supra § 14.1, note 2, comments to § 4; 1987 UAGA, supra § 14.1, note 6, comments to § 2. See forms in § 14.35 this chapter.

3. 1968 UAGA, supra § 14.1, note 2, at § 4(b).

4. 1987 UAGA, supra § 14.1, note 6, comments to § 2.

5. 1987 UAGA, supra § 14.1, note 6, at § 5(c).

6. Id. at § 5(b). Hospital personnel also are to search for a document of gift if a

person arrives at or near death and no information about the person's intent regarding donation is otherwise available. Id. at § 5(c)(2).

§ 14.13

1. See, e.g., Vernon's Ann.Mo.Stat. § 194.240(6) (1983) and Ohio Rev.Code Ann. § 2108.04(c) (Baldwin 1990).

2. 1987 UAGA, supra § 14.1, note 6, at § 2(c).

facilitating utilization of the gift. Many state laws provide that a gift under this subsection is automatically void upon the expiration, cancellation, suspension, or revocation of the license and must be renewed when the license is renewed. The 1987 act, in contrast, specifically states "[r]evocation, suspension, expiration, or cancellation of the license does not invalidate the anatomical gift." [3]

§ 14.14   Testamentary Document

A gift of all or part of one's body, to be effective at death, also may be made by will.[1] While all procedures for the drafting of a will should be followed, any reasonable wording of the donation should be acceptable, since no specific words of donation are required by statute. A gift by will remains valid to the extent relied upon in good faith by a donee even if the document is never offered for or is rejected for probate.[2]

Although an anatomical donation may be made by will, the delay often involved in locating or reading the will of a decedent makes this form of donation likely to be ineffective. Such delay would render an anatomical donation medically useless. Counsel consulted about anatomical donations generally should utilize a document of gift other than a will.

Regardless of the form of donation, counsel for a potential donor should ensure clear and unambiguous drafting of the terms of the donation both with regard to what is donated as well as the use to which the donation may be put. The donation should be executed in full compliance with the statutory requirements of the jurisdiction.

A donor should be told to discuss the decision to make an anatomical donation with family members in both 1968 and 1987 UAGA jurisdictions. Although family members need not consent to an anatomical donation and although they do not have the power to veto a valid donation, the practice of hospitals and organ procurement centers is to seek such consent.[3] To address this problem, the 1987 UAGA specifies that "an anatomical gift that is not revoked by the donor before death is irrevocable and does not require the consent or concurrence of any person after the donor's death."[4] A donation's effectiveness is likely to be enhanced if the donor's physician is notified of the

---

3. Id. [Emphasis added]

§ 14.14

1. 1968 UAGA supra, § 14.1, note 2, at § 4(a); 1987 UAGA, supra § 14.1, note 6, at § 2(e).

2. Id.

3. See, e.g., Comment, Liability Issues Arising out of Hospitals' and Organ Procurement Organizations' Rejection of Valid Anatomical Gifts: The Truth and Consequences, 1990 Wisc.L.Rev. 1655 (1990) (WESTLAW: WILR database, ci(1990 +5 1655)).

4. 1987 UAGA, supra § 14.1, note 6, at § 2(h).

donation. It also may be helpful to inform the donee of the pendency of a gift if a particular donee is specified.

§ 14.15 Oral Expression

Under both the 1968 and 1987 acts, a person may not make a donation of his or her own tissue, organ, or body by mere oral expression. The overwhelming weight of judicial decisions would strongly militate against upholding a "bequest" of the body not in writing, despite the growing recognition of decedents' ability to control postmortem disposition of their bodies.[1] However, under the 1987 UAGA, a donor may amend or revoke an anatomical gift not made by will either in writing or orally.[2] In addition, an anatomical donation may be made orally by the spouse, family member, or guardian of a decedent.[3]

§ 14.16 Proxy Donors

Relatively few individuals make anatomical donations during their lives. Because of the resulting shortage of organs, both the 1968 and 1987 acts authorize anatomical donations by members of a decedent's family, by the decedent's guardian, and by certain public health officials.[1] Indeed, most states now direct hospitals to inform surviving family members of the option of donating the organs of their decedent, and federal law directs hospitals participating in Medicare or Medicaid to inform family members of this option.[2]

Both the 1968 and the 1987 acts establish a hierarchy of individuals authorized to make an anatomical donation of all or part of a decedent's body unless the decedent has indicated opposition to such a donation.[3] Authorized to make a donation are the surviving spouse, adult children, either parent, adult sibling, grandparent (1987 UAGA only), and the guardian of the decedent. A donation may *not* be made by any of these individuals if a member of a prior class is available at

---

§ 14.15

1. See general discussion in Rosenblum v. New Mt. Sinai Cemetery Association, 481 S.W.2d 593 (Mo.App.1972), annotated in 54 A.L.R.3d 1031, 1037.

2. 1987 UAGA, supra § 14.1, note 6, at § 2(f).

3. 1968 UAGA, supra § 14.1, note 2, at § 4(e); 1987 UAGA, supra § 14.1, note 6, at § 3(c).

2. 42 U.S.C.A. § 1320b–8(a)(1)(A); see generally Martyn, Wright & Clark, Required Request for Organ Donation: Moral, Clinical and Legal Problems, 18 Hastings Center Rep., Apr.–May 1988, at 27.

3. 1968 UAGA, supra § 14.1, note 2, at § 2(b); 1987 UAGA, supra § 14.1, note 6, at § 3(a).

§ 14.16

1. 1968 UAGA, supra § 14.1, note 2, at § 2(b); 1987 UAGA, supra § 14.1, note 6, at § 3(a).

the time of death to make a donation or if a member of the same or prior class objects to a donation. Thus, a decedent's spouse could make a donation despite the opposition of the children, but a child could not donate if the surviving spouse was available at the time of death and opposed the donation. Nor could a child donate if another child objected to the donation. An anatomical gift under this provision may be made by document of gift, by telegraph, by phone (if recorded), or, under the 1987 version, by other form of communication if contemporaneously reduced to writing and signed by the recipient.[4]

In addition to donations by the family or guardian, the UAGA permits the coroner, medical examiner, or other public health officer to make donations under limited circumstances.[5] Although proxy donations are permitted, both the 1987 UAGA and federal law forbid the sale of body parts.[6]

§§ 14.17–14.20 are reserved for supplementary material.

C. DELIVERY, AMENDMENT, REFUSAL, AND REVOCATION OF DONATIONS

§ 14.21 Delivery

Delivery of a document of donation is not necessary to make an anatomical gift valid and binding.[1] However, delivery of the document or an executed copy thereof is permitted to facilitate the utilization of the body after death. Delivery is especially advisable if a specific donee is intended. Any documents of gift delivered to a donee should be stored in a suitable manner and must be available for inspection by any interested person after death of the donor.[2]

4. 1968 UAGA, supra § 14.1, note 2, at § 4(b); 1987 UAGA, supra § 14.1, note 6, at § 3(c).

5. 1987 UAGA, supra § 14.1, note 6, at § 4; see also 1968 UAGA, supra § 14.1, note 2, at § 2(b)(6). Statutes authorizing such action were upheld by the Georgia Supreme Court in a suit based on due process, Georgia Lions Eye Bank, Inc. v. Lavant, 255 Ga. 60, 335 S.E.2d 127, 129 (1985), *cert. denied,* 475 U.S. 1084, 106 S.Ct. 1464, 89 L.Ed.2d 721 (1986), and by the Florida Supreme Court in a suit based on due process and equal protection, Florida v. Powell, 497 So.2d 1188 (Fla.1986), *cert. denied* 481 U.S. 1059, 107 S.Ct. 2202, 95 L.Ed.2d 856 (1987). For arguments concerning the legality of nonconsensual re-moval of organs, see Comment, "She's Got Bette Davis['s] Eyes": Assessing the Nonconsensual Removal of Cadaver Organs under the Takings and Due Process Clauses, 90 Colum L.Rev. 528 (1990) (WESTLAW: CLMLR database, **ci(90 + 5 528)**).

6. 1987 UAGA, supra § 14.1, note 7, at § 10; 42 U.S.C.A. § 247e.

§ 14.21

1. See 1968 UAGA, supra § 14.1, note 2, at § 5; 1987 UAGA, supra § 14.1, note 6, at § 7(a).

2. 1968 UAGA, supra § 14.1, note 2, at § 5; 1987 UAGA, supra § 14.1, note 6, at § 7(b).

§ 14.22 Amendment, Revocation, and Refusal to Donate

A donor retains the power to amend or revoke a gift at any time.[1] Under the 1968 UAGA, if the document of gift or a copy thereof has been delivered to a donee, the donor may select any of the following forms of revocation or amendment: (1) execution and delivery to the donee of a signed statement of changes; (2) an oral statement of changes made in the presence of at least two witnesses and communicated to the donee; (3) a statement made during terminal illness to an attending physician and communicated to the donee; or (4) a signed statement found on the person of the donor. Under the 1968 act, to be effective, all these methods of revocation require actual knowledge of revocation to be communicated to a donee to whom a document of gift has been delivered.[2]

The 1987 UAGA modifies the 1968 act's four forms of revocation and amendment. The first three forms of revocation and amendment are modified by dropping the necessity of communication to the donee.[3] The 1987 act makes actual knowledge of communication to the donee an option, rather than a requirement.[4] From the donor's perspective, the 1987 UAGA simplifies both the revocation and the amendment procedures.

If a document of gift has not been delivered to a donee, a donor may elect any of the above methods of revocation or amendment, or may choose to destroy, cancel, or mutilate all executed copies of the undelivered document and the document itself.[5]

The 1987 act does not differentiate between documents that have and have not been delivered.[6] It offers as an alternative, not a requirement, the option of the delivery of a signed statement of revocation or amendment to a specified donee to whom a document of gift has been delivered.[7]

Although the 1987 act, unlike the 1968 act, does not discuss destruction, cancellation, or mutilation of a document of gift and its copies as a method of revocation, such methods are likely to be read into the 1987 act. A gift made by will may be altered or revoked in any

§ 14.22

1. 1968 UAGA, supra § 14.1, note 2, at § 6(a); 1987 UAGA, supra note 6, at § 2(f).

2. 1968 UAGA, supra § 14.1, note 2, at § 6(a).

3. 1987 UAGA, supra § 14.1, note 6, at § 2(f).

4. Id. at 2(f)(4).

5. 1968 UAGA, supra § 14.1, note 2, at § 6(b).

6. *Compare* 1968 UAGA, supra § 14.1, note 2, at § 6 *and* 1987 UAGA, supra § 14.1, note 6, at § 2(f), (g).

7. 1987 UAGA, supra § 14.1, note 6, at § 2(f)(4).

manner pertaining to the amendment or revocation of wills generally in addition to methods specified above.[8]

Because the burden of changing the effect of anatomical donations falls upon the donor, care should be exercised in the original drafting to ensure that it actually reflects the desires of the client, and frequent amendment should be discouraged.

The 1987 act clarifies the effect of an anatomical gift or amendment or revocation of such a gift.[9] A gift of a part is not a refusal to give other parts, nor is a revocation or amendment of a gift a refusal to make another gift. If a person wishes to refuse to make a gift or to ensure that no gift will be made by the person's family, guardian, or by public health officials, the proper course is to expressly refuse to make a gift. Such refusal is permitted by the 1987 act which introduced a new concept of *refusal to make* an anatomical gift.[10] Under the relevant provision, a party may expressly "refuse to make an anatomical gift."[11] A party refuses to make such a gift in the same manner in which a party makes such a gift—a writing specifically stating the party's desire not to make an anatomical gift, or a like statement attached or imprinted on the donor's motor vehicle operator's license.[12]

A donor can limit an anatomical gift to a specific purpose, or to a specific part, by stating the limitation clearly, e.g., "transplantation only" or "eyes only."[13]

§§ 14.23–14.30 are reserved for supplementary material.

D. ACCEPTANCE AND DISPOSITION OF DONATED BODY OR PARTS

§ **14.31** Eligible Donees

Under both the 1968 and 1987 acts, a broad class of persons and institutions are eligible to receive anatomical donations.[1] Virtually any scientific organization may be a beneficiary: hospitals, physicians and surgeons, medical and dental schools, colleges and universities, the state anatomical board, and designated banks and storage facilities. A

---

8. 1968 UAGA, supra § 14.1, note 2, at § 6(c); 1987 UAGA, supra § 14.1, note 6, at § 2(g).

9. 1987 UAGA, supra § 14.1, note 6, at § 2(j), (k).

10. Begleiter, supra § 14.1, note 8, at 52.

11. 1987 UAGA, supra § 14.1, note 6, at § 2(a)(iii).

12. 1987 UAGA, supra § 14.1, note 6, at § 2(i).

13. Id.

§ 14.31

1. 1968 UAGA, supra § 14.1, note 2, at § 3; 1987 UAGA, supra § 14.1, note 6, at § 6.

specified individual may even be the recipient of a donation if it is to be used for transplant or therapy needed by that person.

An anatomical donation may be made with or without specifying a donee. If a certain donee is named, it is advisable to inform the donee so that the donee may better take advantage of the offer. If a specified donee is not named or is not available, the attending physician at death or the hospital may accept the gift as donee, absent an objection on the part of the donor.[2]

The NCCUSL does not adopt a definition of death to be used in conjunction with the gift procedures. Under the 1968 UAGA, the physician who tends the donor at death shall determine time of death, but may not participate in the procedures for removal or transplantation of any body parts.[3] The 1987 UAGA, by contrast, allows the physician who tends to the donor at death to perform the removal or transplantation procedure if the document of gift designates that physician or surgeon as the individual to perform the procedure.[4]

§ 14.32 Rejection

An important point in the UAGA is that the donee may accept or reject the gift.[1] Provision for this possibility should be made at the time the gift document is drafted. The problems of donee rejection and the need for legal planning in the matter are seen in the leading case on this point, *Holland v. Metalious.*[2] The decedent had left her body by will to the Dartmouth Medical School or, should they not accept, to Harvard, with any remains to be cremated. The decedent left instructions that no funeral services were to be held. Both schools declined to accept her body, whereupon a dispute arose between the decedent's family and the administrator of the estate over what should be done with the body. The family desired to hold a funeral. The Supreme Court of New Hampshire held that if the decedent's "primary" testamentary instructions could not be carried out, the desires of her family would prevail over her "secondary" instructions, the primary instructions being donation to science, the secondary cremation. The family was permitted to hold a "brief and simple" funeral, though the court recognized that normally the desires of the decedent are to be given priority over the desires of the family.

2. 1968 UAGA, supra § 14.1, note 2, at § 3; 1987 UAGA, supra § 14.1, note 6, at § 6.

3. 1968 UAGA, supra § 14.1, note 2, at § 7(b).

4. 1987 UAGA, supra § 14.1, note 6, at § 8(b).

§ 14.32

1. 1968 UAGA, supra § 14.1, note 2, at § 7(a); 1987 UAGA, supra § 14.1, note 6, at § 8(a).

2. 105 N.H. 290, 198 A.2d 654, 7 A.L.R.3d 742 (1964).

§ 14.33 Utilization and Funeral Services

The use to which anatomical parts may be put is wide-ranging: education, research, therapy, transplantation, or other advancement of medical or dental science.[1] By statute, the rights of donees are paramount to those of all others,[2] except insofar as the state interest in autopsies is affected.[3] If a gift of all of a body is made, there is no duty on the part of the donee to return the body to the relatives after use. However, if a gift of only parts of a body is made, the donee shall remove the parts with as little mutilation as possible. Custody of the remainder of the body then vests in next of kin or others responsible for disposing of the body.[4]

Most objections to anatomical gifts come from family members who fear they will be deprived of the opportunity to attend a funeral for the deceased, risking emotional and religious complications. By informing family members that many forms of anatomical gifts allow a funeral to be held within a short time after death, counsel can alleviate this objection in most cases.

§ 14.34 Receiving Organs

The focus of this chapter has been the older client as organ donor, but it is possible that an older client may be a potential recipient of a donated organ. The law governing receipt of organs is not as well developed as that governing organ donation. A number of issues that affect the potential recipient of a donated organ are unresolved.[1] Because there are more potential recipients of organs than organs available, access to donated organs raises numerous questions that are as yet unanswered. How do transplant teams decide who will receive an organ? What role do money, age, race, and other factors play in deciding among potential recipients? What constitutional constraints or private law remedies govern these choices?[2] Should these choices be

§ 14.33

1. 1968 UAGA, supra § 14.1, note 2, at § 3; 1987 UAGA, supra § 14.1, note 6, at § 6.

2. 1968 UAGA, supra § 14.1, note 2, at § 2(e); 1987 UAGA, supra § 14.1, note 6, at § 8(a).

3. 1968 UAGA, supra § 14.1, note 2, at § 7(d); 1987 UAGA, supra § 14.1, note 6, at § 11(b).

4. 1968 UAGA, supra § 14.1, note 2, at § 7(a); 1987 UAGA, supra § 14.1, note 6, at § 8(a).

§ 14.34

1. G. Calabresi & P. Bobbitt, Tragic Choices (1978); Comment, Developments in the Law—Medical Technology and the Law, 103 Harv.L.Rev. 1519, 1630–43 (1990). (WESTLAW: HVLR database, ci(103 +5 1519)).

2. See, e.g. Medical Technology, supra note 1, at 1637; Merriken & Overcast, Patient Selection for Heart Transplantation: When Is a Discriminating Choice Discrimination?, 10 J.Health Pol.Pol'y & L. 7 (1985).

subjected to more extensive state or federal regulation?[3]

At present, state and federal funding for transplants is uneven, with Medicare and Medicaid sometimes available and other times not. Sources to pay for organs raise another set of unresolved issues. Should transplants be viewed as entitlements with broader funding available?[4] What role should private health insurance play?

Older clients may be affected by possible future alterations in the method of supplying organs. We have moved from a supply system that relied almost exclusively on organs donated by the source of the organs to one that increasingly solicits family members to donate the organs of a decedent and allows organ donation without consent. Despite these changes, the demand for organs outstrips the supply. Among future possibilities are: requiring hospitals to request donations from patients, allowing the sale of organs from cadavers or living donors, and increasing the government role in organ procurement.[5] It is difficult to predict future developments that will affect older clients. Lawyers should monitor developments as they occur and be creative in serving their clients' interests.

§ 14.35 Forms

The National Conference of Commissioners on Uniform State Laws (NCCUSL) recommends the use of the following forms in states that have adopted the 1968 act. Some states have adopted their own forms.

Anatomical Gift by a Living Donor

I am of sound mind and 18 years or more of age.

I hereby make this anatomical gift to take effect upon my death.

The marks in the appropriate squares and words filled into the blanks below indicate my desires.

I give: ☐ my body; ☐ any needed organs or parts; ☐ the following organs or parts _____;

To the following person (or institution):

☐ the physician in attendance at my death; ☐ the hospital in which I die; ☐ the following named physician, hospital, storage bank or other medical institution _____; ☐ the following individual for treatment _____;

---

3. See, e.g., National Organ Transplantation Act of 1984, 42 U.S.C.A. § 274; Blumstein, Government's Role in Organ Transplantation Policy, 14 J.Health Pol. Pol'y & L. 5 (1989).

4. Schuck, Government Funding for Organ Transplants, 14 J.Health, Pol.Pol'y & L. 169 (1989).

5. See, e.g. Hansmann, The Economics and Ethics of Markets for Human Organs, 14 J.Health Pol.Pol'y & L. 57 (1990).

for the following purposes: ☐ any purpose authorized by law; ☐ transplantation; ☐ therapy; ☐ research; ☐ medical education.

Dated _____   City and State _____

Signed by the Donor in the presence of the following who sign as witnesses:

_____
Signature of Donor

_____
Address of Donor

_____
Witness

_____
Witness

Anatomical Gift by Next of Kin or Other Authorized Person

I hereby make this anatomical gift of or from the body of _____ who died on _____ at the _____ in _____. The marks in the appropriate squares and the words filled into the blanks below indicate my relationship to the deceased and my desires respecting the gift.

I am the surviving: ☐ spouse; ☐ adult son or daughter; ☐ parent; ☐ adult brother or sister; ☐ guardian; ☐ _____, authorized to dispose of the body;

I give ☐ the body of deceased; ☐ any needed organs or parts; ☐ the following organs or parts _____;

To the following person (or institution) _____ (insert the name of a physician, hospital, research or educational institution, storage bank or individual),

for the following purposes: ☐ any purpose authorized by law; ☐ transplantation; ☐ therapy; ☐ research; ☐ medical education.

Dated _____   City and State _____

_____
Signature of Survivor

_____
Address of Survivor

The NCCUSL recommends the use of the following forms in jurisdictions that have adopted the 1987 act. Some states have adopted their own forms.

ANATOMICAL GIFT BY A LIVING DONOR

Pursuant to the Anatomical Gift Act, upon my death, I hereby give (check boxes applicable):

1. [   ]   Any needed organs, tissues, or parts;
2. [   ]   The following organs, tissues, or parts only _____
3. [   ]   For the following purposes only

_____
(transplant-therapy-research-education)

_____	_____
Date of Birth	Signature of Donor
_____	_____
Date Signed	Address of Donor

INSTRUCTIONS

Check box 1 if the gift is unrestricted, i.e., of any organ, tissue, or part for any purpose specified in the Act; do not check box 2 or box 3. If the gift is restricted to specific organ(s), tissue(s), or part(s) only, e.g., heart, cornea, etc., check box 2 and write in the organ or tissue to be given. If the gift is restricted to one or more of the purposes listed, e.g., transplant, therapy, etc., check box 3 and write in the purpose for which the gift is made.

A gift category included in some forms "of my body for anatomical study if needed" has not been included. Although a gift of the entire body is authorized by the Act, the exercise of this option usually requires an agreement with a medical school before a gift is made.

A simple form of refusal under the Act could provide:

Pursuant to the Anatomical Gift Act, I hereby refuse to make any anatomical gift.

_____	_____
Date of Birth	Signature of Declarant
_____	_____
Date of Signing	Address of Declarant

Subsection (c) incorporates an amendment to the original Act in many states providing that an anatomical gift may be made by an attachment to the driver's license. The cross reference to subsection (b) incorporates the concept that a signature is required. A signature on the driv-er's license or on the card attached to the driver's license is sufficient. The hospital or other donee may rely on the anatomical gift even though the license has expired or has been terminated by official act.

The following form is suggested for attachment to the driver's license:

_____
Print or Type Name of Donor

Pursuant to the Anatomical Gift Act, upon my death, I hereby give (check boxes applicable):

1. [   ]   Any needed organs, tissues, or parts;
2. [   ]   The following organs, tissues, or parts only _____;
3. [   ]   For the following purposes only

_____;
(transplant-therapy-research-education)

Refusal:
4. [   ]   I refuse to make any anatomical gift.

_____
Signature

Anatomical Gift by Next of Kin
or Guardian of the Person

Pursuant to the Uniform Anatomical Gift Act, I hereby make this anatomical gift from the body of _____ who died on

Name of Decedent
_____ at
Date
_____ in _____
Place   City and State

The marks in the appropriate squares and the words filled into the blanks below indicate my relationship to the decedent and my wishes respecting the gift.

I survive the decedent as [ ] spouse; [ ] adult son or daughter; [ ] parent; [ ] adult brother or sister; [ ] grandparent; [ ] guardian of the person.

I hereby give (check boxes applicable):

[ ] Any needed organs, tissues, or parts;
[ ] The following organs, tissues, or parts only _____;
[ ] For the following purposes only

_____   _____
Date   Signature of Survivor

                                            _____
                                            Address of Survivor

§ **14.36** Table of Jurisdictions in Which the Act Has Been Adopted

UNIFORM ANATOMICAL GIFT ACT
1968 ACT

Table of Jurisdictions Wherein Act Has Been Adopted

Jurisdiction	Laws	Effective Date	Statutory Citation
Alabama..........	1969, Sp.Sess. No. 164	5–14–1969 [1]	Code 1975, §§ 22–19–40 to 22–19–47, 22–19–60.
Alaska	1972, c. 78	1–1–1973	AS 13.50.010 to 13.50.090.
Arizona..........	1970, c. 147, § 3	8–11–1970	A.R.S. §§ 36–841 to 36–849.
Colorado..........	1969, c. 239	4–24–1969	West's C.R.S.A. §§ 12–34–101 to 12–34–109.
Delaware	57 Del.Laws c. 445, § 2	5–20–1970	16 Del.C. §§ 2710 to 2719.
District of Columbia	P.L. 91–268, §§ 1 to 8	5–26–1970	D.C.Code 1981, §§ 2–1501 to 2–1511.
Florida	1969, c. 69–88	6–14–1969	West's F.S.A. §§ 732.910 to 732.922.
Georgia..........	1969, No. 82	6–14–1969	O.C.G.A. §§ 44–5–140 to 44–5–151.
Guam	P.L. 12–16		10 G.C.A. §§ 83101 to 83109.
Illinois...........	P.A. 76–1209	10–1–1969	S.H.A. ch. 110½, ¶¶ 301 to 311.
Indiana	1969, c. 166	3–13–1969[1]	West's A.I.C. 29–2–16–1 to 29–2–16–11.
Iowa	1969 (63 G.A.) c. 137	7–1–1969	I.C.A. § 142A.1 et seq.
Kansas	1969, c. 301	7–1–1969	K.S.A. 65–3209 to 65–3217.
Kentucky	1970, c. 68	6–18–1970	KRS 311.165 to 311.235.
Louisiana	1968, No. 651	7–31–1968	LSA–R.S. 17:2351 to 17:2359.
Maine	1969, c. 193	10–2–1969	22 M.R.S.A. §§ 2901 to 2910.

Jurisdiction	Laws	Effective Date	Statutory Citation
Maryland	1968, c. 467	7–1–1968	Code, Estates and Trusts, §§ 4–501 to 4–512.
Massachusetts.....	1971, c. 653	8–12–1971 [1]	M.G.L.A. c. 113, §§ 7 to 14.
Michigan	1969, No. 189	3–20–1970	M.C.L.A. §§ 333.10101 to 333.10109.
Mississippi	1970, c. 413	4–6–1970	Code 1972, §§ 41–39–11, 41–39–31 to 41–39–53.
Missouri	1969, S.B. No. 43	5–28–1969	V.A.M.S. §§ 194.210 to 194.290.
Nebraska	1971, LB 799, § 12	8–27–1971	R.R.S.1943, §§ 71–4801 to 71–4818.
New Hampshire....	1969, c. 345	8–29–1969	RSA 291–A:1 to 291–A:9.
New Jersey	1969, c. 161	9–9–1969	N.J.S.A. 26:6–57 to 26:6–65.
New Mexico	1969, c. 105	3–29–1969	NMSA 1978, §§ 24–6–1 to 24–6–11.
New York........	1970, c. 466	5–5–1970	McKinney's Public Health Law §§ 4300 to 4308.
North Carolina	1969, c. 84	10–1–1969	G.S. §§ 130A–402 to 130A–412.1.
Ohio	1969, p. 1796	11–6–1969	R.C. §§ 2108.01 to 2108.10.
Oklahoma	1969, c. 13	7–29–1969	63 Okl.St.Ann. §§ 2201 to 2209.
Oregon	1969, c. 175	8–22–1969	ORS 97.250 to 97.295.
Pennsylvania	1972, P.L. 508, No. 164	7–1–1972	20 Pa.C.S.A. §§ 8601 to 8607.
South Carolina	1969, No. 356	7–1–1969	Code 1976, §§ 44–43–310 to 44–43–400.
South Dakota	1969, c. 111	3–14–1969	SDCL 34–26–20 to 34–26–41.
Tennessee.........	1969, c. 35	3–25–1969	T.C.A. §§ 68–30–101 to 68–30–111.
Texas	1969, c. 375	5–29–1969	V.T.C.A. Health & Safety Code, §§ 692.001 to 692.016.
Virgin Islands	1984, No. 4890	1–19–1984	19 V.I.C. §§ 401 to 409.
Washington	1969, c. 80	6–12–1969	West's RCWA 68.50.340 to 68.50.510.
West Virginia	1969, c. 62	3–10–1969	Code, 16–19–1 to 16–19–9.
Wyoming	1969, c. 80	2–19–1969	W.S.1977, §§ 35–5–101 to 35–5–117.

[1] Date of approval.

UNIFORM ANATOMICAL GIFT ACT (1987)
1987 ACT

Table of Jurisdictions Wherein Act Has Been Adopted

Jurisdiction	Laws	Effective Date	Statutory Citation
Arkansas	1989, No. 436	3–9–1989	A.C.A. §§ 20–17–601 to 20–17–617.
California	1988, c. 1095	1–1–1989	West's Ann.Cal. Health & Safety Code, §§ 7150 to 7156.5.
Connecticut	P.A. 88–318	7–1–1988	C.G.S.A. §§ 19a–279a to 19a–280a.
Hawaii	1988, No. 267	6–13–1988	HRS §§ 327–1 to 327–14.
Idaho	1989, c. 237		I.C. §§ 39–3401 to 39–3417.
Minnesota	1991, c. 202	8–1–1991	M.S.A. §§ 525.921 to 525.9224.
Montana	1989, c. 540	10–1–1989	MCA 72–17–101 to 72–17–312.
Nevada...........	1989, c. 200	10–31–1989	NRS 451.500 to 451.590.
North Dakota	1989, c. 303	7–12–1989	NDCC 23–06.2–01 to 23–06.2–12.
Rhode Island	1989, c. 268	7–1–1989	Gen.Laws 1956 §§ 23–18.6–1 to 23–18.6–15.
Utah	1990, c. 131	4–23–1990	U.C.A.1953, 26–28–1 to 26–28–12.
Vermont	1989, No. 273	6–21–1990	18 V.S.A. §§ 5238 to 5247.
Virginia..........	1990, c. 959		Code 1950, §§ 32.1–289 to 32.1–297.1.
Wisconsin.........	1989, Act 298	5–8–1990	W.S.A. 157.06.

CHAPTER 15

SOCIAL SECURITY RETIREMENT BENEFITS

Table of Sections

A. GENERALLY

WESTLAW Electronic Research

See WESTLAW Electronic Research Guide preceding the Summary of Contents.

A. GENERALLY

§ 15.1 Introduction

The Old Age, Survivors, and Disability Insurance Program (OAS-DI), more commonly known as the Social Security Act, provides cash benefits to retired and disabled workers, and their dependents and survivors, as part of a federal social insurance program administered by the Social Security Administration (SSA).[1] In 1989, more than 39 million retired and disabled workers and their families received social security benefits. More than 90% of persons 65 or older receive social security benefits, and for more than 60% of these individuals, social security is their major source of income. The average social security benefit in 1989 for a retired worker living alone was $552, and for a retired worker and his spouse, it was $966.[2]

The statutory basis for OASDI is found in 42 U.S.C.A. § 401 et seq.; regulations appear at 20 C.F.R. § 404 et seq. The SSA issued the

---

§ 15.1

1. Social Sec.Admin., U.S.Dept. of Health and Human Services, Social Security Handbook § 101 (1988) (Social Security Handbook).

2. United States Department of Health and Human Services, Fast Facts and Figures About Social Security (1990) (Fast Facts).

Program Operation Manual System (POMS) as the guideline for day-to-day operations, and SSA district offices rely on POMS as final authority for their decisions. Because POMS does not always conform to the requirements of the Social Security Act and applicable regulations, attorneys should use care in relying on the guideline. Administrative law judges are not bound by the POMS and may disregard POMS sections that do not conform to the Social Security Act and regulations. Also useful are Social Security Rulings issued by the Social Security Administration and available in West's Social Security Reporting Service.[3]

§§ 15.2–15.10 are reserved for supplementary material.

B. "RETIREMENT" OR "OLD AGE" ELIGIBILITY

Library References:

C.J.S. Social Security and Public Welfare §§ 19, 24, 29, 37.
West's Key No. Digests, Social Security and Public Welfare ☜125.1, 128.1, 135.1.

§ 15.11 Persons Who Could Be Eligible

Persons eligible for cash old age insurance (retirement) or dependent's benefits are: a fully insured individual[1] (see definition in § 15.-13, *infra.*); a wife or divorced wife of an individual entitled to benefits;[2] a husband or a divorced husband of an individual entitled to benefits;[3] an uninsured individual who has attained age 72;[4] and a child of an individual entitled to benefits.[5]

Eligibility for social security depends on work in employment "covered" by the social security system. Nearly all work (including self-employment and part-time work) counts toward eligibility for social security benefits. Major exceptions to "covered" employment are:[6]

1. federal civilian employees hired before 1984;

---

3. See also McCormick, Social Security Claims & Procedures (4th Ed. West, 1991); West's Social Security Reporting Service, and the Unemployment Insurance Reporter (CCH).

§ 15.11

1. 42 U.S.C.A. § 402(a); 20 C.F.R. § 404.310. The formal name for the benefits paid to retired workers is Old–Age Insurance Benefits. The popular name for these benefits is social security retirement benefits. This chapter refers to these benefits as retirement benefits.

2. 42 U.S.C.A. § 402(b); 20 C.F.R. § 404.330.

3. 42 U.S.C.A. § 402(c); 20 C.F.R. § 404.330.

4. 42 U.S.C.A. § 428(a); 20 C.F.R. § 404.380.

5. 42 U.S.C.A. § 402(d); 20 C.F.R. § 404.350.

6. 42 U.S.C.A. § 410; Social Security Handbook, supra § 15.1, note 1, at §§ 900–971.

2. employees of state or local governments not covered by a federal-state agreement; and

3. certain agricultural and domestic workers.

Although most work is covered and most workers are aware when they are in uncovered employment, some workers, such as farmworkers and domestics, are employed in jobs that are covered, but their employers may not pay social security taxes on their behalf and may not comply with social security reporting requirements. As a result, these individuals may be denied benefits at retirement or disability because their work has not been credited to them.[7] In addition, spouses working together (e.g., in small family businesses such as stores and farms) often do not report the income of each spouse separately. Consequently, some spouses may find that they do not have coverage when they apply for benefits.

§ 15.12 Requirements for Eligibility—Overview

To be eligible to receive retirement benefits, a person must:[1] (1) be fully insured; (2) have attained the age of 62; and (3) have filed an application for retirement benefits. The formula for determining the amount of benefits a retired worker will receive is described in § 15.51 infra.

§ 15.13 Requirements for Eligibility—Fully Insured

The requirement that the individual be fully insured is designed to ensure that the individual has worked in covered employment long enough to receive retirement benefits. A "fully insured individual" is one who has earned:[1]

1. quarters of coverage (see § 15.14, infra, for the definition of quarter of coverage) equal to the number of elapsed years between 1950 (or the year the individual reached age 21, if after 1950) and the year the individual reached age 62, became disabled, or died; or

2. 40 quarters of coverage for individuals born January 2, 1929, or later; or

3. in the case of an individual who died prior to 1951, six quarters of coverage.

---

7. See § 15.51 for a discussion of ways to ensure that work is credited.

§ 15.12

1. 42 U.S.C.A. § 402(a); 20 C.F.R. § 404.310.

§ 15.13

1. 42 U.S.C.A. § 414(a); 20 C.F.R. § 404.110(b). One must be "currently insured" for certain survivor's benefits to be paid. See § 15.31 infra.

Years in which an individual had a period of disability are not used in computing the number of quarters needed to qualify for benefits.[2]

§ 15.14 Requirements for Eligibility—Quarter of Coverage

A quarter of coverage (QC) is a period of three months ending March 31, June 30, September 30, and December 31.[1] Before 1978, a self-employed individual was required to make $100 to earn a quarter of coverage (QC), whereas an employee in covered employment earned a QC in any calendar quarter in which the employee earned $50.[2] There is no longer a disparity between the requirements of a self-employed individual and an employee. Every year since 1977, the amount required to earn a QC has increased, and since 1977, quarters of coverage have been based upon annual income.[3] Thus, a person who earns the amount required to earn four quarters of coverage in a particular year may do so by earning it all in one month even if no work is performed after that month. For example, Susan, an editor, earned $2,000 in January 1989. Since the amount needed to earn a quarter of coverage in 1989 was $500, Susan earned four quarters of coverage for 1989, even if she did not work again during 1989. The following chart indicates the earnings required to be credited with a quarter of coverage.

QUARTERS OF COVERAGE [4]

1978	One quarter of coverage for each $250 in annual earnings up to a maximum of four QCs:
1979	for each $260
1980	for each $290
1981	for each $310
1982	for each $340
1983	for each $370
1984	for each $390
1985	for each $410
1986	for each $440
1987	for each $460
1988	for each $470
1989	for each $500
1990	for each $520
1991	for each $540

2. 42 U.S.C.A. § 414(a); 20 C.F.R. § 404.110(c).

§ 15.14

1. 42 U.S.C.A. § 413(a)(1); 20 C.F.R. § 404.102.

2. 42 U.S.C.A. § 413(a)(2)(A)(i); 20 C.F.R. § 404.141(b).

3. 42 U.S.C.A. § 413(a)(2)(A)(ii); 20 C.F.R. § 404.143(a).

4. 42 U.S.C.A. § 413(d)(1); 20 C.F.R. 404.143.

1992..............................for each $570
1993..............................for each $590* [5]
* Will rise in future years in relation to increases in average earnings. The amount required is announced each November for the following year.

A QC will not be credited for any of the following: [6]

1. a calendar quarter that has not begun (that is, prospectively);

2. a calendar quarter beginning after the quarter of the individual's death;

3. a calendar quarter previously credited with a QC;

4. a calendar quarter included in a "period of disability" established for the individual unless:

     a. the quarter is the first *or* last quarter of the "period of disability," or

     b. benefits payable on the individual's earnings record would be denied or reduced because of the period of disability.

§ 15.15   Requirements for Eligibility—Age 65 or 62

The Social Security Act defines retirement age as 65.[1] To be eligible to receive retirement benefits, an individual must be at least 62 years old, the age that is designated as the "early retirement age." [2] One who applies at age 65 is entitled to the full amount of retirement benefits.[3] If application is made at age 62, the amount to which the individual is entitled is actuarially reduced.[4] Similarly, deferring application increases benefits. "Delayed retirement credits" (DRCs) increase the monthly benefit rate for individuals who do not receive benefits for the month they attain age 65 or for any month after that before age 70.[5]

A person born on the first or second day of the month may receive retirement benefits for the month age 62 is attained as that person is deemed to be age 62 throughout that month. All others receive benefits for the following month, the first month they are deemed to be age 62 for the entire month.

5. Social Security Administration 1991 Facts and Figures; 57 Fed.Reg. 48619–01.

6. 42 U.S.C.A. § 413(a)(2)(B); 20 C.F.R. § 404.146; Social Security Handbook, supra § 15.1, note 1, at § 212 (1988).

§ 15.15

1. 42 U.S.C.A. § 416(*l*)(1). The retirement age will increase beginning in 2000. Id.

2. 42 U.S.C.A. § 416(*l*)(2).

3. 42 U.S.C.A. §§ 402(a), 415(a); 20 C.F.R. § 404.312(a).

4. 42 U.S.C.A. § 402(q); 20 C.F.R. § 404.312(c).

5. 42 U.S.C.A. § 402(w); 20 C.F.R. § 404.313. See §§ 15.60–.61 infra.

§ 15.16   Requirements for Eligibility—Filing

An application is a condition precedent to entitlement and must be made before benefits can be paid.

There is limited retroactivity to retirement benefits. If an individual files an application for retirement benefits after the first month the individual is entitled to them, he or she may receive benefits for up to six months preceding the month of application, unless the effect would be to reduce the monthly benefit to which the individual otherwise would be entitled.[1]

Applications for retirement and survivorship benefits filed before the first month in which the claimant meets all requirements of eligibility are considered valid if all the conditions of entitlement are met before a final decision is reached on the application.[2]

In general, an individual must be alive at the time an application for benefits is filed, although application after death is permitted in certain circumstances.[3]

If a fully insured wage earner who is 62 or older files an application for retirement benefits but dies before the claim is processed, the individual's estate is entitled to benefits up to the date of death.[4]

§ 15.17   Dependents and Eligibility—The Benefit

The spouse, divorced spouse, and children of a fully insured individual may be entitled to benefits on that individual's earnings record. The amount of the payment that dependents receive for each month generally is equal to one-half of the insured individual's primary insurance amount if the insured individual is alive, and three-fourths of the primary amount if that individual has died.[1]

§ 15.18   Dependents and Eligibility—Spouse

To qualify for wife's or husband's benefits, one must: be the spouse (according to the marriage laws of the applicable state) or be the "deemed spouse" of an individual receiving retirement or disability benefits.[1] In addition, *one* of the following requirements must be met: [2]

§ 15.16

1. 42 U.S.C.A. § 402(j)(1); 20 C.F.R. § 404.621(a)(1)(ii), (iii).

2. 42 U.S.C.A. § 402(j); 20 C.F.R. § 404.620.

3. 20 C.F.R. § 404.615.

4. Guarino v. Celebrezze, 336 F.2d 336 (3d Cir.1964).

§ 15.17

1. 42 U.S.C.A. § 416(b), (d), (e); 20 C.F.R. § 404.333; 20 C.F.R. § 404.353; see § 15.51 for a discussion of the primary insurance amount.

§ 15.18

1. 42 U.S.C.A. § 416(h)(1); 20 C.F.R. §§ 404.345–404.346.

——

2. See note 2 on page 25.

1. The insured and the spouse have been married not less than one year immediately preceding the day on which the application was filed; or

2. The insured and the spouse are the natural parents of a child; or

3. In the month prior to the marriage, the spouse either was entitled to or, had the spouse been old enough, could have been entitled to wife's, husband's, widow's, widower's, or parent's insurance benefits, disabled child's benefits, or annuity payments under the Railroad Retirement Act for widows, widowers, parents, or children 18 years or older.

An applicant for spouse's benefits must be at least 62 years old or be caring for a child (under 16 or disabled) of the insured and must file an application for benefits. The applicant cannot be entitled to a retirement or disability benefit that equals or exceeds one-half the insured's primary insurance amount.

For a "deemed" relationship to exist, the "deemed spouse" must have gone in good faith through a marriage ceremony with the insured that would have resulted in a valid marriage except for a legal impediment (either an unterminated previous marriage of the insured, or a defect in the marriage procedure).[3] To qualify for benefits, the deemed spouse and the insured must be living in the same household at the time the application is filed or the deemed widow(er) must have been living in the same household as the deceased insured individual at the time of death.

Prior to January 1, 1991, a deemed spouse's entitlement ended when the "legal spouse" became entitled; a deemed spouse's application would be denied if the legal spouse was already entitled.[4] The Omnibus Budget Reconciliation Act of 1990[5] allows for simultaneous entitlement of both deemed and legal spouses for claims filed after December 1990.

§ 15.19   Dependents and Eligibility—Divorced Spouse

To be entitled as a divorced spouse of an individual receiving retirement or disability benefits, a person must meet the following

---

2. 42 U.S.C.A. § 416(b), (f); 20 C.F.R. § 404.330.

3. 42 U.S.C.A. § 416(h)(1)(B); 20 C.F.R. § 404.346(b).

4. 42 U.S.C.A. § 416(h)(1)(B); 20 C.F.R. § 404.346(b).

5. Omnibus Budget Reconciliation Act of 1990, Pub.L. No. 101–508, § 5119, 104 Stat. 1388 (1990), codified at 42 U.S.C.A. § 416(h)(1)(B)(i).

requirements: [1]

1. file an application;

2. have attained age 62;

3. not be married at the time the application is filed;

4. not be entitled to old retirement benefits that equal or exceed one-half of the primary insurance amount of the insured;

5. have been married to the insured for at least ten years before the divorce became final; and

6. have been divorced from the insured individual for at least two years.[2]

To protect economically vulnerable ex-spouses, the Social Security Act allows a divorced spouse satisfying these requirements to receive benefits even if his or her former spouse is not receiving retirement or disability benefits. In contrast, the insured's entitlement is a condition precedent to his or her current spouse's and minor or disabled children's entitlement to benefits.

§ 15.20   Dependents and Eligibility—Children's Benefits

A child of a wage earner entitled to retirement or disability benefits, or of an individual who dies fully or currently insured, is entitled to monthly cash payments where the following conditions are met: [1]

1. The child is the child of the insured person. The term "child" includes adopted children, stepchildren, and grandchildren under some circumstances; [2]

2. The child is dependent upon the insured; [3]

3. An application is filed on the child's behalf;

4. The child is unmarried; and

5. The child has not attained age 18, or is age 18 or older and has a disability that began before age 22, or is age 18 and is in full-time attendance at an educational institution.

§ 15.19

1. 42 U.S.C.A. §§ 416(d), 405(b)(1), 405(c)(1); 20 C.F.R. § 404.331.

2. 42 U.S.C.A. §§ 402(b)(5)(A), 402 (c)(5)(A); 20 C.F.R. § 404.331(f).

§ 15.20

1. 42 U.S.C.A. § 416(e); 20 C.F.R. § 404.350.

2. 20 C.F.R. §§ 404.355–404.359.

3. 20 C.F.R. §§ 404.360–404.365.

The relationship of the child, like that of the spouse, is determined by the law of the state where the insured is domiciled.[4] Because of the diversity of applicable state laws, a child may meet the relationship requirements of one state, but not those of another.

§ 15.21 Special Age 72 Payments

This extremely rare benefit was enacted to protect older persons with little or no work in covered employment who cannot qualify for regular retirement benefits. The requirements are:[1]

1. attainment of age 72 before 1968 or accumulation of at least three QCs in each calendar year between 1966 and the year the individual became age 72;

2. an application; and

3. residence in the United States and status as a United States citizen or an alien lawfully admitted for permanent residence who has resided in the United States continuously during the five years immediately preceding application for benefits.

Special age 72 benefits may not be paid for any month in which the beneficiary receives public assistance or supplemental security income.[2] Limited-income clients potentially eligible for special age 72 benefits should explore eligibility for SSI and Medicaid because of the more generous financial protection offered by those programs.

§§ 15.22–15.30 are reserved for supplementary material.

C. SURVIVOR'S BENEFITS

Library References:

C.J.S. Social Security and Public Welfare § 36.
West's Key No. Digests, Social Security and Public Welfare ⬩140.

§ 15.31 Lump Sum Death Payment

Social security pays a lump sum death payment upon the death of a fully or currently[1] insured individual. The amount of the payment is

---

4. 42 U.S.C.A. § 416(h)(2)(A); 20 C.F.R. § 404.354(b).

§ 15.21

1. 42 U.S.C.A. § 428(a); 20 C.F.R. § 404.381.

2. 42 U.S.C.A. § 428(d); 20 C.F.R. § 404.384(b).

§ 15.31

1. Fully insured status was defined in § 15.13 supra. Currently insured status is required for certain survivor's benefits. One is currently insured if one has six quarters of coverage during the full 13–quarter period ending with the calendar quarter in which one died, became entitled to retirement benefits or most recently be-

$255 or three times the individual's primary insurance amount, whichever is less.[2] The Social Security Administration (SSA) pays the benefit to the surviving spouse living in the same household as the insured. If no same-residence spouse survives, then SSA pays the benefit to a person entitled to widow(er)'s benefits or mother's/father's benefits for the month of the insured's death.[3] The SSA will also pay the benefit to a widow(er) or mother/father who would have been entitled to the benefit if a timely application had been filed.

Where no such person exists, the lump sum death payment is divided equally among persons entitled to child's benefits, or children who would have been entitled had a timely application been filed, for the month of the insured's death.[4]

An application must be filed within two years of the insured spouse's death, except that no application is required when the surviving spouse is entitled to husband's or wife's benefits for the month preceding the month in which the spouse dies.[5]

§ 15.32 Widow's and Widower's Insurance Benefits—The Benefit

Widows and widowers of persons who died fully insured are entitled to survivor's benefits. The amount of the benefit is roughly equal to the primary insurance amount received by the decedent, subject to certain reductions.[1]

Library References:

C.J.S. Social Security and Public Welfare § 39.

West's Key No. Digests, Social Security and Public Welfare ⚷136.

§ 15.33 Widow's and Widower's Insurance Benefits—Persons Eligible

A widow or widower must be a surviving spouse according to the marriage laws of the applicable state or be a survivor of a "deemed valid marriage." [1]

came entitled to disability benefits. 42 U.S.C.A. § 414(b); 20 C.F.R. § 404.120.

2. 42 U.S.C.A. § 402(i); 20 C.F.R. § 404.390.

3. 42 U.S.C.A. § 402(i); 20 C.F.R. § 404.392(a)(1).

4. 42 U.S.C.A. § 402(i); 20 C.F.R. § 404.392(a)(2).

5. 42 U.S.C.A. § 402(i); 20 C.F.R. § 404.392(b).

§ 15.32
1. 42 U.S.C.A. § 416(c), (g); 20 C.F.R. §§ 404.335, 404.338.

§ 15.33
1. 42 U.S.C.A. § 416(c), (g); 20 C.F.R. § 404.335.

§ 15.34　Widow's and Widower's Insurance Benefits—Requirements

To be entitled to survivor's benefits, a widow or widower must meet one of the following conditions: [1]

1. The marital relationship lasted at least nine months immediately prior to the insured's death; or

2. The marital relationship lasted less than nine months immediately prior to the insured's death but either (a) the insured's death was accidental or in the line of duty in military service, or (b) the survivor and the insured had been previously married for at least nine months; or

3. The survivor and the insured were the natural or adoptive parents of a child; or

4. The survivor in the month preceding marriage to the insured was entitled to or receiving one of the benefits listed in 20 C.F.R. § 404.335(a)(4).

In addition to being a spouse and meeting one of the above conditions, to be entitled to survivor's benefits, a widow or widower must: [2]

1. apply, unless the widow(er) was previously entitled to receive spouse's benefits for the month before the insured's death and is at least age 65 and not entitled to either old age or retirement benefits; or the widow(er) was entitled to mother's/father's benefits in the month before attaining age 65;

2. be at least 60 years old; or be at least 50 years old and have been disabled within seven years of the insured's death or termination of mother's/father's benefits, whichever occurred last;

3. not be entitled to a retirement benefit equal to or exceeding the insured's primary insurance amount; and

4. be unmarried unless the remarriage occurred after the widow(er) became 60 years old.

§ 15.35　Surviving Divorced Spouse's Benefits—The Benefit

Benefits for surviving divorced spouses are the same as widow or widower's benefits, roughly equal to the primary insurance amount of

§ 15.34

1. 20 C.F.R. § 404.335(a).

2. 42 U.S.C.A. § 402(e) and (f); 20 C.F.R. § 404.335(b)–(e).

the decedent.[1]

Library References:

C.J.S. Social Security and Public Welfare § 39.

West's Key No. Digests, Social Security and Public Welfare ⚏136.

§ 15.36 Surviving Divorced Spouse's Benefits—Persons Eligible

To be eligible for surviving divorced spouse's benefits, the person must have been validly married to the insured, according to the pertinent state law, for at least ten years before the final divorce.[1]

§ 15.37 Surviving Divorced Spouse's Benefits—Requirements

The surviving divorced spouse must meet the following requirements: [1]

1. apply, unless previously receiving benefits;
2. be at least 60 years old or be at least 50 years old and disabled;
3. not be entitled to a retirement benefit equal to or larger than the insured's primary insurance amount, and
4. be unmarried, unless the remarriage occurred after age 60; or where the surviving divorced spouse was entitled to disabled widow(er)'s benefits, the remarriage must have occurred after age 50 but prior to age 60. The remarriage must have occurred after the insured's death.

§ 15.38 Disabled Widow's and Widower's Insurance Benefits

The disabled widow or widower of an individual who died fully insured, if he or she meets the applicable requirements, can qualify for survivor's benefits.[1] Similarly, a surviving divorced spouse of an individual who died fully insured, if he or she meets the applicable requirements, can qualify for disability benefits on the basis of the fully insured status of the deceased spouse.[2]

To qualify for social security benefits as a disabled survivor, the claimant is required to establish that he or she is at least 50 years of

§ 15.35

1. 42 U.S.C.A. § 402(e) and (f); 20 C.F.R. §§ 404.336, 404.338.

§ 15.36

1. 42 U.S.C.A. § 416(d)(2) and (5); 20 C.F.R. § 404.336(a).

§ 15.37

1. 42 U.S.C.A. § 402(e) and (f); 20 C.F.R. § 404.336(b)–(e).

§ 15.38

1. 42 U.S.C.A. § 402(e); 20 C.F.R. § 404.335(c).

2. 42 U.S.C.A. § 402(e); 20 C.F.R. § 404.336(c).

age, that he or she has physical or mental impairments that are of such severity as to preclude engagement in any substantial gainful activity, and that the impairments were manifest within the specified period.[3]

The Social Security Administration (SSA) now treats the claims of disabled survivors the same as claims of disabled wage earners. However before 1990, the test to determine if a widow(er), or surviving divorced spouse, had a disability entitling him or her to survivor's benefits was stricter than the test for a wage earner.[4] The SSA required the claimant to demonstrate an inability to engage in *any* gainful activity, whereas the wage earner had to show an inability to engage in any *substantial* gainful activity. In addition, although SSA considered factors such as age, education, and work experience in deciding claims of disability by wage earners, such nonmedical factors were ignored in disabled survivor's claims.[5] This disparity no longer exists.

Library References:

C.J.S. Social Security and Public Welfare § 39.
West's Key No. Digests, Social Security and Public Welfare ⊶136.

§ 15.39   Mother's and Father's Insurance Benefits

A widow, widower, or surviving divorced spouse of an individual who died fully or currently insured, as defined at 42 U.S.C.A. § 414, is entitled to survivor's benefits, regardless of whether he or she is 60 years of age, based upon the deceased's earning record if he or she has one or more children of the deceased, under age 16 or disabled before age 22, in his or her care. The requirements for mother's/father's insurance benefits are set out at 42 U.S.C.A. § 402(g)(1) and 20 C.F.R. §§ 404.339 and 404.340.

The mother's/father's insurance benefit for each month will be equal to three-fourths of the primary insurance amount of the deceased, subject to certain reductions.[1]

Library References:

C.J.S. Social Security and Public Welfare § 40.
West's Key No. Digests, Social Security and Public Welfare ⊶136.5.

§§ 15.40–15.50 are reserved for supplementary material.

3. 42 U.S.C.A. § 423; 20 C.F.R. §§ 404.-315 and 404.1505.

4. Sullivan v. Weinberger, 493 F.2d 855 (5th Cir.1974), certiorari denied 421 U.S. 967, 95 S.Ct. 1958, 44 L.Ed.2d 455 (1975); 20 C.F.R. §§ 404.335, 404.336.

5. See e.g. Dorton v. Heckler, 789 F.2d 363, 13 Soc.Sec.Rep.Ser. 315 (6th Cir.1986).

§ 15.39

1. 42 U.S.C.A. § 402(g)(4); 20 C.F.R. § 404.342.

D. COMPUTATION, REDUCTIONS, AND OVERPAYMENTS

Library References:

> C.J.S. Social Security and Public Welfare § 45.
>
> West's Key No. Digests, Social Security and Public Welfare ⊗140.1.

§ 15.51 Computing Amount of Primary Benefit

The monthly benefits a disabled or retired worker receives are intended to replace a portion of the wages previously earned from work. The benefits that an individual and the individual's survivors or dependents receive are based upon the worker's primary insurance amount (PIA), a figure calculated from the worker's average monthly earnings (AME) or average indexed monthly earnings (AIME).[1] The monthly benefit of a worker retiring at 65 usually will be 100% of the worker's PIA. The monthly benefit of a worker retiring between 62 and 64 is reduced actuarially and will be a percentage of the worker's PIA. Similarly, the monthly benefit of a worker who retires after 65 is increased and will be more than the worker's PIA.[2] The monthly benefits of a worker's spouse, children, and other dependents and those of survivors also are based on the worker's PIA and are expressed as a percentage of the PIA.[3]

Computation of a worker's primary insurance amount is complex.[4] Slightly different formulas are used in this computation, depending on the year the worker turned 62, was disabled, or died. In general, for workers who were 62, disabled, or died before 1979, the AME method is employed, whereas the AIME, intended to yield higher benefits, is used for those reaching 62, dying, or becoming disabled in 1979 or later. The purpose of using indexed earnings is to reduce the disparity between benefit amounts based only on recent earnings (such as those of a young disabled worker) and amounts based on earnings for older individuals whose earnings were lower during the early years of social security coverage. Other factors also influence the formula used, and the formulas are adjusted annually.[5] A client wishing to estimate the

---

§ 15.51

1. 20 C.F.R. § 404.204.

2. 20 C.F.R. § 404.312. See §§ 15.60–.61 infra.

3. See, e.g., 20 C.F.R. § 404.333.

4. To illustrate, for a worker attaining 62, dying, or becoming disabled in 1993, the PIA equals 90% of the first $401 of AIME, plus 32% of AIME over $401 through $2,420, plus 15% of AIME over $2,420. These figures change annually.

5. For a detailed discussion of computation of primary insurance amounts, see 20 C.F.R. §§ 404.201–.290.

benefit he or she will receive can obtain a pamphlet for this purpose from a Social Security Administration (SSA) District Office.

Since benefit amounts depend on earnings, it is important that the SSA have accurate earnings records. Clients should be encouraged to request a copy of their earnings record every three years by requesting Form SSA–7004, "Personal Earnings Benefit Estimate Statement." [6] A person who believes earnings have been reported or credited incorrectly should contact the SSA District Office. The SSA will attempt to locate missing reports and, if unsuccessful, will accept evidence of wages paid to the worker, including pay stubs, affidavits of coemployees or of employers, or a Treasury Form W–2.

§ 15.52 Deductions From Monthly Insurance Benefits—Excess Annual Earnings Deduction—The "Retirement" Test

Social security retirement benefits are designed to replace earnings lost as a result of retirement. Therefore, a recipient of retirement benefits is permitted to earn only a limited amount and still retain full social security retirement benefits. The test used in this situation is referred to as the "retirement test." Annual earnings in excess of the "retirement test" level for that year reduce or eliminate benefits otherwise payable to the insured individual and certain dependents.[1] After the exempt amount is earned by beneficiaries under age 65, one dollar of benefit is reduced for each two dollars of "excess income" earned.

Since the beginning of 1990, the Social Security Administration (SSA) has reduced monthly benefits for working beneficiaries aged 65 to 69 one dollar for every three dollars of "excess income" earned.[2] An individual age 70 or over may earn an unlimited amount and still receive social security benefits.[3] For example, during 1993, a person aged 65 to 69 could earn up to $10,560 per year, or $880 per month, without suffering any loss of social security benefits; a person between 62 and 65 could earn up to $7,680 per year, or $640 per month. These figures are based on the level of social security benefits for that year, which changes each year.

---

6. Earnings should be requested regularly, since corrections in earnings records are more difficult to make if the correction is requested more than 3 years, 3 months, and 15 days after the year in which the error occurred. 20 C.F.R. §§ 404.802, 404.-822.

§ 15.52

1. 42 U.S.C.A. § 402(q); 20 C.F.R. § 404.415.

2. 42 U.S.C.A. § 403(f)(3).

3. 42 U.S.C.A. § 403(f)(1); 20 C.F.R. §§ 404.415, 404.428.

"Earnings" means the sum of an individual's wages for services and net earnings from self-employment in the same year.[4]　Therefore, earnings does not include payments made under an employer's pension plan or retirement, sickness, or accidental disability plan.　Nor will payments made under an annuity plan be included as earnings.[5]

Furthermore, income from investment is not earnings from services or self-employment; thus, income from investments such as stock dividends or building and land rentals is not counted.　Further, advance planning may convert that which would otherwise be "earnings" into investment income that can be received in an unlimited amount without affecting entitlement to retirement benefits.　For example, if a business or property, including a farm, is managed or rented by another, the individual's income from it would be investment income rather than earnings.　In the case of a business, payments from it will be investment return as long as the individual does not perform substantial services in the business.　Services include both physical work and planning or managing activities.　As detailed below, services of less than fifteen hours a month are never considered substantial, whereas services of more than 45 hours monthly usually are considered substantial.[6]　The SSA considers farm rental income to be investment income if the lessor does not participate materially in the production or management of the farm.[7]

§ 15.53　Deductions From Monthly Insurance Benefits—Excess Annual Earnings Deduction—Exempt Amount and Amount Deducted

In general, the retirement test is based on annual earnings.　Benefits are reduced if earnings exceed the allowable exempt amount regardless of when they were earned during a year.　However, special rules apply to a recipient's "grace year," usually the year in which the recipient first receives retirement benefits.　During this year, benefits are not reduced in months in which earned income does not exceed the monthly limit, regardless of the total earned during the year.

The grace year allows people to receive benefits for the remainder of the year during which they retire, regardless of their earnings before retirement.　It also allows a person who has retired to do special projects or consult in one or a few months and lose benefits only for those months.　Under this rule, a person can get a full benefit for any month the person's wages do not exceed the monthly exempt amount

---

4.　42 U.S.C.A. § 403(f)(5)(A); 20 C.F.R. § 404.429.

5.　42　U.S.C.A.　§ 403(f)(5)(C)(i);　20 C.F.R. § 404.429.

6.　20 C.F.R. § 404.447(a).

7.　20 C.F.R. § 404.1082(c).

and if the person does not perform substantial services in self-employment. The monthly exempt amount in 1993 is $880 per month for those 65 or older and $640 per month for those under 65.[1] This monthly test also applies during the year benefits begin for children or for mothers or fathers who receive benefits because they have been caring for a young child. And it applies in the first year of entitlement to a second type of benefit, such as retirement or widow(er)'s benefits. However, there must be a break in entitlement of at least one month before an individual becomes entitled to a different benefit.[2] The special monthly test can apply only in the first year in which a person has little or no earnings for one or more months. In all other years, the amount of benefits payable depends on a person's total annual earnings, except as explained above.

The special monthly test differs depending on whether the person works as an employee or is self-employed. For an employee, it does not matter when the wages are actually paid; the controlling factor is when the money is earned. For the self-employed, the main consideration is whether the person is active in his or her business and is performing "substantial services."[3] Unlike employees, who usually know how much they earn each month, self-employed people often do not know whether they will have a profit or a loss until the end of the year. The money a self-employed person receives from his or her business in a given month may vary considerably and often may be for work during some earlier month. For these reasons, the SSA does not use monthly earnings to decide how work affects payments for self-employed people. Self-employed people can get unreduced benefits if they do not perform "substantial services."

The Social Security Administration (SSA) decides whether the services of a self-employed person are substantial by looking at the amount of time the individual devotes to the business, the kind of services performed, and how the services compare with what the individual did in the past. In general, more than forty-five hours of self-employment service in a month is considered substantial, and less than forty-five hours in a month is not considered substantial service. However, forty-five hours of work or less may be considered substantial if it involves the management of a sizeable business or is in a highly skilled occupation. Fewer than fifteen hours a month is never consid-

§ 15.53

1. 42 U.S.C.A. § 403(f)(8); 20 C.F.R. §§ 404.430–404.447; U.S. Department of Health and Human Services, "How work affects your Social Security check". The exempt amounts are redetermined each year. 20 C.F.R. § 404.430.

2. 20 C.F.R. § 404.435(c)(4).

3. 20 C.F.R. § 404.446.

ered substantial, regardless of the size of the business or the value of the service.[4]

§ 15.54 Deductions From Monthly Insurance Benefits—Excess Annual Earnings Deduction—Reporting

An individual entitled to retirement or survivor's benefits during any taxable year in which the individual has earnings in excess of the applicable monthly exempt amount must report the earnings to the Social Security Administration (SSA).[1] No report is necessary for a taxable year beginning with or after the month the individual attains age 70. Generally, the annual earnings report is done after the beneficiary receives a W2 form from the employer, but before April 15th of the year subsequent to that in which the earnings were paid. The annual earnings report form requires the beneficiary to state the earnings for the prior year and an estimate of the earnings for that year. Benefits are paid based upon the estimate. The annual earnings report also validates the prior year's estimate. If the individual fails to report earnings without good cause, penalty deductions will be imposed against the individual's benefits in addition to the deductions required because of excess earnings.[2]

If the report predicts excess earnings, benefits will be reduced or suspended until the excess has been collected.[3] For example, a 64–year–old beneficiary who informs the SSA that he or she will earn $9,000 during 1993 by earning over $750 per month will have excess earnings of $660 for the year. The term "excess earnings" includes only the portion of earnings that results in a reduction of social security benefits, not the entire sum in excess of the yearly maximum. Since SSA reduces benefits by one dollar for every two dollars earned over the allowable limit, the excess earnings in this example are $660, one-half of the $1,320 earned in excess of the allowable limit of $7,680. If this person's social security benefits were $350 per month, the SSA would collect the excess earnings of $660 by suspending benefits for January, and by reducing the February benefit.[4] Beginning in March, the SSA would pay full benefits for the balance of the year.

---

4. 20 C.F.R. § 404.447.

§ 15.54

1. 42 U.S.C.A. § 403(h); 20 C.F.R. § 404.452.

2. 20 C.F.R. §§ 404.453–.454.

3. 20 C.F.R. § 404.456.

4. Slightly different rules apply during the calendar year in which a person retires. During the first year of retirement,

benefits will be reduced only for months in which an employee earns more than one-twelfth of the applicable yearly maximum. 42 U.S.C.A. § 403(f). For self-employed individuals, benefits will be reduced during the first year of retirement only during months in which the self-employed person renders substantial services in self-employment. Id. For example, if a person at age 65 retires on June 30 and receives benefits

The SSA deducts the excess earnings of the retired individual from the total monthly family benefit, i.e., the benefits of the retired individual, spouse, and child. But the SSA does not charge excess earnings against disability insurance benefits or the benefits of an entitled divorced spouse who had been divorced from the retired individual at least two years.[5]

The SSA may require an individual to file another report at the end of the year if no original report was filed or if the original report was inaccurate, i.e., the person earned more or less than predicted in the original report. In addition, the SSA checks with the Internal Revenue Service (IRS) to make sure that earnings reports are accurate and to catch persons who earned money but failed to file a report with the SSA. As a result of the second report or the check with the IRS, the SSA may determine that a person has been overpaid, i.e., that a person received full benefits in a month(s) in which excess earnings occurred. When this happens, the SSA will attempt to collect the overpayment by reducing or terminating future benefits.[6]

§ 15.55 Deductions From Monthly Insurance Benefits—Reductions Due to Family Maximum

Congress has established a maximum amount, called the family maximum, that generally can be paid a family, regardless of the number of entitled beneficiaries on a worker's record. The family maximum is determined according to the method of computing the primary insurance amount (PIA) (usually the amount received for retirement at age 65) and the kind of benefits payable to the worker. For example, if a worker first became eligible or died in 1979 or later, the family maximum is computed by adding fixed percentages of predetermined dollar amounts (called "bend points") that are part of the PIA. The formula in effect for 1993 was 150% of the first $513 of the PIA, plus 272% of the excess of PIA over $513 through $740, plus 134% of the excess PIA over $740 through $966, plus 175% of the excess PIA over $966. These "bend points" usually change each year.

The family maximum for disability benefits is 85% of the average indexed monthly earnings of the worker, but not less than the PIA nor more than 150% of the PIA.

from July through October but returns to work during November and December, earning over the exempt amount each month, benefits would be reduced only for November and December, since these are the only months after retirement during which more than the monthly exempt amount was earned.

5. 20 C.F.R. §§ 404.415–.416, 404.434–.441.

6. 20 C.F.R. §§ 404.501–.502.

All the benefit rates, except the retirement or disability insurance benefits and benefits payable to a divorced spouse or surviving divorced spouse, are subject to reduction to bring the total monthly benefits payable within the family maximum.[1] Note that the total benefits payable to the family group are not necessarily reduced when monthly benefits are not payable to one member of the group. For example, if a spouse continues to work, his or her benefit can be used to increase the benefits of others in the family group, usually eligible children.[2]

§ 15.56 Deductions From Monthly Insurance Benefits—Deductions Because Beneficiary Failed to Have Child in Care

One of the requirements for a person to receive spouse's benefits based upon the insured's fully insured status is that the spouse either be age 62 or have in care a child entitled to child's insurance benefits.[1] The Social Security Administration (SSA) will deduct an amount from the spouse's insurance benefit for any month in which the spouse is under age 65 and does not have in care a child entitled to a child's insurance benefit.[2] However, a deduction is not made for any month in which the spouse is age 62 or over but under age 65, and there is in effect a certification of election for the spouse to receive an actuarially reduced spouse's insurance benefit for that month.[3]

The amount to be deducted from the spouse's insurance benefit equals the amount of the benefit that is otherwise payable for the month in which the spouse did not have a child in care.[4] A similar deduction is made from survivor's benefits.[5]

§ 15.57 Deductions From Monthly Insurance Benefits—Deductions Due to Refusal to Accept Rehabilitation Services

Widows or widowers entitled to disability insurance benefits can lose some of their benefits if they are under age 60 and refuse, without

§ 15.55

1. 42 U.S.C.A. § 403(a); 20 C.F.R. § 404.403.

2. For a discussion of the family maximum, see the Social Security Handbook, 10th edition, §§ 730–38 and 20 C.F.R. §§ 404.403–.406.

§ 15.56

1. 42 U.S.C.A. § 402(b); 20 C.F.R. § 404.330.

2. 42 U.S.C.A. § 403(c); 20 C.F.R. § 404.421.

3. 20 C.F.R. § 404.421(a).

4. 20 C.F.R. § 404.421(c).

5. 20 C.F.R. § 404.421(b).

good cause, to accept rehabilitation services available under a state plan approved under the Vocational Rehabilitation Act.[1]

§ 15.58 Deductions From Monthly Insurance Benefits—Reduction Due to Entitlement to Other Social Security Benefits

If an individual is entitled to a retirement insurance benefit or disability insurance benefit and to any other Old Age, Survivors, and Disability Insurance Program (OASDI) monthly benefit for the same month, the other benefit is reduced by an amount equal to such retirement insurance benefit or such disability insurance benefit.[1]

> Example # 1—John receives $250 per month in childhood disability benefits when he becomes entitled to disability benefits of $100 per month. His net monthly benefits will be $250, of which $100 is allocated to his disability record and the remaining $150 to his childhood disability benefit record. His childhood disability benefits are offset by the payment of disability benefits.

If an individual is entitled for any month to a widow's or widower's insurance benefit and to any other monthly OASDI benefit for the same month, except a retirement benefit, the other insurance benefit (after any reductions under 42 U.S.C.A. §§ 402(q) and 403(a)) is reduced, but not below zero, by an amount equal to the widow's or widower's insurance benefit.[2]

> Example # 2—Alice receives surviving divorced spouse benefits of $450 per month when she becomes entitled to a disability benefit of $620 per month. Her net monthly benefit will be $620 per month, of which $170 is allocated to the disability record and $450 to her surviving divorced spouse's record.

Any individual who is entitled to both a retirement benefit and a disability insurance benefit is entitled to only the larger benefit amount for that month unless the individual elects to take the smaller benefit.[3]

§ 15.59 Deductions From Monthly Insurance Benefits—Reduction Due to Receipt of Government Pension

Social security benefits payable to a spouse, divorced spouse, surviving spouse, or surviving divorced spouse may be reduced if the

---

§ 15.57

1. 42 U.S.C.A. § 422(b); 20 C.F.R. § 404.422.

§ 15.58

1. 42 U.S.C.A. § 402(k)(3)(A); 20 C.F.R. § 404.407(a). Any reduction under 42 U.S.C.A. § 402(q) (entitlement to benefit before retirement age) and any reduction under 42 U.S.C.A. § 403(a) (exceeding the family maximum) will occur before the reduction attributable to dual entitlement.

2. 42 U.S.C.A. § 402(k)(3)(B); 20 C.F.R. § 404.407(b).

3. 42 U.S.C.A. § 402(k)(4); 20 C.F.R. § 404.407(c).

claimant receives a pension resulting from his or her employment for the federal government, a state, or a political subdivision of a state.[1] This government pension offset reduces the amount of a claimant's social security spouse's (including divorced spouse's) or surviving spouse's benefits by two-thirds of the amount of the claimant's pension. For example, if a claimant receives a monthly civil service pension of $900, two-thirds of that, or $600, must be used to offset the claimant's spouse's or surviving spouse's benefits. Therefore, a spouse who is eligible for a $700 surviving spouse's benefit will receive $100 from social security ($700 − $600 = $100).

Certain claimants are exempt from the government pension offset:[2]

1. any federal, state, or local employee whose government pension is from a job where he or she was paying social security taxes on the last day of employment;

2. any claimant who received or was eligible to receive a government pension before December 1982 and who meets all the requirements for social security spouse's benefits in effect in January 1977. This exemption applies to a divorced woman whose marriage lasted 20 years or more and to a husband or widower who received one-half or more of his support from his spouse; and

3. any claimant who received or was eligible to receive a federal, state, or local government pension before July 1, 1983, and was receiving one-half support from his or her spouse.

§ 15.60 Changes in Primary Benefits Due to Receipt of Social Security Benefits Before or After Age 65—Reduction Due to Early Retirement

The Social Security Administration (SSA) will reduce the benefits of retirees, spouses, widows, or widowers who receive them prior to age 65. However, in the case of an individual entitled to spouse's benefits, there is no reduction in benefits for any month the spouse has in care a child of the insured individual, if the child is entitled to child's insurance benefits.[1] In the case of retirement benefits, the individual's primary insurance amount is reduced by $5/9$ of one percent (or $1/180$) for each month of entitlement before age 65. In the case of wife's or husband's benefits, the individual's benefit amount is reduced first for the family maximum (described in § 15.55 supra) and then further

§ 15.59

1. 20 C.F.R. § 404.408a.
2. 20 C.F.R. § 404.408a(b).

§ 15.60

1. 42 U.S.C.A. § 402(q)(1); 20 C.F.R. § 404.410.

by $^{25}/_{36}$ of one percent (or $^{1}/_{144}$) for each month of entitlement before age 65. In the case of widow's or widower's benefits, the individual's benefit amount is first reduced for the family maximum and is then further reduced by $^{19}/_{40}$ of one percent (or $^{19}/_{4000}$) for each month of entitlement between age 60 and 65.[2] For individuals attaining age 62 on January 1, 1990, or later, SSA does not carry over a reduction when the individual files for retirement benefits after receiving widow(er)'s benefits before age 62.[3]

Example # 1—Marsha, born January 4, 1931, becomes entitled to retirement benefits effective May 1993. Her benefits are reduced for the 32 months between May 1993, her entitlement date, and January 1996, the month she attains age 65. Her reduction is therefore $\frac{180-32}{180}$ or $\frac{148}{180}$, which equals 82.2%. If her benefits would be $615 at age 65, her reduced benefits in May 1993 would be $505 per month.

Example # 2—Timothy, born May 18, 1930, becomes entitled to husband's benefits effective November 1993. He does not have an entitled child in his care, nor is he entitled to retirement benefits on his own record. His reduction is therefore $\frac{144-18}{144}$ or $\frac{126}{144}$, which equals 87.5%. If his benefits would be $365 at age 65, his reduced husband's benefits in November 1993 would be $319 per month. If he had an entitled child in his care, his benefits would be $365 and would not be subject to reduction for age.

§ 15.61   Changes in Primary Benefits Due to Receipt of Social Security Benefits Before or After Age 65—Increase Due to Delayed Retirement [1]

A person who delays applying for retirement benefits beyond the month in which the person turns 65 earns a "delayed retirement credit" (DRC) for each month after attaining 65 in which the person does not apply for benefits. Similarly, a person entitled to retirement benefits who does not receive them because of income from work (see §§ 15.52–.54 supra) receives a DRC for each month in which benefits were not received. Delayed retirement credits are available until the month in which a beneficiary turns 70, after which time full retirement benefits are paid without reduction for earned income. Delayed retirement credits are added to a person's benefit amount beginning in

2. 42 U.S.C.A. § 402(q); 20 C.F.R. § 404.410.

3. Omnibus Budget Reconciliation Act of 1989, Pub.L. No. 101–239, § 102–03, 103 Stat. 2473 (1989), codified at 42 U.S.C.A. § 402(d)(8)(E), (F), (G).

§ 15.61

1. 20 C.F.R. § 404.313.

January of the year after the year in which the DRC was earned, except that DRCs earned in year(s) prior to the year in which an application for retirement benefits is filed are included in the beneficiary's first check.

For months during 1982 to 1989, the delayed retirement credit was one-fourth of one percent for each month in which an individual was eligible for but did not receive a retirement benefit. For months beginning with 1990, the delayed retirement credit depends on the year in which it occurs.

Year age 65 is reached	Delayed retirement credit percent
1990	$^7/_{24}$ of 1%
1991	$^7/_{24}$ of 1%
1992	$^1/_3$ of 1%
1993	$^1/_3$ of 1%
1994	$^3/_8$ of 1%
1995	$^3/_8$ of 1%
1996	$^5/_{12}$ of 1%
1997	$^5/_{12}$ of 1%
1998	$^{11}/_{24}$ of 1%
1999	$^{11}/_{24}$ of 1%
2000	$^1/_2$ of 1%
2001	$^1/_2$ of 1%
2002	$^{13}/_{24}$ of 1%
2003	$^{13}/_{24}$ of 1%
2004	$^7/_{12}$ of 1%
2005	$^7/_{12}$ of 1%
2006	$^5/_8$ of 1%
2007	$^5/_8$ of 1%
2008 and later	$^2/_3$ of 1%

For example, Alan was qualified for retirement benefits when he reached age 65 in January 1993 but decided not to apply for retirement benefits immediately because he was still working. When he became age 66 in January 1994, he stopped working and applied for these benefits beginning with that month. Based on his earnings, his primary insurance amount was $326.60, and his monthly retirement benefit was $326.60 if no delayed retirement credits were added. However, he did not receive benefits for the 12 months from the month in which he became 65 (January 1993) until the first month in which he stopped working (January 1994). Therefore, his monthly retirement benefit of $326.60 was increased by four percent (one-third of one percent times 12 months) to yield a total $339.67, which rounded to the next lower multiple of $0.10 is $339.60.[2]

2. See 20 C.F.R. § 404.313(e) for a dis-   cussion of the effect of DRCs on depen-

§ 15.62   Effect of Remarriage of Widow, Widower, or Divorced Spouse Receiving Survivor's Benefits

Widow's and widower's benefits are not affected when the beneficiary remarries after age 60.[1] In the case of a surviving divorced spouse or a widow or widower under age 60, remarriage generally terminates benefits.[2] However, benefits are not automatically terminated if the remarriage is to a person entitled to husband's, wife's, widow's, widower's, mother's, father's, parent's, or disabled child's benefits. When the subsequent remarriage ends, the widow(er) may become entitled or re-entitled on the prior deceased spouse's earnings record beginning with the month the subsequent marriage ends.[3]

§ 15.63   Overpayments—Recoupment

A recipient may receive an overpayment either because of an error by the Social Security Administration (SSA) or because SSA is unaware of a fact that should cause a reduction in the amount of the benefit, such as receipt of excess earned income. Regardless of the cause of the overpayment, SSA may require that it be repaid.[1]

The SSA can request voluntary payment in the form of a direct refund, either from the recipient or from the assets of the recipient's estate. However, involuntary repayment may be made only by deductions from the monthly benefits due the recipient and from monthly benefits due any other contingently liable individual on the record.[2] Monthly benefits can be withheld altogether until the overpayment has been repaid, or only part of the monthly benefit will be withheld if withholding the full amount each month would defeat the purpose of such monthly payments or deprive the person of income required for ordinary and necessary living expenses.[3]

In determining the amount of an overpayment, SSA "nets" the amount of any underpayments that have occurred against overpay-

---

dent's benefits and on the family maximum.

§ 15.62

1. 42 U.S.C.A. § 402(e)(3)(A) and (f)(4)(A); 20 C.F.R. § 404.335(e); 20 C.F.R. § 404.337(b)(1).

2. 42 U.S.C.A. § 402(e)(3)(A); 20 C.F.R. § 404.336(e)(2)(ii).

3. Social Security Handbook, supra § 15.1, note 1, at § 406.

§ 15.63

1. 42 U.S.C.A. § 404(a); 20 C.F.R. § 404.502.

2. SSA regulations forbid involuntary cross-program recovery. Thus, an overpayment of retirement benefits should not result in a reduction of SSI benefits, nor should an SSI overpayment cause retirement benefits to be reduced unless the recipient consents. 20 C.F.R. § 416.570.

3. 42 U.S.C.A. § 404(b); 20 C.F.R. § 404.502.

ments to determine the "net" overpayment.[4] Although this practice may help a recipient by reducing the size of an alleged overpayment, it also may harm the recipient, since it deprives the recipient of the opportunity to obtain a waiver of recovery of the larger amount under the procedures described in this section.[5]

Whenever SSA determines that an overpayment has been made, the SSA will send the overpaid individual a notice of the alleged overpayment, the proposed recovery, and the right to request reconsideration or seek waiver of recoupment. The SSA will also notify any other contingently liable individual from whom SSA may seek an adjustment or recovery of the overpayment.[6] The initial determination that an overpayment has been made is final and binding upon all parties unless the recipient requests review.[7]

A recipient may appeal the determination that the recipient has been overpaid or may seek waiver of recovery of the overpayment, or both. Although counsel often combine a request for reconsideration of the initial determination that an overpayment has occurred with a request for waiver of recovery, it is not necessary that the requests be combined. In some instances, it may be preferable first to contest whether an overpayment has occurred, then to ask for waiver of recovery.

A recipient has 60 days from the date of receipt of notice (presumed to be five days after date of notice) to make a written request for reconsideration or waiver.[8] If the recipient requests reconsideration or waiver within 30 days of the notice, the agency will continue to pay benefits until a reconsideration determination is issued. Reconsiderations of the initial determinations are paper reviews. A personal conference is available when waiver of overpayment is sought.[9]

Library References:

C.J.S. Social Security and Public Welfare § 47.

West's Key No. Digests, Social Security and Public Welfare ⟴140.3.

4. 20 C.F.R. § 404.504; S.S. Ruling 81–19a.

5. SSA's "netting" policy was sustained in Sullivan v. Everhart, 494 U.S. 83, 110 S.Ct. 960, 108 L.Ed.2d 72, 28 Soc.Sec.Rep. Ser. 383 (1990), *on remand* 901 F.2d 838 (10th Cir.1990).

6. 20 C.F.R. § 404.502a.

7. 20 C.F.R. § 404.905.

8. 20 C.F.R. § 404.909.

9. SSA Program Operations Manual System (POMS) §§ GN 02210.006 (4/90), GN 02270.001–GN 02270.020 (Part 2) (10/89); Califano v. Yamasaki, 442 U.S. 682, 99 S.Ct. 2545, 611 L.Ed.2d 176, *on remand* 607 F.2d 329 (9th Cir.1979); Yamasaki v. Schweiker, 680 F.2d 588 (9th Cir. 1982).

§ 15.64 Overpayments—Waiver of Recovery

The Social Security Act mandates that the Social Security Administration (SSA) cannot recoup overpayments from "any person who is without fault if such adjustment or recovery would defeat the purpose of [the Social Security Act] or would be against equity and good conscience."[1] To benefit from this provision, a claimant must request a waiver. Following this request, the SSA must provide an oral hearing[2] at which the claimant can present evidence that the overpayments were not the claimant's fault and that it would violate equity and good conscience or defeat the purpose of the Social Security Act to recover these overpayments from the claimant.

§ 15.65 Overpayments—Without Fault—In General

In determining whether a person is at fault, the Social Security Administration (SSA) considers all relevant circumstances, including the person's age, intelligence, education, physical and mental condition, and language difficulty.[1] The SSA considers a person to be at fault if:

1. The person has given the SSA an incorrect statement concerning eligibility for benefits or amount of benefits that the person knew (or should have known) to be incorrect;[2]

2. The person failed to give the SSA information the person knew (or should have known) to be important;[3] or

3. The person accepted a payment that the person knew (or should have known) was incorrect.[4]

Furthermore, the SSA may consider a person to be at fault even though the SSA itself was partially to blame for the overpayment.

It is important to provide the SSA with a plausible explanation of why the error occurred. Examples of circumstances that have been held not to be the fault of the recipient include reliance upon erroneous information from an official source with the SSA with respect to an interpretation of the Social Security Act or regulations,[5] reasonable

§ 15.64

1. 42 U.S.C.A. § 404(b); 20 C.F.R. § 404.506.

2. Califano v. Yamasaki, 442 U.S. 682, 99 S.Ct. 2545, 61 L.Ed.2d 176, *on remand* 607 F.2d 329 (9th Cir.1979) (the Supreme Court held that an oral hearing is necessary to guard against error in deciding issues regarding recoupment and that a claimant is entitled to an oral hearing prior to recoupment).

§ 15.65

1. 20 C.F.R. § 404.507.

2. 20 C.F.R. § 404.507(a).

3. 20 C.F.R. § 404.507(b).

4. 20 C.F.R. § 404.507(c).

5. 20 C.F.R. § 404.510(b). See Michalak v. Weinberger, 416 F.Supp. 1213 (S.D.Tex.1976). See Valente v. Secretary of Health and Human Services, 733 F.2d 1037, 5 Soc.Sec.Rep.Ser. 125 (2d Cir.1984)

belief that only take-home pay is used to compute compliance with the retirement test,[6] mistakes in computing earnings resulting from inaccurate reporting by the employer,[7] and earnings at a higher rate than expected.[8]

The burden of proving "without fault" is always on the claimant, so credibility is important.

§ 15.66   Overpayments—Without Fault—Recovery Against Equity and Good Conscience

Even if one establishes that one was not at fault in receiving an overpayment, the Social Security Administration (SSA) will seek to recover the overpayments unless one also establishes that such a recovery would be "against equity and good conscience" or that the "purpose of [the Social Security Act]" would be defeated by a recovery. Repayment of social security benefits is against equity and good conscience when a person has given up a valuable right or has changed his or her financial position for the worse in reliance upon receiving the benefits that now are alleged to have been improperly paid.[1]

The individual must establish that he or she relied, to his or her financial detriment, upon the correctness of the SSA's determination of the individual's entitlement to benefits. An example of such reliance is a person who quits a job after being notified of entitlement to retirement benefits and is now unable to find employment.[2] Another example is a widow who, having been awarded benefits for herself and her daughter, enrolls her daughter in a private school because the monthly benefits make this possible. If the SSA determines, a year later, that the deceased worker was not insured and that all payments were incorrect, recovery from the widow would not be in equity and good conscience, since she has incurred a financial obligation in reliance on continued receipt of the benefits.[3]

The critical ingredient in establishing that recovery would be against equity and good conscience is that one has changed one's

(the court remanded for SSA's reconsideration of finding of fault where Chat's wife testified SSA advised her to cash check and the administrative law judge made no finding that she was not credible).

6. 20 C.F.R. § 404.510(a).

7. 20 C.F.R. § 404.510(f)(3).

8. 20 C.F.R. § 404.510(f)(2).

§ 15.66

1. 42 U.S.C.A. § 404(b); 20 C.F.R. § 404.509. One court has extended the

meaning of "against equity and good conscience" to include situations in which the insured had no knowledge that benefits were being incorrectly paid. Groseclose v. Bowen, 809 F.2d 502, 16 Soc.Sec.Rep.Ser. 151 (8th Cir.1987) (daughter who lived away from home received incorrectly paid benefits). Accord, 20 C.F.R. § 404.509 (example 4).

2. 20 C.F.R. § 404.509 (example 2).

3. 20 C.F.R. § 404.509 (example 1).

financial situation for the worse in reliance upon the correctness of payments or was unaware that someone else received incorrect payments on the same work record. Financial worth is not a critical ingredient in this determination.

§ 15.67 Overpayments—Without Fault—Recovery Defeating Purpose of Social Security Act

Another way to avoid repaying an overpaid amount is to establish that recovery of the overpayment would "defeat the purpose of Title II of the Social Security Act."[1] The purpose of the act is to provide necessary income to retirees, disabled workers, and their dependents and survivors. If an individual can establish that he or she has limited income and assets and needs continued payment of social security benefits to meet the ordinary and necessary expenses of life, recovery will be inappropriate.[2] To establish need for continued payment of benefits, a person should provide the Social Security Administration (SSA) with a statement of living expenses such as food, clothing, rent, mortgage payments, utility payments, medical expenses, and other necessary expenses of living.[3] Once it has been established that payment of benefits is essential to meeting the individual's necessary expenses, the purpose of the act would be defeated were the person required to repay the overpaid amount.

A person unable to establish that recovery should not take place may nevertheless be able to persuade the SSA to recover the overpayment over a period of time by deducting a small amount each month from the monthly benefits. The SSA may spread out the repayment if withholding the full amount each month would defeat the purpose of Title II, that is, if the individual is dependent on social security benefits as the primary source of income. However, these partial deductions must be made within a reasonable time period, and the overpayment cannot have been the product of willful false statements or misrepresentation.[4]

§ 15.68 Underpayments

If an individual to whom an underpayment is due is living, the amount of the underpayment will be paid to the individual in a single payment or by increasing one or more monthly benefits or a lump sum

---

§ 15.67

1. 42 U.S.C.A. § 404(b); 20 C.F.R. § 404.508(b).

2. See, e.g., Sierakowski v. Weinberger, 504 F.2d 831 (6th Cir.1974); Hatfield v. Richardson, 380 F.Supp. 1048 (D.Kan. 1974).

3. 20 C.F.R. § 404.508.

4. 20 C.F.R. § 404.502(c).

death payment to which the individual is or becomes entitled.[1] If an individual to whom an underpayment is due dies before receiving payment, the underpayment will be distributed to the deceased's spouse, children, or parents in the order of priority set forth in 42 U.S.C.A. § 404(d).

§ 15.69   Lost Checks and Returned Benefits

In cases where the post office cannot deliver a monthly check, either because a recipient has moved or for any other reason, the check will be returned to Social Security. If the beneficiary has the benefits directly deposited into a bank, the bank will return the money to Social Security if the account has been closed. These returned benefits become an underpayment.

A recipient should notify the Social Security Administration (SSA) of an underpayment or lost check by the fourth day after it was due. The SSA will ask for the Social Security number under which the benefit is paid, the name and address of the recipient, and the month for which a reduced payment or no payment was received. To illustrate, a person expecting to receive a check for March benefits on April 3 can report it as missing on or after April 7th. Recipients usually receive replacement checks within two weeks of the initial report. In addition, SSA will make an "expedited benefit payment" when the conditions described in 20 C.F.R. § 404.1810(c) are met.

§§ 15.70–15.80 are reserved for supplementary material.

E.   APPLICATION FOR AND RECEIPT OF BENEFITS

Library References:

C.J.S. Social Security and Public Welfare § 34.
West's Key No. Digests, Social Security and Public Welfare ☞124.16.

§ 15.81   Filing Process—Where to File

Applications are filed at a Social Security Administration (SSA) District Office, but applications are not considered filed until the district office actually receives the application. The application may be filed in person or by phone; most district offices schedule appointments to eliminate lengthy waiting.

Some applications, although not filed at an SSA District Office, nevertheless will be treated as valid applications. Examples include

§ 15.68
1. 42 U.S.C.A. § 404(a)(1)(B); 20 C.F.R. § 404.503(a).

applications for retirement or survivor's benefits filed with the Railroad Retirement Board or the Veteran's Administration.[1]

§ 15.82 Filing Process—Who Can File

Generally an application must be filed by the individual claiming benefits. Although an applicant may accept assistance in completing the application, the applicant is required to sign it. However, if a person is mentally or physically incapable of signing an application, a legal guardian, caregiver, or other interested person may complete and sign the application. Where the claimant is in the care of an institution and is not mentally competent or physically able to execute an application, the manager or principal officer of the institution may execute the application.[1]

When the application is executed by a person other than the claimant, that person must, at the time of filing the application or within a reasonable time thereafter, file evidence of authority to execute the application on behalf of the claimant. If the person executing the application is the legally appointed guardian, committee, or other legal representative, the evidence should be a certificate executed by the proper official of the court of appointment. If the person executing the application is not such a legal representative, the evidence should be a statement describing the person's relationship to the claimant. Except in the case of a child living with a parent, the statement should also include a description of the extent to which the person is responsible for the care of the claimant.[2]

§ 15.83 Filing Process—Written Statement Considered Application

When an individual files a written statement such as a letter with the Social Security Administration (SSA) indicating an intention to claim monthly benefits or a lump sum death payment, or to establish a period of disability, and that statement bears the individual's signature or the individual's mark properly witnessed, the statement is considered to be the filing of an application. However, for the statement to continue to be effective as an application on the date the statement was filed, the individual must file a prescribed application form within six months of that date. The SSA will send the individual a notice advising the individual of the need to file an application within six

§ 15.81

1. 20 C.F.R. § 404.611(c).

§ 15.82

1. 20 C.F.R. § 404.612. To protect a claimant from losing benefits, when there is good cause for the claimant not signing the application, SSA may accept an application from another, such as a neighbor. Id.

2. 20 C.F.R. § 404.613.

months. If a prescribed application form is not filed within six months, the filing of the written statement will not be considered the filing of an application.[1] A telephone inquiry stating an intent to file for benefits will be treated as a written statement to prevent loss of benefits if the individual cannot file an application before the end of the month.[2]

§ 15.84 Filing Process—When to File

Generally, those filing for retirement, wife's, husband's, widow's, or widower's benefits are not entitled to benefits before the month in which the application is filed unless they meet certain exceptions.[1] Furthermore, persons who delay in filing for benefits for which they are eligible may forfeit some benefits due for the months or years before application. For example, the Social Security Administration (SSA) allows a maximum of six months of retroactive benefits to an applicant for retirement and survivor's benefits who files any time after the first month for which the person would have been entitled to the benefits.[2] As a consequence, benefit applications should be filed promptly. In addition, a time limit exists on filing applications for certain benefits.

An application for a lump sum death payment must be filed within two years of the date of death of the individual upon whose wages and self-employment income the lump sum claim is filed.[3] An application for disability benefits on the record of a deceased person who could have been entitled to disability but for the person's death must be filed within three months of the disabled individual's death.[4]

§ 15.85 Filing Process—Evidence to File With Application— Overview

The applicant has the burden of establishing eligibility for social security benefits, so the applicant must submit evidence of eligibility. The Social Security Administration (SSA) regulations specify certain evidence as "preferred." If submitted, such evidence will be accepted as "convincing" evidence of the fact asserted and no further evidence will be needed unless SSA records raise a doubt about the evidence. If "preferred" evidence is unavailable, other evidence may be submitted

§ 15.83
1. 20 C.F.R. § 404.630(c).
2. 20 C.F.R. § 404.630(b).

§ 15.84
1. 20 C.F.R. § 404.621(a)(1)(iii).

2. 42 U.S.C.A. § 402(j); 20 C.F.R. § 404.621(a).

3. 20 C.F.R. § 404.621(b).

4. 20 C.F.R. § 404.621(e).

and may be found "convincing" either alone or in combination with other evidence.[1]

The Evidence Usually Required to Be Submitted to the Social Security Administration in Claims for Monthly Benefits or the Lump–Sum Death Payment

		Evidence to be submitted by claimant						
		Relationship						
Beneficiary	Age	Marriage	Divorce	Parent-child	Dependency or support	School attendance	Child in care	Death of a worker
Insured person	X							
Spouse (62 or over)	X	X						
Spouse under 62 (child in care)		X					X	
Divorced spouse (62 or over)	X	X	X					
Child	X			X	X	X		In survivor claims
Widow(er) (60 or over, 50 or over if disabled)	X	X						X
Surviving divorced spouse	X	X	X					X
Widow(er) under 62 or surviving divorced mother or father (child in care)		X	X	X			X	X
Parent	X			X	X			X
Lump-sum death payment: A. Surviving spouse living in same household		X						X
B. Eligible surviving spouse, excluding divorced spouse	X	X						X
C. Eligible children	X			X	X	X		X

Source: Social Security Handbook, 10th edition (1988), p. 258. This is merely a summary of requirements. See text for details.

§ 15.86   Filing Process—Evidence to File With Application—Age

An applicant for retirement, wife's, husband's, widow's, or widower's benefits should file supporting evidence showing the date of birth if the applicant's age is a condition of entitlement or is otherwise relevant to the payment of such benefits. "Preferred evidence" is a birth certificate or hospital record established before age five, or a religious record showing date of birth that was established before age five.[1] Other acceptable evidence of age includes: a family bible record, school records, census records, the applicant's child's birth record, voter's records, or passports.[2]

If there is a conflict in establishing age—some documents indicating one age, others another age—the applicant should attempt to corroborate the applicant's claim with as many documents and statements as possible. In general, the Social Security Administration (SSA)

§ 15.85
1. 20 C.F.R. §§ 404.703–404.709.

§ 15.86
1. 20 C.F.R. § 404.716(a).

2. 20 C.F.R. § 404.716(b).

gives more weight to old documents than to recent documents.[3] However, in one case in which an age dispute arose, SSA determined the claimant was 61 based on her original birth certificate, a census record, and her son's birth certificate, even though she submitted a corrected birth certificate showing her age as 62. But the court reversed SSA, discounting the census record because of errors on its face, and holding that the correction on the birth certificate must be given full faith and credit.[4]

§ 15.87 Filing Process—Evidence to File With Application— Death

An applicant for monthly benefits or a lump sum death payment based upon the earnings of a deceased individual must file supporting evidence of the death of that individual including the time and place of the death. The applicant should furnish:[1]

1. a certified copy of the public record of death, coroner's report, or verdict of the coroner's jury of the state or community where death occurred;

2. a statement of the funeral director, attending physician, or intern of the institution where death occurred; or

3. a certified copy of an official report or finding of death made by an agency or department of the United States that is authorized to make such a report or finding.

If this evidence cannot be obtained, the applicant should state the reason and submit the signed statements of two or more persons having personal knowledge of the death, setting forth the facts and circumstances regarding the place, date, cause of death, and other evidence of probative value. Furthermore, if an individual has been absent without explanation from the individual's residence and unheard of for seven years, the Social Security Administration (SSA), upon satisfactory establishment of those facts and in the absence of any evidence to the contrary, will presume that the individual has died.[2]

§ 15.88 Filing Process—Evidence to File With Application— Marriage

A spouse or surviving spouse applying for benefits is required to submit proof of marriage. The type of evidence required to prove marriage depends upon whether there was a valid ceremonial mar-

---

3. Social Security Handbook, supra § 15.1, note 1, at 238–44.

4. Bennett v. Schweiker, 532 F.Supp. 837 (D.D.C.1982).

§ 15.87

1. 20 C.F.R. § 404.720.

2. 20 C.F.R. § 404.721.

riage, a common law marriage, or a marriage that the Social Security Administration (SSA) deems to be valid.[1] The law of the state where the insured person was domiciled is used to determine the validity of a marriage.[2]

When a couple follows the procedures set by law in the state where the marriage takes place, a valid ceremonial marriage exists. If the applicant is applying for wife's or husband's benefits, both the insured and the spouse should submit signed statements telling where and when the marriage took place. Such statements are preferred evidence.[3] If the claimant is applying for a lump sum death payment, the surviving spouse should submit a signed statement telling the time and place of the marriage. If preferred evidence is not available, convincing evidence such as the signed statement of the official who performed the marriage may be submitted.[4]

If there is evidence that raises doubt about whether there was a ceremonial marriage, a wife, husband, widow, or widower who applies for monthly benefits or for a lump sum death payment based upon the earnings of a husband, wife, deceased husband, or deceased wife, may be requested to submit supporting evidence of the time and place of marriage, such as an original certificate of marriage or a certified copy of the public or church record of the marriage. If these records are not available, an affidavit signed by the person who performed the marriage ceremony or statements from persons who witnessed the marriage may serve as proof of marriage.[5] Evidence may also be required as to the termination of any former marriage.

Some states recognize common law marriages. A common law marriage will be accepted by the SSA as a valid marriage if the state in which the agreement was made recognizes such marriages.[6] If the SSA requires proof of a common law marriage, such proof may be established in the following ways.[7] If both husband and wife are living, each should submit an affidavit confirming the agreement to live together as husband and wife, and each should obtain a statement from a blood relative confirming the agreement. If one spouse is no longer living, the surviving spouse should submit an affidavit attesting the marriage and should obtain statements from two persons with knowledge of the marriage, preferably blood relatives of the deceased spouse.

§ 15.88

1. 20 C.F.R. § 404.723.
2. Id.
3. 20 C.F.R. § 404.725.
4. 20 C.F.R. § 404.725.

5. 20 C.F.R. § 404.725.
6. 20 C.F.R. § 404.726.
7. Id.

If state procedures are not properly followed and no common law marriage exists, the SSA may still find a deemed valid marriage. Preferred evidence of a deemed valid marriage includes: [8]

1. evidence of a ceremonial marriage;

2. if the insured person is alive, a signed statement from that person which states that the other party had reason to believe that the marriage was valid;

3. a signed statement from the other party stating his or her reasons for believing the marriage was valid;

4. the signed statements of others showing that the other party went through the marriage in good faith; or

5. evidence that the two parties were living together at the time of application, if the insured is living, or at the time of death if the insured is deceased.

If preferred evidence is not available, other evidence may be submitted.

A divorced spouse who applies for benefits based upon the earnings of a deceased former spouse will be requested to submit supporting evidence of the marriage to that individual and of the divorce from the spouse.[9] Preferred evidence of divorce or annulment is a certified copy of the divorce decree or annulment. If these documents are not available, other convincing evidence may be submitted.

§ 15.89 Filing Process—Evidence to File With Application— Parental Relationship

When an individual is applying for parent's or child's benefits, the individual must submit evidence showing the individual's relationship to the insured person. The evidence required depends on whether the relationship to the insured is that of natural parent, natural child, stepparent, stepchild, grandchild, stepgrandchild, adopting parent, or adopted child.[1]

An individual claiming benefits for the natural child of the insured must establish parentage.[2] If the child was born while the parents were married, a birth or baptismal certificate will suffice. If, however, the child was born out of wedlock, parentage can be established by submitting one of the following documents: a written acknowledgment of paternity by the insured, a court decree declaring that the insured is the parent of the child, or a court decree ordering the insured to support the child because he is the child's father. If none of these

---

8. 20 C.F.R. § 404.727.

9. 20 C.F.R. § 404.728.

§ 15.89

1. 20 C.F.R. § 404.730.

2. 20 C.F.R. § 404.731.

documents are available, other evidence that the insured is or was the parent of the child and lived with the child or contributed to the child's support can be submitted.

A written acknowledgment of parentage by the insured can be an income tax return listing the child, a will referring to the child as his, an application for insurance naming the child as his, or a letter acknowledging parentage. If a court decree of paternity is used, the decree must identify the worker and the child and must include a specific finding of paternity. If a court order for support is used, the order must identify the child and the insured as the parent and must direct the worker to contribute to the child's support.

Other evidence might include hospital, church, or school records; court orders not meeting the requirements just mentioned; or statements from physicians, relatives, or others acknowledging the relationship between the child and the insured. Such statements should include the basis for the person's knowledge of the relationship. Evidence that the insured and the child's parent were living together when the child was conceived is also relevant. Another way to establish eligibility is to demonstrate that the child could inherit the insured's (i.e., the parent's) personal property in the state where the parent has his permanent home at the time the child applies for benefits, if the parent dies without a will. If the parent is deceased, the SSA will look at the laws that were in effect at the time the parent died in the state where the parent had his permanent home.[3]

An example of sufficient evidence of paternity to determine that a child born out of wedlock was eligible for survivor's benefits can be found in the case of *Becker v. Secretary of Health & Human Services.*[4] In *Becker,* the court found clear and convincing evidence that the child's mother and the insured were living together at the time the child was conceived, the insured stated that he was the child's father, he helped to support the child monetarily, and he had visited the child. The court found eligibility even though the insured had undergone a vasectomy prior to the child's birth that he later attempted to have reversed and his relationship with the child's mother had been stormy.

The United States Courts of Appeals are divided regarding whether an acknowledgment of paternity is sufficient to establish a child's eligibility for benefits. In *Luke v. Bowen,*[5] the Eighth Circuit held that a child seeking surviving child's insurance benefits must be the biological child of the wage earner to be eligible. However, in *Patterson v.*

---

3. 20 C.F.R. §§ 404.354–.355.

4. 895 F.2d 34, 28 Soc.Sec.Rep.Ser. 444 (1st Cir.1990).

5. 868 F.2d 974, 25 Soc.Sec.Rep.Ser. 35 (8th Cir.1989).

Bowen, the Fourth Circuit held that a father's voluntary admission that he is the child's father is sufficient.[6]

A case in which the court held that a child born out of wedlock was not eligible for child's benefits is *Kinney v. Sullivan.*[7] Even though the putative father acknowledged that the child was his, the court found the child ineligible because the mother failed to show that the child would be entitled to share in the putative father's property under Oklahoma's law of intestate succession. In addition, the putative father did not treat the child as his own.

An individual seeking benefits for an adopted child must submit a copy of the court decree of adoption or a copy of the amended birth certificate issued after the adoption.[8]

When benefits are sought for a stepchild, an individual may need to establish that the child is the natural or adopted child of the spouse of the insured and prove that the child's parent is validly married to the insured.

To obtain child's benefits for a grandchild, it is necessary to demonstrate that the grandchild was living with and receiving support from the grandparent and that the child's parents were dead or disabled when the grandparent became eligible for social security benefits or—in the case of survivor's benefits—that the grandchild has been adopted by the surviving grandparent.

§ 15.90   Filing Process—Estoppel

Generally, Social Security Administration (SSA) employees give accurate advice to the elderly about eligibility for benefits. However, errors sometimes are made and those receiving advice should be wary. Although a reasonable person might believe that an agency would be bound by the advice of its employees, the Supreme Court has ruled repeatedly that a person harmed by erroneous advice may not estop the agency from disavowing advice that is inconsistent with the statute governing the agency.[1]

---

6. Patterson v. Bowen, 839 F.2d 221, 20 Soc.Sec.Rep.Ser. 495 (4th Cir.1988).

7. 746 F.Supp. 1067, 31 Soc.Sec.Rep.Ser. 406 (W.D.Okl.1990).

8. Children who are adopted after the worker has become entitled to benefits must meet a special dependency test. 42 U.S.C.A. § 416(e), (h); 20 C.F.R. § 404.-362(b).

denied 451 U.S. 1032, 101 S.Ct. 3023, 69 L.Ed.2d 401 (1981); Heckler v. Community Health Services, 467 U.S. 51, 104 S.Ct. 2218, 81 L.Ed.2d 42, 5 Soc.Sec.Rep.Ser. 29 (1984); Office of Personnel Management v. Richmond, 496 U.S. 414, 110 S.Ct. 2465, 110 L.Ed.2d 387, *rehearing denied* 497 U.S. 1046, 111 S.Ct. 5, 111 L.Ed.2d 821 (1990).

§ 15.90

1. Schweiker v. Hansen, 450 U.S. 785, 101 S.Ct. 1468, 67 L.Ed.2d 685, *rehearing*

The importance of not relying upon informal employee advice regarding eligibility for benefits can be seen from *Schweiker v. Hanson,*[2] a case that involved a woman who inquired whether she was eligible for "mother's insurance benefits." An SSA employee erroneously told her that she was not eligible. The woman left the SSA office without filing a written application. Subsequently, after learning that she was in fact eligible, she filed a written application. She received retroactive benefits only from the date of her written application, not from the date of the oral inquiry. The Supreme Court upheld denial of retroactive payments to the date of original inquiry, stating that the SSA worker's error did not excuse the woman's failure to file a written application.

To protect claimants from harm resulting from erroneous advice concerning eligibility for benefits, the Social Security Act provides that benefits may be paid to a claimant misinformed about eligibility for benefits from the date of such misinformation if the Secretary is satisfied that the failure to apply resulted from the misinformation.[3] This statute only partially alleviates the Court's harsh estoppel doctrine. Clients may be harmed by erroneous advice in a variety of circumstances. To avoid such harm, one should confirm the accuracy of oral advice and insist that an initial determination be rendered on matters affecting benefit eligibility or amount, thereby preserving a right to appeal agency errors.

§ 15.91   Application Accepted

At the conclusion of the interview where an application has been accepted, the applicant should be given a receipt stating the name of the interviewer/adjudicator and phone numbers for follow-up questions. The applicant will be notified by an "award letter" when the application has been approved. The letter will state the amount of the recipient's regular monthly payment and the time when the first payment will be made. The first payment includes all the benefits a recipient is entitled to for the period between the date of the application and the date of the award.

Award letters often are not sent, however, and thus overpayments may not be detected. Recipients often assume that the Social Security Administration (SSA) is sending them a check for the correct amount. However, for purposes of finding "fault" and "cause" in an overpayment hearing, SSA contends that the recipient has the responsibility

---

2. 450 U.S. 785, 101 S.Ct. 1468, 67 L.Ed.2d 685 (1981), *rehearing denied* 451 U.S. 1032, 101 S.Ct. 3023, 69 L.Ed.2d 401 (1981).

3. 42 U.S.C.A. § 402(j)(5); see also 57 Fed.Reg. 47,415, 58 Fed.Reg. 5687 (proposed regulations implementing § 402(j)(5)).

for verifying the correct amount of the check.[1] As noted in § 15.90 supra, the clients should be instructed not to trust an anonymous voice on the telephone at the local office who assures the client that the check is correct. If there is a question, the client should request written confirmation.

§ 15.92 Receipt of Benefits—Mailing of Benefit Check

Monthly benefit checks are usually mailed for receipt on the third day of the month following the month for which payment is due. For example, checks for January are received on February 3.[1]

Monthly benefit payments to a husband and wife who are entitled to benefits on the same social security record and are living at the same address are usually combined in one check made out to them jointly.[2] However, individual checks will be sent to a husband and wife upon request.

Library References:

C.J.S. Social Security and Public Welfare § 47.

West's Key No. Digests, Social Security and Public Welfare ☞140.3.

§ 15.93 Receipt of Benefits—Direct Deposit of Check

A social security beneficiary may elect to have the benefit check mailed directly to a bank, savings and loan association, credit union, or other financial institution. This election may be made at the initial interview or anytime thereafter by calling the local district office. Direct deposit may be advantageous to the beneficiary, since it diminishes the possibility of loss, is more convenient, and provides assurance that deposits will be uninterrupted during periods of absence or temporary relocation.[1]

§ 15.94 Receipt of Benefits—Representative Payee

Social Security presumes that each adult beneficiary is capable of handling his or her own funds.[1] However, where there is competent medical, legal, or lay evidence that a beneficiary is legally incompetent or mentally or physically incapable of managing his or her affairs, the Social Security Administration (SSA) may determine that it is in the

§ 15.91
1. But see 42 C.F.R. § 404.510a.

§ 15.92
1. Social Security Handbook, supra § 15.1, note 1, at § 131.
2. 20 C.F.R. § 404.1825(a).

§ 15.93
1. Social Security Handbook, supra § 15.1, note 1, at § 134.

§ 15.94
1. 20 C.F.R. § 404.2001(b).

beneficiary's best interest that payment be made to a "representative payee."[2]

A representative payee must apply these payments exclusively for the use and benefit of the beneficiary. The SSA considers the payments used properly when they are spent on the beneficiary's "current maintenance," which includes food, shelter, clothing, medical care, and personal comfort items.[3]

Although SSA intended that the representative payee system benefit recipients, problems in the system have undermined its effectiveness and harmed beneficiaries. Such problems have included the selection of inappropriate representative payees, lack of adequate monitoring of payee performance, and procedural deficiencies in the process by which payees have been selected, including inadequate opportunity for beneficiaries to object to the appointment or identity of a payee.[4]

Congress in 1990 changed the Social Security Act[5] so that now all representative payee applicants must submit proof of their identity, and SSA staff must conduct a face-to-face interview with the applicant. The Agency must verify the applicant's social security number, inquire about employment or other sources of income, and inquire about any prior experience as a representative payee and whether that arrangement was terminated due to misuse of funds.[6]

In the selection of a payee, preference is given to the beneficiary's legal guardian, spouse, or family who have custody of the beneficiary or who demonstrate concern for the beneficiary. Friends satisfying these requirements may serve as representative payees, as may nonprofit organizations or residential facilities.[7] The SSA has ruled that qualified organizations serving as representative payees may collect a monthly fee from the disability beneficiary for expenses incurred in providing representative services.[8] A creditor of a beneficiary who provides the beneficiary with goods or services usually will not qualify as a representative payee.[9]

2. 20 C.F.R. §§ 404.2001, 404.2010.

3. 20 C.F.R. § 404.2040.

4. See generally, Komlos–Hrobsky, Representative Payee Issues in the Social Security and Supplemental Security Income Programs, 23 Clearinghouse Rev. 412 (1989); Stiegel, Proposed Solutions to Social Security Representative Payee Problems, 24 Clearinghouse Rev. 570 (1990).

5. Pub.L. No. 101–508, § 5105, 104 Stat. 1388–254, codified at 42 U.S.C.A. § 405(j).

6. 42 U.S.C.A. § 405(j)(2)(A), (B).

7. 20 C.F.R. § 404.2021.

8. 20 C.F.R. §§ 404.903, 404.2040a, 416.-640a, 416.1403.

9. A creditor may receive benefits, however, if creditor is a relative residing with beneficiary, a legal guardian or legal representative, a licensed care facility, an administrator in a licensed care facility, or a creditor with the Secretary's approval. 42 U.S.C.A. § 405(j)(2)(C)(iii).

The SSA must notify the beneficiary in advance of both the decision to send payments to the representative payee and the name of the potential representative. The beneficiary may object either to the need for an appointment or to the choice of the representative.[10] The Secretary is to review the objection and any additional evidence and make a determination.[11] If a beneficiary is not satisfied with the determination, the beneficiary may request a hearing with the Secretary.[12] The beneficiary also is entitled to judicial review of the Secretary's final decision.[13]

To avoid misuse of funds by the representative payee, the Secretary is required to keep a centralized file of all past and present representative payees that includes information about any past misuse of funds.[14] In addition, the Secretary is required to establish a system of monitoring representative payees under which payees are to report annually regarding their use of payments.[15] The Secretary may require that any representative provide an accounting if misuse of funds is suspected.[16] Misuse of funds results in the suspension of payment to that representative and appointment of another.[17] If the Secretary's negligence in selecting or monitoring a representative payee results in misuse of funds, the Secretary is to pay the beneficiary or new representative payee an amount equal to the misused funds and attempt to recover the misused funds from the former payee.[18]

If the Secretary determines that payment to the selected representative payee would result in substantial harm to the beneficiary, payment shall be suspended until a new representative is certified. To avoid substantial hardship to the beneficiary, payments may not be suspended for more than one month. After a month, the payments will go directly to the beneficiary until a new representative is found.[19]

§ 15.95 Receipt of Benefits—Attachment of Social Security Benefits

The Social Security Act, § 407, prohibits the transfer or assignment to any person of any future social security benefits and provides that "none of the monies paid or payable . . . shall be subject to execution levy, attachment, garnishment, or other legal process, or to

---

10. 20 C.F.R. § 404.2030(a).

11. 20 C.F.R. § 404.2030(b).

12. 20 C.F.R. § 404.2030(b).

13. 42 U.S.C.A. § 405(j)(2)(E).

14. 42 U.S.C.A. § 405(j)(2)(B)(ii).

15. 42 U.S.C.A. § 405(j)(3)(A).

16. 42 U.S.C.A. § 405(j)(3)(E).

17. 42 U.S.C.A. § 1383(a)(2)(III).

18. 42 U.S.C.A. § 405(j)(5).

19. 42 U.S.C.A. § 405(j)(2)(D).

the operation of any bankruptcy or insolvency law."[1] Therefore, a creditor cannot garnish or attach social security benefits.

The rule against attachment extends to money of a recipient that can be traced directly to social security checks, such as money in a bank account.[2] However, goods such as a car or a television paid for by a recipient's social security benefits may be attached by a creditor.

In 1973, the Supreme Court applied the rule forbidding attachment of social security benefits to creditors that are state or local governments.[3] Similarly, the Court invalidated an Arkansas statute that allowed the state to attach a prisoner's estate in order to help defray the cost of maintaining its prison system as barred by § 407.[4]

The Social Security Administration (SSA) has attempted to invoke § 407 to escape the operation of the bankruptcy laws, but the courts have held that the section does not immunize SSA from complying with orders issued by a bankruptcy court. Thus, SSA's right to recover overpayment of benefits has been held to be discharged in a Chapter 7 proceeding,[5] and SSA has been required to forward social security benefits to a trustee in bankruptcy in a voluntary Chapter 13 proceeding.[6]

Important exceptions to the rule that social security benefits cannot be attached are proceedings to enforce a court order obligating a recipient to pay child support or alimony,[7] or to collect back taxes owed to the United States.[8] In addition, § 407 does not forbid a state from taxing income attributable to social security.[9] And courts have allowed

§ 15.95

1. 42 U.S.C.A. § 407.

2. Finberg v. Sullivan, 634 F.2d 50 (3d Cir.1980).

3. Philpott v. Essex County Welfare Board, 409 U.S. 413, 93 S.Ct. 590, 34 L.Ed.2d 608 (1973) (the Court ruled that a county welfare department could not sue a social security recipient to recover welfare payments made to the recipient even though the recipient had promised the welfare he would repay them if he was declared eligible for social security benefits).

4. Bennett v. Arkansas, 485 U.S. 395, 108 S.Ct. 1204, 99 L.Ed.2d 455, 21 Soc.Sec. Rep.Ser. 3 (1988), *on remand* 295 Ark. 472, 748 S.W.2d 668 (1988); see also Brinkman v. Rahm, 878 F.2d 263, 26 Soc.Sec.Rep.Ser. 198 (9th Cir.1989) (Social Security Act preempts Washington's effort to obtain reimbursement for involuntarily committed mental patient); but see Fetterusso v. State of N.Y., 898 F.2d 322 (2d Cir.1990) (voluntary payment for mental health services does not violate Social Security Act).

5. Rowan v. Morgan, 747 F.2d 1052, 7 Soc.Sec.Rep.Ser. 219 (6th Cir.1984).

6. United States v. Devall, 704 F.2d 1513, 1 Soc.Sec.Rep.Ser. 389 (11th Cir.), *rehearing denied* 714 F.2d 1068 (1983).

7. 42 U.S.C.A. § 659; see e.g., Kirk v. Kirk, 577 A.2d 976 (R.I.1990).

8. 26 U.S.C.A. § 6331.

9. Boersma v. Karnes, 227 Neb. 329, 417 N.W.2d 341, 20 Soc.Sec.Rep.Ser. 433, appeal dismissed 488 U.S. 801, 109 S.Ct. 29, 102 L.Ed.2d 9 (1988).

payments from the estates of social security recipients.[10]

§ 15.96 Taxation of Social Security Benefits

A social security beneficiary who receives income in addition to social security benefits will have to pay federal income tax on a portion of his or her Social Security benefits if his or her income exceeds the following base amounts:

1. $25,000 for an individual ($34,000 beginning January 1, 1994);

2. $25,000 for a married individual who did not file a joint return and did not live with his or her spouse at any time during the entire taxable year ($34,000 beginning in 1994);

3. $32,000 for a married couple who filed a joint return ($44,000 beginning in 1994); and

4. $0 for a married individual who did not file a joint return but who did live with his or her spouse at any time during the entire taxable year.[1]

A beneficiary's income attributable to social security is taxable if the adjusted gross income combined with 50% of the social security benefits plus any tax-exempt interest and certain Foreign-source income exceeds the base amount.

Through 1993, up to 50% of an individual's Social Security (or Tier 1 Rail Road Retirement) benefits are subject to federal income tax at ordinary tax rates. Beginning in 1994, up to 85% of these benefits are subject to federal income tax at ordinary tax rates.

For example, John Ash, who is single, received $8,000 in social security benefits in 1993. His adjusted gross income for 1993 was $24,000. He received $2,000 in tax exempt interest. The calculations for 1993 are as follows (the calculations will be different beginning in 1994):

1. Total net benefits for year (the amount shown in Box 5 of Form SSA–1099 and Box 5 of Form RRB–1099 or, if a claimant received more than one form, the total amount of the amounts in Box 5 of each form) . . . . $ 8,000
2. One-half of line 1 amount . . . . $ 4,000

---

10. See, e.g., Matter of Estate of Vary, 401 Mich. 340, 258 N.W.2d 11 (1977), *cert. denied* 434 U.S. 1087, 98 S.Ct. 1283, 55 L.Ed.2d 793 (1978); Conservatorship of Estate of Lambert, 143 Cal.App.3d 239, 191 Cal.Rptr. 725, 2 Soc.Sec.Rep.Ser. 1311 (1983).

§ 15.96

1. 26 U.S.C.A. § 86 as amended by § 14.215 of the Omnibus Budget Reconciliation Act of 1993, Pub.L. No. 103–66, 107 Stat. 312; Internal Revenue Service Publication 915, Social Security Benefits and equivalent Railroad Retirement Benefits (1991).

3.	Modified adjusted gross income (the sum of the claimant's adjusted gross income plus any tax-exempt interest received in the entire taxable year)	$26,000
4.	Add amounts on lines 2 and 3	$30,000
5.	Base amount	$25,000
6.	Subtract line 5 amount from line 4 amount	$ 5,000
7.	One-half of line 6 amount	$ 2,500
8.	Taxable benefit is the smaller of line 2 amount or line 7 amount	$ 2,500.

When determining what to count as social security benefits for income tax purposes, a beneficiary can use the figure in Box 5 of the Form SSA–1099 that each social security beneficiary receives or determine it manually. The beneficiary should count benefits actually received (after reductions for early retirement or because of the family maximum or retirement test). Amounts deducted from disability benefits under the workers' compensation offset, Medicare premium deductions, and amounts withheld to recover an overpayment are included as benefits received for purposes of the income tax.

Library References:

C.J.S. Internal Revenue §§ 76–83; Taxation §§ 1090, 1091.
West's Key No. Digests, Internal Revenue ⊆3119; Taxation ⊆933.

§§ 15.97–15.100 are reserved for supplementary material.

F. APPEAL PROCESS IN SOCIAL SECURITY ADMINISTRATION

Library References:

C.J.S. Social Security and Public Welfare §§ 73–79.
West's Key No. Digests, Social Security and Public Welfare ⊆142.5, 145.

§ 15.101 Appeal of Decisions Affecting Benefits—Overview [1]

The first stage of decision-making in the Social Security System is the initial determination. If a client is dissatisfied with an initial determination, the first level of appeal to seek is reconsideration of the initial determination. A person dissatisfied with the reconsideration determination may seek a hearing before an administrative law judge (ALJ). An appeal of the decision of the ALJ lies with the Appeals Council, an appellate body within the Social Security Administration (SSA) Office of Hearings and Appeals. To appeal an Appeals Council decision, a person may seek judicial review in federal district court.

§ 15.101

1. 20 C.F.R. §§ 404.906, 404.911.

New evidence is freely admitted during the SSA appeals process, with the exception of the Appeals Council review where some restrictions exist. New evidence generally may not be admitted during judicial review.

All of these decisions become final and binding unless appealed. SSA appeals must be in writing and filed within 60 days of receipt of the determination, unless there is good cause for delay. Notice is presumed to have been received five days after it was sent. Circumstances constituting good cause for delay include: death or serious illness in claimant's immediate family; records accidentally damaged; claimant was misled by a representative of the SSA about his or her rights; and unusual circumstances that show that claimant could not reasonably be expected to have been aware of the time limits for filing or that prevented claimant from filing on time. Slightly different rules govern filing in federal court.

§ 15.102 Appeal of Decisions Affecting Benefits—Initial Determinations [1]

Most decisions concerning social security benefits are initial determinations that may be appealed. Examples include entitlement to benefits, amount of benefits, termination of benefits, whether to appoint a representative payee, who should serve as payee, and whether adjustment or recovery of overpaid benefits should occur.[2]

A few decisions concerning social security benefits are not considered initial determinations. Although review of these decisions may be sought, the decisions are not subject to the full Social Security Administration (SSA) appellate process and judicial review. Examples of decisions not viewed as initial determinations are: some temporary suspensions of benefits, some determinations concerning representation and fees, some requests for extensions, and requests to reopen determinations.[3] The SSA will send the claimant or beneficiary written notice of an initial determination that will include the basis for the determination, its effect, and the right to seek reconsideration.

If not appealed, an initial determination becomes a final and binding determination of the SSA.[4] Clients should be made aware of this effect of an initial determination. Often a client will fail to appeal a denial of benefits, then later reapply. To the extent that the facts underlying the applications are the same, the SSA can treat the original denial as res judicata and deny the second application. The

§ 15.102
1. 20 C.F.R. §§ 404.902–.905.
2. 20 C.F.R. § 404.902.
3. 20 C.F.R. § 404.903.
4. 20 C.F.R. § 404.905.

SSA's failure to explain adequately the consequences of failing to appeal adverse initial determinations led Congress to amend the Social Security Act to require the SSA to describe the consequences of not appealing an adverse initial determination in "clear and specific language." A claimant misled into not appealing an adverse initial determination by the SSA's failure to comply with this obligation may reapply.[5] A claimant also may request that an initial determination be reopened.[6]

Library References:

C.J.S. Social Security and Public Welfare § 63.

West's Key No. Digests, Social Security and Public Welfare ☞142.

§ 15.103　Appeal of Decisions Affecting Benefits—Reconsiderations[1]

Reconsideration may be sought of any initial determination of the Social Security Administration (SSA) by any person "adversely affected" by the determination. Generally, a claimant seeks reconsideration, but another party such as a dependent "adversely affected" by the determination can also seek reconsideration. With the exception of disability "cessation" cases (see § 16.43 infra) and waiver of recovery cases (see §§ 15.63–.67 supra), reconsideration consists of a case or "paper" review in which the file may be reviewed and additional evidence may be submitted, but in which no right of personal appearance exists. Reconsideration is conducted by an SSA employee not previously involved in the claim. To prevail, the individual seeking review must show that the initial determination was erroneous due to missing facts, evidence, or an erroneous application of social security law.

A written request for reconsideration must be submitted to an SSA office within 60 days of receipt of the initial determination unless there is reason for delay, in which case an extension must be requested. A beneficiary seeking continuation of benefits pending reconsideration in a disability cessation case must file for reconsideration within 10 days of the date notice is received from the SSA office concerning its decision to terminate benefits.

The SSA will issue a reconsideration determination based on the claimant's file and additional information supplied during reconsideration. Notice of the decision, of the reasons for it, and of the right to

5. 42 U.S.C.A. § 405(b)(3). See also Gonzalez v. Sullivan, 914 F.2d 1197, 31 Soc.Sec.Rep.Ser. 188 (9th Cir.1990).

6. See § 15.109 infra.

§ 15.103

1. 20 C.F.R. 404.907 et seq.

appeal will be sent to the claimant and any other parties. The reconsideration becomes final and binding unless appealed.

Library References:

C.J.S. Social Security and Public Welfare § 77.

West's Key No. Digests, Social Security and Public Welfare ☞142.25.

§ 15.104 Appeal of Decisions Affecting Benefits—Hearing [1]

To appeal a reconsideration determination, a claimant should request a hearing before an administrative law judge (ALJ) by submitting SSA Form HA–501, "Request for Hearing," or other writing containing: [2]

1. the name and social security number of the claimant;

2. the reasons for disagreeing with the reconsidered decision;

3. a statement of additional evidence to be submitted; and

4. the name and address of the claimant's representative, if any.

The request should be filed within 60 days of receipt of the reconsideration determination unless there is good cause for delay, in which case an extension should be sought.

The hearing is a crucial element in the appeal process, since it constitutes the claimant's "day in court" and, in most cases, the hearing record forms the sole basis for subsequent judicial review. The hearing is the first formal opportunity for the claimant to appear personally or by representative; [3] to present and object to the introduction of evidence (formal evidence rules do not apply); [4] to present legal arguments, orally or in writing; [5] and to subpoena, examine, and cross-examine witnesses. [6] Written requests for subpoenas must be filed at least five days before the date of the hearing. [7] The Social Security Administration (SSA) will pay the fees and mileage of any witness so subpoenaed. [8] The SSA is not represented by counsel at the hearing.

The SSA will send notice of the time and place of the hearing and of the issues to be heard at the hearing to the parties at least 20 days prior to the hearing. Objections to the timing or location of the hearing or to the issues should be filed promptly with reasons for the objections. Similarly, a request to disqualify the ALJ for prejudice

§ 15.104

1. 20 C.F.R. §§ 404.929–.961.
2. 20 C.F.R. § 404.933.
3. 20 C.F.R. § 404.950(a).
4. 20 C.F.R. § 404.950(c).
5. 20 C.F.R. § 404.950(d).
6. 20 C.F.R. § 404.950(e).
7. 20 C.F.R. § 404.950(d)(2).
8. Id. at (d)(4).

should be filed promptly.[9] New issues may be introduced by either the ALJ or the parties on proper notice.[10] An ALJ may invoke the doctrine of collateral estoppel and decline to allow a claimant to introduce evidence concerning an issue of fact (e.g., the age or marital status of a claimant) decided in a prior social security case.[11] The hearing may be dismissed if either the claimant or the claimant's representative fails to appear.[12] Such a dismissal may be vacated if good cause is shown in a motion filed within 60 days after receipt of such dismissal.[13]

An ALJ may adjourn, consolidate, or reopen a hearing and may hold a prehearing or posthearing conference to facilitate the handling of a case.[14] Where the parties have submitted new evidence or Congress has changed the law after a hearing has been requested but before it has been held, SSA may issue a revised determination. Parties will be notified if a revised determination is under consideration, and can agree to defer the hearing to allow the revised determination to be issued. Absent consent, the hearing will proceed unless the revised determination is entirely favorable to claimant.[15]

The ALJ will send the parties a written decision that will be based on the record and will contain findings of fact, reasons for the decision, and an explanation of how to appeal. Unless appealed, the decision is final and binding. Section 16.44, infra, contains suggestions for preparing for and presenting a case at an ALJ hearing.

Library References:
> C.J.S. Social Security and Public Welfare §§ 73–78.
> West's Key No. Digests, Social Security and Public Welfare ☜142.5.

§ 15.105 Appeal of Decisions Affecting Benefits—Appeals Council Review [1]

The Appeals Council is the appellate body of the Social Security Administration (SSA) Office of Hearings and Appeals. A claimant dissatisfied with a hearing decision may seek review with the Appeals Council by filing a written request with the SSA (or the Railroad Retirement Board) within 60 days of receipt of notice of the decision.[2] The claimant may make the request on SSA Form HA–520 or by other writing and can seek an extension if there is good cause for delay. In addition to responding to appeals requested by parties to a hearing, the

9. 20 C.F.R. §§ 404.938–.940.

10. 20 C.F.R. § 404.956(b).

11. 20 C.F.R. § 404.950(f).

12. 20 C.F.R. § 404.957(b).

13. 20 C.F.R. § 404.960.

14. 20 C.F.R. §§ 404.944, 404.961.

15. 20 C.F.R. § 404.941.

§ 15.105

1. 20 C.F.R. § 404.967 et seq.

2. 20 C.F.R. § 404.968.

Appeals Council itself may initiate review of a hearing decision by notifying the parties of its intention to do so within 60 days of the decision.

The grounds for Appeals Council review of a hearing decision are:

1. an abuse of discretion by an ALJ;

2. an error of law;

3. the action, findings, or conclusions of the ALJ are not supported by substantial evidence; or

4. the presence of a policy or procedural issue affecting the public interest.

Appeals Council review is of the hearing record, supplemented by any evidence relating to events prior to the date of the hearing decision submitted by the parties. The parties also may submit briefs or other statements relating to the facts and law of the case. Oral argument may be requested, but rarely is granted.

The Appeals Council has discretion whether to grant review of a hearing decision.[3] The Appeals Council may deny or dismiss a request for review or may grant the request and issue a decision or remand the case to an ALJ for further hearing. A decision of the Appeals Council affirming, modifying, or reversing an ALJ decision constitutes a final decision of the SSA. Similarly, a decision of the Appeals Council denying a request for review results in the ALJ decision being the final decision of the SSA. Dismissal of a request as untimely is also a final decision. Judicial review may be sought of all these final decisions.

In contrast, a decision by the Appeals Council to remand a case to an ALJ to consider additional evidence or take other action is not a final decision of which judicial review may be sought. The administrative process continues until a decision or recommended decision is issued by the ALJ, at which point further review by the Appeals Council may be sought and a final decision rendered.

Advocates have criticized the Appeals Council's conduct of its review function.[4] An important problem has been the Appeals Council's use of the reopening regulations (see § 15.109 infra) to lengthen its review period. Unlike the Appeals Council regulations, which require the Council to act in 60 days, the reopening regulations allow a case to be reopened years later. The Appeals Council repeatedly has relied on the reopening regulations as the basis for reviewing a case long after the period for review has passed. The circuit courts are divided on the

3. 20 C.F.R. § 404.967.

4. Wilson, Procedural Challenges to Social Security Appeals Council Practices, 20 Clearinghouse Rev. 937 (1986).

legality of this practice, with some permitting either claimant or the SSA to reopen cases,[5] while others forbid or limit the SSA from doing so.[6] Another important issue is whether the Appeals Council is authorized to reverse an ALJ decision for which substantial evidence exists. A majority of courts considering the issue have permitted such reversals.[7]

Library References:

    C.J.S. Social Security and Public Welfare §§ 73–78.

    West's Key No. Digests, Social Security and Public Welfare ⊕142.5.

§ 15.106   Appeal of Decisions Affecting Benefits—Judicial Review—Normal Process [1]

A dissatisfied claimant who has exhausted the administrative appeals described in the previous sections may file a civil action in federal district court for the district in which the claimant resides or has a principal place of business.[2] The action must be filed within 60 days of receipt of the decision of the Appeals Council, either denial of review or decision on the claim, unless an extension has been granted. The Secretary of the Department of Health and Human Services (HHS) is the defendant, and service may be made on the local United States Attorney.

There is no trial *de novo* on the facts. The district court's review is limited to the questions of whether the Secretary had substantial evidence for the findings of fact, whether substantive or procedural legal errors occurred, and whether the Secretary correctly applied the law to the facts. The hearing record constitutes the basis for review.[3] The government has 60 days in which to answer and is required to file the transcript when it answers. Motions for summary judgment usually form the basis of review, with each party claiming that it is entitled to a judgment as a matter or law and that no genuine dispute exists

5. Zimmermann v. Heckler, 774 F.2d 615, 11 Soc.Sec.Rep.Serv. 143 (4th Cir. 1985); Higginbotham v. Heckler, 767 F.2d 408, 10 Soc.Sec.Rep.Ser. 217 (8th Cir.1985).

6. McCuin v. Secretary of Health & Human Services, 817 F.2d 161, 174, 17 Soc. Sec.Rep.Ser. 691 (1st Cir.1987); Butterworth v. Bowen, 796 F.2d 1379, 1385–87, 14 Soc.Sec.Rep.Ser. 290 (11th Cir.1986) (SSA may reopen in limited circumstances); see also 56 Fed.Reg. 55477 (10/28/91) (proposal to clarify authority of SSA to reopen under 20 C.F.R. §§ 404.987 and 416.1487).

7. e.g., Kellough v. Heckler, 785 F.2d 1147, 13 Soc.Sec.Rep.Ser. 58 (4th Cir.1986); Mullen v. Bowen, 800 F.2d 535, 15 Soc.Sec. Rep.Ser. 34 (6th Cir.1986); Parker v. Bowen, 788 F.2d 1512, 13 Soc.Sec.Rep.Ser. 298 (11th Cir.), *on remand* 793 F.2d 1177, 14 Soc.Sec.Rep.Ser. 106 (1986); contra Powell v. Heckler, 783 F.2d 396 (3d Cir.1986).

§ 15.106

1. 42 U.S.C.A. § 405(g), 20 C.F.R. § 404.981.

2. 42 U.S.C.A. § 405(g).

3. 42 U.S.C.A. § 405(g).

concerning any material facts. Claimant's attorney should file a memorandum supporting the request for judgment.

Library References:

C.J.S. Social Security and Public Welfare § 79.

West's Key No. Digests, Social Security and Public Welfare ⚷145.

§ 15.107   Appeal of Decisions Affecting Benefits—Judicial Review—Special Problems

The court is authorized, under 42 U.S.C.A. § 405(g), to affirm, modify, or reverse the HHS Secretary's decision or to remand the case to the Secretary for further proceedings. Remands may be ordered in conjunction with entry of a judgment affirming, modifying, or reversing a Social Security Administration (SSA) decision (called a sentence four remand) or to allow consideration of material new evidence (called a sentence six remand). The distinction between these remands is important. The Supreme Court has held that a sentence four remand is a final judgment that the Secretary may appeal, while a sentence six remand is not.[1] The distinction also affects counsel's ability to obtain attorney fees under the Equal Access to Justice Act (EAJA).[2] The filing period for seeking fees begins after entry of judgment in sentence four remands, but not until entry of judgment following postremand proceedings in sentence six remands.[3] Additional details concerning judicial review, and practice suggestions are found in § 16.49, infra.

---

§ 15.107

1. Sullivan v. Finkelstein, 496 U.S. 617, 110 S.Ct. 2658, 110 L.Ed.2d 563, 30 Soc.Sec. Rep.Ser. 118 (1990), *on remand* 924 F.2d 483, 32 Soc.Sec.Rep.Ser. 276 (3d Cir.1991). A party seeking a sentence six remand must demonstrate the evidence is material and show good cause why the evidence was not available previously. A sentence six remand becomes final judgment upon entry of judgment after the case is returned to it following remand. Several important issues were left open by the Court, including whether claimant may appeal a sentence four remand and whether a new petition for review must be filed following a sentence four remand. For a discussion of these issues, see Deford, Two Late–Term Sleepers from the Supreme Court Pose Questions for Advocates, 24 Clearinghouse Rev. 705 (1990).

2. 28 U.S.C.A. § 2412(d).

3. Melkonyan v. Sullivan, __ U.S. __, __, 111 S.Ct. 2157, 2165, 115 L.Ed.2d 78, 94, 33 Soc.Sec.Rep.Ser. 363, *on remand* 943 F.2d 1476 (9th Cir.1991); Shalala v. Schaefer, __ U.S. __, 113 S.Ct. 2625, 125 L.Ed.2d 239, 41 Soc.Sec.Rep.Ser. 334 (1993). The Court earlier ruled that attorney fees could be obtained under EAJA for work done in conjunction with a remand "where a court orders a remand ... and retains continuing jurisdiction ... pending a decision from the Secretary which will determine the claimant's entitlement to benefits." Sullivan v. Hudson, 490 U.S. 877, 892, 109 S.Ct. 2248, 2258, 104 L.Ed.2d 941, 955, 25 Soc.Sec.Rep.Ser. 401 (1989). For a discussion of these issues, see Deford, Melkonyan v. Sullivan: What Hath the Supreme Court Wrought?, 25 Clearinghouse Rev. 662 (1991).

Additional discussion of attorney fees under the EAJA is found in §§ 15.137–.145 infra.

Most SSA litigation involves an individual claimant seeking benefits, but a considerable volume of litigation has been filed in recent years challenging SSA practices as violative of the Social Security Act or the Constitution. In these cases, complex questions of jurisdiction are common. Although litigants ordinarily are required to exhaust their administrative remedies before seeking judicial review and a claim filed more than 60 days after an Appeals Council decision will be dismissed, the courts may waive these requirements in appropriate cases. A leading example is *Bowen v. City of New York*,[4] a class action challenging a "secret policy" of the SSA that resulted in termination of benefits to a large number of disability recipients. Over the objection of SSA, the class included individuals who failed to complete the SSA appeals process and others who completed the process but failed to seek judicial review within 60 days of the Appeals Council decision. The Supreme Court concluded that the exhaustion requirement should be waived and the filing period "equitably tolled" because SSA's conduct made compliance with the requirements difficult and hardship would result from enforcing the requirements.

The Social Security Act specifies that "no ... decision of the Secretary shall be reviewed" except by the judicial review method described above.[5] The Supreme Court has interpreted this provision to preclude challenges brought against the Secretary under federal question jurisdiction and the Administrative Procedure Act.[6] Despite this provision, claims challenging SSA procedures have been allowed under mandamus jurisdiction.[7]

A final issue is that of delay. Despite the promulgation of performance standards for claims processing,[8] SSA's adjudication and appeals process, particularly for disability cases, often is very slow. Months, even years, can pass before SSA concludes its consideration of a claim.

---

4. 476 U.S. 467, 106 S.Ct. 2022, 90 L.Ed.2d 462, 13 Soc.Sec.Rep.Ser. 14 (1986); see also Briggs v. Sullivan, 886 F.2d 1132, 27 Soc.Sec.Rep.Ser. 313 (9th Cir.1989), *appeal after remand* 957 F.2d 534, 36 Soc.Sec. Rep.Ser. 203 (1992) (9th Cir.1989) (waiver and tolling allowed); Bailey v. Sullivan, 885 F.2d 52, 27 Soc.Sec.Rep.Ser. 59 (3d Cir.1989) (only partially allowed); Deford, One Year Later: City of New York Begins to Bear Fruit, 21 Clearinghouse Rev. 132 (1987).

5. 42 U.S.C.A. § 405(h).

6. Weinberger v. Salfi, 422 U.S. 749, 95 S.Ct. 2457, 45 L.Ed. 522 (1975) (28 U.S.C.A. § 1331—federal question); Califano v. Sanders, 430 U.S. 99, 97 S.Ct. 980, 51 L.Ed.2d 192 (1977) (5 U.S.C.A. § 702—administrative procedure act).

7. 28 U.S.C.A. § 1361; see e.g., Mathews v. Eldridge, 424 U.S. 319, 96 S.Ct. 893, 47 L.Ed.2d 18 (1976); Briggs v. Sullivan, 886 F.2d 1132, 27 Soc.Sec.Rep.Ser. 313 (9th Cir.1989), *appeal after remand* 954 F.2d 534, 36 Soc.Sec.Rep.Ser. 203 (1992).

8. 20 C.F.R. §§ 404.1640–404.1694.

When this situation occurs, litigation may be required to obtain relief. Although the Supreme Court has disallowed the imposition of classwide mandatory deadlines as a remedy for this problem, it has indicated that individual injunctive relief may be available to speed claims processing.[9]

§ 15.108 Expedited Appeal Process [1]

If the claimant and the Social Security Administration (SSA) agree that the only reason for denying a claim is a provision in the law alleged by the claimant to be unconstitutional, an expedited process of appeal to the courts is available. The claimant may request an expedited appeal within 60 days of a reconsideration determination or an administrative law judge (ALJ) decision. The claimant also may request an expedited appeal after seeking review by an ALJ or the Appeals Council until these reviews are held. If the request is granted, the claimant may seek judicial review without further appeal within the SSA. If a request for expedited appeal is denied, the case is treated as an appeal to the next level of review within the SSA.

§ 15.109 Reopening [1]

An administrative decision may be reopened for any reason within 12 months of the date of the notice of the initial determination and within four years if there is good cause.[2] Good cause will be found where material new evidence is furnished, where a clerical error was made in computing benefits, or where an error is obvious from the face of the evidence on which the decision was based. A change in legal interpretation or administrative ruling is not good cause to reopen a decision.[3] In addition, a determination may be reopened at any time in certain circumstances, including proof of the use of fraud or the commission of a crime to obtain benefits; the occurrence of subsequent events affecting entitlement to benefits, such as proof that a person believed to be dead is alive or vice versa; or action to correct obvious or clerical errors.

9. Heckler v. Day, 467 U.S. 104, 104 S.Ct. 2249, 81 L.Ed.2d 88, 5 Soc.Sec.Rep. Ser. 40 (1984), *appeal after remand* 794 F.2d 17, 14 Soc.Sec.Rep.Ser. 115 (1986); Hasen, Delay in the Social Security Appeals Process: The Potential for Individual Litigation After Heckler v. Day, 20 Clearinghouse Rev. 523 (1986).

§ 15.108

1. 20 C.F.R. §§ 404.923–.928.

§ 15.109

1. 20 C.F.R. §§ 404.987–404.996; see 56 Fed.Reg. 55477 (proposal to amend 20 C.F.R. § 404.987 to clarify authority of secretary to reopen). See Komlos–Hrobsky, Administrative Finality in Disability Proceedings, 23 Clearinghouse Rev. 147 (1989).

2. 20 C.F.R. § 404.988.

3. 20 C.F.R. § 404.989.

As noted in § 15.105 supra, controversy surrounds the question of whether the Social Security Administration as well as claimants may reopen a case. Denial of a person's request to reopen a determination is not an initial determination and may not be appealed.[4]

§ 15.110   Nonacquiescence—Introduction

Judicial review of administrative decision-making has at least two important functions. The first is to protect individuals harmed by errors made by the agency in handling individuals' cases. The second is to ensure that "the rule of law" is maintained by ensuring that an agency implementing a statute does not exceed the limits of its power. A court can correct agency errors of statutory construction and require that agency procedures be fair and consistent with the requirements of the statute.

Judicial review of Social Security Administration (SSA) decisions usually accomplishes the first goal of "individual justice," in that claimants wrongly denied benefits can obtain relief from the courts. Because SSA refuses to implement many decisions of the federal judiciary construing the Social Security Act, however, it is less clear whether "the rule of law" rationale of judicial review is succeeding. The SSA does not view all judicial decisions as binding precedent on it, even those of Circuit Courts of Appeal and even within the circuit in which a decision was rendered. This practice of choosing not to follow circuit court precedent is known as "nonacquiescence."

"Intracircuit nonacquiescence,"[1] in which the SSA refuses to follow federal circuit court precedent with which it disagrees in all factually similar cases arising within the circuit issuing the decision, has been criticized widely.[2] The SSA's intracircuit nonacquiescence practice can be seen as a way for the agency to have its cake and eat it too. By not appealing an adverse circuit court decision, the agency

---

4. 20 C.F.R. § 404.903(f); Califano v. Sanders, 430 U.S. 99, 97 S.Ct. 980, 51 L.Ed.2d 192 (1977).

§ 15.110

1. See generally Kubitschek, Social Security Administration Nonacquiescence: The Need for Legislative Curbs on Agency Discretion, 50 U.Pitt.L.Rev. 399 (1980) [Kubitschek] (WESTLAW: UPTLR database, ci(50 + 5 399)). See Diller & Morawetz, Intracircuit Nonacquiescence and the Breakdown of the Rule of Law: A Response to Estreicher and Revesz, 99 Yale L.J. 801 (1990) [Diller & Morawetz].

(WESTLAW: YLJ database, ci(99 + 5 801)).

2. Federal courts have been clear in their distaste for agency nonacquiescence. See, e.g., Stieberger v. Heckler, 615 F.Supp. 1315, 1353, 11 Soc.Sec.Rep.Ser. 383 (S.D.N.Y.1985) ("[T]he SSA's nonacquiescence policy has been the subject of almost universal condemnation by those courts which have considered its legality."); Anderson v. Heckler, 756 F.2d 1011, 1013, 9 Soc.Sec.Rep.Ser. 91 (4th Cir.1985); Douglas v. Schweiker, 734 F.2d 399, 400, 5 Soc. Sec.Rep.Ser. 195 (8th Cir.1984).

avoids the risk of a nationally binding ruling by the Supreme Court on an issue concerning the Social Security Act. By not acquiescing to adverse circuit court judgments, the agency avoids adherence to circuit court precedents it considers "wrongly" decided. Intracircuit nonacquiescence is distinguishable from "intercircuit nonacquiescence," in which the SSA follows the decisions of a particular circuit within that circuit but does not recognize the decision as binding in other circuits.[3]

The SSA's nonacquiescence to a circuit's precedent can be either formal or informal. Formal nonacquiescence occurs when the SSA publishes an acquiescence ruling (AR) in the Federal Register,[4] describing SSA's dispute with a circuit court decision that SSA regards as contrary to the Social Security Act and explaining the SSA's position on the particular issues and how the agency will apply the adverse holding.[5] Informal nonacquiescence is more difficult to detect and, therefore, more pernicious. Informal nonacquiescence occurs when an agency, without public announcement of its intent to do so, simply nonacquiesces or refuses to follow to unfavorable precedent. Agency personnel ignore a judicial decision, deciding claims and appeals under a standard declared unlawful by the court.

§ 15.111 Nonacquiescence—SSA's Defense of Nonacquiescence

The Social Security Administration (SSA) views itself as the primary body responsible for interpreting the Social Security Act and believes that it is important that social security programs be administered uniformly.[1] It cannot accomplish these goals, SSA argues, if it must acquiesce in each circuit court interpretation of the act or regulation, because each of the circuits may interpret a law or regulation differently. The SSA also argues that nonacquiescence is "necessary" to allow it to relitigate issues of importance to it, rather than being bound by the judgment of the first circuit to consider a question. In the future, another circuit may agree with the SSA's view. The SSA also argues that it should be free to interpret a court decision in a way that is consistent with the SSA's view of the act and regulations. Thus, the SSA believes that "the Secretary is bound only by the provisions of

3. Intercircuit nonacquiescence is not controversial in that it allows an agency to relitigate an issue it believes wrongly decided by a circuit. This process may enable an agency to obtain a favorable ruling on an issue from other circuits. See Diller & Morawetz, supra note 1, at 802 n. 8.

4. See 20 C.F.R. § 404.985(b); 20 C.F.R. § 410.670c(b); 20 C.F.R. § 416.1485(b).

5. Id.

§ 15.111

1. See generally Kuhl, The Social Security Administration's Nonacquiescence Policy, 4 Det.C.L.Rev. 913 (1984).

the Social Security Act, regulations and rulings, and by United States Supreme Court decisions. A district or circuit court decision is binding only in the specific case it decides."[2]

§ 15.112   Nonacquiescence—Consequences   of   Nonacquiescence

Agency nonacquiescence is a costly practice. Persons most hurt by it are unrepresented claimants whose claims are denied by the Social Security Administration (SSA) under an interpretation of the Social Security Act ruled erroneous by the Court of Appeals of that circuit. Most of these individuals will not appeal the determination denying benefits and will lose benefits to which they arguably are "entitled." Also harmed are the numerous claimants who appeal the denial of benefits and eventually prevail in court, but who must endure a long and expensive appeal process. Harmed, too, is the judicial branch inundated with "unnecessary" appeals by those claimants able to appeal.

The practice of nonacquiescence arguably violates separation of powers. When it purposely refuses to follow the controlling decisional law of a circuit, the SSA takes upon itself the judicial function to "say what the law is."[1] In addition, nonacquiescence has been condemned as violative of *stare decisis,*[2] and at least one court has found the practice to violate equal protection.[3] Courts have responded to nonacquiescence by, among other actions, enjoining it,[4] waiving exhaustion of administrative remedies,[5] tolling the period in which to seek judicial review,[6] and awarding fees and costs under the Equal Access to Justice

---

2. Hillhouse v. Harris, 715 F.2d 428, 430, 2 Soc.Sec.Rep.Ser. 475 (8th Cir.1983) (quoting Social Security Appeals Council), *affirming* 547 F.Supp. 88 (W.D.Ark.1982).

§ 15.112

1. See, e.g., Stieberger, supra § 15.110, note 2, at 1350; Hyatt v. Heckler, 807 F.2d 376, 16 Soc.Sec.Rep.Ser. 52 (4th Cir.1986), *cert. denied* 484 U.S. 820, 108 S.Ct. 79, 98 L.Ed.2d 41 (1987).

2. See e.g., Anderson v. Heckler, 756 F.2d 1011, 9 Soc.Sec.Rep.Ser. 91 (4th Cir. 1985); Kubitschek, supra § 15.110, note 1, at 399. Collateral estoppel, or issue preclusion, is not involved in these cases. Although private litigants may employ collateral estoppel offensively to prevent a party from relitigating an issue, the Supreme Court has held that the federal govern-

ment may not be so estopped. United States v. Mendoza, 464 U.S. 154, 104 S.Ct. 568, 78 L.Ed.2d 379, *on remand* 737 F.2d 824 (9th Cir.1984).

3. Stieberger, supra § 15.110, note 2, at 1362; see also Stieberger v. Sullivan, 738 F.Supp. 716, 30 Soc.Sec.Rep.Ser. 361 (S.D.N.Y.1990).

4. Stieberger v. Sullivan, 738 F.Supp. 716, 30 Soc.Sec.Rep.Ser. 361 (S.D.N.Y. 1990).

5. Wilkerson v. Bowen, 828 F.2d 117, 19 Soc.Sec.Rep.Ser. 16 (3d Cir.1987).

6. Stieberger v. Heckler, 615 F.Supp. 1315, 11 Soc.Sec.Rep.Ser. 383 (S.D.N.Y. 1985), vacated on other grounds sub nom. Stieberger v. Bowen, 801 F.2d 29, 15 Soc. Sec.Rep.Ser. 104 (2d Cir.1986).

Act.[7]

§ 15.113 Nonacquiescence—SSA's Current Nonacquiescence Policy

The Code of Federal Regulations codifies the current nonacquiescence practice of the Social Security Administration (SSA).[1] Under the policy, the SSA generally will apply circuit court precedent that the SSA believes conflicts with the SSA's interpretation "of a provision of the Social Security Act or regulations,"[2] but the SSA will not acquiesce in such a precedent until the agency issues an acquiescence ruling (AR). The SSA will not acquiesce in circuit law, however, if the SSA "seeks further review,"[3] or if it relitigates the issue in accordance with other provisions of the nonacquiescence policy.[4]

The nonacquiescence regulations provide that the SSA may "relitigate" (i.e., can nonacquiesce in) an issue despite the issuance of an AR when:[5] (1) the General Counsel of the Department of Health and Human Services, in consultation with the Department of Justice, decides that relitigation (nonacquiescence) is "appropriate"; *and* (2) notice is given in the Federal Register. In addition to numbers (1) and (2) being met, one of the following must exist: (3)(a) Congressional action "indicates" that the adverse circuit precedent is inconsistent with legislative intent; (3)(b) a "statement" in a majority opinion of the same circuit "indicates the court might no longer follow" its previous precedent; (3)(c) subsequent precedent from other circuits supports the SSA's interpretation of the relevant statute or regulation; or (3)(d) a subsequent Supreme Court decision "presents a reasonable legal basis" for disregarding the controlling circuit's precedent.[6]

---

7. Hyatt v. Heckler, 807 F.2d 376, 16 Soc.Sec.Rep.Ser. 52 (4th Cir.1986), *cert. denied* 484 U.S. 820, 108 S.Ct. 79, 98 L.Ed.2d 41 (1987).

§ 15.113

1. See 20 C.F.R. § 404.985; 20 C.F.R. § 410.670c; 20 C.F.R. § 416.1485. The language used in these sections varies slightly. The difference in the language appears not to have any bearing on the effect of the sections. The SSA's prior nonacquiescence policy can be found in Interim Circular ("I.C.") 185 (which has been appended as Appendix C to Stieberger v. Heckler, 615 F.Supp. 1315, 1403, 11 Soc. Sec.Rep.Ser. 383 (S.D.N.Y.1985)), and in Transmittal X-7. See Stieberger v. Sullivan, 738 F.Supp. 716, 750-55, 30 Soc.Sec.

Rep.Ser. 361 (S.D.N.Y.1990) for a discussion of I.C. 185 and Transmittal X-7.

2. 20 C.F.R. § 404.985(a); 20 C.F.R. § 410.670c(a); 20 C.F.R. § 416.1485(a).

3. Id. The SSA notes that the issue is not settled until the appeal process is exhausted. 55 Fed.Reg. 1013.

4. Id.

5. 20 C.F.R. § 404.985(c); 20 C.F.R. § 410.670c(c); 20 C.F.R. § 416.1485(c).

6. 20 C.F.R. § 404.985(c)(1)(iv); 20 C.F.R. § 410.670c(c)(1)(iv); 20 C.F.R. § 416.-1485(c)(1)(iv). When the agency relitigates an issue to which it previously acquiesced, the agency must provide notice to all affected parties. 20 C.F.R. § 404.985(d); 20

The regulations provide a means by which a claimant can have an adverse agency ruling readjudicated if the adverse ruling was issued after the favorable circuit court decision but before the issuance of an applicable AR.[7] The burden is on the claimant to show that the adverse ruling is worthy of reconsideration in light of the AR. The SSA's "denial of a request for readjudication will not be subject to further administrative or judicial review."[8] The nonacquiescence policy also gives the SSA the power to revoke "obsolete" ARs in certain circumstances.[9]

§ 15.114 Nonacquiescence—Conclusion

A lawyer representing a claimant should carefully monitor circuit court decisions and Social Security Administration (SSA) implementation of them and should be aware that SSA personnel may disregard circuit court precedent in handling a client's claim. Where this situation occurs, counsel should inform SSA personnel of the precedent and request that it be applied. In addition, where an acquiescence ruling (AR) has been issued, counsel should insist that it be followed if SSA personnel fail to do so. Counsel should seek to have a claim reopened if it was decided before the issuance of an AR governing the claim. Finally, counsel should seek judicial review of a claim denied as a result of nonacquiescence and should seek fees and costs under the Equal Access to Justice Act.

§§ 15.115–15.120 are reserved for supplementary material.

G. ATTORNEY FEES

Library References:

    C.J.S. Social Security and Public Welfare §§ 63, 84.

    West's Key No. Digests, Social Security and Public Welfare ⚷142.30.

C.F.R. § 410.670c(d); 20 C.F.R. § 416.-1485(d). Those whose cases were relitigated will be provided with written determinations of how the case would have been decided if the agency applied the circuit's precedent to which it previously acquiesced. Id.

    7. 20 C.F.R. § 404.985(b); 20 C.F.R. § 410.670c(b); 20 C.F.R. § 416.1485(b).

    8. Id.

    9. 20 C.F.R. § 404.985(e); 20 C.F.R. § 410.670c(e); 20 C.F.R. § 416.1485(e). Those reasons include the Supreme Court overruling or limiting the circuit precedent that was the basis of the AR (20 C.F.R.

§ 404.985(e)(1); 20 C.F.R. § 410.670c(e)(1); 20 C.F.R. § 416.1485(e)(1)), or the circuit overruling or limiting its own decision that was the basis of the AR (20 C.F.R. § 404.-985(e)(2); 20 C.F.R. § 410.670c(e)(2); 20 C.F.R. § 416.1485(e)(2)); or a federal law removing the basis of the circuit court decision that was the basis for the AR (20 C.F.R. § 404.985(e)(3); 20 C.F.R. § 410.-670c(e)(3); 20 C.F.R. § 416.1485(e)(3)). Finally, SSA may conclude that an AR is obsolete when the rule interpreted by a court is modified or replaced. 20 C.F.R. § 404.985(e)(4).

§ 15.121 Claimant Representation—Generally

A claimant has a statutory right to appoint a representative in any dealings with the Social Security Administration (SSA).[1] The HHS Secretary is required to notify a claimant of the right to counsel in administrative hearings, including the claimant's options for obtaining an attorney and the availability of legal services organizations providing free legal assistance.[2] When a claimant is not represented, especially if there is a possibility that the claimant may be incompetent or mentally ill, the administrative law judge (ALJ) should explain the right to counsel and the role of an attorney in even greater detail to ensure that the claimant understands these issues.[3] Such safeguards ensure that the ALJ conducts a full, fair hearing.[4]

§ 15.122 Claimant Representation—Qualification of Representative

Any attorney in good standing may represent a claimant in a proceeding against the Social Security Administration (SSA) if the attorney: (1) is admitted to practice before a court of a state, territory, or district or before the U.S. Supreme Court; (2) has not been disqualified or suspended from acting as a representative in a proceeding before the SSA; and (3) is not otherwise prohibited from acting as a representative.[1] The claimant's representative may be someone other than an attorney, but the representative must be known to have a good character and reputation, capable of giving valuable help, not disqualified from acting as a representative in dealings with the SSA, and not prohibited by any law from acting as a representative.[2]

§ 15.123 Claimant Representation—Appointment and Authority of Representative

When appointing a representative, the claimant must sign and file a written notice, using Form SSA–1696, stating that the claimant wants

§ 15.121

1. 42 U.S.C.A. § 406(a); 20 C.F.R. § 404.1700. However, there is no constitutional right to counsel at a Social Security Administrative hearing. See, e.g., Holland v. Heckler, 764 F.2d 1560, 1562, 10 Soc.Sec. Rep.Ser. 110 (11th Cir.1985) citing Clark v. Schweiker, 652 F.2d 399 (5th Cir.1981); Garcia v. Califano, 625 F.2d 354 (10th Cir. 1980) citing Lonzollo v. Weinberger, 387 F.Supp. 892 (N.D.Ill.1974), *reversed* 534 F.2d 712 (7th Cir.1976).

2. 42 U.S.C.A. § 406(c). See Smith v. Schweiker, 677 F.2d 826 (11th Cir.1982).

3. See Vance v. Heckler, 579 F.Supp. 318, 4 Soc.Sec.Rep.Ser. 571 (N.D.Ill.1984); Clark v. Schweiker, 652 F.2d 399 (5th Cir. 1981).

4. Kelley v. Heckler, 761 F.2d 1538, 1540, 9 Soc.Sec.Rep.Ser. 387 (11th Cir. 1985); see also Vance, 579 F.Supp. at 318.

§ 15.122

1. 20 C.F.R. § 404.1705.

2. 20 C.F.R. § 404.1705.

a person to be his or her representative in dealings with the Social Security Administration.[1] Additionally, if the representative is not an attorney, the person must sign a statement agreeing to the representation.[2] An appointed representative has the authority to obtain information about the claim, submit evidence, make statements about facts and law, and make any requests or give any notice about the proceedings.[3] However, the representative generally may not sign an application for social security benefits.

§ 15.124 Claimant Representation—Representative Prohibitions and Penalties

A representative owes certain obligations to the claimant or prospective claimant. Violation of these duties results in penalties to the representative. The HHS Secretary's regulations provide that a representative shall not:[1]

1. intentionally defraud or knowingly deceive a claimant or beneficiary about statutory benefits or rights;

2. knowingly charge or collect, or make an agreement to charge or collect, any fee in excess of that allowed by Social Security Administration (SSA) or by a court;

3. knowingly make a false statement about any material fact affecting the rights of any person under Title II of the act; or

4. divulge any SSA-supplied information about another person's claim.

If a representative violates these rules, SSA may suspend or disqualify the representative from acting as a representative in proceedings before the SSA and may charge the representative with a misdemeanor.[2]

§ 15.125 Attorney Fee Limits and Payments—Generally

An attorney representing a claimant under the Social Security Act may receive a fee for rendering services in a proceeding before the Social Security Administration (SSA).[1] When no fee agreement is submitted in writing prior to the SSA's favorable determination of the claim, the HHS Secretary shall "fix ... a reasonable fee to compensate such attorney for the services performed by him in connection with

§ 15.123

1. 20 C.F.R. § 404.1707.
2. Id.
3. 20 C.F.R. § 404.1710(a).

§ 15.124

1. 20 C.F.R. § 404.1740.

2. 42 U.S.C.A. § 406(a)(5).

§ 15.125

1. 20 C.F.R. § 404.1720.

such claim." [2]   In any case where the SSA decides for the claimant and the SSA must pay past-due benefits, the SSA will certify for direct payment to the attorney, out of such benefits, the smallest of the following:

1.   25% of the total of past-due benefits;

2.   the amount of the fee set by the SSA, or the amount agreed on between the attorney and claimant represented.[3]

§ 15.126 Attorney Fee Limits and Payments—Automatic Approval Payment Process

The Omnibus Budget Reconciliation Act of 1990 [1] simplified the process of determining a "reasonable" fee whenever the HHS Secretary makes a determination favorable to the claimant. An automatic fee approval process eliminates the need for an attorney to file a fee petition for payment for services rendered in administrative proceedings, except in rare cases. Under this system, the Secretary approves a fee agreed to by a claimant and the claimant's representative in a written fee agreement if: (1) they present the agreement to the Secretary before the Social Security Administration determines the claim, (2) the specified fee does not exceed the lesser of 25% of the past-due benefits or $4,000, and (3) the determination is favorable to the claimant.[2]

When a written fee agreement has been approved, the Secretary is to notify the claimant and representative in writing of:

1.   the dollar amount of the past-due benefits (as determined before any applicable reduction under 42 U.S.C.A. § 1320a–6(a)) and the dollar amount of the past-due benefits payable to the claimant;

2.   the dollar amount of the maximum fee that may be charged or recovered; and

3.   a description of the procedures for review.[3]

When no written fee agreement is submitted prior to a determination, or when the amount due under a fee agreement is greater than 25% of the past-due benefits or $4,000, or when the claimant, representative, administrative law judge, or other decision-maker contests the

2. 42 U.S.C.A. § 406(a)(1).

3. 20 C.F.R. § 404.1730(b).

§ 15.126

1. Public Law 101–508, § 5106, 104 Stat. 1388, codified at 42 U.S.C.A. § 406(a).

2. 42 U.S.C.A. § 406(a)(2).

3. 42 U.S.C.A. § 406(a)(2)(C).

fee, then the automatic approval procedure does not apply and a fee petition must be submitted.[4]

§ 15.127   Attorney Fee Limits and Payments—SSA Approval Necessary for Representative's Fees

Most cases are handled through the automatic approval payment process. If that process is not applicable,[1] the attorney, after the Social Security Administration (SSA) or a district court provides a favorable determination, must seek approval of the fee by submitting Form SSA–1560. The written request is filed after the proceedings are completed.

The following information should be provided when requesting fee approval:

1. the dates the representative's services began and ended;

2. a list of the services given and the amount of time spent on each type of service;

3. the amount of the fee the representative wants to charge for the services;

4. the amount of the fee the representative wants to request for services in the same matter before any state or federal court;

5. the amount and a list of any expenses incurred for which the attorney has been paid or expects to be paid;

6. a description of the special qualifications that enabled a representative, who is not an attorney, to give valuable help in connection with the claim; and

7. a statement showing that the representative sent the claimant a copy of the request for approval of a fee.[2]

The SSA has established criteria by which to judge fee requests. In evaluating a request for approval of a fee, SSA considers the purpose of the Social Security program, which is to provide a measure of economic security for the beneficiaries, along with the following factors:

1. the extent and type of services performed;

2. the complexity of the case;

3. the level of skill and competence required in rendition of services;

4. the amount of time spent on the case;

---

4. 42 U.S.C.A. § 406(a)(2).   **2.** 20 C.F.R. § 404.1725(a).

§ 15.127

1. 42 U.S.C.A. § 406(a)(2).

5. the results achieved;

6. the level of administrative review to which the claim was carried within the SSA and the level of review at which the attorney entered the proceedings; and

7. the amount of fee requested, excluding the amount of any expenses incurred, but including any amount previously authorized or requested.[3]

§ 15.128   Fees in Special Circumstances—At Initial Determination and Where No Benefits Are Recovered

A claimant may be awarded benefits upon an initial determination without having a hearing before an administrative law judge. In a Title II claim, the Social Security Administration (SSA) office that will authorize the payment of the claimant's benefits will review the attorney's fee petition. The fee petition may be submitted to the SSA District Office.[1] Also, the SSA "may authorize a fee even if no benefits are payable."[2] Therefore, although the Social Security Act (see 42 U.S.C.A. § 406) only authorizes attorney fees out of past-due benefits, an attorney may be able to collect a fee even when the claimant has not recovered benefits.

§ 15.129   Fees in Special Circumstances—Nonattorney Representative Fees

A representative who is not an attorney also is required to request approval of fees.[1] The representative has the responsibility of collecting an approved fee from the claimant, however, because the HHS Secretary will "assume no responsibility for the payment of any fee" that the SSA has authorized, nor "deduct the fee from any benefits payable to the claimant represented."[2]

§ 15.130   Notice and Review—Generally

When a fee is authorized, both the representative and the claimant are notified and allowed 30 days from the date of notification in which to request an administrative review. If a request for review is filed in a timely manner, the Social Security Administration (SSA) will grant a review, and an SSA official who did not participate in the fee determination will perform the review. The SSA will mail a written notice of

3. Id. at § 404.1725(b).

§ 15.128

1. For further discussion, see McCormick, Social Security Claims and Procedures, § 549 (4th ed. 1991).

2. 20 C.F.R. § 404.1725(b)(2).

§ 15.129

1. 20 C.F.R. § 404.1725.

2. 20 C.F.R. § 404.1730(b)(2).

the decision to the representative and the claimant. If the request for review is not filed in a timely manner, SSA will grant review only if it determines that there was good cause for the delay.[1]

§ 15.131   Notice and Review—Review of Automatic Approval of Fee

The following persons may seek review of an automatically approved fee award by written request within 15 days of receipt of notice of approval of the fee:

1. The claimant, or the administrative law judge (ALJ) or other adjudicator who made the favorable determination, may seek to reduce the maximum fee;

2. The representative may seek to increase the maximum fee.[1]

Before a review of the maximum fee can be conducted, the representative and the adjudicator must have reasonable notice and an opportunity to submit written information in favor of or in opposition to the request. The adjudicator can ask the HHS Secretary to reduce the maximum fee only if there is evidence of the failure of the representative to represent adequately the claimant's interest, or if there is evidence that the fee clearly is excessive for the services provided.[2]

When a claimant or a representative requests a review, the ALJ who made the favorable determination ordinarily will conduct the review. When the adjudicator requests the review, another ALJ ordinarily conducts the review.[3] When the review is completed, the reviewer will affirm or modify the amount of the maximum fee. This decision is not subject to further review.[4]

§ 15.132   Favorable Court Proceeding

If a federal court proceeding under the Social Security Act results in a judgment for a claimant, the court may allow the attorney a fee not in excess of 25% of the total past-due benefits to which the claimant is entitled by reason of the judgment.[1] The court may certify a direct payment to the attorney.

The fee for any services rendered in the court must be approved by the court, as the HHS Secretary's regulations provide, "[w]e shall not

§ 15.130

1. 20 C.F.R. § 404.1720(c), (d).

§ 15.131

1. 42 U.S.C.A. § 406(a)(3)(A).
2. 42 U.S.C.A. § 406(a)(3)(A).

3. 42 U.S.C.A. § 406(a)(3)(B).

4. 42 U.S.C.A. § 406(a)(3)(C).

§ 15.132

1. 42 U.S.C.A. § 406(b).

consider any service the representative gave you in any proceeding before a State or Federal court to be services as a representative in dealings with the SSA." [2]   Conversely, most circuits have concluded that a federal court lacks authority to award attorney fees for work done by an attorney before the SSA.   If more than one forum (i.e. agency or court) is involved, the attorney should petition for a fee separately to each forum.[3]   The Sixth Circuit has held, however, that whatever forum is making the favorable determination for benefits may provide for attorney fees for all aspects of representation involved in the claim.[4]   The total amount of the fee awarded should not exceed 25% of past-due benefits.   Thus, in most circuits, a case involving work before both the SSA and the district court requires two fee requests:

1.   After a favorable determination (unless the automatic fee approval process described in § 15.126 supra applies) the attorney submits Form SSA–1560 to the administrative body making the decision;

2.   HA–530 is sent to the attorney, authorizing the attorney to charge and receive a fee; and

3.   The attorney then submits a motion to the highest court before which the attorney appeared, requesting approval of a fee for work done before the court.[5]

§ 15.133   Issues Often Litigated in Social Security Fee Cases— Past–Due Benefits

"Past-due benefits" is defined as the total accumulated amount of benefits payable by reason of the favorable determination, through the month prior to the month the determination is effectuated.[1]   Past-due benefits include the amount due the claimant and any amount due members of the claimant's family.[2]   When the claimant is entitled to both Title II and SSI benefits, any SSI benefits the claimant receives

2.   20 C.F.R. § 404.1728(a); See also MacDonald v. Weinberger, 512 F.2d 144 (9th Cir.1975).

3.   Harris v. Secretary of Health and Human Services, 836 F.2d 496, 20 Soc.Sec. Rep.Ser. 247 (10th Cir.1987); Guido v. Schweiker, 775 F.2d 107, 11 Soc.Sec.Rep. Ser. 173 (3d Cir.1985); Gardner v. Menendez, 373 F.2d 488, 490 (1st Cir.1967); McKittrick v. Gardner, 378 F.2d 872, 866 (4th Cir.1967).

4.   Webb v. Richardson, 472 F.2d 529 (6th Cir.1972).

5.   For details regarding fee requests, see McCormick, Social Security Claims and Procedures,   §§ 761–783   (4th   ed.1991); Hall, Social Security Disability Practice, §§ 6.1–6.94 (2d ed.1992).

§ 15.133

1.   20 C.F.R. § 404.1703.

2.   See Shinn by Shinn v. Sullivan, 915 F.2d 1186, 1188, 31 Soc.Sec.Rep.Ser. 284 (8th Cir.1990), citing Hopkins v. Cohen, 390 U.S. 530, 88 S.Ct. 1146, 20 L.Ed.2d 87 (1968).

must be subtracted from the total recovery before past-due benefits are calculated.[3]

§ 15.134 Issues Often Litigated in Social Security Fee Cases—Lodestar Method

Many courts compute attorney fees with the "lodestar method," which is a determination of attorney fees based on hourly rates, allowing for increases depending on the facts of each case. Following this method, the number of hours expended are multiplied by a reasonable hourly rate for the type of litigation, with the potential for adjustment based on the contingency of the claim.[1]

§ 15.135 Issues Often Litigated in Social Security Fee Cases—Interim Benefits

Interim benefits are those elected to be paid, pending a final determination, when a disability benefits recipient appeals a decision terminating benefits. These interim benefits must be repaid if the final determination is adverse. There is disagreement on whether these interim benefits are included in the definition of past-due benefits for purposes of determining attorney fees when the claimant is successful. The Eighth and Eleventh Circuits have held that interim benefits payments are past-due benefits includable when determining attorney fees.[1] The First Circuit has held the opposite.[2]

§ 15.136 Issues Often Litigated in Social Security Fee Cases—Supplemental Security Income Cases

An attorney representing a claimant for Supplemental Security Income (SSI) benefits may petition the SSA for a fee for such represen-

3. See McCormick, Social Security Claims and Procedures, § 762, at 351 (4th ed. 1991).

§ 15.134

1. See generally, McCormick, Social Security Claims and Procedures, § 762 (4th ed. 1991); see also, Brown v. Sullivan, 917 F.2d 189, 31 Soc.Sec.Rep.Ser. 419 (5th Cir. 1990).

§ 15.135

1. See Gowen v. Bowen, 855 F.2d 613, 22 Soc.Sec.Rep.Ser. 691 (8th Cir.1988); Shoemaker v Bowen, 853 F.2d 858, 22 Soc.

Sec.Rep.Ser. 563 (11th Cir.1988); but see Pittman v. Sullivan, 911 F.2d 42 (8th Cir. 1990); Davis v. Bowen, 894 F.2d 271, 28 Soc.Sec.Rep.Ser. 291 (8th Cir.1989), *cert. denied* 495 U.S. 904, 110 S.Ct. 1922, 109 L.Ed.2d 286 (1990) (Secretary held not in contempt when he failed to include interim benefits as part of past-due benefits to be withheld for payment of attorney fees, even though subsequent opinion in another case ruled that interim benefits had to be included.).

2. See Rodriguez v. Secretary of Health and Human Serv., 856 F.2d 338 (1st Cir. 1988).

tation.[1] Unlike the process for social security retirement or disability benefits, the SSA is not authorized to withhold a portion of an award of past-due benefits as a fee award for the representative.[2] As a result, the attorney must obtain payment from the client. Federal courts are divided as to whether a fee petition must be submitted for work done in federal court on behalf of a client in an SSI case.[3] As with fees for representation before the SSA, a court is not authorized to order that a fee award be withheld from an award of past-due benefits ordered by the court.

Some social security disability cases involve concurrent applications for SSI disability benefits. In these cases, errors can occur in determining the total amount of the award and the amount allocable to each program, in calculating the required "windfall offset"[4] and in ascertaining whether the representative's fee award has been withheld from an award of past-due benefits. The attorney should be alert to these problems.[5]

§ 15.137 Equal Access to Justice Act—Introduction

Congress enacted the Equal Access to Justice Act (EAJA)[1] to remove the financial barriers that litigants confront when pursuing valid claims against the government. The act allows claimants to recover attorney fees from the government if certain conditions under the EAJA are satisfied. Ninety percent of all EAJA petitions for attorney fees and awards are filed against the Department of Health and Human Services.[2]

Like the Social Security Act, the EAJA can be employed to obtain attorney fees. The primary difference between the EAJA and the Social Security Act is in the source of fees. Under the EAJA, a prevailing claimant's counsel obtains a fee from the government, whereas under the Social Security Act, the fee is taken from the past-due benefits awarded to the claimant.

§ 15.136

1. 42 U.S.C.A. § 1383(d)(2)(A); 20 C.F.R. § 416.1520.

2. Bowen v. Galbreath, 485 U.S. 74, 108 S.Ct. 892, 99 L.Ed.2d 68 (1988), on remand 845 F.2d 760 (8th Cir.1988).

3. See e.g., McGuire v. Sullivan, 873 F.2d 974 (7th Cir.1989); McCarthy v. Secretary of H.H.S., 793 F.2d 741 (6th Cir.1986).

4. See 42 U.S.C.A. § 1320a-6.

5. For details, see Hall, Social Security Disability Practice, Chapter 6 (2d ed. 1992).

§ 15.137

1. 5 U.S.C.A. § 504; 28 U.S.C.A. §§ 2412(b), 2412(d).

2. Commissioner, INS v. Jean, 496 U.S. 154, 165 n. 12, 110 S.Ct. 2316, 2322 n. 12, 110 L.Ed.2d 134 (1990), citing Annual Report of the Director of U.S. Courts, Report of Fees and Expenses Awarded Under the Equal Access to Justice Act 100, table 32 (1989).

28 U.S.C.A. § 2412(d)(1)(A), the EAJA section most often used to obtain fees in social security proceedings, provides that a prevailing party in an adversary adjudication may obtain fees as long as the government's position is not substantially justified and there are no special circumstances to make an award unjust. Section 2412(b) makes the government responsible for attorney fees and expenses under the common law doctrines of bad faith, common fund, or common benefit.[3] Definitions of terms concerning costs and fees of parties and other matters relevant to the EAJA are found in 5 U.S.C.A. § 504.

Library References:

C.J.S. United States § 209.

West's Key No. Digests, United States ⊛147(18).

§ 15.138   Equal Access to Justice Act—Requirements—Overview

To obtain fees under 28 U.S.C.A. § 2412(d)(1)(A) of the Equal Access to Justice Act (EAJA), counsel must meet the following requirements:

1. The work must have been performed in an adversarial proceeding;

2. The claimant must be a prevailing party;[1]

3. The government's position must not be substantially justified or have any special circumstances to make the award unjust; and

---

3. Under the bad faith section, the prevailing party may be awarded fees when the government's behavior has caused undue delay, needless litigation, or deliberate defiance of the law. Wells v. Bowen, 855 F.2d 37, 46, 22 Soc.Sec.Rep.Ser. 650 (2d Cir.1988); Blue v. Bureau of Prisons, 570 F.2d 529 (5th Cir.1978). Since the awarding of fees is under the court's discretion, the award may exceed the $75 an hour cap provided in § 2412(d)(2)(A). The bad faith section is a narrow exception to the normal rule for awarding fees as provided in § 2412(d)(2)(A). See Brown v. Sullivan, 916 F.2d 492, 31 Soc.Sec.Rep.Ser. 296 (9th Cir.1990). The common fund or common benefit sections are also narrow exceptions to obtaining fees. A prevailing party may

be awarded attorney fees when his or her action creates a common fund or benefit in which others may share. Blue v. Bureau of Prisons, 570 F.2d 529 (5th Cir.1978). (An example is when the action benefits an identifiable class.)

§ 15.138

1. To be eligible, a party must be (1) an individual whose net worth did not exceed $2 million at the time of civil action; (2) a business or entity whose net worth did not exceed $7 million at time of civil action and did not have more than 500 employees; (3) a nonprofit corporation under § 501(c)(3) of the Internal Revenue Code, regardless of net worth. 28 U.S.C.A. § 2412(d)(2)(B).

4. Counsel must file for attorney fees within 30 days of a final judgment.[2]

§ 15.139 Equal Access to Justice Act—Requirements—Adversarial Proceeding

The scope of the Equal Access to Justice Act (EAJA) is limited to work performed in an "adversarial proceeding."[1] An adversarial proceeding is an adjudication in which "the position of the United States is represented by counsel or otherwise."[2] Since the Social Security Administration (SSA) operates as an "adjudicator," proceedings before it are not "adversarial."[3] As a consequence, EAJA fees in social security cases are available primarily for work performed in federal court seeking modification or reversal of an adverse decision by SSA concerning a client's right to benefits.

Attorneys for claimants whose cases are remanded by a district court to the HHS Secretary may obtain fees for work that they perform during that administrative proceeding provided other requirements are met.[4] When a court orders a remand to the Secretary yet retains jurisdiction over the action, the proceedings on remand are considered an integral part of the "civil action" for judicial review.[5] Thus, attorney fees for representation on remand may be available.[6]

§ 15.140 Equal Access to Justice Act—Requirements—Prevailing Party

The claimant has the burden of proving that he or she is a "prevailing party."[1] Under 28 U.S.C.A. § 2412(d)(2)(H), a prevailing party "means a party who obtains a final judgment (other than by settlement)" on the merits of the case.[2] Generally, the courts have defined "prevailing party" as a claimant who has succeeded on any

2. 28 U.S.C.A. § 2412(d)(1)(A); See generally Deford, Melkonyan v. Sullivan: What Hath the Supreme Court Wrought?, 25 Clearinghouse Rev. 663 (1991); Bohr, The Equal Access to Justice Act, 37 Soc.Sec.Rep.Ser.Commentary 5 (7/9/92) (WESTLAW: SSRS database, ci(37 + 5 1)).

§ 15.139

1. 5 U.S.C.A. § 504; 28 U.S.C.A. §§ 2412(b), 2412(d).

2. 5 U.S.C.A. § 504(b)(1)(c).

3. See Hull v. Bowen, 748 F.Supp. 514, 518, 31 Soc.Sec.Rep.Ser. 484 (N.D.Ohio 1990); Brown v. Secretary of Health and Human Services, 747 F.2d 878, 880, 7 Soc. Sec.Rep.Ser. 211 (3d Cir.1984).

4. Sullivan v. Hudson, 490 U.S. 877, 109 S.Ct. 2248, 404 L.Ed.2d 941, 25 Soc.Sec.Rep. Ser. 401 (1989).

5. Sullivan v. Hudson, 490 U.S. 877, 892, 109 S.Ct. 2248, 2258, 104 L.Ed.2d 941, 25 Soc.Sec.Rep.Ser. 401 (1989).

6. See §§ 15.138–.142 and 15.144 for further discussion of fees in cases involving remands.

§ 15.140

1. Fincke v. Heckler, 596 F.Supp. 125, 7 Soc.Sec.Rep.Ser. 668 (D.Nev.1984).

2. 28 U.S.C.A. § 2412(d)(2)(H).

significant issue involved in the litigation.[3] Receipt of the desired relief may not be sufficient; courts also may require that the lawsuit act as a catalyst in securing the desired relief.[4] Ordinarily, in Social Security Act cases, a claimant prevails by obtaining an award of benefits, but other victories also can result in the claimant being viewed as a prevailing party.[5]

It is common in social security cases to request the district court to remand the case to the Secretary. Whether a claimant becomes a prevailing party by obtaining a remand order depends on the statutory basis for the remand and the relief obtained.

In Sullivan v. Hudson, the Supreme Court indicated that since "a claimant will not normally attain prevailing party status until after the result of the administrative proceedings is known;" a claimant generally does not obtain status as a prevailing party merely by obtaining a remand order.[6] The Supreme Court stated in Melkonyan v. Sullivan, that in a remand pursuant to sentence six of 28 U.S.C.A. § 405(g), the court retains jurisdiction; therefore, there is no final judgment from which to obtain prevailing party status.[7] The Court also indicated that if there is a joint stipulation to voluntarily dismiss an appeal and consent to a remand, the claimant would not be a prevailing party.[8] In Shalala v. Schaefer, the Court held that a claimant who obtains a remand pursuant to sentence four of the section is a prevailing party and that the judgment of remand is a final judgment for EAJA purposes.[9]

---

3. Brown v. Secretary of Health and Human Services, 747 F.2d 878, 883, 7 Soc. Sec.Rep.Ser. 211 (3d Cir.1984); Fincke v. Heckler, 596 F.Supp. 125, 7 Soc.Sec.Rep. Ser. 668 (D.Nev.1984); Shepard v. Sullivan, 898 F.2d 1267, 29 Soc.Sec.Rep.Ser. 165 (7th Cir.1990); Petrone v. Secretary of Health and Human Services, 936 F.2d 428 (9th Cir.1991).

4. Fincke v. Heckler, 596 F.Supp. 125, 7 Soc.Sec.Rep.Ser. 668 (D.Nev.1984); See also Petrone v. Secretary of Health and Human Services, 936 F.2d 428 (9th Cir.1991), *cert. denied* __ U.S. __, 112 S.Ct. 1161, 117 L.Ed.2d 409, 36 Soc.Sec.Rep.Ser. 274 (1992) (a claimant whose victory resulted from the change in law was not a "prevailing party" under the EAJA); But see Perket v. Secretary of Health and Human Services, 905 F.2d 129, 30 Soc.Sec.Rep.Ser. 155 (6th Cir.1990) (claimant whose victory resulted

from change in law was a "prevailing party" under the EAJA).

5. E.g. Bradley v. Heckler, 785 F.2d 954, 13 Soc.Sec.Rep.Ser. 48 (11th Cir.1986) (EAJA fees awarded for procedural victory).

6. Sullivan v. Hudson, 490 U.S. 877, 886, 109 S.Ct. 2248, 2255, 104 L.Ed.2d 941 (1989).

7. Melkonyan v. Sullivan, __ U.S. __, 111 S.Ct. 2157, 2165, 115 L.Ed.2d 78, 33 Soc.Sec.Rep.Ser. 363, *on remand* 943 F.2d 1476 (9th Cir.1991). See §§ 15.142 and 15.-144 for further discussion.

8. Id.

9. Shalala v. Schaefer, __ U.S. __, 113 S.Ct. 2625, 125 L.Ed.2d 239, 41 Soc.Sec.Rep. Ser. 334 (1993).

§ 15.141 Equal Access to Justice Act—Requirements—Substantially Justified

After the claimant has proven that he or she is a prevailing party, the burden shifts to the government to show that its position was substantially justified.[1] Generally, "position" encompasses both the prelitigation conduct of the Social Security Administration (SSA) and the Department of Justice's subsequent litigation position before the district court.[2] Because the Equal Access to Justice Act (EAJA) favors treating a case as a whole rather than as separate items, the statute requires a single finding that the government's position either has or lacks substantial justification.[3] To establish that substantial justification exists, the government must demonstrate a reasonable basis in both law and fact for its position.[4] The government's loss of the case creates no presumption that its position was not substantially justified,[5] so long as the government's position was taken in good faith. The government also may argue that there are special circumstances that would make an award of attorney fees unjust. Generally, this provision acts as a safety net to protect the government's good faith advancement of different yet credible interpretations of the law and to allow the court, at its discretion, to rely upon equitable considerations in denying a fee award.[6]

§ 15.142 Equal Access to Justice Act—Requirements—Final Judgment

A party is required to seek fees within 30 days of a "final judgment." "Final judgment" is a judgment that is not appealable from any court.[1] Administrative decisions are not final judgments under the

§ 15.141

1. Fincke v. Heckler, 596 F.Supp. 125, 7 Soc.Sec.Rep.Ser. 668 (D.Nev.1984).

2. Commissioner, I.N.S. v. Jean, 496 U.S. 154, 110 S.Ct. 2316, 110 L.Ed.2d 134 (1990); Andrew v. Bowen, 837 F.2d 875, 20 Soc.Sec.Rep.Ser. 314 (9th Cir.1988).

3. Commissioner, I.N.S. v. Jean, 496 U.S. 154, 110 S.Ct. 2316, 110 L.Ed.2d 134 (1990); Andrew v. Bowen, 837 F.2d 875, 20 Soc.Sec.Rep.Ser. 314 (9th Cir.1988).

4. Thomason v. Sullivan, 777 F.Supp. 1277, 1280, 35 Soc.Sec.Rep.Ser. 661 (D.S.C. 1991); Broussard v. Bowen, 828 F.2d 310, 312, 19 Soc.Sec.Rep.Ser. 26 (5th Cir.1987); Fincke v. Heckler, 596 F.Supp. 125, 128, 7 Soc.Sec.Rep.Ser. 668 (D.Nev.1984); Pierce v. Underwood, 487 U.S. 552, 108 S.Ct. 2541,

101 L.Ed.2d 490 (1988) (once the court makes a determination for or against the government, its finding is subject only to an abuse of discretion standard of review rather than a *de novo* standard).

5. Broussard v. Bowen, 828 F.2d 310, 312, 19 Soc.Sec.Rep.Ser. 26 (5th Cir.1987).

6. Brinker v. Guiffrida, 798 F.2d 661 (3d Cir.1986) (An example is when the claimant is the prevailing party, yet has "unclean" hands in the action. In such a case, the Court may deny attorney fees under the EAJA.).

§ 15.142

1. 28 U.S.C.A. § 2412(d)(2)(G); Melkonyan v. Sullivan, ___ U.S. ___, 111 S.Ct. 2157, 115 L.Ed.2d 78, 33 Soc.Sec.Rep.Ser.

Equal Access to Justice Act (EAJA). Generally, the 30–day EAJA limit does not begin to run until after expiration of the 60–day period in which to file a notice of appeal or a petition for a writ of certiorari.[2]

In cases involving remands, the type of remand entered by the district court under 42 U.S.C.A. § 405(g) determines when a fee application must be filed. A sentence four remand, defined as "where a court can enter a judgment affirming, modifying, or reversing the secretary's decision with or without remanding the case for a rehearing," is a final judgment. A sentence six remand, defined as "where the court may order a remand for the taking of additional evidence but only upon a showing that there is new evidence which is material and there is good cause for the failure to incorporate such evidence into the record in a prior proceeding," is not final.[3]

The final judgment occurs, and therefore the 30–day filing period begins, as follows:

1. A judgment reversing the Secretary and awarding benefits is a final judgment. The filing period begins after the 60–day appeal period has expired.

2. In a sentence four remand, the remand order itself generally is a final judgment. Consequently, the filing period generally begins after the 60–day appeal period following the district court order directing remand. Several circuits held that a sentence four remand order is not a final judgment for the purpose of filing an EAJA fee petition where the district court intended to retain jurisdiction of the matter.[4] Under this approach, no final judgment would occur until the district court

363, *on remand* 943 F.2d 1476 (9th Cir. 1991) (a "final judgment in the action" in § 2412(d)(1)(B) refers to "civil action . . . in any court" in § 2412(d)(1)(A)).

2. Shalala v. Schaefer, ___ U.S. ___, 113 S.Ct. 2625, 125 L.Ed.2d 239, 41 Soc.Sec.Rep. Ser. 334 (1993). See also Hudson v. Sullivan, 779 F.Supp. 37, 35 Soc.Sec.Rep.Ser. 771 (W.D.Pa.1991); Martindale v. Sullivan, 890 F.2d 410, 27 Soc.Sec.Rep.Ser. 573 (11th Cir.1989); but see Myers v. Sullivan, 916 F.2d 659, 672, 31 Soc.Sec.Rep.Ser. 313 (11th Cir.1990) (when the Secretary presented clear and unequivocal notice that he was waiving his right to appeal the postremand judgment, the 30–day limit began immediately).

3. 42 U.S.C.A. § 405(g); Melkonyan v. Sullivan, ___ U.S. ___, 111 S.Ct. 2157, 2164,

115 L.Ed.2d 78, 33 Soc.Sec.Rep.Ser. 363, *on remand* 943 F.2d 1476 (9th Cir.1991). See also, Sullivan v. Finkelstein, 496 U.S. 617, 622, 625, 110 S.Ct. 2658, 2663, 2664, 110 L.Ed.2d 563, 30 Soc.Sec.Rep.Ser. 118 (1990), *on remand* 924 F.2d 483, 32 Soc.Sec.Rep. Ser. 276 (3d Cir.1991) (sentence four remand is a final judgment that the Secretary may appeal under 28 U.S.C.A. § 405(g)).

4. Labrie v. Secretary of Health and Human Services, 976 F.2d 779, 785 (1st Cir.1992); Hafner v. Sullivan, 972 F.2d 249, 252 (8th Cir.1992); Scanlon v. Sullivan, 974 F.2d 107, 108 (9th Cir.1992); Gutierrez v. Sullivan, 953 F.2d 579, 584 (10th Cir.1992).

enters a judgment in the matter following completion of the proceedings on remand. However, in Shalala v. Schaefer,[5] the Supreme Court held that a sentence four remand order is a final judgment for purposes of filing an EAJA fee petition.

3. In a sentence six remand, the 30–day filing period does not begin until after the following sequence of events:

a. the postremand proceedings are completed and the Secretary returns to the court;

b. the court enters a final judgment; and

c. the 60–day appeal period runs.[6]

The courts are divided on the exact date of the final judgment when the Court of Appeals remands the case to the district court,[7] and the Supreme Court has declined to reach a decision on whether a fee petition can be filed before the 30–day period begins or before judgment is entered.[8] Some lower courts have permitted claimants to file for fees before entry of the final judgment.[9]

§ 15.143 Equal Access to Justice Act—Fees and Fee Requests

A prevailing party under 28 U.S.C.A. § 2412(d) is entitled to an award of fees based on "prevailing market rates for the kind and quality of the services furnished."[1] Fees are capped at $75 per hour "unless the court determines that an increase in the cost of living or a special factor, such as the limited availability of qualified attorneys for

---

5. __ U.S. __, 113 S.Ct. 2625, 125 L.Ed.2d 239, 41 Soc.Sec.Rep.Ser. 334 (1993). The Court disapproved of district court retention of jurisdiction in sentence four remands. The Court did note however, that the appeal period does not run until a final judgment *is entered.* Since no judgment has been entered in *Schaefer,* the EAJA fee petition was timely. Id.

6. Melkonyan v. Sullivan, __ U.S. __, 111 S.Ct. 2157, 2164, 115 L.Ed.2d 78, 33 Soc.Sec.Rep.Ser. 363, *on remand* 943 F.2d 1476 (9th Cir.1991).

7. See Luna v. U.S. Department of Health and Human Services, 948 F.2d 169, 35 Soc.Sec.Rep.Ser. 416 (5th Cir.1991) (held circuit court's remand was not the final judgment); but see Taylor v. Sullivan, 1992

WL 367993 (S.D.Ga.1992) (circuit order to remand was a final judgment).

8. Melkonyan v. Sullivan, __ U.S. __, 111 S.Ct. 2157, 115 L.Ed.2d 78, 33 Soc.Sec. Rep.Ser. 363 (1991), *on remand* 943 F.2d 1476 (9th Cir.1991) (the Court suggested that the claimant would not be prejudiced by filing early).

9. Cf. Kowalick v. Sullivan, 812 F.Supp. 534, 40 Soc.Sec.Rep.Ser. 171 (E.D.Pa.1993); Haitian Refugee Center v. Meese, 791 F.2d 1489, 1495 (11th Cir.1991), *vacated in part on other grounds on rehearing,* 804 F.2d 1573 (1986) (fee petitions may be filed before final judgment in order to obtain interim fee awards in appropriate circumstances).

§ 15.143

1. 28 U.S.C.A. § 2412(d)(2)(A).

the proceedings involved, justifies a higher fee."[2]　Because Congress intended that attorney fees should be paid under the Equal Access to Justice Act (EAJA) regardless of the fee arrangements between the attorney and client, courts have held that fee awards are appropriate for services performed *pro bono* or by a legal services program.[3]　In addition, other representatives are entitled to fees under the EAJA.[4] The work that law clerks and paralegals perform is also compensable.[5]

The EAJA authorizes recovery of costs[6] and expenses.[7]　Filing and service fees, costs of expert witnesses, travel, postage, and phone calls are among the items that can be recovered.[8]

An attorney may apply for fees under both the Social Security Administration (SSA) and the EAJA, and an award under one statute does not preclude an award under the other.[9]　Some courts encourage simultaneous applications on the same case.[10]　When dual awards are obtained, the EAJA award must be used to reduce the payment the

2. 28 U.S.C.A. § 2412(d)(1)(A); see also Kelly v. Bowen, 862 F.2d 1333, 1336, 24 Soc.Sec.Rep.Ser. 77 (8th Cir.1988) (fees can be enhanced due to cost of living); Scavone v. Sullivan, 780 F.Supp. 976, 36 Soc.Sec. Rep.Ser. 180 (E.D.N.Y.), *affirmed* 970 F.2d 896 (2d Cir.1992) (cost of living index is the "legal services" category under the Consumer Price Index); Pirus v. Bowen, 869 F.2d 536, 541–42, 25 Soc.Sec.Rep.Ser. 81 (9th Cir.1989) (special expertise is a factor justifying a larger fee); Garcia v. Schweiker, 829 F.2d 396, 402, 19 Soc.Sec.Rep.Ser. 65 (3d Cir.1987) (Court should use current not historical rate calculations in awarding fees).

3. See H.R.Rep. No. 1418, 96th Cong., Admin.News 4953, 4984, 4994 (Congress's intent in passing the EAJA); Cornella v. Schweiker, 728 F.2d 978, 985–87, 4 Soc.Sec. Rep.Ser. 204 (8th Cir.1984) (fee award for *pro bono* work or work done by a legal services program).

4. See e.g., DiGennaro v. Bowen, 666 F.Supp. 426, 430, 19 Soc.Sec.Rep.Ser. 105 (E.D.N.Y.1987) (fee award appropriate for unpaid law student); Celeste v. Sullivan, 734 F.Supp. 1009, 29 Soc.Sec.Rep.Ser. 472 (S.D.Fla.1990), *reversed in part, vacated in part* 972 F.2d 1349 (11th Cir.1992) (claimant's proceeding *pro se* may be eligible for a fee award); Hoffman v. Heckler, 656 F.Supp. 1136, 1137, 17 Soc.Sec.Rep.Ser. 563 (E.D.Pa.1987) (personal representative of a

deceased claimant's estate may file for fees on behalf of the estate).

5. See e.g., Kopunec v. Nelson, 801 F.2d 1226, 1229 (10th Cir.1986); Hoopa Valley Tribe v. Watt, 569 F.Supp. 943, 947 (N.D.Cal.1983); United States v. Boeing Co., Inc., 747 F.Supp. 319, 323 (E.D.Va. 1990) (law clerks and paralegals are generally compensated at rates between $25 to $50 per hour).

6. 28 U.S.C.A. § 2412(a).　A prevailing party can obtain fees even if the government's position was substantially justified.

7. 28 U.S.C.A. § 2412(b), (d)(2)(A).

8. Kelly v. Bowen, 862 F.2d 1333, 24 Soc.Sec.Rep.Ser. 77 (8th Cir.1988).

9. Russell v. Sullivan, 930 F.2d 1443, 33 Soc.Sec.Rep.Ser. 210 (9th Cir.1991); Hull v. Bowen, 748 F.Supp. 514, 31 Soc.Sec.Rep. Ser. 484 (N.D.Ohio 1990); Secatore v. Bowen, 732 F.Supp. 1569, 29 Soc.Sec.Rep.Ser. 257 (S.D.Fla.1990); O'Grady v. Secretary of U.S. Dept. of HHS, 661 F.Supp. 1030, 18 Soc.Sec.Rep.Ser. 340 (E.D.N.Y.1987); Petrella v. Secretary of Health and Human Services, 654 F.Supp. 174, 17 Soc.Sec.Rep. Ser. 160 (M.D.Pa.1987).

10. E.g. Hull v. Bowen, 748 F.Supp. 514, 525, 31 Soc.Sec.Rep.Ser. 484 (N.D.Ohio 1990) (to promote judicial economy).

claimant would otherwise owe the attorney.[11] Because an EAJA award can result in a reduced Social Security Act fee paid from a claimant's award of back benefits, some courts have said that an attorney has an obligation to seek EAJA fees and that an attorney should notify the client of the reason the attorney thought an EAJA fee petition was not justified.[12]

§ 15.144 Equal Access to Justice Act—Remand Cases

In *Sullivan v. Hudson,*[1] the Supreme Court held that counsel can obtain fees for work done during the court proceeding and for work done at the administrative level following a remand, if the district court retains jurisdiction of the case. Such fees are available in sentence six remands, but until recently it was unclear whether a district court could retain jurisdiction over a sentence four remand. If the court is precluded from retaining jurisdiction, it would seem that counsel would be precluded from obtaining attorney fees for work on remand. Because *Melkonyan v. Sullivan*[2] did not limit district court retention of jurisdiction to sentence six remands, some courts held that a district court could retain jurisdiction over a sentence four remand.[3] In *Shalala v. Schaefer,*[4] the court rejected this possibility, indicating that retention of jurisdiction is not proper in a sentence four remand, which, in the court's view, is a judgment terminating the litigation. As a result of *Schaefer,* it will be difficult for an advocate to obtain an EAJA fee for representation before SSA in a sentence four remand. The decision also makes it clear that an advocate should file an EAJA fee petition

11. Russell v. Sullivan, 930 F.2d 1443, 33 Soc.Sec.Rep.Ser. 210 (9th Cir.1991); Hull v. Bowen, 748 F.Supp. 514, 31 Soc.Sec. Rep.Ser. 484 (N.D.Ohio 1990); Secatore v. Bowen, 732 F.Supp. 1569, 29 Soc.Sec.Rep. Ser. 257 (S.D.Fla.1990).

12. Knagge v. Sullivan, 735 F.Supp. 411, 29 Soc.Sec.Rep.Ser. 510 (M.D.Fla. 1990).

§ 15.144

1. 490 U.S. 877, 109 S.Ct. 2248, 104 L.Ed.2d 941, 25 Soc.Sec.Rep.Ser. 401 (1989).

2. ___ U.S. ___, 111 S.Ct. 2157, 115 L.Ed.2d 78, 33 Soc.Sec.Rep.Ser. 363, *on remand* 943 F.2d 1476 (9th Cir.1991).

3. See Deford, Melkonyan v. Sullivan: What Hath the Supreme Court Wrought?, 25 Clearinghouse Rev. 663 (1991). The 1st, 8th, 9th, and 10th Circuits have so held. See § 15.142, note 4 supra. See also, Gu-

tierrez v. Sullivan, 953 F.2d 579, 584, 36 Soc.Sec.Rep.Ser. 129 (10th Cir.1992) (recognizes a subcategory of cases in which the district court may retain jurisdiction over a sentence four remand until after the administrative proceedings are complete); Burr v. Bowen, 782 F.Supp. 1285, 1289, 36 Soc.Sec.Rep.Ser. 324 (N.D.Ill.1992) (gives a liberal construction to sentence six remands so that a remand for the taking of medical tests was a sentence six remand); Boronat v. Sullivan, 788 F.Supp. 557, 37 Soc.Sec.Rep.Ser. 136 (S.D.Fla.1992) (refusing to retrospectively label its fourth sentence remand order as a final judgment when it clearly was not intended as such). See also Bohr, The Equal Access to Justice Act, 37 Soc.Sec.Rep.Ser. Commentary 5 (7/9/92) (WESTLAW: SSRS database, ci(37 +5 1)).

4. ___ U.S. ___, 113 S.Ct. 2625, 125 L.Ed.2d 239, 41 Soc.Sec.Rep.Ser. 334 (1993).

promptly upon obtaining a judgment in a sentence four case, even when the relief obtained is a remand to SSA.

§ 15.145 Equal Access to Justice Act—Retroactivity and Tolling

Since *Melkonyan v. Sullivan* [1] altered widely utilized Equal Access to Justice Act (EAJA) practices, the issue of its retroactive application is important. Courts are divided on whether the decision should be applied retroactively.[2] The problem is that prior to *Melkonyan*, the appropriate time for filing a petition for EAJA fees was after final judgment by the district court, following positive resolution of the merits, including postremand administrative proceedings. If *Melkonyan* is applied retroactively, then for sentence four remands, the 30–day filing period begins after the 60–day appeal period following the district court's remand. As a result, some claimants with sentence four remands have missed the time limit to file for EAJA attorney fees.

Another issue is whether the EAJA 30–day limit is jurisdictional or a statute of limitations. If the 30–day limit is a statute of limitations, it may be subject to equitable tolling.[3] However, if the 30–day limit is jurisdictional, the claimant's failure to file timely application precludes the district court from considering the merits of the application.[4]

§ 15.146 Information

Social Security Administration local offices suggest that an individual call the Teleservice Center at 1–800–772–1213 to find out what information the individual needs in order to file an application. The Teleservice Center also may be able to schedule a face-to-face or telephone appointment for the individual and can answer questions.

§ 15.45

1. ___ U.S. ___, 111 S.Ct. 2157, 115 L.Ed.2d 78, 33 Soc.Sec.Rep.Ser. 363, *on remand* 943 F.2d 1476 (9th Cir.1991).

2. See Butts v. Bowen, 775 F.Supp. 1167, 35 Soc.Sec.Rep.Ser. 449 (N.D.Ill.1991) (not retroactively applied); Fergason v. Sullivan, 771 F.Supp. 1008, 35 Soc.Sec.Rep. Ser. 53 (W.D.Mo.1991); Sargent v. Sullivan, 941 F.2d 1207 (4th Cir.1991); But see Audette v. Secretary of Health and Human Services, 776 F.Supp. 84, 35 Soc.Sec.Rep. Ser. 468 (D.R.I.1991) (retroactively applied); Welter v. Sullivan, 941 F.2d 674, 675, 34 Soc.Sec.Rep.Ser. 375 (8th Cir.1991).

3. Golbach v. Sullivan, 779 F.Supp. 9, 35 Soc.Sec.Rep.Ser. 761 (N.D.N.Y.1991) (30–day limit is a statute of limitations that can be waived).

4. Myers v. Sullivan, 916 F.2d 659, 31 Soc.Sec.Rep.Ser. 313 (11th Cir.1990) (if *Melkonyan* is applied retroactively, claimant would most likely have already missed the time limit to file).

CHAPTER 16

SOCIAL SECURITY DISABILITY

Table of Sections

A. GENERAL INFORMATION

A. GENERAL INFORMATION

§ 16.1 Introduction

The Social Security Act provides disability benefits to individuals unable to work due to illness or injury under two programs. This chapter discusses social security disability benefits available to disabled persons who meet the "disability," "waiting period," and "insured status" requirements of the act (see below).[1] The Supplemental Security Income (SSI) program (see Chapter 17, infra) provides benefits to disabled individuals who are impoverished.

The programs utilize the same definition of "disability." Disability benefits are particularly important for persons between the ages of 50 and 65 because of their difficulty in becoming reemployed after illness or injury. Since Department of Health and Human Services (HHS) regulations, commonly referred to as "Grids," are weighted in favor of persons over age 55,[2] an attorney representing a seriously ill or injured client over 55 should examine closely the possibility of a social security disability claim.

A client between the ages of 62 through 65 generally should file a concurrent social security retirement claim (see Chapter 15, supra) along with a disability claim, thereby enhancing the likelihood that the client will have income while the disability claim is processed. The retirement claim is not a substitute for a disability claim, however, since disability benefits usually are greater than retirement benefits for persons under 65.

A person who has become disabled long after the termination of the person's employment, or who has not worked long enough to meet disability insured status (see §§ 16.12–.13, infra), should explore the possibility of receiving SSI.

§ 16.2 Administration

The Social Security Administration (SSA) administers social security disability. Applicants may file at the local District Office or by telephone. An agency of the state in which the claimant resides, the

---

§ 16.1   2. 20 C.F.R. Pt. 404, Subpt. P, App. 2.

1. 42 U.S.C.A. § 423.

Disability Determination Service (DDS), generally makes the medical determination of eligibility for SSA. This state agency also makes the medical determinations for Supplemental Security Income claimants.

§ 16.3 Authority

The statutory authority for the social security disability program is found in Title II of the Social Security Act, 42 U.S.C.A. §§ 423–425. The HHS regulations implementing the program are found at 20 C.F.R. § 404.1 et seq. Social Security Administration (SSA) employees use the Program Operations Manual System (POMS) to administer the Retirement, Survivors, Health, and Disability Insurance (RSHDI) program as well as the Supplemental Security Income (SSI) program. Attorneys may review POMS at the local District Office or a federal depository library. The POMS provisions sometimes conflict with the Social Security Act and the HHS regulations. Attorneys should rely on POMS with caution and be aware that administrative law judges may disregard POMS provisions that conflict with the act and the regulations. Also useful are Social Security Rulings issued by SSA and available in West's Social Security Reporting Service.

Additional sources of assistance include C. Hall, Social Security Disability Practice (West Annual edition) and H. McCormick, Social Security Claims and Procedures (4th ed. West, 1991).

§§ 16.4–16.10 are reserved for supplementary material.

B. ELIGIBILITY

Library References:

C.J.S. Social Security and Public Welfare §§ 48, 49.
West's Key No. Digests, Social Security and Public Welfare ⊕140.5.

§ 16.11 Persons Entitled [1]

To receive disability insurance benefits, an individual must:

1. meet the disability insured status requirements,

2. not have attained age 65,

3. file an application for disability benefits,

4. have fulfilled the waiting period if applicable, and

5. be under a disability (see below).

§ 16.11

1. 42 U.S.C.A. § 423(a)(1); 20 C.F.R. § 404.315.

Spouses and children may receive monthly benefits while the disabled worker is entitled to disability benefits provided certain criteria are met. The first four requirements shown above are routine administrative actions. The bulk of social security disability litigation centers on the issue of "disability."

§ 16.12 Disability Insured Status [1]—Worker Age 31 and Over

To achieve disability insured status, a disabled worker age 31 and over must meet two earnings requirements. First, the worker must earn at least one quarter of coverage (QC), whenever acquired, for each calendar year after 1950 or the year the worker attains age 21 (whichever occurs later) until the year the worker becomes disabled.[2] For example, Sheila, born in 1957, becomes disabled in 1993. Sheila attains age 21 in 1978, so the next year is 1979. She must have at least one QC for each subsequent year until 1993, or 14 QCs.

The second requirement is that the disabled worker must earn 20 QCs during the 40–quarter period ending with the quarter in which the worker becomes disabled.[3] For example, Sheila, born July 1, 1957, becomes disabled on June 21, 1993. Counting 40 quarters back from the quarter of disability means Sheila must have 20 QCs from July 1, 1983, through June 30, 1993. For various reasons, Sheila did not work for 16 of the 40 periods. However, she has earned 24 QCs, so she meets the 20/40 requirement.

§ 16.13 Disability Insured Status—Worker Before Age 31

A worker disabled before age 31 also has two earnings requirements to meet. The worker must have earned one quarter of coverage (QC) for each year after the year the worker attained age 21 until the year the worker became disabled, but at least six QCs.[1] The worker then has what is called fully insured status. For example, Jason, born in 1971, becomes disabled in 1994. He attains age 21 in 1992, so the next year is 1993. Ordinarily only one QC for each subsequent year up to the year of disability is required; in Jason's case, this would be one quarter. However, the minimum requirement is six QCs, so Jason must have six quarters to be "fully insured."

The second requirement the worker disabled before age 31 must meet is to earn QCs in at least one-half of the quarters after the quarter during which the worker attains age 21 until the worker becomes

§ 16.12

1. 42 U.S.C.A. § 423(c)(1); 20 C.F.R. §§ 404.130–404.133.

2. See § 15.14 for a discussion of quarters of coverage.

3. 20 C.F.R. § 404.130(b).

§ 16.13

1. 20 C.F.R. § 404.130(c).

disabled. If this number of quarters is an odd number, the necessary number is reduced by one quarter. If the period is less than 12 quarters, the worker must have earned six quarters in the 12–quarter period ending with the quarter of disability. For example, Jason, born December 26, 1971, becomes disabled on February 14, 1994. Since he is under age 31 on the date he becomes disabled, the special-age-31 requirement applies. Jason attains age 21 in the last quarter of 1992. Since there are less than 12 quarters from December 1992 until February 1994, Jason needs six QCs in the 12–quarter period ending in February 1994 (4/91 to 1/94). If Jason has earned fewer than six QCs in that period, he fails to meet insured status. If he has earned six or more quarters, he is insured.

A disabled individual who does not meet disability insured status may be eligible for Supplemental Security Income (SSI) disability benefits.

§ 16.14 Waiting Period

A disabled individual must serve a waiting period before monthly cash benefits will be paid. The waiting period consists of five consecutive months beginning with the first full month of disability.[1] Prior to the Social Security Amendments of 1972,[2] the waiting period was six months. Technically, the waiting period is now five months,[3] but as a practical matter, the Social Security Administration's (SSA's) interpretation, which counts only full months of disability, effectively requires disabled individuals to wait six months. For example, if George's application of April 10, 1993, is approved, and he is determined to have become disabled on February 2, 1993, his waiting period begins March 1, 1993, which is the first full month he was disabled. George's waiting period continues through July 31, 1993, and his benefits are payable beginning in August 1993. The SSA's construction of the act has been upheld against challenges by advocates who argued that only claimants disabled on the first day of a month avoid waiting six months.[4]

The waiting period can begin no earlier than the first day of the 17th month preceding the month in which the application was filed if the individual is insured for disability in such month.[5] In the previous

§ 16.14

1. 42 U.S.C.A. § 423(c)(2); 20 C.F.R. § 404.315(d).

2. Pub.L. No. 92–603 § 104(d), 118(a)(4), 86 Stat. 1329, codified at 42 U.S.C.A. § 423(c)(2).

3. 42 U.S.C.A. § 402(e)(5)(A); 42 U.S.C.A. § 402(f)(4).

4. Sanchez v. Schweiker, 656 F.2d 966 (5th Cir.1981), cert. denied 456 U.S. 943, 102 S.Ct. 2008, 72 L.Ed.2d 465 (1982); Robbins v. Schweiker, 708 F.2d 340, 342, 2 Soc.Sec.Rep.Ser. 116 (8th Cir.1983).

5. 42 U.S.C.A. § 423(c)(2); 20 C.F.R. § 404.315(d).

example, if George filed his application April 10, 1993, and was found to be disabled as of February 15, 1991, his waiting period would begin November 11, 1991, and continue through March 31, 1992, with benefits payable effective April 1992.

No waiting period is required when the disabled individual becomes re-entitled to disability benefits within five years of the termination of a prior entitlement.[6] For example, Bret's disability application of October 1, 1993, is approved with an onset date of June 2, 1992. Since the onset date is not the first day of the month, the next month is the first full month under disability. Thus Bret's waiting period is July 1992 to November 1992, and cash benefits are payable from December 1992 on. If Bret had received disability benefits until July 1987, his waiting period for his subsequent application would be waived, since he would have become re-entitled within five years.

A waiting period is required for disabled workers, disabled widows,[7] and disabled widowers,[8] unless the re-entitlement exception is met. Disabled childhood beneficiaries [9] and Supplemental Security Income (SSI) beneficiaries do not serve waiting periods. Counsel should advise their clients who otherwise meet the criteria for SSI to file concurrent social security disability and SSI disability claims. This ensures that the client will receive some income during the waiting period, particularly if the disability occurred within six months of the date of the application.

§§ 16.15–16.20 are reserved for supplementary material.

C. DISABILITY

§ 16.21 Disability Defined [1]

Disability means the "inability to engage in any substantial gainful activity by reason of any medically determinable physical or mental impairment" which can be expected to result in death or which has lasted or is expected to last for twelve consecutive months. An individual not only must be unable to perform his or her previous work due to this impairment but, considering age, education, and work experience, also cannot be expected to engage in any other substantial gainful work existing in the national economy, regardless of whether such work

---

6. 20 C.F.R. § 404.315(d).

7. 42 U.S.C.A. § 402(e)(1)(F); 20 C.F.R. § 404.335(c).

8. 42 U.S.C.A. § 402(f)(1)(F); 20 C.F.R. § 404.335(c).

9. 42 U.S.C.A. § 402(d)(1)(G); 20 C.F.R. § 404.352.

§ 16.21

1. 42 U.S.C.A. § 423(d).

exists in the immediate area in which the individual lives, whether a specific job vacancy exists, or whether the individual would be hired if he or she applied for work.[2] "Work which exists in the national economy" is work that exists in significant numbers in the region where the individual lives, or in several regions of the country.[3]

This definition of disability applies to individuals applying for disability insurance benefits, Supplemental Security Income (SSI) disability benefits, disabled children's benefits, and disabled widow's benefits (filed or pending on January 1, 1991). There are different rules for determining disability for statutorily blind individuals and disabled widows whose claims were filed before January 1, 1991.[4]

Many disability claims turn on the determination of whether medical or vocational evidence establishes "an inability to engage in substantial gainful activity" or a "medically determinable physical or mental impairment."[5]

Library References:

C.J.S. Social Security and Public Welfare § 50.

West's Key No. Digests, Social Security and Public Welfare ☜140.10.

§ 16.22 Substantial Gainful Activity

Substantial gainful activity (SGA) refers to work activity that is both substantial and gainful. Gainful work activity is for remuneration or profit (or intended for profit, whether or not a profit is realized, or of a nature generally performed for remuneration or profit).[1] Substantial work activity involves the performance of significant physical or mental duties, or a combination of both. In order for work activity to be substantial, it is not necessary that it be performed on a full-time basis; work activity performed on a part-time basis also may be substantial. It is immaterial that the work activity of an individual may be less, or less responsible, or less gainful, than that in which the individual was engaged before the onset of the impairment.

Thus, performing functions, utilizing skills or experience, or assuming responsibilities that contribute substantially to an enterprise may be evidence of an individual's ability to engage in SGA.[2] However,

2. 42 U.S.C.A. § 423(d)(1)(A); 20 C.F.R. § 404.1505.

3. 42 U.S.C.A. § 423(d)(2)(A); 20 C.F.R. § 404.1566.

4. Omnibus Budget Reconciliation Act of 1990, Pub.L. No. 101–508, § 5103, 104 Stat. 1388, codified at 42 U.S.C.A. § 423(d).

5. See §§ 16.22–.23, infra.

§ 16.22

1. 20 C.F.R. § 404.1572(b).

2. 20 C.F.R. §§ 404.1572–404.1573.

activities or work that produce no profit or involve minimal duties may demonstrate an inability to perform SGA.

Activities such as taking care of one's self, household tasks, hobbies, and school attendance are not considered SGA. Similarly, work under special conditions such as in a sheltered workshop generally will not be considered SGA, although it can constitute evidence of skills needed to perform SGA.[3]

The Department of Health and Human Services (HHS) regulations presume that a person whose wages as an employee average less than $300 a month is not engaged in SGA, while a person whose wages exceed $500 a month is presumed to be engaged in SGA. A person whose wages are between these figures may be found to be engaged in SGA, depending on consideration of such factors as the time, energy, skill, and value of the work.[4] The procedure employed for determining whether a self-employed individual is engaged in SGA is similar to that described above for employees.[5]

§ **16.23** Impairment

A "physical or mental impairment" is an impairment resulting from anatomical, physiological, or psychological abnormalities that are demonstrated through medically acceptable clinical and laboratory diagnostic techniques.[1] The impairment must be established by medical evidence consisting of signs, symptoms, and laboratory findings, not merely by the individual's statement of symptoms.[2] If the impairment is not expected to result in the individual's death, it must have lasted or be expected to last 12 consecutive months.[3]

If the alleged impairment is not a "medically determinable physical or mental impairment," the individual is not disabled. Likewise, even though the impairment is "medically determinable," if it is not expected to last 12 consecutive months or result in the individual's death, the individual is not disabled. Multiple, unrelated severe impairments cannot be combined to meet the 12–month duration test. If

---

3. 20 C.F.R. §§ 404.1572–404.1574.

4. 20 C.F.R. § 404.1574. These figures are for years after 1989. The amounts may change. Impairment-related work expenses are deducted from these figures.

5. 20 C.F.R. § 404.1575.

§ **16.23**

1. 42 U.S.C.A. § 423(d)(3). Several circuits require that SSA defer to the opinion of a claimant's treating physician. See

e.g., Schisler v. Bowen, 851 F.2d 43 (2d Cir.1988). SSA issued rules on the weight to be given medical evidence, including reports from treating physicians. 56 Fed. Reg. 36, 931 (Aug. 1, 1991), codified at 20 C.F.R., parts 400–499. For a discussion of these issues, see Zelenske, Treating Physician Evidence in Social Security Disability Cases: What Does the Future Hold?, 27 Clearinghouse Rev. 31 (1993).

2. 20 C.F.R. § 404.1508.

3. 20 C.F.R. § 404.1509.

none of the impairments alone meet the duration test, the individual is not disabled.[4]

However, if a claimant has two or more concurrent impairments that in combination are severe, the Social Security Administration (SSA) must determine whether that combination of impairments can be expected to remain severe for the 12–month period. If one of the impairments is expected to or does improve so that the combination of impairments is no longer severe, the individual is not disabled.[5]

Administrative provisions specifically provide that *all* symptoms, including pain, be considered in the determination of a disability.[6] However, an individual's statement as to pain or other symptoms alone is not conclusive evidence of an impairment. The claimant must prove objective medical signs and findings established by medically acceptable clinical or laboratory diagnostic techniques that show an impairment capable of producing the pain or symptoms alleged.[7] When such an impairment is found to exist, the intensity and persistence of the symptoms will be evaluated to determine the extent to which they limit the claimant's capacity to work.[8] Courts have relied upon statutory wording to find that pain without objective evidence of its source may be disabling and that subjective complaints must be considered in demonstrating impairment.[9] Further, when an administrative law judge (ALJ) rejects an individual's testimony concerning pain, the ALJ must state specific reasons for questioning the individual's credibility.[10]

§ 16.24　Disability Determinations [1]—Sequential Evaluation— Overview

The Social Security Administration (SSA) must consider all material factors when making a disability determination. A five-step sequential evaluation is used to determine whether an individual is disabled (see chart, infra).[2]

Step 1. Is the applicant working? If "yes," the claim is denied if the work is considered substantial gainful activity regard-

4. 20 C.F.R. § 404.1522(a).

5. 20 C.F.R. § 404.1522(b).

6. 20 C.F.R. § 404.1529.

7. 42 U.S.C.A. § 423(d)(5)(A).

8. 20 C.F.R. § 404.1529(c)(1).

9. Polaski v. Heckler, 739 F.2d 1320, 6 Soc.Sec.Rep.Ser. 123 (8th Cir.1984), *vacated on other grounds* 476 U.S. 1167, 106 S.Ct. 2885, 90 L.Ed.2d 974 (1986); Avery v. Secretary of Health and Human Services, 797

F.2d 19, 14 Soc.Sec.Rep.Ser. 301 (1st Cir. 1986); Bunnell v. Sullivan, 947 F.2d 341, 35 Soc.Sec.Rep.Ser. 299 (9th Cir.1991).

10. Walker v. Bowen, 826 F.2d 996, 1004, 18 Soc.Sec.Rep.Ser. 725 (11th Cir. 1987).

§ 16.24

1. 20 C.F.R. § 404.1525.

2. 20 C.F.R. § 404.1520.

less of vocational factors, i.e., the applicant's age, education, and work experience. If "no," the second factor is considered.

Step 2. Does the applicant have a "severe impairment"? If "no," the claim is denied regardless of vocational factors. If "yes," the third factor is considered.

Step 3. Does the severity of the impairment meet or equal an impairment listed in Appendix 1 of 20 C.F.R. part 404, subpart P, so as to automatically qualify as a disability? If "yes," the applicant is disabled regardless of vocational factors. If "no," the fourth factor is considered.

Step 4. Does the impairment prevent the applicant from performing past relevant work? If "no," the claim is denied; if "yes," the final factor is considered.

Step 5. Does the impairment prevent the applicant from performing any other work? If "yes," the applicant may be found disabled after considering vocational factors. If "no," certain applicants still may be found disabled if they are only marginally educated unskilled laborers and can no longer perform that kind of work. Otherwise, the applicant's claim is denied.

THE 5 STEPS IN SEQUENTIAL EVALUATION

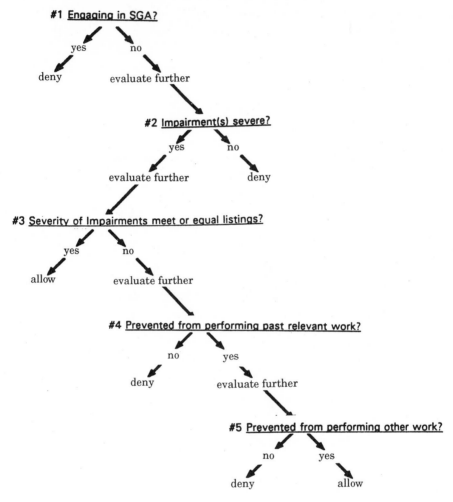

#1 Engaging in SGA?

yes   no

deny   evaluate further

#2 Impairment(s) severe?

yes   no

evaluate further   deny

#3 Severity of Impairments meet or equal listings?

yes   no

allow   evaluate further

#4 Prevented from performing past relevant work?

no   yes

deny   evaluate further

#5 Prevented from performing other work?

no   yes

deny   allow

[G13788]

§ 16.25 Disability Determinations—Sequential Evaluation— Step 1

The Social Security Administration (SSA) denies very few claims because the person is engaging in substantial gainful activity (SGA) either at the time of the application or prior to the disability determination by the state agency. Generally, where the claimant is working at the time the disability claim is taken, the District Office employee dissuades the claimant from filing. As a result, the first step in the sequential evaluation does not lead to many disability claim denials.

Clients should be made aware, however, that failure to file a claim on the oral advice of SSA employees can have undesirable consequences.[1] Because no initial determination is reached, no appeal is available from an oral denial. A client who believes that he or she is not engaging in SGA should file a claim and appeal the denial of benefits. If the applicant is found not to be engaging in SGA, the evaluation proceeds to step 2.

§ 16.26 Disability Determinations—Sequential Evaluation—Step 2

In the second step, the Social Security Administration (SSA) inquires whether there is an impairment or combination of impairments that is severe. The SSA does not consider an impairment to be severe if it does not significantly limit the claimant's physical or mental capacity to do basic work-related functions.[1] To be determined severe, an impairment must last at least 12 months.[2]

Claimants have challenged this step, asserting that it is inconsistent with the Social Security Act, since it permits the SSA to deny an application by determining on medical factors alone that the impairment is not severe. In *Bowen v. Yuckert,*[3] the Supreme Court upheld the severe impairment regulation, stating that it is consistent with the Social Security Act. It now appears that the SSA may require a *de minimis* showing of severity in step 2 to identify claimants whose impairments are "so slight that it is unlikely they would be found to be disabled even, if their age, education, and experience were taken into account." [4]

If the impairment or combination of impairments is determined not to be severe, the claim is denied. If, however, the impairment is determined to be severe, the evaluation proceeds to step 3.

§ 16.27 Disability Determinations—Sequential Evaluation—Step 3

Because of the requirement that an impairment last at least 12 months, most of the impairments listed in Appendix 1 of 20 C.F.R. part 404, subpart P, are permanent or expected to result in death.[1] In addition to the 12–month requirement, each impairment listed in

§ 16.25

1. See § 15.90 supra.

§ 16.26

1. 20 C.F.R. § 404.1520(c).

2. 20 C.F.R. § 404.1509.

3. 482 U.S. 137, 107 S.Ct. 2287, 96 L.Ed.2d 119, 17 Soc.Sec.Rep.Ser. 661 (1987).

4. 482 U.S. at 153, 107 S.Ct. at 2297, 96 L.Ed.2d at 134.

§ 16.27

1. 20 C.F.R. § 404.1525(a).

Appendix 1 includes specific clinical findings which must support the diagnosis in order to establish that impairment.[2] Additional medical findings beyond those listed may not be imposed by the Secretary.[3]

When an individual has an impairment that equals or meets the listed impairments in Appendix 1, SSA will determine the individual is disabled regardless of vocational factors, i.e., age, education, or work experience. Appendix 1 should be the standard against which an attorney should measure whether the client's impairment is disabling. Using the appendix, a medical opinion alone could suffice to establish that the applicant meets social security's definition of disability.

Appendix 1 is lengthy and detailed and is divided into parts A and B.[4] Part A gives the criteria used when the individual is over age 18 or when the individual is under 18 and the disease has similar effects on children as on adults. Part B contains the medical criteria for the evaluation of impairments of children under age 18 when part A does not apply.

If the individual's impairment is not listed, the impairment will be compared to the listed impairment most similar to that alleged, to determine if the alleged impairment is medically equal to the listed impairment. If the applicant has more than one impairment, none of which meets or equals the listed impairment, the Social Security Administration (SSA) will review the signs, symptoms, and laboratory findings of the impairments to determine if they are medically equal.[5]

An additional procedure is used to evaluate whether mental impairments are disabling.[6] The SSA is required to indicate whether certain findings relevant to the ability to work are present, and to rate the degree of functional loss due to the impairment. The SSA considers four areas essential to work: activities of daily living, social functioning, concentration, and deterioration/decompensation in work or work-like settings. Each area is rated on a scale ranging from "no limitation" to a severity level that is incompatible with the ability to perform work-related functions.

If the applicant's impairment meets or equals an impairment listed in Appendix 1, disability is established and the claim is allowed. If not, the applicant's residual functional capacity must be determined in step 4.

---

2. 20 C.F.R. § 404.18525(d).

3. See e.g. Gambill v. Bowen, 823 F.2d 1009, 18 Soc.Sec.Rep.Ser. 462 (6th Cir. 1987).

4. 20 C.F.R. § 404.1525.

5. 20 C.F.R. § 404.1526.

6. 20 C.F.R. § 404.1520a.

§ 16.28 Disability Determinations—Sequential Evaluation—Step 4

An applicant who cannot establish in step 3 that his or her severe impairment meets or equals an impairment listed in Appendix 1 of 20 C.F.R. part 404, subpart P, must demonstrate disability to the extent that the applicant can no longer perform the duties required by his or her former job. At this point, the claimant's "residual functional capacity" (RFC) becomes relevant. The claimant must show that he or she cannot perform his or her former job despite the limitations of the impairment. The RFC is what the individual can do despite the limitations.[1] The RFC is a medical assessment that may include a description of limitations beyond the symptoms necessary to diagnose and treat the medical condition. The RFC is determined by the state agency, the administrative law judge, or the Appeals Council, depending upon the level at which the claim is denied.[2]

If an applicant with a severe impairment establishes that he or she is unable to perform past relevant work, the evaluation proceeds to step 5.

§ 16.29 Disability Determinations—Sequential Evaluation—Step 5

In step 5, the burden of proof shifts to the Social Security Administration (SSA) which must prove that the applicant can do a job that exists in the national economy. The "Grids" are used for that purpose. The applicant's residual functional capacity (RFC) and impairment are applied to the Grids to make an automatic finding of "disabled" or "not disabled."

Formerly, a vocational expert testified at the hearing in each case in response to hypothetical questions from the administrative law judge (ALJ) as to what jobs were available in the national economy that the claimant was physically and mentally capable of performing. However, the SSA decided to simplify its task by adopting the "Grids." The Department of Health and Human Services (HHS) formulated the Grid rules in light of information about jobs existing in the national econo-

§ 16.28   2. 20 C.F.R. § 404.1546.
1. 20 C.F.R. § 404.1545.

my.[1]

There are two tables in the Grids that match combinations of functional abilities to the ability to perform a job.[2] The client is classified according to the client's RFC[3] on one of these tables: Table No. 1, for claimants capable of doing sedentary work, and Table No. 2, for those capable of doing light work. Only if an exact match with a Grid disabled category is found will the SSA find the client disabled. If the client fits a not disabled category, the SSA will consider all the relevant facts to determine whether the person's RFC is equivalent to the rule to decide whether the person is disabled.[4] Therefore, counsel should be prepared to convince the ALJ that the client cannot perform either sedentary or light work and does not fall into a not disabled category.

Claimants have argued that the Grid regulations are unconstitutional and that they violate the congressional mandate, which seems to require a case-by-case evaluation.[5] In *Heckler v. Campbell*,[6] the regulations were upheld. The Court found that although the act contemplates individualized determinations, certain classes of issues may be resolved through the HHS Secretary's rulemaking authority. The Court indicated that the regulations allow the claimant to present evidence regarding the claimant's abilities or to show that the guidelines are inapplicable to the claimant.

Several cautionary remarks must be made about the Grids. First, they are predicated on the existence of exertional impairments[7] and may not fully apply where nonstrength limitations such as mental, sensory, or skin impairments are present. Second, if the findings of fact do not exactly coincide with the rule, the rule is inapplicable and there is no directed conclusion that the individual is disabled or not disabled.[8] Finally, the SSA may not apply the correct Grid or Grid category in its determination when the individual's education level or

---

§ 16.29

1. 20 C.F.R. § 404.1569. The Grids are reproduced in § 16.32, infra.

2. This excerpt shows the portion of the Grids that illustrates how claims will be resolved for those persons of advanced age (55 and older) who are capable of doing only sedentary work. Other portions of the Grids show how claims will be resolved for those individuals who are younger than advanced age or who are capable of doing light work. The Grids are located at 20 C.F.R. Pt. 404, Subpt. P, App. 2, and are reproduced at § 16.32, infra.

3. 20 C.F.R. § 404.1545. See also Hall, Social Security Disability Practice, § 1.11 (West 1992).

4. 20 C.F.R. § 404.1569.

5. See 42 U.S.C.A. § 423(d)(2)(A).

6. 461 U.S. 458, 103 S.Ct. 1952, 76 L.Ed.2d 66, 1 Soc.Sec.Rep.Ser. 3 (1983).

7. 20 C.F.R. Pt. 404, Subpt. P, App. 2 § 200.00(e).

8. 20 C.F.R. Pt. 404, Subpt. P, App. 2 § 200.00(a).

job title does not accurately reflect the individual's job skills or the transferability of those skills into other types of jobs.

In step 5, vocational factors, i.e., the individual's age, education, and work experience, are relevant to the disability determination.[9]

"Age" is the chronological age of the individual, but it is also a consideration affecting the individual's ability to adapt to new work or to do work in competition with others. Generally, those under age 50 are assumed to be adaptable to a new work situation, but those over age 55 are not.[10]

"Education" is the formal schooling or other training contributing to the individual's ability to perform certain activities such as reasoning, communication skills, and arithmetic ability. The educational background is important when the time period between the end of formal schooling and the onset cf the severe impairment is considered. Formal education that was completed many years prior to the onset may no longer be meaningful in determining present ability to work.[11]

"Work experience" includes the skills and abilities the applicant acquired through work experiences which show the type of work the applicant may be expected to perform. Work experience within the last 15 years applies if it lasted long enough for the individual to acquire the skills required by the job.[12]

The SSA does not consider an individual to be disabled due to an inability to get work, lack of work in the locale, employers' hiring practices, or the fact that he or she is not hired to do work the individual's RFC and impairment otherwise would make it possible for the individual to perform, as long as such work exists in the national economy.[13] The SSA reviews publications from various governmental agencies such as the Department of Labor, Census Bureau, state employment agencies, and the Bureau of Labor Statistics to determine if work exists in the national economy.[14]

§ 16.30 Disability Benefits Based on Blindness

An individual is considered to be disabled for social security and Supplemental Security Income (SSI) purposes if the individual is statutorily blind. Statutorily blind is "central visual acuity of 20/200 or less in the better eye with the use of a correcting lens." This measure of acuity means that the widest diameter of the visual field subtends an

9. 20 C.F.R. § 404.1560(b).

10. 20 C.F.R. § 404.1563.

11. 20 C.F.R. § 404.1564.

12. 20 C.F.R. § 404.1565.

13. 20 C.F.R. § 404.1566(c).

14. 20 C.F.R. § 404.1566(d).

angle no greater than 20 degrees.[1] A person who is statutorily blind must meet the 12–month duration requirement.[2]

The Social Security Administration (SSA) evaluates the work activity of blind people differently than that of sighted, disabled people. Sighted people who perform substantial gainful activity are not considered disabled, regardless of the severity of the impairment.[3] However, blind persons under age 55 can be disabled even though they earn a monthly average equal to the amount allowed to retired social security beneficiaries between the ages of 65 and 69. In 1992, this amount was $850; the amount changes each year with the cost of living. Blind individuals over age 55 with this level of earnings are doing work that is substantial gainful activity only if their current work involves skills and abilities that are about the same as those they used while working before becoming blind.[4] If the new work for the age 55 or over blind individual requires less or different skills or abilities than work done before becoming blind, disability benefits will be paid, except for months in which the substantial gainful activity level was exceeded.[5]

§ 16.31   Disabled Widow(er)s, Disabled Former Spouses, and Disabled Children

Every widow and surviving divorced wife of an individual who dies fully insured can qualify for disability benefits on the basis of the fully insured status of the deceased spouse if she meets the applicable requirements.[1] Similarly, a widower and surviving divorced husband of a fully insured deceased individual, who otherwise meets the applicable requirements, can receive benefits on his deceased spouse's record.[2]

The applicant must be at least age 50, but younger than age 60, and have become disabled within seven years of the insured wage earner's death or his or her own entitlement to mother's or father's benefits or to widow(er)'s benefits based upon a disability. Also, the widow(er) must be disabled throughout a five-month waiting period unless a waiting period has been served due to a prior entitlement to disabled widow(er)'s benefits.[3] In addition, a disabled surviving divorced spouse must have been married to the deceased wage earner for at least ten years before their divorce became effective.[4]

§ 16.30

1. 42 U.S.C.A. § 416(i)(1)(B); 20 C.F.R. § 404.1581.

2. 20 C.F.R. §§ 404.1581, 404.1509.

3. 20 C.F.R. § 404.1520(b).

4. 20 C.F.R. § 404.1584(c).

5. 20 C.F.R. § 404.1584(c).

§ 16.31

1. 42 U.S.C.A. § 402(e); 20 C.F.R. §§ 404.335, 404.336.

2. 42 U.S.C.A. § 402(f); 20 C.F.R. §§ 404.335, 404.336.

3. 20 C.F.R. § 404.335.

4. 20 C.F.R. § 404.336.

Prior to January 1991, disabled widow(er)s and disabled surviving divorced spouses had to meet a stricter standard of disability than did disabled workers, or the disabled children of a retired or deceased wage earner.[5] The widow(er) or surviving divorced spouse had to demonstrate an inability to perform *any* gainful activity.[6] This was a harder standard to meet than the "inability to engage in any substantial gainful activity" standard for disabled wage earners and disabled children.[7] Also, vocational factors were not considered in evaluating the widow(er)'s or surviving divorced spouse's disability.[8] Effective January 1991, the standard of disability is the same for disabled widow(er)s and disabled workers. Applications for disabled widow(er)'s or disabled surviving divorced spouse's benefits that were pending as of January 1, 1991, are adjudicated under the new standards.

A disabled adult child of an individual entitled to old age or disability insurance benefits of an insured deceased wage earner can receive monthly cash benefits if certain conditions are met. The disabled adult child must show that he or she is related to the wage earner, dependent upon the wage earner, unmarried, and became disabled before he or she attained age 22.[9] Often, the childhood disability is based upon a developmental disability such as mental retardation, making it easier to prove a disability onset prior to age 22.[10]

§ 16.32 Residual Functional Capacity—Tables (20 C.F.R. Part 404, Subpart P, Appendix 2) ("The Grids")

TABLE No. 1—Residual Functional Capacity: Maximum Sustained Work Capability Limited to Sedentary Work as a Result of Severe Medically Determinable Impairment(s)

Rule	Age	Education	Previous work experience	Decision
201.01	Advanced age	Limited or less	Unskilled or none	Disabled.
201.02	do	do	Skilled or semiskilled—skills not transferable 1	Do.
201.03	do	do	Skilled or semiskilled—skills transferable 1	Not disabled.
201.04	do	High school graduate or more—does not provide for direct entry into skilled work 2.	Unskilled or none	Disabled.
201.05	do	High school graduate or more—provides for direct entry into skilled work 2.	do	Not disabled.
201.06	do	High school graduate or more—does not provide for direct entry into skilled work 2.	Skilled or semiskilled—skills not transferable 1	Disabled.

5. Omnibus Budget Reconciliation Act of 1990, Pub.L. No. 101–508, § 5103, 104 Stat. 1388, codified at 42 U.S.C.A. § 423(d)(2)(B).

6. 20 C.F.R. § 404.1577; Sullivan v. Weinberger, 493 F.2d 855 (5th Cir.1974), *cert. denied* 421 U.S. 967, 95 S.Ct. 1958, 44 L.Ed.2d 455 (1975).

7. 42 U.S.C.A. § 423(d)(1)(A); 20 C.F.R. § 404.1505.

8. 42 U.S.C.A. § 423(d)(2)(B); 20 C.F.R. § 404.1577.

9. 42 U.S.C.A. § 402(d)(1); 20 C.F.R. § 404.350.

10. Hall, Social Security Disability Practice § 1.19 (1992).

Rule	Age	Education	Previous work experience	Decision
201.07 ....do		...do	Skilled or semiskilled—skills transferable 1.	Not disabled.
201.08 ...... do		High school graduate or more— provides for direct entry into skilled work 2.	Skilled or semiskilled—skills not transferable 1........	Do.
201.09 ....Closely approaching	advanced age......	Limited or less	Unskilled or none	Disabled.
201.10 ....do		...do	Skilled or semiskilled—skills not transferable.	Do.
201.11 ....do		...do	Skilled or semiskilled—skills transferable.	Not disabled.
201.12 ....do		High school graduate or more— does not provide for direct entry into skilled work 3.	Unskilled or none	Disabled.
201.13 ....do		High school graduate or more— provides for direct entry into skilled work 2.	...do	Not disabled.
201.14 ....do		High school graduate or more— does not provide for direct entry into skilled work 3.	Skilled or semiskilled—skills not transferable.	Disabled.
201.15 ....do		...do	Skilled or semiskilled—skills transferable.	Not disabled.
201.16 ....do		High school graduate or more— provides for direct entry into skilled work 3.	Skilled or semiskilled—skills not transferable.	Do.
201.17 ....Younger individual	age 45–49.	Illiterate or unable to communicate in English.	Unskilled or none	Disabled.
201.18 ....do		Limited or less—at least literate and able to communicate in English.	...do	Not disabled.
201.19 ....do		Limited or less	Skilled or semiskilled—skills not transferable.	Do.
201.20 ....do		...do	Skilled or semiskilled—skills transferable.	Do.
201.21 ....do		High school graduate or more	Skilled or semiskilled—skills not transferable.	Do.
201.22 ....do		...do	Skilled or semiskilled—skills transferable.	Do.
201.23 ....Younger individual	age 18–44.	Illiterate or unable to communicate in English.	Unskilled or none	Do.4
201.24 ....do		Limited or less—at least literate and able to communicate in English.	...do	Do.4
201.25 ....do		Limited or less	Skilled or semiskilled—skills not transferable.	Do.4
201.26 ....do		...do	Skilled or semiskilled—skills transferable.	Do.4
201.27 ....do		High school graduate or more	Unskilled or none	Do.4
201.28 ....do		...do	Skilled or semiskilled—skills not transferable.	Do.4
201.29 ....do		...do	Skilled or semiskilled—skills transferable.	Do.4

1 See 201.00(f).
2 See 201.00(d).
3 See 201.00(g).
4 See 201.00(h).

TABLE No. 2—Residual Functional Capacity: Maximum Sustained Work Capability Limited to Light Work as a Result of Severe Medically Determinable Impairment(s)

Rule	Age	Education	Previous work experience	Decision
202.01 ....Advanced age		Limited or less	Unskilled or none	Disabled.
202.02 ....do		...do	Skilled or semiskilled—skills not transferable.	Do.
202.03 ....do		...do	Skilled or semiskilled—skills transferable.1	Not disabled.
202.04 ....do		High school graduate or more— does not provide for direct entry into skilled work.2	Unskilled or none	Disabled.
202.05 ....do		High school graduate or more— provides for direct entry into skilled work.2	...do	Not disabled.

Rule	Age	Education	Previous work experience	Decision
202.06 ...... do		High school graduate or more—does not provide for direct entry into skilled work.2	Skilled or semiskilled—skills not transferable.	Disabled.
202.07 ...... do		...do	Skilled or semiskilled—skills transferable.2	Not disabled.
202.08 ...... do		High school graduate or more—provides for direct entry into skilled work.2	Skilled or semiskilled—skills not transferable.	Do.
202.09 ....Closely approaching advanced age.		Illiterate or unable to communicate in English.	Unskilled or none	Disabled.
202.10 ...... do		Limited or less—At least literate and able to communicate in English.	...do	Not disabled.
202.11 ...... do		Limited or less	Skilled or semiskilled—skills not transferable.	Do.
202.12 ...... do		...do	Skilled or semiskilled—skills transferable.	Do.
202.13 ...... do		High school graduate or more	Unskilled or none	Do.
202.14 ...... do		...do	Skilled or semiskilled—skills not transferable.	Do.
202.15 ...... do		...do	Skilled or semiskilled—skills transferable.	Do.
202.16 ....Younger individual ..		Illiterate or unable to communicate in English.	Unskilled or none	Do.
202.17 ...... do		Limited or less—At least literate and able to communicate in English.	...do	Do.
202.18 ...... do		Limited or less	Skilled or semiskilled—skills not transferable.	Do.
202.19 ...... do		...do	Skilled or semiskilled—skills transferable.	Do.
202.20 ...... do		High school graduate or more	Unskilled or none	Do.
202.21 ...... do		do	Skilled or semiskilled—skills not transferable.	Do.
202.22 ...... do		do	Skilled or semiskilled—skills transferable.	Do.

1 See 202.00(f).
2 See 202.00(c).

TABLE No. 3—Residual Functional Capacity: Maximum Sustained Work Capability Limited to Medium Work as a Result of Severe Medically Determinable Impairment(s)

Rule	Age	Education	Previous work experience	Decision
203.01 ....Closely approaching retirement age		Marginal or none................	Unskilled or none	Disabled.
203.02 ...... do		Limited or less	None	Do.
203.03 ...... do		Limited	Unskilled	Not disabled.
203.04 ...... do		Limited or less	Skilled or semiskilled—skills not transferable.	Do.
203.05 ...... do		...do	Skilled or semiskilled—skills transferable.	Do.
203.06 ...... do		High school graduate or more	Unskilled or none	Do.
203.07 ...... do		High school graduate or more—does not provide for direct entry into skilled work.	Skilled or semiskilled—skills not transferable.	Do.
203.08 ...... do		...do	Skilled or semiskilled—skills transferable.	Do.
203.09 ...... do		High school graduate or more—provides for direct entry into skilled work.	Skilled or semiskilled—skills not transferable.	Do.
203.10 ...... do		Limited or less	None	Disabled.
203.11 ...... do		...do	Unskilled	Not disabled.
203.12 ...... do		...do	Skilled or semiskilled—skills not transferable.	Do.
203.13 ...... do		...do	Skilled or semiskilled—skills transferable.	Do.
203.14 ...... do		High school graduate or more	Unskilled or none	Do.
203.15 ...... do		High school graduate or more—does not provide for direct entry into skilled work.	Skilled or semiskilled—skills not transferable.	Do.
203.16 ...... do		...do	Skilled or semiskilled—skills transferable.	Do.

Note: In the 203 table, the Age entries read: 203.01 "Closely approaching retirement age", 203.10 through 203.16 "Advanced age".

Rule	Age	Education	Previous work experience	Decision
203.17 ... ...do		High school graduate or more—provides for direct entry into skilled work.	Skilled or semiskilled—skills not transferable.	Do.
203.18 ....Closely approaching advanced age.		Limited or less	Unskilled or none	Do.
203.19 ... ...do		...do	Skilled or semiskilled—skills not transferable.	Do.
203.20 ... ...do		...do	Skilled or semiskilled—skills transferable.	Do.
203.21 ... ...do		High school graduate or more	Unskilled or none	Do.
203.22 ... ...do		High school graduate or more—does not provide for direct entry into skilled work.	Skilled or semiskilled—skills not transferable.	Do.
203.23 ... ...do		...do	Skilled or semiskilled—skills transferable.	Do.
203.24 ... ...do		High school graduate or more—provides for direct entry into skilled work.	Skilled or semiskilled—skills not transferable.	Do.
203.25 ....Younger individual ..		Limited or less	Unskilled or none	Do.
203.26 ... ...do		...do	Skilled or semiskilled—skills not transferable.	Do.
203.27 ... ...do		...do	Skilled or semiskilled—skills transferable.	Do.
203.28 ... ...do		High school graduate or more	Unskilled or none	Do.
203.29 ... ...do		High school graduate or more—does not provide for direct entry into skilled work.	Skilled or semiskilled—skills not transferable.	Do.
203.30 ... ...do		...do	Skilled or semiskilled—skills transferable.	Do.
203.31 ... ...do		High school graduate or more—provides for direct entry into skilled work.	Skilled or semiskilled—skills not transferable.	Do.

§§ 16.33–16.40 are reserved for supplementary material.

D. PROCEDURE

Library References:

C.J.S. Social Security and Public Welfare §§ 73–78.

West's Key No. Digests, Social Security and Public Welfare ☞142.5.

§ 16.41 Initial Determination

The administrative process begins with the filing of the claim. In most cases, the attorney is not present at the time the claim is filed. An employee in the District Office or branch office interviews the claimant and fills out the application for the claimant as he or she answers questions. The employee also attempts to develop evidence of the disability by inquiring as to specific facts relating to the illness or injury such as the physical or mental limitations of the claimant and when the condition became disabling. The District Office employee, a claims representative, also will inquire as to the names and addresses of physicians or hospitals that have treated the claimant, and information concerning family relationships that may determine what parties are eligible to receive benefits.

The employee writes his or her observations on a medical form. Typically, these observations are similar to "walked with a cane," or "did not appear to be in pain," or "did not have any trouble reading the forms." Counsel should carefully examine the official file of the Social Security Administration (SSA) before the hearing to determine whether such a judgment regarding medical evidence was made by a nonmedical person, which might affect the decision of the administrative law judge. In the event that an erroneous assumption or comment was made, the attorney should be prepared to present evidence to refute it.

In recent years, in response to staff cuts, the SSA has been promoting the use of "tele-claims," in which a claimant calls a nation-wide toll-free number and speaks to an SSA employee. The employee fills out the application for disability benefits for the claimant by interviewing the claimant over the phone. When telephone applications are made, observations by the claims representative are rarely complete. Counsel should ask the client about the manner in which the application was filed. If a disability claim was taken by telephone interview, there is no assumption that the claimant was unable to complete the application in the Social Security Office, and a notation is added to the application that the individual was not observed.

The initial determination of disability in most states is made by a state agency.[1] At this level, a "medical review team" of physicians and agency employees review the medical records from physicians and hospitals. They make a determination and issue a Disability Determination and Transmittal Report to the SSA. The recommendation of the state agency will be signed by a physician who is part of the "medical review team."

If the individual's medical sources fail to provide their records, or if the SSA requires more information, the SSA may request a consultative examination, which is an SSA-provided examination or test.[2] Generally, the individual is notified that he or she will have to submit to an examination at a site and time arranged by the SSA. The examination is provided at no cost to the individual, who must provide his or her own transportation. Failure to appear at the consultative examination may result in a denial of the individual's claim absent a good reason for the failure.[3]

§ 16.42 Reconsideration

After an adverse decision, the claimant must file a request for reconsideration with the Social Security Administration (SSA) within

§ 16.41

1. 42 U.S.C.A. § 421(a); 20 C.F.R. § 404.1613(a).

2. 20 C.F.R. § 404.1517.

3. 20 C.F.R. § 404.158.

60 days of the receipt of the initial determination.[1] A different medical review team considers the evidence in the file; they may request new evidence, and they can consider new information submitted by the claimant.

At this stage, if the medical evidence shows a medically determinable impairment listed in Appendix 1,[2] the SSA will decide for the claimant. Consequently, an attorney entering the proceeding after the initial determination should review the medical evidence that has been submitted. If a claimant's supplementary medical evidence is sufficient to list the claimant in Appendix 1, the claimant may be awarded benefits prior to the hearing stage. If there is any possibility of meeting the requirements of Appendix 1 at the hearing stage, preparation should be directed toward that goal. However, most hearings involve claimants whose disability will not come within Appendix 1. Therefore, in the sequential evaluation,[3] most of the evidence at the hearing is directed toward steps 2 and 4.[4]

§ 16.43 Disability Benefit Continuation

Once the Social Security Administration (SSA) has approved a claimant for disability benefits, SSA will review the claimant's case from time to time, usually every three to seven years. These reviews ensure that the claimant is still disabled.[1]

Benefits are continued where the person has not had any medical improvement in condition and is still unable to engage in substantial gainful activity. Even where there has been some medical improvement, benefits may be continued absent a showing that the claimant has the functional capacity to perform basic work activities, i.e., the abilities and aptitudes needed to do most jobs.[2]

Upon completion of the disability review, the SSA determines whether to continue or terminate benefits, and sends the client written notification of the decision. If the SSA decides to terminate benefits, it sends information on appeal rights, advance notice of when benefits cease, and a summary of the evidence used to make the determination.[3] The claimant must appeal the decision by requesting a reconsideration within ten days of receipt of the advance notice.[4] When a claimant requests reconsideration, the claimant may request that his or her benefits, and/or the benefits for anyone else entitled on his or her

---

§ 16.42	§ 16.43
1. 20 C.F.R. § 404.909.	1. 20 C.F.R. § 404.1594(a).
2. 20 C.F.R. Pt. 404, Subpt. P, App. 1.	2. 20 C.F.R. § 404.1594(b).
3. See §§ 12.43–.47, supra.	3. 20 C.F.R. § 404.1597(b).
4. See §§ 16.26–.27 supra.	4. 20 C.F.R. § 404.1595(c).

record, be continued pending the outcome of the reconsideration request.[5]

Once the state agency receives the reconsideration request, it schedules a disability hearing[6] and sends a notice of the time and place of the hearing to the individual, who is expected to travel to the hearing site. At the disability hearing, the individual may introduce evidence and present his or her views to a disability hearing officer, who was not involved in the disability cessation decision.[7] Counsel may accompany their clients and may review the evidence either at the hearing itself, or at an earlier date upon request. The attorney may present and question witnesses at the disability hearing. After the hearing, counsel or their clients may review and comment on any evidence the state agency obtained or developed prior to the issuance of the reconsidered determination. If the reconsidered determination is unfavorable, the next appeal is the hearing before the administrative law judge.[8]

§ 16.44 Administrative Hearing—Request and Preparation

If the claimant, after application or after a disability review, receives an unfavorable decision at the reconsideration level, the request for hearing must be filed within 60 days.[1] The request is made on the HA–501–U5 form which may be obtained from the Social Security Administration (SSA) and can be signed by either the claimant or the claimant's attorney. The request may be filed at any District Office where it will be forwarded, along with medical form HA–4486, to the Office of Hearings and Appeals, the appellate division of the SSA. The case is docketed by the administrative law judge (ALJ) to whom it is assigned, and the claimant and the claimant's attorney are notified of the hearing at least 20 days prior to the hearing date.[2] Written requests for continuances should be sent to the ALJ immediately upon receipt of the notice of hearing.

The claimant and the claimant's attorney should plan to arrive at the hearing site before the hearing early enough to allow sufficient time to examine the file. Ordinarily this is the first time the attorney will have access to the claimant's official file. The attorney should closely examine all exhibits in the file, which are marked with numbers, since the attorney will need to refer to exhibit numbers later when writing a brief.

---

5. 20 C.F.R. § 404.1597(a).

6. 20 C.F.R. § 404.914.

7. 20 C.F.R. § 404.916.

8. See §§ 16.44–.47 infra.

§ 16.44

1. 42 U.S.C.A. §§ 405(h), 421(d); 20 C.F.R. § 404.933.

2. 20 C.F.R. § 404.938; Social Security Handbook 1988 (10th Ed.) § 2009.

§ 16.45   Administrative Hearing—Procedure—Preliminaries

The hearing ordinarily will begin with a statement of the issues to be considered by the administrative law judge (ALJ). The ALJ will admit all exhibits previously marked, subject to the objection of the claimant's attorney, and will admit any new medical reports filed immediately prior to the hearing. In general, most evidence is admissible, since the disability hearing is not an adversarial proceeding.[1] Lay witnesses are entitled to comment upon observable medical problems; and unsworn medical reports, normally not admissible in a civil court, are admissible at social security disability hearings.[2] Counsel should object whenever the evidence or the ALJ's questioning is legally improper, since some courts have held that the admission of objectionable hearsay evidence not objected to may form the basis for an ALJ's finding of fact.[3] Since many disability claimants fail to seek legal representation prior to the hearing stage, it is suggested that counsel review the claims file for any legally improper statements or evidence.

The ALJ will ordinarily ask counsel whether counsel wishes to examine his or her client before the ALJ examines the client. The better practice is for the attorney to conduct his or her own examination. On occasion, some ALJs will proceed with their examination of the client before the attorney has the opportunity to do so. Should this occur, counsel should proceed at the appropriate time with a complete examination as though the ALJ's examination had not taken place.

§ 16.46   Administrative Hearing—Procedure—Testimony

When handling direct examination of the client at a hearing, counsel should remember that one purpose of the hearing is to provide a record for the Appeals Council or District Court on appeal. For that reason, the examiner should have the areas of examination well-developed before the hearing and should proceed to develop evidence in chronological order. Hearings are normally recorded by the hearing assistant to the administrative law judge (ALJ) on a cassette recorder. In the event the case eventually is filed in District Court, the cassette is transcribed by a central transcribing agency in the Social Security Administration (SSA). Any proper names that might be subject to misinterpretation by the transcribers should be spelled out by client's counsel.

One suggested format for the examination includes preliminary questions dealing with the age, marital and family status, and education of the client. Marital and family status are sometimes impor-

---

§ 16.45

1. 20 C.F.R. § 404.944.
2. 20 C.F.R. § 404.950(c).

3. McCormick, Social Security Claims and Procedures § 594.

tant to show what work the claimant does or does not do around the house, which may reflect upon his or her ability to engage in substantial employment. The educational background of the client is particularly important in view of the "Grid" regulations.[1] Attorneys should give special attention to developing evidence in regard to a client whose abilities may not measure up to the amount of education the client has received, such as a client who attended school through the eighth grade but is functionally illiterate. The attorney also should ask about any special training that the client has received and show the limited value of the training—whether it was ever used by the client, or is relevant to any job the client is presently able to perform.

A complete chronological work history is very important. The easiest method for making a logical record for appeal is to go through each job held by the client, beginning with the first job held after the termination of regular education. In developing the record of the client's job experience, counsel should remember it is counsel's burden to show that the client cannot return to his or her prior employment. The attorney should go into the approximate dates the client worked, the physical duties involved, and the skill or training involved. It is necessary to develop the information about each job completely, since partial discussion of a job may result in the ALJ seizing upon a particular job as one to which the client could return. For example, one decision read, "Claimant can return to his prior employment as a bait shop operator." In this particular case, the claimant was not represented at the hearing and mentioned to the ALJ that he had worked in a bait shop. The actual facts were that this was a summer job for a relative when the claimant was 17 years old and that he was paid less than minimum wage for three weeks of digging worms and selling minnows.

After a work history is completed, a detailed medical history should be given, again in chronological order whenever possible. If the claim for disability centers around an injury, the facts of the particular injury should be brought out. Medical treatment and hospitalization should be listed, and the medication taken by the claimant within the time of disability should be presented by name, frequency, and dosage. In many cases, it is easiest to have the claimant bring the medication to the hearing. All the medical evidence presented by the claimant should be supported by medical evidence previously filed with the ALJ in the form of affidavits.

Counsel should then develop for the ALJ an accurate picture of what the client does during an average day: what time the client wakes up, whether the client gets washed, what the client eats for meals, what

§ 16.46

1. See §§ 16.24–.29 supra.

chores the client performs, and whether any assistance is required for these activities. The client should explain any physical or mental activity used: how much time is spent and what difficulties are incurred in an average day standing, walking, sitting, or concentrating. Any particular medical problems that occur on a regular basis, e.g., dizzy spells, pain, or swelling, should be presented as part of the client's typical day. Counsel should then refer to the prior employment of the client, job by job, to make a record showing the inability of the client to resume any of the prior jobs. Counsel should ask hypothetical questions to the client concerning his or her ability to perform jobs involving light or sedentary work.[2]

Counsel may present testimony of the client's spouse, coworkers, or employer. Each individual situation must be weighed, and counsel should ensure that the witness provides accurate and unbiased testimony. A spouse is usually very helpful in presenting evidence of pain or inability to do certain things that the client does not like to admit or discuss. A coworker or employer can be very persuasive in testifying as to the client's inability to perform work that is required for a particular job.

§ 16.47 Administrative Hearing—Procedure—Conclusion

Once counsel has presented a prima facie case showing that the client cannot return to his or her prior employment, the burden shifts to the Social Security Administration (SSA) to show that the client is capable of substantial gainful employment within the national economy.[1] The "Grids" are used for that purpose.[2]

Counsel should present evidence to show that the client is not properly placed in a Grid category requiring the administrative law judge (ALJ) to determine that the client is not disabled. The Grids are predicated on conditions that limit strength; thus, they reflect exertional requirements for jobs and might not be applicable where the condition involves nonexertional limitations, such as mental, sensory, or skin impairments.[3] If the Grids cannot be used to force a finding, the attorney may choose to present the testimony of a vocational expert. To prevent a finding of disabled, the SSA must show that jobs exist which the client can do. A vocational expert's testimony for the client can demonstrate that the client cannot do those jobs.

However, vocational experts are seldom used until remand, after the District Court has found that the claimant has met the burden of

2. 20 C.F.R. § 404.1510.

    § 16.47

1. 20 C.F.R. § 404.1566.

2. See §§ 16.24–.32 supra.

3. 20 C.F.R. § 404.1545(d).

proof in showing that the claimant cannot return to his or her prior job, but that additional evidence is needed to show what employment the claimant is capable of performing. At the remand hearing, the client again presents testimony as to his or her educational background, vocational background, and medical problems. The vocational expert will testify in response to hypothetical questions from the ALJ, incorporating the facts presented by the testimony. Opportunity for reversal often results from a question by the ALJ that fails to incorporate a medically or vocationally significant fact.[4]

At the conclusion of the hearing, counsel should request time in which to present additional medical reports and to file a brief and suggested conclusions of law.[5] Normally, an extension of 30 days is considered reasonable. The brief should develop the facts presented to the ALJ with reference to medical exhibits by their exhibit numbers and should present suggested findings based on social security regulations.

§ 16.48   Appeals Council Review

If the Administrative Law Judge (ALJ) rules against the claimant, the ALJ will communicate the decision by letter to the claimant and the claimant's attorney. In order to preserve an appeal to District Court, a request for review by the Appeals Council must be made in writing and be filed with the Social Security Administration (SSA) within 60 days after the date of the notice.[1] The Appeals Council is located outside of Washington, D.C. in Arlington, Virginia. Although hearings can be held, the claimant and attorney must appear at their own expense. Most reviews conducted by the Appeals Council are simply reviews of the prior record and any additional medical evidence or a legal brief submitted by the attorney relating to the period on or before the date of the ALJ's decision.[2]

The Appeals Council is unable to provide a detailed review of every case presented to it. For this reason, many attorneys look upon the Appeals Council simply as a prerequisite to filing suit in the District Court. The Appeals Council also can review a hearing decision or dismissal on its own motion.[3] If the Appeals Council decides to review a case, notice of the action is mailed to all parties. The Appeals Council may decide to remand the case to an ALJ, or it may affirm,

---

4. Haskins v. Finch, 307 F.Supp. 1272 (W.D.Mo.1969).

5. 20 C.F.R. § 404.949.

§ 16.48

1. 20 C.F.R. § 404.968.

2. 20 C.F.R. § 404.976(b)(1).

3. 20 C.F.R. § 404.969.

modify, or reverse the ALJ. If the Appeals Council reviews the ALJ's decision, its decision is binding. If the Appeals Council refuses to review the ALJ's decision, the ALJ's decision is binding.[4] A decision of the Appeals Council is a final decision of the HHS Secretary, and a suit must be filed within 60 days after the mailing of the decision.[5]

The Appeals Council or the claimant may reopen the prior decision under limited conditions. A determination may be reopened within 12 months of the date of the initial determination notice for any reason, within four years of that date if "good cause" is found, or at any time if obtained by fraud or similar fault, or in other limited circumstances.[6] Recently, the Appeals Council has been criticized for using the reopening regulation to lengthen its review period. Some circuits agree with the SSA that either the Appeals Council or the claimant can request that a determination be reopened,[7] while others forbid or limit the Appeals Council from so doing.[8]

§ 16.49 Judicial Review

Judicial review commences upon the filing of a complaint that requests that the United States District Court review the decision of the Health and Human Services (HHS) Secretary.[1] The complaint is filed in the district in which the claimant lives, and service should be made on the United States Attorney for the district, the Attorney General of the United States, and the HHS Secretary.[2] The court may only review the record as it exists below; most cases turn on whether the Secretary's decision is based upon substantial evidence.[3] The review is not a trial *de novo,* and the Secretary's factual determinations will be sustained if supported by substantial evidence.[4]

The court's scope of review includes the legal standards used by the Secretary as well as constitutional challenges. Review in the District Court also may be used to challenge the validity of regulations promulgated by the Secretary or the Secretary's application of incorrect

4. 20 C.F.R. § 404.981.

5. 42 U.S.C.A. § 405(g); 20 C.F.R. § 404.981.

6. 20 C.F.R. § 404.988. See § 15.108 for a discussion of reopening.

7. Zimmermann v. Heckler, 774 F.2d 615, 617, 11 Soc.Sec.Rep.Ser. 143 (4th Cir. 1985); Higginbotham v. Heckler, 767 F.2d 408, 410, 10 Soc.Sec.Rep.Ser. 217 (8th Cir. 1985).

8. McCuin v. Secretary of Health and Human Services, 817 F.2d 161, 174, 17 Soc.Sec.Rep.Ser. 691 (1st Cir.1987); Butterworth v. Bowen, 796 F.2d 1379, 1385–87, 14 Soc.Sec.Rep.Ser. 290 (11th Cir.1986).

§ 16.49

1. 42 U.S.C.A. § 405(g).

2. Fed.R.Civ.P. 4(d)(4).

3. 42 U.S.C.A. § 405(g); 5 U.S.C.A. § 706.

4. Alston v. Sullivan, 904 F.2d 122, 30 Soc.Sec.Rep.Ser. 34 (2d Cir.1990).

standards.[5]

As part of the complaint, the attorney should allege the jurisdiction of the court, the history of the case below, the claimant's insured status, the claimant's disability, the final decision of the Secretary, and the error of the Secretary. The relief requested should include: a certified copy of the transcript of the earlier proceedings to be filed with the Secretary's answer, reversal of the Secretary's decision, or in the alternative, an order for a rehearing, and a prayer for attorney fees as agreed upon by the parties.

The Secretary is represented in the judicial review by the Justice Department, usually the United States Attorney for the district in which the suit is filed. Since the United States is the defendant, it has 60 days in which to file an answer.[6] With the answer and transcript (at no charge) the United States Attorney will often file a motion for summary judgment or a motion for a judgment on the pleadings. The plaintiff/claimant should be prepared to answer either motion filed by the United States Attorney and should file a similar motion within a very short time after the case is at issue. In conjunction with the plaintiff/claimant's motion, a brief should be filed setting forth the facts in the case by reference to the transcript and the law involved.

As in other cases, most United States district courts are reluctant to grant oral arguments on motions. The request for oral argument may be filed, but the plaintiff/claimant should prepare the motion and brief believing that this will be the only argument that the court will consider. The court will take the case under advisement and will rule on both motions.

The court may affirm, reverse, modify, or remand the decision back to the Secretary for further proceedings.[7] The usual entries are either affirmation or remand. Remand is made to the Appeals Council, which in turn certifies the case back to an administrative law judge (ALJ) for the taking of further evidence. The policy of the Social Security Administration (SSA) is to remand the case back to the ALJ who issued the decision that is being appealed.

On remand, the court's order will set out the type of testimony to be taken or evidence needed, which often will be additional medical or vocational evidence. The attorney will receive a notice of the hearing, which will be held in usual manner.

Another ground for remand involves new medical evidence that was not available to the SSA. The District Court has authority to

---

5. Johnson v. Bowen, 817 F.2d 983, 17 Soc.Sec.Rep.Ser. 729 (2d Cir.1987).

6. Fed.R.Civ.P. 12(a).

7. 42 U.S.C.A. § 405(g); 20 C.F.R. § 404.983.

remand any social security appeal at any time, on "good cause" shown, or order additional evidence to be taken before the Secretary.[8] The submission of new medical evidence has been found to be "good cause." However, the medical evidence must be new, not cumulative, and must bear directly upon the disputed matter. There also must be a reasonable chance that the SSA would have reached a different result, and the SSA would not be prejudiced by a remand for the purposes of accepting and considering the evidence.[9]

The Supreme Court has distinguished between remands ordered in conjunction with entry of a judgment modifying or reversing an SSA decision (sentence four remand) or to allow consideration of material new evidence (sentence six remand). According to the Supreme Court, a sentence four remand is a final judgment that the Secretary may appeal, while a sentence six remand is not.[10] The distinction affects counsel's ability to obtain attorney fees under the Equal Access to Justice Act (EAJA).[11] The filing period for seeking fees begins after entry of judgment in sentence four remands, but not until entry of judgment following postremand proceedings in sentence six remands.[12] (Additional details concerning this distinction may be found in §§ 15.-101–.107, supra; additional discussion of attorney fees under the EAJA is found in §§ 15.137–.145, supra.)

Library References:

C.J.S. Social Security and Public Welfare § 79.

West's Key No. Digests, Social Security and Public Welfare ⚖145.

8. 42 U.S.C.A. § 405(g).

9. Simonsen v. Secretary of Health and Human Services, 512 F.Supp. 1064 (S.D.Cal.1981).

10. Sullivan v. Finkelstein, 496 U.S. 617, 110 S.Ct. 2658, 110 L.Ed.2d 563, 30 Soc.Sec.Rep.Ser. 118 (1990), on remand 924 F.2d 483, 32 Soc.Sec.Rep.Ser. 276 (3d Cir. 1991). A sentence six remand becomes final judgment upon entry of judgment after the case is returned to it following remand. Several important issues were left open by the court, including whether the claimant may appeal a sentence four remand and whether a new petition for review must be filed following a sentence four remand. For a discussion of these issues, see Deford, Two Late–Term Sleepers from the Supreme Court Poses Questions for Advocates, 24 Clearinghouse Rev. 705 (1990).

11. 28 U.S.C.A. 2412(d); Shalala v. Schaefer, ___ U.S. ___, 113 S.Ct. 2625, 125 L.Ed.2d 239, 41 Soc.Sec.Rep.Ser. 334 (1993).

12. Melkonyan v. Sullivan, ___ U.S. ___, ___, 111 S.Ct. 2157, 2165, 115 L.Ed.2d 78, ___, 33 Soc.Sec.Rep.Ser. 363 (1991), on remand 943 F.2d 1476 (9th Cir.1991); the court earlier ruled that attorney fees could be obtained under EAJA for work done in conjunction with a remand "where a court orders a remand ... and retains continuing jurisdiction ... pending a decision from the Secretary which will determine the claimant's entitlement to benefits." Sullivan v. Hudson, 490 U.S. 877, 892, 109 S.Ct. 2248, 2258, 104 L.Ed.2d 941, ___, 25 Soc.Sec.Rep.Ser. 401 (1989). For a discussion of these cases, see Deford, Melkonyan v. Sullivan: What Hath the Supreme Court Wrought?, 25 Clearinghouse Rev. 662 (1991).

§ 16.50 Attorney Fees

The Social Security Act authorizes payment of "a reasonable fee" to an attorney who obtains benefits for a claimant.[1] Similarly, the attorney for a "prevailing party" in litigation against the United States may obtain fees under the Equal Access to Justice Act.[2]

Library References:

C.J.S. Social Security and Public Welfare § 53.
West's Key No. Digests, Social Security and Public Welfare ⊗142.30.

§§ 16.51–16.60 are reserved for supplementary material.

E. SPECIAL CONSIDERATIONS

§ 16.61 Worker Compensation/Public Disability Offset

Many claimants have been injured in the course of their employment and will have received workers' compensation benefits for the injury for which they have claimed social security disability. In the event the social security claim is approved, the total monthly benefits received from both workers' compensation payments and social security disability payments cannot exceed 80% of the claimant's "average current earnings" before the claimant became disabled.[1]

Public disability benefits—cash payments made to a worker under a law or plan of the United States, a state, a political subdivision, or an instrumentality—are also considered in the determination of whether the worker's social security disability benefits should be offset. However, where the public disability benefits or state workers' compensation law states that it will be offset by the worker's entitlement to social security disability benefits, there is no offset to the social security disability benefits.[2] This situation is called a "reverse offset."

The workers' compensation/public disability benefits offset ends when the claimant attains age 65, if the claimant's onset was after February 1981 and the claimant became entitled to social security after August 1981.[3] Where the claimant's onset was prior to March 1981 and entitlement was before September 1981, the offset will continue until the claimant attains age 62.[4]

§ 16.50

1. 42 U.S.C.A. § 406.

2. 28 U.S.C.A. § 2412(d). See §§ 15.-125–.146, supra, for a detailed discussion of these topics.

§ 16.61

1. 42 U.S.C.A. § 424a; 20 C.F.R. § 404.-408(c)(3).

2. 20 C.F.R. § 404.408(b)(1).

3. 20 C.F.R. § 404.408(a)(2).

4. 20 C.F.R. § 404.408(a)(1).

Counsel should be careful to instruct clients that social security benefits may be offset by receipt of workers' compensation payments even where there are two different disabilities or injuries involved.[5] The Social Security Administration ordinarily will have a claimant sign a statement acknowledging the potential overpayment at the time a claim is taken when a workers' compensation claim is pending.

Library References:

C.J.S. Workmen's Compensation § 330.

West's Key No. Digests, Workers' Compensation ⬉907.

§ 16.62 Rehabilitation Services and Trial Work Period

The Secretary of Health and Human Services (HHS) is directed to develop and conduct experiments and work incentive projects designed to encourage disabled beneficiaries to return to work. Beneficiaries are selected to participate in the work-incentive plans, notably vocational rehabilitation. A beneficiary who refuses to accept vocational rehabilitation services without good cause may have his or her benefits withheld.[1]

A disabled individual may test his or her ability to work through a trial work period.[2] This trial work period is a period of up to nine months in which the person may render services but still continue to receive benefits. The nine months do not have to be consecutive, and the services are not evaluated as being indicative of a disability cessation until all nine months have been utilized. "Services" means any activity performed for remuneration or gain or which is determined by the HHS Secretary to be of a type normally performed for remuneration or gain.[3]

A trial work period begins in a month the individual is entitled to disability, but not before the application for benefits is filed. A trial work period closes at the earliest of (1) the ninth month in which the individual renders services, or (2) the month the individual's disability ceases, without regard to work performed during the period of trial work.

An individual is limited to one trial work period during a period of entitlement to disability benefits.[4] However, effective January 1992, a

---

5. Shabazz v. Bowen, 912 F.2d 532, 31 Soc.Sec.Rep.Ser. 29 (2d Cir.1990).

§ 16.62

1. 42 U.S.C.A. § 422(b).

2. 20 C.F.R. § 404.1592.

3. 42 U.S.C.A. § 422(c)(2); 20 C.F.R. § 404.1592(b).

4. 42 U.S.C.A. § 422(c)(3); 20 C.F.R. § 404.1592(c).

disability beneficiary's trial work period continues until the beneficiary performs services in nine months of any 60 consecutive months.[5]

§ **16.63** Table of Forms

The following forms are used frequently by advocates in social security disability matters:

— Application for Disability Insurance Benefits: Form SSA–16–F6

— Disability Report: Form SSA–3368–Bk

— Request for Reconsideration: Form SSA–561–U2

— Reconsideration Disability Report: Form SSA–3441–F6

— Request for Hearing by Administrative Law Judge: Form HA–501–U5

— Claimant's Statement When Request for Hearing is Filed and the Issue is Disability: Form HA–4486

— Request for Review of Hearing Decision/Order: Form HA–520–U5

— Appointment of a Representative: Form SSA–1696–U4

— Petition to Obtain Approval of a Fee for Representing a Claimant Before the Social Security Administration: Form SSA–1560–U4

— Report of Continuing Disability Interview: Form SSA–454–Bk

— Request for Reconsideration—Disability Cessation: Form SSA–789–U4

— Reconsideration Report for Disability Cessation: Form SSA–782–Bk

— Work Activity Report—Employee: Form SSA–821–F4

---

5. Omnibus Reconciliation Act of 1990,   codified at 42 U.S.C.A. § 422(c)(4).
Pub.L. No. 101–508, § 5112, 104 Stat. 1388,

CHAPTER 17

SUPPLEMENTAL SECURITY INCOME

Table of Sections

A. GENERALLY

WESTLAW Electronic Research

See WESTLAW Electronic Research Guide preceding the Summary of Contents.

A. GENERALLY

Library References:

C.J.S. Social Security and Public Welfare § 95.
West's Key No. Digests, Social Security and Public Welfare ⏝175.5.

§ 17.1 Introduction

Supplemental Security Income (SSI) is a federal program of cash assistance for aged, blind, and disabled individuals who have little income and few assets. The program provides monthly checks from the federal government of (in 1993) up to $434 for an individual and up to $652 for a couple. Most states supplement this basic federal grant by paying an additional amount to eligible individuals and couples. In 1989, approximately $14.6 billion was paid to people enrolled in the SSI program—about $11.6 billion by the federal government and about $2.95 billion by the states. The SSI program provides an important source of income for the elderly poor. It also is important because in most states, eligibility for SSI automatically qualifies a person for Medicaid (see Chapter 11).

The basic purpose of the SSI program is to ensure a minimum level of income to people who are age 65 or over or who are blind or disabled and do not have sufficient income and resources to maintain a standard of living at the established federal minimum income level. In 1989, that level was about $5,950 annually for one individual. The SSI program, effective January 1, 1974, replaced the former federally funded programs that had been administered by each state for the aged (Old Age Assistance—OAA), blind (Aid to the Blind—AB), and disabled (Aid to the Permanently and Totally Disabled—PTD).

Eligibility requirements and benefit payments for federal SSI benefits are identical throughout the 50 states and the District of Columbia.

Eligibility requirements and payments for state supplements vary from state to state. Federal payments are financed from the general funds of the United States Treasury.[1] In states that supplement SSI, state supplemental payments are from the state treasury.

§ 17.2 Administration

The SSI program is administered by the Social Security Administration (SSA), although in 24 states the state welfare department has primary responsibility for administering the state's supplemental benefits program. When SSI eligibility is based on disability, the state disability determination agency also will be involved.[1]

§ 17.3 Authority

The legal authority for the Supplemental Security Income (SSI) program is contained in Title XVI of the Social Security Act, 42 U.S.C.A. §§ 1381–1385. The United States Department of Health and Human Services (HHS) regulations implementing the program are found in 20 C.F.R. §§ 416.101–416.2227.

The Program Operation Manual System (POMS) is the guideline for day-to-day operations issued by the Social Security Administration (SSA) and relied on by SSA district offices as final authority for their decisions. Because POMS does not always conform to the requirements of the Social Security Act and applicable regulations, attorneys should use care in relying on it. Administrative law judges (ALJs) are not bound by the POMS and may disregard POMS sections that do not conform to the Social Security Act and regulations. Also useful are Social Security Rulings issued by the Social Security Administration and available in West's Social Security Reporting Service.

§§ 17.4–17.10 are reserved for supplementary material.

B. ELIGIBILITY FOR SSI PAYMENTS

Library References:

C.J.S. Social Security and Public Welfare § 95.
West's Key No. Digests, Social Security and Public Welfare ⊕175.15, 175.20.

§ 17.1

1. 20 C.F.R. § 416.110.

§ 17.2

1. In the following states, the state supplementation program is state-administered: Alabama, Alaska, Arizona, Colorado, Connecticut, Florida, Idaho, Illinois, Indiana, Kentucky, Maryland, Minnesota, Missouri, Nebraska, New Hampshire, New Mexico, North Carolina, North Dakota, Oklahoma, Oregon, South Carolina, South Dakota, Virginia, Wyoming. Fast Facts and Figures About Social Security, 50 Soc. Sec.Bull. 18 (May 1987); Current Operating Statistics, 53 Soc.Sec.Bull. 46 (January 1990).

§ 17.11   Basic Requirements—Financial Need

To be eligible for Supplemental Security Income (SSI), an individual must meet the financial requirements established by Congress. An individual may not have *countable* income exceeding $434 a month. A couple's countable income cannot exceed $652 a month.[1] The countable resources of an individual cannot exceed $2,000, and the countable resources of a couple cannot exceed $3,000.[2] As is explained in §§ 17.-21–.33 infra, countable income and resources differ substantially from actual income and resources, and a person or couple may be eligible for SSI even though their actual income and resources exceed these figures.

§ 17.12   Basic Requirements—Nonfinancial Requirements—Age or Physical Condition

To be eligible for Supplemental Security Income (SSI), an individual must be 65 years old or older, or blind, or disabled. Age is proved by the same methods used to establish eligibility for social security benefits discussed in Chapter 15.[1]

The definitions of blindness and disability for SSI are essentially the same as the social security definitions discussed in Chapter 16.[2]

§ 17.13   Basic Requirements—Nonfinancial Requirements—Resident, Citizen, Alien

An individual, in order to be eligible for Supplemental Security Income (SSI), is required to be a resident of the United States[1] and either (1) a citizen of the United States,[2] or (2) an alien lawfully

§ 17.11

1. 42 U.S.C.A. §§ 1382(a)(1), 1382f; 57 Fed.Reg. 48619. These figures are for 1993 and are adjusted annually.

2. 42 U.S.C.A. § 1382(a)(1); 20 C.F.R. § 416.1205(c).

§ 17.12

1. 20 C.F.R. §§ 416.804–416.806.

2. Blindness: 42 U.S.C.A. § 1382c(a)(2); 20 C.F.R. §§ 416.981–416.986; Disability: 42 U.S.C.A. § 1382c(a)(3); 20 C.F.R. §§ 416.905–416.911. More liberal standards of blindness and disability are used for persons who were eligible in December 1973 for aid to the blind benefits or aid to the disabled benefits. 20 C.F.R. § 416.982 (blindness), § 416.907 (disability). To obtain the benefits of this more liberal standard of disability, a person also must have

been disabled at least one month prior to July 1973. 20 C.F.R. § 416.907.

§ 17.13

1. Residence in the United States means residence in one of the 50 states, the District of Columbia, and the Northern Mariana Islands. Other U.S. territories and possessions including Puerto Rico are excluded for this purpose. 20 C.F.R. § 416.603. The documents required to establish residence are described in 20 C.F.R. § 416.603.

2. The definition of the United States for citizenship purposes is broader than for purposes of residence. It includes the 50 states, the District of Columbia, Puerto Rico, Guam, the U.S. Virgin Islands, American Samoa, Swain's Island, and the Northern Mariana Islands. 20 C.F.R. § 416.-

admitted for permanent residence [3] or otherwise permanently residing in the United States under color of law of the Immigration and Nationality Act.[4]

§ 17.14 Basic Requirements—Nonfinancial Requirements—Eligible Individuals and Couples

An individual's eligibility for Supplemental Security Income (SSI) payments and the amount of SSI payments received are affected by whether that individual is married and living with a spouse. The rules for countable resources and income are different for a couple than for an individual living alone or with a person other than a spouse. In addition, SSI payment levels differ for an eligible individual living outside of a marriage and for one or more eligible individuals living as a couple.[1] A change in the living arrangements of a couple, such as institutionalization of one or both of them, will affect the payments they receive.[2]

A person is married for SSI purposes if the person is married under the law of the state in which that person is domiciled or has been determined eligible for social security spouse's benefits. A person also may be considered married for SSI purposes if living in a household with another person of the opposite sex and both persons lead others to believe they are married.[3]

1610. Documents required to establish citizenship are set forth in 20 C.F.R. § 416.1610.

3. 20 C.F.R. § 416.1615.

4. An alien residing in the United States with the knowledge and permission of the Immigration and Naturalization Service (INS) satisfies the requirement of permanently residing in the United States under color of law if INS does not contemplate enforcing the departure of that individual. A decision not to enforce the departure of an alien can result from the policy or practice of INS not to enforce the departure of aliens in a particular category, or from the facts and circumstances of individual cases. 20 C.F.R. § 416.1618. Beneficiaries of this provision include some Cuban and Haitian refugees as well as refugees from other countries and some aliens granted asylum under the provisions of the Immigration and Nationality Act. 8 U.S.C.A. § 1158; 8 C.F.R. §§ 208.1–208.24. For the proof required to establish such status, see § 416.1618. Also eligible under this provision as a result of the Immigration Reform and Control Act of 1986 are aliens over 65 who have resided continuously and illegally in the United States since January 1, 1982, who are granted temporary residence status. 8 U.S.C.A. § 1255a(a)(2)(A).

§ 17.14

1. 20 C.F.R. § 416.1802.

2. 20 C.F.R. § 416.432. Until October 1990, a couple in which both members were eligible for benefits continued to be treated as a couple until they had lived apart for six months. They are now treated as a couple only for months in which they are living together. 42 U.S.C.A. § 1382c(b), amended by Pub.L. No. 101–239, § 8012, 103 Stat. 2464.

3. 20 C.F.R. § 416.1806(c); for details concerning proof of marital status, see id. at §§ 416.1806–416.1835.

§ 17.15 Basic Requirements—Precluding Conditions—In General

Certain conditions preclude eligibility for Supplemental Security Income (SSI) benefits. A person otherwise eligible for SSI will not receive SSI payment (or may be viewed as having been overpaid) for the period (usually a month or more) in which the condition precluding eligibility exists.

§ 17.16 Basic Requirements—Precluding Conditions—Inmate of Public Institution

A person is not eligible for Supplemental Security Income (SSI) benefits for any month throughout which the person is an inmate of a public institution.[1] Exceptions to this rule exist for residents of certain public institutions. A resident of a publicly operated community residence serving no more than sixteen may be eligible for SSI benefits. To qualify as a community residence, a facility must provide food and shelter and some additional services such as social services, incidental medical or remedial care, help with personal living activities, or training in socialization and life skills.[2] Since December 31, 1987, residents of public emergency shelters for the homeless may be eligible for SSI benefits for any six months of a nine-month period in which they reside in such a shelter.[3] In addition, if the public institution is a medical care facility and Medicaid pays more than 50% of the cost of a person's care, the person is eligible for a reduced SSI payment of $30 per month.[4]

§ 17.17 Basic Requirements—Precluding Conditions—Other Benefits

An individual who fails to apply for other benefits for which the individual may be eligible, within 30 days of receiving written notice

---

§ 17.16

1. 42 U.S.C.A. § 1382(e)(1)(A); 20 C.F.R. § 416.211(a)(1). A person is regarded as an inmate or resident of a public institution even if that person or a third party pays for his or her care and is regarded as present throughout a month even if absent not more than 14 consecutive days during the month. 20 C.F.R. §§ 416.201, 416.211. See also Dougherty on Behalf of Dougherty v. Bowen, 685 F.Supp. 104, 22 Soc.Sec.Rep. Ser. 185 (M.D.Pa.1988) and McCauley v. Bowen, 659 F.Supp. 292, 17 Soc.Sec.Rep. Ser. 863 (D.Kan.1986), but see Levings v. Califano, 604 F.2d 591 (8th Cir.1979).

2. 20 C.F.R. § 416.211(c).

3. 20 C.F.R. § 416.211(d).

4. 20 C.F.R. §§ 416.211(b), 416.414. This provision was sustained in Schweiker v. Wilson, 450 U.S. 221, 101 S.Ct. 1074, 67 L.Ed.2d 186 (1981). A related rule results in the reduction of SSI benefits for residents of private medical care facilities. 20 C.F.R. § 416.414. See also Albanese on Behalf of Albanese v. Sullivan, 724 F.Supp. 1083, 27 Soc.Sec.Rep.Ser. 653 (E.D.N.Y. 1989).

from the Social Security Administration (SSA) of such eligibility, is ineligible for Supplemental Security Income (SSI) benefits. Other benefits include annuities, pensions, retirement or disability benefits, veterans' compensation, retirement, survivors' and disability insurance benefits, workers' compensation payments, and unemployment insurance.[1]

§ 17.18 Basic Requirements—Precluding Conditions—Drug or Alcohol Treatment

A disabled individual is ineligible for Supplemental Security Income (SSI) payments for any month that the individual is medically determined to be a drug addict or an alcoholic unless the individual is undergoing appropriate treatment for the condition at an institution or facility approved by the Department of Health and Human Services and is complying with the terms, conditions, and requirements of that treatment.[1]

§ 17.19 Basic Requirements—Precluding Conditions—Vocational Rehabilitation

The Social Security Administration (SSA) will refer any blind or disabled individual who is under 65 and is receiving Supplemental Security Income (SSI) benefits to the appropriate state agency administering the state plan for vocational rehabilitation services approved under the Vocational Rehabilitation Act. An individual who fails to accept these services without good cause is ineligible for SSI payments.[1]

§ 17.20 Basic Requirements—Precluding Conditions—Outside United States

An individual is ineligible for Supplemental Security Income (SSI) benefits for any month during all of which the individual is outside the United States. After an individual has been outside the United States for any period of 30 consecutive days, the individual shall be treated as remaining outside the United States until he or she has been in the United States for a period of 30 consecutive days.[1]

§ 17.17

1. 42 U.S.C.A. § 1382(e)(2); 20 C.F.R. § 416.210.

§ 17.18

1. 42 U.S.C.A. § 1382(e)(3); 20 C.F.R. § 416.213.

§ 17.19

1. 42 U.S.C.A. § 1382d(a), (c); 20 C.F.R. § 416.212. For this purpose, United States means the 50 states, the District of Columbia, and the Northern Mariana Islands.

§ 17.20

1. 42 U.S.C.A. § 1382(f); 20 C.F.R. § 416.214.

§ 17.21 Financial Requirements—Resource Limitations—In General

The Social Security Administration defines resources as "cash or other liquid assets or any real or personal property that an individual owns and could convert to cash to be used for support and maintenance." [1] To be eligible for Supplemental Security Income (SSI), a single person cannot have countable resources worth more than $2,000, and a couple cannot have countable resources worth more than $3,000. [2] The higher limit for couples applies even if only one spouse is eligible for SSI (for example, if the husband is 65 and the wife is 60).

§ 17.22 Financial Requirements—Resource Limitations—Liquid and Nonliquid Resources

Only property that a person has a right to liquidate is considered a resource. An interest in property that a person cannot liquidate is not regarded as a resource of that individual. [1] Liquid resources are cash and other property that can be converted to cash within 20 days. Resources ordinarily viewed as liquid are stocks, bonds, mutual fund shares, promissory notes, mortgages, life insurance policies, bank accounts, certificates of deposits, and similar items. [2]

Jointly owned property may or may not be counted as a resource. If an individual has the right, authority, or power to sell the individual's share, it will be considered a resource. [3] However, if the sale of the property would cause the other owner undue hardship, such as the loss of that owner's only available place of principal residence, it may not be a countable resource. [4]

The Social Security Administration (SSA) *conclusively* presumes that a checking or savings account, certificate of deposit, or other financial institution account held in a Supplemental Security Income (SSI) applicant's or recipient's own name belongs to that individual. [5] A *rebuttable* presumption exists that an account jointly owned by the SSI applicant or recipient belongs to that individual. [6] *All* of the funds in the jointly owned account are presumed to belong to the applicant or recipient, but this presumption can be rebutted by proof that the funds (or a portion of them) do not belong to the applicant or recipient. The

---

§ 17.21

1. 20 C.F.R. § 416.120(c)(3).

2. 20 C.F.R. § 416.1205.

§ 17.22

1. 20 C.F.R. § 416.1201(a)(1).

2. 20 C.F.R. § 416.1201(b).

3. 20 C.F.R. § 416.1201(a)(1).

4. 42 U.S.C.A. § 1382b(b)(2), 20 C.F.R. § 416.1245(a).

5. 57 Fed.Reg. 22187 (May 27, 1992) (proposed rule codifying SSA practice, to be codified at 20 C.F.R. § 416.1208).

6. Id.

rebuttable presumption of ownership extends to persons such as the spouse of an applicant whose income and resources are "deemed" to belong to the applicant. Even an account jointly owned by a third party, such as an adult child, and the noneligible spouse of an applicant would be presumed to belong to the applicant.

Nonliquid resources are property, other than cash, that cannot be converted to cash within 20 days. Examples include household goods, automobiles and other vehicles, machinery, livestock, buildings, and land.[7]

The general rule regarding resources is that if an individual has a resource, the resource is not excluded, and if the resource is one that a claimant or recipient can liquidate, the resource is counted for determining SSI eligibility. This rule has a number of exceptions, so caution must be exercised in handling resource questions and problems. If doubt exists about whether applicable rules treat something as a resource, consider whether the claimant can convert the resource into a liquid resource to obtain food, clothing, or shelter. Because of the complexity of SSI resource rules, careful attention to the statute, regulations, and POMS is required.[8]

Careful planning can enable a client to obtain or retain eligibility for SSI benefits (and often for Medicaid as well, which may provide critically needed medical care), despite the presence of resources that normally would disqualify the client from eligibility.[9]

Library References:

C.J.S. Social Security and Public Welfare § 95.

West's Key No. Digests, Social Security and Public Welfare ⊕175.20.

§ 17.23 Financial Requirements—Resource Limitations—"Deeming"

In addition to resources belonging to an applicant for Supplemental Security Income (SSI), the Social Security Administration (SSA) treats resources belonging to certain other persons as available to the applicant and, thus, counts these resources in determining SSI eligibility. The process of counting these resources is called "deeming" because

---

7. 20 C.F.R. § 416.1201(c).

8. See generally Deford and Sweeney, SSI Resource Rules: An Update 23 Clearinghouse Rev. 465 (1989).

9. See e.g., Navarro v. Sullivan, 751 F.Supp. 349, 32 Soc.Sec.Rep.Ser. 52 (E.D.N.Y.1990) (court reversed termination

of SSI benefits to disabled adult because of "excess" resources consisting of malpractice settlement structured so that funds could only be used for limited purposes; court concluded that settlement was not a resource owned by recipient that could be used for his support or maintenance).

these resources are deemed available to an applicant even though legally they belong to another. Deeming occurs in three situations—the resources of a spouse are deemed available to a spouse living in the same household, the resources of a parent are deemed available to a child under 18, and the resources of a sponsor are deemed available to an alien for three years after the alien's admission.[1] Deeming occurs only with countable resources. In addition to resources that generally are not counted in determining eligibility for SSI (see § 17.24, infra), some third-party resources are not deemed available to an applicant for SSI. An important example is that pension funds of an ineligible spouse or parent (of a minor under 18) are excluded from deeming.[2]

§ 17.24 Financial Requirements—Resource Limitations—Excluded Resources

A number of valuable assets are not counted by the Social Security Administration (SSA) in determining eligibility for Supplemental Security Income (SSI):

1. Homestead (family home). The value of a person's family home and the land surrounding it is ignored completely by the SSA in determining eligibility for SSI.[1] An individual can have a house worth any amount of money and still be eligible for SSI as long as the individual is using the house as his or her residence and meets the other requirements. Even if a person is not currently living in the home, it will be considered an excluded resource as long as the person intends to return to it or if a spouse or dependent relative continues to live in the home. If a home is sold, the proceeds are exempt as long as they are used to purchase a replacement residence within three months.[2]

2. Household goods and personal effects. A person can have household goods such as furniture and personal effects such as jewelry and clothing worth up to a total of $2,000 in equity value without having these items counted in determining eligibility for SSI. If a person's goods and effects exceed $2,000 in

§ 17.23

1. 42 U.S.C.A. § 1382c(f); 20 C.F.R. §§ 416.1202–416.1204. A fourth situation of deeming occurs between an essential person and a qualified individual. Relatively few individuals are covered by this rule. 20 C.F.R. § 416.1203.

2. 20 C.F.R. § 416.1202(a), (b). Pension funds include IRAs, Keogh plans, and work-related pension plans.

§ 17.24

1. 42 U.S.C.A. § 1382b(a)(1); 20 C.F.R. § 416.1212.

2. 20 C.F.R. § 416.1212(d). See e.g., Hart v. Bowen, 799 F.2d 567, 14 Soc.Sec.

value, only the excess is counted.[3] Furthermore, certain goods and effects are excluded altogether in determining eligibility. Totally excluded are wedding and engagement rings and personal property acquired for medical reasons such as prosthetic devices and wheelchairs.[4]

3. Automobiles and other vehicles. An individual or married couple may own one car, and it will not be counted as a resource as long as its current value (retail market value) is $4,500 or less.[5] If its value exceeds $4,500, only the excess over $4,500 is counted against the 1993 resource maximums of $2,000 and $3,000. However, if the car is used for transportation to employment or to obtain medical services for a specific medical problem or is specially equipped for a handicapped person, it is not counted as a resource at all regardless of its market value.[6] Any additional automobile is treated as a nonliquid resource and an individual's equity in the car is counted against the resource limit.[7]

4. Life insurance. Some life insurance policies are excluded altogether in determining SSI eligibility, and others are excluded if their value does not exceed $1,500. Excluded altogether are burial policies and policies having no cash surrender value, such as term life insurance policies. Policies with a cash surrender value are excluded if their face value does not exceed $1,500.[8]

5. Property essential for self-support. Property of a trade or business (such as land, buildings, equipment, and inventory) or nonbusiness income-producing property (such as land that produces rents) "essential to self-support" is excluded by up to $6,000 of a person's equity in the income-producing property if it produces a net annual income of at least six percent of the excluded equity. For example, Sharon has a small business in her home making hand-woven rugs. The looms and other equipment used in the business have a current market value of $7,000. The value of her equity is $5,500, since she owes $1,500 on the looms. Sharon's net earnings from self-employment are $400. Since Sharon's equity in the looms and other equipment ($5,500) is under the $6,000 limit for property essential to self-support and her net income after expenses ($400) is greater than six percent of her equity, her income-producing property is excluded from countable resources. The home is not considered in any way in valuing property essential to self-support.

Rep.Ser. 438 (9th Cir.1986).

3. 20 C.F.R. § 416.1216(b). Equity value equals the fair market value of the item, minus any encumbrances.

4. 20 C.F.R. § 416.1216(c).

5. 20 C.F.R. § 416.1218(b)(2).

6. 20 C.F.R. § 416.1218(b)(1).

7. 20 C.F.R. § 416.1216(b).

8. 20 C.F.R. § 416.1230.

Nonbusiness property used to produce goods or services necessary for an individual's daily activities (such as land used to produce vegetables or livestock only for personal consumption) is excluded if the individual's equity in the property does not exceed $6,000. For example, Bill owns a small, unimproved lot several blocks from his home. He uses the lot, which is valued at $4,800, to grow vegetables and fruit only for his own consumption. Since his equity in the property is less than $6,000, the property is excluded as necessary to self-support.

Personal property required by the individual's employer for work (such as tools, safety equipment, or uniforms) is excluded, regardless of value, while the individual is working. Property is regarded as essential for self-support if it is a significant factor in producing income necessary for one's support.[9] These rules are complex and often harmful to older persons with small farms or businesses. In addition to trying to satisfy these requirements, it may be possible to challenge the $6,000/6% rule.[10]

6. Cash received from an insurance company or another source to replace lost or damaged excluded property, as long as it is used to replace the lost or damaged property. Replacements normally should occur within nine months of receipt of the cash.[11]

7. Burial spaces for an individual, the individual's spouse, and members of the individual's immediate family (children, siblings, parents, and the spouses of these individuals). The definition of burial spaces includes a cemetery plot, improvements such as gravestones, and even some funeral expenses, such as opening and closing the gravesite for burial. Also excluded are funds (up to $1,500 for an individual and $3,000 for a couple plus accrued interest) separately set aside for burial expenses. Interest accrued on the excluded funds is excluded as long as it is retained as part of the fund.[12]

8. Retroactive payments of social security retirement or disability benefits or SSI benefits. These are excluded for six months following the month of their receipt. To qualify for this exclusion, the funds must be identifiable as resulting from such retroactive payments. The rule applies only to unspent funds, not to property purchased with such money. However, if the money is used to acquire exempt resources, the rules governing

---

9. 20 C.F.R. §§ 416.1220–416.1224; SSA POMS §§ SI 01140.001 et seq. (12/87).

10. Cf. Derrer v. Sullivan, 768 F.Supp. 765, 34 Soc.Sec.Rep.Ser. 350 (D.Colo.1991) (termination of SSI benefits because of excess resources not supported by substantial evidence); Maine Association of Interdependent Neighborhoods v. Petit, 659 F.Supp. 1309, 18 Soc.Sec.Rep.Ser. 187 (D.Me.1987) ($6,000/6% rule invalidated as arbitrary, capricious, and in excess of statutory authority).

11. 20 C.F.R. § 416.1232.

12. 42 U.S.C.A. § 1382b(d); 20 C.F.R. § 416.1231.

such resources would apply. The SSA is to notify beneficiaries of this exclusion when making retroactive payments.[13]

9. Payments received under certain federal statutes. To be excluded, the relevant statute must require that a payment or benefit not count as a resource for SSI purposes. Examples include relocation assistance payments, the value of federally donated foods, excess value of food stamp coupon allotments, and disaster relief payments.[14]

§ 17.25 Financial Requirements—Resource Limitations—Excess Resources

Normally, if an applicant for Supplemental Security Income (SSI) has excess countable resources, the application is denied. Similarly, a recipient of SSI who is determined to have excess resources is declared ineligible for benefits for each month in which there are excess resources, and the Social Security Administration (SSA) will attempt to recoup SSI payments made during months of ineligibility.[1]

The SSI resource rules count assets at the beginning of the month. Changes in resources or changes in their value occurring during a month are calculated as occurring at the beginning of the next month. Cash and other items countable as income received during a month are treated as income for the month (see income rules in §§ 17.26–.33, infra). If unexpended, the cash becomes a resource at the beginning of the next month.[2]

A person contemplating application for SSI whose countable resources exceed allowable limits has several options.

1. Convert excess countable assets into excluded assets. For example, excess cash could be used to purchase burial plots and gravestones or to prepay for certain funeral expenses, or insurance with a cash surrender value could be exchanged for a term policy, or improvements or repairs on a home could be made.

2. If the resource is liquid, spend the excess. For example, bills may be paid. Caution must be exercised, since such expenditures may affect the value of resources (i.e., increase an applicant's equity), and expenditure on behalf of others (e.g., children) will be treated as a transfer of the asset.

3. Transfer the asset. The effect of selling or transferring a nonexcluded asset for less than fair market value depends on

---

13. 20 C.F.R. § 416.1233. For retroactive payments received between October 1, 1987, and September 30, 1989, the period of exemption is nine months, rather than the six-month period otherwise applicable.

14. 20 C.F.R. § 416.1236.

§ 17.25

1. 20 C.F.R. § 416.1324.

2. 20 C.F.R. § 416.1207(b), (c).

when it occurred. Such transfers made on or after July 1, 1988, have no effect on SSI eligibility.[3] *More restrictive rules govern Medicaid eligibility, however, so no transfer of an asset should be made without consulting the rules governing Medicaid.*

Transfers made prior to July 1, 1988, are subject to different rules. These rules are important primarily for existing SSI beneficiaries who may have transferred assets in violation of these rules and whose benefits may be terminated or reduced as a result (see §§ 17.43–53, infra). Prior to July 1, 1988, countable resources owned or partially owned by an individual or eligible spouse could not be given away or sold for less than fair market value for purposes of establishing SSI eligibility. The fair market value of resources so disposed of (less the amount of compensation received) was included in the individual's total resources for a period of 24 months after the transaction. Any gift or sale for less than fair market value was presumed to have been made for the purpose of establishing eligibility, unless convincing evidence established that the transaction was exclusively for some other purpose.[4] Convincing evidence may be documentary or nondocumentary evidence that shows that the transfer was ordered by a court (e.g., a support order) or that at the time of transfer, the individual "could not have anticipated becoming eligible due to the existence of other circumstances which would have precluded eligibility" (e.g., the individual had ample income and resources on which to live.[5]

4. Qualify for conditional payments. If an applicant's total countable liquid resources (i.e., cash, stocks, bonds, etc.) do not exceed three times the monthly SSI federal benefit rate for an individual ($1,302 in 1993) or for a couple ($1,956 in 1993), the applicant can be eligible to receive SSI benefits immediately if he or she complies with certain conditions.[6] The SSI payments under this rule are called "conditional payments."

To qualify for conditional payments, an applicant must agree in writing to sell enough "nonliquid" resources to bring the applicant within the basic resources maximum. Second, the applicant must agree to repay the government the difference between the SSI payments received from the time the applicant agreed to sell the resources until the time of sale and the amount of SSI benefits the applicant would have received

---

3. 42 U.S.C.A. § 1382b(b), (c); 20 C.F.R. § 416.1246(f).

4. 20 C.F.R. § 416.1246(e).

5. 20 C.F.R. § 416.1246(e). For transfers occurring after April 1, 1988, this anti-

transfer rule will be suspended if its application would cause "undue hardship." Id. at § 416.1246(d)(2), (3).

6. 42 U.S.C.A. § 1382b(b)(1); 20 C.F.R. § 416.1240.

during the same period had the proceeds from the sale been included as available at the beginning of that period. In effect, this agreement often amounts to a repayment by the applicant of the net proceeds of the sale minus any amount of the proceeds necessary to raise the applicant's available nonexempt resources up to the maximum allowed under the basic resources rule. The third condition is that the sale generally must be made within nine months if real property is being sold, or three months for all other types of property. The time period can be extended if there is a valid reason.[7]

An applicant is not required to dispose of real property when it cannot be sold because (1) it is jointly owned and its sale would cause undue hardship, due to loss of housing, for the other owner(s); (2) its sale is barred by legal impediment; or (3) the owner's reasonable efforts to sell it have been unsuccessful.[8] In some cases, it may be better not to receive conditional payments. For example, where property can be easily disposed of, an applicant may prefer to lower the total resources to within the maximums allowed by independently spending the sale proceeds, thereby enjoying a temporarily higher standard of living. Another possibility is to spend the excess countable resources to purchase an excluded resource.

§ 17.26 Financial   Requirements—Income   Limitations—In General

The Social Security Administration (SSA) defines income as "anything you receive in cash or in kind that you can use to meet your needs for food, clothing, and shelter."[1] Under this definition, income includes both earned and unearned income,[2] and it includes both cash and noncash income such as food or clothing.[3] Noncash income is referred to by the SSA as income "in-kind."[4]

To be eligible for federal Supplemental Security Income (SSI) benefits in 1993, an individual's countable monthly income could not exceed $434 (or $652 for a couple). However, since many kinds of income are not counted in determining SSI eligibility, a person may be eligible for SSI even though the person's actual income is considerably higher than these figures. Furthermore, a person who lives in a state

7. 42 U.S.C.A. § 1382b(b)(1); 20 C.F.R. §§ 416.1240–416.1244.

8. 42 U.S.C.A. § 1382b(b)(2); 20 C.F.R. § 416.1245. For details, see Deford and Sweeney, supra § 17.22, note 8. See also Freedman and Berlow, SSI Benefits for Individuals and Couples Who Own Excess Nonliquid Resources, 23 Clearinghouse Rev. 474 (1989).

§ 17.26

1. 20 C.F.R. § 416.1102.

2. 20 C.F.R. § 416.1102.

3. Id.

4. 20 C.F.R. § 416.1130.

that supplements SSI by paying additional benefits may be eligible for state supplemental benefits even though the person's income is too high to be eligible for federal SSI benefits.

§ 17.27 Financial   Requirements—Income   Limitations— Earned Income

The Social Security Administration (SSA) regards as earned income the gross wages a person receives from a job and net earnings from self-employment.[1] Earned income is usually money, but it also can be income in-kind, such as food or clothing.

§ 17.28 Financial   Requirements—Income   Limitations—Unearned Income

Any income received other than earned income is treated by the Social Security Administration (SSA) as unearned income.[1] Common examples of unearned income include social security, veterans' benefits, workers' compensation benefits, unemployment insurance benefits, pensions,[2] gifts, alimony, inheritances,[3] and lottery winnings and other prizes.[4]

§ 17.29 Financial   Requirements—Income   Limitations—Income In–Kind

Income is not limited to cash received by an individual or couple; it includes noncash items such as food, clothing, and shelter. Payments in-kind can be either earned or unearned income. For example, if a person works for another and receives food rather than cash, the noncash payment is regarded as earned income.[1] Unearned income in-kind includes gifts of food, clothing, or shelter.

In determining the value of earned income in-kind, the Social Security Administration (SSA) assesses the current market value of the income in-kind received.[2] For example, if a person works as a hotel clerk, earning $100 per month and use of a room, the person's monthly income will be $100 plus the current market value of the room.

§ 17.27

1. 42 U.S.C.A. § 1382a(a)(1); 20 C.F.R. § 416.1110.

§ 17.28

1. 42 U.S.C.A. § 1382a(a)(2); 20 C.F.R. § 416.1120.

2. 20 C.F.R. § 416.1121(a).

3. 20 C.F.R. § 416.1121(b), (g).

4. 20 C.F.R. § 416.1121(f).

§ 17.29

1. 20 C.F.R. § 416.1110(a). However, payments in-kind for certain kinds of work, including work as a domestic or as a farm-worker, are treated as unearned income. Id.; SSA Program Operations Manual System POMS § SI 00830.530 (2/93).

2. SSA POMS § SI 00820.010C (12/91).

Because determining the current market value of income in-kind is difficult, the SSA does not actually determine unearned income in-kind. The SSA presumes that the income is worth $164.67 (1993) per month for one person and $237.33 (1993) per month for a couple.[3] This presumption is rebuttable. If an individual believes that this "presumed value" is wrong, the individual must prove that the value of the food, clothing, housing, etc., that he or she is receiving is worth less than its "presumed value," which is done by supplying the SSA with documents establishing the actual value of the unearned income. For example, if a person's daughter buys all of her food for each month, the SSA will presume that this food is worth $164.67 a month and will treat the person as having $164.67 of unearned income each month. However, if the food is worth only $60 per month and this can be proven by presenting the daughter's grocery bills, only $60 per month of unearned income will be attributed to the individual.

A particularly complicated problem involving income in-kind arises when a person lives in the household of another. If a person receives both room and board, the SSA does not determine the actual value of this room and board; instead, it presumes that the value of the room and board is equal to one-third of the maximum Supplemental Security Income (SSI) payment ($144.67 in 1993) available to an individual.[4] If a person lives with her daughter and receives both room and board, her SSI payment will be reduced by one-third even if the value of the room and board is less than this amount. Unlike the normal rule for unearned income in-kind, the one-third rule involves an *irrebuttable* presumption.

This rule substantially harms SSI applicants who are unable to pay their full share of living costs until they start receiving their SSI benefits. Although the reduction may apply to them in the month in which they first receive benefits, they should return to the local SSA office in the next month and show that they are now paying a fair share of the household expenses and have the one-third reduction removed. In cases where the one-third reduction prevents applicants from paying their fair share of living expenses, they can argue that the remainder of their share is being paid for them as a loan, and they should document this "loan" in writing.[5]

---

3. 20 C.F.R. § 416.1140. The presumed value actually is one-third of the maximum federal SSI payment plus $20. At 1993 payment levels, the amounts specified in the text would be applicable.

4. 20 C.F.R. § 416.1131.

5. See, Hickman v. Bowen, 803 F.2d 1377, 15 Soc.Sec.Rep.Ser. 285 (5th Cir.1986)

(an applicant can receive a loan of in-kind food and shelter while waiting for application to be approved); Ceguerra v. Secretary of Health and Human Services, 933 F.2d 735, 33 Soc.Sec.Rep.Ser. 482 (9th Cir.1991) (room and board received from son while appealing termination of SSI benefits found to be a loan). SSA has abandoned

The one-third reduction rule does not apply to all situations in which a person is living with family or friends. The rule does not apply, for example, if a person is receiving only room or board, but not both.[6] However, in this situation, the SSA will presume that the value of the room or board that is received is worth $164.67 (1993) per month ($237.33 per month in 1993 for a couple). This presumption is rebuttable. Evidence that the value of the room or board is less than $164.67 (or $237.33) per month may be presented.

The one-third reduction rule also does not apply if a person lives in his or her own home with friends or family members, or in a commercial establishment such as a hotel, or if the person is paying his or her pro-rata share of the household expenses (food, rent, utilities, etc.).[7] Thus, if a person and her daughter are living in an apartment the person has rented or if her daughter is staying in the mother's home, the one-third reduction rule does not apply. However, the SSA will include as income any rent or help with the cost of groceries that the daughter provides and will presume that its value is $164.67 (in 1993) per month. The presumption is rebuttable. Proof that the contribution is not worth this much or that the mother is paying her pro-rata share of household expenses can be supplied.

§ 17.30 Financial Requirements—Income Limitations—Excluded Income

Eligibility for Supplemental Security Income (SSI) is based on how much countable income one has. For a variety of reasons, many kinds of income are excluded completely in determining countable income. Also excluded completely is the first $20 of income (earned or unearned) one receives each month.[1] In addition, only part of one's earned income is counted in determining whether one is eligible for SSI.

The following kinds of income are not countable in determining one's eligibility for SSI:

1. income tax refunds;[2]

2. property tax or food sales tax refunds;[3]

3. Medicare Part B premium paid by an insurance company or by Medicaid;[4]

its argument that only loans of cash qualify as a loan. See POMS § GN E00835.481.

6. 20 C.F.R. § 416.1131(a)(2).

7. 20 C.F.R. §§ 416.1132–416.1133.

§ 17.30

1. 42 U.S.C.A. § 1382a(b)(2); 20 C.F.R. § 416.1124(c)(12).

2. 20 C.F.R. § 416.1103(d).

3. 20 C.F.R. § 416.1124(c)(1).

4. 20 C.F.R. § 416.1103(a)(6).

4. wages received from VISTA, the Foster Grandparent Program, the Retired Senior Volunteer Program, or the Senior Companion Program;[5]

5. the value of home produce consumed by one's family;[6]

6. the value of free meals provided under Title 7 of the Older Americans Act;[7]

7. certain payments for foster care of children;[8]

8. medical care or services (including incidental room and board) paid by an insurance company or by Medicaid[9] and noncash social services (such as advice or training or cash given by the Veterans Administration to purchase aid and attendance);[10]

9. cash or other property received from the sale or exchange of a resource (although this cash or property will be treated as a resource and, thus, may affect one's eligibility);[11]

10. insurance payments for the replacement of a resource (again, these payments may be treated as a resource and so may affect eligiblity);[12]

11. cash payments by a state or local government agency that are based upon need;[13]

12. the value of housing assistance from the federal government;[14]

13. up to $10 per month of infrequently received earned income and up to $20 per month of infrequently received unearned income;[15]

14. cash provided by a nongovernmental social services program under certain circumstances;[16]

15. any support or maintenance assistance (e.g., food, clothing, and shelter) provided in-kind by a private nonprofit organization;[17]

5. 20 C.F.R. pt. 416, subpt. K, app.

6. 20 C.F.R. § 416.1124(c)(4).

7. 20 C.F.R. pt. 416, subpt. K, app.

8. 20 C.F.R. § 416.1124(c)(8).

9. 20 C.F.R. § 416.1103(a).

10. 20 C.F.R. § 416.1103(b).

11. 20 C.F.R. § 416.1103(c).

12. Id.

13. 20 C.F.R. § 416.1124(c)(2).

14. 20 C.F.R. pt. 416, subpt. K. app.

15. 20 C.F.R. §§ 416.1112(c)(1), 1124(c)(6).

16. 20 C.F.R. § 416.1103(b)(3).

17. 42 U.S.C.A. § 1382a(b)(4)(C)(13); 20 C.F.R. § 416.1157.

16. income excluded as provided by federal laws other than the Social Security Act (e.g., food stamps and grants to certain Indian Tribes); [18]

17. the value of commercial transportation tickets received as a gift and not converted to cash; [19] and

18. payments to certain groups (e.g., reparations from West Germany to Holocaust survivors and payments to individuals of Japanese ancestry interned by the United States during World War II).[20]

The list of uncountable income is subject to change. Counsel should carefully review the appropriate statute and regulations to ensure that uncountable income received by a client is not overlooked.

§ 17.31 Financial Requirements—Income Limitations—Partially Excluded Income

In addition to forms of income that are excluded altogether in determining one's eligibility for Supplemental Security Income (SSI), other income is partially excluded in making this determination. The principal example is earned income. The first $20 of unearned income one receives each month is excluded altogether in determining SSI eligibility. Also excluded is the first $65 ($85 if one has only earned income) earned each month.[1] In addition, one-half of a person's monthly earnings in excess of $65 is excluded in determining eligibility.[2] Because of these exclusions, a person can earn up to $952, and a couple up to $1388, per month (in 1993) and still be eligible for some SSI benefits.

§ 17.32 Financial Requirements—Income Limitations—Rules for Couples

If a person is single, only that person's income will be counted in determining whether he or she is eligible for Supplemental Security Income (SSI).[1] However, if a person is married and living with a spouse, both spouses' incomes will be counted.[2] If both spouses are

18. See 20 C.F.R. pt. 416, subpt. K, app.

19. 42 U.S.C.A. § 1382a(b)(15).

20. Grunfeder v. Heckler, 748 F.2d 503, 7 Soc.Sec.Rep.Ser. 266 (9th Cir.1984) (reparations payments); 50 U.S.C.A. § 19896–4(f) (Japanese internees).

§ 17.31

1. 42 U.S.C.A. § 1382a(b)(4).

2. Id.

§ 17.32

1. 20 C.F.R. § 416.1102. However, the income of a spouse or parent will be counted for eligible children and spouses, and the income of an "essential person" is counted. 20 C.F.R. §§ 416.220–416.223, 416.1160–416.1169.

2. 42 U.S.C.A. § 1382a(b).

applying for SSI, the normal rules governing income exclusions apply, and the countable incomes will be added together to determine whether both spouses are eligible for benefits. If both spouses are eligible, they will receive the level of benefits (federal benefit rate) paid to a couple (up to $652 per month in 1993).

Slightly different rules apply if only one member of a couple is applying for SSI benefits.[3] For example, if a husband is applying for benefits but his wife is not, the determination of whether he is eligible for SSI will work as follows. His income will be counted in the normal way—that is, the regular income exclusions will be utilized in determining his income. If his wife has any income, the Social Security Administration (SSA) will determine how much of this income can be counted by applying slightly different exclusion rules than it normally uses to determine countable income. Once SSA has decided how much countable income she has, it will add this income to his countable income to determine whether he is eligible for SSI benefits. He will be eligible for benefits if their combined countable income does not exceed the maximum income couples are allowed to have. However, the amount of benefits he will receive will never be more than he would have received were he living alone. The process of including the income of an ineligible spouse in counting how much income the eligible spouse has is called "deeming." [4]

To illustrate, John is 65 and has no income. Jane, his wife, is 58 and not eligible for SSI. She works and regularly makes $300 per month (before taxes). To determine John's SSI payment amount in light of Jane's income, which is deemed available to him, a three-step calculation must be done. First, the monthly earned and unearned income of Jane must be determined (i.e., $300). As this is more than the difference between the monthly SSI federal benefit for a couple and the federal benefit for an individual ($218), Jane's income cannot be ignored. Second, as Jane and John have no unearned income, the calculations involve only earned income. Jane's monthly earned income is added to John's ($300 + 0 = $300). The first $20 is disregarded ($300 − 20 = $280). Also disregarded is $65 of earned income ($280 − 65 = $215). The remainder is divided in half ($215 ÷ 2) to get the countable earned income ($107.50). Third, this countable income is subtracted from the monthly federal benefit rate for a couple ($652 − 107.50 = $544.50). Had this figure been below $434 (the amount John would receive if he were applying as an individual), then it would have been John's monthly SSI payment amount. Because it exceeds that

3. 20 C.F.R. § 416.1163.   4. Id.

amount, John will simply receive $434 for that month.[5]

§ 17.33 Financial Requirements—Income Limitations—Sponsor–Alien Deeming

Under recent changes to the Social Security Act, the income and resources of sponsors are deemed to aliens for three years beginning with the month the alien is admitted to the United States for permanent resident status. Before any income and resources are deemed, certain "allocations" are made for the sponsor, the sponsor's spouse, and their dependents.[1] The sponsor-to-alien deeming provisions supplement rather than replace other deeming rules. For example, if the alien's ineligible spouse is also his or her sponsor, the spouse-to-spouse deeming rules apply, not the sponsor-to-alien deeming rules. In addition, if the sponsor and the alien are married and both are eligible for Supplemental Security Income (SSI), the Social Security Administration (SSA) will treat them as a couple. In sponsor-to-alien deeming, the allocation for the sponsor is equal to the SSI federal benefit rate ($434 in 1993), and the allocations for the sponsor's spouse and dependents are one-half the federal benefit rate each ($217 in 1993). The countable resources deemed to an alien are those in excess of the amount allowable under SSI for an individual ($2,000 in 1993).[2]

To illustrate, John, an alien who has no income, has been sponsored by Herbert who has monthly earned income of $1,600 and unearned income of $200. Herbert's wife and three children have no income. The SSA adds Herbert's earned and unearned income for a total of $1,800 and applies the allocations for the sponsor and his dependents. Allocations total $1,302. These are made up of $434 (the federal benefit rate for an eligible individual) for the sponsor, plus $868 (one-half the benefit rate for an eligible individual, $217 each) for Herbert's wife and three children. The $1,302 is subtracted from Herbert's total income of $1,800 which leaves $498 to be deemed to John as his unearned income. John's only exclusion is the $20 general income exclusion. Since the $478 balance exceeds the $434 federal benefit rate, John is ineligible.

If Herbert's income had been $1,700 instead of $1,800, John would have been eligible for a small SSI benefit, since the income deemed to him would have been $414, or $8 less than the federal payment amount. This example assumes that John has no resources and that

5. 20 C.F.R. § 416.1163(d); see also § 416.1163(g), example 3.

§ 17.33

1. 42 U.S.C.A. § 1382j; 20 C.F.R. §§ 416.1160, 1166a.

2. 20 C.F.R. § 416.1204. If an alien's sponsor is living with a spouse, the resource limits for a couple are used. Id.

Herbert does not have countable resources exceeding $3,000. If Herbert had resources exceeding $3,000, they would be allocated to John, who would be ineligible if his countable resources, together with Herbert's excess resources, exceeded the resource limit for an individual ($2,000 in 1993).

§§ 17.34–17.40 are reserved for supplementary material.

C. PROGRAM ADMINISTRATION

Library References:

> C.J.S. Social Security and Public Welfare § 95.
>
> West's Key No. Digests, Social Security and Public Welfare ☜175.25.

§ 17.41 Applications—Process

The process for applying for Supplemental Security Income (SSI) benefits is similar to the process for applying for social security benefits. Application normally is made on a written form provided by the Social Security Administration (SSA),[1] but one can initiate an application by contacting a social security office and requesting an application form.[2] An application is considered effective on the date it is received at the social security office, or if it is mailed, on the date it was postmarked.[3] Benefits will be paid from the date an application is filed, unless the applicant was not eligible for SSI on that date. Thus, the SSI payment for the first month of eligibility will be prorated by the number of days in the month for which there is an effective application.[4]

As with social security benefits, the burden of establishing eligibility for SSI rests with the applicant. The applicant must prove that he or she is 65 or older, blind, or disabled; and the applicant will have to supply the SSA with proof concerning income, resources, and living situation. The SSA is required to help obtain proof needed to establish eligibility for SSI.[5] For the most part, the process of applying for SSI benefits is similar to applying for social security. The same documents

---

§ 17.41

1. 20 C.F.R. § 416.310.

2. Cf. 20 C.F.R. § 416.340. If a person writes or makes an oral inquiry to the SSA expressing an intention to apply for SSI benefits, the person will be treated as having applied as of the date of this first communication if the person then completes an official application within 60 days of the SSA notice to file a formal application. Id.; 20 C.F.R. § 416.345.

3. 20 C.F.R. § 416.325.

4. 42 U.S.C.A. § 1382(c)(2), (5); 20 C.F.R. §§ 416.330, 416.335, 416.421.

5. SSA Program Operations Manual System (POMS) § SI 00601.110B (9/92).

used to prove age,[6] blindness, or disability for social security benefits can be used when applying for SSI benefits.[7] Because SSI eligibility is based partly on income and assets, detailed proof regarding these matters also is required. For this reason, a client should collect documents concerning income, resources, citizenship, marital status, and living arrangements before going to the social security office to apply for SSI. Documents that may be useful are checking and savings account statements, rent receipts, deeds, and certificates of title for automobiles and other property. However, the client should not delay in submitting an application until all of these documents are assembled. If there is difficulty in obtaining any of these documents, the applicant should apply first and obtain the documents later, so as not to lose benefits as a result of delay in submitting an application.

The Internal Revenue Service (IRS) is authorized to release tax information to the SSA for the purpose of determining a person's income and assets to determine SSI eligibility. The IRS also is authorized to release information to other government agencies administering AFDC, Medicaid, unemployment compensation, and food stamps. The SSA (or other government agency) "may [not] terminate, deny, suspend, or reduce any benefits of an individual" until it has "taken appropriate steps to independently verify information relating to:

- the amount of the asset or income involved; whether the individual actually has (or had) access to such asset or income for his [or her] own use; and
- the period or periods when the individual actually had such asset or income."

Furthermore, a person must be afforded the opportunity to contest the SSA's findings "in the same manner as applies to other information and findings relating to eligibility factors under the program." [8]

§ 17.42 Applications—Obtaining Benefits While SSI Application Is Pending

Because of the delay in processing Supplemental Security Income (SSI) applications, Congress and the Social Security Administration (SSA) have provided several ways in which a person may obtain some help while his or her application is pending.[1] For example, SSI applicants sometimes have difficulty establishing their age. If one

---

6. 20 C.F.R. §§ 416.801–416.806. However, the proof-of-age requirements for persons claiming to be at least 68 years old are relaxed. 20 C.F.R. § 416.806.

7. 20 C.F.R. § 416.901.

8. 42 U.S.C.A. § 1320b–7.

§ 17.42

1. See Leyser, The SSI Emergency Advance Payment System, 23 Clearinghouse Rev. 478 (1989).

establishes financial eligibility for SSI and provides the SSA with a document (at least three years old) indicating that one is at least 65 years old, one can obtain advance payments even if the SSA wants further proof of age.[2]

A person who applies for SSI based upon disability can obtain benefits while the application is processed if he or she is determined to be "presumptively disabled."[3] To be eligible for special benefits because of presumptive disability, one must establish financial eligibility for SSI and that one is suffering from a disability so severe that eligibility for benefits is extremely likely.[4] If one establishes financial eligibility as well as a serious disability of this type, one is eligible for up to three months of SSI benefits while the application for benefits is pending. If later determined not to be eligible for SSI because one is found not to be disabled, one does not have to repay the benefits received in the meantime.[5]

In addition to these specialized forms of temporary assistance, an applicant for SSI in 1993 is entitled to up to $434 (or $652 for a couple), plus any federally administered state supplementary payment, if the applicant shows a strong likelihood that he or she will be eligible for benefits (i.e., that he or she is poor enough) and if a financial emergency exists that requires immediate assistance.[6] An example of such a financial emergency is lack of food, clothing, shelter, or medical care.[7]

Moreover, the SSA has implemented an "immediate payment" program under which the SSA will issue an immediate payment of up to $200 to (1) an individual who is currently eligible for either social security insurance or SSI benefits but has not received his or her check, or (2) an individual who has been approved for either social security or SSI but has not started receiving his or her monthly checks. These payments are made when the eligible individual cannot wait the seven- to ten-day time period required for having a critical payment processed and when further delay in payment would deprive the individual of food and/or shelter, endanger the individual's health, or cause the SSA

---

2. 20 C.F.R. § 416.806. If one later is determined not to be eligible for SSI, payments received in the meantime are treated as overpayments. Id.

3. 20 C.F.R. §§ 416.931–416.934.

4. 20 C.F.R. § 416.934; Examples of impairments that are sufficient in this case are amputation of two limbs, or of a leg at the hip, or of a foot as a result of diabetes; allegation of total deafness; confinement to a bed or immobility without a wheel-chair, walker, or crutches because of a longstanding condition; allegation of a stroke of at least four months ago or of cerebral palsy, muscular dystrophy, or AIDS as defined by the Centers for Disease Control.

5. 20 C.F.R. § 416.931.

6. 42 U.S.C.A. § 1383(a)(4)(A); 20 C.F.R. § 416.520.

7. 20 C.F.R. § 416.520(b)(2).

extremely adverse public relations. Only one emergency payment can be issued under each program every thirty days.[8]

§ 17.43 Payments—SSI Benefits Payments—In General

Supplemental Security Income (SSI) benefits are paid monthly in the form of multicolored United States Treasury checks that usually arrive soon after the first of the month. When both members of a couple are eligible for SSI, each receives a check for one-half of the monthly amount the couple is entitled to receive.[1]

The monthly federal SSI benefit of $652 for a couple and of $434 for an individual may be increased by state supplements, which vary from state to state. Also, the federal portion of SSI benefits may be increased periodically by cost-of-living adjustments.[2]

§ 17.44 Payments—SSI Benefits Payments—Benefit Computations [1]

Supplemental Security Income (SSI) benefits are computed monthly. The amount of the monthly payment is computed by reducing the federal benefit rate by the amount of countable income an individual or couple receives. In general, the Social Security Administration (SSA) uses the amount of countable income in the second month prior to the current month (the month for which a benefit is payable) to determine how much a persons's benefit amount will be for the current month. For example, a person's countable income in July is used to determine the benefit amount for September.

The SSA uses a person's countable income in the current month to determine the benefit amount for the first month the person is eligible for SSI benefits or for the first month the person becomes eligible for SSI benefits after at least a month of ineligibility. Payment for that month is prorated according to the number of days in the month that the person is eligible, beginning with the date of application or the date on which the person attains (or reattains) eligibility, whichever is later. For example, a person applies for SSI benefits in September. The SSA uses that person's countable income in September to determine the amount of the benefit for September. The same would be true if that person had been ineligible for SSI benefits in August and again became eligible for such benefits in September.

8. SSA POMS §§ SI E02004.100, et seq. (10/92); RS E02801.030, et seq. (8/85).

§ 17.43

1. 20 C.F.R. § 416.502.

2. 42 U.S.C.A. § 1382f.

§ 17.44

1. 20 C.F.R. § 416.420. See 20 C.F.R. §§ 416.421–416.435 for additional details.

The SSA uses a person's countable income in the first month prior to the current month to determine how much the benefit amount will be for the current month when the current month is the second month of initial eligibility or the second month following at least a month of ineligibility. For example, a person was initially eligible for SSI benefits in September. The benefit amount for October will be based on the person's countable income in September (first prior month). For the third month of eligibility and beyond, the general rule described above is used to determine the payment a person will receive. Thus, for a person who was initially eligible for SSI benefits in September, the benefit amount for November will be based on the person's countable income in September (second prior month).

The SSA uses a person's income from certain assistance payments in the current month to determine that person's SSI benefit amount for that same month.[2] If a person has been receiving an SSI benefit and receiving a social security insurance benefit and the latter is increased on the basis of a cost-of-living adjustment or because the person's benefit is recomputed, SSA will compute the amount of the SSI benefit for January (the month of any SSI benefit increase) by including in the person's income the amount by which the social security benefit in January exceeds the amount of the social security benefit in November. Similarly, SSA will compute the amount of the person's SSI benefit for February by including in the person's income the amount by which the social security benefit in February exceeds the amount of the social security benefit in December. For example, a person's SSI benefit amount is being determined for January (the current month). This person has social security income of $100 in November, $100 in December, and $105 in January. The SSA finds the amount by which the person's social security income in January exceeds the social security income in November ($5) and adds that to the person's income in November to determine the SSI benefit amount for January.

§ 17.45 Payments—Representative Payees

As with social security checks, if a person is determined to be unable to care for himself or herself, the checks may be sent to a "representative payee."[1] The rules governing representative payees for SSI beneficiaries are similar to those of representative payees for social security recipients. Certain SSI recipients, however, do not receive their SSI checks directly. The SSI checks of individuals deter-

---

2. Examples include Aid to Families with Dependent Children, Foster Care, Refugee Cash Assistance and Bureau of Indian Affairs Cash Assistance. See 20 C.F.R. § 416.420(b)(4).

§ 17.45

1. 20 C.F.R. §§ 416.601–416.665.

mined by the SSA to be alcoholics or drug addicts are sent automatically to a representative payee regardless of the ability of the individual to take care of his or her own needs.[2]

§ 17.46 Payments—Lost and Stolen Checks

Lost or stolen Supplemental Security Income (SSI) checks are handled much like lost or stolen social security checks. One should promptly notify the local social security office if one's check does not arrive on time. As with social security checks, if the Social Security Administration (SSA) determines that no check has been issued and that one is entitled to a check for that month, a check will be issued, which should be received in about ten to fifteen days. However, if it appears that the check has been cashed, replacement of the check will take a long time because of the need to contact the Treasury Department to determine whether a forgery has occurred.[1] A person who needs temporary assistance while waiting for an SSI check to be replaced can apply to the local welfare department for emergency assistance.

In order to prevent checks from being stolen or lost, clients should have their checks deposited directly into their bank accounts. One can apply for "direct deposit" of one's check by signing Form SF–1199, which is sent to a social security office by the financial institution. One should discuss the procedure for direct deposit with one's financial institution to learn its procedures and conditions.

§ 17.47 Payments—Required Reports

A Supplemental Security Income (SSI) recipient is required to report any changes in income or living situation that may affect eligibility for SSI or the amount of SSI benefits.[1] Examples of events that must be reported are: [2]

    1. a change of address;

2. 42 U.S.C.A. § 1383(a)(2)(ii); 20 C.F.R. § 416.601(b)(1). See e.g., Briggs v. Sullivan, 886 F.2d 1132, 27 Soc.Sec.Rep.Ser. 313 (9th Cir.1989), *appeal after remand* 954 F.2d 534, 36 Soc.Sec.Rep.Ser. 203 (1992). See §§ 15.92–.95 supra, for a detailed discussion of representative payee issues, including the extensive changes adopted in 1990.

lost checks are replaced. Moore v. Matthews, 69 F.R.D. 406, 23 F.R.Serv.2d 88 (D.Mass.1975); for an attempt to respond to nonreceipt of checks due to problems relating to representation payees, see Briggs v. Sullivan, 886 F.2d 1132, 27 Soc. Sec.Rep.Ser. 313 (9th Cir.1989), *appeal after remand* 954 F.2d 534, 36 Soc.Sec.Rep. Ser. 203 (1992).

§ 17.46

1. At least one suit has been filed attempting to speed up the process by which

§ 17.47

1. 20 C.F.R. §§ 416.704–416.712.

2. 20 C.F.R. § 416.708.

2. a change in living arrangements—additions to and departures from the household;

3. a change in the income of a beneficiary, ineligible spouse, essential person, or child;

4. a change in resources of a beneficiary, ineligible spouse, or essential person;

5. eligibility for other benefits;

6. the death of a beneficiary, spouse, or other person living with a beneficiary;

7. a change in the marital status of a beneficiary, and the death of a representative payee;

8. medical improvements in disabled beneficiaries;

9. refusal to accept vocational rehabilitation services;

10. refusal to accept treatment for drug addiction or alcoholism, or discontinuance of treatment by beneficiaries determined to be drug addicts or alcoholics;

11. admission to or discharge from a medical facility, public institution, or private institution;

12. a change in school attendance by an eligible child;

13. a termination of residence in the United States; and

14. leaving the United States for 30 days or more.

This report must be filed not later than ten days after the month in which the change of circumstances occurred.[3] Failure to make such a report can result in a client being overpaid and can lead to an effort by the Social Security Administration (SSA) to recover the overpayment.[4] The SSA can impose a penalty of between $25 and $100 for failure to make a required report on time. The penalties are collected by reducing one's SSI check in the amount of the penalty. The SSA will not collect the penalty if there is good cause for failing to report on time.[5]

In addition, the SSA will redetermine every year whether a recipient is still eligible for SSI.[6] The redetermination process requires one to fill out forms similar to the application forms. The SSA may require that these forms be filled out more often than every year if it believes a change in circumstances has occurred that affects one's benefits.[7]

3. 20 C.F.R. § 416.714(a); SSA POMS § SI 02301.400 D (pt. 5) (6/88).

4. Cf. 20 C.F.R. §§ 416.537–416.538.

5. 20 C.F.R. §§ 416.724, 416.732.

6. 20 C.F.R. § 416.204.

7. 20 C.F.R. §§ 416.204, 416.714(b).

§ 17.48 Payments—Underpayments [1]

A beneficiary may receive less than he or she was entitled to or may not be paid for a period in which payments were due. A beneficiary who believes he or she has been underpaid should notify the Social Security Administration (SSA) of this fact and request that the underpayment be corrected. If SSA agrees that an underpayment has occurred, it will notify the beneficiary and adjust for the underpayment by sending a separate check or by increasing subsequent monthly payments. If the beneficiary has been overpaid for a different period, SSA may retain the underpayment to offset the overpayment.[2] A beneficiary who disagrees with an SSA decision concerning the existence or amount of an underpayment may appeal the decision by requesting a reconsideration.

If the beneficiary no longer is alive, the underpaid amount will be paid only to a surviving spouse also eligible for Supplemental Security Income (SSI) payments who was living with the beneficiary (or was not separated from the beneficiary for six months) at the time of death. Payment will not be made to the beneficiary's estate or other survivors.

§ 17.49 Payments—Overpayments [1]—In General

The Social Security Administration (SSA) may decide a person has been receiving larger benefit checks than he or she is entitled to, or that a person should not be receiving Supplemental Security Income (SSI) checks at all. If this happens, the SSA must notify the person in writing of its conclusion regarding overpayment.[2] A client can contact the SSA to try to persuade it informally that it is wrong. If informal discussions are unsuccessful, a client should appeal the decision through the usual SSI appeals process.[3] If a person notifies the SSA promptly (within thirty days of receipt of the notice) that the person disagrees with the SSA's determination, he or she is entitled to have benefits continued until a hearing is held by the SSA.[4]

The SSA usually attempts to recover overpaid benefits by reducing future SSI checks each month until the overpaid amount has been

§ 17.48

1. 20 C.F.R. §§ 416.535, 416.536, 416.-538–416.543.

2. 20 C.F.R. §§ 416.538, 416.543; SSA's practice of "netting" underpayments against overpayments was sustained in Sullivan v. Everhart, 494 U.S. 83, 110 S.Ct. 960, 108 L.Ed.2d 72, 28 Soc.Sec.Rep.Ser. 383 (1990), *on remand* 901 F.2d 838 (10th Cir.1990).

§ 17.49

1. 42 U.S.C.A. § 1383(b); 20 C.F.R. §§ 416.535–416.571.

2. 20 C.F.R. § 416.558.

3. 20 C.F.R. §§ 416.1401–416.1482.

4. SSA POMS § GN 02220.050B.

recovered.[5] However, one can ask the SSA to waive recovery of the overpaid amount.[6] As with social security benefits, waiver will be granted only if a beneficiary establishes that the error was not his or her fault and that recovery of the overpayment would either "defeat the purpose of the Supplemental Security Income program" or be "against equity and good conscience" or that the overpaid amount is so small as to be inefficient to recover.[7]

Although most standards governing waiver of recovery of overpayment apply to both the social security and SSI programs, several standards apply specifically to SSI. For example, recovery will be waived for a current SSI recipient whose income does not exceed the current monthly federal benefit rate, plus applicable income exclusions, and the amount of any state supplemental payment.[8] Similarly, recovery will be waived for an SSI recipient who is a member of a couple separated less than six months for any portion of an overpayment he or she did not receive.[9]

If a beneficiary requests a waiver within thirty days of receipt of the notice of overpayment, benefits will continue to be paid pending the waiver determination, and a personal conference will be held.[10]

§ 17.50   Payments—Overpayments—Benefit Reductions [1]

The Social Security Administration (SSA) is limited in the amount of adjustment or recovery of a Supplemental Security Income (SSI) overpayment in any month to the lesser of (1) the amount of the benefit for the month, or (2) an amount equal to 10% of the person's countable income (including SSI) for that month. The 10% limitation does not apply where the overpayment resulted from "fraud, willful misrepresentation, or concealment of material information" or from misuse of a burial fund under 20 C.F.R. § 416.1240. The limitation also does not apply when the recipient requests a different rate at which income may be withheld or recovered. And recovery is suspended altogether if a beneficiary is receiving a reduced benefit rate because he or she is a resident of a medical facility and his or her care is being paid by

---

5. 20 C.F.R. § 416.570. The SSA's practice of "netting" underpayments against overpayments to determine the amount of overpayment has been sustained by the Supreme Court.

6. 20 C.F.R. § 416.550.

7. 20 C.F.R. §§ 416.550–416.556; SSA POMS § GN 02260.030 (pt. 2) (8/82). See also Harrison v. Heckler, 746 F.2d 480, 7 Soc.Sec.Rep.Ser. 138 (9th Cir.1984); Hinton v. Sullivan, 737 F.Supp. 232, 30 Soc.Sec.

Rep.Ser. 241 (S.D.N.Y.1990). For a detailed discussion of these requirements, see Chapter 15, supra.

8. 20 C.F.R. § 416.553(b).

9. 20 C.F.R. § 416.554.

10. SSA POMS §§ GN 02201.011 (7/90) GN 02270.001–02270.017 (10/89).

§ 17.50

1. 20 C.F.R. § 416.571.

Medicaid.[2] The SSA must clearly notify claimants that the 10% rate of withholding is the norm and that a higher rate of repayment is not expected or required.[3]

§ 17.51 Payments—Overpayments—Due to Excess Resources

Where a person's assets exceed the Supplemental Security Income (SSI) resource limit ($2,000 in 1993) by $50 or less, the person will be deemed to be without fault for purposes of waiving the overpayment, unless the Social Security Administration (SSA) finds that the failure to report the excess was "knowing and willful." This will help some SSI recipients who unknowingly permit their bank accounts to creep over the limit. When the individual's assets exceed the resource limit by more than $50, the existing Social Security Act provision on waiver may warrant a waiver of all or part of the resulting overpayment.[1]

§ 17.52 Payments—Protections Against Creditors

Just as creditors are forbidden by the Social Security Act from attaching social security benefits, creditors are prohibited from attaching Supplemental Security Income (SSI) benefits.[1] However, Congress has authorized a procedure under which state governments are repaid for interim assistance provided while an application for SSI was pending.[2]

§ 17.53 Payments—Dual Benefits

Over half of the persons receiving Supplemental Security Income (SSI) also receive social security benefits. A person whose social security benefits are less (in 1993) than $454 (plus the state supplement, if any) per month for an individual or $672 (plus the state supplement, if any) per month for a couple can receive some SSI benefits.[1]

A person can receive both SSI and Medicaid.[2] In fact, in many states a person who is eligible for SSI is automatically eligible for

2. Id.

3. 42 U.S.C.A. § 1383(b)(1)(B).

§ 17.51

1. "The managers recognize that there can be cases where large amounts of excess assets can exist in circumstances where it would be inappropriate to require full repayment of SSI benefits...." H.R.Rep. No. 98–369, 98th Cong., 2d Sess. 1390, reprinted in 1984 Vol. 3 U.S.Code Cong. & Adm.News 2078.

§ 17.52

1. 42 U.S.C.A. § 1383(d)(1). See e.g., Tennessee D.H.S. ex rel. Young v. Young, 802 S.W.2d 594, 32 Soc.Sec.Rep.Ser. 475 (Tenn.1990) (state court may not attach SSI benefits for child support).

2. 42 U.S.C.A. § 1383(g)(1).

§ 17.53

1. 42 U.S.C.A. § 1382a(b)(2); 20 C.F.R. §§ 416.1121(a), 416.1124(c)(12).

2. 42 U.S.C.A. § 1383c.

Medicaid. In other states, only some persons eligible for SSI are also eligible for Medicaid. This is explained in more detail in Chapter 11, supra.

§ 17.54 SSI Appeals System—In General

The system for Supplemental Security Income (SSI) appeals is similar to the system explained in Chapter 15 for appealing decisions concerning social security benefits. Likewise, many of the suggestions in that chapter on how to handle a social security appeal apply to the SSI process. However, there are important differences between the two systems. The following sections provide a description of the SSI system.

Library References:

C.J.S. Social Security and Public Welfare § 95.

West's Key No. Digests, Social Security and Public Welfare ⬄175.25, 175.30.

§ 17.55 SSI Appeals System—Initial Determination

As with social security benefits, most decisions by the Social Security Administration (SSA) affecting Supplemental Security Income (SSI) benefits are called "initial determinations." Included within the definition of initial determinations are decisions to reduce, suspend, or terminate benefits. As is true with social security benefits, one should appeal adverse initial determinations because the determination becomes final unless appealed.[1]

§ 17.56 SSI Appeals System—Reconsideration

The first stage in the Supplemental Security Income (SSI) appeals process is called "reconsideration," as it is in social security appeals. If one wishes to appeal an adverse initial determination, one should file a request for a reconsideration within 60 days of receiving notice of the initial determination by the Social Security Administration (SSA) on one's benefits.[1] This request should be in writing, either on an SSA form or by letter sent to any SSA District Office. The SSA must acknowledge receipt of this request, and if appropriate, it should schedule a conference within 15 days of the request for reconsideration.[2]

§ 17.55

1. 20 C.F.R. § 416.1405.

§ 17.56

1. 20 C.F.R. § 416.1409. One may be able to request a reconsideration later than 60 days after receiving notice of the initial determination if there is good cause for the delay. 20 C.F.R. § 416.1411.

2. 20 C.F.R. § 416.1413c(c).

The SSA has established three different methods of reconsideration. The first, called "case review," provides an opportunity to submit additional evidence of eligibility for SSI (such as additional evidence that one is 65) and an opportunity to discuss one's situation with an SSA employee, who will review the file and decide whether the initial determination concerning benefits was correct.[3]

An "informal conference" is also available.[4] In an informal conference, one can bring witnesses to testify regarding one's eligibility for SSI, and the SSA employee is required to keep a record of the conference and include it in the file. This employee cannot have had anything to do with the case prior to the request for reconsideration.[5]

A third type of conference available is called a "formal conference."[6] In the formal conference, one can subpoena documents and witnesses to help prove eligibility for SSI, and one can cross-examine witnesses whose testimony is unfavorable. A record is kept of the formal conference and is made a part of the SSA file.[7]

The type of reconsideration to which a client is entitled depends upon the basis for the initial determination. If the initial determination was that an applicant was not entitled to benefits, the applicant may choose either a case review or an informal conference.[8] It is usually advantageous to request an informal conference because of the additional rights available. However, if an application for SSI benefits was based on a claim that one is blind or disabled, and the denial of the application was based on a medical issue, the only form of reconsideration available is case review.[9]

A person who is appealing a decision to reduce, suspend, or terminate SSI benefits is entitled to choose case review, informal conference, or formal conference.[10] In addition, if one appeals any SSA determination to suspend, reduce, or terminate SSI benefits (except for disability cessations based on medical factors) within ten days of the receipt of the SSA notice, benefits will be continued until a decision on such initial appeal is issued.[11] The request for appeal should include a request to continue benefits during the appeal. A person failing to specify the type of reconsideration desired will receive a case review.

3. 20 C.F.R. § 416.1413(a). This employee is not supposed to have had any previous connection with the case. 20 C.F.R. § 416.1420.

4. 20 C.F.R. § 416.1413(b).

5. 20 C.F.R. § 416.1420.

6. 20 C.F.R. § 416.1413(c).

7. 20 C.F.R. §§ 416.1413(c), 416.1420.

8. 20 C.F.R. § 416.1413a(a); SSA POMS § GN 03110.070 (pt. 2) (9/83).

9. 20 C.F.R. § 416.1413a(b).

10. 20 C.F.R. § 416.1413b.

11. Id.; 20 C.F.R. § 416.1336(b).

§ 17.57 SSI Appeals System—Hearings

When the reconsideration determination upholds the earlier decision of ineligibility or finds that benefits are to be reduced, suspended, or terminated, one may appeal this determination by filing a written request for a hearing within 60 days of receiving the notice of the reconsideration determination.[1] This request should be sent to the local social security office. Unless one files such a request, the reconsideration determination will become final.[2]

Supplemental Security Income (SSI) hearings are quite similar to hearings involving social security benefits. One should prepare for an SSI hearing in the same way that one would prepare for a hearing in connection with a claim for social security benefits.[3] The Social Security Act requires that a hearing decision be reached within 90 days of the date it was requested, except in disability cases, for which there is no deadline.[4] After a decision has been reached, the administrative law judge will send written notice.[5]

§ 17.58 SSI Appeals System—Appeals of Unfavorable Hearing Decisions

A decision by the administrative law judge that a person is not eligible for benefits or that benefits should be reduced, suspended, or terminated can be appealed to Social Security Administration's (SSA's) Appeals Council.[1] Written appeal should be sent to the local SSA office or to the Appeals Council within 60 days of receiving the adverse hearing decision.[2] Unless such an appeal is filed, the decision of the hearing officer becomes final.[3] Appeals Council review in Supplemental Security Income (SSI) cases proceeds in the same way as in social security cases. One is notified in writing of the decision by the Appeals Council.[4]

§ 17.59 SSI Appeals System—Judicial Review

If dissatisfied with the Appeals Council's decision, one may appeal the decision by filing suit in a federal court within 60 days of receiving

§ 17.57

1. 20 C.F.R. § 416.1433(b). An extension of time in which to request a hearing may be obtained for good cause. 20 C.F.R. §§ 416.1411, 416.1433(c).

2. 20 C.F.R. § 416.1421.

3. 20 C.F.R. §§ 416.1444–416.1453.

4. 42 U.S.C.A. § 1383(c)(2); 20 C.F.R. § 416.1453(b).

5. 20 C.F.R. § 416.1453(a).

§ 17.58

1. 20 C.F.R. § 416.1467.

2. 20 C.F.R. § 416.1468. An extension of time in which to appeal may be obtained for good cause. 20 C.F.R. §§ 416.1411, 416.1468(b).

3. 20 C.F.R. § 416.1455.

4. 20 C.F.R. § 416.1479.

the adverse Appeals Council decision.[1] Judicial review of adverse Supplemental Security Income (SSI) decisions is the same as in social security cases.

§ 17.60 SSI Appeals System—Continuation of Benefits

A Supplemental Security Income (SSI) recipient notified that the Social Security Administration (SSA) believes benefits should be reduced, suspended, or terminated is entitled to continue to receive benefits until a reconsideration determination (or hearing decision in medical cessation cases) has been reached.[1] If one sends a notice to the SSA requesting reconsideration within ten days of being notified of SSA's intention to reduce, suspend, or terminate benefits, SSA must continue to pay benefits until it reaches a decision after the reconsideration conference or hearing.[2]

Benefits do not continue during the remaining stages of appeal beyond reconsideration. If it is determined that the unfavorable decision was erroneous, benefits will be restored for the future and a check will be sent containing back benefits for the months between the reconsideration determination or hearing decision and the time the favorable decision was reached on appeal.

In disability cases where the SSA has determined that a beneficiary no longer is disabled or blind because the beneficiary's medical condition has improved, the beneficiary is entitled to a "face-to-face" reconsideration.[3] If the beneficiary wants benefits continued during this appeal, the beneficiary must file both a request for reconsideration and a request to have benefits continued within ten days of receipt of the notice of termination.[4] A beneficiary who misses this 10-day deadline or who does not want benefits continued has 60 days from receipt of the notice of termination or reconsideration notice to request either a reconsideration or a hearing.[5] As with all SSI appeals, a

---

§ 17.59

1. 42 U.S.C.A. § 1383(c)(3). An extension of time in which to appeal may be obtained for good cause. 20 C.F.R. §§ 416.-1411, 416.1482.

§ 17.60

1. 20 C.F.R. § 416.1336(b). The only exceptions to this rule are when benefits are terminated because the recipient is dead, the recipient is receiving more than one check per month, or the amount received is impossibly high. In the latter two situations, one will continue to receive benefits but at a lower amount. 20 C.F.R. §§ 416.1334, 416.1337.

2. 20 C.F.R. § 416.1336(b); 20 C.F.R. §§ 416.966(c)(1), (d)(1).

3. 42 U.S.C.A. § 405(b)(2); 20 C.F.R. §§ 416.1414–416.1418.

4. 20 C.F.R. § 416.996(c)(1).

5. 20 C.F.R. §§ 416.996(c)(1), (d)(1); 20 C.F.R. §§ 416.1409, 416.1433.

person who misses either the 10–day or 60–day deadline can show "good cause" to excuse the failure to file on time.[6]

It is almost always to one's advantage to ask that benefits be continued pending a reconsideration determination. The only disadvantage of insisting that benefits be continued pending appeal is that if the appeal is unsuccessful, the benefits received between the time one was notified of the SSA's intention to cut off benefits and the time of the reconsideration decision can be treated as an overpayment.[7]

§ **17.61** Attorney Fees

An attorney who obtains a favorable determination for a claimant for SSI benefits may obtain a "reasonable fee" for his or her services.[1] An attorney for a "prevailing party" in litigation against the United States also may be eligible for costs and fees under the Equal Access to Justice Act.[2]

6. 20 C.F.R. §§ 416.996(c)(2), (d)(2); 20 C.F.R. § 416.1411.

7. 20 C.F.R. § 416.537. 20 C.F.R. § 416.996(f) ("Waiver of recovery of an overpayment resulting from continued benefits to you may be considered as long as the cessation determination was appealed in good faith." 20 C.F.R. § 416.996(g)(2).)

§ **17.61**

1. 42 U.S.C.A. § 1383(d)(2)(A); 20 C.F.R. § 416.1520.

2. 28 U.S.C.A. § 2412(d). See § 15.121–.146 for a detailed discussion of these topics.

CHAPTER 18

FOOD STAMPS

Table of Sections

WESTLAW Electronic Research

See WESTLAW Electronic Research Guide preceding the Summary of Contents.

---

§ 18.1 Introduction

The Food Stamp Program was established by the federal government,[1] is directed by the United States Department of Agriculture

§ 18.1

1. 7 U.S.C.A. § 2011 et seq.

(USDA), and is administered within the various states by state agencies, usually the same agency administering other means-based benefit programs. Until October 1, 1992, benefits varied from a household monthly maximum of $111 for one person to $203 for two persons to $667 for eight persons.

Each state agency has its own manual that local administrators use for routine procedures and as a source of authority when conferring with recipients or their attorneys. These manuals are required by federal law to conform to federal regulations;[2] therefore, the state officials must bow to the national requirements in case of conflict. Courts recognize a private right of action to enforce the Food Stamp Act and regulations in federal courts.[3] Violations of the state plan, which must have received USDA approval in order to operate a food stamp program, create a cause of action against responsible state officials.[4]

This chapter is not intended to be a comprehensive manual on the Food Stamp Program for two reasons. First, the precise income and allocation amounts are subject to change each October. Second, because the program is administered by state agencies, variations in state practice must be determined by contacting the particular agency involved. The federally required framework is discussed in the following sections.[5]

§ 18.2 Procedures—Application

Food Stamp (FS) applications are processed on a household, rather than on an individual, basis.[1] Applications may be filed with the local agency office by any member of the household in person, by an authorized representative or by mail. Households in which all persons are Supplemental Security Income (SSI) applicants or recipients may

---

2. See, 7 C.F.R. Pt. 273 et seq.

3. Gonzalez v. Pingree, 821 F.2d 1526 (11th Cir.1987); Victorian v. Miller, 813 F.2d 718 (5th Cir.1987); Haskins v. Stanton, 794 F.2d 1273 (7th Cir.1986).

4. Barnes v. Cohen, 749 F.2d 1009 (3d Cir.1984), *cert. denied* 471 U.S. 1061, 105 S.Ct. 2126, 85 L.Ed.2d 490 (1985); Super and Lewis, Introduction to the Food Stamp Program, 25 Clearinghouse Rev. 905 (Nov. 1991).

5. Super, Introduction to the Food Stamp Program, 23 Clearinghouse Rev. 870 (Nov. 1989) and Super and Lewis, Introduc-

tion to the Food Stamp Program, 25 Clearinghouse Rev. 905 (Nov. 1991) have been valuable sources of information for this chapter. For more detailed information and arguments opposing some USDA policies, see the Food Research and Action Center's Guide to the Food Stamp Program (Oct. 1988); available for $12.00 from FRAC, 1319 F St., N.W., Ste. 500, Washington, D.C. 20004; (202) 393–5060.

§ 18.2

1. See § 18.8 infra, for definition of household.

apply at a Social Security District Office.[2] Households in which all persons are recipients of SSI or public assistance are categorically eligible.[3]

All applicant households will have a personal interview with an eligibility worker before initial certification and all recertifications.[4] Interviews are generally scheduled within ten days of the filing of an application.

If a household fails to appear for the interview, the agency must schedule another interview without requiring the household to show good cause for its failure to appear.

The application interview serves a twofold purpose:

1. to obtain information to establish the household's eligibility, and

2. to give the household information about the program and its responsibilities.[5]

Library References:

C.J.S. Agriculture § 27.

West's Key No. Digests, Agriculture ☞2.6(1).

§ 18.3 Procedures—Verification

The household has the responsibility to furnish information necessary to determine its eligibility, both initially and on a continuing basis. The household has primary responsibility for providing documentary evidence to support its income statements and to resolve any questionable information in instances where verification is required.

"Food stamp offices generally prefer written verification such as pay stubs, social security award letters, utility bills, or rent receipts; food stamp offices may not insist on any one particular piece of verification or reject anything probative that the household offers as verification. If written verification is not available, the food stamp office must accept the statement of someone outside of the household (a 'collateral contact'), such as a landlord or employer, who can support the truth of what the household has reported."[1]

---

2. 7 C.F.R. § 273.2(k)(1).

3. Id. This does not include persons in California or Wisconsin where SSI payments specifically cover food needs. 7 C.F.R. § 273.20.

4. 7 C.F.R. § 273.2(e).

5. Id.

§ 18.3

1. Super and Lewis, supra § 18.1, note 4, at 907.

§ 18.4 Procedures—Certification

For each application and reapplication, a definite certification period will be set. This period will never exceed 12 months.

Eligibility for food stamps ends at the expiration of each certification period. To continue to receive benefits, a household must reapply and re-establish eligibility. Benefits will not be continued beyond the end of a certification period without a new determination of eligibility.

§ 18.5 Procedures—Obtaining Coupons

Upon certification, households will be assigned a coupon allotment based on their monthly net income. An Authorization to Purchase card will be mailed to each eligible household. This card shows the allotment of food stamps the household is entitled to receive from a coupon vendor (bank, post office) during a limited period of time.

Each certified household will be issued a validated identification ID card. The household or authorized representative must present the card on request to the food store or meal service when obtaining food by coupon.

An authorized representative may be designated to obtain coupons. He or she also may use coupons to purchase food for the household with its knowledge and consent and the household's ID card.

Under direct mail issuance, all certified households receive their coupon allotment by mail directly from the state office. Direct mail issuance is available in large cities of a few states and, since 1992, all states may provide it in specially designated rural areas.[1] No cards are issued to households in mail issuance areas.

Elderly [2] and disabled persons are entitled to help in obtaining their stamps if they are unable to travel.[3] For these persons, stamps may be given at the food stamp office.

§ 18.6 Nonfinancial Eligibility Requirements—Overview

Five requirements may affect an elderly person's food stamp eligibility: citizenship and residency, household determination, work registration, resources and income. (Tax dependency, a requirement basically aimed at college students, is omitted from this summary.)

§ 18.5

1. Id. at 908.

2. Elderly is defined as 60 years old or older. 7 C.F.R. § 271.2.

3. Super and Lewis, supra § 18.1, note 4, at 908.

Library References:

C.J.S. Agriculture §§ 27, 28.
West's Key No. Digests, Agriculture ☞2.6(2).

§ 18.7 Nonfinancial Eligibility Requirements—Residency and Citizenship [1]

There is no durational residency requirement for food stamps. Applicants must live in the county in which they are applying; however, intent to permanently remain in the county or state is not a condition of eligibility. Applicants who maintain a residence in the county for any purpose *other than a vacation,* regardless of the length of time they have resided in the area, meet the residence requirement.

To be eligible for food stamps, household members must be either U.S. citizens, or aliens lawfully present in this country on a permanent basis. The applicant may sign a statement to this effect for all members of the household.[2]

§ 18.8 Nonfinancial Eligibility Requirements—Household Determination [1]

A person living alone or persons living together who purchase food and prepare meals together constitute a food stamp (FS) household. A household, which must apply as a unit, may be composed of any of the following individuals or groups of individuals, provided they are not residents of a commercial boarding house or an institution not authorized to participate in the FS program:

1. an individual who:
    a. lives alone and purchases and prepares food for home consumption,
    b. lives with others but customarily purchases food and prepares meals separate and apart from the others,
    c. is a boarder in a noncommercial boarding house and pays reasonable compensation for meals,
    d. is eligible for delivered meals and/or a communal dining program, or
    e. resides with his or her spouse who is eligible for delivered meals and/or a communal dining program;
2. a group of individuals who:
    a. live together and customarily purchase and prepare food together for home consumption, or

---

§ 18.7

1. 7 C.F.R. §§ 273.3–273.4.
2. 7 U.S.C.A. § 2020(e)(2).

§ 18.8

1. 7 C.F.R. § 273.1.

    b.   are boarders in a noncommercial boarding house and pay reasonable compensation to the others for meals;

  3.   other individuals living together who must be considered household members whether they, in fact, purchase and prepare food together are:

    a.   boarders paying less than reasonable compensation,[2] and

    b.   persons related as siblings, parents and children, children under the control of an adult (including foster and grandchildren) and spouses.[3]

Elderly or disabled persons may be accorded separate household status even if otherwise considered a household member.[4]

Persons who do not purchase food and prepare meals together, or individuals who do these activities with others, but are boarders by virtue of paying reasonable compensation for such meals, constitute separate households.

§ 18.9   Nonfinancial Eligibility Requirements—Work Registration [1]

The Food Stamp Act requires all able-bodied adults who are members of households applying for food stamps to register for work unless otherwise exempt, and to accept suitable employment if referred.

Persons exempt from the registration requirement include persons age 60 or older and persons who are physically or mentally incapable of gainful employment.

§ 18.10   Financial Eligibility Requirements—Overview

In addition to the nonfinancial requirements for food stamps, both the *resources* and *income* of an applicant household must fall within certain limitations.

Library References:

  C.J.S. Agriculture §§ 27, 28.

  West's Key No. Digests, Agriculture ⬤⟳2.6(2).

2. Id. at § 273.1(c)(4).

3. Id. at § 273.1(a)(2).

4. Id. See, for application to grandparents, Wilson v. Department of Health & Rehabilitative Serv., 561 So.2d 660 (Fla. App.1990).

§ 18.9

1. 7 C.F.R. § 273.7.

§ 18.11   Financial Eligibility Requirements—Resource Limitations—In General

"Resources"[1] includes both liquid and nonliquid resources. Liquid resources are readily negotiable assets such as cash, bank accounts, stocks, bonds, notes receivable, prizes, tax refunds, and full cash value of individual retirement accounts. Nonliquid assets are fixed assets such as real property and personal property (including boats, cars, etc.).

Limits[2] are applied to all households, including those receiving Supplemental Security Income (SSI) unless every member is a recipient. The value of a nonexempt resource is its equity value, i.e., fair market value minus encumbrances. A household will not be eligible for food stamps if the total nonexempt resources owned by all of its members exceeds:

1. $3,000 for households with two or more persons that include at least one member age 60 or over, or

2. $2,000 for all other households.

Resources[3] of the household are taken into consideration in the following ways. All nonexempt resources of all persons determined to be household members are considered. Resources held jointly by separate households or members of separate households will be considered available in total to each household unless it can be demonstrated by the applicant household that such resources are inaccessible to that household. If the household can demonstrate that it has access to only a portion of the resources, the value of that portion of the resources shall be counted toward the household's resource level. The resources shall be considered totally inaccessible to that household if the resources cannot practically be subdivided and the household's access to the value of the resources is dependent on the agreement of a joint owner who refuses to comply.[4]

For example, if two people have a savings account shared as joint tenants, either of them can withdraw any amount without the other's signature. This is a resource held jointly for food stamp purposes. The total value of the savings account is considered an available liquid resource for each person. If a group of people have an undivided interest in a piece of property, one person cannot sell another's interest in the property. Even though the resource is contained in one place, it is not a resource held jointly for food stamp purposes because each person has access only to the portion of the interest that belongs to that person.

§ 18.11

1. 7 C.F.R. § 273.8(c).
2. Id. at § 273.8(a)–(c).
3. Id. at § 273.8(c).
4. Id. at § 273.8(d).

§ 18.12   Financial Eligibility Requirements—Resource Limitations—Exempt Resources [1]

The following types of assets will not be counted as resources:

1. the home and surrounding property, regardless of the number of lots or acres. This exemption applies even when the property is temporarily unoccupied because of employment, illness, damage, or natural disaster, if the household intends to return;

2. personal property, including household goods and personal effects;

3. vehicles will be treated as follows:

   a. the entire value of any licensed vehicle is excluded if the vehicle is:

      (1) used primarily for income-producing purposes, e.g., taxi or commercial fishing boat;

      (2) annually producing gross income consistent with its fair market value, even if used only on a seasonal basis;

      (3) necessary for long distance travel essential to employment; or

      (4) specially equipped to transport a physically disabled member;

   b. the following licensed vehicles (unless exempted above) will have only that portion of the vehicle's fair market value (according to the used car Blue Book) that exceeds $4,500 considered in the household's resources:

      (1) one licensed vehicle per household, regardless of the use of the vehicle;

      (2) any other licensed vehicles used to transport household members to seek or maintain employment or education that is preparatory to employment; and

   c. for all other licensed vehicles not excluded above, that portion of the vehicle's fair market value that exceeds $4,500 is compared to the vehicle equity value. Only the greater of these two amounts will be counted as a resource;

4. one burial plot per household member;

5. cash surrender value of life insurance policies and pension funds (Keogh plans and IRAs are not excluded); [2]

---

§ 18.12

1. Id. at § 273.8(e)–(h).

2. Id. at § 273.8(e)(2).

6. investment property that annually produces gross income consistent with its fair market value, even if used only on a seasonal basis;

7. assets necessary for conducting a business or otherwise producing income;

8. marketable assets, including livestock, crops, merchandise, produce, and lumber. These will be counted as income at the time of their sale;

9. real property that the household is making a good faith effort to sell at a reasonable price and that has not been sold; and

10. inaccessible resources such as irrevocable trust funds, property in probate, and notes receivable that cannot be easily liquidated.

Exempt funds will remain exempt indefinitely if kept in a separate account. Exempt funds commingled in an account with nonexempt funds will remain exempt for six months. After six months, all funds in the commingled account are counted as a resource.

§ 18.13 Financial Eligibility Requirements—Resource Limitations—Transfer of Resources [1]

Upon application and reapplication, households must provide information regarding any resources transferred by any member within three months preceding the date of application/reapplication, including property transferred during a certification period.

The following transfers will not affect eligibility:

1. resources that would not otherwise affect eligibility, e.g., transfers of excluded personal property;

2. resources sold or traded at or near their fair market value;

3. transfers within the same food stamp household; and

4. transfers for reasons other than food stamp eligibility, e.g., repayment of a bona fide loan.

With the exceptions above, households that have transferred resources knowingly for the purpose of qualifying for food stamps may be held ineligible for up to one year. An administrative fraud hearing is not required to impose the ineligibility period. However, the burden of establishing that the transfer was "knowingly" done is on the state agency, which must send notice of denial or disqualification.[2]

§ 18.13   2. Id. at § 273.8(i)(3).

1. Id. at § 273.8(i).

§ 18.14 Financial Eligibility Requirements—Income Limitations [1]—In General

Generally, households with a net monthly income over the poverty limit cannot qualify for food stamps.[2] In addition, unless someone in the household is elderly [3] or disabled, a gross household income over 130% of the poverty line prevents qualification. Only the net income limit applies to a household with an elderly person.

The combined monthly net food stamp income of all household members could not exceed the maximums shown until October 1, 1992:

Household Size	48 States District of Columbia and Puerto Rico
1	$ 552
2	740
3	929
4	1,117
5	1,305
6	1,494
7	1,682
8	1,870

§ 18.15 Financial Eligibility Requirements—Income Limitations—Income Defined [1]

Household income means all income, earned or unearned, from whatever source, excluding only items specified under income exclusions. Earned income [2] includes:

1. wages;

2. gross income from self-employment;

3. payments from roomers and boarders; and

4. Agricultural Stabilization and Conservation Service payments.

Unearned income [3] includes (but is not limited to):

1. public assistance (AFDC, SSI, and other assistance programs based on need);

§ 18.14

1. Id. at § 273.9.
2. Id. at §§ 273.11, 273.21.
3. Elderly is defined as 60 years old or older. 7 C.F.R. § 271.2.

§ 18.15

1. Id. at § 273.9.
2. Id. at § 273.9(b)(1).
3. Id. at § 273.9(b)(2).

2. annuities and pensions (retirement and disability benefits, VA benefits, workers' or unemployment compensation, strike benefits, social security benefits, etc.);

3. support or alimony from nonhousehold members;

4. payments from government-sponsored programs that can be construed to be a gain or benefit;

5. recurring lump sums from insurance policies, sales of property, etc., which will be considered income when received;

6. all other payments (except loans) that may be construed to be a gain or benefit (dividends, interest, royalties, proceeds from trust funds, etc.); and

7. contributions (e.g., money paid directly to the household by a person outside the household).

§ 18.16 Financial Eligibility Requirements—Income Limitations—Excluded Income [1]

Only the following items may be excluded from household income:

1. income in-kind, i.e., any gain or benefit not in the form of money (meals, clothing, public housing, garden produce, etc.);

2. vendor payments, i.e., when a person or organization outside the household uses its own funds to make a direct money payment on behalf of the household to creditors or persons providing services to the household, including governmental subsidies and gift payments by friends or relatives. For example, when a son gives his mother money to pay her rent, the money from the son is unearned income. On the other hand, if the son pays the money directly to the landlord, the payment would be excluded from income as a vendor payment.[2] Obviously, vendor contributions are more helpful than direct aid to those seeking eligibility.

3. irregular income, provided such income of all household members will not exceed $30 in a three-month period;

4. loans;

5. reimbursements for past or future expenses;

6. representative payments. A "representative payee" is a third-party payee receiving income on behalf of a beneficiary. Such payments are made most commonly in social security programs to payees where the beneficiary is unable to manage the payments. Representative payees who meet the following

---

§ 18.16   **2.** Id. at § 273.9(c)(1)(i).

1. Id. at § 273.9(c).

conditions will have the representative payments excluded from their income:

    a.   the beneficiary is not a member of the payee's household,

    b.   the payee uses the payment only for the beneficiary's care and maintenance, and

    c.   the payee cannot legally use the payment for any purpose other than the care and maintenance of the beneficiary;

7.   nonrecurring lump sums, including (but not limited to) lump sum insurance settlements; cash prizes, awards, and gifts (except those for support, maintenance, or educational expenses); inheritances; retroactive lump sum social security, railroad retirement, and pension payments; income tax refunds; reimbursed funeral expenses; etc.;

8.   up to $300 in three months from private charities;

9.   self-employment business expenses; and

10.   senior citizens' pay for work under Title V of the Older American's Act.

§ 18.17 Financial Eligibility Requirements—Income Limitations—Income Deductions [1]

Deductions will be allowed only for the following items:

1.   20% of gross earned income (whether or not actual expenses are greater);

2.   standard deduction—$122 per household per month (until October 1, 1992);

3.   dependent care, i.e., payment for care of a child or other dependent when necessary for a household member to seek, accept, or continue employment, or to attend training or pursue education preparatory to employment—up to $160 per month;

4.   shelter cost—persons disabled or 60 or over may deduct all monthly shelter costs exceeding 50% of the household's income after all other deductions have been taken. For others, the shelter deduction may not exceed $194 minus the dependent care deduction taken (until October 1, 1992); and

5.   elderly or disabled persons may deduct all unreimbursed amounts over $35 actually spent for medical care in a month.[2]

---

§ 18.17

1. 7 C.F.R. § 273.9(d).

2. Pub.Law 96–58, 93 Stat. 389 (1979). Procedures were simplified in 1990. See, 7 U.S.C.A. § 2020. (1990 Farm Bill, Pub.L. No. 101–624, § 1736(2)).

§ 18.18   Meal Services

Certain individuals may use food stamps to purchase meals prepared for and delivered to them by a nonprofit meal delivery service authorized by the Food and Nutrition Service (FNS) of the USDA.[1] To be eligible, a recipient must be:

1. 60 years of age or older, or

2. housebound, physically handicapped, or otherwise disabled to the extent that the person is unable to adequately prepare all meals.

The spouse of a qualified recipient also may purchase such meals with food stamps regardless of age or disability.

"Communal dining facilities"[2] include senior citizens' centers, apartment buildings occupied primarily by elderly persons, and certain public or nonprofit private schools and organizations (tax exempt) that prepare and serve meals for the elderly. Such facilities also include private establishments under government contract to offer meals prepared especially for the elderly. A food stamp recipient may be approved to purchase meals at a communal dining facility, authorized by FNS, if the person is:

1. age 60 or over or a Supplemental Security Income (SSI) recipient, and

2. not a resident of an institution or commercial boarding house.

The spouse of such a recipient also may purchase meals from the facility regardless of age.

§ 18.19   Restoration of Benefits [1]

Whenever a household receives fewer benefits than it is entitled to receive and the loss was not caused by the household, the agency must restore those lost benefits to the household retroactively. However, benefits will not be restored if lost more than 12 months prior to:

1. the month in which the agency discovers or is notified of the loss; or

2. the date the household requested a hearing to contest the adverse action that caused the loss.

If the household believes it is eligible for restoration of benefits but the agency disagrees, the household has 90 days from the date of the agency's determination to request a hearing.

---

§ 18.18

1. 7 C.F.R. § 274.10(e).
2. Id. at §§ 274.10(e), (f), 278.1(d).

§ 18.19

1. 7 C.F.R. § 273.17.

If the household and agency agree that the household is eligible for restoration of benefits but disagree on the amount to be restored or on any other agency action, the household has 90 days from the date of notice of entitlement to request a hearing.

§ 18.20   Right to Hearing—Overview

The Food Stamp Act of 1977 requires a fair hearing for any household aggrieved by agency action that affects the household's participation in the Food Stamp Program including initial denial, reduction, or discontinuance of stamps.[1] Since 1986, a separate set of regulations requires the agency to take action, either by referral for criminal prosecution or by an administrative disqualification hearing, when the agency has sufficient documentary evidence to substantiate that an individual has committed an intentional program violation (fraud).[2]

Either type of hearing will be provided within a state administrative structure that can differ from state to state as long as the basic requirements of the regulations are met. The major difference between the two hearings is that the applicant or recipient initiates the fair hearing, but the agency initiates the disqualification hearing and has the burden of proof. The respective sections of the regulations must be consulted for details.

Library References:

C.J.S. Agriculture §§ 28, 29.
West's Key No. Digests, Agriculture ☞2.6(4).

§ 18.21   Right to Hearing—Fair Hearing—Notice and Request [1]

Certified households will receive a ten-day advance notice before food stamp benefits are discontinued or reduced during the certification period. A household may request a hearing within 90 days after any agency action or loss of benefits.

Any clear expression, oral or written, by the household or its authorized representative, friend, relative, or legal representative, that the household wishes to present its case to a higher authority will constitute a request for a hearing.

After the request, the household must fill out an application for hearing. The form may be completed at home, or the household may request a caseworker to help it complete the form at the agency office.

§ 18.20

1. 7 U.S.C.A. § 2020(e)(10); 7 C.F.R. § 273.15.

2. 7 C.F.R. § 273.16.

§ 18.21

1. Id. at §§ 273.13(a), 273.15(g)–(h).

§ 18.22　Right to Hearing—Fair Hearing—Continuation of Benefits [1]

Food stamp benefits will be continued, pending a hearing, in the following circumstances:

1. a household requests a hearing within the ten-day advance notice period and before its certification period has expired. The application for hearing form contains space for the household to indicate whether or not continued benefits are waived. If the household does not positively request a waiver, benefits will be continued.

2. a household fails to request a hearing within the required ten-day time period but establishes "good cause" for its delay. Benefits will be reinstated at their former level, i.e., before the benefits were reduced or terminated, absent a specific waiver by the household.

If the agency action is upheld at the hearing, a claim may be established against the household for all overissuances.

§ 18.23　Right to Hearing—Fair Hearing—Conferences and Information [1]

Aggrieved households will be offered a conference either before or after the request for a hearing. An agency conference is optional and will not delay or replace the fair hearing process. The conference may lead to an informal resolution of the dispute. However, a hearing must still be held, if the household has requested one, unless the household makes a written withdrawal of its request.

Upon request, the agency will provide, without charge, the materials necessary for the household to determine whether to request a hearing and/or to prepare for the hearing, including copies of case record materials that directly relate to the disputed issue and an opportunity to inspect the case record.

§ 18.24　Right to Hearing—Disqualification Hearing [1]—Notice and Consolidation

The agency must give written notice 30 days in advance of the date for a disqualification hearing.[2] The notice must include a summary of the evidence, a warning that disqualification will result, advice of

---

§ 18.22

1. 7 C.F.R. § 273.15(k).

§ 18.23

1. Id. at § 273.15(d), (i).

§ 18.24

1. Id at § 273.16.

2. Id. at § 273.16(e)(3).

available free legal services, and a statement that the hearing does not preclude criminal prosecution.

The agency may combine a disqualification hearing and fair hearing into a single hearing if the factual issues are related and notice of consolidation has been given.[3] In case of consolidation, the household may waive the 30–day advance notice period.

§ 18.25 Right to Hearing—Disqualification Hearing—Waiver [1]

An individual may waive the right to a hearing or sign a disqualification consent agreement.[2] According to Super, writing in 1989, "Some food stamp agencies also try to coerce households into signing forms consenting to be disqualified or waiving their right to a hearing. Because states receive extra funds from the USDA for investigating and prosecuting recipients for IPVs [intentional program violations], some advocates believe that, in many cases, where little evidence has been collected, their states allege that overissuances have resulted from IPVs rather than from inadvertent household errors (or even an agency error)." [3]

§ 18.26 Right to Hearing—Disqualification Hearing—Continuation of Benefits [1]

Because the disqualification hearing is for the purpose of disqualification, benefits may not be terminated or reduced due to the alleged intentional program violation until the hearing process is completed. However, any other reasons for reduction or termination of benefits may suffice.

§ 18.27 Right to Hearing—Disqualification Hearing—Periods of Disqualification [1]

The first intentional program violation, whether found in court, through an administrative disqualification hearing, or by consent, disqualifies the individual from receiving food stamps for six months. On the second offense, the disqualification is for a year, and on the third offense, it is permanent. In addition, 20% of the remaining household

3. Id. at § 273.16(e)(1).

§ 18.25

1. Id. at § 273.16(a)(3).
2. Id.
3. Super, Introduction to the Food Stamp Program, 23 Clearinghouse Rev. 870, 876 (Nov. 1989).

§ 18.26

1. 7 C.F.R. § 273.16(e)(5).

§ 18.27

1. Id. at § 273.16(b).

members' current food stamp allotment may be recouped each month until the overissuance obtained in violation is recovered.

§ 18.28   Claims   and   Collection   Procedures—Overissuance Claim [1]

Federal regulations require state agencies to establish a claim for reimbursement against a household that has received more food stamp benefits than it was entitled to receive. Claims may result from (but are not limited to) the following situations:

1. a household's failure to give correct and complete information;
2. a household's failure to timely report changes in its circumstances;
3. a caseworker's erroneous computation of a household's income, deductions, or coupon allotment;
4. a caseworker's failure to take prompt action on a change reported by the household; or
5. the household was found to be ineligible pending a hearing decision.

There are different limitations on stamp reduction and monetary collection efforts depending upon the cause of the overissuance. Nonfraud claims are for overissuance due to agency error and due to household misunderstanding or unintentional error. Fraud claims are for overissuance due to intentional violation.

§ 18.29   Claims and Collection Procedures—Repayment and Collection—Reduction in Stamp Allotments [1]

Overissuance due to agency error may not be offset or recouped from future stamp entitlements without consent of the household. This puts a premium on asserting agency error and not consenting to recoupment. The agency will then have to negotiate a repayment schedule and, perhaps, compromise the claim.

A reduction of $10 or 10% of current food stamp allotments is permitted to collect overissuances resulting from a misunderstanding or unintentional error by the household.

A claim is handled as a fraud claim only if an administrative fraud hearing or an appropriate court finds that a household member has committed an intentional program violation. A reduction of 20% of the household's food stamp allotment or $10 per month is authorized.

§ 18.28   § 18.29

1. 7 C.F.R. § 273.18(a)–(b).   1. Id. at § 273.18(d)(4).

§ 18.30 Claims and Collection Procedures—Repayment and Collection—Monetary Collection [1]

No action [2] will be taken if the total amount of a nonfraud claim is less than $35 and cannot be recovered by reduction in stamp allotment.

Claims are collected in one of the following ways: [3]

1. lump sum—payments are collected in one lump sum if the household is financially able to pay in this manner; or

2. installments—payments are accepted in regular installments if the household is unable to afford a lump sum payment. Installments should be large enough to liquidate the claim in three years or less.

The regulations contemplate negotiation of acceptable repayment schedules. Claims that cannot be liquidated in three years may be reduced by the agency to an amount that the household can pay off in three years or the full amount can be used to offset stamp benefits due.

§ 18.30

1. Id. at § 273.18(d), (g).
2. Id. at § 273.18(d), (e).

3. Id. at § 273.18(d), (g).

CHAPTER 19

ASSISTANCE FOR RENTAL HOUSING

Table of Sections

A. FEDERALLY FINANCED HOUSING PROGRAMS

WESTLAW Electronic Research

See WESTLAW Electronic Research Guide preceding the Summary of Contents.

A. FEDERALLY FINANCED HOUSING PROGRAMS

Library References:

C.J.S. United States § 122.

West's Key No. Digests, United States ☞82(3).

§ 19.1 Type of Programs—Publicly Owned Housing

The 1937 Housing Act,[1] the first major federally supported housing program for low income persons, financed local government construc-

§ 19.1

1. United States Housing Act of 1937, Pub.L. No. 75–412, 50 Stat. 888 (codified as amended at 42 U.S.C.A. §§ 1437–1437aaa–6).

tion of publicly owned housing. Conventional public housing is owned by a Public Housing Authority (PHA). The PHA contracts with the Department of Housing and Urban Development for contributions to finance the rental charges. Since a PHA is a governmental unit, its actions constitute governmental action for purposes of the fourteenth amendment. A tenant's interest in a public housing unit is entitled to due process protections, including good cause for eviction [2] and grievance procedures providing opportunity for fair hearing.[3]

Both the quality and quantity of public housing has deteriorated during the past two decades. The Reagan Administration's policy was to phase out public housing entirely. Congress kept public housing alive in the Housing and Community Development Act of 1987 [4] with authorization of $1.5 billion for operating subsidies and funds for new construction of 5,000 units.[5]

However, the role of public housing may continue to diminish if federal government programs increasingly favor home ownership. As part of the Cranston–Gonzalez National Affordable Housing Act,[6] Congress enacted the Housing Opportunities for People Everywhere (HOPE) program. This program facilitates the purchase of public housing by tenants by limiting the mortgage payments to 30% of a family's adjusted gross income.[7] The HOPE programs are an indication of the federal government's inclination toward privatizing public housing and delegating the task of public housing programs to state and local governments.

Among experts and planners there is an apparent consensus that current public housing that is not privatized should be retained. The more heated debate is over whether to build additional publicly owned housing.[8]

2. Caulder v. Durham Housing Authority, 433 F.2d 998 (4th Cir.1970), cert. denied 401 U.S. 1003, 91 S.Ct. 1228, 28 L.Ed.2d 539 (1971). See also, 42 U.S.C.A. § 1437d(1)(4).

3. Samuels v. District of Columbia, 770 F.2d 184 (D.C.Cir.1985), *on remand* 650 F.Supp. 482 (D.D.C.1986). See, 42 U.S.C.A. § 1437d(k); 24 C.F.R. § 966.55.

4. Housing and Community Development Act of 1987, Pub.L. No. 100–242, 101 Stat. 1815 (1988) (codified at 12 U.S.C.A. § 1715, 42 U.S.C.A. §§ 1437–1437aaa–6, 42 U.S.C.A. §§ 5301–5310).

5. McDougall, Affordable Housing for the 1990's, 20 U.Mich.J.L.Ref. 727, 729 (1987).

6. Pub.L. No. 101–625, 104 Stat. 4079 (1990) (codified at 42 U.S.C.A. § 12701 et seq.).

7. Cranston–Gonzalez National Affordable Housing Act, Pub.L. No. 101–625, § 444, 104 Stat. 4079, 4176 (1990) (hereinafter NAHA).

8. Diesenhouse, Public Housing: Why the Bad Rap?, 48 J. of Housing 293, 296 (1991). For detailed information and list of resource materials, see, Fuchs, Introduction to HUD Conventional Public Housing, Section 8 Existing Housing, Voucher, and Subsidized Housing Programs, 25 Clearinghouse Review 782 (Nov.1991). Local Housing and Urban Development or Public

§ 19.2 Type of Programs—Developer Subsidized Housing

There are numerous federal, state, and local programs to subsidize the cost of private construction of moderate and low priced housing. These are administered by the Department of Housing and Urban Development, often through a local Public Housing Authority.

The major source of these subsidies to project developers has been the National Housing Act of 1959 [1] and, for rural areas, §§ 515 and 521 of the Housing Act of 1949.[2] With the decreasing supply of government-owned public housing, project-based programs under these acts have gained increased importance in providing a sufficient supply of low-income housing.[3] These programs loan capital and subsidize and insure mortgage payments for qualifying developments. Section 221(d)(3), § 231, and § 236 programs of the National Housing Act, each with its own technical requirements, are mortgage insurance and interest reduction programs enacted to encourage development of multifamily units with reduced rentals for lower income families.[4]

Most significant for the elderly are National Housing Act of 1959 § 202 programs, which provide direct federal loans at low interest rates to private nonprofit corporations or consumer cooperatives for housing projects serving elderly or handicapped families and individuals.[5] Not only must rentals be low, but direct tenant subsidies under § 8 are available for lower income persons as well.[6] "Older people occupy almost half of all federally-assisted housing units. . . . The 'Section 202' program is a proven success limited only by the resources committed to it." [7]

The National Affordable Housing Act of 1990 not only allows state and local governments to receive funding for construction, reconstruction, and moderate or substantial rehabilitation, with a preference for rehabilitation, but it also provides tenant rental assistance.[8] In particular, the act addresses the need for supportive housing for the elderly

Housing Administration offices should be consulted for information.

§ 19.2

1. Pub.L. No. 86–372, 73 Stat. 667 (codified at 12 U.S.C.A. §§ 1701q and 1715).

2. Pub.L. No. 8, 42 U.S.C.A. § 1485 et seq.; 7 C.F.R. § 1994.205.

3. See generally, McDougall, Affordable Housing for the 1990's, 20 U.Mich.J.Law Ref. 727, 745 (1987).

4. See, Fuchs, Introduction to HUD Conventional Public Housing, Section 8 Ex-

isting Housing, Voucher, and Subsidized Housing Programs, 25 Clearinghouse Review 990 (Dec.1991).

5. 12 U.S.C.A. § 1701q. Federal regulations are currently located at 24 C.F.R. § 885.1 et seq.

6. Section 202 and § 8 eligibility is discussed in §§ 19.7–19.15, infra.

7. Pollach and Howard, Justice for America's Elders, Winning America 179 (M. Raskin and C. Hartman, eds. 1988).

8. NAHA, Pub.L. No. 101–625, § 212, 104 Stat. 4079, 4097 (1990).

in Title VIII, subtitle A.[9] Under Title VIII, § 801 amends § 202 of the Housing Act of 1959 [10] and provides that assistance may be given to local and state agencies in the form of capital advances and rental assistance.[11]

§ 19.3 Type of Programs—Tenant–Based Rental Assistance

The federal government funds local and state rental assistance programs that provide assistance for tenants in many types of housing.[1] When operating expenses of developer-subsidized projects grew, Congress in 1965 responded by creating rent supplements for tenants in housing under § 221(d)(5) and § 236 of the National Housing Act.[2] This program was superseded later by the Set–Aside Program which provides assistance for existing multifamily § 221(d)(5), § 236, and § 202 projects.[3]

The major tenant-based program, known as the § 8 Housing or Rental Assistance Program, was created in § 8 of the Housing and Community Development Act of 1974, amending the Housing Act of 1937. *Section 8 provides rental assistance for tenants in both private and developer-subsidized housing.*[4] The program is administered by the Department of Housing and Urban Development (HUD) through local Public Housing Agencies (PHAs). Within the scope of § 8 funding, the

---

9. Id. at 4297.

10. 12 U.S.C.A. § 1701q.

11. NAHA, Pub.L. No. 101–625, § 801, 104 Stat. 4079, 4298 (1990). For detailed information, See, Fuchs, Introduction to HUD Conventional Public Housing, Section 8 Existing Housing, Voucher, and Subsidized Housing Programs, 25 Clearinghouse Review 990 (Dec.1991). Also contact the National Housing Law Project, 1950 Addison Street, Berkeley, California 94704, (510) 548–9400, for updated information. The project's publication, The Subsidized Housing Handbook (1982), was designed for advising developers. HUD Housing Programs: Tenants' Rights (1981) describes all the housing programs in existence at that time and is a litigation-oriented book. Preserving HUD–Assisted Housing for Use by Low–Income Tenants: An Advocates Guide (1985) develops strategies for preventing the loss of units from subsidized housing when developers seek to sell or are threatened with foreclosures.

§ 19.3

1. Taub, The Future of Affordable Housing, 22 The Urban Lawyer 659, 660 (Fall 1990) (WESTLAW: URBLAW database, **ci(22 + 5 659)**).

2. McDougall, supra § 19.1, note 5, at 753; 12 U.S.C.A. § 1701s.

3. Fuchs, Introduction to HUD Conventional Public Housing, Section 8 Existing Housing, Voucher, and Subsidized Housing Programs, 25 Clearinghouse Review 990 (Dec. 1991).

4. 42 U.S.C.A. § 1437. For further discussion with respect to the general nature of § 8 rental assistance, see the pamphlet published by HUD, Housing for Low Income Families, HUD's New Section 8 Housing Assistance Payments Program, available from HUD offices. Also helpful is HUD Handbook 4350.3, Occupancy Requirements of Subsidized Multifamily Housing Programs.

federal government has developed several methods to supplement the rent payments of low income families and individuals who qualify.[5]

Although § 8 programs have suffered due to a lack of funding in recent years, the Cranston–Gonzalez National Affordable Housing Act [6] committed federal funding to state and local programs for rental assistance.[7] Also, a 1990 appropriations act for Veterans' Affairs and HUD provided funding for rental assistance.[8]

§ 19.4 Advantages of Subsidized Housing for Elderly—Design

The publicly subsidized housing developed under programs for increasing housing for elderly and disabled tenants requires features designed to assist elderly and disabled tenants. In these units, there may be additional facilities such as railings in the hallways, elevators, wheelchair cabinets for the kitchen and bathroom sinks, lower cabinets for shorter people, railings in the showers, and alarms that sound in the main office and set off a light over the individual's door. Consequently, an elderly person who moves into subsidized housing often moves a step up in housing quality.[1]

Library References:

C.J.S. United States § 122.
West's Key No. Digests, United States ⟐82(3, 4).

§ 19.5 Advantages of Subsidized Housing for Elderly—Meals

Under authority of various provisions of the National Housing Act,[1] the Department of Housing and Urban Development (HUD) has established regulations [2] governing mandatory meals programs in certain HUD-assisted congregate housing projects for the elderly or handicapped where the project is equipped with central dining facilities.[3] Meals may be provided by the Area Agency on Aging in cooperation with the Department of Agriculture.

---

5. See §§ 19.7–.15, infra.

6. NAHA, Pub.L. No. 101–625, 104 Stat. 4079 (1990).

7. NAHA, Pub.L. No. 101–625, § 203, 104 Stat. 4079, 4095.

8. Departments of Veterans Affairs and Housing and Urban Development, and Independent Agencies Appropriation Act 1991, Pub.L. No. 101–507, 104 Stat. 1351 (1990).

§ 19.4

1. Struyk and Soldo, Improving the Elderly's Housing 200, 201 (1980).

§ 19.5

1. Section 202 of the National Housing Act of 1959, 12 U.S.C.A. § 1701q; § 101 of the Housing and Urban Development Act of 1965, 12 U.S.C.A. § 1701s; § 211 of the National Housing Act, 12 U.S.C.A. § 1715b; § 8 of the United States Housing Act of 1937, 42 U.S.C.A., § 1437f; § 7(d) of the Department of Housing and Urban Development Act, 12 U.S.C.A. § 3535(d).

2. 24 C.F.R. § 278.1 et seq.

3. Projects covered under the regulations are defined in 24 C.F.R. § 278.3.

Approval by HUD of the mandatory meals program is required and, where obtained, project owners are permitted to require as a condition of occupancy that one meal (or more) per day be purchased by tenants residing in the project.[4] Regulations require that project owners grant an exemption from purchasing meals under the program to persons with a medical condition that requires a special diet that the project cannot provide,[5] persons with paying jobs that require their absence during meal time,[6] persons who will be absent from the project for one week or more,[7] and persons who are permanently immobile.[8]

§ **19.6** Advantages of Subsidized Housing for Elderly—Services

As part of the increased emphasis on allowing older persons to age in place, § 802 of the Cranston–Gonzalez National Affordable Housing Act (NAHA) has an important requirement that congregate housing under that section must offer other services in addition to meals, such as transportation, personal care, housekeeping, counseling, and group activities which may prevent unnecessary institutionalization of eligible residents.[1] The NAHA requires resident fees sufficient to provide 10% of the cost of services.[2] In addition, projects under § 202 may use project funds to provide a service coordinator. Attorneys should contact the Department of Housing and Urban Development (HUD) to obtain handbooks concerning these services in assisted housing.

Local agencies should be contacted for details concerning eligibility and availability of new housing programs. Local offices to contact for inquiry about programs include: Housing and Urban Development Public Housing; Area Agency on Aging; Welfare or Family Services; Community Action Agency; and Farmers Home Administration.

4. Id. at § 278.10.
5. Id. at § 278.12(a)(1).
6. Id. at § 278.12(a)(2).
7. Id. at § 278.12(a)(3).
8. Id. at § 278.12(a)(4).

2. Id. at Pub.L. No. 101–625, § 802(d)(7), 104 Stat. 4079 at 4308 (codified at 42 U.S.C.A. § 8011).

§ **19.6**
1. NAHA, Pub.L. No. 101–625, § 802(d), 104 Stat. 4079, 4308 (1990) (codified at 42 U.S.C.A. § 8011).

B. FEDERAL RENTAL ASSISTANCE

§ 19.7 Tenant Eligibility for Rental Assistance—Administration

The Department of Housing and Urban Development (HUD) allocates funding for rental assistance, including § 202 subsidized units, to the local Public Housing Agency (PHA). A PHA is any state, county, municipal, or other governmental entity or public body that is authorized to engage in or assist in the development or operation of low income housing and is determined by HUD to be eligible.

All contracts to enter the program with the owners of existing housing are made with the PHA.[1] The PHA will invite owners of local housing to make dwelling units available by publishing a notice in an area newspaper. The PHA also has a list of landlords they believe would be willing to participate in the program.

If the owner of housing is willing to lease to a § 8 participant, that housing will be available if the unit is decent, safe, and sanitary. In addition, the gross rent must be within the HUD-established "fair market rent" for existing housing.[2] Regulations are issued each year by HUD establishing the fair market rent for each county in the state. This schedule of fair market rent is listed each March in the *Federal Register*. If the proposed unit does not include utilities in its rent, the figure appearing in the schedule for that type of housing will be reduced by the local PHA.

Contracts to enter the program with developers or owners of newly constructed or substantially rehabilitated units could be served through HUD field offices or through a PHA.[3] The housing agency enters into long-term assistance payment contracts with developers and landlords who will build or substantially rehabilitate existing units to meet the program standards. The owner agrees to build or rehabilitate a property and to rent it to low and moderate income families.

When the rehabilitation is completed and low and moderate income families are occupying the units, HUD will pay the difference between what the families pay and the agreed upon rent. In general, the assistance payments will be sufficient to limit the total tenant rent payment to the highest of (1) 30% of the tenant's monthly adjusted income, (2) 10% of monthly income, or (3) the amount of welfare assistance payments specifically designated for housing.[4]

The owner retains all responsibility for managing the property, subject to HUD review to ensure that the owner is keeping units in

---

§ 19.7

1. 24 C.F.R. §§ 882.101, 882.102.

2. 24 C.F.R. § 882.106.

3. 24 C.F.R. §§ 880.101(g), 880.102 (new construction); 24 C.F.R. §§ 881.101(g), 881.-102 (rehabilitation).

4. 24 C.F.R. § 813.107. See 24 C.F.R. § 813.107(b) for different percentages applied to leases prior to August 1, 1982.

decent, safe, and sanitary condition and is fulfilling the owner's responsibilities under the contract with HUD. The term of the contract with HUD may be for twenty, thirty, or forty years, depending upon specific circumstances.

§ 19.8 Tenant Eligibility for Rental Assistance—Procedure for Renters—Lease and Contract for Existing Housing

For existing housing, the applicant will contact either the Public Housing Agency (PHA) or the owner of the housing initially. The owner, if contacted first, will refer the applicant to the local PHA. At the PHA, the applicant will fill out an application for tenant eligibility and certification. If the PHA determines that the applicant is eligible for rental assistance, the PHA will give a certificate of family participation to the applicant.[1] With the certificate, the applicant will be given information about properties available to rent, including the location of housing and the applicable fair market rent, and a request for lease approval.

After certification to participate in the program, the applicant has 60 days to find suitable housing and an owner who agrees to lease to the applicant.[2] If a certificate expires or is about to expire, the applicant may submit the certificate to the PHA with a request for an extension.

After finding an available unit, the applicant must submit to the PHA a request for lease approval signed by the owner of the unit and the applicant, and a copy of the proposed lease.[3] The unit in which the applicant is already living may qualify if the owner agrees to participate in the program.

If the PHA determines that the proposed lease complies with the Department of Housing and Urban Development (HUD) requirements, the PHA will approve the lease. The PHA will then execute a contract with the property owner, agreeing to pay a portion of the total rent on behalf of the tenant. The tenant pays a monthly amount for rent, which is determined by examination of income, family size, etc., and the PHA pays the difference between the family contribution and the total amount of rent due. The tenant pays no more than 30% of the gross family income for rent. Both the tenant and the PHA make the monthly payments directly to the property owner or landlord.

§ 19.8

1. 24 C.F.R. § 882.209. See 24 C.F.R. § 882.210(b) for permitted reasons to deny participation of an otherwise eligible applicant.

2. 24 C.F.R. § 882.209(d).

3. Id. at § 882.209(e).

§ 19.9   Tenant Eligibility for Rental Assistance—Procedure for Renters—Housing Vouchers

Housing vouchers are issued directly to eligible individuals and families by the local Public Housing Authorities (PHAs). Accordingly, applicants must apply directly to the PHA for a housing voucher.

Once the housing voucher is issued, the holder must find rental housing within the state of the issuing PHA. The unit may be the one the holder is currently occupying [1] which meets the § 8 housing quality standards.[2] If the housing owner agrees to enter into a housing voucher contract with the PHA, the PHA will agree to make housing assistance payments to the owner on behalf of the housing voucher holder.[3] The primary difference between the certification and voucher programs is that the voucher landlords may charge more than the fair market rent according to Department of Housing and Urban Development (HUD). Since assistance is only to pay the difference between 30% of the tenant's income and the fair market rent, tenants have to pay the shortfall.[4]

Those eligible are families that have been continuously assisted under the Housing Act of 1937, low income families that have been displaced by rehabilitation, and very low income families.[5]

§ 19.10   Tenant Eligibility for Rental Assistance—Procedure for Renters—Special Allocations Under Set–Aside Programs

Only projects with serious financial difficulties or foreclosed Department of Housing and Urban Development, (HUD)-insured and HUD-held mortgages are eligible for this project-based § 8 assistance. The purpose of this Loan Management Set–Aside Project is to protect the insurance funds.[1] A housing assistance payments contract is executed between the housing owner and HUD that provides, *inter alia,* that certain units within the project qualify for § 8 assistance. Section 8 payments will be paid to the project owner for units under lease by eligible families.

Applicants must apply directly to the project for a unit. If a resident vacates the unit, payments in the amount of 80% of the

---

§ 19.9

1. Id. at § 887.203.

2. Id. at § 887.251.

3. Id. at § 887.301.

4. 24 C.F.R. §§ 887.351–887.353. Fuchs, supra § 19.3, note 3.

5. 24 C.F.R. 887.151. A very low income family, depending on size, is one with an income 50% or less than the median income in the area. Id. at § 887.7.

§ 19.10

1. 24 C.F.R. § 886.101 et seq.

contract rent may be paid to the subsequent eligible occupant for 60 days.[2]

§ 19.11 Tenant Eligibility for Rental Assistance—Procedure for Renters—New Construction/Substantial Rehabilitation

Mortgages are insured under various sections of the National Housing Act for either new construction or substantial rehabilitation. Some or all of the units in the project are also covered by a housing assistance payments contract with the owner under which Department of Housing and Urban Development (HUD) pays the difference between the tenant's contribution and the agreed upon rent. The contract administrator may be HUD, a Housing Finance Agency, or a Public Housing Authority (PHA).

An applicant for housing with substantial rehabilitation or new construction assistance must apply directly to the housing owner under the § 8 programs.[1] The owner determines eligibility.

§ 19.12 Tenant Eligibility for Rental Assistance—Persons Eligible [1]

In order to be eligible for § 8 rental assistance, either in privately financed or publicly subsidized,[2] existing, substantially rehabilitated, or newly constructed housing programs, the applicant must be:

1. a family consisting of the applicant and one or more family members who do not have to be related by blood or marriage;[3] or

2. an individual at least 62 years of age or older; or

3. a physically handicapped individual; or

4. a person with a developmental disability (mentally retarded, caused by cerebral palsy, epilepsy, or other neurological disorder prior to age 18); or

5. two or more elderly, disabled, or handicapped persons living together, or one or more of such individuals living with another person needed to care for them; or

2. Id. at § 886.109(c).

§ 19.11

1. 24 C.F.R. §§ 880.603 and 881.603.

§ 19.12

1. 24 C.F.R. Pts. 812–813. These are also the basic eligibility criteria for publicly owned housing.

2. These include § 202 housing for elderly and handicapped.

3. 24 C.F.R. § 912.2; Fuchs, supra § 19.3, note 3.

6. a person displaced by disaster or by governmental action; or

7. a single person authorized by HUD, so long as no more than 15% of leases are held by single persons; and

8. within the required income limits.

§ 19.13 Tenant Eligibility for Rental Assistance—Low-Income Qualification—Income Limitations

The § 8 program helps low income and very low income families.[1] A "low income" family is one whose annual income does not exceed 80% of the median income in the area. A "very low income" family is one whose annual income does not exceed 50% of the median income in the area. The precise income limits are figured on a local basis and take into account the size of the family. They are available from area Department of Housing and Urban Development (HUD) offices.

Appendix I to the Application for Tenant Eligibility and Recertification Form HUD–52659 sets out the definition of income, what is included in figuring an applicant's income and what is excluded.

§ 19.14 Tenant Eligibility for Rental Assistance—Low-Income Qualification—Annual Income [1] and Exclusions

Annual income includes total income of all family members. However, certain income is excluded. The following items are excluded from income:

1. casual gifts;

2. medical expenses reimbursement;

3. lump sum additions to family assets, such as inheritance, insurance payments, capital gains, and settlement for personal or property losses;

4. educational scholarships and governmental veterans' payments paid directly to a student or to the educational institution;

5. hostile fire pay to a serviceperson;

6. government relocation payments;

7. foster child care payments;

8. the value of food stamp coupon allotments; and

9. payments received for participation in national volunteer programs including VISTA and programs for persons aged 60 and over, such as Retired Senior Volunteer Programs, Foster

§ 19.13

1. 24 C.F.R. § 813.102.

§ 19.14

1. Id. at § 813.106.

Grandparent Program, Older American Community Services Program, National Volunteer Program to Assist Small Business Experience, Service Corps of Retired Executives (SCORE) and Active Corps of Executives (ACE).

§ 19.15 Tenant Eligibility for Rental Assistance—Low–Income Qualification—Adjusted Income

Adjusted income is annual income minus certain allowances. The deductible allowances include $400 for any elderly family and specific allowances for handicapped members and for medical expenses.[1]

One-twelfth of adjusted income is adjusted monthly income, which is used in determining the amount of rental assistance that will be paid. Assistance should ensure that the tenant does not pay more than 30% of monthly adjusted income for rent.[2]

§ 19.16 Eviction

In order for an owner to evict a § 8 tenant, the owner must comply with the requirements of the local law *and* the Department of Housing and Urban Development (HUD) requirements.[1] Under leases executed since 1981, the owner must use court action, giving notice to both the tenant and the Public Housing Authority (PHA), to force eviction.[2] During the first year, only family malfeasance or nonfeasance warrant eviction; under longer leases, "other good cause[s]" suffice, such as owner wishing to use the premises, business reasons or refusal of the tenant to accept the offer of a new lease.[3]

Under pre-October 1981 leases, the owner must give the PHA written notice of the proposed eviction, and the owner must obtain the PHA's authorization for an eviction.[4] The PHA will examine the grounds for eviction and will authorize the eviction unless it finds the grounds to be insufficient under the lease. The PHA has the sole right to give notice to the tenant.

The protections for tenants living in subsidized housing but without rental assistance are less specific, but similar.[5]

§ 19.15
1. 24 C.F.R. § 813.102.
2. 24 C.F.R. § 813.107.

§ 19.16
1. 24 C.F.R. § 882.215.

2. Id. at § 882.215(c)(4).

3. Id. at § 882.215(c).

4. Id. at § 882.215(d).

5. See Fuchs, supra § 19.3, note 3.

CHAPTER 20

FEDERAL EMPLOYEES AND RAILROAD RETIREMENT PROGRAMS

Table of Sections

A. FEDERAL EMPLOYEES RETIREMENT

B. RAILROAD RETIREMENT

WESTLAW Electronic Research

See WESTLAW Electronic Research Guide preceding the Summary of Contents.

A. FEDERAL EMPLOYEES RETIREMENT

Library References:

C.J.S. Officers and Public Employees §§ 243–249.

West's Key No. Digests, Officers and Public Employees ⊕101.5(1, 2).

§ 20.1 Civil Service Retirement System (CSRS) and Federal Employees Retirement System (FERS) Overview

Since 1984 when newly hired federal workers were brought into the social security system for the first time, there have been major changes to the retirement system applicable to federal employees. In fact, there are now two retirement systems. One system is known as the Civil Service Retirement System (CSRS).[1] The other system is known as the Federal Employees Retirement System (FERS).[2]

The CSRS, in general, covers federal employees hired prior to 1984; the FERS covers all new federal employees hired after December 31, 1986. There are special rules applicable to certain employees hired or rehired between January 1, 1984, and December 31, 1986.[3] Also, all employees covered by CSRS have a limited opportunity to elect to be covered by FERS. Both programs coexist under, and for the most part are administered by, the Office of Personnel Management (OPM).[4]

The statute governing the CSRS is set out at 5 U.S.C.A. § 8301 et seq. with the applicable regulations being set out at 5 C.F.R. § 831.101 et seq. The statute governing the FERS set out at 5 U.S.C.A. § 8401 et seq. with the applicable regulations being set out at 5 C.F.R. § 841.401 et seq.

The rules applicable to CSRS and FERS are complicated. For more detailed information concerning these programs, the OPM or the personnel office of the agency for which the claimant works or worked can be consulted. Retirees (or their survivors) and their attorneys also can contact the personnel office of the agency that formerly employed them, or they can contact the OPM's Retirement Information Office in Washington D.C., which gives advice and information to retirees or their representatives. However, there are many questions concerning the proper interpretation of CSRS and FERS that may require litigation to resolve.

§ 20.1

1. 5 U.S.C.A. § 8301 et seq.; 5 C.F.R. § 831.101 et seq.

2. 5 U.S.C.A. § 8401 et seq.; 5 C.F.R. § 841.401 et seq.

3. 5 U.S.C.A. § 8402; 5 C.F.R. § 842.-104.

4. 5 U.S.C.A. §§ 8347, 8461.

§ 20.2 Key Elements of CSRS—Financing and Benefits

The Civil Service Retirement System (CSRS) is financed by mandatory payroll deductions and employing agency contributions. The employing agency obtains the funds that it is required to contribute through the federal budget appropriation process. The employee's annuity (or pension) paid pursuant to CSRS is in lieu of social security benefits. Annuities or lump sum benefits are payable under CSRS to employees or their survivors on the basis of age, years of service, and other criteria. Generally speaking, the amount of a CSRS annuity is based on: (1) the employee's average wage for the three consecutive years of highest pay, and (2) the length of employment.[1] An alternative formula is permitted if it provides a higher annuity.[2]

§ 20.3 Key Elements of CSRS—Eligibility Requirements

To be eligible for Civil Service Retirement System (CSRS) benefits, an employee must have worked a specific number of years in a CSRS-covered job category. If an employee has made the required annual contributions, CSRS credit generally will be given both for civilian government service and military service.[1] Unused sick leave days also can be counted in calculating the length of service.[2] There are also provisions that enable some employees to receive additional CSRS credit by purchasing additional annuities or by making voluntary contributions for prior years of military or civilian service for which no contribution was made to CSRS.[3]

§ 20.4 Key Elements of CSRS—Types of Annuities

Depending on the length of federal employment, a person may be eligible for either of two types of Civil Service Retirement System (CSRS) annuities: (1) immediate, or (2) deferred. Both types of annuity require at least five years of civilian service.

Immediate annuities are payable 30 days after voluntary retirement from federal employment to persons who qualify under a formula based on age and length of employment. Immediate annuities are available to persons who are age 62 or older and have five years of

§ 20.2

1. 5 U.S.C.A. §§ 8339, 8331(4).

2. 5 U.S.C.A. §§ 8339, 8331(4).

§ 20.3

1. 5 U.S.C.A. § 8332; 5 C.F.R. §§ 831.-301–831.303.

2. 5 C.F.R. § 831.302.

3. 5 U.S.C.A. § 8334; 5 C.F.R. §§ 831.-401–831.402.

employment, age 60 to 62 and have twenty years of employment, or age 55 to 60 and have thirty years of employment.[1]

Persons who leave the CSRS before qualifying for an immediate annuity may still be eligible for a deferred annuity. Persons who have served five years or more are entitled to an annuity payable beginning at the age of 62.[2]

§ 20.5 Key Elements of CSRS—Special Provisions

Special retirement provisions exist for certain classes of employees such as law enforcement officers, fire fighters, and air-traffic controllers.[1] Also, employees who leave federal employment under special circumstances (such as a reduction of the work force, a major reorganization of the agency, or a transfer of function) are entitled to immediate annuities if they have worked at least 25 years for the federal government or if they are 50 years of age and have 20 years of federal employment.[2] Persons separated from employment with the federal government for at least 31 days have the option to receive a lump sum payment of all accrued benefits in lieu of an annuity[3] if they would not be entitled to receive an annuity commencing within 31 days after the application for a refund is filed. Also, lump sum death benefits are payable when an employee or retiree dies without survivors or when a former employee dies before retirement.[4] Finally, the Civil Service Retirement System (CSRS) has an optional thrift savings plan that allows most employees to save up to five percent of their salary and receive a tax break.[5]

§ 20.6 Key Elements of FERS—Sources of Benefits—Overview

The Federal Employees Retirement System (FERS) provides retirement benefits from three different sources: (1) a basic benefit plan, (2) social security, and (3) the thrift savings plan.

§ 20.7 Key Elements of FERS—Sources of Benefits—Basic Benefit Plan

The basic benefit plan is funded through contributions from federal employees and the federal government. To be eligible to receive the

§ 20.4

1. 5 U.S.C.A. § 8336(a), (b), (f).

2. 5 U.S.C.A. § 8338(a).

§ 20.5

1. See, e.g., 5 U.S.C.A. § 8336(c), (e).

2. 5 U.S.C.A. § 8336(d); 5 C.F.R. §§ 831.108, 831.504.

3. 5 U.S.C.A. § 8342; 5 C.F.R. §§ 831.2002–831.2010 (1989).

4. 5 U.S.C.A. § 8342(c)–(f); 5 C.F.R. § 831.2003.

5. 5 U.S.C.A. § 8351.

basic benefit plan, one must have at least five years of creditable civilian service with the federal government.[1] Survivor and disability benefits are available after eighteen months of creditable service.[2] Creditable civilian service generally includes federal civil service and military service for which a contribution has been paid.[3]

A person can retire with a basic benefit as soon as the person reaches the "minimum retirement age" (MRA) and has ten years of creditable civilian service.[4] The MRA is the first year in which a person can receive benefits and varies according to the year in which the person was born.[5] For example, for anyone born before 1948, the MRA is age 55. A person can also retire when his or her age and years of federal service match one of another set of retirement combinations—for example, for five years of service, benefits begin at age 62; for 20 years of service at age 60 years; and for 30 years of service at the MRA.[6]

For persons who leave federal service before they meet these requirements for immediate retirement benefits, there are provisions for deferred retirement benefits.[7] Individuals with at least five years of service can begin receiving benefits at age 62.[8] Moreover, individuals with at least 10 years of service who leave federal service before their MRA may designate a date after their MRA and before their 62nd birthday on which the annuity is to begin.[9]

The Federal Employees Retirement System (FERS) provides a special retirement supplement for those who retire after 30 years of service at their MRA and those who retire at age 60 after 20 or more years of service.[10] This special retirement supplement is paid until age 62 when a person is eligible for social security benefits;[11] however, the amount of the special retirement supplement may be reduced if the individual's earnings from work performed while the individual is entitled to the supplement exceed an allowable amount.[12]

The FERS also permits withdrawal of contributions to the basic benefit plan when an employee leaves federal employment for at least 31 consecutive days and will not become eligible to receive an annuity

§ 20.7

1. 5 U.S.C.A. § 8410.
2. 5 U.S.C.A. §§ 8442(b), 8451(a)(1)(A).
3. 5 U.S.C.A. § 8411.
4. 5 U.S.C.A. § 8412(g).
5. 5 U.S.C.A. § 8412(h).
6. 5 U.S.C.A. § 8412(a), (b), (c).
7. 5 U.S.C.A. §§ 8413, 8415(f).

8. 5 U.S.C.A. § 8413(a).
9. 5 U.S.C.A. § 8413(b).
10. 5 U.S.C.A. § 8421.
11. 5 U.S.C.A. § 8421(a)(3)(B).
12. 5 U.S.C.A. § 8421a. For a discussion of the handling of a similar issue in the social security retirement system, see §§ 15.52–.59, supra.

within 31 days after applying for the withdrawal.[13]   If this option is exercised, that person will not be eligible to receive basic benefits based on service covered by the refund.[14]

§ 20.8   Key Elements of FERS—Sources of Benefits—Social Security

In general, benefits payable under the Federal Employees Retirement System (FERS) are in addition to benefits payable under the Social Security Act.[1]   For purposes of FERS, "social security" means benefit payments provided to workers and their dependents who qualify as beneficiaries under Old–Age, Survivors, and Disability Insurance (OASDI) programs of the Social Security Act.   The rules applicable to persons receiving social security under FERS are the same as those applicable to any person receiving benefits under the Social Security Act.

§ 20.9   Key Elements of FERS—Sources of Benefits—Thrift Savings Plan

The third part of the Federal Employees Retirement System (FERS) package is a tax-deferred savings plan.   All federal employees covered by FERS are eligible to participate in the thrift savings plan (usually within six to twelve months after hire).[1]   The employing government agency automatically contributes an amount equal to one percent of the employee's basic pay to a savings account each pay period, even if the employee does not contribute each pay period.[2] Additionally, if an employee chooses, he or she may contribute up to ten percent of his or her pay to the savings plan through payroll deductions, and the government will match a portion of those savings according to a sliding schedule.   The agency must match one dollar for each dollar the employee contributes up to three percent of the employee's basic pay and 50 cents for each dollar the employee contributes over three percent of his or her basic pay.   However, the agency may not match employee contributions that exceed five percent of the basic pay.[3]

Funds may be withdrawn from the thrift savings fund when the employee retires, becomes disabled, or leaves federal employment if at that time the employee's right to those funds has become vested.[4]

---

13. 5 U.S.C.A. § 8424(a).

14. 5 U.S.C.A. § 8424(a).

§ 20.8

1. 5 U.S.C.A. § 8403.

§ 20.9

1. 5 U.S.C.A. § 8432.

2. 5 U.S.C.A. § 8432(c)(1)(A).

3. 5 U.S.C.A. § 8432(c)(2)(B).

4. 5 U.S.C.A. §§ 8432(g) and 8433(a).

Employee contributions are vested and nonforfeitable when made.[5] Matching contributions of the employing agency are not vested and, therefore, are forfeitable if employment is terminated, until the employee completes either two or three years of service, depending on the nature of the position.[6] However, matching contributions will not be forfeited regardless of length of service if the employee dies while still employed in civil service.[7]

Depending upon length of service and age, an employee (or that employee's beneficiaries) may elect to receive thrift fund savings in the form of an annuity or a lump sum payment or to roll savings over into an individual retirement account (IRA) or similar retirement plan.[8] However, an employee who leaves government employment before becoming entitled to a deferred annuity has no such choice: the employee's account balance is automatically transferred to an eligible retirement plan.[9] In some circumstances, the employee may borrow from the savings plan account for serious financial needs such as the purchase of a home, medical expenses, educational expenses, and financial hardship.[10]

§ 20.10 Disability Benefits Under CSRS and FERS—Availability

Both the Civil Service Retirement System (CSRS) and the Federal Employees Retirement System (FERS) provide disability benefits; however, the disability benefits offered by the two plans differ in several respects. The CSRS requires a minimum of five years employment in a CSRS-covered position to qualify for disability benefits,[1] while FERS requires only eighteen months of FERS-covered service to qualify for disability benefits.[2] If a person applies for disability benefits under FERS, that person also must apply for social security disability insurance benefits or show that he or she is not eligible for those benefits.[3]

§ 20.11 Disability Benefits Under CSRS and FERS—Disability Defined

The Civil Service Retirement System (CSRS) and the Federal Employees Retirement System (FERS) use essentially the same definition of disability. To be found disabled under either system, an

---

5. 5 U.S.C.A. §§ 8432(g) and 8433(a).

6. 5 U.S.C.A. § 8432(g)(2).

7. 5 U.S.C.A. § 8432(g)(4).

8. 5 U.S.C.A. §§ 8433, 8434.

9. 5 U.S.C.A. § 8433(d).

10. 5 U.S.C.A. § 8433(i).

§ 20.10

1. 5 U.S.C.A. § 8337(a).

2. 5 U.S.C.A. § 8451(a)(1)(A).

3. See 5 U.S.C.A. § 8452(a)(2); 5 C.F.R. § 844.201(b).

employee must be unable, because of disease or injury, to render "useful and efficient service" either in the employee's current position or in a vacant position in the same agency at the same grade or pay level for which that employee is qualified to render useful and efficient service.[1] "Useful and efficient service" is defined as acceptable performance of critical or essential elements of the position and satisfactory conduct and attendance.[2] In general, it is easier to establish disability under CSRS and FERS than to establish disability under social security.

The determination of entitlement to disability benefits is based on the following factors: objective clinical findings, diagnostic and expert medical opinions, subjective evidence of pain and suffering, and other evidence of the effect of the condition on the applicants' ability to perform the work required.[3] Moreover, disability benefits may be awarded where disability arises from the aggravation of a preexisting condition.[4] However, disability benefits may be denied if the employee's condition continues because of the employee's refusal or failure to follow medical advice.[5]

§ 20.12 Disability Benefits Under CSRS and FERS—Benefit Amounts

Under the Civil Service Retirement System (CSRS), disability benefits will generally be equal to the employee's projected pension benefits at age 60 or to 40% of the employee's average salary for the three consecutive highest salary years.[1] Cost-of-living benefits will be added annually in conjunction with the rate of inflation.

Under the Federal Employees Retirement System (FERS), during the first year of disability, an employee generally will be paid 60% of his or her average salary for the three consecutive highest salary years minus 100% of an approximation of any social security insurance benefit for which that person qualifies. After the first year and until age 62, if a person remains disabled and does not qualify for social security, the FERS disability benefit will be 40% of the person's average salary for the three consecutive highest salary years. If the

§ 20.11

1. 5 U.S.C.A. §§ 8337(a), 8451.

2. 5 C.F.R. §§ 831.502(a), 844.102.

3. Baumann v. Office of Personnel Management, 42 M.S.P.R. 257, 1989 WL 145463 (MSPB 1989) (WESTLAW: **fi 42 mspr 257**).

4. McDuffie v. Office of Personnel Management, 26 M.S.P.R. 106 (MSPB 1985)

(WESTLAW: **fi 26 mspr 106**); Swanson v. Office of Personnel Management, 25 M.S.P.R. 492 (MSPB 1984) (WESTLAW: **fi 25 mspr 492**).

5. Baker v. Office of Personnel Management, 782 F.2d 993 (Fed.Cir.1986).

§ 20.12

1. 5 U.S.C.A. § 8339(g).

disabled person qualifies for social security insurance benefits, during this period, the FERS disability benefits will be reduced by 60% of the initial social security benefit to which that person is entitled.[2] Cost-of-living benefits will be added annually only after the first year of the annuity, and this benefit may be somewhat less than the rate of inflation.[3] When the disabled person reaches age 62, the disability benefit is "redetermined," so that the person receives essentially the same retirement annuity he or she would have received had he or she not been disabled and had he or she worked continuously until age 62.[4]

§ 20.13 Survivors' Benefits Under CSRS and FERS—In General

Both the Civil Service Retirement System (CSRS) and the Federal Employees Retirement System (FERS) provide for survivors' benefits. If a federal employee covered by the CSRS program or the FERS program dies after completing at least 18 months of covered service, that employee's surviving spouse is entitled to survivor benefits.[1]

§ 20.14 Survivors' Benefits Under CSRS and FERS—Eligibility

Under both the Civil Service Retirement System (CSRS) and the Federal Employees Retirement System (FERS), surviving spouses must either have been married to the employee at least nine months immediately before the death or be the parent of a child of the marriage.[1] These requirements need not be satisfied if the employee's death was "accidental" and not caused by disease or illness.[2] An election must be made in order for a spouse who marries after the employee retires to receive survivor benefits.[3]

Former spouses also may be entitled to survivor benefits if the employee elects to provide them through reductions in the employee's annuity, or if the terms of a divorce decree or court-approved property settlement expressly provide them.[4] Former spouses of individuals who retired before May 7, 1985 must meet additional requirements, including a length of marriage requirement of at least ten years of the employee's creditable service.[5] The annuity of the retiree is reduced in

---

2. 5 U.S.C.A. § 8452(a).

3. 5 U.S.C.A. § 8452(a).

4. 5 U.S.C.A. § 8452(b)(1).

§ 20.13

1. 5 U.S.C.A. §§ 8341(d), 8442(b). 5 C.F.R. §§ 831.618, 842.602.

§ 20.14

1. 5 U.S.C.A. §§ 8341(a), 8441.

2. 5 U.S.C.A. § 8442(e), 5 C.F.R. § 831.-618.

3. 5 U.S.C.A. §§ 8341(b)(3), 8442(a)(2).

4. 5 U.S.C.A. §§ 8341(h), 8445.

5. 5 C.F.R. § 831.622.

order to provide survivor benefits for the employee's spouse or former spouse, unless the employee and the spouse waive this benefit.[6]

The rights of surviving spouses and former spouses to receive survivor benefits terminate when the surviving spouse or former spouse dies or remarries before turning 55 years old.[7] A divorce decree may provide an earlier termination date for the survivor benefits of a former spouse.

Children of the employee are also entitled to survivor benefits if they are: (1) unmarried, dependent, and less than 18 years old; (2) unmarried, dependent, between 18 and 22 years old, and a full-time student; or (3) unmarried, dependent, and incapable of self-support because of a mental or physical disability incurred before age 18.[8] A child's right to receive survivor benefits terminates when the child dies or ceases to meet the above eligibility requirements.[9] The shares of the remaining eligible children are then recomputed and paid as if the terminated child had predeceased the employee.[10]

§ 20.15 Survivors' Benefits Under CSRS and FERS—Benefit Amounts—CSRS

In general, if an employee dies while working for the government, the employee's surviving spouse will receive at least 55% of the employee's accrued benefit.[1] If a person dies while the person is a Civil Service Retirement System (CSRS) retiree, an eligible spouse will be paid 55% of the amount the deceased retiree was receiving in benefits or a lesser amount that the retiree and spouse agreed on at the time of retirement.[2] The benefits of a surviving spouse are reduced by any survivor annuity payable to a former spouse.[3] The benefits of a former spouse are equal to the benefits of a surviving spouse minus any survivor benefits payable to any other former spouses of the employee.[4] The benefits to which eligible children of a deceased employee covered by CSRS will be entitled depend on how many children that employee had and on whether the spouse is still living.[5]

If a person dies while the person is a federal civilian employee with more than 18 months of service covered by the Federal Employees Retirement System (FERS) but less than ten years of total service, an

---

6. 5 U.S.C.A. §§ 8339(j), 8416, 8417.

7. 5 U.S.C.A. §§ 8341(b)(3), 8341(d), 8442(d) (surviving spouse), 8341(h)(3), 8445(c) (former spouse).

8. 5 U.S.C.A. §§ 8341(a)(4), 8441(4).

9. 5 U.S.C.A. §§ 8341(e)(3), 8443(b).

10. Id.

§ 20.15

1. 5 U.S.C.A. § 8341(d).

2. 5 U.S.C.A. § 8341(b).

3. 5 U.S.C.A. §§ 8341(b)(4), 8341(d).

4. 5 U.S.C.A. § 8341(h)(2).

5. 5 U.S.C.A. § 8341(e).

eligible spouse will receive a lump sum payment of $15,000 plus the higher of either half of the deceased employee's annual salary at the time of death or half of the average pay for the three consecutive years of highest pay.[6] If the deceased employee had at least ten years of covered service, an eligible spouse also will receive an annuity equal to one-half of the accrued basic benefit plan.[7]

§ **20.16** Survivors' Benefits Under CSRS and FERS—Benefit Amounts—FERS

If a person is a Federal Employees Retirement System (FERS) retiree at the time of death, an eligible surviving spouse will be paid 50% of the retiree's annuity and possibly a special retirement supplement.[1] As under the Civil Service Retirement System (CSRS), the benefits of a surviving spouse are reduced by any survivor annuity payable to a former spouse, and the benefits of a former spouse are equal to those of a surviving spouse minus any survivor benefits payable to any other former spouses.[2] If an employee met the social security eligibility requirements at the time of death, the employee's survivors also may be entitled to social security survivors' benefits. Under FERS, surviving children (of employees and retirees) will receive the amount of the total children's annuity payable under CSRS reduced by the amount of social security benefits those surviving children are paid.[3]

§ **20.17** Divisibility of Retirement and Disability Benefits in Divorce Proceedings

Both the Civil Service Retirement System (CSRS) and the Federal Employees Retirement System (FERS) permit retirement and disability payments to be made directly to a former spouse pursuant to a valid divorce decree or court-approved property settlement.[1] Although these provisions do not speak to when and how such benefits should be partitioned, they do indicate a congressional intent to allow CSRS and FERS benefits to be divided in divorce proceedings according to state law.[2]

---

6. 5 U.S.C.A. § 8442(b). The $15,000 lump sum payment will be adjusted annually according to a prescribed formula.

7. 5 U.S.C.A. § 8442(b).

§ **20.16**

1. 5 U.S.C.A. § 8442(f).

2. 5 U.S.C.A. §§ 8442(h), 8445(b).

3. 5 U.S.C.A. § 8443(a).

§ **20.17**

1. 5 U.S.C.A. §§ 8345(j), 8467.

2. This is important in light of the decisions of the United States Supreme Court in McCarty v. McCarty, 453 U.S. 210, 101 S.Ct. 2728, 69 L.Ed.2d 589 (1981), and Hisquierdo v. Hisquierdo, 439 U.S. 572, 99 S.Ct. 802, 59 L.Ed.2d 1 (1979).

The Court in these cases held that military nondisability retirement benefits and

In both community property and common law property states, pension rights of a worker upon divorce generally are property subject to division at divorce. Generally, if an employee spouse's right to pension benefits accrued during the marriage, the benefits are property includable as a marital asset,[3] since the money the employer paid into a retirement fund otherwise would have been available to the husband and wife during the marriage, and employer contributions are a significant part of an employee's compensation package and may represent the most valuable asset acquired during marriage.[4]

Even if the employee's pension interests are deemed "nonvested" during the course of his or her marriage, so long as there is a contractual right to those interests, they are likely to be included as marital property and divided between the spouses.[5] Nonvested public pension rights usually are viewed not as mere expectancy, but as a contractual right that is a form of property.[6] Since social security is a taxation program subject to retroactive changes by Congress, social security benefits are not property. Therefore, only those CSRS and/or FERS benefits representing earned pension rights not substituting for social security should be divisible.

Because of differences among state laws, there is no nationally applicable law on the subject of how or if a civil service pension should be divided between spouses upon the dissolution of their marriage. When confronted with the situation, an attorney must look at the statutes and court decisions in the state where the divorce is to take place.

Railroad Retirement Act retirement benefits, respectively, may not be divided in divorce proceedings because Congress intended the employee spouses to receive these benefits intact. Therefore, the Court held that federal law preempted state divorce laws under the supremacy clause.

Congress legislatively overruled the result in *McCarty* by passing the Uniformed Services Former Spouses' Protection Act, 10 U.S.C.A. § 1408, which provides that military pensions may be included in marital estates and divided in divorce pursuant to state law. Similarly after *Hisquierdo*, Congress amended the Railroad Retirement Act to allow railroad retirement benefits to be paid to a former spouse. 45 U.S.C.A. §§ 231a(c)(2), 231a(c)(4), 231m; 20 C.F.R. Pt. 295.

3. Pulliam v. Pulliam, 796 P.2d 623 (Okl.1990); Kis v. Kis, 639 P.2d 1151 (Mont.1982); In re Marriage of Pryor, 224 Mont. 488, 731 P.2d 895 (1986); Deering v. Deering, 292 Md. 115, 437 A.2d 883 (1981).

4. Copeland v. Copeland, 91 N.M. 409, 575 P.2d 99 (1978); In re Marriage of Brown, 15 Cal.3d 838, 126 Cal.Rptr. 633, 544 P.2d 561 (1976); Heisterberg v. Standridge, 656 S.W.2d 138 (Tex.App.—Austin 1983); Shill v. Shill, 100 Idaho 433, 599 P.2d 1004 (1979), *appeal after remand* 115 Idaho 115, 765 P.2d 140 (1988); Carpenter v. Carpenter, 657 P.2d 646 (Okl.1983); Woodward v. Woodward, 656 P.2d 431 (Utah 1982). Barbour v. Barbour, 464 A.2d 915 (D.C.App.1983).

5. Janssen v. Janssen, 331 N.W.2d 752 (Minn.1983); Reed v. Reed, 93 A.D.2d 105, 462 N.Y.S.2d 73 (3d Dept.1983); Hebron v. Hebron, 116 Misc.2d 803, 456 N.Y.S.2d 957, 4 E.B.C. 1025 (1982).

6. See note 5, supra.

Disability benefits under CSRS and FERS are treated differently than retirement benefits under state property division laws. Some courts treat disability benefits the same as retirement benefits, so that the portion of the benefits earned during marriage is deemed to be property subject to division in divorce.[7] However, other courts apportion disability retirement benefits into two components: (1) compensation to the employee for pain and suffering and loss of earning capacity, and (2) retirement support.[8] To the extent that the first component is analogous to future personal injury damages or workers' compensation awards, it is separate property and not subject to partition in divorce.[9] The second component, as deferred compensation for retirement support, is divisible property to the extent it is attributable to employment during the marriage. Therefore, these courts hold that the amount the disabled retiree receives each month over and above what he or she would have received as retirement benefits based on longevity is excluded from any partition in divorce.

The Office of Personnel Management (OPM) has issued regulations to improve its processing of court orders affecting retirement benefits under the Civil Service Retirement System (CSRS) and the Federal Employees Retirement System (FERS). The regulations establish rules of interpretation and procedures for processing court orders that divide retirement benefits or award survivor annuities, provide model paragraphs for use in preparing court orders, and create a single uniform set of procedures for processing court orders under FERS and CSRS.[10]

---

7. Busby v. Busby, 457 S.W.2d 551 (Tex. 1970); Johnson v. Johnson, 532 So.2d 503 (La.App. 1st Cir.1988); Gilbert v. Gilbert, 422 So.2d 1330 (La.App. 3d Cir.1983), *writ denied* 445 So.2d 1231 (La.1984) (applying Georgia law).

8. Levy v. Office of Personnel Management, 902 F.2d 1550 (Fed.Cir.1990) (applying California law); Villasenor v. Villasenor, 134 Ariz. 476, 657 P.2d 889 (App.1982).

9. The Louisiana appellate court, in Gilbert v. Gilbert, 422 So.2d 1330, 1332 (La.App. 3d Cir.1983), *writ denied* 445 So.2d 1231 (La.1984), refused to recognize such a personal injury component, reasoning that, because CSRS "disability retirement" benefits are found in a separate chapter than federal workers' compensation benefits, disability retirement benefits "are more in the nature of a retirement scheme than compensation for disability."

10. 57 Fed.Reg. 33570 (July 29, 1992), codified at 5 C.F.R. §§ 838.101–838.1018. OPM has issued a handbook designed to assist lawyers seeking OPM implementation of state decrees of divorce or separation. The handbook is available from the Superintendent of Documents, P.O. Box 371953, Pittsburgh, PA 15250–7954 for $13/copy. These regulations apply only to court orders affecting CSRS and FERS basic benefits administered by OPM, not to court orders affecting the Thrift Savings Plan. The Federal Retirement Thrift Investment Board administers the Thrift Savings Plan. The Board processes court orders relating to the Thrift Savings Plan pursuant to regulations found at subpart I of 5 C.F.R. part 1650. Court orders relating to the Thrift Savings Plan must be submitted directly to the Board's recordkeeper, the National Finance Center in New Orleans.

Under the regulations court orders affecting CSRS or FERS benefits should be mailed to the Office of Personnel Management, Retirement and Insurance Group, P.O. Box 17, Washington, DC 20044; or delivered to the Court-ordered Benefits Section, Allotments Branch, Retirement and Insurance Group, Office of Personnel Management, 1900 E Street, NW., Washington, DC.

§ 20.18   Application Process Under CSRS and FERS

A federal employee who is eligible for retirement and who is applying for Civil Service Retirement System (CSRS) or Federal Employees Retirement System (FERS) retirement benefits must file an application for retirement with his or her department or agency within 30 days before, on, or any time after that employee reaches the requisite retirement age.[1] A former federal employee who is eligible for retirement must file an application for retirement with the Office of Personnel Management (OPM) within 30 days before, on, or after that former employee meets the requisite retirement age.[2]

Survivors of deceased employees must file for survivor benefits with the OPM at any time within 30 years after the death of the employee.[3] Applicants should use the proper form presented by OPM when filing for these benefits.[4]

An applicant for disability retirement must submit an application for retirement (and an application for an annuity) with the OPM before separation from service or within one year after separation from service, but this time limit may be extended in the case of an employee who is found to be incompetent on the date of separation or within one year thereafter.[5] The application must include supporting documentation that the eligibility requirements are satisfied, including: deficiency in performance, causal connection between the deficiency and a medical condition, and inability of the agency to accommodate the condition or find another available position.[6] An applicant under FERS must, in addition, provide the OPM certain documents and statements with respect to social security applications relating to the same disability.[7] The OPM may require the applicant to submit to a medical examination if an independent evaluation is needed to determine eligibility.[8]

§ 20.18

1. 5 C.F.R. §§ 831.501, 841.303(a).

2. 5 C.F.R. §§ 831.501, 841.304(a).

3. 5 C.F.R. §§ 831.619, 843.103, 843.302.

4. 5 C.F.R. §§ 831.104, 841.202.

5. 5 U.S.C.A. §§ 8337(b), 8453, 5 C.F.R. §§ 831.501, 844.201.

6. 5 C.F.R. §§ 831.502(b), 844.203(a).

7. 5 C.F.R. §§ 844.201(b).

8. 5 C.F.R. §§ 831.502(c), 844.203(b).

§ 20.19 Claim and Review Process Under CSRS and FERS

The Office of Personnel Management (OPM) considers all applications for benefits and adjudicates all claims.[1] After an unfavorable initial decision, the applicant may file a written request for reconsideration with the OPM within 30 days of the initial decision.[2] After an unfavorable final decision of the OPM, the applicant may appeal to the Merit Systems Protection Board (MSPB).[3]

The MSPB provides an opportunity for a hearing on whether the applicant is entitled to benefits.[4] Decisions of the OPM generally will be sustained if they are supported by a preponderance of the evidence.[5]

After a final unfavorable decision of the MSPB, the applicant may seek judicial review by filing in the United States Court of Appeals for the Federal Circuit within 30 days of receiving notice of the final decision of the MSPB.[6] The decision of the MSPB will be upheld on appeal unless it is arbitrary, capricious, or an abuse of discretion; obtained without following the required procedures; or unsupported by substantial evidence.[7]

§ 20.20 Health Benefits Plan Procedures

The health benefits plan [1] for federal employees and retirees generally is the group health insurance program applicable to federal employees, retirees, their families, and survivors. The Office of Personnel Management (OPM) contracts with various qualified group health insurance carriers (such as Blue Cross–Blue Shield) around the country for group health insurance plan coverage. Individual claims for payment or service initially are handled by the health benefits plan carrier in which the employee or retiree is enrolled.[2] If a claim (or portion of a claim) or a service is initially denied by a health benefits plan carrier, the carrier will reconsider its denial if a written request for reconsideration is made within one year of the denial.[3] Such a written request should set forth the reasons why the enrollee believes the denied claim or service should have been paid or provided. The plan carrier must affirm the denial in writing to the enrollee—setting out in detail the reasons—within 30 days after receipt of the request for reconsideration, or it must pay or provide the claim or service within such time, unless

§ 20.19

1. 5 U.S.C.A. §§ 8347, 8461(c).

2. 5 C.F.R. §§ 831.109, 841.305, 841.306.

3. 5 U.S.C.A. §§ 8347(d), 8461(e); 5 C.F.R. §§ 831.110, 844.104.

4. 5 U.S.C.A. § 7701(a).

5. 5 U.S.C.A. § 7701(c).

6. 5 U.S.C.A. § 7703(b)(1).

7. 5 U.S.C.A. § 7703(b)(1).

§ 20.20

1. 5 U.S.C.A. § 8901 et seq.; 5 C.F.R. § 890.101 et seq.

2. 5 C.F.R. § 890.105(a).

3. 5 C.F.R. § 890.105(b).

it specifically requests additional information reasonably necessary to a determination.[4]

If a plan carrier affirms its denial of a claim or fails to respond to a written request for reconsideration within 30 days of the request or within 30 days after it receives requested additional information, the enrollee may make a written request to the OPM for a review of the plan carrier's decision.[5] A request for review will be considered only if it is received by the OPM within 90 days of the date of the carrier's affirmation of the denial or within 120 days of a timely request for reconsideration if the carrier fails to respond.[6] Under some limited circumstances, this time requirement can be extended by the OPM.[7] In reviewing a claim denied by a plan carrier, the OPM may review copies of all original evidence and findings upon which the plan carrier denied the claim and any additional evidence (including an advisory opinion from an independent physician) it deems appropriate.[8] Within 30 days after all evidence requested by the OPM has been received, it must notify the enrollee and the plan carrier in writing of its findings upon review.[9]

Litigation to recover on a claim for health benefits should be brought against the carrier of the health benefits plan. An action to review the legality of the OPM's regulations applicable to the health benefits plan or a decision made by the OPM should be brought against the OPM.[10] According to the applicable federal regulations, an enrollee's dispute of an OPM decision solely because the OPM concurs in a health plan carrier's denial of a claim is not a challenge to the legality of the OPM's decision; therefore, any subsequent litigation to recover on the claim should be brought against the carrier, not the OPM.[11]

§ 20.21 Sources of Additional Information

Current employees seeking information about benefits should contact the personnel office of the agency for which they work. Persons who have left federal employment and are now eligible for an annuity (if, for example, they are 62 years of age) can contact the Retirement Information Office for information and application forms. The Retirement Information Office can be contacted to report the death of a retiree or someone receiving survivors' benefits. If the Retirement Information Office cannot handle a problem immediately, it will refer the matter to other divisions (such as an advisory services division

4. 5 C.F.R. § 890.105(b).

5. 5 C.F.R. § 890.105(a).

6. 5 C.F.R. § 890.105(d)(1).

7. 5 C.F.R. § 890.105(d)(1).

8. 5 C.F.R. § 890.105(d)(2).

9. 5 C.F.R. § 890.105(d)(4).

10. 5 C.F.R. § 890.107.

11. Id.

which handles very technical problems and emergencies or a medical claims dispute division which will assist retirees in disputes regarding health insurance benefits).

§§ 20.22–20.30 are reserved for supplementary material.

B. RAILROAD RETIREMENT

Library References:

C.J.S. Social Security and Public Welfare § 85.

West's Key No. Digests, Social Security and Public Welfare ☞161.

§ 20.31 Introduction

The railroad retirement system covers nearly all types of railroad employment in the United States. Employees of railroad labor unions and consolidated railroad terminal stations are included in the plan, but employees of local or intercity street rail systems and employees of railroad lines that operate within the confines of a mine or industrial plant are not covered.[1] If certain vesting and work record requirements are met, the spouses and dependent survivors of these employees also may receive benefits.

The statute governing the railroad retirement system is the Railroad Retirement Act of 1974, 45 U.S.C.A. § 231 et seq., with the applicable regulations of the Railroad Retirement Board (RRB) found at 20 C.F.R. §§ 200.1–295.7. The RRB is an independent agency of the executive branch of the federal government created by the Railroad Retirement Act. It is composed of three members appointed by the President with the advice and consent of the Senate.[2] The RRB is responsible for the determination and payment of benefits.[3] The RRB also administers social security benefits to certain retired railroad employees, their spouses, former spouses, and survivors who are entitled to social security benefits.[4] When the RRB pays social security benefits, the benefits are combined with any Railroad Retirement Act annuity payable and paid in one check.[5] However, the Social Security Administration still adjudicates all claims regarding social security benefits as well as making all determinations regarding entitlement,

---

§ 20.31

1. 20 C.F.R. §§ 202.1–202.15; 203.1.

2. 45 U.S.C.A. § 231f(a), 20 C.F.R. § 200.1(a).

3. 45 U.S.C.A. § 231f(b)(1), 20 C.F.R. § 200.1(a)(2).

4. 45 U.S.C.A. § 231f(b)(2)(D), 20 C.F.R. § 235.3.

5. RRB—SSA Coordination Guide, U.S. Railroad Retirement Board, Chicago, Illinois 60611, RB–31 (10–89), p. 12.

benefit amounts, termination and suspension actions, recovery of overpayments, and awarding of underpayments.[6]

§ 20.32 Benefits Available—Overview

The railroad retirement program provides benefits similar to those available under social security. Specifically, it provides for retirement,[1] disability,[2] spouse's,[3] survivors',[4] lump sum death,[5] and supplemental annuity benefits.[6] In most respects eligibility for these benefits is determined by standards and procedures similar to those used to determine eligibility for social security benefits. The railroad retirement program frequently overlaps and is very similar to the social security program. However, some features of the railroad retirement program are unique, and railroad retirees may encounter difficulties not experienced by beneficiaries of other programs.[7] In particular, because many railroad retirees or their spouses may also qualify for benefits from social security, the Civil Service Retirement System, the Federal Employees Retirement System, or state public employee pension programs, processing delays are common, and errors in eligibility determinations and benefit calculations occur frequently.

Library References:
C.J.S. Social Security and Public Welfare § 89.
West's Key No. Digests, Social Security and Public Welfare ☞166.

§ 20.33 Benefits Available—Employee Benefits—Age Benefits

A railroad employee is eligible for an age annuity under the Railroad Retirement Act if he or she has attained retirement age under the Social Security Act, or is at least age 60 with 30 years of service, or is age 62 with at least ten years of service.[1] In addition, the employee must apply for the annuity, stop all work for pay for any railroad or nonrailroad employer, and give up the right to return to work for a railroad employer. The employee may, however, engage in unincorporated self-employment or work as an independent contractor or consultant, as long as he or she is not supervised by an employer and is not a regular member of an employer's staff.[2] If the employee has less than

---

6. Id.

§ 20.32

1. 45 U.S.C.A. § 231a(a)(1).

2. 45 U.S.C.A. § 231a(a)(1)(iv), (v).

3. 45 U.S.C.A. § 231a(c).

4. 45 U.S.C.A. § 231a(d)(1).

5. 45 U.S.C.A. § 231e.

6. 45 U.S.C.A. § 231a(b).

7. See generally, "The Railroad Retirement Act" in National Senior Citizens Law Center, Representing Older Persons (1985).

§ 20.33

1. 45 U.S.C.A. § 231a(a)(1); 20 C.F.R. § 216.5.

2. 20 C.F.R. §§ 216.7, 216.8.

ten years of creditable railroad service when the employee reaches the retirement age, the employee's railroad credits are transferred to the social security system and treated as social security credits.[3]

§ 20.34 Benefits Available—Employee Benefits—Disability Benefits

A railroad employee also may be eligible for either a total disability annuity or an occupational disability annuity under the Railroad Retirement Act. An employee is eligible for a total disability annuity if the employee is permanently disabled for all regular work (including nonrailroad work), is younger than 65 years old with at least ten years of railroad service, and stops all work for pay.[1] An employee is eligible for an occupational disability annuity if the employee is permanently disabled for work in his or her regular railroad occupation, is younger than 65 years old, stops all work for pay, has a "current connection" with the railroad industry, and has either 20 years of service or ten years of service and is 60 years old or older.[2] A "current connection" is defined as work in the railroad industry in at least 12 months out of the 30 consecutive months preceding the month in which the annuity begins or the month in which the employee dies.[3] Self-employment will not break a current connection. When the disabled employee turns 65 years old, the disability annuity automatically becomes an age annuity.[4]

Library References:

C.J.S. Social Security and Public Welfare § 90.

West's Key No. Digests, Social Security and Public Welfare ⊸167.

§ 20.35 Benefits Available—Employee Benefits—Supplemental Annuity

In addition to these age and disability annuities, an employee will also be eligible for a supplemental annuity if the employee retires on or before his or her supplemental annuity closing date,[1] qualifies for either

3. 45 U.S.C.A. § 231q(2).

§ 20.34

1. 45 U.S.C.A. § 231a(a)(1)(v); 20 C.F.R. § 216.6(b).

2. 45 U.S.C.A. § 231a(a)(1)(iv); 20 C.F.R. § 216.6(a).

3. 20 C.F.R. § 216.97. A "current connection" with the railroad industry is also required for a supplemental annuity, a survivor annuity, a spouse windfall annuity,

and a lump sum death payment. 20 C.F.R. § 216.96(a).

4. 20 C.F.R. § 216.5(b).

§ 20.35

1. Generally, the closing date is the last day an employee can work for a railroad employer and still be entitled to a supplemental annuity. There are two types of closing dates: (1) regular—the last day of the first month after the employee turns age 65, if an employee has 25 years of

an age or disability annuity, has a current connection with the railroad industry when the annuity begins, and is either 65 or older with 25 years of service or 60 or older with 30 years of service.[2] The amount of the supplemental annuity is $23 plus $4 for each year of service in excess of 25 years.[3]

§ 20.36 Benefits Available—Spouse's Benefits

The spouse of a railroad employee is generally eligible for an annuity under the Railroad Retirement Act, provided that the eligible spouse is currently living with and has been married to an employee who is eligible for an age or disability annuity at least one year before the date the employee spouse applied for the annuity, or is the natural parent of the employee's child. In addition, the spouse must stop the same type of work for pay that an employee must stop and meet certain age requirements based on the employee's age, date of retirement, and years of railroad service.[1]

A former spouse is eligible for benefits if he or she was married to an employee who is at least 62 years old and entitled to an age or disability annuity, is presently not married, has attained the retirement age of the Social Security Act, and would be entitled to social security benefits as a divorced spouse if the employee's railroad service was treated as creditable service under the Social Security Act.[2]

Furthermore, annuity benefits are considered marital property subject to division and distribution at divorce. The Railroad Retirement Board must comply with a court decree of divorce, annulment, or legal separation awarding annuity benefits.[3]

§ 20.37 Benefits Available—Survivors' Benefits

Survivors of a deceased employee are eligible for survivors' annuities if they meet certain requirements and if the deceased employee had completed at least ten years of railroad service and had a current

service and is eligible for an old age benefit under SSA, and (2) special—the last day of the month before an employee is eligible for an old age benefit under SSA or the last day of the first month an employee meets the service requirement to be entitled to a supplemental annuity, if an employee has completed at least 23 but less than 25 years of service and is not eligible for an old age benefit under SSA at the regular closing date. 20 C.F.R. § 216.13.

2. 45 U.S.C.A. § 231a(b); 20 C.F.R. § 216.12.

3. 45 U.S.C.A. § 231b(e).

§ 20.36

1. 45 U.S.C.A. § 231a(c); 20 C.F.R. §§ 216.20, 216.22.

2. 45 U.S.C.A. § 231a(c)(4).

3. 45 U.S.C.A. § 231m(2); 20 C.F.R. §§ 295.1, 295.2.

connection with the railroad industry at the time of death.[1] The Social Security Administration will have jurisdiction over survivors' benefits if the deceased employee had less than ten years of creditable railroad service or had no current connection at retirement or death.

A surviving spouse generally is eligible if he or she (1) was married to the employee for at least nine months prior to the employee's death or was married for less than nine months and was the natural parent of the employee's child, (2) has not remarried, and (3) is at least 60 years old, at least 50 years old with a disability, or less than 65 years old and caring for the deceased employee's child who is eligible for survivors' benefits.[2]

A surviving child generally is eligible if he or she is the natural child, legally adopted child, stepchild, grandchild, stepgrandchild, or equitably adopted child of the qualified employee.[3] In addition, the child must be unmarried, dependent on the employee, and either less than 18 years old, 18 years old or older and disabled, or less than 22 years old and a full-time student.[4]

If there is no spouse or child who is or could ever be entitled to a survivors' annuity, the surviving parent of a qualified railroad employee may be entitled to an annuity. To be eligible, the parent must be at least 60 years old, unmarried since the death of the employee, and dependent on the employee for at least one-half support at the time the employee died.[5]

§ **20.38**   Dual Benefits

Many railroad employees have spent a portion of their lives working for nonrailroad employers, thereby earning quarters of coverage for social security or similar credits for benefits under the Civil Service Retirement System or a state public employee retirement program. Similarly, a railroad retiree's spouse may have qualified for benefits under one of these programs as a result of his or her own work. A railroad retiree or his or her spouse also may be eligible for veterans' benefits. Further, in addition to being eligible for benefits as a result of their own work, a railroad retiree and his or her spouse may qualify for spouses' or dependents' benefits under one of these programs.

A railroad retiree and his or her spouse may receive benefits from more than one program, depending on the benefit for which there is

§ 20.37

1. 45 U.S.C.A. § 231a(d).

2. 45 U.S.C.A. § 231a(d); 20 C.F.R. §§ 216.30, 216.32.

3. 20 C.F.R. § 216.49.

4. 45 U.S.C.A. § 231a(d); 20 C.F.R. § 216.46.

5. 45 U.S.C.A. § 231a(d)(iv); 20 C.F.R. § 216.70.

dual eligibility and the date on which eligibility vested. In most cases, a railroad retiree and his or her spouse will not receive the full value of all of the benefits for which they qualify. Usually a person eligible for more than a single benefit either receives the higher of the benefits to which he or she is entitled or has one benefit set off against another and thus receives less than the sum of the benefits to which he or she is entitled.[1] An example of the former may occur when a person is eligible for railroad retirement benefits both as a survivor (as a child or parent) and as a spouse.[2] An example of the latter is when, as a result of his or her own work, a person is eligible for both railroad retirement and social security benefits.[3]

There are a number of exceptions to the general rule against full receipt of dual benefits, however, and some railroad retirees and their spouses are eligible to receive multiple benefits with little or no reduction. For example, persons receiving railroad retirement and social security benefits on January 1, 1975, continue to receive dual benefits (called vested dual benefits). Eligibility for vested dual benefits also was extended to certain individuals who had not retired by January 1, 1975, but who had worked long enough to be fully qualified under both systems: those who (1) had a "current connection" to the industry (12 months of railroad service in the previous 30 months); (2) had 25 or more years of railroad service before January 1, 1975; (3) had performed some railroad service in 1974; or (4) had fully qualified for social security by the close of the year (prior to 1975) in which they left railroad employment.[4] Vested dual benefits are not available to individuals fully qualified on January 1, 1975, who lacked these characteristics, nor to the individuals who lacked sufficient credits on December 31, 1974, to be fully qualified under both systems. Despite the harsh consequences of the act for some railroaders, the act was sustained by the Supreme Court.[5]

Thus, while some railroad retirees and their spouses are eligible for unreduced dual benefits from social security and railroad retirement, most dual beneficiaries from these programs have their benefits reduced. Similarly, many dual beneficiaries from federal and state public retirement programs have their benefits reduced. But dual

---

§ 20.38

1. See generally, U.S. Railroad Retirement Board, Railroad Retirement and Survivor Benefits for Railroad Workers and their Families (1992) [Railroad Retirement Benefits].

2. 45 U.S.C.A. § 231a(h)(4); 20 C.F.R. § 216.90.

3. 45 U.S.C.A. § 231b(m).

4. 45 U.S.C.A. § 231b(h). Technically the benefits of these individuals are reduced, then most of the reduction is restored. Id.

5. U.S. Railroad Retirement Bd. v. Fritz, 449 U.S. 166, 101 S.Ct. 453, 66 L.Ed.2d 368 (1980), rehearing denied 450 U.S. 960, 101 S.Ct. 1421, 67 L.Ed.2d 385 (1981).

receipt of veterans' and railroad retirement benefits does not affect one's railroad retirement benefits.

Railroad retirement benefits are divided into two parts: Tier 1 benefits (calculated very similarly to social security benefits), and Tier 2 benefits (based solely on railroad service).[6] Technically what occurs in many dual benefit cases is that the railroad retiree's Tier 1 benefit is reduced or eliminated due to his or her receipt of a benefit from one of the other programs, which can cause confusion and delay when application for benefits is first made, and also can result in errors and delay if an individual or couple's circumstances later change. For example, underpayment or overpayment of one's railroad retirement benefits can occur as a result of changes in the size of one's social security benefit. Divorce, death of a spouse, or other change in family circumstances can affect both eligibility for benefits and payment levels. Similarly, post-retirement employment by one spouse can affect the family's eligibility for benefits and the payment levels. Because of the legal and factual complexities and the frequent involvement of two or more bureaucracies in dual benefit cases, the possibility of error is high.

Consequently, dual beneficiaries need to consider whether it is advantageous to receive social security benefits and railroad retirement benefits. It may be disadvantageous, for instance, in some retirement cases and in all survivor cases, where an individual is receiving two Railroad Retirement Act (RRA) annuities, as in the case of an employee annuitant who is also entitled to a spouse's annuity. An individual's total benefits could be less than if the individual had not filed for social security benefits in addition to his or her railroad retirement benefits.[7]

On the other hand, a dual beneficiary may find it advantageous to file for social security benefits where (1) the social security benefit is larger than the portion of the railroad retirement benefit to be reduced for social security entitlement; (2) there are children or other family members who are not eligible for a RRA benefit but who are eligible for a social security benefit; (3) the employee annuitant or his or her spouse began receiving an annuity before October 1, 1981, that was reduced for early retirement; or (4) a surviving spouse was awarded an insurance annuity before August 31, 1981, is over age 70 and does not expect to have excess earnings, was entitled to social security, and the

---

6. The social security equivalent portion of the benefits is treated as a social security benefit, while the railroad retirement benefits over and above social security levels are treated like private and public pensions for federal income tax purposes. Pocket Guide to Railroad Retirement and

Survivor Benefits, U.S. Railroad Retirement Board, Chicago, Illinois 60611, Form RB–4 (Jan. 1991).

7. RRB–SSA Coordination Guide, U.S. Railroad Retirement Board, Chicago, Illinois 60611, RB–31, (10–89), p. 14.

employee had ten years of service before 1975.[8] An individual's total benefits may increase under these circumstances. In order to determine the effect of social security benefits on their annuities, clients should be advised to contact a Railroad Retirement Board field office before filing for social security benefits.

§ 20.39 Application and Appeals

An application for benefits may be submitted at any office of the Railroad Retirement Board (RRB).[1] The process for applying for railroad retirement benefits, including the evidence needed to prove eligibility for benefits, is very similar to the process of applying for social security benefits described in Chapter 15. The application will be reviewed by the board's Bureau of Retirement Claims, which notifies claimants in writing of its decisions on applications.[2]

To appeal the decision on an application or other decisions affecting benefits, one must file a written request for reconsideration.[3] Ordinarily one has 60 days in which to file this request,[4] but a person seeking reconsideration of a decision that the person has been overpaid or seeking waiver of recovery of an overpayment, must file a request so that it is received by the board within 30 days of the date the notice of overpayment was sent.[5] Most reconsiderations are written reviews of the initial decision; but in overpayment cases, one may request an oral hearing, which will be conducted by a disinterested board employee who will report to the Director of Retirement Claims who, in turn, will issue a written decision.[6]

Appeals from reconsiderations lie with the Bureau of Hearings and Appeals and must be filed in writing within 60 days of the date of the reconsideration decision.[7] The hearing is conducted by a referee and closely resembles a Social Security Administration hearing. The referee is to issue a decision within 45 days if evidence was heard; otherwise within 90 days.[8]

An appeal from the referee's decision lies with the RRB itself. The appeal must be filed within 60 days of receiving notice of the referee's decision, and the board is to issue its decision within 90 days.[9]

To appeal the board's decision, a person may file an appeal within one year in one of three federal courts: the U.S. Court of Appeals in the

---

8. Id., 45 U.S.C.A. § 231b(h).

§ 20.39

1. See generally, 20 C.F.R. Pt. 217.
2. 20 C.F.R. § 260.1.
3. 20 C.F.R. § 260.3.
4. Id.

5. 20 C.F.R. § 260.4.
6. Id.
7. 20 C.F.R. § 260.5.
8. Id. at §§ 260.6, 260.7.
9. Id. at § 260.9.

area in which the person resides, the U.S. Circuit Court of Appeals for the Seventh Circuit (in Chicago, Illinois), or the U.S. Court of Appeals for the District of Columbia.[10]

Library References:

C.J.S. Social Security and Public Welfare §§ 91, 93.

West's Key No. Digests, Social Security and Public Welfare ⇐169.1, 171.1.

10. 45 U.S.C.A. §§ 231g, 355(f).

CHAPTER 21

VETERANS' BENEFITS

Table of Sections

A. VETERANS' BENEFITS GENERALLY

B. BENEFITS FOR SERVICE–CONNECTED DISABILITY AND DEATH

C. NONSERVICE–CONNECTED DISABILITY (PENSIONS)

D. MEDICAL BENEFITS

E. MISCELLANEOUS BENEFITS

F. APPLYING FOR VETERANS' ADMINISTRATION BENEFITS

WESTLAW Electronic Research

See WESTLAW Electronic Research Guide preceding the Summary of Contents.

A. VETERANS' BENEFITS GENERALLY

§ 21.1   Introduction—Over–65 Population in VA System

Although the American population is growing older, this change is pronounced among veterans.[1] As veterans who served in the Korean

---

§ 21.1

1. A veteran is "a person who served in the active military, naval or air service, and who was discharged or released therefrom under conditions other than dishonorable." 38 U.S.C.A. § 101(2). See also 38

War and World War II reach retirement age, a large population of mostly male veterans will be relying on the Department of Veterans Affairs (VA) for income support and health care services. By the year 2000, veterans over 65 will make up over one-third of the veteran population, and 63% of all American males over 65 will be veterans.[2]

Two critical changes in the VA have enabled attorneys to serve their clients more effectively. Until recently, Veterans Administration decisions were not subject to judicial review. In 1988 Congress enacted the Veterans' Judicial Review Act, which authorized judicial review of these decisions.[3] In addition, Congress repealed a provision forbidding an attorney from charging more than $10 to represent a client in a veterans case. An attorney now can charge a fee that is not "excessive or unreasonable."[4]

§ 21.2 Introduction—Where to Find Law

Title 38 of the United States Code lists the basic provisions covering veterans' benefits.[1] Regulations governing the VA are in volume 38 of the Code of Federal Regulations.[2] Also useful are VA decisions reported both in the Secretary's Decisions of the Department of Veterans Affairs and in Department of Veterans Affairs General Counsel Opinions (DVA–GCO).[3] The VA also publishes a booklet entitled Federal Benefits for Veterans and Dependents, which summarizes eligibility requirements for benefits and basic procedures and which contains other helpful information.[4]

C.F.R. § 3.1(d). The veteran must have served in the "active military" service. Congress and the VA established detailed criteria for determining whether a veteran served in the "active military." See 38 U.S.C.A. § 101; 38 C.F.R. § 3.6. See also 1 Wildhaber, Abrams, Stichman & Addlestone, *Veterans Benefits Manual* (1991) at 2–4. The specific personnel who can qualify as being a veteran in the active military are listed at 38 C.F.R. § 3.7. The type of service (wartime or peace time) and the length of service (where the veteran served after September 8, 1980) are also relevant to the type of benefits to which a claimant may be entitled. 38 U.S.C.A. §§ 1521 and 5303A, respectively. See generally Veterans Benefits Manual (1991) at Chp. 2.

2. Department of Veterans Affairs, Caring for the Older Veteran (1984).

3. Veterans Judicial Review Act, Pub.L. No. 100–687, 102 Stat. 4105 (1988).

4. 38 U.S.C.A. § 7263(c)–(d).

§ 21.2

1. 38 U.S.C.A. § 101 et seq.; 38 U.S.C.A. § 1110.

2. 38 C.F.R. § 3.1 et seq.

3. The district counsel at each Regional Office will provide decisions on request. The general counsel prepares an index to opinions. The VA decisions are available in paper or on computer. To arrange for computer access to the index and text of decisions, contact the Office of the General Counsel, 810 Vermont Ave. N.W., Washington, D.C. 20420.

4. The federal benefits booklet can be ordered through the Department of Veterans Affairs Office of Public Affairs (80D), 810 Vermont Ave. N.W., Washington, D.C. 20420.

A comprehensive discussion of veterans' matters is found in Wildhaber, Stichman & Addlestone, Veterans Benefits Manual (National Veterans Legal Services Project 1991).

§ 21.3   Who Is Eligible?

Eligibility requirements differ for each type of veterans' benefit. Veterans and members of a veteran's family may qualify for benefits if they meet the statutory requirements for their particular status. Eligible family members include spouse,[1] widow or widower,[2] child,[3] and parent.[4]

§ 21.4   Types of Benefits Offered by VA

The VA offers a broad range of benefits and services for veterans and their dependents or survivors. These benefits include compensation for service-connected disability or death; health care, including hospitalization, nursing home, or domiciliary care; pensions for nonservice connected disability or death; life insurance; benefit programs for survivors and dependents; and burial benefits.

§§ 21.5–21.10 are reserved for supplementary material.

B.   BENEFITS FOR SERVICE–CONNECTED DISABILITY AND DEATH

Library References:

C.J.S. Armed Services §§ 255, 264–267.

West's Key No. Digests, Armed Services ☞104.1.

§ 21.11   Compensation for Service–Connected Disability—Eligibility—Introduction

A veteran is eligible for compensation for a service-connected disability if the veteran:

1. was disabled by injury or disease incurred or aggravated during military service;

2. has a disability that was not the result of willful misconduct; and

3. was discharged under conditions other than dishonorable.

§ 21.3

1. 38 C.F.R. §§ 3.1(j), 3.50(a) and (c), 3.52, 3.55, 3.204–3.207.

2. 38 C.F.R. § 3.50(b).

3. 38 C.F.R. §§ 3.57, 3.209–3.210.

4. 38 C.F.R. § 3.59.

Veterans satisfying these requirements are entitled to benefits that depend on the severity of their disability and may receive additional allowances for their dependents.

§ 21.12 Compensation for Service–Connected Disability—Eligibility—Caused or Aggravated by Military

A veteran who either has a service-connected disability or aggravates a preexisting injury while in the line of duty can apply for benefits.[1] The term "service-connected" means, with respect to disability, "that such disability was incurred or aggravated ... in line of duty in the active military, naval, or air service."[2] The injury or illness must be the primary reason for the disability for which the veteran claims benefits.

To obtain benefits, a veteran must present proof that the disability is service-connected.[3] Proof may consist of service records, official histories from the organizations in which the veteran served, medical records, and relevant lay evidence.[4] Statutes presume that certain disabilities, such as tropical diseases, are service-connected even without a record of evidence of the condition during the period of service.[5] Different statutory presumptions of service connection attach for former prisoners of war, veterans involved in "radiation-risk activity," and veterans exposed to certain herbicide agents.[6]

In determining whether a disability is service-connected, the VA reviews all the evidence of the case. The VA's policy is to administer the law under a broad interpretation, so if a reasonable doubt arises about service connection, the degree of disability, or any other point, the doubt is resolved in the claimant's favor.[7] The VA presumes that a veteran was in sound condition when he or she entered service except in regard to conditions noted at entrance into service, or where clear and unmistakable evidence demonstrates that an injury existed previously.[8] Only conditions recorded in examination reports are to be considered "as noted."

A preexisting injury or disease is considered to have been aggravated by active service if there was an increase in disability during service, absent a specific finding that the increase in disability was due to the disease's natural progression.[9]

§ 21.12

1. 38 U.S.C.A. § 1110; 38 C.F.R. § 3.4(a)–(b).

2. 38 U.S.C.A. § 101(16).

3. 38 C.F.R. §§ 3.1(k), 3.4(a), and 3.303.

4. 38 C.F.R. § 3.303(a).

5. 38 C.F.R. § 3.308(b).

6. 38 C.F.R. § 3.309.

7. 38 C.F.R. § 3.102.

8. 38 U.S.C.A. §§ 1111, 1132.

9. 38 U.S.C.A. § 1153.

When an initial diagnosis of a disease occurs after discharge, a veteran still may be granted service connection if evidence establishes that the disease was contracted in service.[10] The veteran must provide a medical report linking the current disability with a condition incurred or aggravated during service. Certain conditions such as a tropical disease, tuberculosis, Hansen's disease, and multiple sclerosis are presumed to be service-connected unless the VA offers affirmative evidence to the contrary.[11]

A veteran may be denied benefits if evidence establishes that the injury or disease was suffered after separation from service or was due to the veteran's own willful misconduct or abuse of alcohol or drugs.[12] Willful misconduct is "an act involving conscious wrongdoing or known prohibited action." [13] Willful misconduct is disqualifying only if it is the "proximate cause of the injury, disease or death." [14] Claims for compensation in which allegations of willful misconduct often arise include claims for compensation for venereal disease and alcohol or drug-related illnesses.[15] An advocate should be careful in presenting such claims to minimize assertions that the illness was "proximately caused" by the veteran's willful misconduct. For claims filed prior to November 1, 1990, compensation could be obtained for disabilities that were the indirect result or secondary effect of alcohol or drug abuse. This has become more difficult for claims filed since that date as a result of an amendment to the Act that bars compensation for disabilities resulting from abuse of drugs or alcohol.[16]

§ 21.13   Compensation for Service–Connected Disability—Eligibility—Separation Not Under Dishonorable Conditions

In addition to proof of a service-connected disability, the veteran must not have been separated from the service under dishonorable conditions.[1] The VA decides the character of the discharge by considering the facts of each case. A discharge under honorable conditions is binding on the VA as to the character of discharge.[2]

---

10. 38 C.F.R. § 3.303(d).

11. 38 U.S.C.A. §§ 1112, 1113.

12. 38 U.S.C.A. §§ 105, 1110, 1113, 1131; 38 C.F.R. § 3.1(n).

13. 38 C.F.R. § 3.1(n); 38 C.F.R. § 3.301(c)(2)–(3). See further discussion of willful misconduct in § 21.16–.21, infra.

14. 38 C.F.R. § 3.1(n)(3).

15. See 38 C.F.R. § 3.301.

16. COBRA 1990, Pub.L. 101–508, § 8052(a)(3), 104 Stat. 1388–351, codified at 38 U.S.C.A. §§ 1110, 1131.

§ 21.13

1. 38 U.S.C.A. § 101(18); 38 C.F.R. §§ 3.1(d), 3.12.

2. 38 C.F.R. § 3.12(a).

Dishonorable discharges include discharges under conditions such as AWOL, spying, conscientious objection, desertion, etc.[3] The VA denies benefits in such circumstances unless the person was insane at the time of the offense causing discharge or unless otherwise provided for in the regulations.[4]

Discharges can be upgraded as the result of an individual case review.[5] Requests for upgrades must be filed with the Discharge Review Board or Board for Corrections for Military Records for the appropriate service. A veteran may seek review of a less-than-honorable discharge in federal district court.[6]

§ 21.14 Compensation for Service–Connected Disability—Disability Rating and Monthly Compensation

Once a disability is determined to be service-connected, the Secretary must determine the extent of that disability based upon the average diminution of earning capacity that a similar injury would cause in a civilian occupation. The Secretary issues rating tables that assign a rate to the disability, based on a percentage decrease in earning capacity. A rating under 10% receives no compensation.[1] The rating tables found in part IV, 38 C.F.R., are organized according to impaired organs, body systems (e.g., respiratory, digestive, cardiovascular), mental disorders, and impairing conditions. A veteran with more than one service-connected disability may receive a combination rating.[2] The tables place a percentage rating on the degree of disability resulting from impairment or injury to those organs or systems. The VA considers all veterans who are unable to secure a substantially gainful occupation because of service-connected disabilities to be totally (100%) disabled.[3]

The rate of service-connected disability compensation follows: [4]

Disability rating	Monthly compensation
10%	$ 85
20%	162

3. 38 C.F.R. § 3.12(b)–(d).

4. 38 C.F.R. § 3.12.

5. 38 C.F.R. § 3.12(g)(1).

6. 10 U.S.C.A. §§ 1552, 1553; Ogden v. Zuckert, 298 F.2d 312 (D.C.Cir.1961); Neal v. Secretary of the Navy, 639 F.2d 1029 (3d Cir.1981); Blassingame v. Secretary of the Navy, 866 F.2d 556 (2d Cir.1989). See also the Veteran's Self–Help Guide to Discharge Upgrading (National Veteran's Legal Services Project 1990).

§ 21.14

1. 38 U.S.C.A. § 1155.

2. 38 C.F.R. § 4.25.

3. 38 C.F.R. § 4.16(b).

4. 38 U.S.C.A. § 1114. These figures are effective December 1, 1992, and are updated annually in November; 57 Fed. Reg. 56,634 (Nov. 30, 1992).

Disability rating	Monthly compensation
30%	247
40%	352
50%	502
60%	632
70%	799
80%	924
90%	1040
100%	1730

An eligible veteran who is totally (100%) disabled who also has suffered certain injuries such as the loss of a limb, or an eye, will receive $70[5] per month for each such loss independent of any other compensation. A veteran who has suffered more serious injuries, such as deafness, blindness, amputations not correctable by the use of prosthetic appliances, is entitled to a higher monthly compensation. In 1993, this figure can be as high as $3,015 per month.[6]

A veteran entitled to compensation whose disability is not less than 30% is eligible for additional monthly compensation for dependents,[7] including the veteran's spouse, children, and parents. The amount received depends on the number and identity of the dependents. In 1993, the allowance for a spouse is $103 per month with additional compensation available for children and dependent parents, if any.[8]

Library References:

C.J.S. Armed Services §§ 255, 264–267.
West's Key No. Digests, Armed Services ⊱104.2(3).

§ 21.15 Survivors' Payments Due to Service–Connected Death—Monthly Compensation

The survivors (including parents) of a veteran who dies from a service-connected or compensable disability may receive monthly compensation.[1] This compensation is called "dependency and indemnity compensation" (DIC). Congress modified the formula for determining DIC benefits in 1992.[2] Where a veteran died before January 1, 1993,

---

5. 38 U.S.C.A. § 1114(k). This figure was effective December 1, 1992, and is updated annually in November; 57 Fed.Reg. 56,634 (Nov. 30, 1992).

6. 38 U.S.C.A. §§ 1114(k)–(p). This figure went into effect December 1, 1992, and is updated annually in November; 57 Fed. Reg. 56,634 (Nov. 30, 1992).

7. 38 U.S.C.A. § 1115.

8. 38 U.S.C.A. § 1115; 57 Fed.Reg. 56,-634 (Nov. 30, 1992).

§ 21.15

1. 38 U.S.C.A. §§ 1310–1315.

2. 38 U.S.C.A. § 1311.

See Dependency and Indemnity Compensation Reform Act of 1992, of the Veterans' Benefits Act of 1992. Public Law 102–568. ("DIC Reform Act"). This Act modified 38 U.S.C.A. §§ 1310 and 1311. See also 38 C.F.R. § 3.5, which amends the regulations to comply with the statutory changes.

the Reform Act entitles the surviving spouse to receive DIC benefits based upon either the pre-Reform Act formula or under the Reform Act's formula. The spouse is entitled to the calculation that provides the greater monetary benefit. The DIC benefits to which such a spouse is entitled under the pre-Reform Act is based on the veteran's military pay grade.[3] The DIC amounts in force on December 1, 1992, were as follows:

Pay grade	Monthly rate	Pay grade	Monthly rate
E–1	$ 634	W–3	$ 860
E–2	654	W–4	911
E–3	672	O–1	803
E–4	714	O–2	829
E–5	732	O–3	888
E–6	749	O–4	939
E–7	785	O–5	1,035
E–8	829	O–6	1,168
E–9	866	O–7	1,262
W–1	803	O–8	1,383
W–2	835	O–9	1,483
		O–10	1,627

Where a veteran died after January 1, 1993, (or where the veteran died before that date yet the veteran's military pay grade did not entitle the spouse to as much compensation as the spouse would receive under the Reform Act), DIC benefits are $750 per month.[4] The surviving spouse is entitled to a $165 increase of the basic rate if certain criteria are satisfied: (1) at the time of the veteran's death the veteran received, or was entitled to receive, compensation for a service-connected disability; (2) the disability was totally disabling; and (3) the disability lasted for a continuous period of at least eight years immediately prior to the veteran's death. To calculate the period of the veteran's disability, only the time the veteran and spouse were married is considered.[5] Where the veteran died after January 1, 1993, the spouse must receive benefits under the Reform Act's formula.[6]

The monthly DIC payment increases if minors are involved. In addition to the base rate, the surviving spouse is entitled to $100 per child during fiscal year 1993, $150 per child for 1994, and $200 per child thereafter.[7] Monthly DIC payments likewise will increase if the veteran's spouse is permanently home-bound, confined to a nursing

---

3. 38 C.F.R. § 3.5(e).

4. DIC Reform Act, § 102, 38 U.S.C.A. § 1311(a)(1).

5. DIC Reform Act § 102, 38 U.S.C.A. § 1311(a)(2).

6. 38 C.F.R. § 3.5(e)(1).

7. DIC Reform Act § 102, 38 U.S.C.A. § 1311(b).

home, or in need of the regular aid and attendance of another person.[8] A dependent child permanently incapable of self-support after age 18 is entitled to benefits.[9] DIC payments may be available to a surviving dependent in place of social security survivors' benefits. If the dependent is not eligible for social security because the deceased veteran was not fully insured at the time of death, the Secretary will pay an amount equal to the amount of benefits that would have been paid to the survivor.[10]

§ 21.16 Survivors' Payments Due to Service–Connected Death—Eligibility—Service–Connected Requirement

For survivors to be eligible for DIC benefits, the veteran must have died from a service-connected or compensable disability or injury. If a service-connected death occurred after discharge, the discharge must have been other than dishonorable.[1] The determination of whether a service-connected disability contributed to the cause of death is made on the basis of medical evidence, service records, lay evidence, and similar proof.[2]

If death occurred during military service, it must have occurred in the line of duty, and cannot be the result of the veteran's own willful misconduct or abuse of alcohol or drugs.[3] Claims for compensation for deaths that may be viewed as resulting from the veteran's willful misconduct present special problems for the advocate. Claims seeking compensation for suicide are an illustration.

Suicide will be considered willful misconduct if the act of self-destruction was intentional.[4] An essential element of willful misconduct is intent. A person with an unsound mind is incapable of forming an intent.[5] In order for the suicide victim's survivors to receive benefits, the veteran's mental unsoundness that resulted in the suicide must be service-connected.[6] Each case is decided on its merits, with any reasonable doubt being resolved favorably to support a finding of service connection.[7] Similar problems arise when compensation is sought for deaths related to abuse of alcohol or drugs.[8]

8.   38 U.S.C.A. § 1311.

9.   38 U.S.C.A. § 1314.

10.   38 U.S.C.A. § 1312(a).

§ 21.16

1.   38 U.S.C.A. § 1310.

2.   38 C.F.R. §§ 3.303(a), 3.312.

3.   38 U.S.C.A. §§ 105, 1110, 1113, 1310(a); 38 C.F.R. §§ 3.1(n), 3.301, 3.302.

4.   38 C.F.R. § 3.302(a)(1).

5.   38 C.F.R. § 3.302(a)(2).

6.   38 C.F.R. § 3.302(a)(3).

7.   38 C.F.R. § 3.302(c)(2).

8.   38 C.F.R. § 3.301. See also discussion in § 21.12, supra.

If the VA is found liable to a veteran who is injured or dies as a result of hospitalization or other VA medical treatment, the veteran receives benefits as though the disability, aggravated condition, or death were service-connected.[9] If the veteran is awarded a judgment or enters into a settlement or compromise as the result of injury or death from VA hospitalization or treatment, the VA will suspend monthly benefits until the amount of benefits suspended total the award or settlement amount.[10]

§ 21.17 Survivors' Payments Due to Service–Connected Death—Eligibility—Surviving Spouse Qualification

Compensation will be paid to the surviving spouse[1] of a veteran only if the veteran and spouse were married:

1. within 15 years after the termination of the service in which the injury or disease causing the death of the veteran occurred; or

2. for one year or more; or

3. for any period of time, if a child was born of the marriage or born to them before the marriage.[2]

§§ 21.18–21.20 are reserved for supplementary material.

C. NONSERVICE–CONNECTED DISABILITY (PENSIONS)

Library References:

C.J.S. Armed Services §§ 255, 264–267.

West's Key No. Digests, Armed Services ⊕104.1.

§ 21.21 Service and Disability Requirements for Veterans' Pension—Introduction

A veteran is eligible for a pension if the veteran:

1. actively served for 90 days or more during a period of war;[1] and

2. was permanently and totally disabled from a nonservice-connected injury or illness;[2]

9. 38 U.S.C.A. § 1151.

10. 38 U.S.C.A. § 1151.

§ 21.17

1. For a definition of spouse or surviving spouse, see 38 C.F.R. §§ 3.50, 3.1(j).

2. 38 U.S.C.A. § 1102.

§ 21.21

1. 38 U.S.C.A. § 1501(a).

2. 38 U.S.C.A. § 1502(a).

3. has an annual income and net worth below limits established by law;[3] and

4. was discharged under other than dishonorable conditions.[4]

§ 21.22 Service and Disability Requirements for Veterans' Pension—Disability—Medical Rating Plus Age

A veteran is considered disabled if he or she is unemployable as the result of a disability reasonably certain to continue throughout the veteran's life; if he or she suffers from any disability that would render it impossible for the average person to be substantially, gainfully employed for life; or if he or she suffers from certain diseases or disorders determined by the Secretary to render a person permanently and totally disabled.[1] Age is a factor in determining whether a veteran is disabled. To receive a pension, a veteran age 60 or older must have one or more disabilities rated at 50% or higher.[2] A veteran between age 55 and 59 must have one or more disabilities rated at 60% or higher.[3] A veteran under 55 must have either one disability rated at 60% or higher or a combination disability rating of 70% with one disability rated at 40% or more.[4]

In exceptional cases, a veteran who fails to meet the percentage ratings listed above may be awarded a pension if the veteran demonstrates that he meets basic entitlement criteria and is unemployable.[5]

§ 21.23 Service and Disability Requirements for Veterans' Pension—Disability—Evidence Requirements

A veteran must support his or her claim with evidence of a disability that is likely to continue for the remainder of the veteran's life.[1] The evidence should include medical reports that demonstrate the extent of the veteran's disability and the effect of the disability on daily activities.[2] If the evidence submitted establishes a reasonable probability of a valid claim, the Department of Veterans Affairs will authorize the veteran to undergo a mandatory medical examination. However, the VA may rate the pension claim without an examination

3. 38 U.S.C.A. §§ 1521, 1522.

4. 38 C.F.R. § 3.12.

§ 21.22

1. 38 U.S.C.A. § 1502.

2. 38 C.F.R. § 4.17. For claims filed before November 1, 1990, a claimant 65 years of age or older was presumed to be permanently and totally disabled. COBRA 1990, Pub.L. No. 101–508, § 8002(b) amended 38 U.S.C.A. § 1502 to eliminate that presumption.

3. Id.

4. 38 C.F.R. § 4.16.

5. 38 C.F.R. § 3.321(b).

§ 21.23

1. 38 C.F.R. § 3.342.

2. 38 C.F.R. § 3.326.

or further inquiry if it receives statements from a private physician that include the clinical manifestations and substantiations of diagnosis by generally accepted diagnostic techniques.[3]

§ 21.24   Requirements for Veterans' Pension—Pension Benefits

Income requirements for determining eligibility for pensions fall into two categories:[1] "section 306" pensions,[2] effective until December 31, 1978, and "improved pensions,"[3] effective January 1, 1979. The VA will pay compensation to the veteran depending on the veteran's marital status, number of dependents, annual income, and need for aid and attendance.[4]

This chart shows annual pension rates for disabled veterans under the improved pension program. A veteran with no countable income receives the relevant maximum rate. A veteran receiving countable income has his or her rate reduced by the amount of the countable income. A veteran whose countable income exceeds the maximum rate receives no pension for that period. Benefits are paid monthly.[5]

Improved pension maximum Annual Rates[6]

1. Veterans in need of aid and attendance
   Veteran with no dependents $12,187
   Veteran with one dependent 14,548
       Each additional dependent 1,296
2. Veterans permanently and totally disabled
   Veteran with no dependents .... $ 7,619
   Veteran with one dependent 9,980
       Each additional dependent 1,296
3. Veterans who are housebound
   Veteran with no dependents .... $ 9,313
   Veteran with one dependent 11,673
       Each additional dependent 1,296

"Section 306" beneficiaries entitled to benefits as of December 31, 1978, who do not elect the improved pension system, will receive benefits at the rate they received them on December 1, 1978, if they

---

3. 38 C.F.R. § 3.326(b).

§ 21.24

1. A third pension category entitled "old law" is largely outdated as it applied to veterans eligible to receive a pension prior to June 1960. 38 C.F.R. § 3.26.

2. 38 C.F.R. §§ 3.1(u), 3.26, 3.28.

3. 38 C.F.R. § 3.1(w).

4. 38 U.S.C.A. § 1521.

5. 38 C.F.R. § 3.273.

6. 38 C.F.R. § 3.26; 38 U.S.C.A. § 1521. These amounts and the annual income limitations are updated annually consistent with C.O.L.A., 38 U.S.C.A. § 5312 and § 306 of Pub.L. 95–588. 57 Fed.Reg. 56632–03, effective Dec. 1, 1992.

continue to be permanently disabled, do not lose a dependent, or their incomes do not exceed the adjusted limitation. The income limitation increases yearly based on changes in the Consumer Price Index.[7] Following is a table listing section 306 pension income limitations:

Veteran or spouse with no dependents	$ 8,667
Veteran with no dependents in need of aid or attendance . .	$ 9,229
Veteran or surviving spouse with one or more dependents	$11,653
Veteran with one or more dependents in need of aid or attendance	$12,216
Child (no entitled veteran or surviving spouse)	$ 7,084 [8]

A veteran whose countable income exceeds these amounts receives no pension. A veteran with no countable income receives the full amount listed. A veteran with some countable income has his or her pension payment reduced by the amount of the countable income. Benefits are paid monthly.

Veterans receiving benefits under "section 306" pensions can elect to receive benefits under the "improved pension" program.[9] Eligible veterans married to each other must elect to receive the improved pension. These veterans, as well as those becoming entitled to a disability pension after December 31, 1978, must meet the income test used for "improved pensions." With the limited exception of public assistance beneficiaries, an election to receive improved pension benefits is irrevocable.[10]

§ 21.25 Requirements for Veterans' Pension—Resources

The VA determines the amount that would be reasonable for a veteran to use from the corpus of the veteran's and spouse's estate to meet living expenses.[1] A pension may be denied when the agency determines that the corpus of the estate, considering all circumstances including the veteran's and his or her family's income, should be used to support the veteran.[2] The net worth and corpus of estate mean the market value, less mortgages of all property owned by the claimant, excluding dwelling and yard, and reasonable personal effects.[3]

The VA rarely denies a claim for pension benefits when the veteran's net worth, excluding residence and car, is less than $35,000.

---

7. Federal Benefits for Veterans and Dependents. IS–1 Fact Sheet, 10 (1991).

8. 57 Fed.Reg. 56632–03, effective Dec. 1, 1992.

9. 38 C.F.R. § 3.711.

10. 38 C.F.R. §§ 3.711, 3.714.

§ 21.25

1. 38 U.S.C.A. § 1522.

2. 38 C.F.R. § 3.274.

3. 38 C.F.R. § 3.275.

Claimants who have a net worth greater than $35,000 should explain why the claim should not be denied because of excess net worth.[4]

§ 21.26 Requirements for Veterans' Pension—Countable Income

In determining a veteran's annual income, all payments of any kind—from any source including the income of the veteran's spouse and any child for whom a pension is paid—are included in income, with the following exceptions: [1]

1. public or private relief donations—including welfare payments and contributions by friends, family and charitable organizations;

2. veterans' pension benefits;

3. amounts equaling unreimbursed expenditures by spouse or child for veteran's debts, last illness, and burial;

4. amounts equaling expenditures by veteran or spouse for last illness and burial of spouse or child;

5. casualty insurance proceeds;

6. profits from disposition of property other than in course of business;

7. joint accounts transferred by death of joint owner;

8. amounts equal to unreimbursed medical expenses;

9. some costs of education, rehabilitation, and training pursued by veteran or spouse; and

10. current work income of child not exceeding prescribed amounts;

11. payments from certain statutory or court-ordered programs— e.g. Agent Orange Settlement payments.

Both section 306 and the improved pension plans require that a spouse's income be included when determining total income. Under the improved pension plan, all of the spouse's earned and unearned income is included. However, under the section 306 plan, only income of the spouse that is reasonably available to the veteran in excess of the amount of the spouse's income exclusion of $2,764 [2] or the total earned

---

4. 1 Wildhaber, Abrams, Stichman & Addlestone, Veterans Benefits Manual (1991).

§ 21.26

1. 38 U.S.C.A. § 1503; 38 C.F.R. §§ 3.260–3.272.

2. This amount is specified in § 306(a)(2)(B) of Pub.L. 95–588 and in-

income of the spouse, whichever is greater, can be considered income of the veteran, unless to do so would inflict hardship on the veteran.[3] The spouse's income is presumed to be available to the veteran without causing hardship to the veteran. However, this presumption may be rebutted by evidence of unavailability or of expenses beyond usual family costs.[4]

To determine the amount of pension a veteran will receive, the VA determines the maximum annual pension rate (MAPR),[5] then deducts countable income for VA purposes (IVAP). This amount is divided by 12 to determine the veteran's monthly benefit.[6] The VA distinguishes between regular, recurring income and that which is irregular or short-term.[7] Errors in computing a veteran's monthly pension are common.[8]

§ 21.27 Requirements for Veterans' Pension—Special Monthly Pensions

A veteran who is severely and permanently disabled may be eligible for a special monthly pension (SMP) as a person who is "permanently housebound" or in need of the regular "aid and attendance" of another person. The maximum annual pension rate (MAPR) of such a veteran is increased to recognize his or her special needs.[1]

§ 21.28 Requirements for Veterans' Pension—How VA Pensions Affect Other Benefits

Claimants eligible for VA benefits also may be eligible for other benefits programs, including Social Security, Medicaid, or SSI. SSI and Medicaid consider the claimant's income and assets when awarding benefits. Applicants for Medicaid and SSI are required to seek veterans' benefits before applying, but a VA applicant is not required to apply for other programs.

A veteran's monthly pension payment is considered "income" in computing the veteran's eligibility for SSI benefits.[1] Therefore, the amount of SSI benefits will be decreased for veterans receiving pensions. However, certain types of veterans' benefits, such as a depen-

---

creased periodically under § 306(a)(3) of Pub.L. 95–588. 57 Fed.Reg. 56632–03, effective Dec. 1, 1992. 38 U.S.C.A. §§ 1521, 1541, 1542 and 5312.

3. 38 C.F.R. §§ 3.262(b)(2), 3.26.

4. 38 C.F.R. § 3.262(b).

5. § 21.24, supra.

6. 38 C.F.R. § 3.273.

7. 38 C.F.R. § 3.271.

8. See Veterans Benefit Manual, supra § 21.25, note 4 at Chapt. 5.

§ 21.27

1. 38 U.S.C.A. §§ 1502(b), (c); 38 C.F.R. §§ 3.351, 3.352.

§ 21.28

1. 42 U.S.C.A. § 1382a(a)(2)(B); 20 C.F.R. § 416.1102.

dent's portion of benefits, are not counted as income.[2] Aid and attendance benefits for a veteran may not be counted as income for SSI benefits.[3]

A majority of states use SSI entitlement criteria for Medicaid; the remaining states establish their own standards of eligibility under Federal guidelines.[4] In states using SSI standards, VA aid and attendance payments should not be countable income for Medicaid eligibility, and the same principle should apply to other states.[5]

§ 21.29 Death Pensions for Survivors of Wartime Veteran

The VA pays death pension benefits to the survivors of a wartime veteran on the basis of need. Survivors, therefore, must meet income tests established by the VA to be eligible.[1]

The veteran must have served 90 days or more during a period of war, have been separated from service under conditions other than dishonorable, and have left survivors who meet the income test and are otherwise eligible by virtue of their age, marital status, and relationship to the veteran.[2]

The "improved pension" maximum annual rates are as follows:[3]

1. Surviving spouse alone $5,106
   Surviving spouse and one child in custody 6,689
   Each additional child 1,296
2. Surviving spouses who are house-bound
   Surviving spouse alone $6,243
   Surviving spouse and one child in custody 7,822
   Each additional child 1,296
3. Surviving spouse in need of aid or attendance
   Surviving spouse alone $8,167
   Surviving spouse with one child in custody 9,746
   Each additional child .... 1,296 [4]

The rate payable is the applicable maximum rate minus the countable annual income of the eligible person. The type of income and assets

2. Whaley v. Schweiker, 663 F.2d 871 (9th Cir.1981); White v. Sullivan, 813 F.Supp. 1059 (D.Vt.1992).

3. 20 C.F.R. § 416.1103.

4. See Chapter 11; see also Wilder, Abrams, Stichman & Addlestone, Veterans Benefits Manual § 13.2.2 (1991).

5. E.g., Sherman v. Griepentrog, 775 F.Supp. 1383, 35 Soc.Sec.Rep.Ser. 456 (D.Nev.1991).

§ 21.29

1. 38 U.S.C.A. §§ 1541, 1542.

2. 38 U.S.C.A. §§ 1541, 1542.

3. 38 U.S.C.A. §§ 1541, 1542.

4. 38 C.F.R. § 3.26; 38 U.S.C.A. §§ 1541, 1542. These amounts are updated annually consistent with C.O.L.A., 38 U.S.C.A. § 5312. 57 Fed.Reg. 56632–03, effective Dec. 1, 1992.

considered are the same as those considered under the income test for a disability pension.

In addition to qualifying as a widow or widower,[5] the spouse must have been married to the veteran for at least one year. A widow also qualifies if she bore a child fathered by a veteran either during or before the marriage.[6]

Library References:

C.J.S. Armed Services §§ 251–267.

West's Key No. Digests, Armed Services ☞101.

§§ 21.30–21.40 are reserved for supplementary material.

D. MEDICAL BENEFITS

Library References:

C.J.S. Armed Services §§ 257–267.

West's Key No. Digests, Armed Services ☞107.

§ 21.41   Hospital Care—Veterans' Hospitals

The VA provides hospital care in VA hospitals to veterans separated from the service under conditions other than dishonorable. Eligibility is mandatory or discretionary, depending on whether the disability is service-connected and on the veteran's income. Veterans with service-connected disabilities (and older veterans of wartime service) fall into the mandatory category.[1]

Veterans with nonservice-connected disabilities in need of treatment who are unable to defray the expense of necessary hospital care are entitled to care if their incomes are lower than the VA means test for medical care. The VA has the discretion to provide hospital and nursing care to veterans with nonservice-connected disabilities who have incomes higher than the VA thresholds for free care if these veterans pay for the care they receive.[2]

Veterans who are discharged because of disability incurred in the line of duty but who do not receive compensation for service-connected disability should arrange for their official armed forces records to be submitted to determine whether they are eligible for hospital care.[3]

5. 38 C.F.R. §§ 3.50, 3.1(j).

6. 38 U.S.C.A. § 1541(f).

§ 21.41

1. 38 U.S.C.A. § 1710.

2. 38 U.S.C.A. § 1710(a)(2)(f); 38 C.F.R. §§ 17.47, 17.48. In 1993, care is mandatory for a single veteran with a nonservice-connected disability who has no dependents if his income is $19,408 or less.

3. 38 C.F.R. § 17.48.

§ 21.42   Hospital Care—Non–VA Hospitals

A veteran may be eligible for treatment at hospitals operated by the Department of Defense, Public Health Service, or other federal agencies under certain conditions.[1] If the Department of Veterans Affairs has an agreement with a certain agency, a specific number of beds allocated for VA patients' care may be authorized for any eligible veteran described in the previous subsection. A few restrictions apply for military retirees or for veterans suffering from chronic disabilities.[2] Emergency care may be authorized at any hospital operated by a U.S. governmental agency that does not have an agreement for specific beds allocated for veterans.[3]

In addition, the VA also may contract with public or private hospitals to provide hospital care or medical services because of geographical accessibility or if the VA is otherwise unable to provide the care or services required in a given situation.[4]

Veterans must obtain advance authorization from the VA for private hospitalization. In emergency cases, authorization must occur within 72 hours of admission.[5]

§ 21.43   Outpatient Care

Outpatient care is available without charge to eligible veterans and may be provided by outpatient clinics, or in some cases by private physicians who have contracted with the VA. Prescription drugs may be obtained from outpatient clinics or when authorized by a private physician and reimbursed by the VA.[1] Outpatient dental services or treatment and related dental appliances may be covered, subject to limitations more fully described in the statute.[2]

Outpatient care is available for most veterans eligible for hospital care. In addition, it may be authorized if necessary to prepare the veteran for hospitalization or to obviate the need for hospital admission.[3]

§ 21.44   Nursing Home Care

Nursing home care at a VA facility is available to veterans with a service-connected disability and to needy veterans with a disability that

---

§ 21.42

1. 38 C.F.R. § 17.50a.

2. See 38 C.F.R. § 17.50.

3. 38 C.F.R. § 17.50a.

4. See 38 C.F.R. § 17.50b for a complete listing of eligibility requirements for hospital care and medical services in non-VA facilities.

5. 38 C.F.R. § 17.50d.

§ 21.43

1. 38 U.S.C.A. § 1712; 38 C.F.R. § 17.-60.

2. 38 U.S.C.A. § 1712(b).

3. See 38 C.F.R. § 1712 for eligibility criteria.

is not service-connected.[1]

Veterans who have received hospital care, nursing home care, or domiciliary care in a VA facility may receive nursing home care in a non-VA nursing home care unit.[2] The nursing home must meet standards prescribed by the VA. Any reports of inspection are to be made available to all agencies responsible for licensing, regulating, and inspecting such institutions.[3]

Veterans with chronic conditions requiring skilled care, but who no longer need hospital care, are eligible for nursing home care in a contract public or private nursing home facility. Generally, the individual must (1) require nursing home service, supportive health service, and consultant service of a physician; (2) no longer be in need of hospitalization; and (3) be unable to meet the criteria for admission to a VA shelter care facility.[4]

Nursing home care generally is not provided for more than six months.[5] However, a veteran whose hospitalization was primarily for a service-connected disability is not subject to this limitation.[6] In addition, directors of health facilities may authorize, for any veteran whose hospitalization was not primarily for service-connected disability, an extension beyond six months of nursing care in a public or private nursing home care facility under specific circumstances.[7]

§ 21.45   Domiciliary Care

The VA domiciliary care (shelter care) program provides shelter, room and board, and continuing medical care to needy disabled veterans. Because this care is available only in VA domiciliaries or homes, the number of veterans who are able to receive such care is small. Requirements for care in a VA domiciliary are based on service, disability, and financial need. The veteran also must be able to meet certain self-care requirements.[1] The veteran must have been discharged under other than dishonorable conditions. Veterans discharged or released from active service for a service-connected disability, or who receive disability compensation, when suffering from a

§ 21.44

1. 38 U.S.C.A. § 1710. In addition, other veterans may receive nursing home care if there is room and they pay for their care. Id.

2. 38 U.S.C.A. § 1720.

3. 38 U.S.C.A. § 1720(b).

4. 38 C.F.R. § 17.51.

5. 38 U.S.C.A. § 1720.

6. 38 C.F.R. § 17.51(b)(4).

7. 38 C.F.R. § 17.51a.

§ 21.45

1. 38 C.F.R. § 17.47(e)(2).

permanent disability, tuberculosis, or a neuropsychopathic ailment are eligible.[2]

§ 21.46 Domiciliary Care—Disability

To fulfill the domiciliary care requirement for disability, the veteran must have a disease or injury that is chronic and prevents the veteran from earning a living.[1]

§ 21.47 Domiciliary Care—Need

To be eligible for domiciliary care, a veteran must prove that because of his or her disability, the veteran has inadequate income to support himself or herself and finance the care needed.[1]

§ 21.48 Domiciliary Care—Self–Care Ability

The veteran must be able to provide care for himself or herself, including personal hygiene, grooming, and feeding. The veteran is also expected to contribute to the operation of the facility.[1]

§§ 21.49–21.50 are reserved for supplementary material.

E. MISCELLANEOUS BENEFITS

Library References:

C.J.S. Armed Services §§ 251–267.
West's Key No. Digests, Armed Services ☞101.

§ 21.51 Personal Benefits

The VA may allow up to $5,500 as a one-time payment on the purchase of a motor vehicle for a veteran who has a service-connected disability consisting of the loss of use of one or both hands or one or both feet, or permanent extreme impairment of vision.[1] The service-connected disability must have arisen from a period of service during or after World War II.

The VA allows payment for certain adaptive equipment.[2] A trained guide dog is available for a blind veteran entitled to receive

2. 38 C.F.R. § 17.48(c).

§ 21.46
1. 38 C.F.R. § 17.48(c).

§ 21.47
1. 38 C.F.R. § 17.48(b)(2).

§ 21.48
1. 38 C.F.R. § 17.47(e)(2).

§ 21.51

1. This figure went into effect in 1988 and is updated periodically. 38 U.S.C.A. § 3902; 38 C.F.R. § 3.808.

2. 38 C.F.R. § 3.808.

disability compensation for any service-connected condition.[3] Prosthetic devices, sensory rehabilitative aids, and special clothing made necessary by the wearing of such appliances are available, subject to some restrictions, for a veteran who is eligible for outpatient care or is receiving hospital, nursing home, or domiciliary care.[4]

§ 21.52 Medical Supplies and Medicines

A veteran entitled to payments for regular aid and attendance or house-bound allowance may be furnished medical equipment and supplies (excluding medicines) if the device, equipment, or item is determined to be medically necessary.[1] Such a veteran also may have a prescription for drugs and medicines that is ordered by a private or non-VA doctor, filled by a VA pharmacy under certain circumstances.[2]

§ 21.53 Other Benefits—Vocational Rehabilitation

Vocational rehabilitation is available for any veteran who is entitled to service-connected disability compensation.[1]

§ 21.54 Other Benefits—Food Stamps

Certain disabled veterans may receive food stamps for their households. The eligibility standards are more generous than those for nonveterans.[1]

§ 21.55 Other Benefits—Life Insurance

The government has various life insurance plans for veterans. The family has a wide variety of payment options upon death. The government pays premiums while the veteran is on active duty, but the veteran pays premiums after discharge.[1]

3. 38 C.F.R. § 17.118.
4. 38 C.F.R. § 17.115.

§ 21.52

1. 38 C.F.R. § 17.115c.
2. 38 C.F.R. § 17.60d.

§ 21.53

1. 38 U.S.C.A. § 1151.

§ 21.54

1. 7 C.F.R. §§ 271.2, 273.9; see Chapter 18, supra, for details.

§ 21.55

1. See 38 U.S.C.A. §§ 1901–1925; 38 C.F.R. Pts. 6 and 9.

§ 21.56   Other Benefits—Burial Benefits

Deceased veterans may be interred in any open cemetery in the National Cemetery System (immediate family is also eligible).[1]

§§ 21.57–21.60 are reserved for supplementary material.

F.   APPLYING FOR VETERANS' ADMINISTRATION BENEFITS

Library References:

C.J.S. Armed Services § 263.

West's Key No. Digests, Armed Services ⚷132.

§ 21.61   Recognition of Agent or Attorney

The Administrator of Veterans' Affairs can recognize a nonattorney to represent the veteran in the preparation or prosecution of a VA claim. Traditionally, advocates for veterans usually have been nonattorney practitioners from veterans' service organizations. The regulations now provide a method by which an organization can qualify certain persons for such recognition.[1]

An attorney who is a member in good standing of the bar of the highest court of a state may represent a person before the agency after filing a written declaration that he or she is currently qualified and authorized to represent the particular client. The statement must be on the attorney's letterhead with a signed consent from the claimant. Once the VA receives the statement, the agency will give the attorney complete access to the claimant's files.[2] The VA is required to send notice of any VA decision that affects a claimant's benefits to the claimant and his or her representative.[3]

§ 21.62   Application Process

Specific forms for initiating claims are available through the VA.[1] Form 21–526 is used for a veteran's application for compensation or pension. Form 21–534 is the claim for dependency and indemnity compensation or death pension by a widow or child. The application for dependent parents is Form 21–535. Claims usually are filed with a regional office of the VA.

§ 21.56

1. See 38 U.S.C.A. §§ 2400–2410 for additional benefits and details.

§ 21.61

1. 38 C.F.R. § 14.629(a).

2. 5 U.S.C.A. § 500; 38 C.F.R. § 14.-629(c).

3. 38 C.F.R. §§ 3.103(b)(1), (f); 3.105(h)(2).

§ 21.62

1. 38 C.F.R. § 3.150. For helpful suggestions on the applications process, see Snyder, Paralegal's Guide to Veteran's Administration Advocacy, 23 Clearinghouse Rev. 236 (July 1989).

Although the VA generally will not pay benefits unless a formal claim is filed on an appropriate form signed by the applicant, an informal claim can be submitted on the veteran's behalf.[2] If an official claim form is submitted within one year of indicating an intent to apply for a specific benefit, payments will begin when the original intent to apply was made apparent. There must be a record of the initial contact.[3]

A veteran who has applied for some type of VA benefits in the past has been assigned a "claim number," which should be used on the new claim; otherwise, the VA will assign a claim number at the time of application.

If the claim for benefits is based upon injury, illness, or disability where treatment or diagnosis did not occur at a VA facility or during military service, medical evidence should be included with the application. The statement or physician's report should be detailed and explain clearly the extent and severity of the disability.

Medical records of treatment or injury while in the military or at a VA hospital will be obtained by the VA if necessary for the application.[4] The VA also is to share information with the Social Security Administration (SSA) and is required to obtain from the SSA evidence relevant to a claim for VA benefits.[5] The agency will notify an applicant if additional evidence is needed to evaluate an application.

A claimant has the burden of "submitting evidence sufficient to justify a belief by a fair and impartial individual that the claim is well grounded."[6] The VA is required to assist a claimant discharge this burden. Where a reasonable doubt exists as to whether a claimant has discharged this burden, the doubt is to be resolved in favor of the claimant.[7] As a result, a claim should be allowed unless the preponderance of evidence is *against* the claim.[8]

The Court of Veteran's Appeals (CVA) has ruled that the VA is required to consider all relevant medical opinions and diagnoses before denying a claim for benefits.[9] Frequently, the VA's prior practice was

2. 38 C.F.R. § 3.155(c).

3. 38 C.F.R. §§ 3.109, 3.150, 3.400.

4. 38 C.F.R. § 3.200.

5. 38 C.F.R. §§ 3.153, 3.201(a).

6. 38 U.S.C.A. § 5107(a).

7. 38 U.S.C.A. § 5107(b); 38 C.F.R. § 3.102.

8. Gilbert v. Derwinski, 1 Vet.App. 49, 1990 WL 303138 (1990).

9. See, e.g., Godfrey v. Derwinski, 2 Vet.App. 352, 1992 WL 74912 (1992); Futch v. Derwinski, 2 Vet.App. 204, 1992 WL 30151 (1992); Sokowski v. Derwinski, 2 Vet.App. 75, 1991 WL 307255 (1991); Colvin v. Derwinski, 1 Vet.App. 171, 1991 WL 146392 (1991), *appeal after remand* 4 Vet. App. 132, 1993 WL 20431 (1992). See generally National Veterans Legal Services Project, Veterans Law Developments, 26 Clearinghouse Rev. 1043, 1046 (1993) for a

to rely on the agency's own experts in evaluating a claim and dismiss other medical opinions that were favorable to the claimant. Importantly, the CVA has held that the VA's own unsupported medical opinions rendered by Agency personnel lack evidentiary value and cannot be relied upon by the agency when denying benefits.[10] Hence, if the claimant presents medical evidence in support of his claim, the VA is precluded from countering that evidence with the agency's unsupported conclusions. Finally, the CVA held that a spouse's mere submission of lay evidence *could be sufficient* to support an agency finding of service-connection, where the spouse claimed that her husband, a World War II combat veteran, committed suicide as a result of post-traumatic stress disorder.[11]

§ 21.63 Applications for Medical Care

The basic application form for VA hospitalization is VA Form 10–10, Application for Medical Benefits, available at any VA office or hospital. This form certifies need for hospitalization or treatment and should be completed prior to admission. The office receiving the application will determine eligibility, and the hospital admitting the veteran will make the final determination regarding the need for medical care.

The VA can do a complete workup and preparation for hospitalization after the claimant is certified but prior to admission. Thirty days before the scheduled admission, VA personnel may conduct the prehospital workup, including necessary preoperation tests, examinations, X-rays, etc.[1]

In emergency cases, the veteran's doctor can arrange for hospitalization at a VA hospital. The doctor can request authority for admission of the patient and reimbursement of the expense necessary to bring the veteran to the hospital within 72 hours of the veteran's actual admission.[2] The VA usually permits a per-mile, one-way reimbursement when an ambulance is required for transporting a patient to the hospital.[3] A veteran already admitted into a non-VA hospital may not be admitted into a VA hospital on an emergency basis.

more complete discussion of the cases and holdings.

10. Futch v. Derwinski, 2 Vet.App. 204, 1992 WL 30151 (1992); Sokowski v. Derwinski, 2 Vet.App. 75, 1991 WL 307255 (1991).

11. Sheets v. Derwinski, 2 Vet.App. 512, 1992 WL 147362 (1992).

§ 21.63

1. 38 C.F.R. § 17.45(a).

2. 38 C.F.R. § 17.50d.

3. 38 C.F.R. § 17.80.

§ 21.64   Decisions on Claims for Benefits

Most claims for VA benefits are filed with a VA Regional Office (VARO). The process for deciding such claims varies with the nature of the claim, but most claims will be decided by the adjudication division of the VARO. The claimant and his or her representative will be notified of the decision on the claim. If the claim is denied, the VA is required to provide a statement of the reasons for the decision, a summary of evidence considered, a notice of the claimant's appeal rights.[1] If the decision is to reduce or terminate a veteran's DIC or pension benefits, advance notice of this decision must be given to the veteran. If the veteran appeals the decision within 30 days of the notice, benefits cannot be reduced or terminated until after a hearing is held and a decision rendered by the hearing officer.[2]

§ 21.65   Miscellaneous Issues Affecting VA Beneficiaries

A veteran who is receiving VA pension or compensation benefits may encounter actions by third parties or the VA intended to reduce or end his or her receipt of benefits. Creditors may, for example, seek to garnish VA benefits. Most creditors' claims are barred by 38 U.S.C.A. § 5301, "payments of benefits ... shall be exempt from the claim of creditors," but some courts have held that this provision does not preclude reaching VA benefits in the award of child support or alimony payments in a state divorce proceeding.[1]

The VA may conclude that a veteran has been overpaid and seek to recover the overpayment by reducing or terminating future benefits. As is true of a Social Security beneficiary faced with such a claim, a veteran may contest the conclusion that he or she has been overpaid and assert that recovery of the overpaid amount would be "against equity and good conscience."[2]

Although VA benefits generally are paid directly to the veteran, the VA may conclude that the "interest of the beneficiary would be served" by paying the benefit to the veteran's spouse or another person

---

§ 21.64

1. 38 U.S.C.A. § 5104; 38 C.F.R. § 3.103. The appeals process is described in §§ 21.71–.91, infra. See Veterans Benefits Manual, supra § 21.2 for details of handling VA benefit applications and appeals.

2. 38 C.F.R. §§ 3.103, 3.105(h).

§ 21.65

1. E.g. Murphy v. Murphy, 302 Ark. 157, 787 S.W.2d 684 (1990); Repash v. Re-

pash, 148 Vt. 70, 528 A.2d 744 (1987). See also Rose v. Rose, 481 U.S. 619, 107 S.Ct. 2029, 95 L.Ed.2d 599 (1987); Uniformed Services Former Spouses' Protection Act, 10 U.S.C.A. § 1408.

2. 38 U.S.C.A. § 5302; see also 38 C.F.R. §§ 1.963(b)(2), 3.103, 3.105.

because the veteran is incapable of handling the benefits.[3] A veteran's incapacity also may result in the appointment of a guardian or conservator for the veteran under state law.[4]

§§ 21.66–21.70 are reserved for supplementary material.

G. APPEALING VETERANS' ADMINISTRATION DECISION AND VETERANS' JUDICIAL REVIEW ACT OF 1988

Library References:

C.J.S. Armed Services § 262.

West's Key No. Digests, Armed Services ⊷130, 136, 150.

§ 21.71 Initial Review of Adverse VA Decision

Upon notification of an adverse VA decision, the claimant has one year to file a notice of disagreement.[1] Failure to timely file the notice results in the VA decision becoming final. No formal language is required in the notice, but the notice should express that the claimant wishes to have the decision reviewed.[2] It should be sent, along with any supporting evidence, to the regional office that issued the adverse decision.

The claimant's attorney or authorized representative may file the appeal on the claimant's behalf.[3] A claimant who is incompetent may have a notice filed by a guardian or conservator or, in the absence of a fiduciary, by next of kin or a friend.[4]

The Adjudication Division of the regional office reviews the facts and evidence submitted by the claimant. If the claimant has satisfied the burden of submitting the necessary quantum of evidence to show that the claim is well grounded, the VA has an obligation to assist the claimant in developing facts pertinent to the claim.[5]

After completion of the review, the regional office may reverse, revise, or uphold the initial decision. If the initial decision is upheld, a statement of the case is prepared and sent to the claimant and repre-

---

3. 38 U.S.C.A. § 5502; 38 C.F.R. §§ 13.1–13.111.

4. See Uniform Veterans Guardianship Act (U.L.A.) §§ 1–24 (1942) which has been adopted by about ¾ of the states. For a listing of those states, see the Table of Jurisdictions Adopting the 1942 Act. (WESTLAW: ULA database, **ci(veterans /1 guardianship)**).

§ 21.71

1. 38 C.F.R. § 20.302(a).

2. 38 C.F.R. § 20.201.

3. 38 C.F.R. § 20.301(a).

4. 38 C.F.R. § 20.301(b).

5. 38 U.S.C.A. § 5107(a).

sentative.[6] The statement summarizes the decision and includes pertinent facts, applicable laws or regulations, and any other criteria upon which the decision is based. Included with the statement of the case is VA Form 1–9, Appeal to the Board of Veterans Appeals.[7]

§ 21.72 Substantive Appeal From Adverse VA Decision

After receiving the statement of the case, the claimant may file for a substantive appeal.[1] A substantive appeal must be initiated within 60 days of the receipt of the statement of the case or within the remainder of the one-year period beginning with the receipt of initial notice of determination.[2]

VA Form 1–9 must be used for a substantive appeal request and should be mailed to the regional office, which will forward the request to the Board of Veterans Appeals.[3] In the form for appeal, it is important to contest any statement by the VA that the claimant believes to be incorrect, since the BVA considers statements correct if the claimant does not object to them.[4] Specific allegations of error or fact should be identified, as should an error in the application of law. The regional office reviews the case before sending it to the BVA to determine if the claimant has brought in any new evidence or facts upon which the regional office may revise its decision.[5]

The Board of Veterans' Appeals ("BVA") is authorized to: exercise appellate jurisdiction over VA decisions [6]; remand claims where necessary for further agency development of the record [7]; conduct hearings; evaluate evidence; and enter written decisions on issues presented in appeals.[8]

The BVA's jurisdiction is expansive. It can decide "[a]ll questions of law and fact necessary to a decision by the Secretary ... under a law that affects the provision of benefits by the Secretary to veterans [and others entitled to benefits] ...".[9] In addition to following applicable statutes and regulations, the BVA is bound by precedent opinions of the General Counsel of the Department of Veterans Affairs.[10] The BVA is

---

6. 38 C.F.R. §§ 19.26–19.29.

7. 38 C.F.R. § 19.30.

§ 21.72

1. 38 C.F.R. §§ 20.200, 20.202.

2. 38 C.F.R. § 20.302(b).

3. 38 C.F.R. § 20.300.

4. 38 C.F.R. § 20.202.

5. 38 C.F.R. §§ 19.35–19.37.

6. 38 U.S.C.A. §§ 7101–7110; 38 C.F.R. § 20.101 defines the jurisdiction of the

BVA, BVA rules are codified at 38 C.F.R. Part 19, entitled, "Board of Veterans' Appeals: Appeals Regulations," and Part 20, entitled, "Board of Veterans' Appeals: Rules of Practice."

7. 38 C.F.R. § 19.38.

8. 38 C.F.R. § 19.4.

9. 38 C.F.R. § 20.101.

10. 38 C.F.R. § 20.101(a).

not bound by Department manuals or administrative circulars.[11]   The BVA's appellate jurisdiction also extends to issues of a claimant's eligibility or hospitalization, outpatient treatment, and nursing home and domicillary care, as well as whether a claimant is entitled to certain health related devices.[12]   Other examples of the BVA's jurisdiction are set out in the regulation.[13]   The BVA lacks authority, however, to review medical determinations or whether certain medical care is appropriate.[14]

If the appellant or his representative desire a hearing, one will be granted.[15]   The hearings are structured to be non-adversarial in nature.[16]   Unless good cause is shown, a personal hearing will not be granted solely for the purpose of the representative presenting an oral argument.[17]   The rules also allow oral argument to be presented on audio tape.[18]   The appellant has a right to a hearing before the BVA's traveling board.[19]

The appellant can present witness testimony, but such testimony must be under oath.[20]   When necessary, the appellant can move the BVA to issue a subpoena to compel the attendance of a witness(es) residing within 100 miles of the place for the hearing.[21]   The subpoena can likewise be used to compel the production of tangible evidence.[22]   If during the hearing it is determined that additional evidence would be helpful, the presiding Member may direct that the record be left opened for not longer than 60 days so that additional evidence can be obtained.[23]

BVA decisions are to be based on the entire record.[24]   Decisions must be in writing and must set forth the issues under consideration; the decisions also must include separately stated findings of fact and conclusions of law on all material issues of fact and law presented in the record.[25]   The decision must also include the reasons or bases for its findings and conclusions.[26]   The BVA is required to mail its decision to all parties and representatives.[27]

11. 38 C.F.R. § 19.5.

12. 38 C.F.R. § 20.101(b).

13. 38 C.F.R. § 20.101(a).

14. 38 C.F.R. § 20.101(b).

15. 38 C.F.R. § 20.700(a).

16. 38 C.F.R. § 20.700(c).

17. 38 C.F.R. § 20.700(b).

18. Id. See 38 C.F.R. § 20.700(d).

19. 38 C.F.R. §§ 20.703 and 20.704.

20. 38 C.F.R. § 20.710.

21. 38 C.F.R. § 20.711.

22. Id.

23. 38 C.F.R. § 20.709.

24. 38 C.F.R. § 19.7(a).

25. 38 C.F.R. § 19.7(b).

26. Id.

27. 38 C.F.R. § 19.8.

§ 21.73 Appeal From Adverse BVA Decision—Introduction

If after review of the VA disposition the BVA issues an adverse decision, the claimant has three options. First, the claimant can reopen the case if new and material evidence arises. Second, the claimant can request the BVA to reconsider its decision. Third, if jurisdictional requirements are satisfied, the claimant can appeal to the Court of Veterans' Appeals.[1]

§ 21.74 Appeal From Adverse BVA Decision—Reopening Claim

Where the BVA renders an adverse decision, the claimant has a statutory right to request that the case be reopened "if new and material evidence is presented or secured with respect to a claim."[1] Evidence is "new" when the evidence is not merely cumulative of evidence existing in the record.[2] Evidence is "material" when there is a reasonable chance that when the "new" evidence is considered in the context of the existing evidence, the disposition might change.[3] If the BVA determines that the evidence is new and material to the claim, the finality of the decision is removed, and the BVA can review the entire record and make new factual determinations regarding the case.[4]

§ 21.75 Appeal From Adverse BVA Decision—Reconsideration of Claim

The Veterans' Judicial Review Act of 1988 (VJRA) affirmed prior BVA practice of permitting the BVA to reconsider decisions.[1] The regulations at 38 C.F.R. §§ 20.1000 through 20.1003, which existed prior to the VJRA and are currently in force, detail the procedure for initiating BVA reconsideration. The regulations state that reconsideration may be accorded at any time upon an allegation of obvious error of fact or law, or upon discovery of new and material evidence.[2]

Library References:

C.J.S. Armed Services § 263.
West's Key No. Digests, Armed Services ☞134.

§ 21.73

1. This third alternative regarding the Court of Veterans Appeals and the Veterans' Judicial Review Act of 1988 is discussed in § 21.76.

§ 21.74

1. 38 U.S.C.A. § 5108. See also 38 U.S.C.A. § 7104(b) and 38 C.F.R. § 19.194.

2. See, e.g., Colvin v. Derwinski, 1 Vet. App. 171, 1991 WL 146392 (1991), *appeal*

after remand 4 Vet.App. 132, 1993 WL 20431 (1992).

3. See, e.g., Smith v. Derwinski, 1 Vet. App. 178, 1991 WL 148047 (1991).

4. Thompson v. Derwinski, 1 Vet.App. 251, 1991 WL 146472 (1991).

§ 21.75

1. 38 U.S.C.A. § 7103(a).

2. 38 C.F.R. § 19.185(a) & (b). See 38 C.F.R. § 3.156.

§ 21.76   Overview of Veterans' Judicial Review Act of 1988

In creating "a court of record to be known as the United States Court of Veterans' Appeals"[1] (CVA), Congress provided access to the federal judiciary for claimants who are seeking federal appellate court review of an adverse decision by the Board of Veterans Appeals (BVA).[2] This article I court,[3] which has exclusive jurisdiction to review decisions of the BVA,[4] was established in the Veterans' Judicial Review Act of 1988 (VJRA).[5] Furthermore, recognizing that access alone was not sufficient under the system as it then existed, Congress provided an attorney fee provision that replaced an antiquated 1862 provision, which prohibited an attorney from charging a fee of more than $10.

Library References:

C.J.S. Armed Services § 262.

West's Key No. Digests, Armed Services ⌐150.

§ 21.77   Appeal Requirements

The persons who can appeal an adverse BVA decision to the CVA are limited. The Veterans Administration (the Secretary) cannot seek judicial review at the CVA.[1] The fact that the Secretary is precluded from appealing to the CVA reveals that Congress intended judicial review to benefit only claimants. A BVA decision must "adversely affect" the claimant before the claimant can appeal to the CVA.[2] A partially successful claimant can appeal to the CVA.

A claimant can appeal only a final BVA decision.[3] Apparently, if the BVA remands a case, that decision is not "final" within the meaning of the statute and cannot be appealed to the CVA.

§ 21.76

1. 38 U.S.C.A. §§ 7251–7298.

2. For an analysis of the VJRA, see generally Stichman, The Veterans' Judicial Review Act of 1988: Congress Introduces Courts and Attorneys to Veterans' Benefits Proceedings, 23 Clearinghouse Rev. 506 (1989).

3. Unlike the judges in an article III court, where judges and justices are appointed for life unless impeached, the CVA judges are appointed for a 15–year term, 38 U.S.C.A. § 7253(c); and the President may remove a CVA judge only on the grounds of misconduct, neglect of duty, or for engaging in the practice of law, 38 U.S.C.A.

§ 7253(f)(1). Similar to the practice in an article III court, the President, with the advise and consent of the Senate, appoints the CVA judges. 38 U.S.C.A. § 7253(b).

4. 38 U.S.C.A. § 7252(a).

5. Veterans' Judicial Review Act of 1988, Pub.L. No. 100–687, 102 Stat. 4105 (1988).

§ 21.77

1. 38 U.S.C.A. § 7252.

2. 38 U.S.C.A. § 7266(a).

3. 38 U.S.C.A. § 7266(a). However, the All Writs Act affects the final decision requirement.

§ 21.78 Final Decisions and All Writs Act

The All Writs Act provides that courts Congress establishes "may issue all writs necessary or appropriate in aid of their respective jurisdiction and agreeable to the usages and principles of law." [1] This is an exception to the "final decision" requirement, since the act, when used in conjunction with the VJRA,[2] permits the CVA to entertain motions from claimants who seek such a writ. The Rules of Practice and Procedure must be followed when a claimant requests the CVA to issue a writ.[3]

In *Erspamer v. Derwinski*,[4] the CVA held that its power pursuant to the All Writs Act is appropriate where "an alleged refusal to act would forever frustrate the ability of a court to exercise its appellate jurisdiction." [5] There are two requirements a claimant must satisfy before a writ can be issued: (1) the claimant must be "clearly entitled" to the writ's issuance; and (2) the claimant must not have other adequate means to achieve relief.[6] Hence, the CVA has the authority to issue a writ compelling the VA or the BVA to take action the CVA considers appropriate, notwithstanding the fact that the VA or BVA's decision is not final.

§ 21.79 Appeal Process—United States Court of Veterans' Appeals Rules of Practice and Procedure

The Rules of Practice and Procedure govern proceedings before the CVA.[1] Except for appropriate modifications, the rules the CVA ultimately adopted are based largely on the Federal Rules of Appellate Procedure.[2]

Library References:

C.J.S. Armed Services § 262.

West's Key No. Digests, Armed Services ⚖155.

§ 21.78

1. 28 U.S.C.A. § 1651(a). The All Writs Act applies to article I courts. See Noyd v. Bond, 395 U.S. 683, 695 n. 7 (1969).

2. See 38 U.S.C.A. § 7265(b), which permits the CVA to use writs that other United States courts are empowered to use.

3. Court of Veterans Appeals, Rules of Practice and Procedure, Rule 21.

4. Erspamer v. Derwinski, 1 Vet.App. 3, 1990 WL 303127 (1990) (WESTLAW: **fi 1 vet app 3**).

5. Erspamer v. Derwinski, 1 Vet.App. 3, 8, 1990 WL 303127 (1990).

6. Erspamer v. Derwinski, 1 Vet.App. 3, 9, 1990 WL 303127 (1990).

§ 21.79

1. 38 U.S.C.A. § 7264(a).

2. Rules of Practice & Procedure (U.S.Vet.App. Apr. 4, 1991) (order). A copy of the rules can be found in the Appendix of the volume containing 38 U.S.C.A. § 7101 et seq.

§ 21.80 Appeal Process—Notice of Disagreement

Before the CVA can exercise jurisdiction over a claimant's case, the claimant must have filed, on or after November 18, 1988, a notice of disagreement with the VA Regional Office.[1] This notice must have been filed within one year from the date the BVA mailed notice of the result to the claimant.[2] The claimant or other representative, such as an attorney, may file the notice, which must be in writing.[3]

If a notice of disagreement was filed before November 18, 1988, the claimant's case is not within the jurisdiction of CVA. However, under certain situations, a claimant who has a final decision issued before the November 18, 1988, deadline may be within the CVA's jurisdiction. If the claimant presents "new and material evidence" regarding the case, the "Secretary shall reopen the claim and review the former disposition of the claim."[4] First, if the BVA refuses to reopen the case, the CVA can review the BVA's denial under the arbitrary and capricious standard of review and remand the case.[5] Second, if the BVA determines either initially or after remand from the CVA that the claimant's case should be reopened because of "new and material evidence," the CVA can review the BVA's second denial of benefits if the claimant initiates an appeal.[6]

§ 21.81 Appeal Process—Notice of Appeal

In addition to the notice of disagreement requirement, the claimant must file a notice of appeal with the CVA.[1] The claimant also must provide the Secretary of Veterans Affairs with a copy of the notice,[2] although failure to provide the Secretary with a copy will not deprive the CVA of jurisdiction.[3] The notice must be filed with the CVA within 120 days after the BVA mailed its final decision to the claimant.[4] There is a $50 filing fee that must accompany the notice of appeal.[5] However, if the fee requirement would cause "hardship" to the claim-

§ 21.80

1. 38 U.S.C.A. § 7105.

2. 38 U.S.C.A. § 7105(b)(1).

3. 38 U.S.C.A. § 7105(b)(2).

4. 38 U.S.C.A. § 5108.

5. Manio v. Derwinski, 1 Vet.App. 140, 1991 WL 146378 (1991) (WESTLAW: **fi 1 vet app 140**). For the scope of review, see 38 U.S.C.A. § 7261(a)(1)–(3). For scope of review discussion, see § 21.85.

6. Manio v. Derwinski, 1 Vet.App. 140, 1991 WL 146378 (1991). See also Morris v. Derwinski, 1 Vet.App. 260, 1991 WL 146477 (1991) (WESTLAW: **fi 1 vet app 260**).

§ 21.81

1. 38 U.S.C.A. § 7266(a); Rules of Practice and Procedure, Rule 3(a).

2. Rules of Practice and Procedure, Rule 3(b).

3. 38 U.S.C.A. § 7266(b).

4. 38 U.S.C.A. § 7266(a); Rules of Practice and Procedure, Rule 4.

5. 38 U.S.C.A. § 7262(a).

ant, the fee may be waived.[6] The clerk of the court is under a duty to notify all parties of the date the clerk received the notice of appeal.[7]

The notice of appeal "shall" contain the name of the party taking appeal, designate the Board decision appealed from, and include the claimant's address and the address of the claimant's representative, if any.[8] The appendix to the Rules of Practice and Procedure contains a notice of appeal form that the Rules suggest that claimants follow, but a claimant's notice will not be dismissed for mere "informality." Rule 3(c) is liberal in that it permits a notice of appeal to be "filed by facsimile or other printed electronic transmission."

§ 21.82 Appeal Process—Claimant's and Secretary's Duties Once Notice of Appeal Is Filed

After the clerk of the CVA sends notice to the claimant that the court received the notice of appeal, the claimant must file with the CVA and the Secretary a "brief statement of the issue or issues to be raised on appeal."[1]

Thirty days after the claimant files the statement of the issues, the Secretary is under a duty to file with the CVA clerk "a designation of all materials in the record of proceedings before the Secretary and the Board which the Secretary considers relevant to the appeal."[2] The Secretary must serve the claimant with the same materials and provide a list of any materials the Secretary cannot duplicate.

Thirty days after the Secretary provides the materials, the claimant is required to file with the clerk a counterdesignation of any "additional" materials the claimant considers relevant, or a declaration that the claimant agrees with the material the Secretary supplied to the claimant and the clerk. The claimant is to give a copy to the Secretary of any material sent to the clerk. If the claimant does not respond to the materials the Secretary served, a conclusive presumption arises that the claimant agrees with the Secretary's designation of the record.

If the claimant's counterdesignation states that material exists that is not in the claimant's possession, the Secretary must supply, within

---

6. 38 U.S.C.A. § 7262(a). See also Rules of Practice and Procedure, Rule 3(e), Rule 24, and in the Appendix of Forms, Form 4.

7. Court of Veterans Appeals Rules of Practice and Procedure, Rule 4.

8. Court of Veterans Appeals Rules of Practice and Procedure, Rule 3.

§ 21.82

1. Court of Veterans Appeals Rules of Practice and Procedure, Rule 6. The claimant is to follow Rule 25 for service requirements and Rule 26(a) for computation of filing time.

2. Court of Veterans Appeals Rules of Practice and Procedure, Rule 10.

fourteen days after the filing of the counterdesignation, a copy of those materials.

The Secretary is under a duty to send to the clerk, within thirty days after the claimant has filed the counterdesignation, the record on appeal.[3] After the record on appeal is transmitted, all parties will receive a copy. If a party believes the record on appeal is not complete, provision is made to supplement the record. Any corrective action must take place within thirty days after the record has been filed with the clerk.

After receiving the record on appeal, the clerk must immediately notify the parties of the date on which the record was filed.[4]

§ 21.83 Appeal Process—Miscellaneous

The CVA may order the parties to engage in a prehearing conference, which may take place in person or by telephone.[1]

The CVA may order, or a party can request, an oral argument.[2]

§ 21.84 Representation

An attorney is permitted to represent a claimant before the CVA if the attorney is a "person of good moral character and repute" and is generally licensed to practice in another jurisdiction.[1] The attorney is required to file an application with the CVA.

If certain conditions are satisfied, a nonattorney who is not a law student but who is a person of "good moral character and repute" can practice before the CVA.[2] Such a nonattorney will be allowed to represent a claimant under two situations: (1) if the nonattorney is under the direct supervision of an attorney admitted to practice before the court; or (2) if the nonattorney is employed by an organization chartered by Congress and recognized by the Secretary of Veterans Affairs for claims representation.

A law student who has completed at least four semesters of law school work and who attends a law school accredited by the American

3. Court of Veterans Appeals Rules of Practice and Procedure, Rule 11(a).

4. Court of Veterans Appeals Rules of Practice and Procedure, Rule 12(b).

§ 21.83

1. Court of Veterans Appeals Rules of Practice and Procedure, Rule 33(a).

2. Court of Veterans Appeals Rules of Practice and Procedure, Rule 34(a).

§ 21.84

1. Court of Veterans Appeals Rules of Practice and Procedure, Rule 46(a)(1).

2. Court of Veterans Appeals Rules of Practice and Procedure, Rule 46(b).

Bar Association may assist the attorney of record in the representation of a claimant.[3]

Library References:

C.J.S. Armed Services § 262.

West's Key No. Digests, Armed Services ⊯164.

§ 21.85   Scope of Review

The scope of the CVA's review over BVA decisions is governed by 38 U.S.C.A. § 7261. Where issues of law are concerned, the CVA can disregard the BVA's decision if that decision is "arbitrary, capricious, an abuse of discretion, or otherwise not in accordance with law." Further, if the BVA's decision of law does not comply with the Constitution or with any statute, or if it violates a procedure required by law, the CVA can overturn the BVA's decision. The CVA is to employ the "clearly erroneous" standard of review when a "finding of material fact made in reaching a decision" is at issue. The CVA, in *Gilbert v. Derwinski,* stated that a lower tribunal decision of fact is clearly erroneous "when although there is evidence to support [the decision], the reviewing court on the entire evidence is left with a definite and firm conviction that a mistake has been committed." [1] The CVA has applied the clearly erroneous standard in a number of cases.[2]

Where a question of fact is involved, the CVA is not permitted to engage in a trial *de novo.*[3] In its examination of the record, the CVA is limited to the record produced before the BVA and the Secretary.[4] However, if the CVA determines that the Secretary violated the statutory provision requiring the Secretary to "assist such a claimant in developing facts pertinent to the claim," [5] the CVA may order a remand

---

3. Court of Veterans Appeals Rules of Practice and Procedure, Rule (e)(1)–(3).

§ 21.85

1. Vet.App.1990, 1 Vet.App. 49, 1990 WL 303138 (1990) (quoting Anderson v. City of Bessemer City, 470 U.S. 564, 573–74, 105 S.Ct. 1504, ——, 84 L.Ed.2d 518 (1985)).

2. See, e.g. Moore v. Derwinski, 1 Vet. App. 356, 1991 WL 146533 (1991) (WESTLAW: **fi 1 vet app 356**) (a determination on the degrees of disability is a question of fact requiring the clearly erroneous standard); Mense v. Derwinski, 1 Vet.App. 354, 1991 WL 146531 (1991) (WESTLAW: **fi 1 vet app 354**) (question of cause of lower-back disorder is question of fact and subject to clearly erroneous standard); Hillyard v. Derwinski, 1 Vet.App. 349, 1991 WL 146528 (1991) (WESTLAW: **fi 1 vet app 349**) (degree of impairment of disability is question of fact and subject to clearly erroneous standard); Green v. Derwinski, 1 Vet.App. 320, 1991 WL 146507 (1991) (WESTLAW: **fi 1 vet app 320**) (whether claimant's disease worsened in service is question of fact subject to clearly erroneous standard).

3. 38 U.S.C.A. § 7261(c).

4. 38 U.S.C.A. § 7252(b).

5. 38 U.S.C.A. § 5107(a).

and compel the Secretary to develop the record more fully before an appellate determination will take place.[6]

§ 21.86 Appealing Final CVA Decision

Pursuant to 38 U.S.C.A. § 7292, the United States Court of Appeals for the Federal Circuit has exclusive jurisdiction to exercise appellate review over CVA decisions. In addition to a claimant being able to seek federal court review, the statute provides that "any party to a case may obtain review." Thus, the Secretary can seek review of an adverse CVA decision. A party seeking review in the Court of Appeals must file a notice of appeal with the CVA, and the party must follow the Federal Rules of Appellate Procedure for appeals from district courts to the Court of Appeals.

The Court of Appeals is empowered to "decide all relevant questions of law ... and shall hold unlawful and set aside any regulation or any interpretation thereof (other than a determination as to a factual matter)" upon which the CVA relied. The scope of review for questions of law is the arbitrary, capricious, abuse of discretion, and not in accordance with law standard. The court also can strike a CVA decision of law if that decision is contrary to the Constitution, if it violates a statute, or if it is not in accordance with the procedure required by law.

The Court of Appeals is precluded from reviewing any factual determination (unless a constitutional issue is presented), or any challenge to the application of a law or regulation to the facts of a particular case.[1]

Library References:

C.J.S. Armed Services § 283.

West's Key No. Digests, Armed Services ⚷169.

§ 21.87 Fees—For Representation Before BVA

If the Secretary regards an attorney or agent as capable of handling a claimant's case and the person is of good moral character and in

---

6. See, e.g. EF v. Derwinski, 1 Vet.App. 324, 1991 WL 146511 (1991) (WESTLAW: fi 1 vet app 324); Manio v. Derwinski, 1 Vet.App. 140, 1991 WL 146378 (1991) (WESTLAW: fi 1 vet app 140); Akles v. Derwinski, 1 Vet.App. 118, 1991 WL 146359 (1991) (WESTLAW: fi 1 vet app 118); Murphy v. Derwinski, 1 Vet.App. 78, 1990 WL 303142 (1990) (WESTLAW: fi 1 vet app 78); Jolley v. Derwinski, 1 Vet. App. 37, 1990 WL 303136 (1990) (WESTLAW: fi 1 vet app 37).

§ 21.86

1. 38 U.S.C.A. § 7292(d)(2); Fugere v. Derwinski, 972 F.2d 331 (Fed.Cir.1992).

good repute,[1] the VJRA allows that person to collect a fee. An attorney or agent qualified to receive a fee must file with the BVA a copy of the fee agreement.[2] The BVA has the authority to review the agreement on its own motion or at the request of any party, and the BVA may reduce the fee if it is "unreasonable or excessive."[3] The BVA's conclusion as to the reasonableness of the agreement is reviewable by the CVA.[4]

The attorney or agent cannot collect a fee for services rendered before the date on which the BVA first makes a final decision in the case.[5] However, the attorney or agent is allowed to charge a fee for services rendered thereafter so long as the claimant retained the attorney or agent before the end of the one-year period beginning on the date the BVA made its first final decision.[6]

§ 21.88 Fees—For Representation Before CVA

The VJRA permits attorneys or "other persons to practice before the Court who meet standards of proficiency"[1] to charge a claimant for services. The representative must file a "copy of any fee agreement between the appellant and that person with the court at the time the appeal is filed."[2] Hence, an oral agreement about the fee must be reduced to writing. The CVA, either *sua sponte* or on the motion of any party, may review that agreement and "may order a reduction in the fee ... if it finds that the fee is excessive or unreasonable."[3] Any determination of the CVA regarding the fee is conclusive.[4]

§ 21.89 Fees—Limitations

If a contingent fee agreement requires the Veterans Administration to pay the agent or attorney directly from the past-due benefits, the total fee that the agent or attorney can receive under the agreement cannot exceed twenty percent of the total amount of past-due benefits to which the claimant is entitled.[1] The twenty percent limit does not apply to situations in which the claimant pays the attorney or agent, but in such a case, the fee cannot be unreasonable or excessive.

§ 21.87

1. 38 U.S.C.A. § 5904(a).

2. 38 U.S.C.A. § 5904(c)(2).

3. 38 U.S.C.A. § 5904(c)(2).

4. 38 U.S.C.A. § 5904(c)(2).

5. 38 U.S.C.A. § 5904(c)(1).

6. 38 U.S.C.A. § 5904(c)(1).

§ 21.88

1. 38 U.S.C.A. § 7263(b).

2. 38 U.S.C.A. § 7263(c).

3. 38 U.S.C.A. § 7263(d).

4. 38 U.S.C.A. § 7263(d).

§ 21.89

1. 38 U.S.C.A. § 5904(d)(1) and (d)(2)(A).

§ 21.90   Fees—Where Notice of Disagreement Was Filed Before November 18, 1988

If the claimant filed the notice of disagreement prior to November 18, 1988, the attorney fee provision of VJRA may not be applicable; if not, the fee charged cannot exceed $10.[1] If, however, the claimant seeks to reopen the claim by presenting or securing new and material evidence, the new fee provisions apply as long as the claimant refiles a notice of disagreement [2] and abides by the other statutory and regulatory requirements.

§ 21.91   Equal Access to Justice Act

In 1980, Congress enacted the Equal Access to Justice Act ("EAJA"),[1] which provides in part that "a court shall award to a prevailing party . . . fees and other expenses" that the party incurred in a civil suit, "including proceedings for judicial review of agency action" brought against the United States, "unless the court finds that the position of the United States was substantially justified or that special circumstances make an award unjust." [2] Although VJRA's legislative history confirms that Congress intended the EAJA to apply to CVA proceedings,[3] the CVA held that the Act does not apply to proceedings before it.[4] The CVA's position was overruled by the Federal Courts Administration Act of 1992 which amended the EAJA to clarify that costs and fees are available for representation before the CVA.[5]

Library References:

C.J.S. United States §§ 136, 209.

West's Key No. Digests, United States ☜93, 147(20).

§ 21.90

1. 38 U.S.C.A. §§ 3404 & 3405.

2. See discussion at § 21.74, supra.

§ 21.91

1. 28 U.S.C.A. § 2412. See generally 2 Wildhaber, Abrams, Stichman & Addlestone, Veterans Benefits Manual at § 10.3 for a discussion of the EAJA. See also §§ 15.137–15.145, supra.

2. 28 U.S.C.A. § 2412(d)(1)(A).

3. 134 Cong.Rec.Sec. 16650 (daily ed. Oct. 18, 1988); 134 Cong.Rec. H10361 (daily ed. Oct. 19, 1988).

4. Jones v. Derwinski, 2 Vet.App. 231, 1992 WL 50903 (1992), vacated by Jones v. Principi, 985 F.2d 582 (Fed.Cir.1992).

5. Pub.L.No. 102–572, §§ 301(a), 502(b), 506(a), 106 Stat. 4511–4313, amending 28 U.S.C.A. § 2412(d)(2)(F).

§ 21.92   Veterans' Benefits Process—Chart

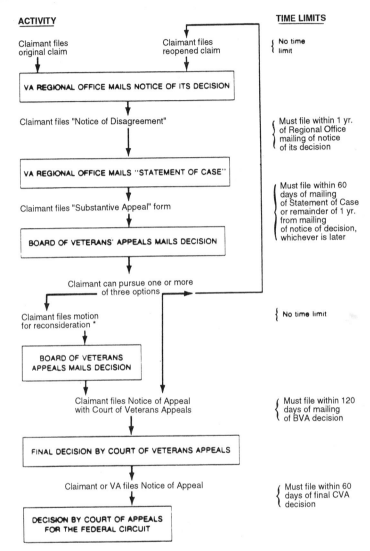

ACTIVITY

TIME LIMITS

Claimant files original claim   Claimant files reopened claim   { No time limit

VA REGIONAL OFFICE MAILS NOTICE OF ITS DECISION

Claimant files "Notice of Disagreement"   { Must file within 1 yr. of Regional Office mailing of notice of its decision

VA REGIONAL OFFICE MAILS "STATEMENT OF CASE"

Claimant files "Substantive Appeal" form   { Must file within 60 days of mailing of Statement of Case or remainder of 1 yr. from mailing of notice of decision, whichever is later

BOARD OF VETERANS' APPEALS MAILS DECISION

Claimant can pursue one or more of three options

Claimant files motion for reconsideration *   { No time limit

BOARD OF VETERANS APPEALS MAILS DECISION

Claimant files Notice of Appeal with Court of Veterans Appeals   { Must file within 120 days of mailing of BVA decision

FINAL DECISION BY COURT OF VETERANS APPEALS

Claimant or VA files Notice of Appeal   { Must file within 60 days of final CVA decision

DECISION BY COURT OF APPEALS FOR THE FEDERAL CIRCUIT

*However, if motion for reconsideration is filed within 120 days of the BVA decision, the appellant gets a fresh 120-day period in which to file a notice of appeal when the BVA notifies the appellant of its decision on the reconsideration issue.

[G13790]

§ **21.93** Court of Veterans' Appeals Process—Chart

MAJOR FILINGS   TIME LIMITS

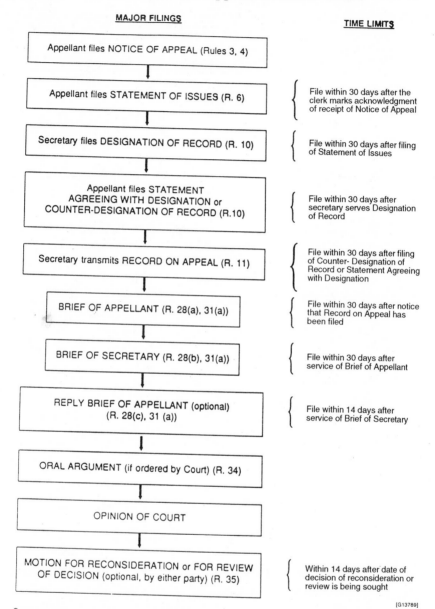

Appellant files NOTICE OF APPEAL (Rules 3, 4)

Appellant files STATEMENT OF ISSUES (R. 6)
    File within 30 days after the clerk marks acknowledgment of receipt of Notice of Appeal

Secretary files DESIGNATION OF RECORD (R. 10)
    File within 30 days after filing of Statement of Issues

Appellant files STATEMENT AGREEING WITH DESIGNATION or COUNTER-DESIGNATION OF RECORD (R.10)
    File within 30 days after secretary serves Designation of Record

Secretary transmits RECORD ON APPEAL (R. 11)
    File within 30 days after filing of Counter- Designation of Record or Statement Agreeing with Designation

BRIEF OF APPELLANT (R. 28(a), 31(a))
    File within 30 days after notice that Record on Appeal has been filed

BRIEF OF SECRETARY (R. 28(b), 31(a))
    File within 30 days after service of Brief of Appellant

REPLY BRIEF OF APPELLANT (optional) (R. 28(c), 31 (a))
    File within 14 days after service of Brief of Secretary

ORAL ARGUMENT (if ordered by Court) (R. 34)

OPINION OF COURT

MOTION FOR RECONSIDERATION or FOR REVIEW OF DECISION (optional, by either party) (R. 35)
    Within 14 days after date of decision of reconsideration or review is being sought

[G13789]

CHAPTER 22

HOME OWNERSHIP

Table of Sections

A. GENERALLY

263

WESTLAW Electronic Research

See WESTLAW Electronic Research Guide preceding the Summary of Contents.

A. GENERALLY

§ 22.1 Introduction

The majority of older persons prefer to and are able to, live independently.[1] This majority includes individuals fully capable of living independently and others who require some assistance in daily housekeeping chores, home maintenance, transportation, and medical care. An independent living environment best serves the psychological well-being of individuals.[2] Increasingly, both private and governmental agency policy is emphasizing *aging in place*.

Unfortunately, the range of choices of housing may be severely limited by unavailability of financial and housing resources. For renters, the existing stock of low-income subsidized housing and affordable unsubsidized rental units is shrinking.[3] Likewise, displacement of the elderly caused by public projects, forced transfer, public or private disinvestment, and private reinvestment may force hasty relocation decisions.[4] Chapter 19, supra, deals with government assistance programs for renters. Utility assistance for both renters and home owners is explained in §§ 22.25–.26, infra. Chapter 4, supra, deals with federally created rights of tenants and home owners against discrimination which particularly affects older persons in both publicly assisted and

---

§ 22.1

1. In 1990, 86% of people aged 60 and older who were surveyed by Market Facts, Inc., for the American Association of Retired Persons reported they would like to stay in their present homes. Over one-fourth of these older people lived alone, and most of the others lived with a spouse. Survey responses indicated that 59% of persons over age 55 owned their homes without mortgage debt, and another 23% owned mortgaged homes. Only 17% were renters, and only 5% lived in a retirement community or complex designed for the elderly. "Understanding Senior Housing for the 1990s." (AARP 1990).

In 1984, approximately 12,500,000 homes were owned by persons over 65 years of age, 80% of those clear of mortgage, Staff of Senate Special Comm. on Aging, 98th Cong., 2d Sess., Turning Home Equity Into Income For Older Homeowners 1 (S. Print 216, 1984). See generally, Hoeflich, Housing the Elderly in a Changing America: Innovation Through Private Sector Initiative, 1985 Univ. of Ill.L.R. 1, 3 (1985).

2. P. Barnett & J. McKenzie, Alternative Mortgage Instruments, § 8.01 (1984).

3. See generally, Simons, Toward a New National Housing Policy, 6 Yale Law & Policy Review, 259, 270–71 (1988).

4. See Comment, Displacement of the Elderly: Policies and Strategies to Combat an Old Problem, 16 Gonzaga L.R. 723 (1981).

private housing. There is no attempt in this book to summarize landlord and tenant law. For particular issues, such as those affecting rental conversions to condominiums, the attorney should determine whether there is special city or state legislation to protect tenants, particularly elderly tenants, from eviction.[5]

Deciding on the most suitable living arrangement for an older person should not take place when a crisis forces the decision. Forced choices may be detrimental financially, psychologically, and physically to the older person. Long-range planning is the key to the provision of suitable living arrangements. A periodic review of an older person's living arrangement, as well as future needs, is imperative. The attorney should consider the present financial, physical, and social needs and should project what these needs will be three, five, and ten years down the road.

The attorney should be knowledgeable not only about the legal matters discussed in this chapter, but also about social and community resources available in the local area for older persons. Increasingly, governmental and private social programs are developing a wide variety of public and private programs to help persons age in place. The Area Agency on Aging is likely to be the most efficient source of directories and referrals for benefits and services ranging from personal care to psychological counseling to meals on wheels to utility assistance to transportation to home weatherizing. Equipped with this information, the attorney can summarize the choices and the client can make an informed decision on what, if any, changes should be made in his or her present living arrangement. This chapter deals with issues related to home ownership.

§§ 22.2–22.10 are reserved for supplementary material.

B. OWNERSHIP HOUSING

§ 22.11   Fee Simple Home Ownership—In General

Many older persons reside in houses they have owned for several years[1] where they desire to remain indefinitely. Owning a home has

---

5. For example, New Jersey law requires a three-year notice for all tenants and protects certain older or disabled tenants from eviction for a 40-year period! See, N.J.S.A. 2A:18–61.1 and 2A:18–61.22 et seq., described in Meiser, Senior Citizens and Condo Conversions, New Jersey Lawyer 26 (Winter 1985).

§ 22.11

1. According to "A Profile of Older Americans: 1990" (American Association of Retired Persons 1990), 19.5 million households are headed by older persons, 75% of which are homeowners, and about 30% of all noninstitutionalized older persons live alone. Two-thirds of them had

advantages: freedom, independence, and continuity. However, it can also pose problems for an older person. The following sections briefly summarize common problems and possible solutions. Although an attempt is made to categorize common housing problems, more often than not a client will be faced with a combination of problems, and resolution of the problems will require a mixture of solutions.

Library References:

C.J.S. Estates § 8.

West's Key No. Digests, Estates in Property ⚷5.

§ 22.12 Fee Simple Home Ownership—Financial Hardship

Owning a home can create a financial hardship on older persons with fixed incomes that do not provide funds for unforeseen expenses such as special assessments, major repairs, and increased taxes. Even routine expenses (monthly mortgage payments, insurance, utilities) can become a financial burden when an older person's income does not keep pace with inflation or when expenses unrelated to housing (medical bills, food, personal needs, transportation, etc.) demand a higher percentage of the income. In such cases, older persons are forced to make choices to pay some expenses and forego others.

Before making any recommendations to a client faced with financial difficulty, the attorney must gather all financial information on the client (income, assets, and expenses). Solutions then may be reviewed to determine if they can provide the financial relief needed. Such solutions include home equity conversion,[1] shared housing, selling and moving to an alternative housing environment, community resources, and government assistance.[2]

§ 22.13 Fee Simple Home Ownership—Physical Limitations

At some point in their lives, most older persons will confront a physical limitation that inhibits their ability to care for themselves or their homes. It is important to consider the duration of the limitation (long-term or only temporary) and whether the severity of the limitation is likely to intensify or remain constant. Solutions that may be

lived in the same region for more than 20 years.

§ 22.12

1. See §§ 22.31–.51, infra, discussing sale-leasebacks and reverse mortgage loans.

2. See Chapter 19, supra, discussing

considered to provide the relief needed include in-home nursing care;[1] government assistance; community resources, including home visitor and telephone reassurance programs; and family and friends.

§ 22.14 Fee Simple Home Ownership—Lack of Social Interaction

Many older persons are faced with a dwindling social circle. Close friends, spouses, and family are no longer available to fill the human need for companionship. Single family home ownership does not provide a built-in network of social activities and opportunities for interaction, a situation that can become devastating for an individual living alone. But this situation need not be devastating; there are solutions such as shared housing, senior citizen centers, church, and social groups.

§ 22.15 Condominiums and Mobile Homes

Condominium housing has become increasingly popular in recent years and is a viable alternative housing option for elderly persons who want to retain the benefits of home ownership without many of its burdens. While holding title to their living units, they will share ownership of the common elements (exterior walls, grounds, parking areas, utility buildings, walkways, and amenities). The purchase of a converted rental unit is ordinarily an option offered at favorable terms when conversion takes place. Unlike those made as a single home owner, many decisions made as a condominium owner must be group-based. An elected board of directors make the decisions about maintenance of the common areas, hire the staff, and discharge the responsibilities. In exchange, the condominium owners pay monthly association and maintenance fees. Thus, the relief from many of the burdens of home ownership comes at a price. The additional cost may range from $150 to $1,000 per month. Prospective purchasers should realize that the fee is likely to increase in the future.

Ownership of a mobile home in a rental or condominium park has many of the same advantages and disadvantages as apartment condominium ownership. However, regulation of common areas will more likely be controlled by the lessor. Since 1976, all manufactured homes in the United States must meet construction standards specified by the Department of Housing and Urban Development so that safety and attractiveness of good quality are expected features of mobile home living. In addition, mobile home communities are appealing because

government assistance available to older persons.

§ 22.13

1. See Chapters 10, 11, and 12, supra, discussing medical care alternatives.

they offer a wide range of recreational and social facilities in a safe atmosphere often limited to older adults. Although financing may be more difficult and expensive than that of a conventional home, the lower total cost may more than make up for the necessity of 15 to 20% down payment. In addition, Veterans Administration (VA) and Federal Housing Administration (FHA) loans are now available.

The major risk of living in a mobile home park is the same as that of living in a building of condominiums—lack of control over increasing monthly fees for lot rental and maintenance. Another risk is eviction, which would be particularly devastating if the resident could not move the mobile home. Some state statutes provide protection against "exorbitant" rent increases and mobile home park eviction.[1]

Library References:
C.J.S. Estates §§ 145, 146.
West's Key No. Digests, Condominium ⚖=1, 13.

§ 22.16   Communal Alternatives—Shared Housing

Shared housing is a way for homeowners to solve both expense and isolation problems while remaining at home. Shared housing is a living arrangement whereby two or more unrelated persons live together, each having their own private space, but sharing common areas. The arrangement offers financial as well as social benefits. When a homeowner shares the home, the other adult provides the owner with services such as meals, transportation, or laundry or pays rent. Income tax consequences will attach, as the rental income must be reported. Accordingly, a homeowner should consider the tax consequences of such an arrangement.

Renters may seek out a "roommate" to share rental and utility expenses. Lease provisions may restrict the arrangement in its entirety or without prior owner approval. Changes in household composition may reduce or terminate public benefits such as Supplemental Security Income (SSI) and Medicaid. Careful consideration of all these issues is important before entering into a shared living arrangement.

It is important that the housemates be compatible. Permitting a stranger to move into the home is not a decision an older person would make casually or without thorough investigation. Referrals for housemates can be obtained from commercial services. In some localities, government-funded programs provide "matching" services with personal counselors to help in making the decisions.

§ 22.15

1. In Kuebler v. City of Escondido, 933 F.2d 1014 (9th Cir.1991), protective city regulations were challenged by the park owner.

Other legal issues that may require consideration are "single family" zoning ordinances and restrictive covenants.

§ 22.17 Communal Alternatives—Congregate Housing

Congregate housing is a form of multifamily housing that offers private, individual units for each resident and some common facilities for all residents such as kitchens, dining areas, and recreational rooms. These in-house facilities provide opportunities and help to older persons not available in a solely owned home, while the individual units provide some degree of independence.

Congregate housing may be a viable alternative for older persons who cannot live independently but who are not in need of the more intensive care of a nursing home. Because additional services are expensive, this living arrangement may be costly. Additionally, the resident is no longer an owner, but rather a tenant. Many facilities are subsidized through the government programs described in Chapter 19, supra. As part of the effort to allow aging persons to stay in place, government regulations will require an increasing variety of services to be offered. Local housing authorities (federal, state, county, municipal) should be contacted for a listing of government-subsidized congregate housing in the client's community.

§ 22.18 Special Purpose Financial Programs—Property Tax Deferrals [1]

A property tax deferral program is a special loan program that allows a senior citizen to avoid paying property taxes on a home until the property is sold or the owner moves. Interest on the deferred taxes, if any, is fixed by statute. The state or local revenue department generally places a lien on the property to secure repayment.

The decision to participate in the program can be made each year, i.e., the program is voluntary. Most programs allow the full amount of the taxes for any one year to be borrowed but limit the total amount of the tax lien that may be placed on the property. Most programs allow full or partial repayment at any time without penalty.

Property tax deferral programs are offered in the following states in some manner: California, Colorado, the District of Columbia, Florida, Illinois, Iowa, Massachusetts, New Hampshire, Oregon, Tennessee, Texas, Utah, Virginia, Washington, and Wisconsin.

---

§ 22.18

1. AARP, Consumer's Guide to Home Equity Conversion 12–14 (Rev. July 1991); Nelson, Home Equity Conversion Plans for House–Rich, Cash–Poor Seniors, 1 Prob. and Prop. 6, 9 (May–June 1987). (WEST-LAW: PROBPROP database, **ci(1   +5   6)** + **au(nelson)**).

Although property tax deferral programs can leave the homeowner with additional cash, there are a few drawbacks. First, the deferment of taxes lowers home equity. Second, deferred tax payments can limit the owner's ability to borrow against the home in later years, whether by equity conversion or by a home equity loan.

Library References:

C.J.S. Social Security and Public Welfare §§ 203–208; Taxation §§ 92–99, 617, 1082.

West's Key No. Digests, Taxation ⚖79, 526.

§ 22.19 Special Purpose Financial Programs—Deferred Payment Loans [1]

With a deferred payment loan (DPL), the proceeds of the loan are used to make repairs or remodel the home, and repayment is deferred until the property is sold or the homeowner dies. Usually there are no loan fees or points, and the interest rate is very low or zero.[2] Typically, DPLs are offered by local governmental or nonprofit agencies, not by banks. In some areas, utility companies offer DPLs for weatherizing homes.

With some types of DPLs, part of the loan is forgiven if the homeowner remains in the home for a number of years. With other types, a certain percentage of the loan, e.g., 20%, is forgiven for each period, e.g., two years, that the senior lives in the home; in this example, the loan would be completely forgiven after ten years.

Each particular program has in its rules the purposes for which the loans may be used. In most programs, the DPL can be used for repairs and improvements that make the home safer, more sound, more accessible, more convenient, more usable, and more energy efficient. Typically, DPLs cannot be used to improve the appearance of the home, i.e., to beautify and redecorate the home.

Generally, DPLs will have income and asset ceilings, limits based on the value or location of the home, and possibly age restrictions. Deferred payment loans are not available in every community. To check for availability, call the Area Agency on Aging, the city or county department of housing, community development agency, community action agency, or housing authority.

§ 22.19

1. AARP, supra § 22.18, note 1, at pp. 10–11.

2. Because the loans are often interest-free and do not have to be repaid until death, the loans may pay themselves off. For example, if $8,000 in improvements made with a DPL increase the value of the home by $5,000, the appreciation in value of the home after several years may earn the homeowner the loan value of $8,000 when the house is sold. AARP, supra § 22.18, note 1, at pp. 10–11.

§ 22.20 Special Purpose Financial Programs—Section 504 Program for Rural Home Owners—In General

The Farmers Home Administration (FmHA) administers rural housing loans and grants under § 504(A) of the Housing Act of 1949.[1] The basic objective of the FmHA in making § 504 loans and grants is to assist owner-occupants in rural areas in repairing or improving their homes in order to make such homes safe and sanitary and remove hazards to the health of the occupants, their families, or the community.

§ 22.21 Special Purpose Financial Programs—Section 504 Program for Rural Home Owners—Eligibility [1]

To be eligible for a § 504 loan or grant, the applicant must own and occupy a home that is in need of repair and that is located in a rural area. In addition, the applicant must:

1. meet residency and legal capacity requirements;

2. have a satisfactory credit history and reasonable ability and willingness to meet financial obligations;

3. be unable to obtain other non-FmHA credit or grant assistance; and

4. have an adjusted annual income that does not exceed very low income limits.

Additionally, loan applicants must show sufficient and dependable income to repay a § 504 loan or obtain a cosigner. Applicants for grant assistance are required to be 62 years of age or older and have an income so low that they could not repay any part of a § 504 loan.

§ 22.22 Special Purpose Financial Programs—Section 504 Program for Rural Home Owners—Purposes and Limitations [1]

Section 504 grants are limited to use for repairs and improvements related to identified health or safety hazards, while § 504 loans have no such restrictions. Examples of uses for § 504 loans or grants are as follows:

1. provision of sanitary water and waste disposal;

§ 22.20

1. 42 U.S.C.A. §§ 1472, 1473, 1474; 7 C.F.R. 1744.451.

§ 22.21

1. 7 C.F.R. § 1944.458.

§ 22.22

1. 7 C.F.R. §§ 1944.456, 1944.457.

2. payment of reasonable connection fees or pro rata installation costs for such things as water, sewer, electricity, or gas;

3. certain energy conservation measures;

4. repair/replacement of deteriorated roofs or siding;

5. certain repairs to mobile/manufactured homes, such as securing of foundation or removal of health or safety hazards; and

6. addition of a room to an existing dwelling in special cases when clearly necessary to remove hazards to the health of the family.

However, there are limitations on the use of § 504 loans and grants. These loans or grants may not be used to:

1. assist in construction of new homes;

2. make repairs to a dwelling of such poor condition and quality that when the repairs were completed, the dwelling would likely continue to be a substantial hazard to the health and safety of the family; or

3. move mobile/manufactured home from one site to another.

In addition, loans are limited to a $15,000 cumulative total, and grants are limited to a $5,000 cumulative total.

§ 22.23 Special Purpose Financial Programs—Section 504 Program for Rural Home Owners—Ownership Evidence and Agreement

Each applicant must submit evidence of ownership [1] of the dwelling in question to the county supervisor. Evidence may be the original or a certified or photostatic copy of the deed, purchase contract, or other instrument evidencing ownership.

In addition, a grant recipient must sign an agreement stating that he or she will not sell the property for a period of three years.[2] Should the property be sold before the end of the three-year period, the grantee must reimburse the government the full amount of the grant.

§ 22.24 Special Purpose Financial Programs—Section 504 Program for Rural Home Owners—Repayment

A § 504 loan is scheduled for repayment in accordance with the applicant's ability to pay. The interest rate for § 504 loans is 1% per annum.[1] Section 504 loans of $2,500 or more will be secured by a

§ 22.23

1. 7 C.F.R. § 1944.461.
2. 7 C.F.R. § 1944.461(d).

§ 22.24

1. 7 C.F.R. § 1944.462.

mortgage on the borrower's real estate.[2]　Real estate security will also be taken for loans of less than $2,500 whenever the loan approval officer determines that the security is needed to reasonably assure repayment of the loan.

§ 22.25　Special Purpose Financial Programs—Utility Assistance—Introduction

Energy costs deplete the low income budgets of elderly persons drastically in winter months.　For example, a survey found that elderly persons living on SSI in all but four states and elderly persons living on Social Security payments in 30 states had less than $125 and $150, respectively, a week for all other household necessities after paying winter energy bills.[1]　Lack of telephone service for older persons is a particular concern related to "aging in place."　The telephone is a crucial link to the outside.　For many older persons, costs of installation and service may be too much.[2]　There is a range of assistance programs offered to elderly low income customers that can help reduce utility costs or conserve energy.　Either renters or home owners may qualify.

Unfortunately, the programs vary widely from state to state.　Information on available programs and on application procedures often is difficult to obtain.[3]　Ordinarily, human services offices, public welfare offices, or Area Agency on Aging offices can provide information.　In addition, each utility supplier should be contacted directly in order to request brochures and application forms.[4]

Library References:

> C.J.S. Social Security and Public Welfare § 12.
> West's Key No. Digests, Social Security and Public Welfare ⚷9.1.

§ 22.26　Special Purpose Financial Programs—Utility Assistance—Types of Programs

There are two general types of programs: *energy assistance* benefit for low income families, which is supported by tax revenues, and *rate reduction* for low income families, which is supported through utility

---

2.　7 C.F.R. § 1944.461(b).

§ 22.25

1.　National Consumer Law Center, Energy and the Poor—The Forgotten Crisis (May 1989).

2.　See, American Association of Retired Persons, Utility Lifeline Programs: Prevalence and Performance 3 (1991) (hereinafter cited as Lifeline).

3.　Id. at 19.

4.　For recent legal developments and advocacy strategies, check Clearinghouse Review and contact the National Consumer Law Center, Inc., 11 Beacon St., Boston, MA, 12108, (617) 523–8010; 236 Massachusetts Ave. N.E., Washington, D.C., 20002, (202) 543–6060.

ratemaking. The two major federally funded assistance benefit programs are the Low–Income Home Energy Assistance Program (LIHEAP) [1] and the Low–Income Weatherization Assistance Program (WAP). [2] State agencies administer both programs and may or may not supplement them with state funding. Both LIHEAP and WAP programs have suffered from federal budget cuts in recent years, but continue. [3] Assistance payments are available to low income families, particularly the elderly. Eligibility requirements differ among the states.

The other programs for utility protection are financed indirectly through general utility rates. "Lifeline" programs reduce the charges for utility service. [4] These include state-mandated emergency service for customers in default: no termination in winter weather; fixed dollar or percentage rate discounts on regular service; and reduced charges for installation of services. The Federal Communication Commission's (FCC's) telecommunications Lifeline program waives federal subscriber line charges if matched by an equal reduction of local telephone charges, and FCC's Link Up plan cuts installation charges by half. [5] Eligibility for reduced charge programs, ordinarily, is limited to families who are currently eligible for or receiving some other social benefit assistance such as SSI or food stamps. [6] However, there may be slightly higher income eligibility standards for persons over 60 or 65 years of age. [7]

Additionally, utility companies may offer a variety of private services. Services available at different locations include (1) no charge service calls, (2) service discounts on labor charges for appliance repairs, (3) discounts on light bulbs, fixtures, and accessories, (4) free or discounted in-home energy analysis conducted by conservation experts who inspect the home and identify steps that can be taken to conserve energy and reduce consumption, (5) low interest loans or rebates for high-efficiency furnaces and/or insulation, and (6) budget payment plans. Elderly persons should familiarize themselves with assistance

§ 22.26

1. P.L. 97–35, Title XXVI, § 2602, 95 Stat. 893 (1981) (codified at 42 U.S.C.A. §§ 8621–8629; 45 C.F.R. § 96.80 et seq.

2. P.L. 94–385, Title IV, § 411 (1976) (codified at 42 U.S.C.A. §§ 6861–6892. 10 C.F.R. § 440.1 et seq.

3. The Augustus F. Hawkins Human Services Reauthorization Act of 1990, P.L. 101–501, § 702, 104 Stat. 1258 (1990) (codified as amended at 42 U.S.C.A. § 8621(b)

reauthorized the programs through fiscal year 1994 with authorized funding for LIHEAP of $2.23 billion for 1992, National Consumer Law Center, Consumer and Energy Developments During 1990, 24 Clearinghouse Rev. 937 (Jan. 1991).

4. See Lifeline, supra § 22.25, note 2, at 1, 13–16.

5. Id. at 13–14.

6. Id. at 15.

7. Id. at 34 et seq.

programs offered by their utility suppliers and should take advantage of the special programs whenever possible.

§§ 22.27–22.30 are reserved for supplementary material.

C. GENERATING INCOME: HOME EQUITY CONVERSION

§ 22.31 Introduction [1]

Older people, especially after retirement, frequently experience a drop in income. Social security benefits, pension payments, and other retirement income may not provide enough money with which to survive. However, many older people have one substantial asset: their home.

A person with substantial equity in a home who wishes to use the equity to increase income has several options. One possibility is to sell the home and move. Upon sale, the person can invest a portion of the proceeds in an income-producing investment and move into a smaller house, condominium, or apartment. However, the person who wishes to remain in the home should consider one of the several forms of home equity conversion that enable the owner to remain in the home and to receive monthly payments.[2]

Typically, a person to whom home equity conversion is attractive has a fixed income, is "'house-rich' but 'cash-poor,'" and desires to keep the home but cannot afford taxes, maintenance, or other living

§ 22.31

1. K. Scholen, "Home–Made Money: Consumer's Guide to Home Equity Conversion" (American Association of Retired Persons, Rev. July 1991) (hereinafter referred to as AARP Guide); Comm'n on Legal Problems of the Elderly, Am. Bar Ass'n, "Attorney's Guide to Home Equity Conversion" (1986) (hereinafter referred to as ABA); Fairbanks, Home Equity Conversion Programs: A Housing Option for the "House–Rich, Cash–Poor" Elderly, 23 Clearinghouse Rev. 482 (Special Issue, Summer 1989) (hereinafter referred to as Fairbanks). Much of the information in this section has been drawn from the AARP Guide, ABA, and Fairbanks.

For updated information, contact National Center for Home Equity Conversion, 1210 East College Drive, # 300, Marshall, Minn. 56258, (507) 532–3230; AARP Home Equity Information Center, Consumer Affairs Section, 601 E. Street, N.W., Washington, D.C. 20049; ABA Commission on Legal Problems of the Elderly, 1800 M Street, Washington, D.C. 20036, (202) 331–2297.

See, also, Options for Elderly Homeowners: A Guide to Revenue Mortgages and Their Alternatives (HUD), available at HUD offices; K. Scholen, Retirement Income on the House (NCHEC 1992), published after completion of this manuscript.

2. A home equity conversion transaction is not the same as either a home equity loan or a home equity line of credit, which require monthly payments from the homeowner to the bank immediately after the loan proceeds are disbursed, are amortized over short periods of time, and are not intended to supply a regular income.

expenses.[3] The amount of monthly income that can be generated in a home equity conversion transaction depends upon the amount of equity in the home, the interest rate, and the age of the homeowner.

Although home equity conversion plans can generate needed income, they have costs to the homeowner in the form of interest, transaction costs, foregone appreciation, and/or ownership. Furthermore, some risk is involved, especially with respect to tax uncertainties. Finally, not all types of plans are available in all communities.

However, for many senior citizens, a form of home equity conversion can make a difference. In addition to having extra money per month for food, medicine, or small luxuries, the homeowner is able to remain in the home—a life-saver for many people.

Basically, two general types of home equity conversion plans exist: sale plans and loan plans. Sale plans contemplate an outright sale of the home, but loan plans do not.

§ 22.32 Sale Plans—Overview

With a home equity conversion sale plan, the homeowner sells the home but retains either a leasehold interest or a life estate in it, allowing the homeowner to remain in the home. Home equity conversion sale plans take two forms: the sale-leaseback and the remainder interest sale.

§ 22.33 Sale Plans—Sale–Leasebacks—Description

A sale-leaseback transaction requires the homeowner to sell the home to a buyer who agrees to lease it back to the seller for life or until the seller moves. Frequently, the buyer is the seller's child or other family member.

The buyer ordinarily will pay the homeowner a portion of the purchase price in cash and the remainder by a note secured by a deed of trust or mortgage. Monthly payments to the seller on the note will be greater than the monthly rent payments from the seller, the difference providing monthly income for the seller. The seller might also use the down payment to purchase a deferred annuity on the seller's life, which would take effect after the final note payment, thereby guaranteeing the seller an income for life.[1]

---

3. Fairbanks, supra note 1, at 481.

§ 22.33

1. AARP Guide, supra § 22.31, note 1, at 35.

Advantages of sale-leasebacks are that the seller, in one transaction, increases his or her income; relinquishes his or her obligations for property taxes, insurance, and repairs; and begins to reduce his or her estate.

A major disadvantage is that in order to attract a buyer who does not want immediate occupancy of the premises and who will agree to contractual limitations on increases in rent, the sale likely will be for less than the home's market value. Also, the seller loses the benefit of the property's appreciation, while the impact of inflation on the buying power of the cash generated cannot be predicted because the proceeds are fixed. Finally, eliminating the home as an asset that may be passed on to heirs may be a disadvantage, although any balance due on the contract would be paid to the seller's estate.

§ 22.34   Sale Plans—Sale–Leasebacks—State Law Issues

Because the former owner becomes a tenant-lessee, state landlord-tenant laws must be considered. Among the most important provisions likely to be encountered are rent control statutes or ordinances and statutory remedies for the lessee if the lessor fails to repair the property as agreed in the lease.[1]

Landlord-tenant laws may also give the landlord remedies if the tenant breaches the lease. Finally, the tenant should know whether he or she has the right to sublet without the permission of the landlord. Statutory or case law might not permit inconsistent terms in the lease agreement, which might inhibit potential buyers.

Along with state landlord-tenant laws, state lender-borrower laws must be considered. States generally give the seller/lessee statutory remedies in the event the buyer defaults on the purchase. If the seller can foreclose, the buyer probably has statutory equity or a right of redemption that can preclude selling to another to produce a needed source of ready income.

Library References:

C.J.S. Taxation § 1097.
West's Key No. Digests, Taxation ☞996.1.

§ 22.35   Sale Plans—Sale–Leasebacks—Federal Income Tax Aspects

The sale-leaseback presents many federal income tax issues, some of which have not been resolved because of the lack of experience in the

§ 22.34

1. ABA, supra § 22.31, note 1, at 12.

area of equity conversion.[1]

Although there is no precedent on the issue, the seller should be able to utilize the Internal Revenue Code § 121 one-time exclusion of gain from income available upon the outright sale of the home.[2] In addition, the installment method of reporting income [3] may be used by the seller-lessee if some portion of the gain on the sale is not excluded by the one-time exclusion, assuming the installment sale is used.[4] If a related buyer sells within two years, he or she may have to show that the sale-leaseback agreement was not for tax purposes.[5]

Since the buyer often will not pay the fair market value for a house subject to a long-term lease, the question arises as to whether the Internal Revenue Service (IRS) will recharacterize the transaction as a bargain purchase, classifying part of the value as a gift. If recharacterized, the buyer's basis for all but loss purposes becomes the greater of the purchase price or the seller's adjusted basis in the home.[6] For loss purposes, the basis is the lesser of the fair market value or the basis for all but loss purposes.[7] In order for the buyer to depreciate the property, the sale must be valid for tax purposes.

The resolution of this issue depends on the arm's length nature of the given transaction. Factors that determine the validity of the agreement include (1) whether the sale price is fair with an economic benefit to the buyer other than tax savings, (2) whether the lessee pays fair market rent,[8] and (3) whether the agreement creates a typical lessor-lessee relationship, meaning that the purchaser-lessor is independent of the seller-lessee,[9] and that the seller-lessee retains a typical level of control over the residence.[10] Hence, a sale-leaseback agreement between relatives may make meeting these requirements a more difficult task. Additionally, in order for the sale-leaseback to be valid in the traditional arm's length transaction, caution should be used in deciding whether to include rent restrictions.

Finally, the buyer in a sale valid for tax purposes should be entitled to investment ownership deductions for taxes, insurance, and

§ 22.35

1. For a discussion of the tax implications of sale-leaseback transactions, see Maule, Taxation of Residence Transactions §§ 36.5–36.9, 41.1 (1985).

2. Id. at § 41.1.

3. I.R.C. § 453.

4. See I.R.C. § 453(b).

5. I.R.C. § 453(e).

6. Treas.Reg. § 1.1015–4(a).

7. Treas.Reg. § 1.1015–4(a)(2).

8. Hilton v. Commissioner, 74 T.C. 305, 356–57 (1980), affirmed, 671 F.2d 316 (9th Cir.1982), cert. denied, 459 U.S. 907, 103 S.Ct. 211, 74 L.Ed.2d 168 (1982).

9. Frank Lyon Co. v. United States, 435 U.S. 561, 584 98 S.Ct. 1291, 1303, 55 L.Ed.2d 550 (1978).

10. Northern Pac. R.R. v. United States, 378 F.2d 686 (Ct.Cl.1967).

repairs that an investor otherwise would be entitled to in connection with rental property. The IRS might challenge the buyer's deductions in excess of the rental income by asserting that § 183 applies. However, at one time, the IRS did concede the inapplicability of § 183.[11]

Library References:

C.J.S. Internal Revenue §§ 96, 111.

West's Key No. Digests, Internal Revenue ☞3193.

§ 22.36 Sale Plans—Sale–Leasebacks—Effect on Receipt of Public Benefits

The transaction may affect determination of resources for eligibility for need-based public benefits such as Supplemental Security Income (SSI) or Medicaid. The value of a home is usually excluded from countable resources.[1] However, after the sale of a home, unless the seller intends to purchase a new home and does purchase a new home within three months, the proceeds of the sale will become a countable resource.[2]

The status of the proceeds from the sale of a home depends on the terms of the agreement and the note held by the seller-lessee. First, if an annuity is purchased with the down payment, payments to the annuitant are considered unearned income, thus reducing or eliminating eligibility for SSI.[3] Second, monthly payments on the note must be broken down into payments of principal and payments of interest. Payments of principal are not income, but rather the conversion of a resource, which could render a person ineligible if retained. Interest received on the interest-bearing note is income,[4] which may reduce the amount of monthly benefit to the recipient or cause ineligibility. The amount to be collected should be carefully geared to the recipient's budget.[5] In addition, if the note is negotiable, it is considered a resource for SSI, Medicaid, and Food Stamp Program purposes.

§ 22.37 Sale Plans—Sale–Leasebacks—Attorney's Role

There are three key components in a sale-leaseback transaction: the home sale; the leaseback to the seller; and if part of the transaction, the acquisition of a deferred payment annuity on the seller's life.

---

11. Priv.Ltr.Rul. 81–32–1017 (Apr. 30, 1981).

§ 22.36

1. 20 C.F.R. § 416.1212(b) (1991).

2. Id. at § 416.1212(d).

3. Id. at § 416.1121(a).

4. Id. at §§ 416.1103(f); § 416.1207(e).

5. See, id. at § 416.1202(b), (c).

Terms of each of these components vary widely. Several recommendations should help to protect the interests of the seller-lessee.[1]

First, resale of the property should be permitted only if the new buyer is obligated to assume all responsibilities under all existing agreements.[2] Therefore, a memorandum of lease should be filed prior to filing the mortgage so that subsequent purchasers take the property subject to the lease. Second, the sale documents should include a due-on-transfer clause. This clause will permit the seller to collect the entire amount of the sale in the event of a later transfer by the buyer. The sale documents should also protect the seller if the buyer is unable to continue making the mortgage payments to the seller or if the buyer dies before the seller.

With respect to the lease, first, the lessee should be ensured lifetime occupancy, and rent increases should be limited with cost-of-living indexing or some similar mechanism. Second, the seller-lessee should be relieved of the rent obligation if the buyer does not pay the mortgage as scheduled. Third, the lessee should be excused from default on the lease if the lessee enters a nursing home or hospital for a specific short period of time. The lessee also should be permitted to sublet for certain periods of time and to have one or two others live with him or her. Fourth, the lessee should be protected in the event of his or her own default. Thus, the lease should require that the lessor notify the lessee of any default in writing and allow the lessee at least 30 days to correct the default.[3] Fifth, the lessee must be protected from the lessor's failure to maintain the property in good condition. The lease should specify duties of the buyer regarding both ordinary maintenance and urgent repairs of the property. Finally, the attorney should be aware of the buyer-lessor's desire to include certain provisions in the transaction, for example, the buyer may wish to place limits on what alterations are permissible by the lessee and to prohibit the lessee from assigning the lease.

§ 22.38 Sale Plans—Remainder Interest Sales—Description

In a remainder interest sale, the homeowner conveys a remainder interest in the property to the buyer, retaining a life estate. In return for the remainder interest, an elderly seller may want a commitment from the buyer to maintain and insure the property and pay taxes in

§ 22.37

1. Because the situation will frequently involve the seller's child or other family member as the buyer, the attorney might be called upon to handle the transaction for both parties. The attorney should be careful not to deviate from ethical consid- erations inherent in representing multiple parties with potentially adverse positions.

2. Fed. Counsel on Aging, House Rich, But Cash Poor 19 (1983).

3. ABA, supra § 22.31, note 1, at 12.

addition to paying the seller a monthly payment for life.[1] The amount of monthly payment received by the seller depends upon the home value, the estimated cost of repairs, and the seller's life expectancy. The seller may be able to elect to receive a lump sum distribution of at least part of the value of the property.

Sale of a remainder interest carries with it obvious financial risks. As in the case of an annuity, if the homeowner dies soon after the transaction is completed, the owner will have sold the remainder interest in the home for much less than its value. Conversely, if the seller lives beyond his or her life expectancy, the seller will receive more than the remainder value in monthly payments.[2]

§ 22.39   Sale Plans—Remainder Interest Sales—Federal Income Tax Aspects

Many federal income tax questions are presented; some are unanswered. For example, the IRS has issued a letter ruling which holds that a taxpayer who wishes to sell a principal place of residence and retain the right to live on the premises rent free until death cannot exclude the gain.[1] The IRS reasoned that § 121 was not available, since the taxpayer did not sell the principal residence, but only part of it. In contrast, the Tax Court has held that the rental value of a rent per period was part of the purchase price and the entire fee had been sold.[2]

§ 22.40   Sale Plans—Remainder Interest Sales—Effect on Receipt of Public Benefits

The effect on eligibility for Supplemental Security Income, Medicaid, and Food Stamps will be similar to that of sale-leaseback transactions. However, the value of repairs, insurance, and property tax paid by the buyer probably will not be counted as income to the seller because the seller is not the remainder owner. If the seller rents the home to others, while in a nursing facility, for example, rental pay-

---

§ 22.38

1. ABA, supra § 22.31, note 1, at 12. See § 22.39, infra, for possible income tax effects.

2. Nelson, "Home Equity Conversion Plans for House–Rich, Cash–Poor Seniors", 1 Prob. and Prop. 6, 9 (May–June 1987) (WESTLAW: PROB PROP database, ci(1 +5 6) + au(nelson)).

§ 22.39

1. Priv.Ltr.Rul. 80–29–088 (Apr. 25, 1980) cited in ABA, supra § 22.31, note 1, at 14.

2. Ramey v. Commissioner, 47 T.C. 363 (1967) (Acq. 1967–2 C.B. 1); Steinway and Sons, Inc. v. Commissioner, 46 T.C. 375 (1966) (Acq. 1967–2 C.B. 3), discussed in J. Smith & A. Samansky, Federal Taxation of Real Estate, § 7.02[3] (1986).

ments can be treated as unearned income.[1]

§ 22.41   Sale Plans—Remainder Interest Sales—Attorney's Role

An attorney representing a homeowner contemplating a remainder interest sale has many of the same concerns as an attorney representing a sale-leaseback client. The agreement should provide for a clear remedy in case of buyer default and should require the buyer to make repairs, pay taxes, and insure the premises.[1] Finally, the agreement should permit others to live in the house and permit the seller to be absent from the house for specified periods of time without being in breach.

§ 22.42   Loan Plans: Reverse Mortgages—In General—Description

In a reverse mortgage transaction, the homeowner does not sell the home, but borrows against the equity in the home, using the home as collateral. The homeowner becomes a borrower rather than a lessee or the holder of a life estate. About 152,000 reverse mortgages had been made by 1991 according to data collected by the National Center for Home Equity Conversion.[1]

Reverse mortgages are "rising debt loans,"[2] i.e., the total amount owed grows larger over time. The lender advances the first monthly loan amount, and the borrower owes only that amount. One month later, the lender adds one month's interest to the first month's advance and delivers the second monthly loan amount. One month later, the lender adds interest on the previous months' total balance and sends the third payment. This pattern continues for the length of the loan period.

Often, the first month's advance, which might be used to pay existing debt or to pay the finance charges on the reverse mortgage, can be substantially larger than the subsequent monthly advances. The amount of monthly payment possible with reverse mortgages is based on (1) the amount of equity in the home, (2) the interest rate on the loan, and (3) the length of the loan term.[3]

§ 22.40

1. 20 C.F.R. §§ 416.1121(d), 416.1102 (1989), 416.1222.

§ 22.41

1. ABA, supra § 22.31, note 1, at 16.

§ 22.42

1. Harney, New Reverse Mortgage Program, The Columbus Dispatch, p. 8J col. 1, Sept. 15, 1991.

2. AARP Guide, supra § 22.31, note 1, at 15–18.

3. ABA, supra § 22.31, note 1, at 1.

§ 22.43 Loan Plans: Reverse Mortgages—In General—Terminology

Several types of reverse mortgages, differing in mode of payment and repayment, have unique appellations.[1]

A *fixed term* reverse mortgage allows the borrower to receive monthly payments from the lender for a fixed period of time, after which the loan must be repaid.

A *split-term* reverse mortgage allows the borrower to receive monthly payments from the lender for a specified time, but repayment is not due until the borrower dies, moves, or sells the home.

A *tenure* reverse mortgage allows the borrower to receive monthly payments from the lender until the borrower dies, moves, or sells the home, at which time the loan must be repaid.

A *line of credit* reverse mortgage allows the borrower to withdraw amounts from an account as needed (no set monthly payment), and repayment is deferred until the borrower dies, moves, or sells the home.

A *reverse annuity* mortgage allows the borrower to receive a lump sum disbursement from the lender to purchase an annuity.

§ 22.44 Loan Plans: Reverse Mortgages—Federal Law—Authority of Lenders to Make Reverse Mortgages

Generally, lenders must be given authority by the agency that granted their charter to make nonamortized loans secured by residential real estate.[1] This authority has been granted to federally chartered banks and federally chartered savings and loan associations.[2]

In 1982, Congress gave state-chartered lenders parity with federally chartered institutions.[3] State-chartered banks, savings and loans, and other nonfederally chartered housing creditors, such as mortgage companies, are allowed to make alternative real estate loans despite existing state law prohibitions, provided that these transactions comply with applicable federal requirements and that the state did not pass

§ 22.43

1. AARP Guide, supra § 22.31, note 1, at 19–20 combines these terms with explanations of method of insurance. For more detailed descriptions, see §§ 22.49–.50, infra.

§ 22.44

1. ABA, supra § 22.31, note 1, at 2.
2. 12 U.S.C.A. §§ 371(a), 1464(c)(1)(B). Such institutions may make real estate loans without regard to state law limitations regarding loan-to-value ratios, repayment schedules, and periods to the maturity of the loan. 12 C.F.R. §§ 34.2(a), 545.33 (1992).

3. 12 U.S.C.A. §§ 3801–3806 (commonly known as the Alternative Mortgage Transaction Parity Act of 1982, Title VIII of the Garn–St. Germain Depositary Institutions Act of 1982, Pub.L. No. 97–320, 96 Stat. 1469); ABA, supra § 22.31, note 1, at 3.

legislation to reject the federal preemption. Only a few states, including New York and Massachusetts, have chosen to override the preemption in whole or in part.[4]

§ 22.45   Loan Plans: Reverse Mortgages—Federal Law—Home Equity Conversion Mortgage (HECM) Insurance [1]

Section 417 of the Housing and Community Development Act of 1987 added a new § 255 to the National Housing Act [2] which authorized a demonstration program for Federal Housing Administration insurance of home equity conversion mortgages for elderly homeowners. The program, which was expanded in 1991, is administered by the Department of Housing and Urban Development (HUD). The HECM program is designed to increase the involvement of mortgage market participants in making HECM for elderly persons and to evaluate data to determine the need and demand among elderly homeowners for HECM mortgages.[3] If a lender is unable to make payments to the borrower, HUD will assume responsibility for making such payments. The mortgage proceeds must be secured by a first mortgage on the property, which allows HUD or the lender to recover any outlays up to the value of the property when the borrower no longer maintains the property as a principal residence.

All borrowers must be 62 years of age or older, and must be able to provide evidence of their age, when signing the application for a HECM.[4] Borrowers cannot have a delinquent or defaulted federal debt that cannot be rectified at closing.[5] Each borrower must occupy the property as a principal residence at closing.[6] The property must be a one-unit dwelling, but may be a condominium.[7] Eligible borrowers must own their homes free and clear, or with liens not exceeding the

4. ABA, supra § 22.31, note 1, at 3.

§ 22.45

1. Housing and Community Development Act of 1987, Pub.L. No. 100–242, Title IV, § 417, 101 Stat. 1815, 1908 (1988) (codified at 12 U.S.C.A. §§ 1715z–1720).

2. 12 U.S.C.A. §§ 1715z–1720.

3. 24 C.F.R. § 206.1. Also, see HUD Handbook § 235.1, Home Equity Conversion Mortgages, p. 1 et seq. (1989).

4. 24 C.F.R. § 206.33.

5. 24 C.F.R. § 206.37.

6. 24 C.F.R. § 206.39. Principal residence is further defined in HUD regulations as the dwelling where the borrower maintains his or her permanent place of abode and typically spends the majority of the calendar year. A person may have only one principal residence at any one time, and such property will be considered to be the principal residence of a borrower who is temporarily or permanently in a health care institution as long as the property is the principal residence of at least one other borrower who is not in a health care institution. See, HUD Handbook, Home Equity Conversion Mortgages, § 235.1 at 5–7 (1989).

7. 24 C.F.R. § 206.45.

principal limit established by HUD regulations.[8]

Loan proceeds from HECMs may be paid out according to one of four payment plans selected by the borrower, who has the option of changing the type of payment plan throughout the life of the loan.[9] The four basic plans or types of reverse mortgages that can be insured are term, tenure, line of credit, and modified term or tenure. The latter plan combines a line of credit with monthly payments. In exchange for reduced monthly payments, the borrower will set aside a specified amount of money at closing for a line of credit, upon which he or she can draw until the line of credit is exhausted.

The maximum amount that a borrower can receive from a HECM is determined by calculating the "principal limit"—the present value of the proceeds available to the borrower.[10] The principal amount is calculated using a formula that considers the age of the youngest borrower, the expected average mortgage interest rate, and the maximum claim amount.[11] The amount increases each month by one-twelfth of the sum of the expected average mortgage interest rate plus the monthly mortgage insurance premium rate.

Repayment of HECMs,[12] unlike that of traditional residential mortgages which are repaid in monthly payments, is due and payable when the borrower dies, the property is no longer the borrower's principal residence, the borrower does not occupy the property for 12 months for health reasons, or the borrower violates the mortgage covenants.[13] When the mortgage becomes due and payable, the property will normally be sold by the borrower or the borrower's estate to pay off the outstanding balance on the mortgage. The lender's recovery will be limited to the value of the home, and there will be no deficiency judgment permitted against the borrower's estate. The insurance operates when the proceeds from the sale of the property are insufficient to pay off the outstanding balance, in which case the lender may file a claim with HUD for the difference.

A borrower may prepay all or part of the outstanding balance at any time without penalty.[14]

Library References:

C.J.S. Mortgages §§ 71, 160 et seq.
West's Key No. Digests, Mortgages ☞9.1, 15.

8. HUD Handbook § 235.1 at 1–1 and 1–2.

9. Id. at 1–3.

10. Id. at 6–2.

11. Id. at 1–2.

12. Id. at 1–6.

13. Uninsured reverse mortgages may be only fixed term mortgages; therefore, the borrower always must plan for repayment at the end of the fixed term. AARP Guide, supra § 22.31, note 1, at 29–32.

14. HUD Handbook § 325.1 at 1–1 and 1–2.

§ 22.46 Loan Plans: Reverse Mortgages—Federal Law—Federal Income Tax Aspects

The major disadvantage of reverse mortgages with respect to federal income taxation is that the interest owed by the borrower is not deductible until paid, which is when the reverse mortgage is paid off in total [1]—usually after the homeowner's death.

If an annuity is acquired, part of the payments received from the annuity are included in gross income.[2] Also, deductions for interest paid on a loan when the loan proceeds are used to purchase an annuity are greatly restricted.[3]

There may be a capital gain when the home is sold at the end of term or when the owner must enter a nursing facility, but there may be insufficient funds to pay the tax after the loan is paid.

§ 22.47 Loan Plans: Reverse Mortgages—Federal Law—Effect on Receipt of Public Benefits

Supplemental Security Income, Medicaid, and Food Stamp Program eligibility may be affected by the proceeds of equity conversion. The Social Security Administration classes reverse mortgage proceeds as a loan; for that reason, the proceeds are not income.[1] However, if the proceeds are held beyond the month of receipt, they will be counted as a resource, which may cause ineligibility or lower benefits.[2] Therefore, the lender should send the monthly payment at the beginning of the month to ensure that it is spent by the end of the month. Further, if the borrower receives a lump sum disbursement at the beginning of the loan, it should be spent in the month of receipt. If the risk of losing public benefits is substantial, a reverse mortgage is not wise.

§ 22.48 Loan Plans: Reverse Mortgages—State Law Issues [1]

Many state law issues arise in a reverse mortgage transaction. First, the state may have exercised its option to override all or part of the federal preemption of state law restrictions on alternative mortgage transactions. If the state has opted to override the federal preemption, there may be state statutory or regulatory restrictions on the ability of

§ 22.46

1. Treas.Reg. § 1.461–1(a)(1).
2. I.R.C. §§ 61(a)(9), 72.
3. I.R.C. § 264.

§ 22.47

1. 20 C.F.R. § 416.1103(f) (1992); S.S.A. Program Circular No. 09–84–OSSI, S.S.A.Pub. No. 17–004 (Aug. 1, 1984).

2. 20 C.F.R. § 416.1201(a).

§ 22.48

1. ABA, supra § 22.31, note 1, at 6–8.

state-chartered lending institutions to make nonamortized real estate loans.

Second, in some states, the disclosure required by the state consumer credit code may be substituted for Truth in Lending disclosures. Although the Truth in Lending Act generally supersedes inconsistent state disclosure requirements, where the state disclosure requirements are equivalent to the federal law, the state law can be followed.

The parties to the transaction should be informed whether a lien filed at the inception of the reverse mortgage secures future advances by the lender to the borrower. The issue may turn on whether the subsequent advances are obligatory or optional in nature.

Foreclosure options for the lender in the event of borrower default must be determined. State law might permit the lender to assess a deficiency if the loan balance is not satisfied by the amount received on sale or foreclosure. The transaction documents should prohibit this type of assessment.

The borrower should be aware of any statutory remedies, in addition to contract remedies, in the event the lender fails to make monthly payments.

§ 22.49   Loan Plans: Reverse Mortgages—Advantages and Disadvantages—Common to All Types

The various types of reverse mortgages have some common advantages and disadvantages. One advantage of a reverse mortgage is that advances of money pursuant to a reverse mortgage are not subject to federal, state, or local taxes. Also, a "nonrecourse" or "limitation of liability" provision is typically included in the terms of the loan, which means that the lender cannot require repayment from assets other than the home.[1] Further, most reverse mortgages allow repayment at any time without penalty.

The most significant disadvantage of a reverse mortgage is the high cost. Interest rates, application fees, points, and closing costs are normally higher for reverse mortgages than for conventional loans. Also, the borrower, as the owner, must pay property taxes and insurance and must maintain the home in good condition.

The reverse mortgage has limited flexibility in that the borrower may have to remain in the home to avoid terminating the transaction and owing the money borrowed.[2] Two California mortgage companies

§ 22.49

1. ABA, supra § 22.31, note 1, at 18–19.

2. Summer or vacation homes and temporary stays in nursing or health care facilities are probably exempted from this

in 1991 were developing plans for lifetime payments even though the owner left the home.[3]

There are other disadvantages: (1) the interest owed is not deductible until paid, which typically is when the borrower dies; and (2) unless the loan term is very short, a significant amount of equity will be consumed in the form of accrued interest on the loan.[4]

§ 22.50 Loan Plans: Reverse Mortgages—Advantages and Disadvantages—Among Different Types

A *term reverse mortgage*[1] is for a fixed period of time, usually between three and ten years.

Term reverse mortgages have two advantages. First, they can be used by a homeowner facing a crisis that requires extensive and costly service such as an extraordinary health condition for an extended but limited time. Second, the borrower retains the benefit of all future appreciation, while the lender, by virtue of the standard nonrecourse provision, risks future depreciation.

The major disadvantage of a term reverse mortgage is that the borrower must pay the debt on the month following the last advance. Unless the borrower has another large source of income or the home has appreciated enough to permit refinancing, the home must be sold. Hence, a term reverse mortgage is only suitable for a borrower who (1) wishes to liquidate a specific amount of equity over a period of time prior to selling; (2) has other sources of income to make amortization payments upon maturity of the loan; or (3) wishes to liquidate only a very small amount of the equity in a home with a high appraisal value.

Like a term reverse mortgage, advances made pursuant to a *split-term reverse mortgage*[2] are for a fixed period. However, a split-term reverse mortgage does not have to be repaid until the borrower dies, moves, or sells the home. Split-term reverse mortgages offer several advantages. First, the borrower may remain in the home long after the monthly payments cease. Second, because some split-term reverse mortgages are offered in conjunction with state agencies, the interest rate can be low. Finally, if the value of the home appreciates, the

requirement. Also, as long as the borrower does not move, he or she may be permitted to have a paying or nonpaying tenant in the home.

3. The companies were Reliance of San Francisco and Freedom Home Equity Partners of Irvine. Harvey, New Reverse Mortgage Program, The Columbus, Dispatch, p. 8J, col. 1, Sept. 15, 1991.

4. Nelson, supra § 22.18, note 1, at 7.

§ 22.50

1. Nelson, *supra* § 22.18, note 1, at 7; AARP Guide, supra § 22.18, note 1, at 29–32.

2. AARP Guide, supra § 22.31, note 1, at 29–32.

borrower might be able to receive monthly payment beyond the scheduled end date.

The *tenure reverse mortgage* [3] provides monthly loan advances until the borrower sells, moves from the home, or dies. Repayment is deferred until that time. Such an unlimited repayment period is possible because the borrower must not only pay principal and accrued monthly interest, but also may agree to surrender some or all of the home's future appreciation to the lender. The amount of payment depends upon home value, the senior's age, and the proportion of future appreciation that is shared (usually between 20 and 100%). Other things being equal, payments are higher when each of these three factors are high.

A tenure reverse mortgage is somewhat like an annuity in that the borrower receives monthly payments regardless of the length of time the borrower lives in the home, but the total repayment is limited to the agreed proportion of the value of the home at the end of the borrower's time in it. Thus, if the borrower lives in the home for a long period and the home does not appreciate, the risk is to the lender.

The tenure reverse mortgage has several advantages. First, because the lender stands to acquire part of the appreciation of the home, lower interest rates and higher monthly payments are possible. Second, payments are made for life or until the borrower moves, guaranteeing a continuous income stream. Third, if the amount of monthly payment that the borrower needs is less than the amount the lender is willing to pay, the borrower can take a smaller monthly payment and preserve some of the home's equity in either of two ways: (1) reduce the percentage of future appreciation the borrower agrees to pay the lender, and/or (2) limit the amount of the value of the home the borrower wishes to reduce to cash, i.e., choose to exempt a fixed amount from the transaction altogether. However, to prevent a windfall, a ceiling needs to be put on the annual appreciation that the lender can receive. Last, some states, e.g., New York, do not allow tenure reverse mortgages.[4]

A major disadvantage is that problems with state usury laws might arise because the lender receives, in addition to interest on the loan, a share in the appreciation of the home. In some jurisdictions, all funds received by the lender, other than administrative fees, are considered interest. Therefore, a violation will occur if the sum of the fixed interest rate plus the amount of the shared appreciation exceeds the

---

3. Id.

4. N.Y.—Real Prop.Law § 280(2)(b) (1989). See Cumby, "Effects of Legislation on the Reverse Annuity Mortgage as a Means of Home Equity Conversion" 13 Fordham Urban Law Journal 869, at 895 (Fall 1985).

usury rate. Running afoul of usury statutes in some states is especially dangerous because the lender may be forced to forfeit all rights to interest as well as the right to repayment of the principal.

A *line of credit reverse mortgage* [5] allows the borrower to request disbursements in the amount and at the times the borrower chooses. Repayment is due when the borrower moves, sells the home, or dies.

This type is ideal for a person who is not interested in generating additional monthly income but who occasionally needs money, for example, for a home repair or a vacation. A line of credit plan would be limited by the number of withdrawals per year, the amount of withdrawal at any one time, and/or the total cumulative withdrawal.

A *reverse annuity mortgage* [6] (RAM) borrower uses the equity in the borrower's home to borrow money with which to buy an annuity on the borrower's life. These varieties of the RAM exist: the *simple RAM*, the *deferred RAM*, and the *refund RAM*. Any of these types of RAMs may disqualify a recipient from public benefits and may trigger tax liabilities to the extent annuity payments constitute income.

With a *simple RAM,* the lender advances the entire loan proceeds to the borrower in a lump sum, and the borrower purchases an annuity on his or her life. A portion of the monthly annuity payment is disbursed to the lender as payment of interest due on the RAM loan, and the remainder is disbursed to the borrower. As an example, assume a 75–year–old woman has a home valued at $125,000. She could get a 10% RAM loan for 80% of the home's value, or $100,000. She would use the $100,000 to purchase an annuity on her life, which would pay her $15,000 per year. Of this sum, $10,000 would be paid directly to the lender as interest on the loan, and the remaining $5,000 would be paid to the borrower-annuitant to use as she wishes. The principal amount of the loan is not payable until the borrower moves, sells the home, or dies.

The simple RAM guarantees a supplemental cash flow to the borrower for the remainder of the borrower's life and eliminates the risk that the homeowner will have to sell the home upon maturity of the RAM loan. Also, accumulated accrued interest is not added to the amount encumbering the property, since all accrued interest is paid monthly with a portion of the annuity payments.

---

5. AARP Guide, supra § 22.31, note 1, at 29–32.

6. The information in this subsection is summarized with the permission of Fordham University from D. Cumby, "Effects of Legislation on the Reverse Annuity Mortgage As A Means of Home Equity Conversion" 13 Fordham Urban Law Journal 869 (Fall 1985).

The disadvantage of this type of RAM is that the amount of payment is determined by the annuitant's age, thus only the very elderly can generate monthly payments sufficient to pay interest on the loan and provide the borrower with a monthly cash supplement. A major risk exists because the annuitant is wagering on the annuitant's own life expectancy; therefore, if the annuitant dies shortly after the transaction, he or she will have received only a small amount of the annuity while owing a large amount on the loan.

With a *delayed annuity RAM,* the lender advances only a portion of the loan in a lump sum at the beginning of the loan term. The borrower uses that sum to purchase an annuity, on which payment to the borrower is deferred for several years. The balance of the loan proceeds are disbursed to the borrower by the lender throughout the remainder of the initial loan term. At the end of the initial loan term, the amount of the principal advanced plus accrued interest will equal the face amount of the mortgage. Then the debt ceases to grow, and payout of the annuity begins. The lender receives a portion of the monthly annuity in repayment of the loan while the borrower receives the balance as an income supplement.

The advantage to the deferred annuity RAM is that the borrower receives some protection in the event that the borrower dies within the initial term of the loan because the borrower, *i.e.,* the borrower's estate, continues to receive payment of the loan proceeds. Also, since the entire amount of the loan is not invested in the annuity, less of the borrower's home equity is subject to the lower rate of interest typically offered on an annuity.

A *refund RAM* is the same as a simple RAM, but the borrower uses the proceeds of the loan to purchase an annuity on the borrower's life payable for a fixed period of years to either the borrower or the borrower's heirs. This type of RAM yields a smaller monthly payment, but limits the risk of a great financial loss due to early death.

§ 22.51 Loan Plans: Reverse Mortgages—Attorney's Role [1]

The attorney for the homeowner should ensure that the reverse mortgage transaction documents provide several protections.

1. No prepayment penalty and no penalty for discontinuing or decreasing the number or amount of payments disbursed should be allowed.

2. The borrower should be protected from acceleration of payments in the event the borrower is absent from the home for specified periods due to medical conditions.

§ 22.51

1. ABA, supra § 22.31, note 1, at 3–4.

3. The borrower should be protected from acceleration of payments if junior liens are placed on the home or if the property is transferred between spouses.

4. The contract should provide that in the event of lender default, interest on the unpaid balance does not continue to accrue, all previously earned interest is forgiven, and this interest-free loan is then not repayable until the long-term maturity date or until the homeowner's occupancy is terminated by death or moving out. The borrower's additional costs incurred due to lender default should be reimbursed by the lender.

5. If the lender transfers the loan, the transferee must be bound by the terms of the original loan.

6. If the interest rate is adjustable, increases in the interest rate should be limited, and the borrower should be allowed to extend the loan term upon an increase in interest.

7. No deficiency judgment should be allowed if the loan amount is not satisfied by the amount received by the lender in foreclosure proceedings or from the sale of the property.

In most areas where reverse mortgages are offered, nonprofit social service agencies are available to assist senior citizens in analyzing their need for a reverse mortgage and determining whether there are alternatives that might be more suitable. These agencies also work to ensure that the senior adequately plans for the home sale at the end of the term.

CHAPTER 23

PRIVATE EMPLOYMENT PENSIONS

Table of Sections

WESTLAW Electronic Research

See WESTLAW Electronic Research Guide preceding the Summary of Contents.

---

§ 23.1 Introduction

Approximately half the private employment jobs in the United States are covered by a pension plan.[1] For those workers, the pension benefits are crucial to being able to cease work and still survive at a decent living standard in their older years. No law requires employers to provide pension benefits. However, the tax code creates incentives to establish pensions, and unions have bargained heavily for them and for laws protecting the rights of potential pension beneficiaries.

§ 23.1

1. R. Brown, The Rights of Older Persons 147 (1989).

Pension benefits are a form of deferred compensation. Employees earn rights to the benefits while employed because of employers' contractual promises to pay the benefits when the employees are eligible for retirement. Once an employer decides to provide a plan, both tax and labor law requirements must be met in order to qualify for special tax treatment.

The Employee Retirement Income Security Act of 1974 (ERISA)[2] has had far reaching effects on private retirement plans and the employees and beneficiaries covered under such plans. The Internal Revenue Service, as in the past, plays a significant role in connection with plans that are qualified under the Internal Revenue Code of 1986, as amended. The ERISA, however, gave significant responsibilities over retirement plans to the Department of Labor. The ERISA also established a corporation, the Pension Benefit Guarantee Corporation (PBGC), to oversee defined benefit plans and to guarantee their financial soundness. The ERISA has provided much needed reform in the pension benefit area.

Many plans prior to ERISA required both lengthy service and employment under the particular plan at the time of retirement; thus, long service alone often failed to achieve eligibility. Under ERISA, however, extended service in covered employment ensures the worker eligibility for at least some benefits. At the foundation of private pensions are the concepts of participation, vesting, and accrual. The ERISA provides stringent guidelines for these aspects of pension plans so that participants have established and protected rights to their retirement benefits.

The ERISA also requires that pension plans provide certain reports to inform participants of these rights. By enactment of the Retirement Equity Act of 1984, ERISA mandates that pension plans offer joint and survivor annuities to protect the interests of participants' spouses.[3] In addition, ERISA preempts all differing state laws that relate to pensions in order to secure a uniform system of providing retirement benefits.[4]

Library References:

C.J.S. Pensions and Retirement Plans and Benefits § 7.
West's Key No. Digests, Pensions ⊃21.

§ 23.2 Establishing Right to Benefit—Application

An employee who desires to begin participating in a pension plan must follow the application procedures provided for by the plan descrip-

---

2. Pub.L. No. 93–406, 88 Stat. 829 (1974). The ERISA's labor provisions are codified at 29 U.S.C.A. §§ 1001–1461.

3. 29 U.S.C.A. § 1055.

4. 29 U.S.C.A. § 1144(a).

tion. Any employee who has correctly followed these procedures is entitled to a decision on the application within a reasonable time. If the application has been declined or no response has been made, the employee must seek review of the application. The employee is entitled to learn the reason for denial and to be told of any additional information needed to support the application. Review by a court will be available only after all administrative procedures provided for by the plan have been exhausted.

Library References:
C.J.S. Pensions and Retirement Plans and Benefits §§ 69–79.
West's Key No. Digests, Pensions ⚯121.

§ 23.3 Establishing Right to Benefit—Participation

Participation standards define who must be allowed to participate (enroll) in a particular pension plan. Although there are some specific exceptions, generally, any employee who has completed one year of service with the employer maintaining the plan or who has attained the age of 21, whichever is later, is entitled to participate in the plan.[1] A year of service is defined as a 12–month period during which the employee has at least 1,000 hours of service.[2] Since 1,000 hours is the equivalent of about 6 months of 40 hour per week employment, not only part-time jobs, but also seasonal jobs, can have pension coverage.

§ 23.4 Establishing Right to Benefit—Breaks in Service

Under both ERISA and prior laws, all periods of service do not count toward the establishment of pension rights. In the past, breaks in service even after many years of employment caused loss of all previous credit. However, recent statutory changes have protected employees from loss of credit when employment temporarily ceases. Currently, only extreme breaks in service can erase established service credits.

A break in service is defined as a 12–consecutive–month period (corresponding to the calendar or plan year) during which an employee has worked 500 or less hours of service.[1] Only when there is no work or less than 500 hours of work can a "break in service" exist that threatens participation or credit. Although all years of service must be taken into account to determine when participation begins,[2] plans may provide a one-year waiting period after a break in service before

§ 23.3
1. 29 U.S.C.A. § 1052(a)(1)(A). Vesting must be retroactive to credit service since age 18 (see § 23.7 infra).
2. 29 U.S.C.A. § 1052(a)(3)(A).

§ 23.4
1. 29 U.S.C.A. § 1053(b)(3)(A).
2. 29 U.S.C.A. § 1052(b)(1).

allowing re-entry into the plan.[3] When the hours worked are between 500 and 1,000, the employer need not give credit for that time, but no break in service occurs that forfeits previously acquired service.

Furthermore, since 1985, no vested benefits can be lost because of a break in service. Even if a nonvested participant has a break in service, prior service credits must count unless the break in service is at least five years and as long as the total aggregate number of years of service before the break.[4] In addition, since 1985, no previous credit may be lost for as much as a year taken off to care for a newborn or adopted child.[5] Thus, ERISA provides substantial protection against the forfeiture of service credits due to periods of nonemployment.[6]

Library References:

C.J.S. Pensions and Retirement Plans and Benefits § 84.

West's Key No. Digests, Pensions ☜125.

§ 23.5   Establishing Right to Benefit—Nondiscrimination

One of the primary purposes of ERISA is to ensure that employers operate their pension plans in a nondiscriminatory manner. Each plan must meet several requirements in order to be considered "qualified" for preferential tax treatment. First, the plan must cover a minimum of 50 employees or 40% of the total number of employees.[1] Second, employers may not discriminate in the persons they allow to participate in their pension plans. For example, prior to 1988, an older employee who began employment within five years of the normal retirement age could be excluded from participation on the basis of age only when the plan was a defined benefit or target benefit plan.[2] Since 1988, these employees cannot be excluded from participation because of age, but they can be required to work a full five years before having any pension rights.[3]

In addition, the plan cannot discriminate by providing coverage in favor of highly compensated individuals.[4] The ERISA also prohibits

3. 29 U.S.C.A. § 1052(b)(3).

4. 29 U.S.C.A. § 1052(b)(4)(A). Breaks between 1976 and 1984 may cause loss of credit if they were as long as the prior period of service.

5. 29 U.S.C.A. § 1052(b)(5).

6. However, in a plan that provides for 100% vesting after two years of service, an employee who has not satisfied the two-year requirement forfeits prior service credit by a break in service. 29 U.S.C.A. § 1052(b)(2).

§ 23.5

1. 26 U.S.C.A. § 401(a)(26).

2. 29 U.S.C.A. § 1052(a)(2).

3. ERISA § 202(a)(2), as amended by the Omnibus Budget Reconciliation Act of 1986, § 9203(a)(1).

4. 26 U.S.C.A. §§ 401(a)(4), 410(b). The plan must pass one of three tests—the percentage test, the ratio test, or the average benefits test. The percentage test requires that at least 70% of non-highly compensat-

pension plans from being discriminatory with respect to the level of contributions or benefits provided to the participants.[5] Thus, employers must provide highly compensated and non-highly compensated employees with contributions and benefits that represent an equal percentage of income to both classes.

Older workers have gained protection from discrimination that denied them pension accruals after a certain age by relying on the Age Discrimination Act.[6]

§ 23.6 Establishing Right to Benefit—Accrual of Benefits: Defined Benefit and Defined Contribution Plans

Accrual of benefits is the rate at which participants accumulate benefits for years of service, although these benefits are not necessarily vested in the employee's account. A "year of service" is a 12–month period during which the employee provides at least 1,000 hours of service.[1] Once an individual has satisfied the requirements for participation in the plan, every year of service must create some credit toward the eventual retirement benefit, although the employer may give only partial credit for less than full-time work.

Benefits accrue under two basic types of pension plans: defined benefit plans and defined contribution plans or individual accounts.[2] Defined contribution plans call for the employer (and sometimes the employee as well) to deposit a specified amount into the employee's retirement plan while the employee is working. The value of the defined contribution plan and, consequently, the amount of each pension benefit upon retirement depends on the success or failure of investments made with the contributions. Defined benefit plans promise to pay a specified amount determined by a formula upon retirement. Under the defined benefit plan, the employer bears the financial risks of funding retirement benefits, while under a defined contribution plan, that risk falls on the employee.

The accrued benefits under both plans must either be kept or be

---

ed employees be covered by the plan. The ratio test requires that the percentage of non-highly compensated employees covered by the plan be at least 70% of the percentage of highly compensated employees covered by the plan. Finally, the average benefit test is a less specific test that hinges upon approval by the Secretary of the Treasury.

5. 26 U.S.C.A. § 401(a)(4).

6. American Association of Retired Persons v. Farmers Group, Inc., 943 F.2d 996 (9th Cir.1991), *cert. denied* Farmers Group Inc. v. American Association of Retired Persons, ___ U.S. ___, 112 S.Ct. 937, 117 L.Ed.2d 108 (1992).

§ 23.6

1. 29 U.S.C.A. § 1052(a)(3)(A).

2. 29 U.S.C.A. § 1054.

determinable by separate accounting.[3] In a defined contribution plan, a separate account must be maintained for the benefits of each employee. The amount that is contributed to this account may be determined by company profits or by the amount of compensation an employee elects to defer. In a defined benefit plan, the funding for all benefits may be lumped together into a single trust that funds all employees' benefits. The level of benefits in this type of plan is determined by a formula that varies between employers, but most often takes into account the employee's years of service and highest average salary for a three- or five-year period. The formula typically multiplies these two variables by a percentage, usually one to two percent, to arrive at a fixed sum.[4] After this calculation, an actuary determines the amount that must be held in the trust to fund this level of benefits upon retirement.

Library References:

C.J.S. Pensions and Retirement Plans and Benefits §§ 16, 19, 69–79.
West's Key No. Digests, Pensions ⊕⇒24.1, 61, 121.

§ 23.7 Establishing Right to Benefit—Vesting

Vested benefits are those accrued retirement benefits to which an employee has earned a nonforfeitable right of receipt upon attaining retirement age. Vesting was a concept introduced by ERISA to preclude employers from revoking pension benefits just before the employee was about to retire. The vesting requirements apply to an employee who works at least 1,000 hours in a plan year after age 18.[1]

Since 1989, pension plans may utilize either a five-year "cliff" vesting schedule or a seven-year graded (graduated) vesting schedule.[2] Cliff vesting provides that after five years of service, an employee must be 100% vested in the accrued benefits under the plan. Prior to that fifth year of service, the employee's benefits are completely forfeitable. In the graded vesting schedule, an employee becomes 20% vested in the accrued benefits after three years of service, with a 20% increase in vested benefits in each year of service thereafter. Under this schedule, the employee will be 100% vested after seven years of service. Only union-negotiated multiemployer plans may continue to require ten years of service before vesting.

3. 29 U.S.C.A. § 1054(b)(3).

4. P. Scott, A National Retirement Income Policy, 44 Tax Notes 913, 919–920 (1989).

2. 29 U.S.C.A. § 1053(a)(2). Persons who ceased employment prior to 1989 cannot change prior ten-year vesting requirements.

§ 23.7

1. 29 U.S.C.A. §§ 1053(b)(1) and (2).

A person retiring after a varied work experience with several employers should reconstruct the entire work history. The employee should inquire about possible pension benefits from any employer which may have a pension program and for which the employee worked five or more years. There may be small amounts payable from several plans.

Library References:

C.J.S. Pensions and Retirement Plans and Benefits §§ 73–83.

West's Key No. Digests, Pensions ⊕62.

§ 23.8 Establishing Right to Benefit—Forfeitability

While ERISA greatly restricts the forfeitability of pension benefits, there are three situations in which ERISA provides no protection. First, vested rights are forfeited upon death of the employee before retirement age provided the employee and the spouse have waived a survivor annuity. Second, although an employee has the right to withdraw employee contributions, an employee who is less than 50% vested forfeits all remaining pension benefits by withdrawal of mandatory employee contributions to the plan.[1] Finally, ERISA provides that retroactive plan amendments may not cause forfeiture of any vested rights to collect at normal retirement age.[2] However, changes can affect earning of future benefits, rights to early retirement, methods of payment, and supplemental benefits, at least, if approved by the Secretary of Labor.[3]

Employers are often concerned about ex-employees working for a business competitor. Ordinarily, no vested benefits can be forfeited because an employee joins a competing workforce. However, if the plan has a noncompetition provision and provides benefits that vest more generously than ERISA requires, vesting that exceeds the minimum required may be forfeited.[4]

Library References:

C.J.S. Pensions and Retirement Plans and Benefits § 80.

West's Key No. Digests, Pensions ⊕127.1.

§ 23.9 Obtaining Information—In General

The ERISA guarantees plan participants and beneficiaries a right to information concerning the provisions of the plan, the financial

---

§ 23.8

1. 29 U.S.C.A. § 1053(a)(3)(D)(i).

2. 29 U.S.C.A. § 1053(a); Brown, supra § 23.1, note 1, at 156.

3. 29 U.S.C.A. § 1053(a)(3)(C).

4. Noell v. American Design, Inc., Profit Sharing Plan, 764 F.2d 827 (11th Cir. 1985).

condition and performance of the plan, and the rights that have accrued to the individual under the plan.

Library References:

C.J.S. Pensions and Retirement Plans and Benefits §§ 31–33.

West's Key No. Digests, Pensions ⚷47.

§ 23.10   Obtaining Information—Plan Description and Appeals

The ERISA requires employers to file with the Secretary of Labor a plan description containing the basic elements of the plan and revealing provisions regarding participation, accrual, vesting, financing, claims procedure, and forfeiture of benefits. In addition, employers are required to furnish participants and beneficiaries with a summary plan description which shall "include the information [required in the plan description] . . . written in a manner calculated to be understood by the average plan participant, and shall be sufficiently accurate and comprehensive to reasonably apprise such participants and beneficiaries of their rights and obligations under the plan." [1]

The summary should explain both procedures for making a claim for pension and for appealing denials.[2] Written notice of denial, ordinarily, must be given within 90 days of claim with the reason for denial stated.[3] The claimant has 60 days in which to file a written appeal and has rights to see pension documents, to know the evidence on which denial was based, and to submit written material, including rebuttal of the evidence, but has no right to appear personally. Ultimately, the claimant may appeal to state or federal court for a review limited to whether there was substantial evidence for denial and whether the law was applied appropriately.[4]

A participant with a detailed question about the plan provisions should not rely solely on the plan summary—it may be misleading in its attempt to simplify. Participants are entitled to a copy of the full plan description, in addition to the summary, without charge within 90 days of becoming participants or receiving first benefits.[5] Any material changes in the subject matter of the plan summary require additional

§ 23.10

1. 29 U.S.C.A. § 1022(a)(1).

2. 29 U.S.C.A. § 1022(b). See Brown, supra § 23.1, note 1, at 157–158 (1989).

3. 29 C.F.R. § 2560.503–1 et seq. contains regulations on the procedural requirements.

4. Mason v. Continental Group, Inc., 763 F.2d 1219 (11th Cir.1985), cert. denied 474 U.S. 1087, 106 S.Ct. 863, 88 L.Ed.2d 902 (1986); Miles v. New York State Teamsters Conference Pension and Retirement Fund Employee Benefit Plan, 698 F.2d 593, 601 (2d Cir.), cert. denied 464 U.S. 829, 104 S.Ct. 105, 78 L.Ed.2d 108 (1983).

5. 29 U.S.C.A. § 1024(b)(1)(A).

notification.[6] Participants can receive underlying documents of the plan, such as collective bargaining agreements and trust agreements, at a reasonable cost or can review them without charge.

§ 23.11 Obtaining Information—Annual Report

Every pension plan is required to produce an annual report that conveys the financial status of the plan, including such items as a financial statement accompanied by the opinion of an independent qualified public accountant, the number of employees covered, and the nature of the services.[1] The annual report is sent to the Secretary of Labor and distributed to any participant or beneficiary who requests it within 210 days of the end of the plan year.[2] The employer is required to provide without charge at least the financial statement portion of the report.

§ 23.12 Obtaining Information—Statement of Individual Benefit Rights

The ERISA entitles individuals to learn the amount of pension to which they will be entitled upon retirement. No more than once a year, a participant/beneficiary may request in writing a statement indicating the total accrued benefits and the total accrued and vested benefits.[1] Plans subject to the vesting provisions of ERISA must also provide participants and the Internal Revenue Service with a pension statement describing the individual's benefits and rights under the plan.

§ 23.13 Benefit Claim Procedure—Methods of Distribution

The statute permits a qualified plan to distribute pension benefits after the employee has reached age 65 (or the normal retirement age specified in the plan), has completed ten years of participation in the plan, or has terminated employment, whichever is later.[1] Three basic

---

6. 29 U.S.C.A. § 1024(b)(1).

§ 23.11

1. For additional report requirements, see 29 U.S.C.A. § 1023.

2. 29 U.S.C.A. § 1024(b)(3).

§ 23.12

1. 29 U.S.C.A. § 1025(a).

§ 23.13

1. 29 U.S.C.A. § 1056(a). 26 U.S.C.A. § 72(t) imposes a ten percent penalty tax on certain distributions including those

made prior to age 59½, unless the participant terminated service after age 55. In addition, the plan must distribute benefits beginning no later than the year after the participant attains age 70½, regardless of whether the employee has retired. 26 U.S.C.A. § 401(a)(9).

payment methods are: annuity, installment, and lump sum.[2] The most common method of distribution is a *straight life annuity*: benefits are paid monthly for the employee's lifetime. Although the benefits may be generous in amount, all risk of forfeiture by death is allocated to the retiree. For married employees who retired after 1985, the most common form of payment may be a *joint and survivor annuity*: benefits are paid monthly for the lifetimes of the employee and one other person, usually the employee's spouse. In order to fund the survivor annuity, the benefits paid during the retired employee's life will be less than without the survivor benefit.

Some plans allow the employee to choose other annuity payment methods. One alternative form is a straight life annuity with period-certain benefits: benefits are paid for the employee's lifetime and for a guaranteed period of time, such as ten years. If the employee dies before the end of the guaranteed period, a second person (the beneficiary) will receive the same sum for the remainder of the period. If the beneficiary has a much longer life expectancy than the employee, this is a dangerous election unless the person has another source of income to commence when the payments cease.

Another variation is fixed-amount, fixed-period installment payments: benefits are paid as a stated amount for a definite number of installments. For example, a stated amount of $75,000 could be paid out in 120 equal monthly installments. This is a method by which a retiree can obtain close to the present value of the expected benefits and invest the proceeds independently. Although it removes risk of forfeiture by premature death, it places risk of a longer life and declining investment value on the retiree.

The third possible payment method is a one-time *lump sum benefit*: payment of the total amount credited to the employee's pension account in a single check. No further payments are made.

Library References:

C.J.S. Pensions and Retirement Plans and Benefits §§ 94–107.

West's Key No. Digests, Pensions ⚌134, 139.

§ 23.14 Benefit Claim Procedure—Assignment of Benefits— Voluntary Assignment

The federal statute discourages voluntary assignments by limiting

---

2. For descriptions and tax consequences, see, A. Gamble, Planning for Distribution from Retirement Plans, 45 (Pt. 1)   N.Y.U.Inst.Fed.Tax'n, Ch. 27, § 27.03 et seq. (1987).

them to a maximum of ten percent of any benefit payment.[1] Most plans forbid voluntary alienation entirely.

Library References:

C.J.S. Pensions and Retirement Plans and Benefits §§ 91–93.

West's Key No. Digests, Pensions ⟜138.

§ 23.15 Benefit Claim Procedure—Assignment of Benefits— QDRO: Qualified Domestic Relations Order

Pension benefit rights may be transferred or assigned involuntarily only by a qualified domestic relations order (QDRO).[1] The QDRO exception was provided by the Retirement Equity Act of 1984 in order to better protect the interests of family members of the employee. A QDRO is any judgment, decree, or order made according to state domestic relations law that "creates or recognizes the existence of an alternate payee's right to, or assigns to an alternate payee the right to, receive all or a portion of the benefits payable with respect to a participant under a plan." The QDRO must relate "to the provision of child support, alimony payments, or marital property rights to a spouse, former spouse, child, or other dependent of a participant."[2] This definition of QDRO has been construed narrowly by the courts.[3]

State laws authorize courts to order a parent to pay support for the benefit of minor children with whom they do not live and, usually, authorize court orders at the time of divorce for support of the ex-spouse and to implement division of the spouses' property. The QDRO contemplated by the Retirement Equity Act is a state-authorized court order entered for one of these purposes. The order is directed to the plan administrator, for payment of a portion of the retirement benefit directly to an alternate payee, someone other than the employee or retiree.[4] The order can require the plan administrator to make payments to the alternate payee either in a lump sum or periodically. The alternate payee has some of the same rights as the employee partici-

§ 23.14

1. 29 U.S.C.A. § 1056(d).

§ 23.15

1. 29 U.S.C.A. § 1056(d)(3)(B).

2. Id.

3. See, e.g., Ablamis v. Roper, 937 F.2d 1450 (9th Cir.1991) (holding that a testamentary transfer of pension rights was not intended by Congress to fall under the QDRO exception to the anti-alienation provisions of ERISA).

4. When state courts divide the value of pension benefits earned during marriage by other methods that do not involve the pension plan itself, a QDRO is not appropriate. For example, the court may accomplish sharing both the value of equity in a house and the value of the pension rights by ordering that the employed spouse keep all pension benefits and the other spouse take the house. No QDRO is needed.

pant, including the right to information about the plan and the individual employee's account. The federal act applies only to direct pay court orders made since January 1, 1985 (although the divorce could have been earlier). The major requisite of a "qualified order" is that it cannot include benefits not provided by the plan. The plan administrator will determine whether the order is qualified, subject to challenge by either the participant or the alternate payee.[5]

A QDRO as part of a property division is based on the state's theory that the married spouses, as partners, contributed to earning the retirement benefits. For that reason, the Retirement Equity Act permits orders to pay either a lump sum or periodic payments to the nonemployee ex-spouse as soon as the employee spouse is eligible to retire, regardless of whether the employee spouse is retiring.[6] This election prior to retirement is dangerous for the nonemployee ex-spouse because most plans subsidize early retirement, but the alternate payee who elects to collect prior to retirement will receive only a portion of the unsubsidized actuarially reduced benefit. If there is no rate for reduction of the subsidy in the plan, a five percent reduction will be made.[7]

Property division QDROs entered while the participant is still employed often order a certain percentage of the portion of the ultimate retirement benefit that was earned during the marriage paid to the nonemployee ex-spouse when the employee retires. Consequently, in planning for retirement income or in checking whether the amount a retiree receives is correct, the attorney should always inquire whether there has been a divorce and should check the court decree for orders to the plan administrator.

§ 23.16 Survivors' Interests in Pensions—Spouses—In General

Pension benefits may be, and must be in some circumstances, distributed through a joint and survivor annuity.[1] The Retirement Equity Act of 1984, viewing marriage as an "economic partnership,"[2] set out to protect the rights of the spouses of pension plan participants by adding this method of distribution to ERISA. The act requires every pension plan to provide survivor annuities to spouses of participants who retire after 1984.

---

5. 29 U.S.C.A. § 1056(d)(3)(G), (H).

6. 26 U.S.C.A. § 414(p)(4)(A)(ii); Troyan, Drafting and Qualifying a Court Order in a Domestic Relations Case, 20 Fam.L.Q. 1 (1986).

7. 26 U.S.C.A. § 414(p)(4)(A).

§ 23.16

1. See, generally, Rose, Why Antenuptial Agreements Cannot Relinquish Survivor Benefits, 43 Fla.L.Rev. 723 (Fall 1991).

2. S.Rep. No. 575, 98th Cong., 2d Session (1) (1984).

Library References:

C.J.S. Pensions and Retirement Plans and Benefits §§ 69–88.

West's Key No. Digests, Pensions ⊕121, 133.

§ 23.17　Survivors' Interests in Pensions—Spouses—Death Before or After Retirement

The survivor requirement takes two forms.　First, a pension plan must provide a preretirement survivor annuity when a vested participant dies before the pension starting date.[1]　A preretirement survivor annuity provides benefits for the life of the surviving spouse payable at the earliest date the participant could have retired.　The value of the annuity will depend upon the length of time between the participant's date of death and the earliest retirement age provided in the pension plan.　The value of the preretirement annuity will decrease as this length of time increases, i.e., the earlier the employee dies, the less the annuity will be.　However, the value of the annuity cannot fall below the value of a comparable joint and survivor annuity.[2]

Second, for participants who retire, i.e., who do not die, before the pension starting date, the pension plan must provide a joint and survivor annuity.[3]　In this situation, a qualified joint and survivor annuity provides an annuity for the life of the participant with a survivor annuity for the life of the spouse.　The spouse's survivor annuity provided by the plan cannot be less than 50% (and not greater than 100%) of the amount payable during the joint lives of the participant and the spouse.[4]

§ 23.18　Survivors' Interests in Pensions—Spouses—Waiver of Survivor Rights

In order for the spouse's rights to be extinguished, both spouses must sign a written consent, witnessed by a plan representative or a notary public,[1] that acknowledges the rights being waived.　Employees and spouses should realize that a waiver results in larger payments during the employee's lifetime but no benefits at all to the surviving spouse.

A waiver of the preretirement survivor annuity must be executed by both spouses within the period starting on the first day of the plan year in which the participant is age 35 and ending on the date of the

---

§ 23.17

1.　29 U.S.C.A. § 1055(d).

2.　29 U.S.C.A. § 1055(e).

3.　29 U.S.C.A. § 1055(a)(1).

4.　29 U.S.C.A. § 1055(d).

§ 23.18

1.　29 U.S.C.A. § 1055(c)(2).

participant's death.[2]   Waiver of the retired employee's survivor rights must be executed by both spouses within a 90–day period ending on the annuity starting date.   The plan administrator should provide forms for these elections at the appropriate times.

§ 23.19 Survivors' Interests in Pensions—Ex–Spouses

Ordinarily, in the absence of a specific court order, a divorced spouse has no survivor rights in the former spouse's pension.[1]   This is true even if the ex-spouse had been an alternate payee receiving monthly payments from the plan from the time of divorce until the retiree's death.   However, the divorce court that has power under state laws to assign pension rights can create survivor rights by a qualified domestic relations order (QDRO).[2]   The terms of the QDRO would determine the ex-spouse's interests.   Survivor benefits can follow after payments to the ex-spouse as alternate payee or can be paid even though no payments were made during the retiree's lifetime.   The rights can include all the benefits of a survivor spouse in the portion of the pension that was earned during the marriage.   The court-ordered survivor rights can exist whether the employee ex-spouse died before or after retirement, provided no waiver had been executed.[3]   If the employee ex-spouse remarried, then two survivors may have rights to different portions of the pension.[4]   The court order must be reviewed to determine these rights.   If the order qualifies, the plan administrator must pay the ordered portion to the ex-spouse as a survivor benefit.

2.   29 U.S.C.A. § 1055(c)(7).

§ 23.19

1.   Retirement Plans, 12 Fam.Adv. 44, 46 (Winter 1990); Kandel, Handling Retirement Plan Benefits When a Couple Divorce, 18 Estate Planning 268 (Sept./Oct. 1991) (WESTLAW: ESTPLN database, ci(18   +5   268)).

2.   29 U.S.C.A. § 1056(d)(3) et seq.; 26 U.S.C.A. § 414(p)(5).

3.   Whether an effective waiver can be made in a prenuptial agreement prior to the marriage is unclear.   Fox Valley & Vicinity Construction Workers Pension Fund v. Brown, 897 F.2d 275 (7th Cir.) (en banc), cert. denied 498 U.S. 820, 111 S.Ct. 67, 112 L.Ed.2d 41 (1990), held that a waiver in an agreement executed at the time of divorce was effective.   In re Estate of Hopkins, 574 N.E.2d 230 (Ill.Ct.App.1991), extended that reasoning to uphold a waiver

in a prenuptial agreement and declined to follow a contrary regulation.   See, Treas. Reg. § 1.401(a)–20, Q & A–28 (1988).   The Hopkins decision is criticized in Rose, Why Antenuptial Agreements Cannot Relinquish Survivor Benefits, 43 Fla.L.Rev. 723 (Fall 1991).   In Hurwitz v. Sher, 789 F.Supp. 134 (S.D.N.Y.), affirmed 982 F.2d 778 (2d Cir.1992), cert. denied, 1993 WL 98245 (Fed.Cir.1993) the Court recognized that a separation agreement executed by the spouses at divorce could constitute a waiver; but the Court declared Hopkins erroneous and held that since the parties were not spouses when executing a premarital agreement, an antenuptial waiver was not accomplished.

4.   Kandel, Handling Retirement Plan Benefits When a Couple Divorce, 18 Estate Planning 268, 271 (Sept./Oct. 1991) (WESTLAW: ESTPLN database, ci(18   +5   268)).

§ **23.20**　Plan Termination

An employer may terminate a pension plan, but an employee has rights to the vested benefits that have accrued to that employee by the time of termination. If a defined contribution plan is terminated, the employee is entitled to receive the amount of vested benefits in that employee's individual account. If a defined benefit plan is terminated, the employee is entitled to receive any employee contributions to the plan and other vested benefits that have accrued under a statutory allocation scheme. Any time a defined benefit plan is insolvent, including upon termination, payments due an employee may be covered by the Pension Benefit Guaranty Corporation.[1]

Library References:

C.J.S. Pensions and Retirement Plans and Benefits §§ 111–117.

West's Key No. Digests, Pensions ☞66.1.

§ **23.20**

1.　29 U.S.C.A. §§ 1321(b), 1322, 1322a, 1431.

CHAPTER 24

TAX BENEFITS

Table of Sections

A. FEDERAL INCOME TAX

WESTLAW Electronic Research

See WESTLAW Electronic Research Guide preceding the Summary of Contents.

A. FEDERAL INCOME TAX

§ 24.1 Filing Requirements—Age 65

An individual will be considered to be 65 years old on the first moment of the day preceding the individual's 65th birthday.[1]

§ 24.1
1. Treas.Reg. § 1.151–1(c)(2) (WEST-LAW: FTX–CFR database, **ci(1.151–1)**).

308

§ 24.2   Filing Requirements—Who Must File

The general rule regarding the obligation to file an income tax return is set out in Internal Revenue Code (IRC) § 6012. Persons age 65 or older are subject to special provisions governing the obligation to file an income tax return. If a person's gross income for the year exceeds the amounts specified in the statute, an income tax return must be filed, even if no tax is owed.[1]

To determine whether a return must be filed, a person first must determine his or her (1) basic standard deduction,[2] (2) additional standard deductions,[3] and (3) exemption amount.[4] A person age 65 or older is required to file a return unless the person falls into one of the following categories:

1. The person is not married,[5] is not a surviving spouse,[6] is not a head of a household,[7] and for the taxable year has a gross income of less than the sum of the taxpayer's exemption amount plus his or her basic standard deductions;[8]

2. The person is the head of a household or a surviving spouse and for the taxable year has a gross income of less than the sum of the taxpayer's exemption amount plus his or her basic standard deduction plus his or her additional standard deduction;[9]

3. The person is entitled to make a joint return and the person's gross income, when combined with the gross income of his or her spouse, is less than the sum of twice the taxpayer's exemption amount plus the basic standard deduction applicable to a joint return plus his or her additional standard deductions, but only if the individual and the individual's spouse, at the close of the taxable year, had the same household as their home;[10] or

4. The person has no other taxable income and had earnings from self-employment of $400 or less for the taxable year, regardless of age.[11]

Note that the exception to the requirement to file does not apply to taxpayers who are dependents (as defined under § 151) and have an

§ 24.2

1. I.R.C. § 6012 et seq.
2. See § 24.4, infra.
3. See § 24.5, infra.
4. See § 24.6, infra.
5. See I.R.C. § 7703 (determining of marital status).
6. See I.R.C. § 2(a) (definition of "surviving spouse").

7. See I.R.C. § 2(b) (definition of "head of household").

8. I.R.C. §§ 6012(a)(1)(A)(i), (a)(1)(B).

9. I.R.C. §§ 6012(a)(1)(A)(ii), (a)(1)(A)(iii), (a)(1)(B).

10. I.R.C. §§ 6012(a)(1)(A)(iv), (a)(1)(B).

11. I.R.C. § 6017.

adjusted gross income greater than the amounts listed under IRC § 6012(a)(1)(C).[12] IRC § 6013, which describes eligibility for filing joint tax returns, sets out special rules regarding the filing of income tax returns where one spouse has died during the tax year.

Library References:

C.J.S. Internal Revenue §§ 17, 19, 67, 82, 323.

West's Key No. Digests, Internal Revenue ☞3560.

§ 24.3   Determining Taxable Income—Nontaxable Income

Some types of income received by older taxpayers are nontaxable and should not be reported in their returns.

1. Certain individuals will be required to include in gross income up to one-half of social security benefits received.[1] These taxpayers are those whose modified adjusted gross income and one-half of the social security benefits exceed:

   a. $25,000;

   b. $32,000 in the case of a joint return; or

   c. zero in the case of a married taxpayer who does not live apart from his or her spouse but who files a separate return.

   For this purpose, modified adjusted gross income includes nontaxable income and is adjusted gross income determined without regard to IRC § 221 (deduction for two-earner married couples), § 911 (U.S. citizens or residents living abroad), § 932 (income from sources within U.S. possessions), or § 933 (income from sources within Puerto Rico).

2. Section 86 of the IRC applies to certain monthly benefits received under the Railroad Retirement Act of 1974.[2] Railroad retirement lump sum payments and the residual payment are not taxable.[3]

3. Public assistance payments from a public welfare fund, such as payments received because of blindness, are not taxable. Longevity bonus payments that are made by a state to its citizens who meet specified age and residency requirements and that are not based on need are not welfare benefits and, therefore,

---

12. I.R.C. § 6012(a)(1)(C).

§ 24.3

1. I.R.C. § 86.

2. I.R.C. § 86(d)(4).

3. Rev.Rul. 74–561, 1974–2 C.B. 24, interpreting I.R.C. § 61 which defines gross income (WESTLAW: FTX–RR database, ci(74–561)).

are taxable to the recipients.[4] Nontaxable public assistance benefits include:

    a. grants under the Disaster Relief Act of 1974;[5]

    b. mortgage assistance payments under § 235 of the National Housing Act (consequently, interest paid on behalf of the homeowner is not deductible by the homeowner);[6] and

    c. grants for home rehabilitation.[7]

  4. Compensation for sickness or injury is generally nontaxable.[8] Nontaxable compensation includes:

    a. workers' compensation received for sickness or injuries. If the worker turns over the workers' compensation payments to his or her employer and all or part of the worker's regular salary continues to be paid, the excess of the salary payments over the amount of the workers' compensation payment is taxable income;[9]

    b. black-lung benefit payments;[10]

    c. damages received for injury or illness;[11]

    d. benefits received under an accident or health insurance policy attributable to premiums paid by the recipient, including a policy provided by an employer to the extent the plan is supported by employee contributions;[12]

    e. disability benefits received for loss of income or earning capacity as a result of injuries under a "no-fault" automobile policy;[13]

    f. compensation received for permanent loss or loss of use of a member or function of the body or for permanent disfigurement;[14] and

    g. Federal Employer's Compensation Act payments for personal injuries or sickness, including payments to beneficiaries in the case of death.

  5. Veterans' benefits are not taxable.[15]

---

4. Rev.Rul. 76–131, 1976–1 C.B. 16 (WESTLAW: FTX–RR database, **ci(76–131)**).

5. Rev.Rul. 76–144, 1976–1 C.B. 17 (WESTLAW: FTX–RR database, **ci(76–144)**).

6. Rev.Rul. 75–271, 1975–2 C.B. 23 (WESTLAW: FTX–RR database, **ci(75–271)**).

7. Rev.Rul. 76–395, 1976–2 C.B. 16 (WESTLAW: FTX–RR database, **ci(76–395)**).

8. I.R.C. § 104.

9. I.R.C. § 104(a)(1).

10. Rev.Rul. 72–400, 1972–1 C.B. 75 (WESTLAW: FTX–RR database, **ci(72–400)**).

11. I.R.C. § 104(a)(2).

12. I.R.C. § 104(a)(3).

13. Rev.Rul. 73–155, 1973–1 C.B. 50 (WESTLAW: FTX–RR database, **ci(73–155)**).

14. I.R.C. § 105(c)(1).

15. 38 U.S.C.A. § 3101.

6. Gifts, bequests, or inheritances received by an individual are not income and, therefore, are nontaxable.[16] However, if such property produces taxable income, such as dividends, interest, or rentals, the income is taxable.[17]

7. Interest on obligations of states and municipalities is generally exempt.[18] However, the Tax Reform Act of 1986 disallows interest exemptions for private activity bonds, arbitrage bonds, and bonds that are not in registered form.[19]

§ 24.4 Determining Taxable Income—Exemption for Age—Basic Standard Deduction

Every taxpayer, regardless of age, is entitled to a basic standard deduction if the taxpayer is not itemizing deductions.[1] The basic standard deduction for the tax year 1992 was as follows: [2]

1. $6,000 if the taxpayer was filing a joint return or was a surviving spouse; [3]

2. $5,250 if the taxpayer was the head of a household; [4]

3. $3,600 if the taxpayer was not married, was not a surviving spouse, and was not the head of a household; [5] and

4. $3,000 if the taxpayer was married and filing a separate return.[6]

Library References:

C.J.S. Internal Revenue § 301.

West's Key No. Digests, Internal Revenue ⊕3295.

§ 24.5 Determining Taxable Income—Exemption for Age—Additional Standard Deduction

Besides the basic standard deduction, older taxpayers and blind taxpayers are entitled to add an additional standard deduction. For 1992, a taxpayer age 65 or older on the last day of the tax year was entitled to an additional standard deduction of $700, and another

16. I.R.C. § 102(a).

17. I.R.C. § 102(b).

18. I.R.C. § 103(a).

19. I.R.C. § 103(b).

§ 24.4

1. I.R.C. § 63(b).

2. These dollar amounts are adjusted annually for inflation. I.R.C. § 63(c)(4).

3. I.R.C. § 63(c)(2)(A). Rev.Proc. 91–65, 1991–50 I.R.B. 12.

4. I.R.C. § 63(c)(2)(B).

5. I.R.C. § 63(c)(2)(C).

6. I.R.C. § 63(c)(2)(D). When married taxpayers file separately, as older remarried taxpayers often do, they must treat their deductions similarly. Therefore, if one itemizes, the other may not take the standard deduction. See, e.g., I.R.C. § 6013, Joint Returns of Income Tax by Husband and Wife.

additional standard deduction of $700 if the taxpayer's spouse was age 65 or older on the last day of the tax year.[1] If the taxpayer was not married and was not a surviving spouse, the amount was $900.[2] A taxpayer was entitled to an additional $700 deduction if he or she was blind, and another $700 deduction if the taxpayer's spouse was blind.[3] If the taxpayer was not married and was not a surviving spouse, the amount was $900.[4]

§ 24.6   Determining Taxable Income—Personal Exemption

Every taxpayer, regardless of age, is also allowed a personal exemption under IRC § 151. For tax year 1992, the personal exemption was $2,300 for the taxpayer and another $2,300 for the taxpayer's spouse if a joint return was not filed and if the spouse had no gross income.[1] This amount is adjusted annually for inflation.[2] Where a joint return is filed, the husband and wife are entitled to a combined personal exemption.

§ 24.7   Determining Taxable Income—Exclusion of Gain from Sale of Residence

A taxpayer who sells or exchanges the taxpayer's principal residence may elect to exclude $125,000 of gain from his or her gross income if the following requirements are met:

1. The taxpayer is age 55 or older before the date of the sale or exchange;

2. The taxpayer owned and used the property sold as his or her principal residence for an aggregate of at least three years within the five-year period ending on the date of the sale or exchange; and

3. Neither the taxpayer nor the taxpayer's spouse have previously elected to exclude gain on the sale or exchange of a residence under this provision.[1]

---

§ 24.5

1. I.R.C. § 63(f)(1). Rev.Proc. 91–65, 1991–50 I.R.B. 12 (WESTLAW: FTX–RP database, **ci(91–65)**).

2. I.R.C. § 63(f)(3). Rev.Proc. 91–65, 1991–50 I.R.B. 12 (WESTLAW: FTX–RP database, **ci(91–65)**).

3. I.R.C. § 63(f)(2).

4. I.R.C. § 63(f)(3). Rev.Proc. 91–65, 1991–50 I.R.B. 12 (WESTLAW: FTX–RP database, **ci(91–65)**).

§ 24.6

1. I.R.C. § 151(b), (d). Rev.Proc. 91–65, 1991–50 I.R.B. 12 (WESTLAW: FTX–RP database, **ci(91–65)**).

2. I.R.C. § 151(d)(4).

§ 24.7

1. I.R.C. § 121, as amended by Public Law 97–34, the Economic Recovery Tax Act of 1981.

If the taxpayer meets the above requirements, the taxpayer may elect to exclude $125,000 of his or her gain on the sale or exchange. However, if the taxpayer is married and filing separately, the taxpayer may elect to exclude only $62,500 of gain on the sale or exchange.[2]

The gain is the excess of the amount realized over the adjusted basis of the residence. The amount realized is the selling price minus the selling expenses; and the adjusted basis is the original cost of the property increased by improvements, additions, and other capital expenditures, and reduced due to fire or other casualty losses and payments for any easements or right-of-ways granted. Internal Revenue Service Form 2119 is the form to use in claiming this exclusion from gross income.

Note that any taxpayer, regardless of age, can avoid the recognition of all or part of the gain on the sale of the taxpayer's residence by buying or building another principal residence within a period beginning two years before the date of the sale and ending two years after that date.[3]

§ 24.8 Determining Taxable Income—Annuities

If a client is receiving income from an annuity contract, a percentage of that income may not have to be included in gross income.[1] Section 72 of the Internal Revenue Code sets out the formula to determine the amount of the income from an annuity that may be excluded from gross income.[2]

An exclusion ratio must be determined to calculate the amount of income from an annuity that may be excluded from gross income.[3] The *exclusion ratio* is the amount of investment in the annuity divided by the expected return from the annuity contract; or:

$$\text{Exclusion ratio} = \frac{\text{Investment in the annuity}}{\text{Taxpayer's expected return}}$$

The *amount invested* in the contract is the aggregate amount of premiums paid, minus any amount returned to the taxpayer before the "stream of income" from the annuity contract begins to flow; or:[4]

$$\begin{array}{l} \text{Amount of premiums paid} \\ - \text{ Any amount returned to taxpayer} \\ = \text{ Investment in the contract} \end{array}$$

2. I.R.C. § 121(b)(1).

3. I.R.C. § 1034.

§ 24.8

1. I.R.C. § 72(a).

2. I.R.C. § 72(b).

3. I.R.C. § 72(b).

4. I.R.C. § 72(c)(1).

The *expected return* is equal to the amount of annual payments multiplied by the length of the payments; or[5]

> Amount of annual payments
> $\times$ Length of payments
> = Taxpayer's expected return

The length of payments either will be stated in the contract or will be "for life." If the payments are "for life," the individual determining the tax must consult the treasury regulations for IRC § 72, which contain actuarial tables that must be used to determine the taxpayer's expected return.[6]

The *amount excluded* from income is determined by multiplying the exclusion ratio by the amount of annual payments to the taxpayer; or:[7]

> Exclusion ratio
> $\times$ Annual payments
> = Amount excluded from gross income

Note, however, that in calculating the tax, the *amount included* in gross income is the important figure. This amount is determined by subtracting the excluded amount from the annual amount of payments; or:

> Annual amount of payments
> − Excluded amount
> = Amount to be included in gross income

Also note that once the amount invested in the contract has been recovered by the taxpayer, the taxpayer may no longer apply the exclusion ratio.[8] After the amount invested in the annuity contract is fully recovered, all of the payments received for an annuity contract must be included in gross income.

In case of death prior to recovering all investment in the annuity, the remaining investment may be excluded in the final tax return.[9]

§ 24.9   Determining Taxable Income—Medical Expense Deductions

Under IRC § 213, medical expenses (not reimbursed by insurance) that exceed seven and one-half percent of the taxpayer's adjusted gross

---

5. I.R.C. § 72(c)(3).
6. I.R.C. § 72(c)(3)(A).
7. I.R.C. § 72(b)(1).
8. I.R.C. § 72(b)(2).

9. I.R.C. § 72(b)(3)(A). However, if the annuity starting date was before July 2, 1986, the rule does not apply. I.R.C. § 1122(b)(2)(B).

income are allowed as a deduction. The deduction is allowed for the taxpayer, his or her spouse, or a dependent (as defined in IRC § 152).[1] If medical expenses are a significant cost to a client, it is important for the attorney to plan other deductions so that the client's adjusted gross income is low enough to meet the seven and one-half percent threshold amount.

"Medical care" that is deductible includes the "[d]iagnosis, care, mitigation, treatment, or prevention of disease ... affecting any structure or function of the body."[2] Deductions may be taken for the following:

1. medicine and drugs, not including toiletries, cosmetics, or sundry items;[3]

2. capital expenditures, such as eye glasses, a seeing-eye dog, artificial teeth and limbs, etc.[4] However, capital expenditures that may increase the value of property are deductible only to the extent they do not increase the value of the property receiving the capital expenditure.[5] For example, if a taxpayer were advised to install an elevator in the home so that he or she would not have to climb stairs, and the cost of the expenditure was $1,000, but the increase in the value of the home was $700, then only $300 would be deductible as a medical expense;[6]

3. transportation "primarily for and essential to the rendition of medical care."[7] However, the cost of meals and lodging while the taxpayer is obtaining medical care are not included;[8] and

4. nursing home costs, to the extent the primary reason for the care is medical treatment.[9] Where the institutionalization of a family member is for custodial purposes, then expenditures for meals, lodging, and personal expenses are not deductible.[10] Essentially, the motivation for placing a family member in a nursing home must be for medical treatment, and not to ease the burden on the family.

§ 24.9

1. I.R.C. § 213.

2. Treas.Reg. § 1.213–1(e) (WESTLAW: FTX–CFR database, ci(1.213–1)).

3. Treas.Reg. § 1.213–1(e)(2) (WESTLAW: FTX–CFR database, ci(1.213–1)).

4. Treas.Reg. § 1.213–1(e)(1)(iii) (WESTLAW: FTX–CFR database, ci(1.213–1)).

5. Id. (WESTLAW: FTX–CFR database, ci(1.213–1)).

6. Id. (WESTLAW: FTX–CFR database, ci(1.213–1)).

7. Treas.Reg. § 1.213–1(e)(1)(iv) (WESTLAW: FTX–CFR database, ci(1.213–1)).

8. Id. (WESTLAW: FTX–CFR database, ci(1.213–1)).

9. Treas Reg. § 1.213–1(e)(1)(v) (WESTLAW: FTX–CFR database, ci(1.213–1)).

10. Id. (WESTLAW: FTX–CFR database, ci(1.213–1)).

Library References:

C.J.S. Internal Revenue §§ 147–183, 259.

West's Key No. Digests, Internal Revenue ☞3352, 3366.

§ 24.10 Determining Taxable Income—Deduction for Expenses to Determine Tax

Under Internal Revenue Code § 212(3), a deduction is allowed for all "ordinary and necessary expenses paid or incurred during the taxable year in connection with the determination, collection, or refund of any tax." [1] This information is crucial for an attorney working in the tax area. The client is allowed to deduct attorney fees that can be attributed to the "determination of any tax"; therefore, any part of a legal matter that involves tax work should be specifically billed as such, so the client may attempt to take the deduction.

Library References:

C.J.S. Internal Revenue §§ 137–156, 260.

West's Key No. Digests, Internal Revenue ☞3370.

§ 24.11 Credits Against Tax—Credits for Older Taxpayers

A person who is age 65 or older before the end of the tax year or who retired on permanent and total disability before the end of the tax year is entitled to a credit against tax.[1] The credit is an amount equal to 15% of the taxpayer's "section 22 amount." [2] In 1989, the credit was figured on Schedule R (Form 1040) of the return, was claimed on line 42 of Form 1040, and could not exceed the tax imposed. Married couples must file jointly to claim the credit unless the spouses have lived apart at all times during the tax year.[3]

The § 22 amount is an initial amount subject to two reductions. The initial amount, set out in § 22(c)(2), is as follows: [4]

§ 24.10

1. I.R.C. § 212(3).

§ 24.11

1. I.R.C. § 22(a), (b).

2. I.R.C. § 22(a).

3. I.R.C. § 22(e)(1).

4. If the taxpayer is not age 65 but qualifies for the credit due to retirement on total and permanent disability, these amounts may not exceed the taxpayer's disability income for the year. I.R.C. § 22(c)(2)(B)(i). Also, special rules apply if the spouses are filing jointly and both spouses are qualified to take the credit but at least one spouse is not age 65. If both spouses are not age 65, the initial amount may not exceed the sum of the spouses' disability income. I.R.C. § 22(c)(2)(B)(ii)(I). If one spouse is age 65, the initial amount may not exceed $5,000 plus the disability income for the spouse who is not age 65. I.R.C. § 22(c)(2)(B)(ii)(II). Disability income is defined as the amount includable in the taxpayer's gross income under § 72 (annuities) or § 105(a) (amounts received from employer-provided accident and health insurance) to the extent such amounts constitute wages. I.R.C. § 22(c)(2)(B)(iii).

1. $5,000 for a single person, or a joint return where only one spouse is qualified to take the credit;

2. $7,500 for spouses filing jointly where both spouses are qualified to take the credit; and

3. $3,750 for a married person filing a separate return.

The initial amount is reduced first by the total amount received by the taxpayer as a pension, annuity, or disability benefit which is excluded from gross income and payable under title II of the Social Security Act, the Railroad Retirement Act of 1974, or a law administered by the Veterans Administration, or which is otherwise excluded from income under any law except the Internal Revenue Code.[5] However, no reduction is made for an amount received as a pension, annuity, or a similar allowance for personal injuries or sickness resulting from active service in the armed forces.[6]

The initial amount is reduced second to account for the amount of the taxpayer's income. If the adjusted gross income of the taxpayer exceeds

1. $7,500 for a single person,

2. $10,000 for a married couple filing jointly, or

3. $5,000 for a married person filing separately,

the § 22 amount is reduced by one-half of the excess of the adjusted gross income over $7,500, $10,000, or $5,000, as the case may be.[7] The available credit for the taxpayer is 15% of this final figure.

Library References:

C.J.S. Internal Revenue §§ 307–319.

West's Key No. Digests, Internal Revenue ⊚⇒3520, 3521.

§ 24.12 Credits Against Tax—Residential Energy Credit

Certain expenditures associated with energy conservation made prior to December 31, 1985, earned the taxpayer a credit on taxes.[1] Such credits can be carried forward, but not to any years beginning after December 31, 1987.[2] Thus, the residential energy credit is no longer available as a practical matter.

---

5. I.R.C. § 22(c)(3)(A).

6. I.R.C. §§ 22(c)(3)(A), 104(a)(4).

7. I.R.C. § 22(d).

§ 24.12

1. I.R.C. § 23 (repealed by Pub.L. No. 101–508, 11–5–90).

2. Id.

Library References:

C.J.S. Internal Revenue § 310.

West's Key No. Digests, Internal Revenue ☞3533.

§§ 24.13–24.20 are reserved for supplementary material.

B. STATE TAX RELIEF

Library References:

C.J.S. Taxation § 1098.

West's Key No. Digests, Taxation ☞1047.

§ 24.21 Generally

At least 95% of the individual states employ a variety of methods for relieving their older citizens of sales, income, and real property tax burdens. The attorney should be familiar with the methods available in his or her state.

§ 24.22 Sales and Income Tax Relief—Refund of Sales Tax Paid

The refund of sales tax method of providing tax relief usually consists of a flat refund amount, reduced on the basis of the annual income for the entire household.

§ 24.23 Sales and Income Tax Relief—Exemption of Certain Products and Services

This method of tax relief exempts from sales tax products that are generally considered necessary, primarily food and drugs; and usually this type of exemption is not limited to elderly persons. Some states also exempt certain types of services from sales tax, the most common of these being meals and housing provided for older citizens.

§ 24.24 Sales and Income Tax Relief—State Income Tax Credit

The credit systems work much like the sales tax refund method of tax relief except the set amount is simply deducted from the income tax liability. The credit may be negative, i.e., it may exceed the income tax liability, in which case a cash refund is paid by the state.

§ 24.25 Sales and Income Tax Relief—Deductions from Income

Many states allow tax relief through the subtraction of both pension and social security payments from income for state income tax purposes. This allowance can effectively eliminate state income tax for older taxpayers.

§ 24.26 Property Tax Relief—Major Types—Relief From Payment of Property Tax

Relief from payment of property tax generally takes the form of either an exemption from taxation of all or part of the assessed value or a deduction from the property tax due. The exemption method is analogous to an income tax deduction, while the latter method is equivalent to a tax credit. Generally this credit may not exceed the tax due, so that no refund is available.

§ 24.27 Property Tax Relief—Major Types—Reduction of State Income Tax Liability

Under the type of system that reduces state income tax liability, the taxpayer is allowed a deduction from the income tax due in an amount up to the amount actually paid as property tax. Some states limit the deductions available, and cash refunds may be allowed when the property tax paid exceeds the income tax liability.

§ 24.28 Property Tax Relief—Eligibility for Relief

The usual eligibility requirements for property tax relief include:

1. The taxpayer must be age 65 or older;

2. The maximum household income must not exceed a certain specified level (other assets also may be included);

3. The taxpayer must reside on the property taxed; and

4. There must be at least a minimum interest in the property.

While ownership in fee is clearly sufficient, many states also provide relief for those who own less than a full interest in the property, and for renters, consider part of the rental payments as equivalent to property tax paid.

CHAPTER 25

FAMILY RIGHTS AND RESPONSIBILITIES

Table of Sections

A. GRANDPARENTS' RIGHTS

B. FINANCIAL RESPONSIBILITY FOR OLDER PERSONS

WESTLAW Electronic Research

See WESTLAW Electronic Research Guide preceding the Summary of Contents.

A. GRANDPARENTS' RIGHTS

Library References:

C.J.S. Infants §§ 5–30; Parent and Child §§ 16, 19.
West's Key No. Digests, Infants ⬅18–19.3; Parent and Child ⬅2.

§ 25.1 Modern Developments

In light of the long-existing legal posture that recognized almost no rights in grandparents toward their grandchildren, the years since 1970 have been revolutionary. Numerous social factors have combined to change the relationship between grandparents and grandchildren. One major development has been the movement of mothers of young children into the work force, creating more pressures and opportunities for grandparents to develop close ties with their grandchildren through caretaking. Another factor has been the high rate of divorce, which has created single parent families requiring more grandparent involvement. Divorce and remarriage also cause more family tension and conflict that may lead to attempts to exclude grandparents who have developed close ties with their grandchildren. A third factor in the increasing recognition of grandparents' rights has been the rapidly growing percentage of the population who are politically active older voters. Senior citizens lobby for legislation protecting their grandparental connections and they litigate to secure their asserted rights.

Every state has passed new legislation regarding grandparents' rights since the late 1970s or early 1980s, and new reported decisions appear day after day. Attorneys for grandparents must constantly check the latest developments, many of which the client will hear about through friends or senior citizen sources.[1]

The most common pattern courts follow is (1) occasionally to grant grandparents custody, but usually defer to parental wishes regarding custody and adoption, and (2) increasingly to recognize grandparental rights by awarding visitation with grandchildren, *provided* the family has been disrupted and the court finds visitation furthers the best interests of the grandchild. The basic tension between parental rights and furthering the best interests of the child through grandparent contact is explored in the following sections dealing with custody. The principles explained there are equally applicable in visitation and adoption disputes.

§ 25.2   Custody—In General

The subject of custody illustrates effectively the extent of parental rights to raise a family free from interference by the state, either independently or on behalf of grandparents. The relatively simple term, custody, means all rights to determine the child's upbringing— where he or she lives, what he or she wears, with whom he or she plays, education, recreation, religion, medical care, and whether the child has contact with grandparents.

§ 25.3   Custody—Presumption for Parent

The parental rights doctrine stands for the proposition that, as against a nonparent, a parent is entitled to the custody of the child unless extraordinary circumstances require that the parent be deprived of custody.[1] Normally, therefore, in a custody dispute between a parent and a grandparent, a parent who is able to care for the child and

---

§ 25.1

1. See, generally, Special Issue on Third–Party Custody, Visitation, and Child Support, 25 Fam.L.Q. 1 et seq. (Spring 1991).

§ 25.3

1. 67A C.J.S. Parent & Child § 18 (1987); Rodriguez v. McFall, 658 S.W.2d 150, 151 (Tex.1983).

desires to do so is entitled to custody.[2]

However, in a child custody case, two distinct relationships are present: (1) the child-state relationship, and (2) the parent-child relationship. The state, in its role as *parens patriae,* has a duty to protect the child. Therefore, the parental rights doctrine is not absolute, but is recognized by case law [3] and statutory law [4] as a rebuttable presumption that the parents should have custody of their children.

Some older cases held that the right of a parent to his or her child vis-a-vis third parties is akin to a property right and paramount to the interests of the child.[5] Today, however, the right of a fit parent to custody of the child should not take precedence over the best interests of the child.[6] Other courts have given the parental rights doctrine constitutional recognition.[7] These courts perceive, however, that the continuing welfare of the child is a legitimate state interest, and as such, parental rights are not beyond limitations made in the public interest.[8] Thus, even constitutional protection for parents' rights is no more than a rebuttable presumption in favor of having custody of their children.

Library References:

C.J.S. Parent and Child §§ 36, 37.
West's Key No. Digests, Parent and Child ⊕2(8).

§ 25.4   Custody—Rebutting Presumption for Parent

In many states, the grandparent facing the presumption that the parent is entitled to custody must rebut the presumption in order to be

2. Shorty v. Scott, 87 N.M. 490, 535 P.2d 1341, 1343 (1975); Bush v. Bush, 684 S.W.2d 89, 93 (Tenn.App.1984).

3. Hao Thi Popp v. Lucas, 182 Conn. 545, 438 A.2d 755, 758 (1980); In re Krause's Custody, 111 Ill.App.3d 604, 67 Ill.Dec. 408, 412, 444 N.E.2d 644, 648 (1982); Ross v. Hoffman, 280 Md. 172, 372 A.2d 582, 586 (1977); Cook v. Cobb, 271 S.C. 136, 245 S.E.2d 612 (1978); Hutchison v. Hutchison, 649 P.2d 38, 40 (Utah 1982).

4. Conn.Gen.Stat.Ann. § 46b–56b (West Supp.1990); Mich.Comp.Laws Ann. § 722.25 (West Supp.1989).

5. Shea v. Shea, 100 Cal.App.2d 60, 223 P.2d 32, 34 (1950).

6. Plemmons v. Stiles, 65 N.C.App. 341, 309 S.E.2d 504, 506 (1983).

7. Hao Thi Popp v. Lucas, 182 Conn. 545, 438 A.2d 755, 758 (1980) (between a

parent and a stranger, the parent's constitutional right to preserve his or her parental right amounts to a presumption that can be overcome only where the child's welfare plainly requires custody to be placed in the stranger); Grier v. West Haven Police Dept., 40 Conn.Sup. 221, 487 A.2d 576, 578 (1984), *affirmed* 8 Conn.App. 142, 510 A.2d 1376 (1986); Ziehm v. Ziehm, 433 A.2d 725, 729 (Me.1981); Wilke v. Culp, 196 N.J.Super. 487, 483 A.2d 420, 425 (App.Div.1984), *cert. denied* 99 N.J. 243, 491 A.2d 728 (1985) (parent has fundamental rights to care and companionship of child, but parent's custody and visitation may be restricted or terminated).

8. In re Juvenile Appeal, 3 Conn.App. 194, 485 A.2d 1369, 1371 (1985), *cert. denied* 196 Conn. 801, 491 A.2d 1105 (1985).

awarded custody. The burden of proof is typically high, often clear and convincing.[1] The standards that a grandparent must establish to overcome the presumption vary as follows:

    1.   the parent must be unfit; [2]

    2.   custody in the parent must be detrimental to the child; [3]

    3.   either the parent must be unfit or custody in the parent must be detrimental to the child; [4]

    4.   the best interests of the child must be served by custody to the grandparent, even though the parent is not unfit; [5]

    5.   there must be a good or compelling reason to overcome the presumption in favor of the parent; [6] or

    6.   the parent has entered into a voluntary agreement that the grandparent have custody.[7]

To what extent the "parental unfitness" and "best interests" requirements differ in application is uncertain. Theoretically, it should be easier for a grandparent to prove that it is in the child's best interests that custody be awarded to the grandparent than to prove that a parent is unfit. The "unfit" criteria usually is equated with that used in dependency or child protection proceedings, i.e., the parent's custodial role is inadequate even by minimal standards tolerated by society. However, these requirements may be distinctions without difference in the face of compelling evidence of strong attachment between grandparent and child, particularly where the grandparent

§ 25.4

1. Gazaway v. Brackett, 241 Ga. 127, 244 S.E.2d 238 (1978); 67A C.J.S. Parent & Child § 19 (1978). However, once the parent has lost custody to a third party, this higher burden may protect the third party rather than the parent. Durden v. Barron, 249 Ga. 686, 290 S.E.2d 923 (1982).

2. Lewis v. Lewis, 523 So.2d 436, 437 (Ala.Civ.App.1988); Harkness v. Harkness, 531 So.2d 749 (Fla.App.1988); Bezio v. Patenaude, 381 Mass. 563, 410 N.E.2d 1207, 1211 (1980); Ruppel v. Lesner, 421 Mich. 559, 364 N.W.2d 665, 667 (1984); Durkin v. Hinich, 431 N.W.2d 553 (Minn.App.1988), *affirmed* 442 N.W.2d 148, 153 (Minn.1989).

3. Conn.Gen.Stat.Ann. § 46b–56b (West Supp.1990); West's Ann.Cal.Civ.Code § 4600 (Supp.1990); Rachal v. Manausa, 483 So.2d 194, 195 (La.App.1986); Nev.Rev. Stat.Ann. § 125.500 (Michie 1986).

4. In re Guardianship of D.A. McW., 460 So.2d 368, 370 (Fla.1984).

5. Lloyd v. Lloyd, 92 Ill.App.3d 124, 47 Ill.Dec. 792, 415 N.E.2d 1105, 1106 (1980); Comer v. Comer, 61 N.C.App. 324, 300 S.E.2d 457, 460 (1983); In re Custody of Townsend, 86 Ill.2d 502, 56 Ill.Dec. 685, 688, 427 N.E.2d 1231, 1234 (1981); In re Custody of Piccirillio, 88 Ill.3d 621, 43 Ill. Dec. 953, 957, 410 N.E.2d 1086, 1090 (1980) (maternal grandparent awarded custody over father); Henrikson v. Gable, 162 Mich.App. 248, 412 N.W.2d 702, 704 (1987).

6. In re Custody of Townsend, 86 Ill.2d 502, 56 Ill.Dec. 685, 427 N.E.2d 1231, 1235 (1981).

7. Raddish v. Raddish, 652 S.W.2d 668, 670 (Ky.App.1983).

has become the "psychological parent." In other words, the stronger the "best interest" evidence is, the more willing a court may be to find the parent "unfit."

§ 25.5   Custody—Best Interests of Child Doctrine—Application

The best interests of the child doctrine requires that the court place custody of the child with the person who will best serve the child's interests.[1] From a grandchild's perspective, the grandparent may serve in many capacities: family historian, teacher, caretaker, role model, friend, and perhaps most importantly, a nonparent with whom the child can confide or who can serve as a negotiator between the child and parent.[2] One psychiatrist described the grandparent/grandchild bond this way: "[T]he connection between grandparents and grandchildren is natural and second in emotional power only to the primordial bond between parent and child.... The instinct to grandparent is as natural as the instinct to parent."[3] A court stated a similar sentiment as follows:

> [A] child not only needs the love, care and attention of his or her parents or parent, but if fortunate enough to have living grandparents, deserves to have the love and association with its grandparents. Particularly is this true in th[e] case where the appellant-grandparents' love and affection for their grandchild is so obviously apparent.[4]

Library References:

C.J.S. Infants §§ 13, 17; Parent and Child §§ 20, 165.

West's Key No. Digests, Infants ☞19.2(2); Parent and Child ☞2(3.1), 17.

§ 25.6   Custody—Best Interests of Child Doctrine—Relevant Factors

Because the best interests of the child test is very general and broad, courts and legislatures have developed many subtests. Trial courts have tremendous discretion in application. Therefore, counsel must be effective in convincing the court of the cumulative effect of all the factors the evidence can establish favoring the grandparents. In

§ 25.5

1. Anno., Award of Custody of Child Where Contest Is Between Child's Parents and Grandparents, 31 A.L.R.3d 1187, 1198 (1970); 67A C.J.S. Parent & Child § 37 (1978). See, e.g., Del.Code tit. 13, § 722 (1981 & 1989 Supp.); Nev.Rev.Stat.Ann. § 125.480 (Michie 1986).

2. A. Kornbaber & K. Woodward, Grandparents/Grandchildren: The Vital Connection 167–178 (1981). See also, A. Cherlin & F. Furstenberg, The New American Grandparent (1985).

3. Id. at 55, 56.

4. Graves v. Graves, 51 Ala.App. 601, 288 So.2d 142, 144–45 (Ala.Civ.App.1973).

demonstrating the child's best interests to the court, the advocate for the grandparent should approach the issue by showing (1) what serves the child's best interests and (2) why the grandparent can satisfy those needs better than the parent.

Typical of the factors used in most states are the following listed in the Minnesota statute:

(1) wishes of the parents;

(2) wishes of the child;

(3) child's primary caretaker;

(4) intimacy of the relationship between each parent and the child;

(5) interaction between the child and any person who may effect the best interests of the child;

(6) child's adjustment to home, school, and community;

(7) length of time the child has lived in a stable, satisfactory environment and the desirability of maintaining continuity;

(8) permanence, as a family unit, of the existing or proposed custodial home;

(9) mental and physical health of all individuals;

(10) capacity and disposition of the parties to give the child love, affection, and guidance and to continue educating and raising the child in the child's culture and religion or creed;

(11) child's cultural background; and

(12) effect on the child of abuse that occurred between the parents.[1]

Courts rely on numerous other factors in determining the best interests of the child, including: the parent's economic and home condition;[2] the interest of the parent in the child after separation;[3] the circumstances surrounding the parent's parting with the child;[4] and the preference of the child.[5] However, the mere fact that a

---

§ 25.6

1. Minn.Stat.Ann. § 518.17 (Supp.1990).

2. Peterson v. Peterson, 224 Neb. 557, 399 N.W.2d 792, 797 (1987); Guardianship of a Minor, 19 Mass.App.Ct. 333, 474 N.E.2d 192, 195 (1985).

3. Conley v. Walden, 166 Mont. 369, 533 P.2d 955, 958 (1975) (maternal grandmother awarded custody over natural par-

ents where parents had abandoned children for six years); Stuckey v. Stuckey, 276 So.2d 408, 411 (La.App.1973) (grandparents awarded custody of child where mother seldom visited).

4. Guardianship of a Minor, 19 Mass. App.Ct. 333, 474 N.E.2d 192, 195 (1985).

5. Mayfield v. Haggard, 490 S.W.2d 777, 780 (Ky.1972); Freeman v. Chaplic, 388 Mass. 398, 446 N.E.2d 1369, 1375 (1983).

grandparent can spend more time with the child than either parent is not a sufficient basis to remove the child from the parents' care.[6] Courts also have held that grandparents of advanced years may be less able than the parents to care for the child, especially where the grandparent is not expected to live to the child's maturity.[7] On the other hand, grandparents in their fifties and sixties have been awarded custody in contests against parents.[8]

§ 25.7 Custody—Best Interests of Child Doctrine—Parental Wishes

Parents' wishes may be influential if the custody dispute is between a grandparent and a nonparent. Custody is usually given to the person with whom the child was placed by the parent who had the power and right to place the child.[1]

After the death of a parent, a person named as testamentary guardian is often given preference, although subject to the child's best interest.[2] Thus, a parent should be informed of this preference at the time of will drafting so that the parent may make the appointment with this fact in mind. A parent may contract to give custody to a grandparent, but such a contract is subject to judicial modification in accordance with the child's best interests.[3]

§ 25.8 Custody—Effects of Differing Contestants—Grandparents vs. Parents

When custody disputes are between a parent and a grandparent, the court will apply both the parental rights doctrine and the best interests of the child doctrine.[1] In many cases, application of either of these doctrines would yield the same result.[2]

6. Mayer v. Mayer, 397 N.W.2d 638, 642 (S.D.1986).

7. Mayfield v. Haggard, 490 S.W.2d 777 (Ky.1972).

8. Alingh v. Alingh, 259 Iowa 219, 144 N.W.2d 134 (1966); In re McGuire, 114 Misc. 81, 186 N.Y.S. 243, 244 (1921); see, also, Fitzgerald v. Jeter, 428 So.2d 84 (Ala. Civ.App.1983); Collins v. Collins, 171 W.Va. 126, 297 S.E.2d 901 (1982).

§ 25.7

1. Freeman v. Chaplic, 388 Mass. 398, 446 N.E.2d 1369, 1374 (1983).

2. Shanks v. Ross, 173 Ga. 55, 159 S.E. 700 (1931) (where contest is between equally qualified maternal and paternal grand-mothers, the grandmother appointed testamentary guardian was entitled to custody); see Minn.Stat.Ann. § 525.6155 (Supp.1990) (a guardian appointed by will is effective when the guardian accepts).

3. Creech v. Lewis, 307 Ky. 799, 211 S.W.2d 812, 815 (1948); In re Adoption of John Doe, 98 N.M. 340, 648 P.2d 798, 804, *cert. denied* Cook v. Brownfield, 98 N.M. 336, 648 P.2d 794 (1982).

§ 25.8

1. Anno., Award of Custody Where Contest Is Between Child's Parents and Grandparents, 31 A.L.R.3d 1187, 1190–91 (1970).

2. Id.

However, if the interests of the child would be best served in the custody of the grandparent, the two doctrines must be balanced in making the decision.[3] To reconcile the two, courts usually coalesce them, which results in a statement that in determining a child's best interests, there is a presumption that the parent should have custody.[4] Thus, rather than two independent tests, courts turn the presumption underlying the parental rights doctrine into a rebuttable presumption in the best interests of the child test.

§ 25.9 Custody—Effects of Differing Contestants—Grandparent vs. Nonparent

If the custody dispute is between a relative of the child, such as a grandparent, and a nonparent, some states give the relative a preference.[1]

If the grandparent is entitled to a preference, the case will be decided much like a custody dispute between a parent and grandparent. If the grandparent is fit and the best interests of the child do not require that the child be placed elsewhere, the grandparent will win. Thus, the presumption is particularly helpful when the best interests of the child test favors neither petitioner.

§ 25.10 Custody—Effects of Differing Contestants—Grandparent vs. Grandparent

If the custody dispute is between the two sets of grandparents, no presumptions in favor of a grandparent or relative tip the scales. However, a preference will be given to the grandparent with whom the child has been living,[1] especially where that grandparent is also in temporary legal custody of the child.[2] Continuity and stability of the

---

3. Campbell v. Campbell, 63 N.C.App. 113, 304 S.E.2d 262, 263, *cert. denied* 309 N.C. 460, 307 S.E.2d 362 (1983).

4. 67A C.J.S. Parent & Child § 36b (1987); Shorty v. Scott, 87 N.M. 490, 535 P.2d 1341, 1344 (1975).

§ 25.9

1. See **California,** West's Ann.Cal.Welf. & Inst.Code § 361.3 (Supp.1990); **Colorado,** West's Colo.Rev.Stat.Ann. § 19–3–605 (Supp.1989); **Georgia,** Official Code Ga. Ann. § 29–4–8 (1986); **Illinois,** 20 ILCS 505/7, formerly Ill.Rev.Stat. Ch. 23, ¶ 5007(b) (Smith-Hurd Supp.1989); **Kan-**

sas, Kan.Stat.Ann. 38–1563 (1986); **Oklahoma,** Okla.Stat.Ann. tit. 10, § 21.1 (West 1987 & Supp.1990); **South Dakota,** S.D.Codified Laws § 30–27–23 (Supp.1991). But, see, Ruppel v. Lesner, 421 Mich. 559, 364 N.W.2d 665, 667 (1984) (except for limited statutory visitation rights, grandparents have no greater claim to custody of child than any other person).

§ 25.10

1. Holland v. Holland, 679 S.W.2d 835 (Ky.App.1984); In re Drew, 637 S.W.2d 772 (Mo.App.1982).

2. Freeman v. Chaplic, 388 Mass. 398, 446 N.E.2d 1369, 1374 (1983).

caretaker relationship is presumptively in the best interests of the child.

§ 25.11   Custody—Procedural Issues—Notice of Custody Disputes

At common law, a grandparent was not entitled to notice of a custody proceeding involving a grandchild.[1] Currently, all states, under some special circumstances, require that the grandparent be given notice of custody proceedings.[2]

The Uniform Child Custody Jurisdiction Act (UCCJA) and the Parental Kidnapping Prevention Act (PKPA)[3] are important sources of the right to notice.[4] The UCCJA sets prerequisites for a court's subject matter jurisdiction of custody disputes, and the PKPA specifies conditions that entitle a custody order to recognition and enforcement in other states. Broadly speaking, both the jurisdictional base and the conditions for recognition depend upon the child's connection with the state.[5] Even if the parties to the dispute reside in the same state, absent proper jurisdiction, the court cannot enter a custody decree that will be effective either in its own state or in another state.

The UCCJA has been adopted in substance by all 50 states and the District of Columbia.[6] Before a decree is made, reasonable notice and opportunity to be heard must be given to the contestants and any person who has physical custody of the child.[7] The term "contestant" is defined as any person who claims a right to custody or visitation with the child.[8] Thus, if the grandparent has physical custody of the child or claims rights of custody or visitation with the child, the grandparent should be given notice and the opportunity to be heard.

The parties in a custody proceeding are required to provide the court with the names and addresses of any person with whom the child has lived during the last five years, any person who presently has

---

§ 25.11

1. 67A C.J.S. Parent & Child § 37 (1978); Hawkins v. Hawkins, 77 Ill.App.3d 873, 33 Ill.Dec. 279, 396 N.E.2d 668 (1979).

2. See, e.g., **Hawaii,** Haw.Rev.Stat. § 560:5–207 (1985 & Supp.1989); **Georgia,** Official Code Ga.Ann. § 19–9–44 (1982).

3. 28 U.S.C.A. § 1728A.

4. See Coombs, Interstate Child Custody: Jurisdiction, Recognition and Enforcement, 66 Minn.L.Rev. 711 (1982). If the child in issue is an American Indian, the Indian Child Welfare Act, 25 U.S.C.A. §§ 1901–1963, must be consulted to determine jurisdictional matters.

5. U.C.C.J.A. § 3; 28 U.S.C.A. § 1738A(c).

6. 12 Fam.Adv. 20 (Fall 1989).

7. U.C.C.J.A. § 4.

8. Id. § 2. The PKPA also imposes notice requirements for nonparents in custody disputes. The notice requirements of the PKPA mirror those of the UCCJA. 28 U.S.C.A. § 1738A(e).

custody of the child, and any person who claims custody or visitation rights with respect to the child.[9] If the court has proper jurisdiction, a custody decree binds all persons who have been served in the state or properly notified and who have had an opportunity to be heard.[10] Since many states have made minor variations in their adoption of the UCCJA, counsel should check the forum's statute.

§ 25.12   Custody—Procedural Issues—Petitioning for Custody

Generally, grandparents do not have standing to petition for custody of a child where the child is living with a parent, separation or marriage dissolution proceedings have not been instituted, and there has been no finding of parental unfitness.[1] Some states have specific statutes on point.[2] In other states, a habeas corpus procedure might be possible even against a parent, but such a procedure is more likely to be the preferred approach only against a nonparent who has physical custody of the child.[3]

§ 25.13   Custody—Procedural Issues—Costs, Attorney Fees, and Other Expenses

A party involved in a child custody dispute occasionally may obtain an award of court costs and attorney fees.[1] Although attorney fees have been awarded without statutory authority where the court found that equity required the award,[2] an award in disputes between parents and grandparents usually requires statutory authorization.[3] Courts will grant costs and fees to either parents or grandparents where

9. U.C.C.J.A. § 9.

10. Id. § 12.

§ 25.12

1. In re Gibson, 61 Ohio St.3d 168, 573 N.E.2d 1074, 1075 (1991); Ruppel v. Lesner, 421 Mich. 559, 364 N.W.2d 665, 667 (1984); Schilling v. Wood, 532 So.2d 12, 14 (Fla.App.1988).

2. E.g., **Illinois,** 750 ILCS 5/601, formerly Ill.Rev.Stat. ch. 40, ¶ 601(b)(2) (Smith–Hurd Supp.1989) (a person may commence a child custody proceeding by petitioning for custody of the child, but only if the child is not in the physical custody of one of the parents).

3. **New Jersey,** N.J.Stat.Ann. 9:2–7 (West 1976); Roberts v. Staples, 79 N.M. 298, 442 P.2d 788, 790 (1968), overruled on other grounds by Shorty v. Scott, 87 N.M.

490, 535 P.2d 1341 (1975); Bartlett v. Hollenbeck, 100 Misc.2d 748, 420 N.Y.S.2d 140, 142 (Fam.Ct.1979); cf. McGaffin v. Roberts, 193 Conn. 393, 479 A.2d 176 (1984), *cert. denied* 470 U.S. 1050, 105 S.Ct. 1747, 84 L.Ed.2d 813 (1985).

§ 25.13

1. See Anno., Attorneys' Fee Awards In Parent–Nonparent Child Custody Cases, 45 A.L.R.4th 212 (1986).

2. Ex parte Handley, 460 So.2d 167, 170 (Ala.), on remand, 460 So.2d 171 (Ala.Civ. App.1984).

3. Snider v. Butler, 278 S.C. 231, 294 S.E.2d 246, 247 (1982); Koch v. Koch, 99 Misc.2d 124, 415 N.Y.S.2d 369 (1979); Carnese v. Carnese, 93 Misc.2d 558, 403 N.Y.S.2d 174, 175 (1978).

permitted by statute.[4]

§ 25.14 Visitation Rights of Grandparents—Traditional Law

Most grandparents who wish to have contact with their grandchild will be either unwilling or unable to adopt or obtain custody of the child. Presumably, this situation is good; as a society, we want parents to raise their own children.[1] However, this situation does not mean that grandparents cannot and should not have a meaningful relationship with their grandchildren. To foster such relationships, grandparent visitation should be encouraged. As one court stated: "Normally, the loving, caring, and reasonable grandparents should be given visitation, and, normally, this visitation should not be restricted...."[2]

If the parent and grandparent have a sound relationship, there should be no reason for a grandparent to seek court-ordered visitation. However, if the parent and grandparent fail to get along, the grandparents can be disenfranchised of the opportunity to interact with their grandchildren.

At common law, the courts nearly unanimously held that grandparents had no right to visit their grandchildren.[3] With a few exceptions,[4] common law courts decided that although the child's parents may have had a moral obligation to allow grandparent visitation, that obligation was not legal.[5]

4. Garner v. Garner, 673 S.W.2d 413, 418 (Tex.App.1984) (paternal grandparents awarded custody and costs against the natural mother); Yancey v. Koonce, 645 S.W.2d 861, 865 (Tex.App.1983) (attorney fees awarded to maternal grandparents against the natural father and the paternal grandparents); Chapman v. Perera, 41 Wash.App. 444, 704 P.2d 1224, 1230 (1985) (court awarded $5,000 to the mother and $13,000 to the father in child custody dispute in which maternal grandparents intervened and petitioned for custody); In re Custody of Thompson, 34 Wash.App. 643, 663 P.2d 164, 167 (1983) (paternal grandparents ordered to pay mother's costs and attorney fees in visitation rights "frivolous" appeal). See also, 67A C.J.S. Parent & Child § 40 (1978).

§ 25.14

1. 67A C.J.S. Parent & Child § 18 (1978).

2. In re Marriage of Lindsey, 158 Ill. App.3d 769, 770, 110 Ill.Dec. 363, 364, 511 N.E.2d 198, 199 (1987).

3. Morris v. Pressley, 494 So.2d 87, 89 (Ala.Civ.App.1986); Tamargo v. Tamargo, 348 So.2d 1163 (Fla.App.1977); Matter of Guardianship of Green, 525 N.E.2d 634, 636 (Ind.Ct.App.1988); Olds v. Olds, 356 N.W.2d 571, 572 (Iowa 1984); Warnecke v. Lane, 75 A. 233 (N.J.Ch.1910); Matter of Geri v. Fanto, 79 Misc.2d 947, 361 N.Y.S.2d 984, 987 (Fam.Ct.1974); Julien v. Gardner, 628 P.2d 1165, 1166 (Okl.1981); See Foster & Freed, Grandparent Visitation: Vagaries & Vicissitudes, 23 St.Louis U.L.J. 634 (1979); 67A C.J.S. Parent & Child § 41(c) (1978).

4. In re Custody of D.M.M., 137 Wis.2d 375, 404 N.W.2d 530, 535 (1987).

5. Morris v. Pressley, 494 So.2d 87, 89 (Ala.Civ.App.1986); Dolman v. Dolman, 586 S.W.2d 606, 607 (Tex.Civ.App.1979).

Library References:

C.J.S. Parent and Child §§ 41, 42.

West's Key No. Digests, Parent and Child ⊚2(17).

§ 25.15 Visitation Rights of Grandparents—State Grandparent Visitation Statutes—In General

In the last 25 years, all 50 states have adopted statutes providing the opportunity for some form of court-ordered grandparent visitation.[1] For the first time, grandparents do have rights. However, grandparents still have no absolute right to visitation. Counsel should advise grandparents at the outset that they have only a right to petition the court for visitation.[2] Because courts value the parent/child relationship more than the grandparent/grandchild relationship, the opportunity for a grandparent to visit with a grandchild is afforded less protection than the right of a parent to visit with the child.[3] Thus, counsel for grandparents seeking a visitation order must exercise diligence and creativity to succeed.

State legislatures have promulgated a wide variety of statutes granting their courts the power to order grandparent visitation.[4] Some of these statutes are very detailed,[5] but others are very simple.[6] The statutes are amended frequently,[7] so counsel should consult the most

§ 25.15

1. E. Segal & N. Karp, Grandparent Visitation Disputes: A Legal Resource Manual 5 (1989); Brown, Grandparent Visitation and the Intact Family, 16 S.Ill. U.L.J. 133 (1991) (WESTLAW: SILULJ database, $ci(16 +5 133)$); Burns, Grandparent Visitation Rights: Is It Time For The Pendulum To Fall?, 25 Fam.L.Q. 59 (1991) (WESTLAW: FAMLQ database, $ci(25 +5 59)$). For interesting discussions of the constitutionality of grandparent visitation statutes, see Note, The Constitutional Constraints on Grandparent Visitation Statutes, 86 Colum.L.Rev. 118 (1986) (WESTLAW: CLMLR database, $ci(86 +5 118)$); Bean, Grandparent Visitation: Can the Parent Refuse? 24 J.Fam.L. 3 (1985–86).

2. Sachs v. Walzer, 242 Ga. 742, 251 S.E.2d 302, 303 (1978); In re Schmidt, 25 Ohio St.3d 331, 496 N.E.2d 952, 957 (1986) (grandparents have neither a right to visit their grandchildren nor a constitutional right of association with their grandchildren).

3. 67A C.J.S. Parent & Child § 41 (1978).

4. Commentators have suggested a number of model grandparent visitation statutes. See Fernandez, Grandparent Access: A Model Statute, 6 Yale L. & Pol'y Rev. 109 (1988) (WESTLAW: YLLPR database, $ci(6 +5 109)$); Zaharoff, Access to Children: Towards A Model Statute For Third parties, 15 Fam.L.Q. 165 (1981). For summary listing, see, Victor, Robbins, and Bassett, Statutory Review of Third–Party Rights Regarding Custody, Visitation, and Support, 25 Fam.L.Q. 19 (1991).

5. See e.g., **Ohio,** Ohio Rev.Code Ann. §§ 2105.18, 3109.051, 3109.11, 3109.12 (Baldwin Supp.1990).

6. See e.g., **Washington,** West's Rev. Code.Wash.Ann. 26.09.240 (Supp.1990).

7. E. Segal & N. Karp, Grandparent Visitation Disputes: A Legal Resource Manual 5 (1989) (at least five state amendments in 1988); Ohio amended its statute effective May 31, 1990.

current version of the relevant statute as an essential prerequisite to a grandparent visitation suit.

The majority of the statutes have a two-prong structure.[8] The threshold "family situation test" must be met first, after which the court must consider the best interests of the child test. In most states, if both tests are answered in favor of the grandparents, the court *may* grant the grandparents visitation. However, some states make the order of visitation mandatory if both tests are met.[9]

§ 25.16   Visitation Rights of Grandparents—State Grandparent Visitation Statutes—Family Situation Test

Few, if any, of the states have adopted identical grandparent visitation statutes. The greatest disparity is found in application of the family situation test, which generally requires that in order for the grandparent to have standing under the statute, a disruptive condition must exist in the family. However, a variety of conditions may satisfy the disruptive condition test and, thus, permit a petition for visitation by the grandparents, including the following:

1. the grandparent was unreasonably denied visitation for more than 90 days;[1]

2. the parents' marriage has terminated;[2]

3. the parents have petitioned for or have been granted a divorce or dissolution of marriage;[3]

---

8. A few exceptions exist to the two-prong structure. Some states do not have a family situation test but merely use the best interests of the child test. E.g., **Washington,** West's Rev.Code Wash.Ann. 26.09.-240 (1990). One state legislature does not even require its courts to ask the best interests question. See **South Carolina,** S.C.Code § 20–7–420(33) (1985).

9. See e.g., **Oklahoma,** Okla.Stat.Ann. tit. 10 § 5 (West 1990); **Vermont,** Vt.Stat. Ann.tit. 15, § 1013 (1989).

§ 25.16

1. **Alabama,** Ala.Code § 30–3–4 (1989); **Missouri,** Vernon's Ann.Mo.Stat. § 452.-402 (1983 & Supp.1990). **Oregon,** Or.Rev. Stat. 109.121 (1990) provides that a grandparent may petition for visitation if the grandparent has established or has attempted to establish ongoing personal contact with the child and the custodian of the child has denied the grandparent reasonable opportunity to visit the child.

2. **Maryland,** Md.Code, Family Law, § 9–102 (1984).

3. **Alabama,** Ala.Code § 30–3–4 (1989); **Alaska,** Alaska Stat. 25.24.150 (Supp. 1989); **Arkansas,** Ark.Code Ann. § 9–13–103 (1989); **California,** West's Ann.Cal. Civ.Code § 4351.5 (1982 & Supp.1990); **Colorado,** West's Colo.Rev.Stat.Ann. § 19–1–117 (Supp.1989); **Connecticut,** Conn. Gen.Stat.Ann. § 46b–56 (West 1986); **Florida,** Fla.Stat.Ann. § 752.01 (Supp.1989); **Georgia,** Official Code Ga.Ann. § 19–7–3 (1989); **Indiana,** West's Ann.Ind.Code 31–1–11.7–2 (1989); **Iowa,** Iowa Code Ann. § 598.35 (West Supp.1990); **Kansas,** Kan. Stat.Ann. 60–1616(b) (Supp.1988); **Louisiana,** LSA–R.S. 9:572 (West Supp.1990); **Massachusetts,** Mass.Ann.Laws ch. 119, § 39D (Law.Co-op.Supp.1990); **Michigan,**

4. the parents' marriage has been dissolved for more than three months;[4]

5. the parents are separated or have petitioned for separation;[5]

6. the parents have petitioned for or have been granted nullification of a void or voidable marriage;[6]

7. one or both parents are deceased;[7]

8. one or both of the parents are deceased and the child is up for placement;[8]

9. the child's parent, who is the child of the grandparent, is deceased;[9]

Mich.Comp.Laws Ann. § 722.27b (West Supp.1989); **Minnesota,** Minn.Stat.Ann. § 257.022 (West Supp.1990); **Missouri,** Vernon's Ann.Mo.Stat. § 452.402 (1983 & Supp.1990); **Montana,** Mont.Code Ann. 40–4–217 (1989); **Nebraska,** Neb.Rev.Stat. § 43–1802 (1988); **Nevada,** Nev.Rev.Stat. § 125A.340 (1978); **New Jersey,** N.J.Stat. Ann. 9:2–7.1 (West Supp.1989); **New Mexico,** N.M.Stat.Ann. § 40–9–1 (1989); **Ohio,** Ohio Rev.Code § 3109.051 (1990); **Oregon,** Or.Rev.Stat. 109.121 (1990); **Rhode Island,** R.I.Gen.Laws § 15–5–24.2 (1988); **Texas,** V.T.C.A., Fam.Code § 14.03(e) (Supp.1990); **Utah,** Utah Code Ann. 30–5–1 (1989); **Virginia,** Va.Code § 20–107.2 (1988 & Supp.1989); **Wyoming,** Wyo.Stat. § 20–2–113(c) (Supp.1989).

4. Arizona, Ariz.Rev.Stat. § 25–337.01 (Supp.1989).

5. Alaska, Alaska Stat. 25.24.150 (Supp.1989); **Arkansas,** Ark.Code Ann. § 9–13–103 (1990); **California,** West's Ann.Cal.Civ.Code § 4351.5 (Supp.1990); **Colorado,** West's Colo.Rev.Stat.Ann. § 19–1–117 (Supp.1989); **Connecticut,** Conn. Gen.Stat.Ann. § 46b–56 (West 1986); **Louisiana,** LSA–R.S. 9:572 (West Supp.1990); **Michigan,** Mich.Comp.Laws Ann. § 722.-27b (West Supp.1989); **Minnesota,** Minn. Stat.Ann. § 257.022 (West Supp.1990); **Montana,** Mont.Code Ann. 40–4–217 (1989); **Nevada,** Nev.Rev.Stat. 125A.340 (1989); **New Jersey,** N.J.Stat.Ann. 9:2–7.1 (West Supp.1989); **New Mexico,** N.M.Stat. Ann. § 40–9–1 (1989); **Ohio,** Ohio Rev. Code § 3109.51 (Supp.1990); **Oregon,** Or. Rev.Stat. 109.121 (1990); **Texas,** V.T.C.A.,

Fam.Code § 14.03(e) (Supp.1990); **Utah,** Utah Code Ann. 30–5–1 (1989); **Wyoming,** Wyo.Stat. § 20–2–113(c) (Supp.1989).

6. California, West's Ann.Cal.Civ.Code § 4351.5 (Supp.1990); **Colorado,** West's Colo.Rev.Stat.Ann. § 19–1–117 (Supp.1989); **Michigan,** Mich.Comp.Laws Ann. § 722.-27b (West Supp.1989); **Oregon,** Or.Rev. Stat. 109.121 (1990).

7. Arkansas, Ark.Code Ann. § 9–13–103 (1989); **California,** West's Ann.Cal. Civ.Code § 197.5 (1982); **Florida,** West's Fla.Stat.Ann. § 752.01 (Supp.1989); **Louisiana,** LSA–Rev.Stat. 9:572 (West Supp. 1990); **Massachusetts,** Mass.Gen.Laws Ann. ch. 119, § 39D (1990); **Nebraska,** Neb.Rev.Stat. § 43–1802 (1988); **Nevada,** Nev.Rev.Stat. 125A.340 (1989); **New Mexico,** N.M.Stat.Ann. § 40–9–2 (1989); **N.Y.—** McKinney's Dom.Rel.Law § 72 (Supp. 1990); **Vermont,** Vt.Stat.Ann.tit. 15, § 1012 (1989); **Wisconsin,** Wis.Stat.Ann. 880.155 (West Supp.1989).

8. Alaska, Alaska Stat. 25.24.150 (Supp.1989).

9. Colorado, West's Colo.Rev.Stat.Ann. § 19–1–117 (Supp.1989); **Indiana,** West's Ann.Ind.Code 31–1–11.7–2 (1989); **Iowa,** Iowa Code Ann. § 598.35 (West Supp.1990); **Michigan,** Mich.Comp.Laws Ann. § 722.-27b (West Supp.1989); **Minnesota,** Minn. Stat.Ann. § 257.022 (West Supp.1990); **Mississippi,** Miss.Code § 93–16–3 (Supp. 1989); **New Jersey,** N.J.Stat.Ann. 9:2–7.1 (West Supp.1989); **Ohio,** Ohio Rev.Code § 3109.11 (1990); **Rhode Island,** R.I.Gen.

10. one parent is deceased and the surviving parent denies the grandparent visitation; [10]

11. a parent has been deceased for more than three months; [11]

12. there is an alimony or child support proceeding; [12]

13. there is a controversy about the custody or care of the child; [13]

14. an award of custody of the child has been made; [14]

15. the child's parent, who is not the child of the grandparent, has been awarded custody; [15]

16. custody of the child has been given to a nonparent; [16]

17. the child has been adopted by a relative; [17]

18. the parents are divorced and the parent who is not the child of the grandparent has custody of the child and the spouse of the child's custodial parent has adopted the child; [18]

19. the child was born out of wedlock; [19]

20. the child was born out of wedlock and paternity has been established; [20]

21. a suit to establish filiation had been commenced; [21]

Laws § 15–5–24.1 (1988); **Texas,** V.T.C.A., Family Code Ann. § 14.03(e) (Supp.1990); **Utah,** Utah Code Ann. 30–5–1 (1989); **Wyoming,** Wyo.Stat. § 20–2–113(c) (Supp. 1989).

10. Alabama, Ala.Code § 30–3–4 (1989); **Missouri,** V.A.M.S. § 452.402 (1983 & Supp.1990).

11. Arizona, Ariz.Rev.Stat. § 25–337.01 (Supp.1989).

12. Ohio, Ohio Rev.Code § 3109.051 (1990).

13. Connecticut, Conn.Gen.Stat.Ann. § 46b–56 (West 1986); **Georgia,** Official Code Ga.Ann. § 19–7–3 (Supp.1989); **Minnesota,** Minn.Stat.Ann. § 257.022 (West Supp.1990); **Oregon,** Or.Rev.Stat. 109.121 (1990).

14. California, West's Ann.Cal.Civ. Code § 4601 (Supp.1990).

15. Mississippi, Miss.Code Ann. § 93–16–3 (Supp.1989).

16. Colorado, West's Colo.Rev.Stat. Ann. § 19–1–117 (Supp.1989); **Michigan,**

Mich.Comp.Laws Ann. § 722.276 (West 1991).

17. Georgia, Official Code Ga.Ann. § 19–7–3 (Supp.1989).

18. Iowa, Iowa Code Ann. § 598.35 (Supp.1990).

19. Florida, West's Fla.Stat.Ann. § 752.01 (1991); **Indiana,** West's Ann.Ind. Code 31–1–11.7–2 (1989); **Iowa,** Iowa Code Ann. § 598.35 (Supp.1990); **Ohio,** Ohio Rev.Code § 3109.12 (Supp.1990); **Oklahoma,** Okl.Stat.Ann. tit. 10, § 5 (West Supp.1990).

20. Indiana, West's Ann.Ind.Code 31–1–11.7–2 (1989); **Iowa,** Iowa Code Ann. § 598.35 (West Supp.1990); **Nebraska,** Neb.Rev.Stat. § 43–18802 (1988); **New Mexico,** N.M.Stat.Ann. § 40–9–1 (1989); **Ohio,** Ohio Rev.Code §§ 2105.18, 3109.12 (1990); **Oklahoma,** Okl.Stat.Ann.tit. 10, § 5 (West Supp.1990).

21. Oregon, Or.Rev.Stat. 109.121 (1990).

22. the child has been placed outside of and does not live in the parents' home; [22]

23. a parent is physically or mentally incapable of making a decision; [23]

24. the child has been placed in a foster home; [24]

25. the child's parent, who is the child of the grandparent, has been declared incompetent; [25]

26. a parent has deserted the child; [26]

27. the child has been abused or neglected by a parent; [27]

28. the child, adjudged dependent, has been removed from custody of parent; [28]

29. the child has been adjudicated to be in need of supervision or a delinquent; [29]

30. visitation rights have been terminated; [30]

31. parental rights have been terminated; [31]

32. the child has lived with the grandparent for more than six months and was removed from the grandparent's home by a parent; [32]

33. the child has resided with the grandparent seeking visitation for more than six months within the 24–month period preceding the petition; [33]

22. Colorado, West's Colo.Rev.Stat. Ann. § 19–1–117 (Supp.1989); **Michigan,** Mich.Comp.Laws Ann. § 722.27b (West Supp.1989).

23. Vermont, Vt.Stat.Ann. tit. 15, § 1012 (1989).

24. Iowa, Iowa Code Ann. § 598.35 (West Supp.1990).

25. Texas, V.T.C.A., Family Code § 14.-03(e) (Supp.1990).

26. Florida, West's Fla.Stat.Ann. § 752.01 (Supp.1989); **Vermont,** Vt.Stat. Ann. tit. 15, § 1012 (1989).

27. Texas, V.T.C.A., Family Code § 14.-03(e) (Supp.1990).

28. California, West's Ann.Cal.Welf. & Inst.Code § 361.2 (Supp.1990).

29. Texas, V.T.C.A., Family Code Ann. § 14.03(e) (Supp.1990).

30. Georgia, Official Code Ga.Ann. § 19–7–3 (1989).

31. Georgia, Official Code Ga.Ann. § 19–7–3 (1989); **Mississippi,** Miss.Code § 93–16–3 (Supp.1989); **Nevada,** Nev.Rev. Stat. 125A.340 (1989); **Oklahoma,** Okl. Stat.Ann. tit. 10, § 5 (West Supp.1990); **Texas,** V.T.C.A., Family Code § 14.03(e) (Supp.1990).

32. Minnesota, Minn.Stat.Ann. § 257.-022 (West 1991) (child had lived with grandparent more than twelve months and was removed from the grandparent's home by a parent); **New Mexico,** N.M.Stat.Ann. § 40–9–2 (1989); **Wyoming,** Wyo.Stat. § 20–7–101 (1991).

33. Texas, V.T.C.A., Family Code § 14.-03(e) (Supp.1990).

34. the child's parent, who is the child of the grandparent, has been incarcerated during the three months preceding the petition;[34] and

35. the parent has been interdicted.[35]

In addition, some states give the grandparents standing under the following circumstances, without regard to the family situation test:

1. if in the child's best interest;[36]

2. if the grandparent has established a substantial relationship with the child;[37] and

3. where equity would see fit.[38]

§ 25.17 Visitation Rights of Grandparents—State Grandparent Visitation Statutes—Best Interests of Child Test

Along with satisfaction of the specific, legislatively prescribed "family situation" test, most states require a finding that grandparent visitation is in the child's best interests before a court can properly grant visitation.[1] If not specifically required by the grandparent visita-

34. **Texas,** V.T.C.A., Family Code § 14.-03(e) (Supp.1990).

35. **Louisiana,** LSA Rev.Stat. § 9:572 (West Supp.1990).

36. **Illinois,** 750 ILCS 5/607, formerly Ill.S.H.A. ch. 40, ¶ 607(b) (Supp.1989) repealed, eff. 7/1/91. For discussion, see, Burns, Grandparent Visitation Rights: Is It Time For The Pendulum To Fall?, 25 Fam.L.Q. 59, 74 (1991). **Kentucky,** Ky. Rev.Stat. § 405.021 (1984 & Supp.1988); **South Dakota,** S.D.Codified Law 25–4–52 (1991); **Washington,** West's Rev.Code Wash.Ann. 26.09.240 (Supp.1990).

37. **Idaho,** Idaho Code § 32–1008 (1983); **Kansas,** Kan.Stat.Ann. 38–129 (1986).

38. **N.Y.**—McKinney's Dom.Rel.Law § 72 (Supp.1990).

§ 25.17

1. **Alaska,** Alaska Stat. 25.24.150, 25.-24.200 (1991); **Arizona,** Ariz.Rev.Stat. § 25–337.01 (Supp.1989); **Arkansas,** Ark. Code Ann. § 9–13–103 (1989); **California,** West's Ann.Cal.Civ.Code §§ 197.5, 4351.5 (1982 & Supp.1990); **California,** West's Ann.Cal.Welf. & Inst.Code § 361.2 (Supp. 1990); **Colorado,** Colo.Rev.Stat.Ann. § 19–

1–117 (Supp.1989); **Connecticut,** Conn. Gen.Stat.Ann. § 46b–56 (West 1986); **Florida,** West's Fla.Stat.Ann. §§ 61.13, 752.01 (Supp.1990); **Georgia,** Official Code Ga. Ann. § 19–7–3 (Supp.1989); **Indiana,** West's Ann.Ind.Code § 31–1–11.7–3 (1989); **Iowa,** Iowa Code Ann. § 598.35 (West Supp.1990); **Kansas,** Kan.Stat.Ann. 38–129 (1986); **Kentucky,** Ky.Rev.Stat. § 405.021 (1984 & Supp.1988); **Louisiana,** LSA–Rev.Stat. § 9:572 (West Supp.1990); **Maryland,** Md.Code, Fam.Law, § 9–102 (1984); **Massachusetts,** Mass.Gen.Laws Ann. c. 119, § 39D (1990); **Michigan,** Mich.Comp.Laws Ann. § 722.27b (West Supp.1989); **Minnesota,** Minn.Stat.Ann. § 257.022 (West Supp.1990); **Mississippi,** Miss.Code § 93–16–5 (Supp.1989); **Missouri,** V.A.M.S. § 452.402 (Supp.1990); **Montana,** Mont.Code Ann. 40–4–217 (1989); **Nebraska,** Neb.Rev.Stat. § 43–1802 (1988); **Nevada,** Nev.Rev.Stat. 125A.330, 125A.340 (1989); **New Hampshire,** N.H.Rev.Stat.Ann. 458:17–d (Supp. 1989); **New Jersey,** N.J.Stat.Ann. 9:2–7.1 (West Supp.1989); **North Dakota,** N.D.Cent.Code 14–09–05.1 (Supp.1989); **Ohio,** Ohio Rev.Code § 3109.051 (1990); **Oklahoma,** Okl.Stat.Ann. tit. 10, § 5

tion statute, the court nonetheless will determine that the best interests standard is to be used.[2]

The burden of proof to establish that visitation is in the child's best interests in grandparent visitation suits is usually proof by a preponderance of the evidence.[3] However, at least one state requires a grandparent to rebut by clear and convincing evidence that the parents' refusal to grant the grandparent visitation privileges was reasonable.[4]

Courts do grant grandparent visitation even though the parent or parents object[5] or the family situation is far from amicable.[6] Authorization and encouragement for visitation over parental objection is the object of the statutes. However, respect for parental wishes is consistent with treatment of parents' wishes when determining the best interests of the child with respect to custody. Some courts view granting visitation to nonparents contrary to the wishes of the custodial parent "with great circumspection."[7] Some statutes increase the grandparents' burden of justification for grandparent visitation in the face of parental objection. For example, California has a rebuttable presumption that visitation by a grandparent is not in the child's best interests if both parties to the marriage agree that the grandparent should not be given visitation rights.[8] Similarly, Rhode Island has a rebuttable presumption that the parents' refusal to permit the grandparent to visit is reasonable.[9]

Besides being one factor used by courts in determining the best

(West Supp.1990); **Oregon,** Or.Rev.Stat. 109.121, 109.123 (1990) (court is to be "guided" by child's best interests); **Rhode Island,** R.I.Gen. Laws § 15–5–24.3 (1988 & Supp.1989); **South Dakota,** S.D.Codified Laws 25–4–52 (1984); **Tennessee,** Tenn. Code Ann. § 36–6–301 (Supp.1989); **Texas,** V.T.C.A., Family Code § 14.03(e) (Supp. 1990); **Utah,** Utah Code Ann. 30–5–2 (1989); **Vermont,** Vt.Stat.Ann. tit. 15 §§ 1011, 1013 (1989); **Virginia,** Va.Code § 63.1–204.1 (1988); **Washington,** West's RCWA 26.09.240 (1990); **West Virginia,** W.Va.Code 48–2b–1 (1986); **Wisconsin,** Wis.Stat.Ann. 880.155 (West Supp.1989); **Wyoming,** Wyo.Stat. §§ 20–2–113(c), 20–7–101 (Supp.1989).

2. Casbergue v. Casbergue, 124 Mich. App. 491, 335 N.W.2d 16, 18 (1983); see Lo Presti v. Lo Presti, 40 N.Y.2d 522, 527, 387 N.Y.S.2d 412, 415, 355 N.E.2d 372 on remand 54 A.D.2d 582, 387 N.Y.S.2d 153

(1976). 67A C.J.S. Parent & Child § 18 (1987).

3. Rosemary E.R. v. Michael G.Q., 471 A.2d 995, 996 (Del.1984).

4. Rhode Island, R.I.Gen.Laws § 15–5–24.3 (1988).

5. Olepa v. Olepa, 151 Mich.App. 690, 391 N.W.2d 446, 453 (1986); Globman v. Globman, 158 N.J.Super. 338, 348, 386 A.2d 390, 395 (App.Div.1978); Matter of Johansen v. Lanphear, 95 A.D.2d 973, 974, 464 N.Y.S.2d 301, 303 (1983).

6. In re Robert D., 151 Cal.App.3d 391, 399, 198 Cal.Rptr. 801, 804 (1984).

7. Wills v. Wills, 399 So.2d 1130, 1131 (Fla.App.1981).

8. West's Ann.Cal.Civ.Code § 4351.5(k) (Supp.1990).

9. R.I.Gen.Laws § 15–5–24.3 (1988).

interests of the child,[10] consideration of the child's wishes is specifically mentioned in the grandparent visitation statutes of several states.[11] However, appellate courts warn the trial judge not to lightly make assumptions with respect to the child's wishes [12] nor give the child's wishes too much weight.[13]

The interactive relationship between the grandparent and grandchild often is the key element in deciding whether to grant the grandparent visitation. In some states, proof of a preexisting interactive grandparent/grandchild relationship is a prerequisite to judicial power to grant visitation.[14] In other states, an interactive relationship is only one of several situations by which a grandparent is given standing under the visitation statute.[15] Other statutes factor the establishment of a significant relationship between the grandparent and grandchild into the best interests visitation determination.[16] Some states have adopted this element by judicial action.[17] Even when not mandatory, a demonstration that visitation will continue a meaningful grandparent/grandchild relationship usually will establish that grandparent visitation is in the best interests of the child.

§ 25.18 Visitation Rights of Grandparents—State Grandparent Visitation Statutes—Great–Grandparents and Step-grandparents

Some state statutes expressly include great-grandparents within

10. See note 3, supra, and accompanying text.

11. **Connecticut,** Conn.Gen.Stat.Ann. § 46b–56 (West 1986); **Minnesota,** Minn. Stat.Ann. § 257.022 (West Supp.1990); **Missouri,** V.A.M.S. § 452.402 (Supp.1990); **New Hampshire,** N.H.Rev.Stat.Ann. 458:17–d (Supp.1989); **Wisconsin,** Wis. Stat.Ann. § 767.245 (West Supp.1989).

12. Matter of Johansen v. Lanphear, 95 A.D.2d 973, 974, 464 N.Y.S.2d 301, 303 (1983) (presumed wishes of child is not a proper reason for denying grandparent visitation).

13. Ehrlich v. Ressner, 55 A.D.2d 953, 391 N.Y.S.2d 152, 153 (1977).

14. **Iowa,** Iowa Code Ann. § 598.35 (West Supp.1990); **Kansas,** Kan.Stat.Ann. 38–129 (1986); **Nebraska,** Neb.Rev.Stat. § 43–1802 (1988); **Oklahoma,** Okla.Stat. Ann. tit. 10, § 5 (West Supp.1990); **Virginia,** Va.Code § 63.1–204.1 (1988); see

North Carolina, N.C.Gen.Stat. § 50–13.2 (1987).

15. **New Mexico,** N.M.Stat.Ann. § 40–9–2 (Michie 1989) (court may order visitation if child has resided with the grandparent for more than six months and is removed from the grandparent's home by a parent); **Texas,** V.T.C.A., Family Code § 14.03(e) (West Supp.1990); **Wisconsin,** Wis.Stat.Ann. 767.245 (West Supp.1989) (any person with a substantial relationship with the child may petition for visitation).

16. **North Dakota,** N.D.Cent.Code 14–09–05.1 (Supp.1989); **Ohio,** Ohio Rev.Code § 3109.051 (1990).

17. Apker v. Malchak, 112 A.D.2d 518, 519, 490 N.Y.S.2d 923, 925 (1985); but, see, Snipes v. Carr, 526 So.2d 591, 592 (Ala.Civ. App.1988) (under Ala.Code § 30–3–4, grandparents do not need to show previously existing or substantial relationship with child in order to seek visitation).

the visitation statutes.[1] Most, however, are silent on this matter.[2] Those statutes that are silent have been interpreted both in favor of [3] and against [4] great-grandparents.

Stepgrandparent visitation issues may also arise, especially where the stepgrandparent came into the child's life at an early age and has had an opportunity to become emotionally attached.[5] Few questions involving stepgrandparent visitation have been decided. One state specifically excludes stepgrandparents from the purview of its grandparent visitation statute.[6]

§ 25.19 Visitation Rights of Grandparents—State Grandparent Visitation Statutes—Presumptions Favoring Grandparent Visitation

Some state courts apply presumptions favoring grandparents when determining whether to grant grandparent visitation.[1] A New Jersey court has interpreted that state's grandparent visitation statute as creating a presumption that the child's best interests are served by maintaining contact with the grandparents.[2] In Illinois, if both of the child's parents are deceased, the court must grant a grandparent appropriate visitation with the grandchild unless the court finds that such visitation would be detrimental to the child's welfare.[3] Thus, an attorney representing grandparents in a visitation case should carefully search statutory and case law for any relevant grandparent visitation presumptions.

§ 25.18

1. **Arizona,** Ariz.Rev.Stat. § 25–337.01 (Supp.1989); **Arkansas,** Ark.Code Ann. § 9–13–103 (1989); **California,** West's Ann.Cal.Civ.Code § 197.5 (1982); **Minnesota,** Minn.Stat.Ann. § 257.022 (West Supp.1990); **Ohio,** Ohio Rev.Code § 3109.-051 (1990); **North Dakota,** N.D.Cent.Code 14–09–05.1 (Supp.1989); **Wisconsin,** Wis.Stat.Ann. 767.245 (West Supp.1989).

2. See e.g., **Alaska,** Alaska Stat. 25.24.-150 (Supp.1989); **Georgia,** Official Code Ga.Ann. § 19–7–3 (Supp.1989) (defining grandparent so as to exclude great-grandparent).

3. Taylor v. Alger, 129 Misc.2d 1054, 495 N.Y.S.2d 120 (Fam.Ct.1985).

4. Cole v. Thomas, 735 S.W.2d 333, 335 (Ky.App.1987).

5. See A. Cherlin & F. Furstenberg, The New American Grandparent 138, 155–162 (1985).

6. Or.Rev.Stat. 109.121 (1990).

§ 25.19

1. But see, Objections of Parents, supra, and Official Code Ga.Ann. § 19–7–3 (Supp. 1989) (stating that there is no presumption in favor of grandparent visitation).

2. Globman v. Globman, 158 N.J.Super. 338, 345, 386 A.2d 390, 394 (App.Div.1978).

3. **Illinois,** 755 ILCS 5/11–7.1, formerly Ill. S.H.A. ch. 110½, ¶ 11–7.1 (Supp.1989).

§ 25.20 Visitation Rights of Grandparents—Effect of Adoption on Grandparent Visitation—Divestment of Rights; Split of Authority

Perhaps second only in importance to the legislated right to petition for visitation with a grandchild is the effect that the adoption of the child has on the grandparent's ability to obtain visitation rights or to continue previously granted visitation rights. Whether the child has been adopted by a new set of parents or by a new spouse of one parent, adoption plays a pivotal role in grandparent visitation matters.

A major concern in granting a biological grandparent visitation privileges after the child has been adopted is the threat that such visitation will undermine the authority of the adoptive parents or create psychological conflicts in the child.[1] However, many of the reasons for giving grandparents visitation rights in the first place often remain after adoption. Thus, courts and legislatures have taken a variety of approaches to answer the question of how adoption affects grandparent visitation.

Traditionally, any rights that a grandparent has with respect to a grandchild can be thought of as derivative of the parent's rights. As a general principle, after adoption, the natural parents and those who claim rights through them are divested of all rights and obligations between them and the child. Thus, because a grandparent's visitation rights are derivative of the rights of their child (the grandchild's parent), if that parent is divested of his or her rights with respect to the child, logically that grandparent would be similarly divested.

As a general rule, therefore, the adoption of a child terminates any rights of the natural grandparents to petition for visitation with the child.[2] Furthermore, in many jurisdictions, statutes require any court-

---

§ 25.20

1. Mimkon v. Ford, 66 N.J. 426, 438, 332 A.2d 199, 205 (1975).

2. Soergel v. Raufman, 154 Wis.2d 564, 453 N.W.2d 624, 625 (1990) (adoption statute overrides general visitation statute, precluding paternal grandparent visitation after adoption by stepfather); In re W.E.G. & J.R.G., 710 P.2d 410, 414 (Alaska 1985) (clear language of the statute precludes granting postadoption visitation to any blood relative, regardless of that relative's bond with the adopted child); In re Marriage of Herreras, 159 Ariz. 511, 512, 768 P.2d 673, 674 (App.1989) (maternal grand-

mother's visitation rights terminated automatically where children were in custody of father and were adopted by the father's new wife); Wilson v. Wallace, 274 Ark. 48, 622 S.W.2d 164, 165 (1981) (court relied on general adoption statute in holding that adoption terminated all legal relationships between the adopted child and his grandparents); Olson v. Flinn, 484 So.2d 1015, 1018 (Miss.1986) (adoption by stepfather terminates grandparent visitation rights, overruled, Howell v. Rogers, 551 So.2d 904, 906 (Miss.1989), interpreting amendment after *Olson*.)

ordered visitation rights already granted to terminate automatically upon adoption.[3]

Parents contemplating placing their child for adoption might want to have the grandparents remain in contact with the child. However, an attempt to contract around the public policy of automatic termination of visitation after adoption probably will be unsuccessful.[4]

In spite of the derivative policy, which is especially strong when strangers adopt, a few courts have allowed grandparent visitation, notably New York[5] and California.[6] In addition, the Oklahoma statute specifically continues court-ordered visitation whenever the adoption occurs subsequent to the grant of visitation.[7]

When a stepparent or close blood relative adopts the child, the derivative policy of enhancing an atmosphere of a totally different family does not apply so strongly.[8] Consequently, a broader split of authority exists, and courts have recognized visitation rights in grandparents more often in this type of situation. One author has noted that most states allow grandparent visitation after stepparent adoptions.[9] That statement is based on both decisions and recently enacted statutes of the type discussed in § 25.21, infra.

Library References:

C.J.S. Adoption of Persons §§ 134–139; Parent and Child §§ 41, 42.

West's Key No. Digests, Adoption ⊜20; Parent and Child ⊜2(17).

3. **Arizona,** Ariz.Rev.Stat. § 25–337.01 (Supp.1989); **California,** West's Ann.Cal. Civ.Code § 197.5 (1982); **Indiana,** West's Ann.Ind.Code 31–1–11.7–2 (1989); **Massachusetts,** Mass.Gen.Laws Ann. ch. 119, § 39D (1990); **Montana,** Mont.Code Ann. 40–9–102 (1989); **North Dakota,** N.D.Cent. Code 14–09–05.1 (Supp.1989); **South Dakota,** S.D.Codified Laws Ann. 25–4–54 (1984); Tenn.Code Ann. § 36–6–301 (Supp. 1989); **Vermont,** Vt.Stat.Ann. tit. 15, § 1016 (1988 & Supp.1989). Both Montana and South Dakota recently provided that previously granted visitation rights terminate only when adoption is by someone other than stepparent or grandparent. **Montana,** Mont.Code Ann. 40.9–102 (1991); **South Dakota,** S.D.Codified Ann. 31–1–11.72 (1991).

4. Matter of Adoption of RDS, 787 P.2d 968, 970 (Wyo.1990).

5. People ex rel. Sibley v. Sheppard, 54 N.Y.2d 320, 445 N.Y.S.2d 420, 429 N.E.2d 1049 (1981).

6. Johnson v. Fallon, 129 Cal.App.3d 71, 181 Cal.Rptr. 414 (1982).

7. Okl.Stat.Ann. tit. 10, §§ 5, 60.16 (West Supp.1990).

8. Kanvick v. Reilly, 233 Mont. 324, 328–329, 760 P.2d 743, 746–747 (1988); Lingwall v. Hoener, 108 Ill.2d 206, 214, 91 Ill.Dec. 166, 170, 483 N.E.2d 512, 516 (1985).

9. Burns, Grandparent Visitation Rights: Is It Time For The Pendulum To Fall?, 25 Fam.L.Q. 59, 68 (1991).

§ 25.21   Visitation Rights of Grandparents—Effect of Adoption on Grandparent Visitation—Continuing Rights Under Specific Exceptions

Many statutes provide specific exceptions to the divestment rule. The apparent public policy is that when a child is adopted within its extended family, members of that familial group should not be automatically denied contact with the child. The allowance of visitation after stepparent adoption is common.[1] This exception has been extended in some states to adoption by grandparents,[2] relatives,[3] blood relatives,[4] close relatives,[5] people biologically related to the child,[6] relatives within the fifth degree of sanguinity,[7] the testamentary guardian,[8] and the baptismal sponsor.[9]

In analyzing statutory exceptions, a distinction should be drawn between a right to petition for visitation and a right to maintain previously granted visitation entitlements. Some states address both issues in the same way. For example, the Missouri statute reads:

> The right of a grandparent to seek or maintain visitation rights under this section may terminate upon the adoption of the child except where the child is adopted by a stepparent, another grandparent or other blood relative.[10]

§ 25.21

1. **California,** West's Ann.Cal.Civ.Code § 197.5 (1982); **Florida,** West's Fla.Stat. Ann. § 757.07 (1986); **Indiana,** West's A.I.C. § 31–1–11.7–2 (1989); **Iowa,** Iowa Code Ann. § 598.35 (West 1991); **Kansas,** Kan.Stat.Ann. 38–129 (1986); **Massachusetts,** Mass.Gen.Laws Ann. ch. 119, § 39D (1990); **Michigan,** Mich.Comp.Laws Ann. § 722.27b (West Supp.1989); **Minnesota,** Minn.Stat.Ann. § 257.022 (West Supp. 1990); **Missouri,** V.A.M.S. § 452.402 (Supp.1990); **New Mexico,** N.M.Stat.Ann. § 40–9–2 (1989); **North Carolina,** N.C.Gen.Stat. § 50–13.2 (1987); **North Dakota,** N.D.Cent.Code 14–09–05.1 (Supp. 1989); **South Dakota,** S.D.Codified Laws 25–4–54 (1984); **Tennessee,** Tenn.Code Ann. § 36–6–301 (Supp.1989); **Vermont,** Vt.Stat.Ann. tit. 15 § 1016 (1989). See also, Howell v. Rogers, 551 So.2d 904, 906 (Miss.1989).

2. **Alabama,** Ala.Code § 26–10A–30 (1986); **California,** West's Ann.Cal.Civ. Code § 197.5 (1982); **Minnesota,** Minn. Stat.Ann. § 257.022 (West Supp.1990); **Missouri,** V.A.M.S. § 452.402 (Supp.1990); **North Dakota,** N.D.Cent.Code 14–09–05.1 (1991); **South Dakota,** S.D.Codified Laws 25–4–54 (1984); **Vermont,** Vt.Stat.Ann. tit. 15, § 1016 (1989); but, see, Bond v. Yount, 47 Wash.App. 181, 734 P.2d 39 (1987). See also, In re Pennington, 55 Ohio App.3d 99, 100–101, 562 N.E.2d 905, 906–907 (1988).

3. **North Carolina,** N.C.Gen.Stat. § 50–13.2 (1987); **Tennessee,** Tenn.Code Ann. § 36–6–301 (Supp.1989); **Vermont,** Vt.Stat.Ann. tit 15, § 1016 (1989).

4. **Georgia,** Official Code Ga.Ann. § 19–7–3, 19–8–15 (Supp.1989); **Missouri,** V.A.M.S. § 452.402 (Supp.1990).

5. **Illinois,** 755 ILCS 5/11–7.1, formerly Ill. S.H.A. ch. 110½, ¶ 11–7.1 (Supp.1989).

6. West's Ann.Ind.Code § 31–1–11.7–2 (1989).

7. N.M.Stat.Ann. § 40–9–4 (1989).

8. Id.

9. Id.

10. V.A.M.S. § 452.402 (Supp.1990).

Thus, in Missouri, neither the right to petition for visitation rights nor the right to maintain previously granted visitation rights is automatically terminated, and it even appears that the court has authority to terminate such rights only if adoption is by persons other than those specified.

Some statutes, however, do not apply the exceptions uniformly to the right to petition for visitation rights and the right to maintain previously granted visitation rights. For example, the Minnesota statute reads:

> This section [the section granting grandparents the right to petition for and receive visitation] shall not apply if the child has been adopted *by a person other than a stepparent or grandparent. Any* visitation rights granted pursuant to this section prior to the adoption of the child shall be automatically terminated upon such adoption.... (emphasis added) [11]

Thus, in Minnesota, a grandparent loses the standing to petition for or receive visitation rights only when adoption occurs by someone other than a stepparent or grandparent. The second sentence, however, is not as gracious; grandparent visitation rights awarded prior to the adoption of a child by a stepparent are terminated. The grandparent would have standing to petition the court again for visitation rights only under the first sentence.

At least one court has addressed a constitutional challenge to the award of grandparent visitation after the adoption of a child and held that such adoption does not by itself preclude visitation.[12] In awarding the grandparents visitation privileges, the court decided that granting visitation would not unconstitutionally invade any privacy rights of the adoptive parents. The intent of the state in furthering the best interests of the child was paramount because the child had previously lived with grandparents and was old enough to comprehend their familial relationship and to remember them. However, the court held that the state may not interfere with family integrity and the family decision-making authority of the adoptive parents in awarding grandparent visitation.

11. Minn.Stat.Ann. § 257.022 (West Supp.1990). See, also, Tenn.Code Ann. § 36–6–301 (Supp.1989).

12. People ex rel. Sibley v. Sheppard, 54 N.Y.2d 320, 327, 445 N.Y.S.2d 420, 423, 429 N.E.2d 1049, 1052 (1981); see Note, Grandparents' Statutory Visitation Rights and the Rights of Adoptive Parents, 49 Brooklyn L.Rev. 149 (1982) (WESTLAW: BKNLR database, ci(49 +5 149)); see also Note, The Constitutional Constraints of Grandparent Visitation Statutes, 86 Colum.L.Rev. 118, 136–37 (1986) (WESTLAW: CLMLR database, ci(86 +5 118)).

§ 25.22   Visitation Rights of Grandparents—Effect of Adoption on Grandparent Visitation—Termination of Parental Rights Without Adoption

If a parent's rights with respect to a child have been terminated but the child has not been adopted, the concern that an award of grandparent visitation would undermine the adoptive parents' authority is not present. Thus, in this situation, a grandparent more likely will retain court-ordered visitation privileges even though the parental rights have ended.[1]

However, a Minnesota court held that a paternal grandparent whose son had voluntarily terminated his parental rights had no visitation rights with the child.[2] In that case, because the statute gave grandparents visitation rights only in specified situations and because the son had no individual visitation rights, the grandparents could have no derivative rights. The court explained that the legislature had created only specific exceptions to the normal policy of respect for autonomy of the adoptive family.[3] A grandparent is more likely to obtain visitation rights where parental rights have been or will be terminated if the grandparent has filed for visitation rights prior to such termination.[4]

§ 25.23   Visitation Rights of Grandparents—Procedural Issues—Jurisdiction and Standing

The Uniform Child Custody Jurisdiction Act (UCCJA) and the Parental Kidnapping Prevention Act (PKPA) apply to child visitation proceedings. Thus, before the court has subject matter jurisdiction over a grandparent visitation proceeding, these statutes must be followed.[1]

Many states permit the petition to be filed either separately or in conjunction with a proceeding that will ultimately affect custody of the child, e.g., a dissolution or divorce proceeding.[2] Mediation may be required on grandparent visitation issues before a court will hear the matter.[3] In Vermont, a grandparent who intervenes in another action

§ 25.22

1. Sands v. Sands, 157 Ariz. 322, 323, 757 P.2d 126, 127 (App.1988).

2. Matter of Welfare of R.A.N., 435 N.W.2d 71 (Minn.App.1989).

3. Id. at 73.

4. See, Nev.Rev.Stat.Ann. 125A.340 (1989).

§ 25.23

1. See § 25.11, supra.

2. E.g., **Arizona,** Ariz.Rev.Stat. § 25–337.01 (Supp.1989); **Georgia,** Official Code Ga.Ann. § 19–7–3 (Supp.1989).

3. West's Ann.Cal.Civ.Code § 4351.5 (Supp.1990); See E. Segal & N. Karp, Grandparent Visitation Disputes: A Legal Resource Manual 79 (1989); Dies, Califor-

does not achieve party status and, thus, may not appeal a court's decision on visitation as it pertains to the grandparent.[4] Some statutes have established a one[5] or two[6] year cooling-off period, during which the grandparent must wait before another petition for visitation can be filed.

§ 25.24　Visitation Rights of Grandparents—Procedural Issues—Visitation Periods and Enforcement

Once a court decides that grandparent visitation is warranted, it has great discretion in granting number and timing of visitation periods. For example, one court granted a grandparent visitation that amounted to four weeks per year plus holidays;[1] another court granted a grandparent one weekend per month;[2] and another court granted biweekly visitation.[3] Courts often are legislatively prohibited from restricting the movement of the child to facilitate grandparent visitation orders.[4]

Once visitation rights are obtained, the enforcement and exercise of those rights becomes important. Some states provide a special remedy[5] or expedited proceeding[6] to encourage cooperation with court-ordered grandparent visitation. For example, Illinois has an expedited procedure for enforcing court-ordered visitation, but permits an award of costs and fees if such an enforcement action is vexatious and

nia's Answer: Mandatory Mediation of Child Custody and Visitation Disputes, 1 Ohio St.J.Dispute Res. 149 (1985).

4. Vt.Stat.Ann. tit. 15, § 1011 (1989), In re S.B.L., 150 Vt. 294, 553 A.2d 1078 (1988) (dicta; holding that grandparents who commence an action under § 1012 may appeal).

5. Vt.Stat.Ann. tit. 15, § 1015 (1989) (exception is made for "substantial and unanticipated change of circumstances").

6. Colorado, West's Colo.Rev.Stat.Ann. § 19–1–117 (Supp.1989); **Georgia,** Official Code Ga.Ann. § 19–7–3 (Supp.1989).

§ 25.24

1. In re Marriage of Jacobson, 228 Mont. 458, 463, 743 P.2d 1025, 1028 (1987).

2. Lyng v. Lyng, 112 A.D.2d 29, 490 N.Y.S.2d 940, 941 (1985).

3. Augustine B.C. v. Michael B., 84 A.D.2d 740, 443 N.Y.S.2d 739 (1981).

4. Colorado, West's Colo.Rev.Stat.Ann. § 19–1–117 (Supp.1989); **Florida,** West's Fla.Stat.Ann. § 61.13 (Supp.1990); **Michigan,** Mich.Comp.Laws Ann. § 722.27b (West Supp.1989).

5. See Alaska Stat. 25.20.140 (1991) (if a parent willfully and without just excuse fails to permit court-ordered grandparent visitation, the grandparent has a separate cause of action for damages. For each such failure, the amount of damages is $200, which may not be increased or decreased once liability has been established. The prevailing party in such an action is entitled to attorney fees. Just excuse does not include the wish of the child not to visit with the person entitled to visitation).

6. See **Illinois** 750 ILCS 5/607.1, formerly Ill.—S.H.A. ch. 40, ¶ 607.1 (Supp. 1989) (A party who has been willfully and without justification denied court-ordered visitation is entitled to an expedited procedure for enforcement of the court order. However, costs and fees are awarded if the

harassing.[7] In Oklahoma, the grandparent is statutorily directed to pay transportation and other costs associated with court-ordered visitation.[8]

§ 25.25 Visitation Rights of Grandparents—Procedural Issues—Costs, Attorney Fees, and Damages

Litigation is expensive, and its costs may dissuade a grandparent with a legitimate claim to visitation from pursuing a remedy in court. As a general rule, court costs and attorney fees are not awarded absent statutory authorization.[1]

Some states provide for costs and fees in the grandparent visitation statute itself.[2] Other states make no specific mention of costs and fees in their grandparent visitation statutes but have general statutes permitting such awards in custody or visitation disputes.[3] However, many states allow costs and fees to be awarded only to specific parties.[4] Some state statutes permit an award of costs and fees only to the respondent in a grandparent visitation suit.[5] Other states permit such an award only to the prevailing party.[6] The statutes may require a finding of bad faith or malicious intent on the part of the petitioner.[7] Vermont courts are authorized to award costs of defending or prosecuting an action to modify or terminate a grandparent visitation order.[8]

Courts have general authority in cases involving a child to appoint

---

enforcement action is vexatious and constitutes harassment).

7. Illinois 750 ILCS 5/607.1, formerly Ill.—S.H.A. ch. 40, ¶ 607.1 (Supp.1989).

8. Okl.Stat.Ann. tit. 10, § 5 (West Supp. 1990).

§ 25.25

1. 67A C.J.S. Parent & Child § 40 (1978).

2. Arkansas, Ark.Code Ann. § 9–13–103 (Supp.1989); **Missouri,** V.A.M.S. § 452.402 (Supp.1990); Ohio Rev.Code § 3109.051 (1990).

3. West's Fla.Stat.Ann. § 61.16 (1986); Enslein v. Gere, 497 So.2d 705 (Fla.App. 1986) (grandparent ordered to pay father's costs and fees).

4. See, e.g., Matter Custody of Mac Harg, 120 Ill.App.3d 753, 76 Ill.Dec. 500, 458 N.E.2d 1154 (1983) (because 750 ILCS 5/508, formerly Ill.—S.H.A. ch. 40, ¶ 508, applies by its terms to a "spouse," it does

not authorize an award of costs and fees unless the parties are or were married).

5. Arkansas, Ark.Stat. § 9–13–103 (Supp.1989) (only if grandparent is denied visitation); **New Hampshire,** N.H.Rev. Stat.Ann. 458:17–d (Supp.1989) (mandatory); **Kansas,** Kan.Stat.Ann. 38–131 (1986) (award to respondent is mandatory unless justice and equity require otherwise).

6. Colorado, West's Colo.Rev.Stat.Ann. § 19–1–117 (Supp.1989); **Louisiana,** LSA Rev.Stat. 9:375 (West Supp.1990); **Missouri,** V.A.M.S. § 452.402 (Supp.1990).

7. Arkansas, Ark.Code Ann. § 9–13–103 (1989). In one case, the paternal grandparents were ordered to pay the mother's costs and attorney fees incurred in defending the grandparent's appeal from an order awarding limited and finite visitation rights to the grandparent. In re Thompson's Custody, 34 Wash.App. 643, 663 P.2d 164, 167 (1983).

8. Vt.Stat.Ann. tit. 15, § 1014 (1989).

a guardian ad litem.[9] Some grandparent visitation statutes specifically authorize appointment of a guardian ad litem.[10] The expenses associated with a guardian ad litem may be awarded against one or more of the parties.[11]

A grandparent whose visitation rights are interfered with may have a claim for tort damages as well as a claim for costs and fees.[12]

§ 25.26   Adoption—Overview

The most total invasion of the parent-child relationship is adoption; after adoption, the parent and child become legal strangers. In addition to its effect on visitation privileges, adoption affects grandparents with respect to three main issues: the ability of a grandparent to adopt the grandchild; the rights of a grandparent to notification of the adoption of the grandchild and the effect of adoption on inheritance.

Library References:

C.J.S. Adoption of Persons §§ 2–4 et seq.
West's Key No. Digests, Adoption ⊂=1 et seq.

§ 25.27   Adoption—Ability of Grandparent to Adopt—Suitability of Grandparent

A grandparent, like any other adult, is legally eligible to be considered to adopt a child;[1] however, special concerns are raised where a grandparent desires to adopt a child. First, the grandparent usually will be older than a typical potential adoptive parent, and the court may be concerned that the grandparent will not live until the child reaches the age of majority.[2] As a general rule, advanced age is an important consideration but does not automatically disqualify a

---

9. See e.g., Mich.Comp.Laws Ann. § 722.27(1)(e) (West 1991).

10. Missouri, V.A.M.S. § 452.402 (Supp.1990); **Montana,** Mont.Code Ann. 40–9–102 (1989); cf. **New Hampshire,** N.H.Rev.Stat.Ann. 458:17–d (1983 & Supp. 1989).

11. Michigan, Mich.Comp.Laws Ann. § 722.27(1)(3) (West 1991); **Missouri,** V.A.M.S. § 452.402 (Supp.1990); but, see Matter of McCuan, 176 Ill.App.3d 421, 427, 125 Ill.Dec. 923, 927, 531 N.E.2d 102, 107 (1988) (party not charged because less able to pay); Minns v. Minns, 615 S.W.2d 893, 898 (Tex.Civ.App.1981) (paternal grandmother not jointly and severally liable with child's father for payment of attorney ad litem fees where the necessity for the

attorney ad litem was not a result of her intervention).

12. Eicke v. Eicke, 517 So.2d 1067, 1072 (La.App.1987) (paternal grandparents awarded damages for abuse of process from mother who had filed petition to terminate court-ordered grandparent visitation where court found petition was obviously designed to obstruct the grandparent's visitation rights at Christmas).

§ 25.27

1. See e.g., Ohio Rev.Code § 3107.03 (1989); 2 C.J.S. Adoption of Persons § 91 (1972).

2. 2 C.J.S. Adoption of Persons § 91 (1972).

potential adoptive parent.[3] Indeed, some grandparents with a relatively short life expectancy have been permitted to adopt their grandchildren.[4]

A second concern relating to grandparent adoption is the health of the grandparent.[5] Like age, health concerns alone may not automatically disqualify a grandparent from consideration but will be an important factor.

Third, a special statute may govern adoption by a grandparent and may even give the grandparents a preference in adoption.[6] In Florida, for example, if a child who is placed for adoption has lived with a grandparent for at least six months, the grandparent is given priority in adoption.[7] Variety in statutory provisions can be crucial. In Illinois, even though a child had lived with the grandparents for a substantial period of time prior to being placed for adoption, the court held that the grandparents were not entitled to intervene in the adoption proceeding.[8]

Fourth, if the parent is voluntarily placing the child for adoption, a private adoption placement with the grandparent is likely to be approved. Private placements for adoption are common. In 1982, only 12% of all adoptions were by "strangers," and 64% were by persons to whom the child was already related.[9]

§ 25.28 Adoption—Ability of Grandparent to Adopt—Parental Objection

If a grandparent wants to adopt a child over the objections of the parents, the grandparent faces the burden of proving the existence of one of the conditions necessary to disperse with parental consent to the adoption.[1] Typically, parental consent to adoption is not required if parental rights have been terminated, the parent has waived consent, the parent is unknown or mentally incompetent, or the parent has

---

3. In re Christian's Adoption, 184 So.2d 657, 658 (Fla.App.1966); Tomlinson v. O'Briant, 634 S.W.2d 546, 549 (Mo.App. 1982).

4. Id.

5. Id.

6. West's Fla.Stat.Ann. § 63.0425 (1992).

7. Id. (preference not applicable if the adoption placement is a result of the death of the child's parent whose will specifies a different preference).

8. In re Adoption of Ruiz, 164 Ill. App.3d 1036, 1040, 115 Ill.Dec. 911, 914, 518 N.E.2d 436, 439 (1987), *rehearing denied* 121 Ill.2d 570, 122 Ill.Dec. 447, 526 N.E.2d 840 (1988).

9. Adoption Factbook, Washington D.C.: National Committee for Adoption (1985).

§ 25.28

1. Tomlinson v. O'Briant, 634 S.W.2d 546, 551 (Mo.App.1982).

neglected or abandoned the child.[2] If the parent objects to the adoption, the grandparent must establish the requisite condition in either an adoption proceeding[3] or a termination of parental rights proceeding,[4] as authorized by statute.

As with visitation and custody, adoption will be decided according to the best interests of the child.[5] Under most statutes, courts will not reach the best interests of the child question until the issue of parental consent has been resolved.[6] However, a few courts have been willing to place the best interests of the child ahead of the rights of both the natural parents and the adoptive parents.[7] The United States Supreme Court approved the best interests basis when the child had been part of the adopting stepfather's *intact* family for some time.[8]

Library References:

C.J.S. Adoption of Persons §§ 51–70 et seq.

West's Key No. Digests, Adoption ☞7–7.8.

§ 25.29 Adoption—Ability of Grandparent to Adopt—Grandparents vs. Grandparents

Where both parents are out of the adoption picture, the paternal

---

2. Id.; Ala.Code § 26–10a–10 (1991); D.S. v. F.A.H., 684 S.W.2d 320, 322 (Ky. App.1985).

3. D.S. v. F.A.H., 684 S.W.2d 320, 322 (Ky.App.1985) (although maternal grandparents had no standing to bring an action to terminate parental rights, their petition to adopt, if granted, would have the same legal effect); In Interest of Unnamed Child, 584 S.W.2d 476 (Tex.Civ.App.1979) (when parental rights did not exist, grandparents who were legal strangers to the child had standing to petition for adoption of their grandchild).

4. North Carolina, N.C.Gen.Stat. § 7A–289.24 (1989) (petition to terminate parental rights may be filed by a judicially appointed guardian or a person with whom the child has lived for more than two years); **Texas,** V.T.C.A., Family Code Ann. § 11.03 (Supp.1989) (suit to terminate parental rights joined with petition to adopt may be brought by a person who has had possession and control of the child for at least two of the last three months immediately preceding the petition or another per-

son with whom the child has had substantial past contact).

5. Connecticut, Conn.Gen.Stat.Ann. § 45a–706 (West 1992); **Missouri,** V.A.M.S. § 453.005 (Supp.1990); In re Interest of A.R.M., 750 S.W.2d 86, 90 (Mo. App.1988) (maternal grandmother allowed to adopt where in child's best interests and where she had been child's sole parent); see 2 C.J.S. Adoption of Persons §§ 88, 90 (1972).

6. See Matter of Adoption of S.T.V., 226 Mont. 18, 20, 733 P.2d 841, 842 (1987).

7. See In re Adcock, 69 N.C.App. 222, 227, 316 S.E.2d 347, 350 (1984) (although severing parental ties is a harsh judicial remedy, the best interests of the child must be considered paramount); Courtney v. Richmond, 55 Md.App. 382, 391, 462 A.2d 1223, 1228 (1983); contra, In Interest of J.A., 283 N.W.2d 83, 92 (N.D.1979).

8. Quilloin v. Walcott, 434 U.S. 246, 254, 98 S.Ct. 549, 554, 54 L.Ed.2d 511 (1978) *rehearing denied* 435 U.S. 918, 98 S.Ct. 1477, 55 L.Ed.2d 511 (1978).

and maternal grandparents may be vying for adoption of the child.[1]　In such a case, the best interests of the child will control.　If the state grandparent visitation statute or another statute does not preserve grandparental ties after adoption, adoption by one set of grandparents will sever any rights of the other set.[2]　On the other hand, if nonadoptive grandparental ties are preserved after adoption, that set of grandparents may be granted visitation privileges even after the other set of grandparents adopts the child.[3]

§ 25.30 Adoption—Right of Grandparent to Notification of Adoption—Ordinarily, No Right to Notice

A grandparent who is not involved in the day-to-day life of the parent and child may not be aware that the parent is considering placing, or has already placed, the child for adoption.　The parent might have any number of reasons for not informing the grandparent of this decision.　The parent might not want to risk being talked out of the adoption by the grandparent, or the parent might feel that the grandparent has no right to know of the adoption.　However, the grandparent might have equally compelling reasons for wanting to be informed.　The grandparent might want to convince the parent to keep the child, to try to adopt the child, or to protect his or her visitation rights with the child, if possible.

As a general rule, the courts and legislatures have sided with the parent and do not require grandparent notice or consent or allow intervention.[1]　Some courts have held this rule applicable even where the grandparent had petitioned for visitation rights or had been granted visitation rights that would terminate automatically upon adoption.[2]

§ 25.29

1. See, e.g., In re Drew, 637 S.W.2d 772 (Mo.App.1982).

2. Ramey v. Thomas, 483 So.2d 747 (Fla.App.1986) (adoption of child by paternal grandparent against maternal grandparent's petition for adoption where parents had been killed completely severed grandchild's family relationship with maternal grandparents).

3. See O'Brien v. Shepley, 451 So.2d 82, 84 (La.App.1984).

§ 25.30

1. In re Jason P., 41 Conn.Sup. 23, 549 A.2d 286, 288 (1988); Mead v. Owens, 149 Ga.App. 303, 254 S.E.2d 431 (1979); Mug-genborg v. Kessler, 630 P.2d 1276 (Okl. 1981); In re Adoption of Ruiz, 164 Ill. App.3d 1036, 1040, 115 Ill.Dec. 911, 914, 518 N.E.2d 436, 439 (1987), *rehearing denied* 121 Ill.2d 570, 122 Ill.Dec. 447, 526 N.E.2d 840 (1988); Aegerter v. Thompson, 610 S.W.2d 308, 309 (Mo.App.1980).

2. Peavy v. Dollar, 515 So.2d 3, 4 (Ala. Civ.App.1987); Browning v. Tarwater, 215 Kan. 501, 524 P.2d 1135, 1139 (1974); Olson v. Flinn, 484 So.2d 1015, 1017 (Miss. 1986); Barriner v. Stedman, 580 P.2d 514, 518 (Okl.1978); contra, **Georgia**, Official Code Ga.Ann. § 19–8–15 (1991) (a grandparent with visitation rights has the right to file objections to a petition for adoption if neither parent has further rights in the child and if the petition has been filed by a blood relative of the child).

Library References:

C.J.S. Adoption of Persons §§ 78–86.

West's Key No. Digests, Adoption ⊕12.

§ 25.31 Adoption—Right of Grandparent to Notification of Adoption—Legal Rights or Actual Custody Entitle Notice

Courts apply the Uniform Child Custody Jurisdiction Act (UCCJA) notice provisions to termination of parental rights proceedings.[1] There is a split of authority on applicability to adoption proceedings.[2] Counsel for grandparents who already have court-ordered visitation rights should argue that the UCCJA entitles the grandparents to notice of and participation in the adoption proceedings.[3]

Even without reliance on the UCCJA, particularly when the child has lived with the grandparent, courts and legislatures occasionally have required that the grandparent be notified of the adoption,[4] or be permitted to participate in the adoption proceedings,[5] or be permitted to challenge the adoption decree.[6]

If the grandparent stands in some other legal relationship to the child, privileges relating to adoption may arise. Notice to the child's guardian may be required;[7] the guardian's consent to adoption may be required;[8] the consent of the person in custody of the child may be

§ 25.31

1. See, S.J. v. L.T., 727 P.2d 789 (Alaska 1986).

2. UCCJA does not apply: Olivo v. Gainey, 185 Ga.App. 427, 364 S.E.2d 279 (1987); In re Johnson, 415 N.E.2d 108 (Ind. App.1981). UCCJA applies: E.E.B. v. D.A., 89 N.J. 595, 446 A.2d 871 (1982), cert. denied 459 U.S. 1210, 75 L.Ed.2d 445 (1983); Matter of K.C.P.'s Adoption, 432 So.2d 620 (Fla.App.1983); Noga v. Noga, 111 Ill. App.3d 328, 67 Ill.Dec. 18, 443 N.E.2d 1142 (1982); Foster v. Stein, 183 Mich.App. 424, 454 N.W.2d 244 (1990); In re Adoption of Baby Boy W., 701 S.W.2d 534 (Mo.App. 1985); In re Adoption of B.E.W.G., 379 Pa.Super. 264, 549 A.2d 1286 (1988).

3. See § 25.23, supra.

4. West's Fla.Stat.Ann. § 63.0425 (1992) (if child has been living with grandparent for more than six months).

5. In re W.E.G. & J.R.G., 710 P.2d 410, 416 (Alaska 1985); West's Fla.Stat.Ann. § 63.0425 (1992); **Georgia,** Official Code Ga.Ann. § 19–8–15 (1991); contra, In re Adoption of Ruiz, 164 Ill.App.3d 1036, 1040, 115 Ill.Dec. 911, 518 N.E.2d 436, 439 (1987), rehearing denied 121 Ill.2d 570, 122 Ill.Dec. 447, 526 N.E.2d 840 (1988).

6. See Hensley v. Wist, 270 Ark. 1004, 607 S.W.2d 80, 82 (1980), reversed on other grounds 274 Ark. 48, 622 S.W.2d 164 (1981) (court indicated that grandparent could challenge an adoption decree if the grandparent stood in loco parentis to the child).

7. In re Duren, 355 Mo. 1222, 1229, 200 S.W.2d 343, 347 (1947) (but guardian's consent to adoption is not required).

8. **New Hampshire,** N.H.Rev.Stat. Ann. 170–B:5(e) (1978); **Rhode Island,** R.I.Gen.Laws § 15–7–5 (1988); **South Carolina,** S.C.Code § 20–7–190 (1989).

required;[9] or the grandparent's consent to adoption may be required if the parent is under the age of majority.[10]

In summary, the grandparent has little right to participate in a grandchild's adoption unless either the child has lived with the grandparent or the grandparent stands in a special legal position with respect to the child. Hence, if the grandparent has reason to believe that the child will be placed for adoption, counsel may want to preempt the move by filing for custody or guardianship of the child.

§ 25.32   Adoption—Effect of Adoption on Inheritance

Because both adoption and intestate succession to property are purely statutory phenomena, the question of whether an adopted child can inherit from natural grandparents is one of statutory construction and may differ from state to state.[1]

After adoption, a natural parent is divested of all legal rights and obligations owed to the child and those owed to the parent by the child.[2] The child and the parent are legal strangers.[3] Those who claim rights and obligations derivative of the parent are similarly divested.[4] Hence, adoption usually terminates the legal relationship between the adopted child and the grandparents.[5]

Conversely, the adoptive parent and the child have all the rights and obligations with respect to each other as a natural parent and child.[6] A parent of the adoptive parent, the adoptive grandparent, is treated legally as a natural grandparent of the child.[7]

These basic principles apply to issues involving intestate inheritance and interpretation of testamentary documents.[8] In all states but one, intestate inheritance from and through both the natural and the adoptive parents is not possible.[9] The adopted child is no longer an

---

9. New York, N.Y.—McKinney's Dom. Rel.Law § 111(f) (Supp.1990); **Ohio,** Ohio Rev.Code § 3107.06(C) (1990).

10. E.g., Okl.Stat.Ann. tit. 10, § 60.5 (West Supp.1990).

§ 25.32

1. Anno., Right of Adopted Child to Inherit from Intestate Natural Grandparent, 60 A.L.R. 3d 631, 633 (1974).

2. Because of this, some statutes specifically retain rights of the natural parent who is the spouse of the adopting parent. See, e.g., Ala.Code § 26–10A–29 (1991).

3. Arkansas, Ark.Code Ann. § 9–9–215 (1987); **Florida,** West's Fla.Stat.Ann. § 63.172 (1985 & Supp.1990).

4. West's Fla.Stat.Ann. § 63.172 (1992).

5. Wilson v. Wallace, 274 Ark. 48, 622 S.W.2d 164, 165 (1981).

6. West's Ann.Cal.Civ.Code § 221.63 (Supp.1992).

7. Rasco v. Moran, 475 P.2d 696, 699 (Alaska 1970).

8. Ark.Code Ann. § 9–9–215 (1987).

9. Wailes v. Curators of Central College, 363 Mo. 932, 254 S.W.2d 645, 649 (1953). Apparently, Illinois is the single exception to the sweeping rule that severs the right of an adopted child to inherit from his or her natural parents. People ex

heir-at-law of the natural parents or of their collateral and lineal relatives,[10] but becomes an heir-at-law of the adoptive family.[11]

Thus, as a general rule, a child adopted by the deceased's child will take if the deceased dies intestate. Similarly, an adopted-away child of the deceased's child will not take from the deceased former grandparent.

However, grandparents can use private documents to create succession rights in their natural grandchildren or to provide for rights in adopted grandchildren.[12] An adopted-away child can take as a named beneficiary from natural relatives by will or trust.[13] The question of whether an adopted child takes by a will or trust that specifies a class of beneficiaries, e.g., issue of children, rather than named beneficiaries, is a question of the testator's or settlor's intent.[14] Courts have reached all conceivable results for a given class designation.[15] Counsel should draft will and trust instruments with specific language covering adoption.

§ 25.33   Relationships With Grandchildren: Books and Other Resources on Grandparenting [1]

Arthur Kornhaber, Grandparents and Grandchildren: The Vital Connection (1981).

David Elkin, Grandparenting: Understanding Today's Children (1982).

Norman H. Birman, The Grandparenting Book (1982).

Miriam Galper Cohen, Long Distance Parenting (1989).

---

rel. Bachleda v. Dean, 48 Ill.2d 16, 19, 268 N.E.2d 11, 13 (1971) (after adoption, the child can still inherit from and through natural parents).

10. Colorado, West's Colo.Rev.Stat. Ann. § 19–3–608 (Supp.1989); **Delaware,** Del.Code. tit. 13, § 920 (Supp.1989); **Florida,** West's Fla.Stat.Ann. § 63.172 (1992); **Maryland** Hall v. Vallandingham, 75 Md. App. 187, 193, 540 A.2d 1162, 1164 (1988).

11. Hawaii, Haw.Rev.Stat. § 578–16 (1985); **New Hampshire,** N.H.Rev.Stat. Ann. 170–B:20 (1991); **Colorado** Wright v. Wysowatcky, 147 Colo. 317, 319, 363 P.2d 1046, 1047 (1961).

12. See Anno., Right of Adopted Child to Inherit from Intestate Natural Grandparent, 60 A.L.R.3d 631 (1974).

13. Maryland, Md.Fam.Law Code, § 5–308 (1984); **New Hampshire,** N.H.Rev. Stat.Ann. § 170–B:20 (1991).

14. Thomas v. Trust Co. Bank, 247 Ga. 693, 279 S.E.2d 440 (1981).

15. See, e.g., **Delaware** Haskell v. Wilmington Trust, 304 A.2d 53 (Del.1973); **Iowa** Cook v. Underwood, 208 Iowa 641, 228 N.W. 629 (1930); **Maryland,** Md.Fam. Law Code, § 5–308 (1984); see also, Annotation, Adoption As Precluding Testamentary Gift Under Natural Relative's Will, 71 A.L.R.4th 374 (1989).

§ 25.33

1. These books and resources were described in Modern Maturity, pp. 41–42, p. 93, Dec. 1990–Jan. 1991 (AARP).

The American Self–Help Clearinghouse is a nationwide computerized database that offers (1) tips on how to start a grandparent self-help group, and (2) a listing of local self-help clearinghouses with resources in the area. Send a legal-sized, self-addressed stamped envelope (SASE) to American Self–Help Clearinghouse, St. Clares–Riverside Medical Center, Denville, NJ 07834, 201–625–7101.

Becoming a Better Grandparent and *Achieving Grandparent Potential* are two 12–session courses developed by Robert and Shirley Strom to help grandparents adjust to their new role. Demonstration and training sessions for course leaders are being offered at selected sites nationwide. Write Robert Strom, Ph.D., ASU College of Education, Tempe, AZ 85287–0611, for the nearest location.

Foundation for Grandparenting offers a free copy of its newsletter, *Vital Connections.* Send a legal-sized, SASE to PO Box 31, Lake Placid, NY 12946. For a brochure on an intergenerational summer camp in the Adirondacks, send a separate SASE to the same address.

Grandparents Against Immorality and Neglect (GAIN) is a grandparents' support/advocacy group. Write Betty Parbs, 720 Kingstown Pl., Shreveport, LA 71108, 318–688–4246.

Grandparents as Parents (GAP) will help grandparents network with other grandparents in their area. Write Sylvie de Toledo, Psychiatric Clinic for Youth, 2801 Atlantic Ave., Long Beach, CA 90801, 213–595–3151.

Grandparents Raising Grandchildren can help grandparents start a self-help group in their area. Send a SASE (45 cents postage) to Barbara Kirkland, PO Box 104, Colleyville, TX 76034.

Second Time Around Parents is a grandparents' support/advocacy group. Write Michele Daly, Family and Community Services of Delaware County, 100 W. Front St., Medina, PA 19063, 215–566–7540.

§§ 25.34–25.40 are reserved for supplementary material.

B.　FINANCIAL RESPONSIBILITY FOR OLDER PERSONS

§ 25.41　Introduction

Most spouses and adult children and parents care for one another. Problems arise when assets and income run low. This part of this chapter discusses legal responsibility of a spouse or other relative to contribute to the support of an older person. There are three basic issues: (1) Can anyone other than the contracting party (usually the recipient) be held liable to the provider of services and supplies? (2)

Can the state require a spouse or other relative to contribute support to an older person? (3) Can the state recoup from a spouse or other relative monies paid by the state on behalf of an elderly recipient?

Federal law that allows the assets and income of an applicant's spouse to be "deemed" or presumed available for the applying spouse when determining eligibility for Medicaid is discussed in Chapter 11, supra.

§ 25.42 Spouse Responsibility for Necessaries—Common Law Necessaries Rule—Husband Liable for Necessaries

The common law rule required a husband to support his wife. Enforcement occurred through the husband's liability to a creditor. The creditor could collect even though the husband had not consented to the purchase, provided the creditor had supplied items to the wife "on the credit" of the husband and those items were necessary to live at the standard the husband had set for the family.[1] The most likely modern situation for application of the necessaries rule is for medical and hospital services, especially of the recipient's last illness.

Library References:

C.J.S. Husband and Wife § 49; Insane Persons §§ 73 et seq.

West's Key No. Digests, Husband and Wife ⊕19; Mental Health ⊕73–80.

§ 25.43 Spouse Responsibility for Necessaries—Common Law Necessaries Rule—Modern Changes

Equal protection attacks on the common law necessaries rule have been successful in either eliminating the rule or extending a similar liability to wives to supply necessaries to the husband.[1] The law of each jurisdiction must be checked. If the husband-only rule has not been repudiated, either defendants or plaintiffs can make an equal

§ 25.42

1. Alamance County Hosp., Inc. v. Neighbors, 315 N.C. 362, 366, 338 S.E.2d 87, 90 (1986); H. Clark, The Law of Domestic Relations in the United States, § 6.3 (West 1968); Krauskopf and Thomas, Partnership Marriage, 35 Ohio St.L.J. 558 (1974); Comment, The Doctrine of Necessaries: Contemporary Application as a Support Remedy, 19 Stetson L.Rev. 661 (1990) (WESTLAW: STETLR database, ci(19 +5 661)); Note, The Unnecessary Doctrine of Necessaries, 82 Mich.L.Rev. 1767 (1984); Ann., 20 A.L.R.4th 196 (1983).

§ 25.43

1. Mahoney, Economic Sharing During Marriage: Equal Protection, Spousal Support and the Doctrine of Necessaries, 22 J.Fam.L. 221 (1983–84); Note, North Carolina Baptist Hospitals, Inc. v. Harris: North Carolina Adopts a Gender–Neutral Approach to the Doctrine of Necessaries, 66 N.C.L.Rev. 1241 (1988) (WESTLAW: NCLR database, ci(66 +5 1241)); Ann., 20 A.L.R.4th 196 (1983).

protection argument. If the husband is sued for necessaries supplied to his wife, he may argue that the rule is invalid as violating equal protection and should be abrogated entirely. In contrast, a supplier of necessaries, such as a hospital, may sue the widow of a man whose last illness and death occurred in the hospital if his estate and insurance are insufficient to cover the bills. The wife could argue no liability under the rule, but the plaintiff would argue that the rule must be extended to impose liability on wives as well as husbands in order to avoid violating equal protection.

Three results are possible. Occasionally, courts have abrogated the rule.[2] More often, decisions have extended the rule by imposing liability on wives for necessaries supplied to their husbands.[3] Some states have statutorily imposed a coequal civil duty of support on both spouses.[4] In addition, some legislatures have modified the criminal nonsupport statute to impose a duty to support one another.[5] These decisions have created a public policy likely to be enforced by the extension of the necessaries doctrine to wives. A few courts have continued to apply the husband-only rule.[6]

§ 25.44 Spouse Responsibility for Necessaries—Common Law Necessaries Rule—Requirements for Liability

If the necessaries rule is applicable, the creditor plaintiff has the burden of proving at least four elements.[1] First, the creditor must have supplied the goods or services "on the credit" of the defendant spouse, i.e., with an intent that the spouse pay. Since there will be no contract with the spouse, this proposition may be difficult to establish. Second, the defendant must not have been providing for the goods or services in some other reasonable way, e.g., paying a different doctor or a clinic. Third, the goods or services must be appropriate or necessary to the spouses' usual standard of living. Fourth, the benefited spouse and the

---

2. Schilling v. Bedford County Memorial Hospital, 225 Va. 539, 544, 303 S.E.2d 905, 908 (1983); Condore v. Prince George's Cty., 289 Md. 516, 532, 425 A.2d 1011, 1019 (1981).

3. Jersey Shore Medical Center–Fitkin Hospital v. Estate of Baum, 84 N.J. 137, 151, 417 A.2d 1003, 1010, 11 A.L.R.4th 1147 (1980); N.C. Baptist Hosp., Inc. v. Harris, 319 N.C. 347, 353, 354 S.E.2d 471, 474 (1987); Richland Memorial Hosp. v. English, 295 S.C. 511, 369 S.E.2d 395 (App. 1988); Cases, Annotation, 11 A.L.R.4th 1147 (1982). See also, Ohio State Universi-

ty Hospital v. Kinkaid, 48 Ohio St.3d 78, 80, 549 N.E.2d 517, 519, *rehearing denied* 49 Ohio St.3d 713, 552 N.E.2d 951 (1990).

4. Va.Code § 55–37 (1991).

5. Ohio, Ohio Rev.Code § 2919.21 (1992); **Virginia,** Va.Code § 20–61 (1983).

6. Shands Teaching Hosp. & Clinics, Inc. v. Smith, 497 So.2d 644 (Fla.1986).

§ 25.44

1. Clark, supra § 25.42, note 1; Krauskopf and Thomas, supra § 25.42, note 1.

defendant must have been residing together or not separated due to the fault of the benefited spouse.

§ 25.45 Spouse Responsibility for Necessaries—Family Expense Statutes

Family expense statutes often impose obligations on both spouses for expenses of the family that are collectible by creditors.[1] Medical care and all other necessaries for family members are included. Therefore, if the common law necessaries rule does not extend to wives, creditors of a husband will try to use family expense statutes to obtain a judgment against the wife for the husband's expenses. Judicial extension of the common law necessaries doctrine to wives has a similar effect.

§ 25.46 Spouse Responsibility for Necessaries—Conditions and Limitations on Liability

Although many courts hold that spouses have joint and several primary liability under family expense and support statutes or the necessaries doctrine,[1] some courts take other approaches. Under either the necessaries doctrine or family expense statutes, two defenses should always be considered. First, the law of the particular state may make the liability of the nonrecipient spouse secondary only,[2] which ordinarily requires that the plaintiff prove the recipient of the services or the recipient's estate is unable to pay.[3] Second, the statute may limit the amount of liability of the nonrecipient spouse to a certain dollar amount of the expense or in excess of a certain amount of assets.[4] The statute or the courts also may impose liability only to the extent that

§ 25.45

1. **Illinois,** 750 ILCS 65/15, formerly Ill.Rev.Stat., ch. 40, ¶ 1015 (1989); **Connecticut,** Conn.Gen.Stat.Ann. § 46b–37 (1988); Iowa Code Ann. § 597.14 (West 1981); **West Virginia,** W.Va.Code 48–3–22 (1986); **Oregon,** Or.Rev.Stat. 108.040 (1990); Utah Code Ann. 30–2–9 (1989).

§ 25.46

1. Cooke v. Adams, 183 So.2d 925, 927 (Miss.1966); Comment, The New Doctrine of Necessaries in Virginia, 19 U.Rich. L.Rev. 317 (1985).

2. Conn.Gen.Stat.Ann. § 46b–37 (1988); Marshfield Clinic v. Discher, 105 Wis.2d 506, 314 N.W.2d 326, 327 (1982) (holding constitutional the requirement that husbands always were primarily liable for both their own and their wives' necessaries). Other cases applying this rule were decided prior to equal protection litigation attacking gender-based differences. See cases, Ann. 20 A.L.R.4th 196 at 202 (1983).

3. Jersey Shore Medical Center–Fitkin Hospital v. Estate of Baum, 84 N.J. 137, 151, 417 A.2d 1003, 1010 (1980); Busch v. Busch Const., Inc., 262 N.W.2d 377, 402 (Minn.1977); Borgess Medical Center v. Smith, 149 Mich.App. 796, 386 N.W.2d 684 (1986), limited by Bronson Methodist Hosp. v. LaRoy, 171 Mich.App. 729, 430 N.W.2d 817 (1988); Comment, supra note 1, recommends this approach.

4. See, e.g., Mass.Gen.Laws Ann. c. 209, § 7 (West 1987).

the spouse is "able to pay," [5] which provides the attorney with opportunity to present arguments of the spouse's inability to pay.

The statutes do not contain guidelines for measuring the standard of living spouses ought to be able to maintain before they are obligated to pay debts of recipient spouses. The courts must determine those amounts without clear criteria. For example, although the defendant wife in one case was not required to surrender and apply her entire life savings of approximately $70,000 to offset Medicaid payments being made by the state on behalf of her husband, the court did require the 85–year–old woman to contribute $440 per month toward the support of her husband. The court recognized that the estate would be depleted in about seven years but apparently assumed the obligor would not live that long.[6]

Defense counsel should argue that the obligor spouse is entitled to live at least as well as the spouse would after a divorce, i.e., that the protected standard ought to be the standard of living of the marriage. Creditors will probably assert that the standard should not be more than the amount permitted to the community spouse from income of a nursing home resident who is receiving Medicaid. Unfortunately, depending on the state's allowance schedule, that amount could be as low as a welfare standard of living. Defense counsel should argue that a standard appropriate for determining payment of public benefits to one's spouse is inappropriately low for determining the amount available to pay a creditor. The statutory medicaid provision that the community spouse's allowance must be no less than the amount of a court order for support buttresses this reasoning.[7]

§ 25.47 Relative Responsibility for Necessaries—Statutes Create Liability

The common law necessaries rule and typical family expense statutes impose obligations for expenses of the family only on spouses. Approximately 28 states also have relative responsibility statutes, usually in the "poor laws" or "general assistance" sections.[1]

5. Ohio State University Hosp. v. Kinkaid, 48 Ohio St.3d 78, 80, 549 N.E.2d 517, 519, *rehearing denied* 49 Ohio St.3d 713, 552 N.E.2d 951 (1990); Cline v. Cline, 92 N.C.App. 257, 262, 374 S.E.2d 462, 465 (1988). Some statutes also limit liability to a percentage of the spouse's income. See, e.g., Neb.Rev.Stat. § 42–201 (1990).

6. Department of Social Services v. Barbara M., 123 Misc.2d 523, 527, 474

N.Y.S.2d 193, 196 (Fam.Ct.1984) (under previous liberal law).

7. See discussion §§ 25.49–.51, infra.

§ 25.47

1. Britton, American's Best Kept Secret: An Adult Child's Duty to Support Aged Parents, 26 Calif.West L.Rev. 351, 358 (1990). Byrd, Relative Responsibility Extended: Requirement of Adult Children to Pay for Their Indigent Parent's Medical

§ 25.48 Relative Responsibility for Necessaries—Enforcement

Relative responsibility statutes may or may not carry criminal penalties. If they do carry such penalties, they are enforceable by the prosecutor. However, it is more likely that an adult child's duty will be taken into account in the determination of the eligibility of the aging parent for public benefits or in attempts to collect reimbursement.[1] State welfare systems may have formulas that enable administrators to determine what percentage of the adult child's income is available for support of the parent.[2] In recent years, welfare administrators have seldom used these statutes.[3] There is a strong consensus among scholars, law enforcement personnel, and welfare authorities that these formulas are useless as a practical matter. Most believe the difficulties in determining how much an adult child with his or her own dependent family can afford to contribute to the support of parents outweigh any amounts collected or saved for the public program. Additionally, taking from the younger family contributes to its impoverishment and increases the probabilities that its members will seek public aid later. These reasons also explain why some states, such as Colorado and Minnesota,[4] do not have adult child support legislation. However,

Needs, 22 Fam.L.Q. 87 (1988). **Alaska** Alaska Stat. 25.20.030 (1985); **California,** West's Ann.Cal.Civ.Code §§ 206, 242 (1982 and Supp.1987); **Connecticut,** Conn.Gen. Stat.Ann. § 46b–215 (West Supp.1986 & Supp.1987); **Delaware,** Del.Code tit. 13, § 503 (1981); **Georgia,** Official Code Ga. Ann. § 36–12–3 (1987); **Idaho** Idaho Code § 32–1002 (1983); **Indiana,** West's Ann. Ind.Code 31–2–9–1 (1987); **Iowa** Iowa Code Ann. § 252.2 (West 1985); **Louisiana** La. Rev.Stat.Ann. 13:4731 (West 1968); **Maine,** Me.Rev.Stat.Ann. tit. 22, § 4319 (1981); **Maryland,** Md.Fam.Law Code, § 13–102 (1991); **Massachusetts** Mass.Gen.Laws Ann. ch. 273, § 20 (West Supp.1987); **Mississippi,** Miss.Code § 43–31–25 (1981); **Montana** Mont.Code Ann. 40–6–214, 301 (1987); **Nevada,** Nev.Rev.Stat. 428.070 (Michie 1986); **New Hampshire,** N.H.Rev. Stat.Ann. 546–A:2 (1974); **New Jersey,** N.J.Stat.Ann. 44:1–140 (West Supp.1987); **North Carolina,** N.C.Gen.Stat. § 14–326.1 (1986); **North Dakota,** N.D.Cent.Code 14–09–10 (1981); **Oregon,** Or.Rev.Stat. 109.-010 (1983); **Pennsylvania,** Pa.Stat.Ann. tit. 62, § 1973 (Supp.1987), limited by § 10 Act of 1976, July 15, P.L. No. 202; **Rhode**

Island, R.I.Gen.Laws § 15–10–1 (1981); **South Dakota,** S.D.Codified Laws 25–7–27 (1984); **Utah,** Utah Code Ann. 17–14–2 (1987); **Vermont,** Vt.Stat.Ann. tit. 15, § 202 (1974 & Supp.1986); **Virginia,** Va. Code § 20–88 (1991); **West Virginia,** W.Va.Code 9–5–9 (1984).

§ 25.48

1. Levy, Supporting the Aged: The Problem of Family Responsibility, An Aging World 253, 254, J. Eckelaar & D. Pearl, eds. (1989).

2. Whitman and Whitney, Are Children Legally Responsible for the Support of Their Parents?, 123 Trusts and Estates 43 (Dec. 1984); Britton, supra § 25.47, note 1, at 360; see, e.g., Swoap v. Superior Ct. of Sacramento Cty., 10 Cal.3d 490, 111 Cal. Rptr. 136, 148, 516 P.2d 840, 852 (1973).

3. Britton, supra § 25.47, note 1, at 360, says that California and Oregon are notable exceptions.

4. In re Marriage of Serdinsky, 740 P.2d 521, 523 (Colo.1987); Minn.Stat.Ann. § 256B.14 (West 1982 and Supp.1990).

when the statutes are used, constitutional challenges generally have not been successful.[5]

Efforts on the part of private providers of goods and services to hold adult children liable on the contract may be authorized by the statute, but like spousal responsibility for necessaries, the liability may be secondary to that of the recipient and may be limited to the "financial ability" of the person charged.[6] Support actually supplied to a parent by another person such as an adult child is properly considered when determining eligibility of the parent for public programs.[7]

§ 25.49 Relative Responsibility for Necessaries—Medical Expenses—Medicaid Eligibility and Support Obligations

In determining eligibility for Medicaid coverage for long-term institutional care, the federal statute requires the states to treat (deem) certain assets and income of the community (non-institutionalized) spouse as though available for the applicant spouse.[1] Once a person is eligible for Medicaid coverage and is institutionalized, no income payable to either spouse alone is "deemed" available to the other. When most of the family income is payable to the institutionalized spouse, for example, when a husband who was the sole wage earner of a family is institutionalized, a certain allowance of assets and income of the institutionalized spouse is not counted in determining the funds available to continue paying part of the costs; otherwise, the community spouse would be left without income for living expenses. Hence, a portion of the institutionalized spouse's income and assets is set aside for the protection of the community spouse.[2]

The allowance is not a federally created obligation of the institutionalized spouse to pay the amount of the allowance to the community spouse. However, if there is a court order imposing a support obligation on the institutionalized spouse under state law, the allowance must not be less than that amount.[3] In this sense, state courts have the ultimate power to determine the amount of the institutionalized spouse's income that should be reasonably allocated to the community spouse rather than being spent for long-term care expenses.

5. Whitman and Whitney, supra note 2, at 44.

6. Id.; **Pennsylvania,** Pa.Stat. tit. 62, § 1973 (1989); **Oregon,** Or.Rev.Stat. 416.-061 (1985).

7. See, e.g., Thornsberry v. State Dept. of Health, 365 Mo. 1217, 1222, 295 S.W.2d 372, 375 (1956). See also, Davis v. Commonwealth, 230 Va. 201, 205, 335 S.E.d

375, 378 (1985) (recognizing contractual duty to care for parent).

§ 25.49

1. See Chapter 11, supra.

2. See explanation in Chapter 11, supra.

3. 42 U.S.C.A. § 1396r–5(d)(5).

Significantly, the allowances in income and assets do not create a federal obligation on the part of the community spouse to actually transfer to the other spouse any income or assets. Nothing in the federal law imposes or requires the states to impose a general obligation of support on spouses. Consequently, state law must always be utilized to determine the extent of spouses' obligations to one another. In the absence of state enforcement efforts, the community spouse could even retain income or assets in excess of the allowable amounts without jeopardizing eligibility of the other spouse.[4]

The federal statute and regulations forbid "deeming" the income and resources of nonspouse relatives as available to an individual applying for Medicaid.[5]　In 1983, the Health Care Financing Administration issued a transmittal letter reinterpreting Medicaid regulations to allow states that imposed general relative support obligations to consider the amount of that relative's obligation when determining Medicaid eligibility.[6]　Although it was expected that states would respond by enacting relative support statutes, especially filial responsibility statutes, little activity has been evident.[7]　Federal courts have invalidated attempts to use state relative support statutes as a basis for "deeming" the amount of the obligations as part of the income of an assistance applicant.　The courts have held that explicit federal statutory language [8] forbids the practice.[9]

Library References:

C.J.S. Social Security and Public Welfare §§ 133.

West's Key No. Digests, Social Security and Public Welfare ⚎241.76.

4.　42 U.S.C.A. § 1396r–5(c)(2) and (3).

5.　42 U.S.C.A. § 1396a(a)(17)(D);　42 C.F.R. § 435.602 (1980).

6.　HCFA–Pub. 45–3, § 3812 "Treatment of Contributions from Relatives to Medicaid Applicants or Recipients," (Feb. 1983), Medicare and Medicaid Guide (CCH) ¶ 32, 457.

7.　National Health Law Program, Health Care for the Poor during 1983: A Time of Reassessment and Transition, 17 Clearinghouse Rev. 977, 979 n. 21 (Jan. 1984), stating that Idaho did respond; Britton, supra § 25.47, note 1, finding no case challenging the transmittal. In 83 Op. Atty.Gen. (1984), the Idaho statute was declared contrary to the Medicaid statute.

8.　42 U.S.C.A. § 1396a(a)(17)(D);　42 C.F.R. § 435.602 (1980).

9.　Mitchell v. Lipscomb, 851 F.2d 734, 736, 22 Soc.Sec.Rep.Ser. 328 (4th Cir.1988); Sundberg v. Mansour, 627 F.Supp. 616, 620, 12 Soc.Sec.Rep.Ser. 723 (W.D.Mich. 1986), *affirmed by* 847 F.2d 1210 (6th Cir. 1988); Childress v. Bowen, 833 F.2d 231, 233, 19 Soc.Sec.Rep.Ser. 573 (10th Cir. 1987); Olson v. Norman, 830 F.2d 811, 820, 19 Soc.Sec.Rep.Ser. 338 (8th Cir.1987); Reed v. Blinzinger, 639 F.Supp. 130, 134, 14 Soc.Sec.Rep.Ser. 764 (S.D.Ind.1986), *opinion adopted by,* 816 F.2d 296, 17 Soc. Sec.Rep.Ser. 411 (7th Cir.1987); Sneede v. Kizer, 728 F.Supp. 607, 610, 28 Soc.Sec. Rep.Ser. 337 (N.D.Cal.1990).

§ 25.50　Relative Responsibility for Necessaries—Medical Expenses—Responsible Party Requirements and Promises

Some medical providers, particularly nursing homes, followed a practice of requiring a resident to have a cosigner who could be held financially responsible for the resident's expenses. Federal law has prohibited such requirements since October 1, 1989.[1] For older contracts, the National Senior Citizens Law Center believes the practice invalid under various federal and state laws.[2] A Kansas Court of Appeals considered an argument that lack of consideration would void an attempted contract with a nephew;[3] however, the decision is ambiguous. Some state statutes make promises to pay for previously furnished necessaries to a parent enforceable without consideration.[4]

§ 25.51　Relative Responsibility for Necessaries—Medical Expenses—Family Supplementation

Family supplementation is a scheme for obtaining relative payments for nursing home care. In 1971, HEW forbade the practice of requiring private payment for various services or upgraded room accommodations, but in the early 1980s, the taboo was interpreted to pertain only to services "covered" by Medicaid. Other private payments for "extras" are permissible and not considered part of the resident's income.[1] However, some states continue to forbid all supplementation.[2] Other states have deliberately reduced types of "covered" services and at the same time allowed family supplementation to pay for any "noncovered" services.[3] The National Senior Citizens Law Center warns that the supplementation practice can rapidly undermine

§ 25.50

1. Edelman, Family Supplementation in Nursing Homes, 18 Clearinghouse Rev. 504, n. 5 (Oct. 1984).

2. Id.; but see, Faith Manor v. Armer, 1991 WL 259567, (Ohio App.1991) (holding that an attorney-in-fact who signs her own name on a contract signature line designated as "for patient or responsible party" is the responsible party).

3. Heritage House Partnership v. Frazier, No. 86C4072 (Kan.Dist.Ct., Johnson Cty., Feb. 8, 1989), cited in 23 Clearinghouse Rev. 1024 (Dec. 1989).

4. **Idaho,** Idaho Code § 32–1002 (Supp. 1989); **Montana,** Mont.Code Ann. 40–6–

214 (1989); **Oklahoma,** Okla.Stat.Ann. tit. 10, § 12 (West Supp.1990).

§ 25.51

1. Resident v. Noot, 305 N.W.2d 311, 314 (Minn.1981); Edelman, supra § 25.50, note 1.

2. Dunlap Care Center v. Iowa Dept. Soc. Serv., 353 N.W.2d 389 (Iowa 1984), Medicare & Medicaid Guide (CCH) ¶ 34,040 (Iowa July 18, 1984).

3. **Georgia,** Official Ga.Code Ann. § 49–4–142 (1984); **Washington,** Wash.Admin.Code § 388–83–010(3)(a)(i), cited in 18 Clearinghouse Rev. 506 (Oct. 1984).

adequate publicly provided benefits by forcing relatives to pay for more and more basic services.[4]

§ 25.52 Recoupment of Public Benefits Paid—In General

After the death of a public benefit recipient, the state may seek to recoup properly paid benefits from the estate of the recipient or the recipient's spouse. Collecting from the estate of the recipient or the survivor has the practical effect of depriving heirs of funds they would otherwise inherit. Attorneys may find it wise to inform potential heirs of this possibility in advance.

Library References:

C.J.S. Insane Persons §§ 73 et seq.; Social Security and Public Welfare §§ 137, 138.

West's Key No. Digests, Mental Health ⬮73–80; Social Security and Public Welfare ⬮241.76.

§ 25.53 Recoupment of Public Benefits Paid—State Laws

State statutes may provide for a lien against the recipient's estate to secure recoupment of state benefits.[1] State statutes also may postpone recoupment attempts until the death of the surviving spouse, but then place a lien against that estate for reimbursement of benefits paid to either spouse.[2]

§ 25.54 Recoupment of Public Benefits Paid—Recoupment of Medicaid Benefits—Estate Recovery

Until October 1, 1993, Federal law permits, but does not require, liens and recoupment in certain circumstances. See § 11.49 supra, footnote 1 amendment requiring estate recovery. States may impose liens, collectible at sale or death, on the beneficiary's property to secure reimbursement of *incorrectly* made payments without restriction.[1] Liens to secure repayment of *correct* Medicaid payments may be made

---

4. Edelman, supra § 25.50, note 1.

§ 25.53

1. **Arizona,** Ariz.Rev.Stat. § 36–2935 (Supp.1990); **Connecticut,** Conn.Gen.Stat. Ann. § 17–82c (West 1988); **Delaware,** Del.Code tit. 31, § 503 (1974 and Supp. 1990); **Florida,** West's Fla.Stat.Ann. § 409.345 (1986); **Hawaii,** Haw.Rev.Stat. § 346–29.5 (1985 and Supp.1990); **Massachusetts,** Mass.Gen.Laws Ann. c. 118E, § 17 (West 1975 and Supp.1990).

2. **Indiana,** West's Ann.Ind.Code § 12–1–19–1 (1982 and Supp.1990); Miss.Code

§ 43–13–7 (1972); **New Hampshire,** N.H.Rev.Stat.Ann. 167:14 (1990); **New Jersey,** N.J.Stat.Ann. 30:4D–7.2 (West 1981 and Supp.1990); **New York,** N.Y.— McKinney's Soc.Serv.Law § 369 (1983 and Supp.1991); **Rhode Island,** R.I.Gen.Laws § 40–8–15 (1990); **Tennessee,** Tenn.Code Ann. § 71–5–116 (1987); **Wyoming,** Wyo. Stat. § 42–4–109 (1988).

§ 25.54

1. 42 U.S.C.A. § 1396p(a)(1)(A).

against real property during the recipient's lifetime only if it is determined at a hearing that the resident cannot reasonably be expected to be discharged from the medicaid financed institution and return home and only if the resident does not have a spouse, minor, or disabled child or specially qualified sibling.[2]

Recovery of correctly paid amounts is permitted in two situations: (1) the situation described immediately above after the death of the beneficiary and his or her surviving spouse,[3] and (2) in the case of a beneficiary who received payments after reaching age 65, but only after the death of both spouses and only if there is no minor or disabled child or specially qualified child or sibling.[4]

Library References:

C.J.S. Social Security and Public Welfare §§ 137, 138.
West's Key No. Digests, Social Security and Public Welfare ☞241.70.

§ 25.55   Recoupment of Public Benefits Paid—Recoupment of Medicaid Benefits—Other Relatives

Medicaid regulations extend the portion of the Medicaid statute that forbids "deeming" from responsible relatives [1] for eligibility purposes to recoupment situations, thus forbidding any reimbursement from any individual or relative other than a spouse or parent.[2] After the 1983 transmittal letter, one New York decision held that recoupment from relatives is different than deeming and that nothing in the federal statute forbids recoveries from relatives who are responsible under a general support law.[3] Absence of other case law indicates that administrative decisions forgo efforts to pursue relatives.[4]

§§ 25.56–25.60 are reserved for supplementary material.

C. THE BROKEN FAMILY

§ 25.61   Introduction

Attorneys who are developing an elder law practice but who are not versed in recent marriage dissolution information and litigation

---

2. 42 U.S.C.A. § 1396p(a)(1)(B); 42 C.F.R. § 433.36 (1980).

3. 42 U.S.C.A. § 1396p(b)(1)(A).

4. 42 U.S.C.A. § 1396p(b)(1)(B); 42 C.F.R. § 433.36(h)(2). See also, In re Estate of Turner, 391 N.W.2d 767, 770 (Minn. 1986), (holding that state statute embodying same provisions did not violate equal protection). See § 11.49 supra for connection to medicaid planning.

§ 25.55

1. 42 U.S.C.A. § 1396a(a)(17)(D).

2. 42 C.F.R. § 435.602(a)(2) (1983).

3. Matter of Estate of Imburgia, 127 Misc.2d 756, 487 N.Y.S.2d 263, 265 (Nassau Cty., 1984).

4. Byrd, supra, § 25.47, note 1, cites 84 Op.Att'y Gen. (Idaho 1984) and 83 Op.Att'y Gen. (Tenn.1983) agreeing with the federal regulation.

may find themselves faced with a dangerous temptation to simplify the decision to end a marriage so that the client is not counseled enough to make a truly informed decision. It is easy in modern culture to assume that persons who have begun to irritate one another or even to actively dislike one another after 15, 27, or 40 years of marriage would be better off independent from each other in their golden years. This discussion is aimed at such temptations; it will briefly describe the law governing economic considerations at marriage dissolution, expose serious disadvantages of dissolving a long-term marriage, and suggest other alternatives that should be considered before a client decides to initiate or accept dissolution of a long-lasting marriage.

§ 25.62 Principles of Marriage Dissolution Affecting Economics—Property Division

Every state now empowers courts to divide property at marriage dissolution. Many states permit all property of the spouses to be divided between them as the court deems equitable, but a majority allow only marital property to be shared. Marital property is that acquired during marriage by marital funds or the efforts of one or both parties. Separate property that may be retained by one spouse usually is that acquired prior to marriage or by gift or inheritance and not converted to marital property by devoting it in some way to the marital partnership. In practice, property likely to be ordered shared is not much different in the two types of jurisdictions. One reason is that courts in jurisdictions with power to divide all property are reluctant to force sharing of property one spouse owned prior to marriage or inherited, provided it has not been devoted to the marital enterprise. In addition, courts in marital property jurisdictions hold that the increase in the value of separate property due to a spouse's efforts is divisible, and sometimes find that separate property was changed, or "transmuted," to marital property when it was jointly titled, commingled with marital property, or used as family property for an extended time.[1]

In any state, a wide range of property is likely to be divided between the spouses. Division might require cash buyouts, in-kind setting off of certain items to one spouse and other items to the other

§ 25.62

1. See, e.g., Whiting v. Whiting, 183 W.Va. 451, 396 S.E.2d 413, 421 (1990); Alston v. Alston, 555 So.2d 1128, 1130 (Ala. Civ.App.1989); In re Marriage of Cullman, 185 Ill.App.3d 1029, 1033, 133 Ill.Dec. 836, 838, 541 N.E.2d 1274, 1276 (1989); cf., Marcum v. Marcum, 779 S.W.2d 209, 210 (Ky. 1989); Walters v. Walters, 782 S.W.2d 607, 608 (Ky.1989).

spouse, or partition.   Courts allocate responsibility for payment of debts, as well.

Although only a few statutes require or presume equal division as equitable, when an average or moderate asset marriage ends, the widespread and increasing judicial trend is to divide the assets equally.[2] This tendency, which is a reflection of the principle that a marriage partnership is being dissolved, is even more likely in marriages of long duration.   The theory is that both spouses through efforts in the marketplace and the home have contributed equally to the accumulation of the assets.   Additionally, a spouse who would otherwise qualify for spousal support may receive an additional share of the property for support purposes.

Values that are considered divisible property run the gamut of all ordinary tangible and intangible interests in realty, personalty, and choses in action: land and buildings, cars, boats, dogs and cats, furniture and housewares, sporting goods, collections, jewelry, bank accounts, Individual Retirement Accounts, burial plots, cash value of insurance, business and professional property individually owned, partnership interests and shares in publicly traded and close corporations, lottery winnings,[3] personal injury and workers' compensation recoveries,[4] future interests, trust interests, contract rights, including vested and unvested rights to collect retirement benefits payable in the future.

Court decisions are more evenly split on the extent to which personal injury claims, professional practice goodwill,[5] and large contingency contracts[6] constitute property subject to division.   The reluctance to divide highly speculative and uncertain values exists because property division, in the absence of fraud, is not modifiable in most states.   When future developments demonstrate a mistaken valuation, there is no chance of correction.   That is why only one state's highest

2. Bobb v. Bobb, 552 So.2d 334, 335 (Fla.App.1989); Sessums, What are Wives' Contributions Worth Upon Divorce? Toward Fully Incorporating Partnership Into Equitable Distribution, 41 U.Fla.L.Rev. 987 (1989) (WESTLAW: FLLR database, ci(41 + 5 987)); Freed & Walker, Family Law in the Fifty States, Chart IV, 24 Fam.L.Q. 309, 335 (1991) (WESTLAW: FAMLQ database, ci(24 + 5 309)).

3. Ullah v. Ullah, 161 A.D.2d 699, 555 N.Y.S.2d 834, 835 (1990).

4. See, Weisfeld v. Weisfeld, 545 So.2d 1341 (Fla.1989) (representing the majority approach in holding compensation for past lost earnings, loss of earning capacity, and

medical expenses paid from marital funds are divisible marital property).

5. See, Johnson v. Johnson, 771 P.2d 696, 698 (Utah App.1989); In re Marriage of Bush, 191 Ill.App.3d 249, 257, 138 Ill. Dec. 423, 427, 547 N.E.2d 590, 594 (1989) (representing the majority approach by dividing it); contra, Travis v. Travis, 795 P.2d 96 (Okl.1990).

6. In re Zells, 197 Ill.App.3d 232, 237, 143 Ill.Dec. 354, 357, 554 N.E.2d 289, 292 (1990) *affirmed in pertinent part by,* 143 Ill.2d 251, 157 Ill.Dec. 480, 572 N.E.2d 944 (1991); *cf.* Kaechele v. Kaechele, 35 Ohio St.3d 93, 96, 518 N.E.2d 1197, 1201 (1988).

court, that in New York, has recognized the increased earning capacity from a professional or graduate education and license to practice as property.[7] Instead, courts consider the value of the contribution from the nonstudent spouse and the amount of increase in the student spouse's earning capacity in determining the proportions of other property and the amount of spousal support to award to the nonstudent spouse.[8]

Difficult problems of preparation for negotiation or trial center on asset discovery and valuation. Discovery must produce information to trace origins of property and intent of the parties in past transactions in order to differentiate marital from separate property.[9] Valuation of partnership and close corporation interests are particularly difficult because of the necessity to establish actual past earnings and an acceptable capitalization rate. This difficulty is compounded when the business was begun prior to a long-term marriage, but the nonowner spouse claims most of its value was developed due to labor or funds of the spouses during the marriage.[10] In order to determine what portion of the value is separate and what marital, the source, timing, and amount of value must be analyzed. Actual division of business interests is especially difficult. Ordinarily, the managing spouse should not have to share co-ownership of the business with the ex-spouse, but arranging a satisfactory buyout plan when there is little other valuable property or cash may seem impossible.

Retirement benefits also present valuation and implementation challenges. Determination of the present value of retirement benefits involves the necessity to discount not only for the time value of money but, more uncertain, for the chance of death. Since retirement benefits are the most valuable assets in a high percentage of long-term marriages, there may not be other property of sufficient value to offset. If a buyout or offset of retirement benefits is not wise or possible, federal legislation specifically allows the states to authorize allocating percentages of both private[11] and military pensions[12] to be paid to the

---

7. O'Brien v. O'Brien, 66 N.Y.2d 576, 584, 498 N.Y.S.2d 743, 746, 489 N.E.2d 712, 715 (1985).

8. See, Freed and Walker, supra note 2, at Chart VI, p. 349.

9. Krauskopf, Classifying Marital and Separate Property—Combinations and Increase in Value of Separate Property, 89 W.Va.L.Rev. 997 (1987); Oldham, Separate Property Businesses that Increase in Value During Marriage, 1990 Wisc.L.Rev. 585

(WESTLAW: WILR database, ci(1990 + 5 585)).

10. Id.

11. In re Marriage of Curfman, 446 N.W.2d 88, 90 (Iowa App.1989); see Chapter 23, supra.

12. Davis v. Davis, 777 S.W.2d 230 (Ky. 1989); Butcher v. Butcher, 178 W.Va. 33, 357 S.E.2d 226, 232 (1987).

nonemployee spouse as the benefits become due, provided the federal requirements are met.[13]

Social security benefits are not property to be divided.[14] The federal law controls and provides that, if the marriage lasted ten years, the nonemployee spouse may collect spousal benefits at age 62 on the employee's earning record.[15] These benefits are payable only to the extent they exceed that spouse's own entitlement from wage earning. These benefits will continue after divorce, and even after remarriage provided the remarriage is not before age 60.

Library References:

C.J.S. Divorce §§ 312–314 et seq.

West's Key No. Digests, Divorce ⊶200 et seq.

§ 25.63 Principles of Marriage Dissolution Affecting Economics—Spousal Support

Contrary to many persons' erroneous beliefs, most divorcing couples, even those in long-term marriages, do not have sufficient assets including retirement benefits to provide adequate support for the ex-spouse who devoted much of her working life to child care and homemaking for the family. For that reason, attorneys for long-term homemakers, including those of the babyboom generation and most of the current generation of middle-class homemakers with children, must consider the laws of spousal support.

Nearly all statutes authorizing alimony, maintenance, or spousal support list numerous factors to be considered in deciding either the amount of support or whether to order any award at all.[1] However, none of the statutes state a purpose to achieve or a theory to justify spousal support. Increasingly, scholars and appellate courts articulate a theory tied to the roles of homemaking and caretaking of children.[2]

---

13. These statutes also permit an order for the pension administration to pay a percentage directly to the nonemployee spouse. See §§ 23.13–.15, supra.

14. Kirk v. Kirk, 577 A.2d 976, 980 (R.I.1990).

15. See Chapter 15, supra.

§ 25.63

1. See Freed and Walker, supra note 2, Table V, p. 343.

2. Beninger and Smith, Career Opportunity Cost: A Factor in Spousal Support Determination, 16 Fam.L.Q. 201 (1982); Carbone and Brinig, Rethinking Marriage:

Feminist Ideology, Economic Change, and Divorce Reform, 65 Tul.L.Rev. 953 (1991) (WESTLAW: TLNLR database, $ci(65 +5 953)$); Carbone, Economics, Feminism and the Reinvention of Alimony or Why the Desire to Remove Distorting Incentives Does Not a Theory Make, 43 Vand.L.Rev. 1463 (1990) (WESTLAW: VNLR database, $ci(43 +5 1463)$) (critique of Ellman); Cohen, Marriage, Divorce, and Quasi–Rents: Or "I Gave Him the Best Years of My Life" 16 J.Legal Stud. 267 (1987); Ellman, The Theory of Alimony, 77 Cal.L.Rev. 3 (1989); Krauskopf, Theories of Property Division/Spousal Support: Searching for

This theory justifies spousal support as a method of equalizing the transfer of earning capacities of the two spouses that occurred during the marriage. The idea is that the caretaker not only provided family homemaking at the expense of her earning capacity, but also enhanced the income producer's earning capacity by freeing him from those limitations on earning. Many of the factors in the statutes are consistent with this theory: relative earning abilities and assets, contribution to the other's earning capacity or education, care of children, duration of marriage, and standard of living of the marriage.

The party seeking spousal support has the burden of producing evidence warranting an award, which means the party must establish: the amount of money needed to maintain the marital standard of living, how much the petitioner is able to earn currently and in the near future, the respondent's current income and earning ability, and the amount needed to live at a comparable standard of living. A careful and complete listing of financial requirements for an adequate standard of living and a well-documented record of attempts to obtain employment should be presented. Both spouses are commonly required to file expense and income statements with the court. Discovery may be required to confirm or deny the accuracy of the other spouse's expense and income statements as well as amounts reported for income tax purposes.

After one spouse establishes evidence warranting spousal support, the other is likely to request a rather short time limit on the award, such as three to five years. Time-limited, short-term, or rehabilitative support is common at the trial level and may constitute the most common award, statistically, because most divorces end relatively short marriages of young people. Appellate courts consistently state that it is *not* appropriate to place unmodifiable time limits on spousal support for long-term homemakers.[3] Most of the decisions require that the evidence show the recipient will be self-supporting at the end of the time in order to justify the limit. Although some states accept a very low level of self-support, increasingly, courts say the ability to support must be in reasonable relation to the standard of living of the marriage in order to limit the award. In the absence of such evidence, long-term homemaker spouses with low earning abilities should obtain indefinite periodic spousal support that can be modified or terminated if circumstances change.

Solutions to the Mystery, 23 Fam.L.Q. 253 (1989); O'Connell, Alimony After No-Fault: A Practice in Search of a Theory, 23 New Eng.L.Rev. 437 (1988); O'Kelly, Entitlements to Spousal Support After Divorce, 61 N.D.L.Rev. 225 (1985); Goldfarb, Marital Partnership and the Case for Permanent Alimony, 27 J.Fam.L. 351 (1989).

3. Krauskopf, Rehabilitative Alimony: Uses and Abuses of Limited Duration Alimony, 21 Fam.L.Q. 573 (1988).

Insurance is a consideration relevant to spousal support. Courts, recognizing that women's life expectancies are longer than men's, sometimes require the obligor spouse to obtain life insurance payable to the recipient of spousal support.[4] Federal legislation, referred to as COBRA, now requires that medical insurance covering dependents of employee spouses be continued for three years after marriage dissolution in order to allow the dependent the advantage of lower rates.[5]

Obligations to pay spousal support may follow the obligor to the grave. Most, but not all, states permit past due arrearages to be asserted as a claim against the obligor's estate.

Library References:

C.J.S. Divorce §§ 369–379 et seq.

West's Key No. Digests, Divorce ⊕231 et seq.

§ 25.64   Principles of Marriage Dissolution Affecting Economics—Child Support

For those long-term marriages that still have children at home or in college, the financial consequences of marriage dissolution include child support. The amount awarded is now strongly influenced by statewide guidelines that seek to achieve a substantial sharing of the parents' incomes for the benefit of minor children. Guidelines have the practical effect of shifting the burden of proof to the potential obligor parent who wants to pay less. The attorney should always check the guidelines because, in the absence of strong reasons to deviate, the amount suggested is the amount that will be ordered. A majority of states do not require support of a child who is no longer a minor but who is enrolled in college, although an increasing number are doing so. The law of the individual state must always be consulted.

Library References:

C.J.S. Divorce §§ 617 et seq., 665–683 et seq.

West's Key No. Digests, Divorce ⊕296 et seq.

§ 25.65   Practical Effects of Marriage Dissolution—Psychological Effects

To conclude a marriage of 15, 20, or 30 years is an emotionally wrenching experience for nearly everyone. Long years of living together create habit patterns and expectations that are not easily shaken.

---

4. See also, discussion of retirement plan survivor's benefits at § 23.16, supra.

5. Consolidated Omnibus Reconciliation Act of 1985, Pub.L. 99–272, 100 Stat. 222 (1986), codified at 29 U.S.C.A. § 1161 et seq.; Gottlich, Koblenz, & Dudontz, Private Pensions and Health Insurance Benefits in Representing Older Persons (Natl. Senior Citizens Law Center 1990).

Extreme anger, guilt, grief, and fear, alone or in combination, may threaten the physical or mental stability of one or both spouses.[1] When expectations of retirement security and enjoyment are dashed and spouses are parted from physical possessions that carry many memories and attachments, all of life may seem shattered for a time.

§ 25.66   Practical Effects of Marriage Dissolution—Financial Effects on Both Spouses

Ending a middle or lower economic level marriage is economically devastating to both spouses after prime earning years have passed. Neither spouse has an opportunity to earn significant money or retirement benefits after age 50 or so. Particularly after retirement age, the loss of the economies of scale from living in the same household and the division of their modest golden years' nest egg, including the wage earner's retirement benefits, is likely to plunge both spouses into unimagined poverty. After a long marriage, courts are more likely to reach a result in which the ex-spouses share equally the sacrifices of a shortfall in funds.

A divorce for people who have been married a long time probably is wise only for those who wish to remarry or for those who wish to legally end a marriage that is already ended by illness or dementia. If the marriage is irretrievably broken due to the physical or mental condition of one spouse, the other may wish a divorce. A divorce may help to qualify the other spouse for Medicaid nursing home coverage without impoverishing both of them. The property division can be done by agreement, although if the ill spouse is incompetent, a guardian may be required.

§ 25.67   Practical Effects of Marriage Dissolution—Disparate Financial Effects on Homemakers

In theory, when an upper middle or upper economic level marriage ends, there is sufficient marital assets for both ex-spouses to live comfortably. But the facts are that after a long-term marriage, the homemaker spouse and children still at home suffer disproportionately.[1]

§ 25.65

1. See, e.g., In re Marriage of Blount, 197 Ill.App.3d 816, 818, 144 Ill.Dec. 217, 555 N.E.2d 114, 115 (1990). Medical expenses for mental health may be shared by the other ex-spouse. See, e.g., Andrews v. Andrews, 27 Mass.App.Ct. 759, 543 N.E.2d 31, 32 (1989), (wife, institutionalized for suicidal depression, was entitled to 65% of marital property and 30% of husband's pension benefits as alimony until wife began collecting all her pension benefits).

§ 25.67

1. See, Pennington, The Economic Implications of Divorce for Older Women, Clearinghouse Rev. 488 (Special Issue Summer 1989).

Following is an eloquent description and suggestions concerning long-term homemakers presented by the American Bar Association Commission on the Legal Problems of the Elderly.[2]

Introduction

What do the majority of older dependent clients emerging from a long-term marriage need most often? What will they most likely lose in the event of a divorce? Unquestionably, it is the long-term security provided through the employment of the other spouse. At a time in life when they face the prospect of declining health and a fixed income, the older client who was supported throughout the marriage by the other spouse is often unable to replace that security after the divorce. In fact, courts have long recognized that the dependent spouse is far more disadvantaged by divorce than the supporting spouse, and that the dependent spouse is almost always the wife.[3]

What are the benefits that are so valuable and so susceptible to loss after a divorce? Simply and broadly stated, they are the tangible and intangible assets acquired during the marriage as an employment benefit. These assets and the long-term security they provide generally consist of a pension and retirement benefits, medical and hospital insurance, license to practice a profession or trade, business goodwill and entitlements to company goods and services.[4] Ending the marriage that counts these "fringes" as assets means two things: (1) the spouse who went to work keeps all job-related benefits and (2) the spouse who stayed at home loses those benefits. Even if the dependent spouse can work, it is unlikely she will find a job with benefits equal to what was lost and, out of necessity, often accepts a job with no benefits. Moreover, if the dependent spouse is over 35, she has passed her peak earning potential in contrast to men who experience their highest earning potential between 40–55 years of age.[5] By definition, the dependent spouse may be too old to earn some benefits because she has too few working years left. Also, even if she receives spousal

2. Wenger, Divorced Dependent Spouses' Plight—Lost Security: An Overview of the Problem and Current Remedies, 10 Bifocal 1 (Winter 1989/90) (edited and footnotes renumbered) copyright 1989, American Bar Association, Chicago, IL. Reprinted by permission of American Bar Association. Lisa Wenger is an attorney in private practice in Detroit, Michigan.

3. Stark, Burning Down the House: Toward a Theory of More Equitable Distribution, 40 Rutgers L.Rev. 1173, 1198–1199 (1988).

4. L. Weitzman, The Divorce Revolution. The Unexpected Social and Economic Consequences for Women and Children in America, 110 (1985).

5. Casey, Getting Support: The Traditional Route, 8 Family Advocate 8 (1985–1986).

support, often judicial assessment of what she has lost, what she needs and when she should be self-supporting has been hopelessly unrealistic. . . .

Identifying the Real Loss

The real measure of wealth for individuals can only be determined by taking into account all of their job-related entitlements, including not only salaries, but health insurance, retirement benefits and similar perquisites.[6] In general, employment has replaced traditional types of property as a primary source of wealth.[7]

Despite strides toward legal equality, for the most part, traditional family patterns exist in marriages wherein couples maintain established roles. They choose to have the wives devote full or part-time to housekeeping and child care valuing the benefits to the family over additional income or because of the lack of acceptable child care.[8] This pattern significantly reduces the lifetime productivity for the woman.[9] Feber and Birnbaum suggest that this traditional division of labor continues because couples are unaware of the long-term costs of wives remaining out of the labor force, and because they tend to be "unrealistically optimistic about the nature and durability of their relationship(s) in the early years when important decisions are made." [10]

Typically, in a marriage where the wife has stayed home, the husband has enhanced his working expertise during the marriage; whereas, the wife upon divorce is less equipped for work than she was when she first married.[11] Even if both spouses worked during the marriage they have probably chosen to give priority to one spouse's career in the expectation that both would share in the benefits of that decision.[12] The fact that one spouse's career (generally the man's) developed more during the course of a marriage is as much the product of the couple's joint efforts and resources as the income earned or property accumulated. In addition, the joint effort results in individual achievement for the man that results in higher lifetime earnings as well as a longer,

---

6. See generally, Reich, The New Property, 73 Yale L.J. 733 (1964).

7. See generally, Glendon, The New Family and the New Property, 53 Tulane L.Rev. 697 (1979).

8. Beninger and Smith, Career Opportunity Cost: A Factor in Spousal Support Determination, 16 Fam.L.Q. 201, 203 (1982).

9. Ferber and Birnbaum, One Job or Two Jobs: The Implication for Young Wives, 7 J. Consumer Research 263, 269 (1980).

10. Id. at 269.

11. Lash v. Lash, Fla.App., 307 So.2d 241 (Fla.App.1975).

12. See Prager, Sharing Principles and the Future of Marital Property Law, 25 UCLA L.Rev. 6–11 (1977).

healthier life than that of an unmarried man.[13] The wife's "home-work" has freed him to concentrate on market work and the acquisition of property for the family.[14] Meanwhile, she has spent considerable time, energy and skills nurturing other family members and has deferred her own ambitions;[15] and, to extend the comparison to her unmarried counterpart, married women have demonstrably less income, earnings and marketability than unmarried women.[16]

Although this traditional division of labor benefits the family by maximizing the husband's earning capacity, when economic and non-economic roles are unevenly divided between spouses essentially a transfer of earning power from one spouse to the other occurs. The wife increases her husband's earning capacity at the expense of her own.[17] Even when both parties work, there is a higher proportion of part-time or part-year workers among women wage earners.[18] A disproportionate number of women remain isolated in the "pink collar ghettos" or gender-determined roles of nursing, teaching and clerical work. They are paid less and have little opportunity for advancement. Often they, too, become uninsured after the divorce because the wife's employer is less likely to offer health insurance than the husband's. Moreover, the husband has more seniority, greater status, and higher salary in his job than the wife in hers.[19] He also has his health insurance—all of which he keeps if the parties divorce. Consequently, divorced women are twice as likely as married women to be without health insurance coverage.[20]

For the past twenty years, one of the most consistent statistics has been the rising divorce rate.[21] (This includes a staggering

13. Landes, Economics of Alimony, 7 J.Legal Studies 35, 40 (1978).

14. Kiker, Divorce Litigation: Valuing the Spouse's Contribution to the Marriage, 16 Trial 48 (1980).

15. Olsen, The Family and the Market: A Study of Ideology and Legal Record, 96 Harv.L.Rev. 1497 (1983) (WESTLAW: HVLR database, **ci(96 +5 1497)**).

16. Women in the American Economy, 36 (1986).

17. Goldfarb, Marital Partnership and the Case for Permanent Alimony, 27 J. of Family Law 351, 359 (1988–89). Benninger and Smith, A Career Opportunity Cost: A Factor in Spousal Support Determination, 16 Fam.L.Q. 201, 203 (1982).

18. Id., 203 18 U.S. Bureau of Labor Statistics, Department of Labor, Special Labor Force Report No. 201, Work Experience of the Population 22 (1976).

19. Stark, Burning Down the House: Toward a Theory of More Equitable Distribution, 40 Rutgers L.Rev. 1173, 1176–1177 (1988).

20. American Journal of Public Health, "Women and Divorce: Health Insurance Coverage, Utilization and Health Care Expenditures," November, 1984, p. 1276.

21. Life Insurance Beneficiaries and Divorce, 65 Texas L.Rev. 635 (1986–87) (WESTLAW: TXLR database, **ci(65 +5 635)**). See e.g., Guadangno, Bickelhaup

increase in midlife divorce.) ... Thirty-five years ago, only 4% of all divorces filed involved marriages of fifteen years or longer. Before the tenth anniversary of no-fault, 25% of divorces involved marriages of that length.[22] ...

Health Care

The Older Women's League recently published a Gray Paper entitled Health Care Financing and Midlife Women: A Sick System, in which the author concludes that access to health care in this country is through Medicare, Medicaid or a tie to the paid labor force. Consider that statement with the following: (1) that women are 80% of all administrative support workers and 69% of all retail and personal service sales employees;[23] and wives who remain in or re-enter the labor force as part-time workers receive few employee benefits such as health care, pensions or vacation time.[24] In contrast eighty-five percent of all persons insured for health expenses have group health plan membership.[25] It follows then, upon divorce, a woman is far more likely than a man to lose health benefits because the insurance was obtained from her husband's employment.

... [T]he Consolidated Omnibus Budget Reconciliation Act of 1985, Pub.L. 00–272, 100 Stat. 222 (1986) (hereinafter referred to as COBRA), ... was to extend to the non-employee spouse the same health coverage available to the employee spouse after the divorce. This legislation provided much needed relief to between four and five million women between ages forty to sixty-five who were uninsured after a divorce or death of an employee.[26] By extending coverage without proof of insurability or qualifying examination, divorced spouses in poor health whose physical condition might have precluded coverage under a private policy were assured of continued insurance coverage for three years. Arguably, these women were most in need of such protection because their illness

and Noecker, Life Insurance in Divorce: Final Considerations for the Divorced Mother, C.L.U., July 1982, at 32, 33 (stating that the divorce rate increased by 96% between March 1970 and March 1979).

22. Lenore J. Weitzman, The Marriage Contract: Spouses, Lovers and the Law, 144 (1981).

23. Goldfarb, Marital Partnership and the Case for Permanent Alimony, 27 J. of Family Law 351, 367 (1988–89).

24. Rowe, Child Care of the 1980's: Traditional Sex Roles or Androgyny?, Women Into Wives: The Legal and Economic Impact of Marriage 169, 181 (J. Chapman and M. Gates eds. 1977); Kulzer, Law and the Housewife: Property, Divorce and Death, 28 U.Fla.L.Rev. 1, 12 (1975).

25. P. Borz, Summary of Health Insurance Coverage Act of 1985, 1 (October 1986).

26. Id. at 255.

or disability could prevent them from ever acquiring individual insurance.

* * *

COBRA was not a complete remedy, however. As noted the premium cost is most often borne by the non-employee spouse and may be prohibitive if she has no income. The cost may be an issue for a substantial number of midlife women and may escalate further because additional administrative costs may be authorized in the future.[27] This seems unfair to the dependent spouse because she may be most in need of the benefit but least able to afford the cost. Further, coverage is extended for the very reason that she is unable to obtain health insurance through her individual efforts. Women over thirty face threats of loss of health coverage unique to their gender. Dependency status exposes them to loss of group insurance; and as shown above, part-time and marginal employment often provides no health fringe benefits; and insurers have a bias against common benign female conditions which can result in total denial of coverage or exclusion from coverage of ordinary reproductive functions or ailments.[28] ... "Until the ex-spouse is suitably covered by another group policy or Medicare, COBRA provides three more years of peace of mind that many ex-spouses could otherwise not afford."[29]

... However, ... COBRA [failed] to provide security for women who are too young for Medicare after expiration of the mandatory extension and who, by their efforts cannot secure individual insurance. For these women compensation for this loss in the form of spousal support has been the traditional remedy but, as shown below, awards of spousal support that assume an older woman will be self-sufficient have been attacked as unrealistic and inappropriate.

Rehabilitative or Transitional Support

As a solution, rehabilitative or transitional alimony, born with the advent of no-fault divorce statutes, was designed to encourage a dependent spouse to become self-supporting by providing alimony for a limited period during which time the woman could be re-

27. S.Rep. No. 146, 99th Cong., 1st Sess. 365 (1985) (WESTLAW: **fi 1985 wl 29974**).

28. Leonard, Gray Paper: Health Care Financing and Midlife Women: A Sick System.

29. Kennedy, The COBRA Strikes at Group Health Insurance Plans: Divorced Women's Rights to Continue Coverage, 92 Dickinson L.Rev. 253, 275 (1987) (WEST-

trained or rehabilitated.[30] It was intended as a temporary subsidy to the dependent spouse designed to make her self-supporting.[31] By definition, rehabilitative alimony presupposes the potential for self-support without which, there is nothing to which one can be rehabilitated.

Despite the obvious need, transitional alimony has often proved insufficient and inappropriate in cases involving older women who are expected to succeed in the job market after many years of absence from the work place. Lawyers, judges and legislators have been overly optimistic and unrealistic regarding the dependent spouse's ability to become self-sufficient. The conclusions reached from an Oregon study of decrees between 1983 and 1984 in marriages lasting 10 years or more were revealing—most policymakers fail to consider all of the economic consequences of divorce, sometimes lacking data, and have not recognized needed changes. Even when rehabilitative alimony is awarded, there is rarely a realistic evaluation of the difficulties women have finding reasonable, fairly compensated employment, especially after a long absence from the labor market.

> The self-sufficiency expected from women after divorce is too great at a time when equality is lacking in employment opportunities, job preparation, and salaries.[32] Without occupation training and labor market experience, women faced divorce with a loss of employment-related benefits, such as health care insurance and pensions and were compelled to take entry level, low paying positions to meet short term necessities.[33] ...

In response to clear signs that a limited award may be an inadequate remedy for an older spouse, courts have begun to refine and limit its application.[34] ... The all too often permanent inability to support oneself, especially with older women, has been recognized as an important consideration.

* * *

LAW: DICKLR database, **ci(92 +5 253)**).

30. Eagerton v. Eagerton, 285 S.C. 279, 328 S.E.2d 912 (App.1985).

31. Goldfarb, Marital Partnership and the Case for Permanent Alimony, 27 J. of Family Law 351, 362 (1988–89). See e.g., Messer v. Messer, 342 So.2d 1076, 1077 (Fla.App.1977); Reback v. Reback, 296 So.2d 541 (Fla.App.1974), *cert. denied* 312 So.2d 737 (Fla.1975); Turner v. Turner, 158 N.J.Super. 313, 314, 385 A.2d 1280

(1978); Molnar v. Molnar, 173 W.Va. 200, 314 S.E.2d 73, 76 (1984).

32. Rowe and Morrow, The Economic Consequences of Divorce in Oregon After Ten or More Years of Marriage, 24 Willamette L.Rev. 463, 484 (1988).

33. Id. at 482.

34. For collection of cases reversing time limits, see, Krauskopf, Rehabilitative Alimony: Uses and abuses of Limited Duration Alimony, 21 Fam.L.Q. 573 (1988). [footnote added]

Thus, the prevailing recurrent theme is that a realistic assessment of the individual older woman's potential work skills and availability of a relevant job market is crucial, since age and health can severely restrict the ability of the dependent spouse to work and is an important factor in job availability. "Many employers are reluctant to hire an older person because of the potential exposure to increased health and pension costs. Furthermore, the cost of training an older employee cannot be amortized over as many years as with a younger person." [35]

Finally, a West Virginia court emphasized the need for continuing jurisdiction particularly with an older dependent spouse with a lengthy marriage unless the record is clear that she is financially self-supporting at the end of the rehabilitative alimony period. This court reversed the rehabilitative alimony award in favor of permanent alimony for want of evidence that the wife, 63 [53 at time of trial], even with a degree could find work at her age as a computer programmer, questioning whether she could realistically achieve a degree after a long absence from academic pursuits. Most important, however, was the rejection of rehabilitative alimony as inappropriate where the older dependent spouse already has a full-time job commensurate with his or her educational background and skills. The court concluded that traditional alimony should be considered to supplement the dependent spouse's present income.[36] The import of this analysis is clear; rehabilitative alimony no matter how tempting, is often inadequate, inappropriate and unrealistic for older women.

Alternative Remedies

Can an award of spousal support be fashioned that adequately compensates the older woman for the benefits lost in the divorce? The answer partly depends upon whether the loss can be quantified and valued....

Several theories for spousal support have been developed that merit review by attorneys who represent older clients in need of compensation after the divorce. One theorist advocates an equalization of the parties' standard of living after divorce arguing that the concept of "self-support" for the dependent spouse should be defined primarily by reference to the standard of living of the other spouse.

---

35. In Re Marriage of Morrison, 20 Cal.3d 437, 452, 143 Cal.Rptr. 139, 149, 573 P.2d 41, 51 (1978).

36. Id. at 78, 79.

[The author argues] If the legal system intends to encourage women to fulfill the socially valuable homemaking role, or intends even to remain neutral in allowing individual women and couples to make the choice, alimony awards that appropriately recognize the effect of the transfer of human capital on women's economic position at divorce must be made available.[37]

The career opportunity cost principle advocates compensation for the difference between the wife's reduced lifetime earning capacity and her husband's increased earning power. This theory utilizes the concept of "human capital" as a marital asset which appreciates with investments in training and market labor experience and depreciates during periods of non-market labor.[38]

Another scholar argues for explicit recognition of the unequal roles played by the parties within the marriage, and [the unequal opportunities which are a consequence as well as a cause of that division of labor] in support of a presumption that awards more than half the marital estate to the woman, if the parties assumed male-breadwinner/female-homemaker roles in the marriage and the husband had the opportunity to benefit from this at the wife's expense. This theory focuses on the wife's lost, or deferred, opportunity to develop her own earning potential as opposed to the husband's enhanced earning capacity.[39] In short, the wife should be compensated if she has effectively lost a job through divorce, and he has not.

* * *

Conclusion

Securing health insurance and adequate support for both spouses after a divorce is an important goal in all dissolution proceedings. For the lawyer representing older people, this objective is paramount and not easily accomplished. With older women, the assumptions that transitional alimony will lead to employment and replacement of benefits lost in the divorce have been wrong. The client is often unemployed, uninsured and virtually incapable of self-support after the alimony stops and COBRA coverage ends.

37. Goldfarb, Marital Partnership and the Case for Permanent Alimony, 27 J. of Fam.Law 351, 361, 363 (1988–89).

38. Beninger and Smith, Career Opportunity Cost: A Factor in Spousal Support Determination, 16 Fam.L.Q. 201, 202, 213 (1982).

39. Stark, Burning Down the House: Toward a Theory of More Equitable Distribution, 40 Rutgers L.Rev. 1173, 1189, 1195 (1988).

Unless COBRA coverage is extended, the gap in coverage will continue to pose a threat to the security of many older divorced women. What is needed is an acknowledgement of this very serious problem by attorneys and parties to the divorce. Support awards should be adequate and should include health care insurance costs if coverage is lost as a result of the divorce. Where necessary, the inability of the dependent spouse to replace these benefits should be recognized as a loss of an asset earned during the marriage for which compensation is in order.

Finally, in all cases with older clients, attorneys, judges and legislators should consider the very real likelihood that the spouse who loses the employment benefits will not be employed at the end of the support term and may not have any health insurance after three years; once considered, it should be the goal of all to give her the security of insurance and support she earned during the marriage and expected for her later years.[40]

§ 25.68   Alternatives to Marriage Dissolution

Alternatives to divorce that may meet the desires of elderly persons include legal separation, which may allow complete economic settlement between the parties but continue valuable medical and death benefits for the dependent spouse stemming from the employee spouse's employment or retirement.[1]

A viable alternative for many older couples is to continue living in the same house or apartment, but live essentially separate lives under agreement. If the agreement spells out their economic entitlements and living arrangements, the spouses may live fairly comfortably without too much interaction and discord. In other words, they may shift to shared housing.

A delay in marriage dissolution can often be achieved by respondent's contesting the petition. If one spouse presents good reasons to continue the marriage, the court may not find marriage breakdown, incompatibility, or grounds.[2] In most states, a divorce could be obtained then only after a year or two delay to establish living separate and apart grounds. During that time, the initiator may change her or his mind.

The key to the adoption of any alternative is adequate counseling of the long-married people. At a minimum, the attorney for either

---

40. Conclusion of Wenger, supra note 2.

§ 25.68

1. A disadvantage is the risk that each might be liable for the other's necessary

expenses including medical care, § 20.18, supra.

2. See, e.g., Buscher v. Buscher, 659 S.W.2d 587 (Mo.App.1983).

party should be sure that the party understands the probable economic consequences of dissolving a long-term marriage. The attorney should help the spouses obtain psychological counseling and financial planning advice so they will be fully informed of the range of alternatives suitable for their situation.

CHAPTER 26

COMPREHENSIVE PLANNING
FOR LONGER LIFE

Table of Sections

WESTLAW Electronic Research

See WESTLAW Electronic Research Guide preceding the Summary of Contents.

---

§ 26.1 Elder Lawyer as Central Planner

The chapters of this book provide details concerning the areas of law that are involved in the practice of elder law. Clients will not have an understanding of the interrelationship of these special areas and their own lives and needs. Clients will probably know that they need assistance in planning for later life and that many of the patterns of living they have developed will change. The pulling together of all these areas for the client is the overall task of the elder lawyer.

Financial life changes in old age for most persons. Earned income often becomes smaller or nonexistent, and people have to rely upon retirement benefits, governmental entitlements, investment income, and savings. With lower earning power, older persons are more vulnerable to inflation and more affected by changes in interest rates that affect their income from savings and investments. Furthermore, the purposes for which money is needed usually change; the house may be paid for, childrearing and educational expenses are no longer concerns, but health care expenses pose potential problems. Preservation of assets to ensure future security becomes more essential when there is no regular income from work. There is, for many elderly, a near total dependence upon governmental benefits, such as social security, or private pensions, many of which have fixed benefits. Exacerbating many of these concerns is the fact that many of today's and tomorrow's elderly who lived through the Depression of the 1930s fear financial collapse.

A substantial industry has grown around financial planning, focusing not only on persons in their income-producing years but also on persons near retirement or already retired. Life for the elderly today is far more complicated than it was for previous generations. Many clients are wise to seek professional assistance in planning for later years and in managing their finite financial resources.

The elder law attorney has an important role in financial planning and management. Even though the attorney may not be an expert on insurance matters, governmental benefits, investments, pensions, or other aspects of financial management, the elder law attorney is often in the best position to act as the central planner, the coordinator, and the unbiased evaluator of the various proposals that may be made by other members of a planning team. The attorney occupies the unique position within a planning team of one who is neither selling any particular financial product nor recommending any particular plan that would benefit the attorney in any way. The attorney, therefore, should have a familiarity with the various financial issues with which the older client is faced. This chapter gives such an overview. Many of the issues discussed are explained in greater detail in other chapters to which reference has been made.

§ 26.2 Comprehensive Estate/Financial Planning—In General

Although "estate planning" is a commonly used term in the practice of law, elder lawyers have expanded the term to mean more than simply planning for the distribution of assets upon death with a minimum amount of taxation. Estate planning for the elderly client must deal not only with death planning but also with planning for extended life. This planning must include preparation of the client and the client's family for the problems of possible disability, consideration of concerns about possible expensive long-term care in or out of an institution, assessment of the income needs of the person during low-earning years, and evaluation of the special insurance needs of the elderly client. In estate planning, the planner must assist the client with both protection of assets during life and transmission of wealth at death.

§ 26.3 Comprehensive Estate/Financial Planning—Gathering Information

The first step in the assessment of the needs of the client is gathering information concerning the client's present financial position. If a client is married, the finances of both spouses have to be taken into consideration. Many older persons are circumspect about divulging such information and must be reassured about the confidentiality of the information and be advised that the data will be used solely for the purpose of recommending a proper plan for the client.

Clients rarely bring all the information that is needed to an initial interview, and very few clients bring copies of documents that must be reviewed to fully assess the client's present position. During the initial interview, the attorney should create a list of documents that will be needed and should supply the client with the list after the meeting. The list may include items such as the current will, current powers of attorney, recent tax returns, and lists of names, addresses, and phone numbers of family members and other important persons to contact. The client also should provide copies of bank statements, securities account reports, stock certificates, deeds, and other evidences of ownership, since the attorney should personally inspect these items to confirm the nature of the ownership—whether the ownership is joint tenancy, sole ownership, tenancy in common, or some other form, which is information the client may not relate reliably without a review of the document itself.

The attorney will find it helpful to give the client a worksheet to complete with comprehensive financial data. A sample life planning questionnaire is set forth in § 26.16. The use of such a questionnaire provides the attorney with a standard source of information that streamlines the process of information gathering and review, thus making the attorney more efficient and the client's process of estate planning more economical.

§ 26.4 Comprehensive Estate/Financial Planning—Routine Considerations

Once the data has been gathered, the elder law attorney has several tasks. This list of tasks should be routine:

1. determine what estate planning documents the client will need, e.g., will, trust, power of attorney, living will;

2. determine whether the nature of ownership of any of the client's assets will need to be changed, e.g., to or from sole ownership, joint tenancy, community property;

3. review the assets owned by the client for suitability as to risk, return on investment, and tax liability;

4. examine the sufficiency of the client's knowledge of the nature and extent of the assets and the client's ability to gather the information requested;

5. consider the property, liability, and health insurance needs of the client and determine whether these are being met; and

6. advise the client on the attorney's observations and make recommendations concerning whether additional professional assistance and advice should be sought.

The elder law attorney does not need to be an expert on each area into which the attorney makes inquiry or offers suggestions; the elder law attorney simply must have an overview of the needs of the elderly client and must be in a position to make necessary referrals so that the client will receive proper attention in regard to his or her needs. It would not be adequate, for example, to prepare estate planning documents for a client without inquiring about the client's present state of health, the need for possible surrogate decision-making, and concerns about long-term care expenses.

§ 26.5 Comprehensive Estate/Financial Planning—Client Income Issues

The elder law attorney, although not a financial planner, should be able to look comprehensively (or holisticly) at the client's financial needs. The financial life of a person changes substantially when the person retires from work and becomes dependent upon savings and upon income from social security and retirement plans. The elder law attorney may be the only professional working with the older client who has a complete picture of the client's legal needs and financial status. The elder law attorney becomes a *de facto* team leader who coordinates all the planning the client needs by pulling together the representatives of the various disciplines that serve the needs of the client, such as insurance sellers, financial advisors, and brokers.

Because of the varied nature of income the elder client could have, the elder law attorney must have some familiarity with such different sources of income as Social Security,[1] Supplemental Security Income,[2] veterans' retirement benefits,[3] private pensions,[4] public service retire-

---

§ 26.5

1. See Chapter 15 for Social Security Retirement and Chapter 16 for Social Security Disability.

2. See Chapter 17.

3. See Chapter 21.

4. See Chapter 23.

ment programs,[5] and government assistance.[6]

The attorney should inventory the income the client has available. After there is no regular paycheck, the client will still need money to pay for the basic expenses of life such as food, clothing, and shelter, as well as money to pay for the things the client wishes to do beyond mere survival, for example, travel, gifts, and entertainment. Taxes still have to be paid on the family residence even though the mortgage may be paid. Utility bills are not likely to decrease substantially and insurance is still required. Transportation expenses continue and medical costs may rise.

When regular paychecks are available, clients may save money in a manner that does not generate income—for example, through investments such as U.S. government savings bonds, long-term certificates of deposit, whole life insurance policies, stocks, and mutual funds that emphasize growth over income. Once the client needs to generate his or her own income, savings and investment strategies must change in focus from long-term growth to dependable income.

The elder law attorney may not have adequate training or experience to advise the client on proper investments or to fully assess the client's needs, in which case the elder law attorney who is doing a comprehensive job will direct the client to a source that will assist the client in meeting the client's income needs from the available resources. The life planning questionnaire set out in § 26.16 will give the attorney adequate information to determine whether the client is apparently generating sufficient income to meet monthly expenses. It is necessary to review the total income shown on the questionnaire, to examine the basic expenses of the client, and to review the client's investments and assets to verify that the client is adequately meeting his or her needs. Once this review is completed, the elder law attorney can decide whether to provide advice or whether to refer the client to a financial planner or investment advisor.

One area with which the elder law attorney should be familiar is home equity conversion, a program that allows a homeowner to borrow against the equity in the home and receive monthly payments that create an indebtedness against that equity.[7] Home equity conversion is an excellent means of increasing the income of a person who may be "house rich and cash poor." A caution is necessary here, however. Home equity conversion may not be necessary or advisable for the client who otherwise would qualify for the state's Medicaid payments

---

5. See Chapter 20.

6. See Chapter 11 for Medicaid, Chapter 18 for food stamps, and Chapter 19 for housing assistance.

7. See Chapter 22.

for home- and community-based services. Those services are provided upon the basis of need and financial eligibility, but the equity in a home of any value is an excluded asset for purposes of determining such eligibility.

§ 26.6 Comprehensive Estate/Financial Planning—Medical Expense Issues

A concern of many elderly persons is whether they have adequate insurance to meet the expenses of an unanticipated illness that may require long periods of time in hospitals and/or nursing homes. Many of them are concerned about their ability to afford extended care in their own homes. In meeting with an elderly client or couple, the elder law attorney should inquire about whether this issue is a concern. The elder law attorney who does estate planning should be familiar with the availability and advisability of long-term care policies and other Medicare supplemental policies [1] and with planning techniques for minimizing the expenses of long-term care.[2] The attorney should respond to the client's concerns in this area by either offering advice or referring the client to an expert in such planning.

Confusion frequently exists among clients as well as some planners about what services are covered by Medicare. The exclusions under Medicare are substantial and include prescription medications, many medical appliances, and most long-term institutional care.[3] Many clients may be inappropriately relying upon Medicare or a combination of Medicare and privately purchased Medicare supplemental policies to cover all their expenses. Clients who have recently retired from employment that provided more comprehensive medical coverage are likely to experience this confusion. The attorney should, in the estate planning conference, at least inquire about whether the client has any questions concerning insurance and offer to do a review or suggest a referral.

§ 26.7 Contents of Comprehensive Plan

The client who visits the elder law attorney and works through the life planning questionnaire will have a complete review of the planning options for later life. The client will have examined the questions of health care decision-making, financial management in the event of disability, the protection of assets from the expenses of possible long-term care, the transfer of assets upon death, and the reduction of taxes

---

§ 26.6

1. See Chapter 10 for supplemental insurance and Chapter 12 for long-term care.

2. See Chapter 11 for Medicaid planning.

3. For information concerning Medicare, see Chapter 10.

to be paid upon death. The client will have reviewed the issue of avoiding the probate process and will have been advised to gather together records so they will be accessible if needed by a surrogate or personal representative. Furthermore, the questions of organ donation, final disposition of remains, and insurance coverage will have been discussed.

As a general rule, every client should be offered and encouraged to have the following documents:

1. a durable health care power of attorney; [1]
2. a durable financial power of attorney; [2]
3. a living will; [3]
4. a last will and testament;
5. a living trust, if needed;
6. autopsy instructions, if desired;
7. final disposition instructions, if desired;
8. a list of separate gifts of personal property in compliance with state law; and
9. an inventory of assets and locations of important documents, insurance policies, and so on.

A client checklist is often a good office practice in order to ensure that clients are presented with all the options available to them. The checklist also is helpful during annual reviews conducted for the client. A copy of the list may be given to the client. Preparation of this form on paper of a distinctive color will make the document readily locatable in the file when annual reviews are conducted and when the attorney needs to review estates because changes in the law require revisions by clients. [4]

§ 26.8 Possession of Documents—Overview

Clients are often uncertain about where to keep the originals of estate planning documents. It is common practice for people to keep important papers in safe deposit boxes in banks or in safes located in their homes or offices. Some people leave important documents with friends, close relatives, or the named agent or personal representative, while other people simply leave these items at home. Another option is to leave the original documents with the client's attorney. Each of

§ 26.7

1. See §§ 8.18–.22.
2. See §§ 8.12–.17.
3. See §§ 8.31–.34 and Chapter 13.

4. Samples of a checklist and letters that can be sent upon an annual or periodic review of client files appear at § 8.61.

these options has benefits and drawbacks that need to be pointed out to the client so the decision can be an informed one best suited to the individual client.

§ 26.9 Possession of Documents—Safe Deposit Box or Safe

Although the placement of important documents in safes or safe deposit boxes provides the documents with adequate protection and also provides the owner with ready access to the documents, the papers are not easily obtained in the absence of the owner. In the case of a disability, it may be nearly impossible (without a court order) for a person named as an agent under a durable health care or financial power of attorney to get into a safe deposit box in order to obtain the documents that give the agent the authority to act. In the case of death of the owner, some states allow entry into the safe deposit box in order to review a will. However, the location of the box and/or the key may be unknown, there may be substantial delay, and there will undoubtedly be inconvenience to all involved.

§ 26.10 Possession of Documents—With Friend, Relative, or Appointee

Since most of the estate planning documents are needed at a time when the principal is not available to provide them (either because of disability or death), it would seem that leaving the documents with a close friend, relative, or even the designated agent or personal representative would be a good idea. If the custodian of the documents survives the principal and the documents are well cared for, they will be accessible when needed. On the other hand, it may be awkward for the principal to recover the documents if the principal is at odds with the custodian or if the principal desires to change the contents of the documents or name a new appointee. Furthermore, placement of the documents in the custody of a third person does not protect the privacy of the documents as well as do other choices that may be available.

§ 26.11 Possession of Documents—At Home

Clients who keep their important documents at home are comfortable that they have control over the documents, that the documents are readily accessible, and that there is complete privacy for the documents. If the client has fireproof security for the documents, the risk of loss from that peril is minimized. Nonetheless, there are significant drawbacks to this option. First, the law in some states provides that a last will and testament in the possession of the testator/testatrix that cannot be located is presumed to have been revoked. People who have valuable papers in their home may not leave them out in plain view, and the documents may never be located or may not be located until after the time when they would be of use. Second, in the event of a disability requiring action by an agent under a health care power of attorney or financial power of attorney, it may be awkward for the agent-designate to obtain the documents while the principal is still in the home, possibly resisting the use of the documents because of the disability.

§ 26.12   Possession of Documents—With Client's Attorney

Leaving the originals of estate planning documents with the client's attorney is becoming an increasingly popular option for many clients. There are good reasons for selecting this option, but there is a significant drawback as well. The lawyer who retains possession of such documents will have safe and accessible storage facilities—these could include a fireproof safe on the premises or perhaps safe deposit box(es) at a nearby bank. The documents will be readily accessible during normal business hours, and the risk of loss is minimal. The client can refer to his or her copies, which can be kept at home without fear of losing valuable originals. The attorney knows that he or she has continuing contact with a client, contact that is likely to result in additional future business. A major drawback is that persons acting in an emergency may not be able to identify the attorney.

§ 26.13   Counseling Clients

An issue that arises frequently in the practice of elder law is the attorney's need to identify who is actually the client that the attorney is representing. For the lawyer who is a litigator involved in lawsuits to resolve disputes, who represents the state or the defendant in cases in criminal matters, or who works with clients who are negotiating contractual agreements, this question generally poses little problem, since the attorney is able to identify the "side" that he or she is representing. Elder law, on the other hand, regularly involves "representation" or advising of the whole family or at least several of its members. Although there can be conflicts of interest among such persons, multiple representation still may be possible. *Potential* conflicts do not always preclude multiple representation, but the attorney must be alert to the issues and be prepared to make other arrangements for the client if the potential conflicts become reality.

The first step in the process of providing services is the identification of the client, i.e., the determination of whom the attorney will be establishing an attorney-client relationship with, to whom the attorney will be relating in a confidential relationship, and to whom the attorney will owe the duty of providing complete information. This identification is not always easily made. For example, in the situation of an adult child bringing a parent to the law firm for the drafting of a will, is the parent or the child the client? What are the responsibilities of the attorney to each? Who is the attorney serving when the parent and the child are considering planning for possible nursing home expense and one solution for protecting assets is to have the parent transfer assets to the child? Can the attorney who has represented a family for an extended time establish a guardianship and conservatorship for the parent by the child even though both have been clients?

In addressing these questions, the attorney should analyze whose interests are being served by the help that is being requested, at whose request the services are being provided, who is paying for the services, and who is directing the representation/service process. None of these factors will necessarily be determinative of the question of who is the client, but consideration of these questions in the total context of the representation will assist the attorney in evaluating possible conflicts. If, for example, a son first consults the attorney requesting information about how to protect his mother's assets in case she needs nursing home care, it is clear that the client is the son, and not the mother. Suppose, however, that the son then brings his mother to the next meeting. Will the attorney give the same advice on the best ways to protect the mother's assets, or will additional information have to be given to the mother regarding the risks and drawbacks associated with such planning techniques? The advice may be different when the attorney is asked to protect assets for the children than when the attorney is asked to ensure the highest quality of care and preserve the widest array of choices for the potential nursing home patient. Similarly, the preparation of a last will and testament is not necessarily a family enterprise. It is not unusual for an elderly client to be brought to an estate planning conference by one or more child(ren). It also is not unusual for the child to answer the questions for the parent and to exert subtle influence upon the parent simply by being present.

In both of the foregoing examples, it would clearly be helpful for the attorney to evaluate the questions of who is benefiting, who is requesting the service, who is paying, and who is directing the process. These questions, however, will not resolve the problem in all cases.

An analysis of who will have a confidential, privileged relationship with the attorney may be an even more helpful measure. In the two examples set forth above, the case involving asset preservation and the case involving estate planning, it would be appropriate for the attorney to have such a relationship with either the child or the parent, but it would probably be inappropriate for the attorney to consider himself or herself to be representing or advising both. In the case involving asset preservation, clearly there are disparate and conflicting interests, and the attorney must choose whether he or she is representing the best interests of the child (preservation and protection of an inheritance) or the best interests of the parent (assurance of quality long-term care). Although these interests may not be mutually exclusive, the considerations clearly are different. At some point, regardless of the identity of the client, a decision will have to be made about whether to transfer the parent's assets, and the client will be looking to the attorney for advice. The attorney must have the greatest degree of allegiance to only one client and must be able to advise the client free of the influence of others, which will require excluding others from the meeting and pointing out clearly the benefits and the drawbacks to the client. In the case of estate planning, the child may have very different intentions and presumptions than the parent regarding what the estate plan should include. If the attorney does not have private communications with the parent alone, there can be subtle or overt undue influence exerted upon the parent (perhaps solely as a result of the child's presence in the room) to consent to an estate plan that is not of the parent's choosing. It is appropriate and perhaps mandatory that the attorney exclude others from the room when discussing estate planning. Once the attorney has decided whom to meet with privately, the question of who is the client is more easily answered.

Finally, in situations in which the attorney serves as the "family attorney," the attorney may be asked by various family members to release documents. It is imperative that the attorney (and the office staff) keep in mind that documents are private to the *individual* and cannot be made available to others without appropriate consent. Even a spouse does not have the right to see the will of the other spouse without the consent of the testator.

In working with families, the attorney may have a tendency to presume that family members are well intentioned with regard to each other. This cannot be presumed, certainly not when family finances are involved. The lawyer must be careful to identify the client and ensure that services and confidences are provided only for that individual.[1]

§ 26.14 Managing Incapacity

Various methods of managing the incapacity of an older person have been described in earlier chapters. The use of durable health care powers of attorney, durable financial powers of attorney, and living wills is discussed in Chapter 8. The role of the guardian of the person and the conservator of the estate and the duties and responsibility of the attorney are discussed in Chapter 9. This section will assist the attorney in advising the fiduciary client about the responsibilities of the appointed agent, guardian or conservator. Instruction sheets for deliv-

§ 26.13

1. See Chapter 9 for further discussion.

ery to the client that are helpful in setting out the parameters of responsibility for the appointee are included in Chapter 9.

First, the attorney should make the client aware of the general duties of a fiduciary by advising the client of reporting requirements, the nature and scope of the authority granted by the appointment, and the limitations on the powers. Strict and clear rules should be set down regarding conflicts of interest between the surrogate and the principal/ward/protected person. The attorney should make clear to the client that questions should be asked before any action is taken about which the client has doubts.

The attorney should not presume that most clients have general information about the necessary recordkeeping requirements and should be clear with the client about the expectations of the lawyer and the court concerning the duty for reporting at specific intervals. The attorney should remind fiduciaries of basic duties such as the responsibility for gathering and managing assets and for segregating the assets of the estate from the fiduciary's personal assets, the types of investments that may be permitted or prohibited, the duty to provide adequate protection for the estate's assets, including physical protection, and the necessity of insurance. The attorney should generally review with the fiduciary the terms of the appointment made by the court or by the power of attorney. This advice serves at least two purposes: first, the client is better equipped to perform his or her duties; second, the attorney is protected from future claims that the fiduciary was not given proper instructions which gave rise to possible losses by the estate.

Finally, the attorney's role, in managing the incapacity of an older person, often will involve work with an entire family. A parent may become incapacitated by virtue of an illness, an injury, or a chronic condition such as Alzheimer's disease. The spouse and/or children may become the "clients" of the attorney who assists them in establishing care for the incapacitated person. These people will look to the attorney for assistance with financial management questions, seek information regarding possible placement alternatives, make inquiries concerning the scope of their authority in making medical decisions, or ask the attorney for advice regarding assets of the adult. In "family representation," numerous conflicts can arise when there are different agendas for the different family members. A child may be concerned about protecting his ultimate inheritance, or a spouse may have anxiety about her economic well-being in light of an expensive illness for the other spouse. The attorney must be ever vigilant to the possibility of such conflicts and be prepared to withdraw from cases as necessary or at least require parties to get independent advice while the attorney is representing the interests of the incapacitated individual.

From a positive perspective, the attorney who assists families in managing the incapacity of a family member has an opportunity to encourage the family to act in a way that maintains the autonomy and dignity of the incapacitated person to the greatest degree possible. This encouragement can be accomplished by being aware of and referring the family to appropriate counsellors and community agencies that can provide supportive and respite services, by encouraging the family to allow the incapacitated person to meaningfully participate in the decision-making process concerning his or her care, and finally, by making certain that the incapacitated person knows that he or she has an advocate in the attorney to turn to when there is need for assistance in asserting specific rights or requests.

Library References:

C.J.S. Insane Persons §§ 11, 58–61.

West's Key No. Digests, Mental Health ⊜31, 107.

§ 26.15 Periodic Review of Documents

Any planning process involves the facts as they are known at the time that the planning occurs. Things, however, change. Family arrangements change by birth, death, and divorce. People change their minds regarding whom they wish to have inherit from them. The financial status of individuals can improve or deteriorate, often requiring a change in a plan that was built on the assumption that the situation would be different. Unfortunately, clients do not always think to contact their attorneys when such changes occur, thus, estate plans may become outdated.

From another perspective, changes in the law, either state or federal, can have a substantial impact upon estate plans that were adequate prior to the changes. A change in a state or federal tax law may have a profound impact on a plan. Changes in state law concerning powers of attorney or living wills may necessitate substantial changes for many clients; when a state adds "persistent vegetative state or irreversible coma" to the list of conditions under which the directives in a living will become effective, this change has a profound impact and may necessitate advising clients concerning the advisability of new documents.

Such potential changes require the attorney not only to review estate plans that are in place for existing clients but also to encourage clients to periodically review the plans they have in place to ensure that such plans continue to accurately reflect the clients' wishes. If the attorney has not made clear to clients that the duties and responsibilities of the attorney end with the preparation and delivery of estate planning documents, the client may rely upon the attorney to advise him or her when changes are necessary.

The attorney may prefer to be responsible for future contact. Information concerning periodic review of documents and appropriate forms for recordkeeping is set forth in § 8.61. Maintaining periodic contact with clients can require a significant commitment of time; however, contact and service builds enormous good will that results in increased referral of new clients with appropriate work in the attorney's field of practice. Periodic review is a service that benefits everyone.

§ 26.16 Life Planning Questionnaire

FIRM NAME
Firm Address
Phone Number

LIFE PLANNING QUESTIONNAIRE

Please complete the following questionnaire to the best of your abilities. This information is most helpful to us so that we may properly plan for you. Do not be upset if you cannot complete all of the questions. We will review this information at our meeting.

	Name	Date of Birth	Social Security Number
Client:	_____	_____	_____
Spouse:	_____	_____	_____

Date of Marriage: _____

Address: _____

_____

Telephone: Home_____   Bus._____

Children common to the marriage:

Name	Date of Birth	Address
_____	_____	_____
_____	_____	_____
_____	_____	_____
_____	_____	_____

Husband's children (prior marriage):

Name	Date of Birth	Address
_____	_____	_____
_____	_____	_____
_____	_____	_____
_____	_____	_____

Wife's children (prior marriage):

Name	Date of Birth	Address

Other persons who are important to your estate plan (grandchildren, siblings, nieces and nephew, etc.)

Name	Date of Birth	Address

General Information	Husband	Wife
Are you covered by Social Security? (Y, N).........	_____	_____
Are you self-employed? (Y, N)	_____	_____
Do you have a Will? (Y, N)	_____	_____
Date of Will.......................................	_____	_____
Are you the beneficiary of any Trust: (Y, N)........	_____	_____
Do you have a Power of Attorney? (Y, N)..........	_____	_____

Comments:

Health Care

Do you have: Medicare Part "A" _____ Part "B" _____
Supplemental Insurance _____
Long–Term Health Care Insurance _____

Do you or any member of your family have any illness or disability that should be considered in planning your estate?

Comments:

Income

Please list your estimated income this year from the following sources:

	Annual or Monthly Amounts	
Source	Client	Spouse
Social Security	_____	_____
Interest	_____	_____
Dividends	_____	_____
Pension Benefits	_____	_____
IRA Benefits	_____	_____
Rental Income	_____	_____

	Annual or Monthly Amounts	
Source	Client	Spouse
Other Income	_____	_____
Subtotal	_____	_____
Total Income	_____	

Do you have any unusual expenses that should be considered in planning your estate?

Comments:

Assets

	(Summary) Value		
	Client's Name	In Joint Names	Spouse's Name
1. Real Estate	_____	_____	_____
2. Stocks and Bonds	_____	_____	_____
3. Bank Accounts	_____	_____	_____
4. Mortgages & Notes	_____	_____	_____
5. Personal Property	_____	_____	_____
6. Life Insurance	_____	_____	_____
7. Retirement Benefits	_____	_____	_____
8. Business Assets	_____	_____	_____
9. Miscellaneous	_____	_____	_____
Subtotal	_____	_____	_____
Total Assets	_____		

ASSETS AND LIABILITIES (Detail)

ASSETS: Complete the appropriate sections or attach separate statements such as bank account or brokerage statements, balance sheet, your own list, etc. If assets are not owned jointly by husband and wife, please indicate.

    1. Real Estate

Location	Estimated Value	Mortgage Balance
_____	_____	_____
_____	_____	_____
_____	_____	_____

Comments:

    2. Stocks and Bonds

Number	Security	Value
	(a) Individually Held	
_____	_____	_____
_____	_____	_____

Number   Security   Value

_____   _____   _____
_____   _____   _____

     (b) Brokerage Accounts

_____   _____   _____
_____   _____   _____
_____   _____   _____

   3. Bank Accounts

Bank and Account Number	Type (checking, CD, money mkt, etc.)	Joint Acct. (if any)	Balance
_____	_____	_____	_____
_____	_____	_____	_____
_____	_____	_____	_____

Do you maintain a safe deposit box?
Bank _____ Branch _____ Number _____

   4. Promissory notes, Mortgages
                    Description   Value

_____   _____
_____   _____
_____   _____

   5. Tangible Personal Property
Estimate the total value of your household furnishings, automobiles, and other personal belongings: _____

Do you have any items of special value that should be considered in planning your estate?

Comments:

(You will have the opportunity to prepare a separate list to designate certain items of tangible personal property for specific persons, but you need not do this now.)

   6. Life Insurance

Insured (H or W?)	Company	Amount	Beneficiary
_____	_____	_____	_____
_____	_____	_____	_____
_____	_____	_____	_____

400

7. <u>Retirement Benefits</u>

Description	Amount	Beneficiary
(a) Pension/Profit–Sharing		
_____	_____	_____
_____	_____	_____
_____	_____	_____
(b) IRA Accounts/401(k)		
_____	_____	_____
_____	_____	_____
(c) Annuities		
_____	_____	_____
_____	_____	_____
_____	_____	_____

8. <u>Business Assets</u>

Description	Value
_____	_____
_____	_____

<u>Comments:</u>

9. <u>Miscellaneous</u>

Description	Value
_____	_____
_____	_____

NOTE: Documents to bring to our meeting, if available and applicable: (a) will(s); (b) deed to residence; (c) latest tax returns; (d) insurance policies; (e) bank or brokerage account statements; and (f) any other documents or information you deem relevant.

<u>Liabilities</u>

Please list any outstanding liabilities (you need not include ordinary monthly expenses) if not shown elsewhere:

Description	Amount	Date Due
_____	_____	_____
_____	_____	_____
_____	_____	_____

CHAPTER 27

COMMUNITY RESOURCES

Table of Sections

WESTLAW Electronic Research

See WESTLAW Electronic Research Guide preceding the Summary of Contents.

---

§ 27.1 Role of Attorney as Coordinator

In working with an older client and/or the client's family, the attorney will often be presented with more than just traditional legal problems involving disputes between discreet, identifiable parties. In earlier chapters, many of these elder law legal issues have been discussed in depth. Frequently the elder law attorney will be asked by the client to assist with a multitude of difficulties that the older person may be experiencing. Some of the issues presented may not involve legal problems. In addition to the need for estate planning or for the management of a present disability that hampers decision-making, the client also may need information about the various services that might be useful in assisting the client deal with problems associated with aging. By being able to provide the client with referrals or by being able to act as a liaison between the client and such services, the attorney serves the client and helps ensure greater independence for the older person. Most persons are unfamiliar with the range of available community services for the elderly unless they already have utilized them; the elder law attorney, on the other hand, will develop substantial familiarity with the community's resources during the course of assisting many clients.

Every community large enough to have an elder law attorney is likely to have a substantial number of services available to elderly persons as well as for those who have assumed responsibility for their care. These services will vary in nature, cost, and availability, but all of them are geared to assisting people to remain as autonomous as possible in the community, to maintain as high a quality of life with dignity as possible, and to ensure that the basic needs of all the population are met.

The elder law attorney must listen to the client during the interview and hear not only those issues that may require legal assistance, such as the preparation of a document or the establishment of a guardianship and conservatorship, but also those problems that may soon give rise to a need for legal help. Such problems may include an inability to get to appointments, a physical disability that limits mobility in the home, confusion about paying bills, multiple physicians prescribing a variety of medications, a need for medical intervention, and other problems with maintaining one's self through the ability to carry out the basic activities of daily living. Proposing the legal remedy (power of attorney, guardianship, etc.) is not complete legal assistance unless the lawyer also counsels the client about how the legal tool can be used to resolve the problem. In many cases, the assistance required will be available from outside sources of which the client may not be aware. The client has come seeking a complete solution to the matter of concern, and the attorney should be prepared to assist the client through such resolution.

§ 27.2 Use of Outside Resources—Overview

There are many types of problems that will be eased by actions such as the establishment of a guardianship, conservatorship, or trust or the appointment of an agent pursuant to a power of attorney. The client who is able to prepare meals, live at home, get to the grocery store, and maintain the home but who cannot remember to pay bills to keep utilities on, to keep the house insured, or to file tax returns either will need a trust or a conservatorship or will need to appoint an agent to act in the client's behalf. The attorney can create the legal relationship that grants someone the power to help, but the power alone is not adequate unless the attorney also ensures that the person empowered knows how to use the document, how to get help, and the limits on the authority granted by the appointment.[1] The client will be grateful for the comprehensive nature of the service provided.

What types of services can be available in the community that can assist the elderly client or someone acting on the client's behalf? The following sections consider, first, the types of services that may be needed or helpful and, second, the best ways of accessing those programs.

§ 27.3   Use of Outside Resources—Types of Services—Basic Needs

Food and shelter are basic needs for the elderly person. There are home delivered meals available, congregate meal programs, and other services that can assist with food needs, such as shopper services that will bring food from the grocery store and transportation services that will assist the client in getting to the store. Housing needs can be met with government-subsidized housing, home repair services, and chore services; and the equity in a home can be used to help meet monthly expenses by means of a reverse annuity mortgage or a home equity conversion.[1]

§ 27.4   Use of Outside Resources—Types of Services—Financial Management

While a conservatorship, trust, or power of attorney may be needed for the client who is so disabled as to not recognize a need for assistance, some clients may suffer from some physical disability that prevents them from handling income and investments, writing checks, or otherwise attending to day-to-day financial chores. Medical insurance claim filing and tracking may be overwhelming to some clients. Other clients may not be able to deal effectively with investments left by a predeceasing spouse. Such clients do not need to give up their authority to a surrogate or trustee; they simply need some regularly available assistance in handling these items. Many communities have "private fiduciaries" who are able to provide just this type of assistance, while other communities have insurance filing services, bookkeeping services, and accountants who are willing to assist with such items. Clients must be cautioned to be certain they are delegating only administrative or clerical duties, and not delegating the right to sign on one's behalf. If authority to sign must be given, the more protective

---

§ 27.2

1. See Chapter 9 for a discussion of managing incapacity and §§ 9.11 and 9.12 for instruction sheets that may be given to guardians and conservators.

§ 27.3

1. See Chapter 22.

arrangements offered by the trust, power of attorney, or conservatorship may be in order. Caution also is to be advised when a family member is to be given signature authority or coownership of assets for purposes of financial management assistance. Aside from the obvious problem of potential mismanagement or defalcation, such an arrangement gives rise to the risk of the loss of one's assets to the creditors, spouse, or poor business decisions of the "helper." Management of a portfolio of substantial assets may require a trust so that an independent trustee can be charged with management and so that the standards to which trustees are held will be clearly applicable.

§ 27.5 Use of Outside Resources—Types of Services—Financial Counseling

Appropriate investments for older persons who are not receiving earned income are different from those of other persons. The recently retired person, the newly widowed person, and the person with sudden wealth will all require help with decisions about how to hold and invest their assets. The attorney is not likely to be able to give such help effectively or economically. There are professional investment advisors and financial planners who can render such assistance, but the attorney should be certain that the referral is to a person who has experience and knowledge concerning the special needs of the elderly, including knowledge of social security, Medicare, Medigap supplemental insurance, Medicaid, long-term care insurance, home equity conversion, private retirement options, and other programs affecting such clients. An important caution in this area is to advise the client to look carefully at any "planner" who is also the seller of a given financial product; the insurance salesperson is likely to place great emphasis on insurance products, the banker is apt to recommend bank investments, the broker is likely to look to products that generate a commission, and so on. An independent financial planner or a registered securities advisor will be more likely to give an unbiased opinion and one that is more tailored to the client's needs than to the benefit of the advisor.

§ 27.6 Use of Outside Resources—Types of Services—Respite Services

Most care given the infirm elderly is given in the family home by family members. When there are great demands made upon the family for such care, the family may be unable to cope. Yet if the family could receive some assistance for several hours per day or per week, the elderly client might be able to remain in the home much longer than if the family had to rely only upon itself. Frequently, the spouse alone is the caregiver and is unable to attend to his or her own basic needs or unable to leave the other spouse alone during the day to get to his or her doctor's appointments, do grocery shopping, or attend to all the other chores of daily living. Acknowledging this situation, public and private services have been developed to provide respite relief to the caretaker in the home so the caregiver can leave, attend to matters, or simply rest without responsibility.

§ 27.7   Use of Outside Resources—Types of Services—Coordinating Care

Considering the panoply of services that can be available for elderly persons, there often is a need for some type of case manager, facilitator, or care coordinator. Such a person has the responsibility of assessing the needs of the elderly person, reviewing the services available, and either making the contacts to arrange the service or giving the family the necessary information concerning eligibility, application requirements, etc. Frequently, such case management services can be a one-time service, but because peoples' needs are fluid, regular reassessments are advised so that changed circumstances can be addressed.

§ 27.8   Use of Outside Resources—Types of Services—Mediation of Family Disputes

There often can be conflicts of interest within the family of an elderly client. Disputes can arise about matters such as who may be entitled to certain items of property, whether a child has a debt to a parent, whose duty it is to care for a parent, or whether a child should be obligated to contribute financially to the parent's needs. There can be questions about whether a family member should be compensated for the time spent caring for a disabled relative. The parent may be receiving more "help" than he or she desires and may want to be left alone. There may be difficulties with neighbors, or family members may disagree about the best type of care to be provided to an older family member. Under these circumstances, mediation by trained professionals may provide the resolution of such issues. The attorney can get into an impossible situation by trying to mediate family disputes while simultaneously maintaining attorney-client privilege; often the attorney will be conflicted out of any representation with resulting unnecessary expense to the client. Services exist that provide mediation in many communities. Many social service agencies provide this assistance, often free of charge. Private practice psychologists and psychiatrists often offer similar services. Private mediation services also are available.

§ 27.9   Use of Outside Resources—Types of Services—Medical/Nursing/Home Health Services

The types of medical care that the elderly family member may need are likely to be substantially different from those that have been required for other family members or at different times of life. There are physicians who are specialists in geriatric medicine, familiar with the interactions of the multiple medications that older persons may be taking, aware of the special dosages needed for older persons, and acquainted with the fears and concerns of persons who are unable to take care of all their personal needs. The family practice physician or internist who has been treating the patient for years may not have the experience or training to meet the special needs of the client who is facing physical and psychological changes associated with the aging process.

Care in the home may be required for some clients, which may involve making arrangements for help with which the client and the family may have had no experience. Choices often include the use of a nursing service or the hiring of private staff to assist in the home. There are benefits and pitfalls to each. The commercial nursing service ensures proper scheduling and staffing but can be very expensive; included in the charges will be the expense of periodic assessment, the cost of employee benefits, and the profits of the agency itself. On the other hand, hiring private in-home staff may be less expensive but involves substantial problems such as finding replacement staff for turnover and illness, interviewing, preparation of payroll, and withholding reporting. For the client already in need of help, these additional responsibilities can be quite onerous. If there is a responsible family member to assist with these requirements, private hiring of staff is a more practicable option. In addition, there often are home health services provided within the community for persons who have modest resources, but these are usually quite limited and do not pose a viable option for the older person who requires even moderate amounts of assistance. Nonetheless, home health services can provide assistance with the administration of medications for the home-bound patient and can assist with respite care and other tasks needed to keep a frail person at home.

Library References:

C.J.S. Asylums and Institutional Care Facilities §§ 2–13.
West's Key No. Digests, Asylums ⊙1, 2, 5, 6.

§ 27.10   Use of Outside Resources—Locating the Services—In General

In providing elder law services, the attorney will often hear information from the older client or the family that describes a wide range of problems, both legal and social as well as financial, medical, and personal. If the practice of elder law is viewed as "holistic," i.e., addressing broader needs of the client than just legal needs, then the attorney should be prepared to provide advice for meeting those wider needs. In doing so, the elder law attorney should have a fair amount of knowledge of the services that are available within the community.[1] Since such a wide range of services is potentially available (and often rapidly changing), the attorney may find it difficult to remain in touch with all the available options.

In making suggestions concerning available resources, the attorney should make referrals to appropriate persons, companies, or agencies with whom the attorney has successfully dealt in the past with prior clients. This is true whether the attorney is referring to an accountant, an insurance seller, a broker, a home health agency, a private fiduciary, or a private duty nurse. Where services or providers are not readily known to the attorney, however, there are many excellent referral services at local, state, and national levels. Familiarity with these referral services will ease the burden of locating proper assistance.

§ 27.11 Use of Outside Resources—Locating the Services—Local Sources

By law, every community must have a local Area Agency on Aging.[1] This agency is charged with the responsibility of being the umbrella agency for all aging services provided within the community. An area agency will have staff familiar with community programs, and generally is responsible for contracting for or providing such services as home delivered meals, congregate meal/day care programs, transportation services, and other services such as home repairs, chore services, respite services, counseling, and mediation. Generally speaking, the Area Agency on Aging will be the single most comprehensive resource for clients who are seeking assistance with the problems of the elderly. Area agencies go by many names; often they are simply called the Area Agency on Aging, but in some communities, the agency may have a different name. The agency can always be located through the state's office on aging.

---

§ 27.10

1. In chapter 2 at §§ 2.11–2.15, there is discussion of the models of law practices available in elder law. These models include the traditional, the clearinghouse, and the umbrella. The traditional model involves the practice of basic law with advice, counseling, and document preparation. The clearinghouse model involves the willingness of the lawyer to make referrals to appropriate agencies or services to meet the wider needs of the client. The umbrella approach presumes that the attorney will have the ability or perhaps the staff to provide most services directly within the law office.

§ 27.11

1. Older Americans Act, 42 U.S.C.A. § 3001 et seq. The National Association of Area Agencies on Aging operates an Eldercare Locator to help identify community resources to assist other persons. The number to contact is 1–800–677–1116.

An additional source of general information about local resources is the local Information and Referral Service. While this service also may be known by different names, it is worthwhile for the attorney to be able to supply access to this resource to the client.[2]

Other local resources include social service agencies that are operated by religious organizations (although services are generally available to persons of any denomination) and public health services operated by cities or counties. Local governmental programs include public guardianship offices and case management services run through public hospitals or local programs for the elderly.

Many local bar associations have formed committees to deal with the legal problems of the elderly. Such committees have arranged educational programs concerning planning for disability, have arranged for low-cost legal services, and have provided forms and other assistance to persons requiring such help. Members of these committees often are available to help with questions concerning services within the community and often have the names of specific persons to contact.

The probate judge and the probate court staff may be able to make appropriate suggestions for ways of dealing with the needs of the elderly client. Having seen a wide variety of cases resolved in a number of often imaginative ways can give the court great insight into options that may exist.

Private fiduciaries and private case management services are becoming more commonly available and often are able to help individuals and families coordinate the various services that enable an older person to remain independent despite various frailties. The attorney's involvement continues so the attorney can ensure that appropriate documents are in place, that there is continuity in care and decision-making, and that contractual arrangements and fees of the company are fair and reasonable.[3]

For the client with substantial resources, local offices of banks and trust companies are willing to assist with financial management through means of a trust or agency account arrangement. The attorney plays an integral part in establishing such a relationship. Frequently, the trust officer will be able to assist the frail client by arranging for services beyond financial management.

---

2. The attorney should caution his or her client to be clear about the information sought and persistent in seeking the information.

3. A good source for referral to such a service would be the National Association of Private Geriatric Case Managers, 655 North Alvernon Way, Suite 108, Tucson, Arizona 85711 (602) 881–8008.

Finally, there is usually a local office of the state's adult protective services program within most cities. This office is charged with the responsibility of investigating and acting upon possible cases of the abuse, neglect, or exploitation of a vulnerable adult. Where the attorney has reason to believe that there may be abuse, neglect, or exploitation, there is often a duty (regardless of privilege) to report to such an agency. In less severe cases, the agency may be able to assist with referrals to other appropriate services.

The attorney will find it helpful to retain a list of local services and their addresses and phone numbers. Preparing such a list and making it available to appropriate clients can be an excellent service that will assist clients in reaching the help needed.

§ 27.12   Use of Outside Resources—Locating the Services—State Resources

The programs that deal with the needs of the elderly at the state and national levels are more likely to be of help to the attorney than to the client. These services can give the attorney insight into the problems faced by this unique client population, will often present excellent educational programs about such problems and their solutions, and will have staff available to provide information about other available services within the local community. These agencies often advocate at the state legislative and administrative levels for the needs of the elderly.

Every state is required to have a state office on aging and a state legal services developer.[1] These offices are required by the Older Americans Act.[2] The state office on aging is charged with overseeing all the programs for the elderly within the state that receive funds from the federal government and will, therefore, be involved with home delivered meals, transportation services, congregate meals, and other programs. These offices will be the funding and oversight agencies for the local Area Agencies on Aging. The state legal services developer is responsible for ensuring that the legal needs of the elderly are met and works with the bar associations and individual attorneys as well as the Area Agencies on Aging to assess the legal needs of the elderly and try to help meet them by continuing legal education programs, pilot projects, encouraging Law Day programs, and by bringing together different elements of the continuum of service providers to work in concert to help foster legal services for the elderly.

§ 27.12

1. The state offices on aging can be found in Appendix A, State Resources for Elderlaw Attorneys and Their Clients.

The legal sources developer can be contacted through the state office on aging.

2. 42 U.S.C.A. § 3025.

Many states have public interest law firms that address, among many other topics, the legal needs and rights of the elderly. Such advocacy programs may represent individual elderly or classes of elderly with regard to access to state services, Medicaid programs, right to treatment (including the right to refuse), housing matters, and other legal issues common to the class. Such programs often have newsletters that address issues of interest to elder law attorneys.[3]

All states have a Long Term Care Ombudsman who is responsible for monitoring nursing homes and other providers of long-term care (LTC) and the government agencies with regulatory responsibility over LTC providers.[4] The ombudsman acts as an advocate for consumers of LTC services and their families. A client with questions or problems with LTC often can receive valuable assistance from the ombudsman. The ombudsman also is a valuable resource for an attorney seeking information about LTC services, providers and financing. In many states, local LTC ombudsmen are available to assist attorneys and clients, as well. In some states, the responsibilities of the ombudsman extend beyond LTC to cover other areas of concern to older clients.

State departments of health services, economic security, welfare, social services, and similar offices operate a wide range of programs geared to assist the elderly and their families. These programs vary from state to state but include income subsidy programs, housing subsidy programs, home equity conversion programs, health programs including Medicaid services, and others. These agencies also are responsible for the adult protective services programs that monitor abuse, neglect, and exploitation of adults. There may be programs that give financial assistance with utility bills, or programs that supervise property tax relief and renters property tax credit.

The state bar association will have an elder law committee or program that serves the state's attorneys with continuing legal education programs, materials, and information about the special needs of the older client. These committees are often active in legislative advocacy for laws affecting the elderly.

§ 27.13　Use of Outside Resources—Locating the Services—National Resources

The programs that address the needs of the elderly on a national level are able to address and advocate on more national issues such as

3. The State Office on Aging or legal sources developer, listed in Appendix A, State Resources for Elderlaw Attorneys and Their Clients, can provide names and addresses of local public interest law firms.

4. See Long Term Care Ombudsman listed in Appendix A, State Resources for Elderlaw Attorneys and Their Clients.

access to health services, revision and funding of the Older Americans Act, Medicaid matters, age discrimination, and other broad issues. These programs are able to assimilate information from the various states and communities and disseminate the information nationally to enable the best programs to be replicated elsewhere. Many of these national programs offer basic information and services that are of great practical use to the elder law practitioner.

The American Association of Retired Persons (AARP), with a membership exceeding 20 million persons, provides a wide range of services to its membership. Such services include monthly publications, insurance programs, prescription medications at a discount, travel benefits, and other discounts. In addition, AARP sponsors a program called Legal Counsel for the Elderly (LCE) which cosponsors the annual Joint Conference on Law and Aging in Washington, D.C., and provides direct legal services to the elderly located in the District of Columbia. Furthermore, LCE has numerous publications for the practitioner and for the public with regard to planning for disability, medical expense issues, and guardianship and conservatorship.[1]

The American Bar Association Commission on the Legal Problems of the Elderly was established by the ABA in 1978 to encourage legal services for the elderly, particularly through involvement of the private bar, and has explored the legal issues surrounding long-term care, home care, guardianship, home equity conversion, surrogate decision-making, and Social Security. The Commission has fifteen members and includes not only lawyers but also judges, physicians, professors, advocates for the elderly, and representatives of major corporations. The Commission, also a sponsor of the Joint Conference on Law and Aging, conducts a wide range of continuing education programs throughout the United States, has a substantial number of publications available to the public and the bar regarding law and aging issues, and acts as a strong advocate for the legal rights of the elderly.[2]

The Legal Services Corporation funds the National Senior Citizens Law Center (NSCLC) as one of its "backup" centers to the local legal services programs. The NSCLC also is a sponsor of the Joint Conference on Law and Aging and provides research and support to legal services attorneys facing problems with the legal issues involving the

§ 27.13

1. Legal Counsel for the Elderly

   601 E Street, NW

   Washington, DC 20049

   (202) 434–2120

2. American Bar Association Commission Commission on the Legal Problems of the Elderly

   1800 M Street, N.W.

   Washington, DC 20036–5886

   (202) 331–2297

elderly client. The NSCLC has several publications that are available, including a weekly legislative report.[3]

The Center for Social Gerontology is another "backup" center for elderlaw. The Center is a sponsor of the Joint Conference on Law and Aging, publishes a newsletter, and is available to assist elderlawyers.[4]

The National Academy of Elder Law Attorneys (NAELA) is an important national organization of attorneys, both public and private as well as academic members, that acts as an advocate for the needs of the elderly as well as for the practitioners of elder law. The Academy sponsors an annual symposium on elder law and an annual Institute that addresses a single topic of elder law with a limited enrollment. The NAELA publishes a monthly NAELA News with information about the practice of elder law and about Academy activities and also publishes the NAELA Quarterly with more extensive articles on elder law issues. There are state and local NAELA chapters, and there are several consumer-oriented publications available for distribution to clients.[5]

Finally, there are numerous periodicals available that address elder law issues. Various publishers have issued monthly newsletters that report on current cases, practice issues, ethical questions, and upcoming programs of continuing legal education.

3. National Senior Citizens Law Center,
  1815 H Street NW, Suite 700
  Washington, D.C. 20006
  202/887–5280

4. Center on Social Gerontology
  2307 Shelby Avenue
  Ann Arbor, MI 34103
  (313) 665–1126

5. National Academy of Elder Law Attorneys

  655 North Alvernon Way,

  Suite 108

  Tucson, Arizona 85711

  (602) 881–4005

*

TABLE OF APPENDICES

APPENDIX A

STATE RESOURCES FOR ELDERLAW ATTORNEYS AND THEIR CLIENTS*

ALABAMA

State Unit on Aging
Alabama Commission on Aging
770 Washington Ave., Suite 470
Montgomery, AL 36130
(205) 242-5743

Long Term Care Ombudsman
Alabama Commission on Aging
770 Washington Ave., Suite 470
Montgomery, AL 36130
(205) 242-5743

Other Resources
Legal Counsel for the Elderly
University of Alabama
P.O. Drawer 870392
Tuscaloosa, AL 35487-0392
(205) 348-4960

ALASKA

State Unit on Aging
Older Alaskans Commission
P.O. Box 110209
Juneau, AK 99811-0209
(907) 465-3250

Long Term Care Ombudsman
3601 C Street, Suite 260
Anchorage, AK 99503-5209
(907) 563-6393
(800) 478-9996

Other Resources
Senior Legal Services Project
Alaska Legal Services Corporation
1016 West 6th Avenue, Suite 200
Anchorage, AK 99501
(907) 272-9431

*Source: American Bar Association Commission on Legal Problems of the Elderly, The Law and Aging Resource Guide. See Appendix C for state listings of Medicare Carriers and Intermediaries, and Appendix D for state listings of Medicaid Agencies and Fiscal Agents.

Elderlaw Project
Alaska Pro Bono Program
1016 West 6th Avenue, Suite 200
Anchorage, AK 99501
(907) 272-9431

ARIZONA

State Unit on Aging
Aging and Adult Administration
Bureau on Aging
Department of Economic Security
1789 West Jefferson
Phoenix, AZ 85007
(602) 542-4446

Long Term Care Ombudsman
Adult and Aging Administration
Department of Economic Security
1789 W. Jefferson
Phoenix, AZ 85007
(602) 542-4446

Other Resources
Elder Abuse Project
Office of the Attorney General
1275 West Washington
Phoenix, AZ 85007
(602) 542-2124

ARKANSAS

State Unit on Aging
Division of Aging and Adult Serv-
ices
Arkansas Department of Human
Services
P.O. Box 1437, Slot 1412
Little Rock, AR 72201
(501) 682-2441

Long Term Care Ombudsman
Office on Aging and Adult Serv-
ices
Donaghey Building
Seventh and Main
Little Rock, AR 72201
(501) 682-2441

Other Resources
Arkansas Volunteer Lawyers for
the Elderly
615 West Markham
Suite 200
Little Rock, AR 72201
(501) 376-8015
(800) 950-5817 (within Arkansas)

CALIFORNIA

State Unit on Aging
Department of Aging and Long–
Term Care
1600 K Street, 4th Floor
Sacramento, CA 95814
(916) 322–5290

Long Term Care Ombudsman
Department of Aging and Long–
Term Care
1600 K Street, 3rd Floor
Sacramento, CA 95814
(916) 323–6681

Other Resources
Committee on Legal Problems of
Aging
California State Bar
555 Franklin Street
San Francisco, CA 94102
(415) 561–8200

California Advocates for Nursing
Home Reform
1610 Bush Street
San Francisco, CA 94109
(415) 474–5171

Los Angeles County Bar Association
Barristers Senior Outreach Committee
P.O. Box 55020
Los Angeles, CA 90055–2020
(213) 896–6446

Clinic for the Elderly
McGeorge School of Law
University of the Pacific
3130 5th Avenue
Sacramento, CA 95817
(916) 739–7161

COLORADO

State Unit on Aging
Aging and Adult Service
Department of Social Services
1575 Sherman Street, 4th Floor
Denver, CO 80203–1714
(303) 866–3851

Long Term Care Ombudsman
The Legal Center
455 Sherman Street, Suite 130
Denver, CO 80203
(303) 722–0300

Other Resources
Pooled Legal Assistance Project
707 17th Street, Suite 2900
Denver, CO 80202
(303) 292–1327

STATE RESOURCES

CONNECTICUT

State Unit on Aging
Department on Aging
175 Main Street
Hartford, CT 06115
(203) 566–3238

Long Term Care Ombudsman
Connecticut Department on Aging
175 Main Street
Hartford, CT 06106
(203) 566–7770

Other Resources
Connecticut Legal Aid to the Elderly Program
Law Department, REAC
151 Farmington Avenue
Hartford, CT 06156
(203) 273–3839

Connecticut Legal Services Inc.
Administrative Office
P.O. Box 841
425 Main Street
Middletown, CT 06457
(203) 347–7237

Legal Assistance to Medicare Patients (LAMP)
P.O. Box 258
872 Main Street
Willimantic, CT 06226

DELAWARE

State Unit on Aging
Division of Aging, Department of Health & Social Services
1909 North Dupont Highway
Administration Building, 2nd Floor Annex
New Castle, DE 19720
(302) 577–4791

Long Term Care Ombudsman
Division of Aging
11–13 Church Street
Milford, DE 19963
(302) 422–1386
Fax: (302) 422–1519

DISTRICT OF COLUMBIA

State Unit on Aging
Office on Aging
1424 K Street, NW
2nd Floor
Washington, DC 20005
(202) 724–5626

Long Term Care Ombudsman
Legal Counsel for the Elderly
601 E Street, N.W., Building 4A
Washington, D.C. 20049
(202) 434–2140

APPENDIX A

Other Resources
Advocates for Older People
2136 Pennsylvania Ave., N.W.
Washington, D.C. 20052
(202) 676–5133

Legal Counsel for the Elderly
601 E Street, N.W., Bldg. 4A
Washington, D.C. 20049
(202) 434–2120
Legal Hotline
(202) 234–0970

FLORIDA

State Unit on Aging
Department of Elder Affairs
Building I, Room 317
1317 Winewood Blvd.
Tallahassee, FL 32301
(904) 922–5297

Long Term Care Ombudsman
Department of Elder Affairs
154 Holland Bldg.
600 South Calhoun Street
Tallahassee, FL 32399–0001
(904) 488–6190
Fax: (904) 488–5657

Other Resources
Elder Law Section
The Florida Bar
c/o The Florida Bar
650 Apalachee Parkway
Tallahassee, FL 32399–2300
(904) 561–5600

Elderly Referral Plan
Lawyer Referral Service
The Florida Bar
650 Apalachee Parkway
Tallahassee, FL 32399–2300
(904) 561–5844
(800) 342–8011

Elderlaw Clinic
Stetson University
College of Law
1401 61st Street South
Gulfport, FL 33707

Nova University Center for the
  Study of Law
Elderlaw Project
74A Lindy Lane
West Palm Beach, FL 33406
(407) 640–9191

GEORGIA

State Unit on Aging
Office of Aging
Department of Human Resources
878 Peachtree Street, Room 632
Atlanta, GA 30309
(404) 894–5333

Long Term Care Ombudsman
Office of Aging
Department of Human Resources
878 Peachtree Street, Room 642
Atlanta, GA 30309
(404) 894–5336
Fax: (404) 853–9096

Other Resources
Committee on Legal Services to
  the Elderly
Young Lawyer Section
State Bar of Georgia
800 The Hurt Building
50 Hurt Plaza
Atlanta, GA 30303
(404) 527–8700
(800) 344–6865

Elderly Legal Referral Panel
SOWEGA Council on Aging
P.O. Box 278
Albany, GA 31702
(912) 432–1124

GUAM

State Unit on Aging
Division of Senior Citizens
Department of Public Health &
  Social Services
Government of Guam
P.O. Box 2816
Agana, Guam 96910
011 (671) 734–4361

HAWAII

State Unit on Aging
Advocacy Assistance Unit
Executive Office on Aging
Office of the Governor
335 Merchant Street, Room 241
Honolulu, HI 96813
(808) 586–0100
Fax: (808) 586–0185

Long Term Care Ombudsman
Executive Office on Aging
Office of the Governor
335 Merchant Street, Room 241
Honolulu, HI 96813
(808) 586–0100

421

Other Resources
University of Hawaii at Manoa
William S. Richardson School of
  Law
Elder Law Program
2515 Dole Street
Honolulu, HI 96822
(808) 956–6544
Fax: (808) 956–6402

IDAHO

State Unit on Aging
Office on Aging
Statehouse, Room 108
Boise, ID 83720
(208) 334–3833

Long Term Care Ombudsman
Office on Aging
Statehouse, Room 108
Boise, ID 83720
(208) 334–2220

ILLINOIS

State Unit on Aging
Department of Aging
421 E. Capitol Avenue
Springfield, IL 62701
(217) 785–2870

Long Term Care Ombudsman
Department on Aging
421 East Capitol Avenue
Springfield, IL 62701
(217) 785–1566

Other Resources
Senior Citizens Advocacy
  Division
Office of Attorney General
100 West Randolf Street, 13th
  Floor
Chicago, IL 60601
(312) 793–3695
(800) 243–5377 (AGE–LESS)

Senior Citizens Wills Program
The Chicago Bar Association
29 South LaSalle Street
Chicago, IL 60603
(312) 782–7348

Springfield Office:
500 South Second Street
Springfield, IL 62706
(217) 782–1090
(800) 252–2518

INDIANA

State Unit on Aging
Choice/Home Care Services
Department of Human Services
251 North Illinois Street
P.O. Box 7083
Indianapolis, IN 46207–7083
(317) 232–7020

Long Term Care Ombudsman
Aging & In–Home Services Section
Family and Social Services Administration
402 West Washington,
P.O. Box 7083
Indianapolis, IN 46207–7083
(317) 232–7134
(800) 622–6122 (Within Indiana)

Other Resources
Senior Law Project
Legal Services Organization
1800 Market Square Center
151 North Delaware
Indianapolis, IN 46204
(317) 631–9424

Vincennes University Older Hoosiers Program
P.O. Box 314
Vincennes, IN 47591
(812) 885–4292

IOWA

State Unit on Aging
Department of Elder Affairs
236 Jewitt Building, 914 Grand Avenue
Des Moines, IA 50319
(515) 281–5187

Long Term Care Ombudsman
Department of Elder Affairs
236 Jewett Building
914 Grand Avenue
Des Moines, IA 50319
(515) 281–4656
Fax: (515) 281–5426

Other Resources
SIMPCO Area Agency on Aging
P.O. Box 447
Sioux City, IA 51102
(712) 279–6286

APPENDIX A

KANSAS

State Unit on Aging
Department on Aging
Docking State Office Building,
  122–S
915 SW Harrison
Topeka, KS 66612–1500
(913) 296–4986
(800) 432–3535 (within Kansas)

Long Term Care Ombudsman
Department on Aging
Docking State Office Building,
  122–S
915 SW Harrison
Topeka, KS 66612–1500
(913) 296–4986
(800) 432–3535 (within Kansas)

KENTUCKY

State Unit on Aging
Cabinet for Human Resources
Department for Social Services
6–W Division of Aging Services
275 East Main Street
Frankfort, KY 40621
(502) 564–6930

Long Term Care Ombudsman
Division of Aging Services
Department for Social Services
Cabinet for Human Resources
275 East Main Street, 6–W
Frankfort, KY 40621
(502) 564–6930
(800) 372–2991 (within Kentucky)

LOUISIANA

State Unit on Aging
Office of Elderly Affairs
4550 No. Boulevard, 2nd Floor
P.O. Box 80374
Baton Rouge, LA 70806
(504) 925–1700

Long Term Care Ombudsman
Office of Elderly Affairs
P.O. Box 80374
Baton Rouge, LA 70898–0374
(504) 925–1700

Other Resources
Louisiana Legal Consortium
1517 Polymnia Street
New Orleans, LA 70130
(504) 522–8111

Gillis Long Poverty Law Center
Loyola University School of Law
7214 St. Charles
New Orleans, LA 70118
(504) 861–5550

STATE RESOURCES

MAINE

State Unit on Aging
Department of Human Services
Bureau of Elder and Adult Serv-
ices
State House-Station # 11
Augusta, ME 04333
(207) 626-5335

Long Term Care Ombudsman
Legal Services for the Elderly
113 Bangor Street
P.O. Box 2723
Augusta, ME 04330
(207) 289-2220

Other Resources
Advocates for Medicare Patients
113 Bangor Street
P.O. Box 2723
Augusta, ME 04338-2723
(207) 289-2287

MARYLAND

State Unit on Aging
Office on Aging
301 West Preston Street
Room 1004
Baltimore, MD 21201
(410) 225-1100

Long Term Care Ombudsman
Office on Aging
301 W. Preston Street
Baltimore, MD 21201
(410) 225-1083

Other Resources
Sixty Plus Legal Program
Maryland State Bar Association
520 West Fayette Street
Baltimore, MD 21201
(410) 685-7878
(800) 492-1993

MASSACHUSETTS

State Unit on Aging
Commonwealth of Massachusetts
Department of Elder Affairs
One Ashton Place
5th Floor
Boston, MA 02108
(617) 727-7750

Long Term Care Ombudsman
Executive Office of Elder Affairs
38 Chauncy Street
Boston, MA 02111
(617) 727-7755
(800) 882-2003

Other Resources
Boston College Legal Assistance
    Bureau
Elder Law Project
24 Crescent Street
Waltham, MA 02154
(617) 893–4793

Greater Boston Elderly Legal Ser-
    vices
102 Norway Street
Boston, MA 02115
(617) 536–0400

Senior Citizens Law and Advocacy
    Project
332 Main Street
Worcester, MA 01608
(800) 649–3718

MICHIGAN

State Unit on Aging
Office of Services to the Aging
P.O. Box 30026
Lansing, MI 48909
(517) 373–8230

Long Term Care Ombudsman
Citizens for Better Care
416 N. Homer St., Suite 101
Lansing, MI 48912
(517) 482–1297
(800) 292–7852

Other Resources
Legal Hotline for Older Michigani-
    ans
115 W. Allegan, Suite 720
Lansing, MI 48933
(800) 347–5297

Sixty Plus Inc. Elderlaw Clinic
Old St. Lawrence Hospital
1201 West Oakland
Lansing, MI 48915
(517) 377–0494

MINNESOTA

State Unit on Aging
Board on Aging
444 Lafayette Road
St. Paul, MN 55155–3843
(612) 296–2770

Long Term Care Ombudsman
444 Lafayette Road
St. Paul, MN 55155–3843
(612) 296–0382
(800) 657–3591
Fax: (612) 296–6624

Other Resources
Minnesota Medicare Advocacy
  Project
906 Minnesota Building
St. Paul, MN 55701
(612) 228–0771

MISSOURI

State Unit on Aging
Division on Aging
Department of Social Services
615 Howerton Court
P.O. Box 1337
Jefferson City, MO 65102–1337
(314) 751–3082

Long Term Care Ombudsman
Division of Aging
Department of Social Services
615 Howerton Court
P.O. Box 1337
Jefferson City, MO 65102
(314) 751–3082
Fax: (314) 751–8493

Other Resources
Gateway Older Adult Legal Service
8420 Delmar, Suite 201
University City, MO 63124
(314) 993–5505

Legal Services of Eastern Missouri
625 North Euclid Avenue
St. Louis, MO 63108
(314) 367–1700

MISSISSIPPI

State Unit on Aging
Aging and Adult Services
421 W. Pascagoula Street
Jackson, MS 39203–3524
(601) 949–2070

Long Term Care Ombudsman
Aging and Adult Services
421 W. Pascagoula Street
Jackson, MS 39204
(601) 949–2070
(601) 366–8757

MONTANA

State Unit on Aging
Governors Office on Aging
State Capitol Building
Capitol Station, Room 219
Helena, MT 59620
(406) 444–3111
(800) 332–2272 (within Montana)

Long Term Care Ombudsman
Governor's Office on Aging
Capitol Station
P.O. Box 232
Helena, MT 59620
(406) 444–4676
Fax: (406) 444–5529

NEBRASKA

State Unit on Aging
Department on Aging
301 Centennial Mall–South
P.O. Box 95044
Lincoln, NE 68509
(402) 471–2306

Long Term Care Ombudsman
Department on Aging
P.O. Box 95044
Lincoln, NE 68509
(402) 471–2307
Fax: (402) 471–2597

NEVADA

State Unit on Aging
Nevada Division for Aging Services
340 North 11th Street, Suite 114
Las Vegas, NV 89101
(702) 486–3545

Long Term Care Ombudsman
NORTHERN NEVADA
Nevada Division for Aging Services
3680 Grant Drive, Suite C–1
Reno, NV 89509
(702) 688–2964

SOUTHERN NEVADA
Nevada Division for Aging Services
340 North 11th Street, Suite 114
Las Vegas, NV 89101
(702) 486–3545

Other Resources
Senior Citizen's Law Project
340 North 11th Street
Las Vegas, NV 89101
(702) 229–6596

NEW HAMPSHIRE

State Unit on Aging
Division of Elderly and Adult
  Services
6 Hazen Drive
Concord, NH 03301–6501
(603) 271–4680

Long Term Care Ombudsman
Division of Elderly and Adult
  Services
6 Hazen Drive
Concord, NH 03301–6508
(603) 271–4375

Other Resources
Senior Citizens Law Project
New Hampshire Legal Assistance
15 Green Street
Concord, NH 03301
(603) 224–3333

NEW JERSEY

State Unit on Aging
Division on Aging
Department of Community Affairs
CN 807, South Broad and Front
  Streets
Trenton, NJ 08625–0807
(609) 292–4833

Long Term Care Ombudsman
Office of the Ombudsman for In-
  stitutionalized Elderly
CN 808, 28 West State Street,
  Room 305
Trenton, NJ 08625–0808
(609) 292–8016
(609) 984–4810

NEW MEXICO

State Unit on Aging
State Agency on Aging
224 East Palace Avenue, 4th Floor
Santa Fe, NM 87501
(505) 827–7640

Long Term Care Ombudsman
Chair, Elder Law Section
State Agency on Aging
224 East Palace Avenue
Santa Fe, NM 87501
(505) 827–7640

Other Resources
Desert State Senior Resources
510 2nd Street, NW
Suite 239
Albuquerque, NM 87102
(505) 843–7535
(505) 988–5550 (Santa Fe)
(505) 527–2081 (Las Cruces)
(505) 622–7780 (Roswell)

State Bar of New Mexico
Lawyer Referral for the Elderly
  Committee
P.O. Box 3587
Albuquerque, NM 87190–3587
(505) 884–5100
Statewide Legal Hotline
(800) 876–6657

NEW YORK

State Unit on Aging
New York State Office for the
  Aging
Agency Building 2
New York State Plaza
Albany, NY 12223–0001
(518) 474–4425
(800) 342–9871

Long Term Care Ombudsman
New York State Office for the
  Aging
Agency Building 2
Empire State Plaza
Albany, NY 12223
(518) 474–7329
(800) 342–9871 (in New York)
Fax: (518) 474–0608

Other Resources
Clinic for the Elderly
Brooklyn Law School
299 Broadway
New York, NY 10007
(718) 780–7944

Institute on Law and Rights of
  Older Adults
Brookdale Center on Aging of
  Hunter College
425 East 25th Street
New York, NY 10010
(212) 481–4433

Legal Services for the Elderly
132 West 43rd Street, 3rd Floor
New York, NY
(212) 391–0120

Legal Services for the Elderly
  Clinic
State University of New York
Buffalo Law School
Legal Assistance Program
Room 507, O'Brien Hall
Buffalo, NY 14260
(716) 636–2107

NORTH CAROLINA

State Unit on Aging
Division of Aging
CB 29531
693 Palmer Drive
Raleigh, NC 27626–0531
(919) 733–3983

Long Term Care Ombudsman
Division on Aging
Department of Human Resources
693 Palmer Drive
Raleigh, NC 27603
(919) 733–3983
Fax: (919) 733–0443

Other Resources
Elderly Law Unit
East Central Community Legal
    Services
P.O. Drawer 1731
5 West Hargett St.
Raleigh, NC 27602
(919) 828–4647

Legal Services for the Elderly
737 East Blvd.
Charlotte, NC 28203
(704) 334–0400

NORTH DAKOTA

State Unit on Aging
Aging Services Division
Department of Human Affairs
P.O. Box 7070
Northbrook Shopping Center
North Washington Street
Bismarck, ND 58507–7070
(701) 224–2577

Long Term Care Ombudsman
Aging Services
P.O. Box 7070
Bismarck, ND 58507–7070
(701) 221–5456

Other Resources
Legal Assistance of North Dakota,
    Inc.
P.O. Box 1893
Bismarck, ND 58502–1893
(701) 222–2110

NORTHERN MARIANA ISLANDS

State Unit on Aging
Office of Aging
Department of Community and
    Cultural Affairs
Civic Center—Susupe
Saipan, Northern Mariana Islands
    96950
9411 or 9732

OHIO

State Unit on Aging
Ohio Department of Aging
50 West Broad Street
9th Floor
Columbus, OH 43266–0501
(614) 466–5500
(800) 282–1206 (within Ohio)

Long Term Care Ombudsman
Ohio Department of Aging
50 West Broad Street
8th Floor
Columbus, OH 43266–0501
(614) 466–1221
(800) 282–1206 (within Ohio)

Other Resources
PRO Seniors
Legal Hotline for Older Ohioans
617 Vine Street, Suite 900
Cincinnati, OH 45202
(513) 621–8721
(800) 488–6070

OKLAHOMA

State Unit on Aging
Aging Services Division
Department of Human Services
P.O. Box 25352
Oklahoma City, OK 73125
(405) 521–2327

Long Term Care Ombudsman
Aging Services Division
Department of Human Services
P.O. Box 25352
312 NE 28
Oklahoma City, OK 73125
(405) 521–2281

Other Resources
Senior Citizens Division
Legal Aid of Eastern OK
430 Court Street
Muskogee, OK 74401
(918) 683–5681

Senior Citizens Division
Legal Aid of Western Oklahoma
P.O. Box 1105
Woodward, OK 73802
(405) 256–1297

OREGON

State Unit on Aging
Senior Services Division
Program Assistance Section
313 Public Service Building
Salem, OR 97310
(503) 378–4728

Long Term Care Ombudsman
Office of the Ombudsman
2475 Lancaster Drive, NE
Building B, Suite 9
Salem, OR 97303
(503) 378–6533

PENNSYLVANIA

State Unit on Aging
Department of Aging
Barto Building
231 State Street
Harrisburg, PA 17101–1195
(717) 783–1550

Long Term Care Ombudsman
Department of Aging
Barto Building
231 State Street
Harrisburg, PA 17101
(717) 783–7247

Other Resources
Senior Citizens Judicare Project
1101 Market Street
11th Floor
Philadelphia, PA 19107
(215) 238–8943

PUERTO RICO

State Unit on Aging
Governor's Office for Elderly
 Affairs
Corbian Plaza Stop 23
Ponce de Leon Avenue 1603
U.M. Office C
San Ture, PR 00908
(809) 721–2858

Long Term Care Ombudsman
Governor's Office for Elderly
 Affairs
Call Box 50063
Old San Juan Station
San Juan, PR 00902
(809) 721–8225

RHODE ISLAND

State Unit on Aging
Department of Elderly Affairs
160 Pine Street
Providence, RI 02903–3700
(401) 277–2858

Long Term Care Ombudsman
Department of Elderly Affairs
160 Pine Street
Providence, RI 02903–3708
(401) 277–6880

Other Resources
Elderly Law Unit
Rhode Island Legal Services, Inc.
77 Dorrance Street
Providence, RI 02903
(401) 274–2652

Legal Information and Referral
 Service for the Elderly
115 Cedar St.
Providence, RI 02903
(401) 521–5040

APPENDIX A

SOUTH CAROLINA

State Unit on Aging
South Carolina Commission on
  Aging
Fontaine Business Center
400 Arbor Lake Drive, Suite
  B-500
Columbia, SC 29223
(803) 735-0210

Long Term Care Ombudsman
Governor's Office
1205 Pendleton Street, Room 306
Columbia, SC 29201
(803) 734-0457

SOUTH DAKOTA

State Unit on Aging
Office of Adult Services & Aging
Division of Human Development
Department of Social Services
700 North Illinois Street
Pierre, SD 57501
(605) 773-3656

Long Term Care Ombudsman
Office of Adult Services & Aging
Division of Human Development
Department of Social Services,
  Kneip Building
700 North Illinois Street
Pierre, SD 57501
(605) 773-3656

TENNESSEE

State Unit on Aging
Commission on Aging
706 Church Street, Suite 201
Nashville, TN 37243-0860
(615) 741-2056

Long Term Care Ombudsman
Commission on Aging
703 Tennessee Building
Nashville, TN 37219
(615) 741-2056

TEXAS

State Unit on Aging
Texas Department on Aging
P.O. Box 12786
Capitol Station
1949 I.H. 35, South
Austin, TX 78741-3702
(512) 444-2727
(800) 252-9240

Long Term Care Ombudsman
Texas Department on Aging
P.O. Box 12786
Capitol Station
1949 I.H. 35 South
Austin, TX 78711
(512) 475-2727
(800) 252-9240

Other Resources
Chief, Elder Law Section
Consumer Protection Division
P.O. Box 12548
Austin, TX 78711-2548
(512) 475-4632

Elderly Law Clinic
Thurgood Marshall School of Law
Texas Southern University
31500 Cleburne Avenue
Houston, TX 77004
(713) 527–7275

Legal Hotline for Older Texans
Texas Legal Services Center
815 Brazos, Suite 1100
Austin, TX 78701
(512) 477–3950
(800) 622–2520

UTAH

State Unit on Aging
Division of Aging and Adult
  Services
Department of Social Services
120 North—200 West
Box 45500
Salt Lake City, UT 84145–0500
(801) 538–3910

Long Term Care Ombudsman
Division of Aging and Adult
  Services
P.O. Box 45500
Salt Lake City, UT 84145–0500
(801) 538–3910
Fax: (801) 538–4062

Other Resources
Utah Legal Services
Senior Citizens Law Center
124 South 400 East
Salt Lake City, UT 84111
(801) 328–8891
(800) 662–4245 (within Utah)

VERMONT

State Unit on Aging
State Department of Aging and
  Disabilities
103 South Main Street
Waterbury, VT 05676
(802) 241–2400

Long Term Care Ombudsman
Vermont Department of Aging
  and Disabilities
103 South Main Street
Waterbury, VT 05676
(802) 241–2400

Other Resources
Vermont Senior Citizens Law Pro-
  ject
Vermont Legal Aid, Inc.
P.O. Box 158
18 Main Street
St. Johnsbury, VT 05819
(802) 748–8721

VIRGIN ISLANDS

State Unit on Aging
Senior Citizen Affairs
Department of Human Services
19 Estate Diamond Fredericksted
St. Croix, VI 00840
(809) 772–4950

VIRGINIA

State Unit on Aging
Department for the Aging
700 East Franklin Street
10th Floor
Richmond, VA 23219–2327
(804) 225–2271
Fax: (804) 371–8381

Long Term Care Ombudsman
Department for the Aging
700 East Franklin Street
10th Floor
Richmond, VA 23219–2327
(804) 225–2271
(800) 552–3402 (within Virginia)

WEST VIRGINIA

State Unit on Aging
Commission on Aging
Holly Grove—State Capitol
Charleston, WV 25305
(304) 348–3317

Long Term Care Ombudsman
Commission on Aging
State Capitol Complex
Charleston, WV 25305
(304) 348–3317

WASHINGTON

State Unit on Aging
Aging and Adult Services Administration
Department of Social and Health Services
P.O. Box 45050
Olympia, WA 98504–5050
(206) 586–3768

Long Term Care Ombudsman
Washington State Long–Term Care Ombudsman
S. King County Multi–Service Center
1505 S. 356th Street
Federal Way, WA 98003
(206) 838–6810
(800) 562–6028

Other Resources
Senior Rights Assistance
Senior Services and Centers
1601 Second Avenue
Seattle, WA 98101
(206) 447–7805

University Legal Assistance Senior Citizens Law Project
Gonzaga University
School of Law
P.O. Box 3520
Spokane, WA 99220
(509) 328–4220

WISCONSIN

State Unit on Aging
Bureau of Aging
Division of Community Services
217 So. Hamilton Street, Suite 300
Madison, WI 53707
(608) 266–2536

Long Term Care Ombudsman
Board on Aging and Long Term Care
214 N. Hamilton Street, Suite 300
Madison, WI 53707
(608) 266–8944
(800) 242–1060

Other Resources
Elder Law Center
Coalition of Wisconsin Aging Groups
1245 East Washington Avenue
Madison, WI 53703
(608) 257–5660

Housing Options for the Elderly Project
Center for Public Representation
121 South Pinckney
Madison, WI 53703
(608) 251–4008

WYOMING

State Unit on Aging
Commission on Aging
Hathaway Building—Room 139
Cheyenne, Wyoming 82002–0710
(307) 777–7986

Long Term Care Ombudsman
P.O. Box 94
953 Water Street
Wheatland, WY 82201
(307) 322–5553

Other Resources
Wyoming Senior Citizens, Inc.
1912 Capitol Ave., Ste. 404
P.O. Box 622
Cheyenne, WY 82003
(307) 632–9067

APPENDIX B

NATIONAL RESOURCES FOR ELDERLAW ATTORNEYS AND THEIR CLIENTS *

G = Government department or agency.

L = National legal organizations.

Administration on Aging G
330 Independence Avenue SW
Washington, DC 20201
(202) 245–0641

The Administration on Aging (AoA), an agency of the Department of Health and Human Services, develops Federal Government programs and coordinates community services for older people.

Aging Network Services
Suite 907
4400 East–West Highway
Bethesda, MD 20814
(301) 657–4329

Aging Network Services is a nationwide for-profit network of private-practice geriatric social workers who serve as care managers for older parents who live apart from their adult children.

Alzheimer's Association
70 East Lake Street
Chicago, IL 60601
(312) 853–3060
INFORMATION AND REFERRAL SERVICE
1–800–621–0379 (toll-free)
1–800–572–6037 (toll-free to residents of Illinois)

The Alzheimer's Association is a voluntary organization that sponsors public education programs and offers supportive services to patients and families who are coping with Alzheimer's disease.

American Association for Geriatric Psychiatry
P.O. Box 376–A

---

* Source: National Institute on Aging,
Resource Directory for Older People (1989).

Greenbelt, MD 20770
(301) 220–0952

The American Association for Geriatric Psychiatry is a professional organization of psychiatrists who have a special interest in the mental health care of older people.

American Association of Homes for the Aging
901 E Street, N.W., Suite 500
Washington, D.C. 20004–2037
(202) 783–2242

The American Association of Homes for the Aging (AAHA) is a professional organization of nonprofit nursing homes, independent housing facilities, continuing care communities, and community service agencies.

American Association of Retired Persons
601 E Street, N.W.
Washington, D.C. 20049
(202) 434–2277

The American Association of Retired Persons (AARP) is a consumer organization that seeks to improve the quality of life for older people.

American Bar Association Commission on the Legal Problems of the Elderly L
1800 M Street NW
Washington, DC 20036
(202) 331–2297

The Commission on the Legal Problems of the Elderly, a program of the American Bar Association, analyzes and responds to the legal needs of older people in the United States.

American Cancer Society
1599 Clifton Road
Atlanta, GA 30329
(404) 320–3333
INFORMATION SERVICE
1–800–227–2345

The American Cancer Society (ACS) is a voluntary organization that funds research to find a cure for cancer and carries out programs to educate the public and health professionals about cancer prevention, detection, treatment, and research.

American Diabetes Association
1660 Duke Street
Alexandria, VA 22314
(703) 549–1500

INFORMATION SERVICE
1–800–232–3472

The American Diabetes Association (ADA) is a voluntary organization that supports research to find a cure for diabetes and seeks to improve the well-being of people with diabetes and their families.

American Geriatrics Society
Suite 400
770 Lexington Avenue
New York, NY 10021
(212) 308–1414

The American Geriatrics Society is a professional organization of physicians and other health care providers who specialize in caring for older people.

American Health Care Association
1201 L Street NW
Washington, DC 20005
(202) 842–4444

The American Health Care Association (AHCA) is a professional organization that represents the interests of licensed nursing homes and long-term care facilities to Congress, federal regulatory agencies, and other professional groups. The Association also provides leadership in dealing with long-term care issues.

American Heart Association
7320 Greenville Avenue
Dallas, TX 75231
(214) 750–5397

The American Heart Association is a voluntary organization that funds research and sponsors public education programs to reduce premature death and disability from heart attack, stroke, and other heart and blood vessel diseases.

American Parkinson's Disease Association
Suite 417
116 John Street
New York, NY 10004
(212) 732–9550
INFORMATION HOTLINE
1–800–223–2732

The American Parkinson's Disease Association is a voluntary organization that funds research to find a cure for Parkinson's disease, educates the public about this illness, and offers assistance to patients and their families.

American Red Cross
17th and D Streets NW
Washington, DC 20006
(202) 737–8300

The American Red Cross offers health education programs (wellness courses and home nursing instruction), health services (screening programs), blood services (collection and processing of blood donations), and disaster relief (health care for illness or injury caused by disaster).

American Society on Aging
Suite 512
833 Market Street
San Francisco, CA 94103
(415) 882–2910

The American Society on Aging is a nonprofit, membership organization that informs the public and health professionals about issues that affect the quality of life for older persons and promotes innovative approaches to meeting the needs of these individuals.

American Society for Geriatric Dentistry
Suite 1616
211 East Chicago Avenue
Chicago, IL 60611
(312) 440–2660

The American Society for Geriatric Dentistry is a professional association of dentists who specialize in providing oral health care to older people.

American Tinnitus Association
P.O. Box 5
Portland, OR 97207
(503) 248–9985

The American Tinnitus Association is a voluntary organization that supports research to find a cure for tinnitus (constant ringing or buzzing in the ears or inside the head) and distributes information to the public about this disorder, which is found most often in people 55 years of age and older.

Arthritis Foundation
1314 Spring Street NW
Atlanta, GA 30309
(404) 872–7100

The Arthritis Foundation is a voluntary organization that supports research to find a cure for all forms of arthritis and distributes information to the public about arthritis and rheumatic diseases.

Association for Gerontology in Higher Education
West Wing 204
600 Maryland Avenue SW
Washington, DC 20024
(202) 484–7505

The Association for Gerontology in Higher Education (AGHE) is a professional organization that includes colleges, universities, and other educational institutions that offer training in the field of gerontology (the study of the biological, clinical, economic, and psychosocial aspects of aging).

Center for Social Gerontology   L
2307 Shelby Ave.
Ann Arbor, MI 48103
(313) 665–1126

Center for the Study of Aging
706 Madison Avenue
Albany, NY 12208
(518) 465–6927

The Center for the Study of Aging is a nonprofit organization that promotes research and training in the field of aging.

Children of Aging Parents
2761 Trenton Road
Levittown, PA 19056
(215) 945–6900

Children of Aging Parents is a nonprofit, self-help organization that provides information and emotional support to caregivers of older persons.

Choice in Dying

200 Varick Street

New York, NY 10014

212–366–5540

Congressional Committee

> **Senate Special Committee on Aging**   G
> Room G–31 Dirksen Senate Office Building
> Washington, DC 20510
> (202) 224–5364

Consumer Information Center   G
P.O. Box 100
Pueblo, CO 81009

The Consumer Information Center, a program of the General Services Administration, helps Federal Government agencies promote and distribute useful information to the general public.

Consumer Product Safety Commission G
Office of Information and Public Affairs
5401 Westbard Avenue
Bethesda, MD 20207
(301) 492–6580
CONSUMER PRODUCT SAFETY HOTLINE
1–800–638–2772
1–800–638–8270 (toll-free TDD outside Maryland)
1–800–492–8104 (toll-free TDD for residents of Maryland)

The Consumer Product Safety Commission (CPSC), an agency of the Federal Government, develops safety standards to protect the public against injury from consumer products, helps consumers evaluate product safety, and promotes research into the causes and prevention of product-related injury.

Disabled American Veterans
P.O. Box 14301
Cincinnati, OH 45250
(606) 441–7300

Disabled American Veterans (DAV) is a private, nonprofit organization that represents veterans with service-connected disabilities and their families.

Elderhostel
Suite 400
80 Boylston Street
Boston, MA 02116
(617) 426–8056

Elderhostel is a nonprofit organization that sponsors educational programs for persons 60 years of age and older.

Federal Council on Aging G
Room 4545 HHS–N
330 Independence Avenue SW
Washington, DC 20201
(202) 245–2451

The Federal Council on Aging, an advisory group authorized by the Older Americans Act of 1965, is selected by the President and the Congress. The 15 members represent a cross-section of rural and urban older Americans, national organizations with an interest in aging, business, labor, and the general public.

Food Research and Action Center L
1875 Connecticut Ave., NW
Suite 540
Washington, DC 20009–5728
(202) 986–2200

Foundation for Hospice and Home Care
519 C Street NE
Washington, DC 20002
(202) 547–7424

The Foundation for Hospice and Home Care is made up of community agencies that provide homemaker-home health services. Professional homemaker-home health aides care for individuals in their own homes in times of illness and stress.

Gray Panthers
1424 16th Street, N.W., Suite 602
Washington, D.C. 20036
(202) 387–3111

The Gray Panthers is an advocacy group that works to eliminate ageism, discrimination against older people on the basis of chronologic age.

Health Care Financing Administration G
6325 Security Boulevard
Baltimore, MD 21207
(301) 594–9086
SECOND SURGICAL OPINION HOTLINE
1–800–638–6833
1–800–492–6603 (toll-free to residents of Maryland)

The Health Care Financing Administration (HCFA) coordinates the Federal Government's participation in Medicare (a health insurance program for persons over 65 years of age and certain disabled persons) and Medicaid (a health insurance program for persons who need financial aid for medical expenses). HCFA also sponsors health care quality assurance programs such as the Second Surgical Opinion Hotline.

Hill–Burton Program G
Health Resources and Services Administration
5600 Fishers Lane
Rockville, MD 20857
(301) 443–5656
HOTLINE
1–800–638–0742
1–800–492–0359 (toll-free to residents of Maryland)

Through the Hill–Burton Program, hospitals and other health care facilities provide free or low-cost medical care to patients who cannot afford to pay.

Huntington's Disease Society of America
6th Floor
140 West 22nd Street
New York, NY 10011
(212) 242–1968
HOTLINE
1–800–345–4372
(212) 242–1968 (residents of New York State)

The Huntington's Disease Society is a voluntary organization that serves patients with Huntington's disease, a hereditary, degenerative neurological disease.

Legal Counsel for the Elderly L
601 E Street N.W.
Washington, D.C. 20049
(202) 434–2196

Legal Services for the Elderly L
3rd Floor
132 West 43rd Street
New York, NY 10036
(212) 391–0120

Legal Services for the Elderly (LSE) is an advisory center for lawyers who specialize in the legal problems of older persons.

Medic Alert Foundation
P.O. Box 1009
Turlock, CA 95381–1009
(209) 668–3333
INFORMATION SERVICE
1–800–344–3226

The Medic Alert Foundation is a nonprofit organization that encourages individuals to carry identification of any medical problems that should be known in an emergency.

Mental Health Law Project
1101 15th Street, NW, Suite 1212
Washington, DC 20005
(202) 467–5730

National Academy of Elder Law Attorneys, Inc. L
655 N. Alvernon Way, Suite 108
Tucson, AZ 85711
(602) 881–4005

445

National Action Forum for Midlife and Older Women
c/o Dr. Jane Porcino
P.O. Box 816
Stony Brook, NY 11790–0609

The National Action Forum for Midlife and Older Women (NA-FOW) serves as a clearinghouse of information dealing with issues of special concern to middle-aged and older women.

National Association of Area Agencies on Aging
1112 16th Street, NW, Suite 100
Washington, DC 20036
(202) 296–8130
ELDERCARE LOCATER 1–800–677–1116

The National Association of Area Agencies on Aging (NAAAA) represents the interests of approximately 650 Area Agencies on Aging across the country. The Association operates a hotline to assist families and friends locate community services for older persons.

National Association for Hispanic Elderly Associacion Nacional Pro Personas Mayores
Suite 270
2727 West Sixth Street
Los Angeles, CA 90057
(213) 487–1922

The National Association for Hispanic Elderly works to ensure that older Hispanic citizens are included in all social service programs for older Americans.

National Association for Home Care
519 C Street NE
Washington, DC 20002
(202) 547–7424

The National Association for Home Care (NAHC) is a professional organization that represents a variety of agencies that provide home care services, including home health agencies, hospice programs, and homemaker/home health aid agencies.

National Association of Meal Programs
204 E Street NE
Washington, DC 20002
(202) 547–6340

The National Association of Meal Programs is an association of professionals and volunteers who provide congregate and home-delivered meals to individuals who are frail, disabled, or homebound.

National Association of Retired Federal Employees
1533 New Hampshire Avenue, NW
Washington, DC 20036
(202) 234–0832

National Association of State Units on Aging
Suite 304
2033 K Street NW
Washington, DC 20006
(202) 785–0707

The National Association of State Units on Aging (NASUA) is a public interest group that provides information, technical assistance, and professional development support to State Units on Aging. This organization is funded by the Administration on Aging of the Department of Health and Human Services and by membership dues.

National Bar Association Black Elderly Legal Assistance Project L
1225 11th Street, NW
Washington, DC 20001
(202) 842–3900

National Caucus and Center on Black Aged
Suite 500
1424 K Street NW
Washington, DC 20005
(202) 637–8400

The National Caucus and Center on Black Aged is a nonprofit organization that works to improve the quality of life for older black Americans.

National Center for Health Statistics   G
3700 East–West Highway
Hyattsville, MD 20782
(301) 436–8500

The National Center for Health Statistics (NCHS), part of the Public Health Service, collects, analyzes, and distributes data on health in the United States.

National Center for State Long Term Care Ombudsman Resources
Suite 304
2033 K Street NW
Washington, DC 20006
(202) 785–1925

The National Center for State Long Term Care Ombudsman Resources was established with funding from the Administration on Aging in 1988 to enhance the skills, knowledge and management capacity of the State Long Term Care Ombudsman Programs. The Center pro-

447

vides national technical assistance, training, and information dissemination, serving as a resource on ombudsman related issues for State Agencies on Aging. The Center is administered by the National Association of State Units on Aging in cooperation with the National Citizens' Coalition for Nursing Home Reform.

National Citizens Coalition for Nursing Home Reform
1224 M Street NW, Suite 301
Washington, DC 20006
(202) 393–2018

The National Citizens Coalition for Nursing Home Reform works to improve the quality of life for nursing home and boarding home residents and to ensure that consumers have a voice in the long-term care system.

National Council on the Aging
Suite 200
409 Third Street SW
Washington, DC 20024
(202) 479–1200

The National Council on the Aging (NCOA), a nonprofit, membership organization for professionals and volunteers, serves as a national resource for information, technical assistance, training, and research relating to the field of aging.

National Council of Senior Citizens
1331 F Street, NW
Washington, DC 20004–1171
(202) 347–8800

The National Council of Senior Citizens, a nonprofit association of clubs, councils, and other community groups, works as an advocate on behalf of older Americans.

National Diabetes Information Clearinghouse   G
Box NDIC
Bethesda, MD 20892
(301) 468–2162

The Clearinghouse, a service of the National Institute of Diabetes and Digestive and Kidney Diseases of the National Institutes of Health, offers information about diabetes to health professionals, patients, and the general public.

National Foundation for Long–Term Health Care
Suite 402
1200 15th Street NW
Washington, DC 20005
(202) 659–3148

The National Foundation for Long–Term Health Care is a private, nonprofit organization that works on behalf of professionals who provide long-term care to older people and chronically ill individuals.

National Health Law Program L
1815 H Street, NW, Suite 705
Washington, DC 20006
(202) 887–5310
and
2639 So. La Cienega Blvd.
Los Angeles, CA 90034
(310) 204–6010

National Hispanic Council on Aging
2713 Ontario Road NW
Washington, DC 20009
(202) 265–1288

The National Hispanic Council on Aging is a private, nonprofit organization that works to promote the well-being of older Hispanic individuals.

National Hospice Organization
Suite 307
1901 North Fort Myer Drive
Arlington, VA 22209
(703) 243–5900

The National Hospice Organization (NHO) promotes quality care for terminally ill patients and provides information about hospice services available in the United States. Hospices provide medical care for dying patients, as well as counseling and supportive services for the patient and family members.

National Indian Council on Aging
P.O. Box 2088
Albuquerque, NM 87103
(505) 242–9505

The National Indian Council on Aging, a nonprofit organization funded by the Administration on Aging, works to ensure that older Indian and Alaskan Native Americans have equal access to quality, comprehensive health care, legal assistance, and social services.

National Institute on Aging G
Public Information Office
Federal Building, Room 6C12
9000 Rockville Pike
Bethesda, MD 20892
(301) 496–1752

449

The National Institute on Aging (NIA), part of the National Institutes of Health, is the Federal Government's principal agency for conducting and supporting biomedical, social, and behavioral research related to the aging process and the diseases and special problems of older individuals.

National Legal Center for the Medically Dependent and Disabled, Inc. L
50 So. Meridian, Suite 605
Indianapolis, IN 46204
(317) 632–6245

National Library of Medicine G
8600 Rockville Pike
Bethesda, MD 20894
(301) 496–5501
MEDLARS SERVICE DESK
1–800–638–8480 (toll-free outside Maryland)
(301) 496–6193 (for residents of Maryland)

The National Library of Medicine (NLM), part of the National Institutes of Health, is the world's largest medical research library, containing more than 3.5 million journals, technical reports, books, photographs, and audiovisual materials covering more than 40 biomedical areas and related subjects.

National Osteoporosis Foundation
Suite 822
1625 I Street NW
Washington, DC 20006
(202) 223–2226

The National Osteoporosis Foundation is a voluntary health agency dedicated to reducing the widespread incidence of osteoporosis, a condition seen most often in older women. Osteoporosis causes bone density to decrease, which produces weakness throughout the skeleton and leads to an increased risk of fractures.

National Pacific/Asian Resource Center on Aging
Suite 410
2033 Sixth Avenue
Seattle, WA 98121–2524
(206) 448–0313

The National Pacific/Asian Resource Center on Aging is a private organization that works to improve the delivery of health care and social services to older members of the Pacific/Asian community.

National Senior Citizens Law Center L
1815 H Street, NW, Suite 700

Washington, DC 20006
(202) 887–5280
and
1052 W. 6th Street
Suite 700
Los Angeles, CA 90017
(213) 482–3550

The National Senior Citizens Law Center (NSCLC) is a public interest law firm that specializes in the legal problems of older people.

National Senior Sports Association
Suite 205
10560 Main Street
Fairfax, VA 22030
(703) 385–7540

The National Senior Sports Association is a nonprofit organization that promotes physical and emotional health through active participation in sports activities.

National Veterans Legal Services Project, Inc. L
2001 S Street, NW
Suite 610
Washington, DC 20009
(202) 265–8305

Older Women's League
666—11th Street, NW, Suite 700
Washington, DC 20001
(202) 783–6686

Pension Rights Center
918—16th Street, NW
Washington, DC 20006
(202) 296–3378

Social Security Administration G
Office of Public Inquiries
6401 Security Boulevard
Baltimore, MD 21235
(301) 594–1234

The Social Security Administration is the Federal agency responsible for the Social Security retirement, survivors, and disability program, as well as the Supplemental Security Income program.

United Parkinson Foundation
360 West Superior Street
Chicago, IL 60610
(312) 664–2344

The United Parkinson Foundation is a nonprofit organization that provides supportive services to patients with Parkinson's disease and their families and funds research to find a cure for this progressive neurological condition.

United Seniors Health Cooperative
Suite 500
1334 G Street NW
Washington, DC 20005
(202) 393–6222

The United Seniors Health Cooperative is a private, nonprofit organization that works to improve the quality and reduce the cost of health care and social services for older adults.

Veterans Administration G

(Department of Veterans Affairs) G
Office of Public Affairs
810 Vermont Avenue NW
Washington, DC 20420
(202) 233–2843

The Veterans Administration, now the Department of Veterans Affairs, is the Federal Government agency that provides benefits to veterans of military service and their dependents.

APPENDIX C

MEDICARE CARRIERS AND INTERMEDIARIES *

Blue Cross Association
Blue Cross and Blue Shield Association
676 North St. Clair Street
Chicago, Illinois 60611

Blue Cross plans
Alabama
Blue Cross and Blue Shield of Alabama
450 Riverchase Parkway East
Birmingham, Alabama 35298

Alaska
See Blue Cross of Washington and Alaska

Arizona
Blue Cross and Blue Shield of Arizona, Inc.
2410 W. Royal Palm Drive
Phoenix, Arizona 85021
Mailing address:
P.O. Box 37700
Phoenix, Arizona 85069

Arkansas
Arkansas Blue Cross and Blue Shield, Inc.
601 Gaines Street
Little Rock, Arkansas 72203

California
Blue Cross of California
21555 Oxnard Street
Woodland Hills, California 91367
Mailing address:
P.O. Box 70000
Van Nuys, California 91570

Colorado
See New Mexico Blue Cross and Blue Shield, Inc.

Connecticut
Blue Cross and Blue Shield of Connecticut, Inc.
370 Bassett Road
North Haven, Connecticut 06473

Delaware
Blue Cross and Blue Shield of Delaware, Inc.
One Brandywine Gateway
P.O. Box 1991
Wilmington, Delaware 19899

District of Columbia
See Blue Cross and Blue Shield of Maryland

Florida
Blue Cross and Blue Shield of Florida, Inc.
532 Riverside Avenue
P.O. Box 1798
Jacksonville, Florida 32231

Georgia
Blue Cross and Blue Shield of Georgia, Inc.
2357 Warm Springs Road
P.O. Box 7368
Columbus, Georgia 31908

Hawaii
See Hawaii Medical Service Association

Idaho
See Blue Cross and Blue Shield of Oregon

Illinois
Health Care Service Corp.
233 North Michigan Avenue
Chicago, Illinois 60601

* Source: Health Care Financing Program Statistics, Medicare and Medicaid Data Book, 1990.

453

APPENDIX C

Indiana
Associated Insurance Companies, Inc.
(d.b.a. Blue Cross and Blue Shield of
Indiana)
120 West Market Street
Indianapolis, Indiana 46204–2805

Iowa
IASD Health Services Corp.
636 Grand Avenue, Station 28
Des Moines, Iowa 50309

Kansas
Blue Cross and Blue Shield of Kansas,
Inc.
1133 Topeka Avenue
P.O. Box 239
Topeka, Kansas 66601

Kentucky
Blue Cross and Blue Shield of Kentucky,
Inc.
9901 Linn Station Road
Louisville, Kentucky 40223

Louisiana
Louisiana Health Service and Indemnity
Company
(d.b.a. Blue Cross of Louisiana)
10225 Florida Boulevard
Baton Rouge, Louisiana 70815–1791
Mailing address:
P.O. Box 95021
Baton Rouge, Louisiana 70895–9021

Maine
Associated Hospital Service of Maine
(d.b.a. Maine Blue Cross and Blue Shield)
110 Free Street
Portland, Maine 04101

Maryland
Blue Cross and Blue Shield of Maryland,
Inc.
P.O. Box 4368
1946 Greenspring Drive
Timonium Industrial Park
Timonium, Maryland 21093

Massachusetts
Blue Cross and Blue Shield of Massachusetts, Inc.
100 Summer Street
Boston, Massachusetts 02106

Michigan
Blue Cross and Blue Shield of Michigan
600 Lafayette East
Detroit, Michigan 48226

Minnesota
Blue Cross and Blue Shield of Minnesota
3535 Blue Cross Road
P.O. Box 64357
St. Paul, Minnesota 55164

Mississippi
Blue Cross and Blue Shield of Mississip-
pi, Inc.
3534 Lakeland Drive
P.O. Box 23035
Jackson, Mississippi 39225–3035

Missouri
Blue Cross and Blue Shield of Missouri
4444 Forest Park
St. Louis, Missouri 63108

Montana
Blue Cross and Blue Shield of Montana
Great Falls Division:
3360 10th Avenue, South
P.O. Box 5004
Great Falls, Montana 59403
Helena Division:
404 Fuller Avenue
P.O. Box 4309
Helena, Montana 59601

Nebraska
Blue Cross and Blue Shield of Nebraska
7621 Mercy Road
Omaha, Nebraska 68124
Mailing address:
P.O. Box 3248
Main Post Office Station
Omaha, Nebraska 68180

Nevada
See Aetna Life and Casualty Company

New Hampshire
New Hampshire–Vermont Health Ser-
vice
Two Pillsbury Street
Concord, New Hampshire 03301

New Jersey
Blue Cross and Blue Shield of New Jersey, Inc.
33 Washington Street
Newark, New Jersey 07102

New Mexico
New Mexico Blue Cross and Blue Shield,
Inc.
12800 Indian School Road, NE.
Albuquerque, New Mexico 87112
Mailing address:
P.O. Box 13597
Albuquerque, New Mexico 87192–3597

MEDICARE CARRIERS AND INTERMEDIARIES

New York
Empire Blue Cross and Blue Shield
622 Third Avenue
New York, New York 10017

North Carolina
Blue Cross and Blue Shield of North
Carolina
P.O. Box 2291
Durham, North Carolina 27702

North Dakota
Blue Cross and Blue Shield of North
Dakota
4510 13th Avenue, SW.
Fargo, North Dakota 58121

Ohio
Community Mutual Insurance Company
Medicare operations:
Randall Building, Holiday Office Park
P.O. Box 145482
801 West Eighth Street
Cincinnati, Ohio 45250–5482

Oklahoma
Group Health Service of Oklahoma, Inc.
1215 South Boulder Avenue
Tulsa, Oklahoma 74119

Oregon
Blue Cross and Blue Shield of Oregon
100 SW. Market Street
Portland, Oregon 97201
Mailing address:
P.O. Box 8110
Portland, Oregon 97207–8110

Pennsylvania
Independence Blue Cross
1901 Market Street
Philadelphia, Pennsylvania 19103
Blue Cross of Western Pennsylvania
Fifth Avenue Place
Pittsburgh, Pennsylvania 15222

Rhode Island
Blue Cross and Blue Shield of Rhode
Island
444 Westminster Mall
Providence, Rhode Island 02901

South Carolina
Blue Cross and Blue Shield of South Car-
olina
Fontaine Business Center
300 Arbor Lake Drive, Suite 1300
Columbia, South Carolina 29223

South Dakota
See IASD Health Services Corp.

Tennessee
Blue Cross and Blue Shield of Tennessee
801 Pine Street
Chattanooga, Tennessee 37402

Texas
Blue Cross and Blue Shield of Texas, Inc.
901 South Central Expressway
Richardson, Texas 75080
Mailing address:
P.O. Box 660156
Dallas, Texas 75266–0156

Utah
Blue Cross and Blue Shield of Utah
2455 Parley's Way
P.O. Box 30270
Salt Lake City, Utah 84130

Vermont
See New Hampshire–Vermont Health
Service

Virginia
Blue Cross and Blue Shield of Virginia
602 South Jefferson Street
P.O. Box 12201
Roanoke, Virginia 24023–2201

Washington
Blue Cross of Washington and Alaska
7001–220th SW.
Mountlake Terrace, Washington 98043
Mailing address:
P.O. Box 2847
Seattle, Washington 98111–2847

West Virginia
Blue Cross and Blue Shield of West Vir-
ginia, Inc.
P.O. Box 231
Charleston, West Virginia 25321

Wisconsin
Blue Cross and Blue Shield United of
Wisconsin
1515 N. River Center Drive
Milwaukee, Wisconsin 53212
Mailing address:
P.O. Box 2025
Milwaukee, Wisconsin 53212–2025

Wyoming
Blue Cross and Blue Shield of Wyoming
4000 House Avenue
P.O. Box 2266
Cheyenne, Wyoming 82001

Blue Shield plans

Alabama

Blue Cross and Blue Shield of Alabama
450 Riverchase Parkway East
Birmingham, Alabama 35298

Alaska

See Aetna Life and Casualty Company

Arizona

See Aetna Life and Casualty Company

Arkansas

Arkansas Blue Cross and Blue Shield,
Inc.
601 Gaines Street
Little Rock, Arkansas 72203

California

California Physicians' Service
(d.b.a. Blue Shield of California)
1 Beach Street
San Francisco, California 94133
Mailing address:
P.O. Box 7013
San Francisco, California 94120

Colorado

Rocky Mountain Hospital and Medical
Service
(d.b.a. Blue Cross and Blue Shield of Colorado)
700 Broadway
Denver, Colorado 80273

Connecticut

See The Travelers Insurance Company

Delaware

See Pennsylvania Blue Shield

District of Columbia

See Pennsylvania Blue Shield

Florida

Blue Cross and Blue Shield of Florida,
Inc.
532 Riverside Avenue
P.O. Box 1798
Jacksonville, Florida 32231

Georgia

See Aetna Life and Casualty Company

Hawaii

See Aetna Life and Casualty Company

Idaho

See EQUICOR, Inc.

Illinois

Health Care Service Corporation
233 North Michigan Avenue
Chicago, Illinois 60601

Indiana

Associated Insurance Companies, Inc.
(d.b.a. Blue Cross and Blue Shield of
Indiana)
120 West Market Street
Indianapolis, Indiana 46204–0452

Iowa

IASD Health Services Corp.
636 Grand Avenue, Station 28
Des Moines, Iowa 50309

Kansas

Blue Cross and Blue Shield of Kansas,
Inc.
1133 Topeka Avenue
P.O. Box 239
Topeka, Kansas 66601

Kentucky

Blue Cross and Blue Shield of Kentucky,
Inc.
100 East Vine Street
6th Floor
Lexington, Kentucky 40507

Louisiana

See Arkansas Blue Cross and Blue
Shield, Inc.

Maine

See Blue Cross and Blue Shield of Massachusetts, Inc.

Maryland

Blue Cross and Blue Shield of Maryland,
Inc.
P.O. Box 4368
1946 Greenspring Drive
Timonium Industrial Park
Timonium, Maryland 21093

Massachusetts

Blue Cross and Blue Shield of Massachusetts, Inc.
100 Summer Street
Boston, Massachusetts 02106

MEDICARE CARRIERS AND INTERMEDIARIES

Michigan
Blue Cross and Blue Shield of Michigan
600 Lafayette East
Detroit, Michigan 48226

Minnesota
Blue Cross and Blue Shield of Minnesota
Waterview Office Tower
1200 Yankee Doodle Road
Eagan, Minnesota 55122
  Mailing address:
  P.O. Box 64357
  St. Paul, Minnesota 55164

Mississippi
See The Travelers Insurance Company

Missouri
Blue Cross and Blue Shield of Kansas
  City
2301 Main
P.O. Box 419840
Kansas City, Missouri 64141

Montana
Blue Cross and Blue Shield of Montana,
  Inc.
P.O. Box 4309
404 Fuller Avenue
Helena, Montana 59601

Nebraska
See Blue Cross and Blue Shield of Kansas, Inc.

Nevada
See Aetna Life and Casualty Company

New Hampshire
See Blue Cross and Blue Shield of Massachusetts

New Jersey
See Pennsylvania Blue Shield

New Mexico
See Aetna Life and Casualty Company
New York
Blue Shield of Western New York, Inc.
275 Oak Street
P.O. Box 356
Buffalo, New York 14240–0356

Empire Blue Cross and Blue Shield
622 Third Avenue
New York, New York 10017

North Dakota
Blue Cross and Blue Shield of North
  Dakota
4510 13th Avenue, SW.
Fargo, North Dakota 58121

Ohio
See Nationwide Mutual Insurance Company

Oklahoma
See Aetna Life and Casualty Company

Oregon
See Aetna Life and Casualty Company

Pennsylvania
Pennsylvania Blue Shield
P.O. Box 89065
Camp Hill, Pennsylvania 17089–0065

Puerto Rico
Seguros de Servicio de Salud de Puerto
  Rico, Inc.
G.P.O. Box 3628
San Juan, Puerto Rico 00936–3628

Rhode Island
Blue Cross and Blue Shield of Rhode
  Island
444 Westminster Mall
Providence, Rhode Island 02901

South Carolina
Blue Cross and Blue Shield of South Car-
  olina, Medicare
Fontaine Business Center
300 Arbor Lake Drive
Suite 1300
Columbia, South Carolina 29223

South Dakota
See Blue Shield of North Dakota

Tennessee
See EQUICOR, Inc.

Texas
Blue Cross and Blue Shield of Texas, Inc.
901 South Central Expressway
Richardson, Texas 75080

Utah
Blue Cross and Blue Shield of Utah
2455 Parley's Way
P.O. Box 30270, Medicare B
Salt Lake City, Utah 84130

APPENDIX C

Vermont
 See Blue Cross and Blue Shield of Massachusetts

Virginia
 See The Travelers Insurance Company

Washington
 Washington Physicians' Service
 4th & Battery Building, 6th Floor
 2401 4th Avenue
 Seattle, Washington 98121

West Virginia
 See Nationwide Mutual Insurance Company

Wisconsin
 See Wisconsin Physicians' Service Insurance Corporation

Wyoming
 See EQUICOR, Inc.

Commercial, independent, State, and other
 Aetna Life and Casualty Company
 151 Farmington Avenue
 Hartford, Connecticut 06156

 Blue Cross and Blue Shield of Missouri
 4444 Forest Park
 St. Louis, Missouri 63108

 Cooperativa de Seguros de Vida de Puerto Rico
 G.P.O. Box 3428
 San Juan, Puerto Rico 00936–3428

 EQUICOR, Inc.
 195 Broadway, 11th Floor
 New York, New York 10007

General American Life Insurance Company
13045 Tesson Ferry Road
St. Louis County, Missouri 63128
 Mailing address:
 P.O. Box 505
 St. Louis, Missouri 63166

Group Health Incorporated
88 West End Avenue
New York, New York 10023

Hawaii Medical Service Association
Medicare Administration
818 Keeaumoku
P.O. Box 860
Honolulu, Hawaii 96808

Mutual of Omaha Insurance Company
P.O. Box 1602
Omaha, Nebraska 68101

Nationwide Mutual Insurance Company
Three Nationwide Plaza
P.O. Box 16788 or P.O. Box 16781
Columbus, Ohio 43216

Transamerica Occidental Life Insurance Company
1149 S. Broadway, 3rd Floor
Los Angeles, California 90015
 Mailing address:
 P.O. Box 54905
 Los Angeles, California 90054–0905

The Travelers Insurance Company
2 Riverview Square East
Hartford, Connecticut 06118

Wisconsin Physicians' Service Insurance Corporation
P.O. Box 1787
Madison, Wisconsin 53701

Railroad Retirement Board
Attention: BRCMPS
844 Rush Street
Chicago, Illinois 60611

APPENDIX D
MEDICAID AGENCIES AND FISCAL AGENTS *

Single State agencies and State medical assistance units

Alabama (Region IV):
Single State agency and medical assistance unit:
Alabama Medicaid Agency
2500 Fairlane Drive
Montgomery, Alabama 36130
205 277-2710

Alaska (Region X):
Single State agency:
Alaska Department of Health and Social Services
P.O. Box H-01
Juneau, Alaska 99811-0601
907 465-3355

Medical assistance unit:
Division of Medical Assistance
Alaska Department of Health and Social Services
P.O. Box H-07
Juneau, Alaska 99811-0601

Arizona (Region IX):
Single State agency and medical assistance unit:
Arizona Health Care Cost Containment System Administration
801 East Jefferson Street
Phoenix, Arizona 85034
602 234-3655

Arkansas (Region VI):
Single State agency:
Arkansas Department of Human Services
Seventh and Main Streets
P.O. Box 1437
Little Rock, Arkansas 72203
501 371-1001

Medical assistance unit:
Office of Medical Services
Arkansas Division of Economic and Medical Services
P.O. Box 1437
Little Rock, Arkansas 72203
501 371-1806

California (Region IX):
Single State agency:
California State Department of Health Services
714 P Street, Room 1253
Sacramento, California 95814
916 445-1248

Medical assistance unit:
California State Department of Health Services
714 P Street, Room 1253
Sacramento, California 95814
916 322-5824

Colorado (Region VII):
Single State agency:
Colorado Department of Social Services
P.O. Box 181000
Denver, Colorado 80218-0899
303 294-5800

Medical assistance unit:
Colorado Department of Social Services
P.O. Box 181000
Denver, Colorado 80218-0899
303 294-5901

Connecticut (Region I):
Single State agency:
Connecticut Department of Income Maintenance
110 Bartholomew Avenue
Hartford, Connecticut 06106
203 566-2008

Medical assistance unit:
Medical Care Administration
Connecticut Department of Income Maintenance
110 Bartholomew Avenue
Hartford, Connecticut 06106
203 566-2934

* Source: Health Care Financing Program Statistics, Medicare and Medicaid Data Book, 1990.

APPENDIX D

Delaware (Region III):
Single State agency:
Delaware Department of Health and
Social Services
Administration Building
Delaware State Hospital
P.O. Box 906
New Castle, Delaware 19720
302 421–6705

Medical assistance unit:
Medical Assistance Services
Delaware Department of Health and
Social Services
Delaware State Hospital
P.O. Box 906
New Castle, Delaware 19720
302 421–6139

District of Columbia (Region III):
Single State agency:
Department of Human Services
801 North Capital Street
Room 700
Washington, D.C. 20002
202 727–0450

Medical assistance unit:
Office of Health Care Financing/Office
of the Controller
D.C. Department of Human Services
1331 H Street, NW.
Room 500
Washington, D.C. 20005
202 727–0735

Florida (Region IV):
Single State agency:
Florida Department of Health and Rehabilitative Services
1317 Winewood Boulevard
Tallahassee, Florida 32301
904 488–7721

Medical assistance unit:
Florida Department of Health and Rehabilitative Services
1317 Winewood Boulevard
Building 6, Room 233
Tallahassee, Florida 32301
904 488–3560

Georgia (Region IV):
Single State agency and medical assistance unit:
Georgia Department of Medical Assistance
2 Martin Luther King Drive
1220 West Tower
Atlanta, Georgia 30334
404 656–4479

Guam (Region IX):
Single State agency and medical assis-
tance unit:
Department of Public Health and So-
cial Services
P.O. Box 2816
Agana, Guam 96910
671 734–2083

Hawaii (Region IX):
Single State agency:
Hawaii Department of Social Services
and Housing
P.O. Box 339
Honolulu, Hawaii 96809
808 548–6260

Medical assistance unit:
Health Care Administration Division
Department of Social Services and
Housing
P.O. Box 339
Honolulu, Hawaii 96809
808 548–3855

Idaho (Region X):
Single State agency:
Idaho Department of Health and Wel-
fare
Statehouse
Boise, Idaho 83720
208 334–5500

Medical assistance unit:
Bureau of Medical Assistance
Idaho Department of Health and Wel-
fare
450 W. State Street
Statehouse
Boise, Idaho 83720
208 334–5794

MEDICAID AGENCIES AND FISCAL AGENTS

Illinois (Region V):
Single State agency:
Illinois Department of Public Aid
Jesse B. Harris Building II
2nd Floor
100 South Grand Avenue, East
Springfield, Illinois 62762
217 782–6716

Medical assistance unit:
Illinois Department of Public Aid
628 East Adams Street
3rd Floor
Springfield, Illinois 62761
217 782–2570

Indiana (Region V):
Single State agency:
Indiana Department of Public Welfare
State Office Building
100 North Senate Avenue
Room 701
Indianapolis, Indiana 46204
317 232–4705

Medical assistance unit:
Indiana Department of Public Welfare
100 North Senate Avenue
State Office Building, Room 702
Indianapolis, Indiana 46204
317 232–4324

Iowa (Region VII):
Single State agency:
Iowa Department of Human Services
Hoover State Office Building
5th Floor
Des Moines, Iowa 50319
515 281–5452

Medical assistance unit:
Bureau of Medical Services
Iowa Department of Human Services
Hoover State Office Building
5th Floor
Des Moines, Iowa 50319
515 281–8794

Kansas (Region VII):
Single State agency:
Kansas Department of Social and Rehabilitation Services
State Office Building, 6th Floor
Room 628–S
Topeka, Kansas 66612
913 296–3271

Medical assistance unit:
Kansas Department of Social and Rehabilitation Services
State Office Building, 6th Floor
Room 628–S
Topeka, Kansas 66612
913 296–3981

Kentucky (Region IV):
Single State agency and medical assistance unit:
Kentucky Department for Medicaid Services
CHR Building
275 East Main Street
Frankfort, Kentucky 40621
502 564–4321

Louisiana (Region VI):
Single State agency:
Louisiana Department of Health and Human Resources
P.O. Box 3776
Baton Rouge, Louisiana 70821
504 342–6711

Medical assistance unit:
Medical Assistance Programs
Louisiana Department of Health and Human Resources
P.O. Box 44065
Baton Rouge, Louisiana 70804
504 342–3956

Maine (Region I):
Single State agency:
Maine Department of Human Services
221 State Street
Statehouse, Station II
Augusta, Maine 04333
207 289–2736

Medical assistance unit:
Bureau of Medical Services
Whitten Road
Statehouse, Station II
Augusta, Maine 04333
207 289–2674

Maryland (Region III):
Single State agency:
Maryland Department of Health and Mental Hygiene
Herbert R. O'Connor Building
201 West Preston Street
Baltimore, Maryland 21201
301 225–6500

Medical assistance unit:
Maryland Department of Health and
Mental Hygiene
Herbert R. O'Connor Building
201 West Preston Street
Room 524
Baltimore, Maryland 21201
301 225–6535

Massachusetts (Region I):
Single State agency:
Massachusetts Department of Public
Welfare
180 Tremont Street
Boston, Massachusetts 02111
617 574–0200

Massachusetts Commission for the Blind
110 Tremont Street
Boston, Massachusetts 02108
617 727–5550

Medical assistance unit:
Massachusetts Department of Public
Welfare
180 Tremont Street
Boston, Massachusetts 02111
617 574–0205

Medical assistance:
Massachusetts Commission for the
Blind
110 Tremont Street
Boston, Massachusetts 02108
617 727–5550

Michigan (Region V):
Single State agency:
Michigan Department of Social Servic-
es
300 South Capitol Avenue
P.O. Box 30037
Lansing, Michigan 48909
517 373–2000

Medical assistance unit:
Michigan Department of Social Services
921 West Holmes
P.O. Box 30037
Lansing, Michigan 48909
517 334–7262

Minnesota (Region V):
Single State agency:
Minnesota Department of Human Services
Centennial Office Building
4th Floor
658 Cedar Street
Saint Paul, Minnesota 55155
612 296–2701

Medical assistance unit:
Bureau of Income Maintenance
Minnesota Department of Public Wel-
fare
Space Center Building, 1st Floor
444 Lafayette Road
Saint Paul, Minnesota 55101
612 296–2766

Mississippi (Region IV):
Single State agency and medical assis-
tance unit:
Division of Medicaid
Office of the Governor
4785 1–55 North
P.O. Box 16786
Jackson, Mississippi 39236–0786
601 981–4507

Missouri (Region VII):
Single State agency:
Missouri Department of Social Servic-
es
Broadway State Office Building
Jefferson City, Missouri 65102
314 751–4815

Medical assistance unit:
Division of Medical Services
Missouri Department of Social Servic-
es
308 East High Street
P.O. Box 6500
Jefferson City, Missouri 65103
314 751–6922

Montana (Region VII):
Single State agency:
Montana Department of Social and Re-
habilitative Services
P.O. Box 4210
Helena, Montana 59604
406 444–5622

MEDICAID AGENCIES AND FISCAL AGENTS

Medical assistance unit:
Economic Assistance Division
Montana Department of Social and Rehabilitative Services
P.O. Box 4210
Helena, Montana 59604
406 444-4540

Nebraska (Region VII):
Single State agency:
Nebraska Department of Social Services
301 Centennial Mall South
5th Floor
Lincoln, Nebraska 68509
402 471-3121

Medical assistance unit:
Nebraska Department of Social Services
301 Centennial Mall South
5th Floor
Lincoln, Nebraska 68509
402 471-9330

Nevada (Region IX):
Single State agency:
Nevada Department of Human Resources
Kinkead Building—Capitol Complex
505 East King Street
Carson City, Nevada 89710
702 885-4730

Medical assistance unit:
Welfare Division
Department of Human Resources
Capitol Complex
2527 North Carson Street
Carson City, Nevada 89710
702 885-4698

New Hampshire (Region I):
Single State agency:
New Hampshire Department of Health and Human Services
6 Hazen Drive
Concord, New Hampshire 03301-6521
603 271-4331

Medical assistance unit:
Office of Medical Services
New Hampshire Division of Health and Human Services
6 Hazen Drive
Concord, New Hampshire 03301-6521
603 271-4353

New Jersey (Region II):
Single State agency:
New Jersey Department of Human Services
Capitol Place One
222 South Warren Street
Trenton, New Jersey 08625
609 292-3717

Medical assistance unit:
Division of Medical Assistance and Health Services
New Jersey Department of Human Services
Building No. 7
Quakerbridge Plaza, CN 712
Trenton, New Jersey 08625
609 588-2600

New Mexico (Region VI):
Single State agency:
New Mexico Department of Human Services
P.O. Box 2348
Santa Fe, New Mexico 87503-2348
505 827-4072

Medical assistance unit:
Medical Assistance Division
New Mexico Department of Human Services
P.O. Box 2348
Santa Fe, New Mexico 87503-2348
505 827-4315

New York (Region II):
Single State agency:
New York State Department of Social Services
Ten Eyck Office Building
40 North Pearl Street
Albany, New York 12243
518 474-9475

Medical assistance unit:
Division of Medical Assistance
New York State Department of Social Services
40 North Pearl Street
Albany, New York 12243
518 474-9132

North Carolina (Region IV):
Single State agency:
North Carolina Department of Human Resources
325 North Salisbury Street
Raleigh, North Carolina 27611
919 733-4534

Medical assistance unit:
Division of Medical Assistance
North Carolina Department of Human Resources
1985 Umstead Drive
Raleigh, North Carolina 27603
919 733–2060

North Dakota (Region VIII):
Single State agency:
North Dakota Department of Human Services
State Capitol Building
Bismarck, North Dakota 58505
701 224–2310

Medical assistance unit:
North Dakota Department of Human Services
State Capitol Building
Bismarck, North Dakota 58505
701 224–2321

Ohio (Region V):
Single State agency:
Ohio Department of Human Services
30 East Broad Street, 32nd Floor
Columbus, Ohio 43266–0423
614 466–6282

Medical assistance unit:
Ohio Department of Human Services
30 East Broad Street, 31st Floor
Columbus, Ohio 43266–0423
614 466–3196

Oklahoma (Region VI):
Single State agency:
Oklahoma Department of Human Services
P.O. Box 25352
Oklahoma City, Oklahoma 73125
405 521–3646

Medical assistance unit:
Medical Services Division
Oklahoma Department of Human Services
P.O. Box 25352
Oklahoma City, Oklahoma 73125
405 557–2540

Oregon (Region X):
Single State agency:
Oregon Department of Human Resources
318 Public Service Building
Salem, Oregon 97310
503 378–3034

Medical assistance unit:
Adult and Family Services Division
Oregon Department of Human Resources
203 Public Service Building
Salem, Oregon 97310
503 378–2263

Pennsylvania (Region III):
Single State agency:
Pennsylvania State Department of Public Welfare
Health and Welfare Building
Room 333
Harrisburg, Pennsylvania 17120
717 787–2600

Medical assistance unit:
Pennsylvania State Department of Public Welfare
Health and Welfare Building
Room 515
Harrisburg, Pennsylvania 17120
717 787–1870

Puerto Rico (Region II):
Single State agency:
Puerto Rico Department of Health
P.O. Box 70184
San Juan, Puerto Rico 00936
809 751–8259

Medical assistance unit:
Health Economy Office
Department of Health
P.O. Box 9342
San Juan, Puerto Rico 00936
809 765–9941

Rhode Island (Region I):
Single State agency:
Rhode Island Department of Human Services
Aime J. Forand Building
600 New London Avenue
Cranston, Rhode Island 02920
401 464–2121

Medical assistance unit:
Rhode Island Department of Human Services
Aime J. Forand Building
600 New London Avenue
Cranston, Rhode Island 02920
401 464–3575

South Carolina (Region IV):
Single State agency:
South Carolina State Health and Human Services Finance Commission
P.O. Box 8206
Columbus, South Carolina 29202–8206
803 253–6100

Medical assistance unit:
Bureau of Health Services
South Carolina State Health and Human Services Finance Commission
P.O. Box 8206
Columbus, South Carolina 29202–8206
803 253–6119

South Dakota (Region VIII):
Single State agency:
South Dakota Department of Social Services
Kneip Building
700 North Illinois Street
Pierre, South Dakota 57501
605 773–3165

Medical assistance unit:
Office of Medical Services
South Dakota Department of Social Services
Kneip Building
700 North Illinois Street
Pierre, South Dakota 57501
605 773–3495

Tennessee (Region IV):
Single State agency:
Tennessee Department of Health and Environment
344 Cordell Hull Building
Nashville, Tennessee 37219
615 741–0213

Medical assistance unit:
Bureau of Medicaid
Tennessee Department of Health and Environment
729 Church Street
Nashville, Tennessee 37219
615 741–0213

Texas (Region VI):
Single State agency:
Texas Department of Human Services
P.O. Box 2960
Austin, Texas 78769
512 450–3030

Medical assistance unit:
Texas Department of Human Services
P.O. Box 2960
Austin, Texas 78769
512 450–3050

Utah (Region VIII):
Single State agency:
Utah Department of Health
P.O. Box 16700
Salt Lake City, Utah 84116–0700
801 538–6111

Medical assistance unit:
Division of Health Care Financing
Utah Department of Health
P.O. Box 16580
Salt Lake City, Utah 84116–0580
801 538–6151

Vermont (Region I):
Single State agency:
Vermont Department of Social Welfare
Agency of Human Services
103 South Main Street
Waterbury, Vermont 05676
802 241–2220

Medical assistance unit:
Division of Medical Services
Vermont Department of Social Welfare
Agency of Human Services
103 South Main Street
Waterbury, Vermont 05676
802 241–2880

Virgin Islands (Region II):
Single State agency:
Virgin Islands Department of Health
P.O. Box 7309
Charlotte Amalie
St. Thomas, Virgin Islands 00801
809 774–0117

Medical assistance unit:
Bureau of Health Insurance and Medical Assistance
Virgin Islands Department of Health
P.O. Box 7309
Charlotte Amalie
St. Thomas, Virgin Islands 00801
809 773–2150

Virginia (Region III):
Single State agency and medical assistance unit:
Virginia Department of Medical Assistance Services
600 East Broad Street, Suite 1300
Richmond, Virginia 23219
804 786–7933

Washington (Region X):
Single State agency and medical assistance unit:
Division of Medical Assistance
Washington Department of Social and Health Services
Mail Stop HB–41
Olympia, Washington 98504
206 753–1777

West Virginia (Region III):
Single State agency and medical assistance unit:
West Virginia Department of Human Services
1900 Washington Street, East
Charleston, West Virginia 25305
304 348–8990

Wisconsin (Region V):
Single State agency:
Wisconsin Department of Health and Social Services
1 West Wilson Street, Room 650
P.O. Box 7850
Madison, Wisconsin 53702
608 266–3681

Medical assistance unit:
Bureau of Health Care Financing
Wisconsin Department of Health and Social Services
1 West Wilson Street, Room 250
P.O. Box 309
Madison, Wisconsin 53701
608 266–2522

Wyoming (Region VIII):
Single State agency:
Wyoming Department of Health and Social Services
Hathaway Building
Cheyenne, Wyoming 82002
307 777–7121

Medical assistance unit:
Medical Assistance Services
Division of Health and Social Services
Hathaway Building, Room 450
Cheyenne, Wyoming 82002
307 777–7531

TABLE OF WEST'S® KEY NUMBERS

Tables

TABLE OF WEST KEY NUMBERS

TABLE OF WEST KEY NUMBERS

TABLE OF STATUTES

TABLE OF STATUTES

TABLE OF STATUTES

TABLE OF STATUTES

TABLE OF STATUTES

TABLE OF STATUTES

477

TABLE OF STATUTES

TABLE OF STATUTES

TABLE OF STATUTES

TABLE OF STATUTES

TABLE OF STATUTES

TABLE OF STATUTES

TABLE OF STATUTES

TABLE OF STATUTES

TABLE OF STATUTES

TABLE OF STATUTES

TABLE OF STATUTES

TABLE OF STATUTES

494

TABLE OF STATUTES

TABLE OF STATUTES

TABLE OF STATUTES

499

TABLE OF STATUTES

TABLE OF STATUTES

TABLE OF STATUTES

TABLE OF STATUTES

TABLE OF RULES AND REGULATIONS

FEDERAL RULES OF CIVIL PROCEDURE

Rule	This Work Sec.	Note
4(d)(4)	16.49	2
12(a)	16.49	6
23	3.47	

RULES OF PRACTICE AND PROCEDURE OF THE UNITED STATES COURT OF VETERANS APPEALS

Rule	This Work Sec.	Note
3	21.81	8
3(a)	21.81	1
3(b)	21.81	2
3(c)	21.81	
3(e)	21.81	6
4	21.81	4
	21.81	7
6	21.82	1
10	21.82	2
11(a)	21.82	3
12(b)	21.82	4
21	21.78	3
24	21.81	6
25	21.82	1
26(a)	21.82	1
33(a)	21.83	1
34(a)	21.83	2
46(a)(1)	21.84	1
46(b)	21.84	2
46(e)(1)—(e)(3)	21.84	3

TREASURY REGULATIONS

Sec.	This Work Sec.	Note
1.151–1(c)(2)	24.1	1
1.213–1(e)	24.9	2
1.213–1(e)(1)(iii)	24.9	4
	24.9	5
	24.9	6
1.213–1(e)(1)(iv)	24.9	7
	24.9	8
1.213–1(e)(1)(v)	24.9	9
	24.9	10
1.213–1(e)(2)	24.9	3
1.401(a)–20	23.19	3
1.461–1(a)(1)	22.46	1

TREASURY REGULATIONS

Sec.	This Work Sec.	Note
1.1015–4(a)	22.35	6
1.1015–4(a)(2)	22.35	7

CODE OF FEDERAL REGULATIONS

Tit.	This Work Sec.	Note
3, Pt. 179	3.1	6
3, Pt. 321	3.31	7
4, § 813.107(b)	19.7	4
5, § 831.101 et seq.	20.1	
	20.1	1
5, § 831.104	20.18	4
5, § 831.108	20.5	2
5, § 831.109	20.19	2
5, § 831.110	20.19	3
5, §§ 831.301–831.303	20.3	1
5, § 831.302	20.3	2
5, §§ 831.401–831.402	20.3	3
5, § 831.501	20.18	1
	20.18	2
	20.18	5
5, § 831.502(a)	20.11	2
5, § 831.502(b)	20.18	6
5, § 831.502(c)	20.18	8
5, § 831.504	20.5	2
5, § 831.618	20.13	1
	20.14	2
5, § 831.619	20.18	3
5, § 831.622	20.14	5
5, §§ 831.2002–831.2010	20.5	3
5, § 831.2003	20.5	4
5, §§ 838.101–838.1018	20.17	10
5, § 841.202	20.18	4
5, § 841.303(a)	20.18	1
5, § 841.304(a)	20.18	2
5, § 841.305	20.19	2
5, § 841.306	20.19	2
5, § 841.401 et seq.	20.1	
	20.1	2
5, § 842.104	20.1	3
5, § 842.602	20.13	1
5, § 843.103	20.18	3
5, § 843.302	20.18	3
5, § 844.102	20.11	2
5, § 844.104	20.19	3
5, § 844.201	20.18	5
5, § 844.201(b)	20.10	3

TABLE OF RULES AND REGULATIONS

TABLE OF RULES AND REGULATIONS

TABLE OF RULES AND REGULATIONS

TABLE OF RULES AND REGULATIONS

TABLE OF RULES AND REGULATIONS

TABLE OF RULES AND REGULATIONS

511

TABLE OF RULES AND REGULATIONS

TABLE OF RULES AND REGULATIONS

TABLE OF RULES AND REGULATIONS

TABLE OF RULES AND REGULATIONS

TABLE OF RULES AND REGULATIONS

TABLE OF RULES AND REGULATIONS

518

TABLE OF RULES AND REGULATIONS

TABLE OF RULES AND REGULATIONS

*

521

TABLE OF CASES

A

D

E

I

M

INDEX

References are to Sections

AARP
American Association of Retired Persons, generally, this index

ABILITY TO PAY
Veterans, medical care and treatment, § 21.47

ABUSE
Generally, § 9.6
Drug Abuse, generally, this index
Guardian and ward, §§ 9.23, 9.27
Nursing homes, patients bill of rights, §§ 12.6, 12.7

ACCESSIBILITY
Attorneys, offices and services, § 2.1
Commercial facilities, § 4.62 et seq.
Labor and employment, § 4.61 et seq.
Multifamily dwellings, § 4.43
New construction, § 4.63
Private clubs, exemptions, § 4.62
Public accommodations, §§ 4.61, 4.63
Public entities, § 4.62
Transportation, public and private, § 4.63

ACCIDENT AND HEALTH INSURANCE
Consumer fraud, §§ 7.21, 7.22
Group health plan, Medicare,
    Part B, premium increases for delayed enrollments, exemptions, § 10.21
    Secondary payer, §§ 10.71, 10.72
Long-Term Care, this index
Medigap Insurance, generally, this index

ACCOUNTS AND ACCOUNTING
Guardian and Ward, this index
Nursing homes, patients bill of rights, §§ 12.6, 12.7

ACQUIRED IMMUNE DEFICIENCY SYNDROME (AIDS)
Discrimination, §§ 4.12, 4.62

ACTIONS AND PROCEEDINGS
Age discrimination, enforcement, §§ 3.19 et seq., 3.46 et seq.
    Age Discrimination Act of 1975, this index
    Age Discrimination in Employment Act of 1967, this index
    Consumer credit, § 5.11 et seq.
    Limitation of Actions, this index
Breach of warranty, federal law, § 6.21 et seq.
Class Actions, generally, this index

INDEX

INDEX

547

AGE
Defined, § 1.1

AGE DISCRIMINATION
Generally, § 3.1 et seq.
Actions and Proceedings, this index
Administrative Law and Procedure, this index
Attorney Fees, this index
Consumer credit. Equal Credit Opportunity Act, generally, this index
Consumer Fraud, generally, this index
Costs, this index
Exemplary Damages, this index
Federally assisted programs, § 3.11 et seq.
Labor and employment, § 3.1 et seq.
Age Discrimination Act of 1975, generally, this index
Age Discrimination in Employment Act of 1967, generally, this index
Limitation of Actions, this index
Social attitudes, § 1.2

AGE DISCRIMINATION ACT OF 1975
Generally, § 3.11 et seq.
Actions and proceedings, § 3.19 et seq.
Attorney general, § 3.19
Burden of proof, § 3.21
Limitation of actions, § 3.22
Private right of action, § 3.20
Burden of proof, § 3.21
Compliance, § 3.18
Defenses and exceptions, § 3.15 et seq.
Enforcement, § 3.18 et seq.
Exemptions, §§ 3.13, 3.14
Limitation of actions, § 3.22
Private right of action, § 3.20
Remedies, § 3.23

AGE DISCRIMINATION IN EMPLOYMENT ACT OF 1967
Generally, § 3.31 et seq.
Actions and proceedings, § 3.46 et seq.
Attorney general, § 3.19
Burden of proof, generally, post
Limitation of actions, generally, post
Private right of action, generally, post
Application of law, § 3.39 et seq.
Attorney fees and costs, § 3.70
Back pay, § 3.67
Burden of proof, § 3.56 et seq.
Disparate impact, statistical proof, § 3.58
Disparate treatment, § 3.57
Class actions, § 3.47
Damages, § 3.68
Defenses and exceptions, § 3.59 et seq.
Employer, defined, § 3.40
Enforcement, § 3.31
Equitable relief, § 3.69
Evidence. Burden of proof, generally, ante
Exemplary damages, § 3.68
Federal employees, § 3.33
Jury, § 3.48
Limitation of actions,
Equal employment opportunity commission, filing charge, § 3.52 et seq.
Private right of action, § 3.49

INDEX

549

INDEX

ASSAULT AND BATTERY
Medical care and treatment, consent, § 13.11
Nursing homes, patients bill of rights, §§ 12.6, 12.7

ASSIGNMENTS
Medicare,
    Part A, fiscal intermediaries, § 10.81
    Part B, payments, claims, § 10.85 et seq.

ASSOCIATIONS AND SOCIETIES
American Association of Retired Persons, generally, this index
Charities, fraudulent solicitation, § 7.111
Consumer credit, truth in lending, § 5.31
Disability discrimination, application of law, § 4.62
National Academy of Elder Law Attorneys, generally, this index
National Association of Insurance Commissioners, generally, this index

ATTORNEY GENERAL ENFORCEMENT
Age discrimination, § 3.19
Consumer fraud, §§ 7.12, 7.122
Disability discrimination §§ 4.18, 4.48, 4.65

ATTORNEY IN FACT
Power of Attorney, generally, this index

ATTORNEY FEES
Age discrimination, enforcement, awards,
    Consumer credit, § 5.23
    Housing, § 4.50
    Labor and employment, § 3.70
Agreement, § 2.32
Breach of warranty, awards, § 6.26
Consumer credit, awards,
    Age discrimination, § 5.23
    Debt collection practices, generally, post
    Real estate transactions, § 5.61
    Truth in lending, § 5.38
Consumer protection,
    Breach of warranty, awards, § 6.26
    Franchises, awards, § 7.58
    Unfair and deceptive trade practices, generally, post
Custody of children, awards, § 25.13
Debt collection practices,
    Application of law, § 5.71
    Awards, § 5.80
Disability discrimination, awards, §§ 4.20, 4.65
Discrimination, §§ 4.20, 4.65
    Age discrimination, generally, ante
    Disability discrimination, §§ 4.20, 4.65
Federal aid for legal services, § 1.35
Franchises, consumer fraud, awards, § 7.58
Housing discrimination, awards, § 4.50
Labor and employment, age discrimination, awards, § 3.70
Medicare, awards, § 10.121
Office practice, § 2.31 et seq.
Real estate transactions, awards, § 5.61
Retainer agreement, § 2.32
Social Security Disability, this index
Social Security Retirement Benefits, this index
Truth in lending, awards, § 5.38

INDEX

INDEX

CHILDREN AND MINORS—Continued
Medicaid, generally, this index
Railroad retirement, § 20.32
    Spouses benefits, natural parent of employee's child, § 20.36
    Survivors benefits, § 20.37
Social security disability,
    Dependents benefits, § 15.20
    Disabled children, § 16.31
Social security retirement benefits,
    Dependents benefits, § 15.20
    Spouses benefits, deductions, child not in care, § 15.56
Supplemental security income, foster care payments, income limits, § 17.30
Support, § 25.64
Veterans,
    Disability compensation, dependents, § 21.14
    Survivors payments, § 21.15
Visitation of Children, generally, this index

CHIROPRACTORS
Consumer fraud, § 7.11

CHURCH RECORDS
Social security, filing for benefits, § 15.86

CIRCUMSTANTIAL EVIDENCE
Labor and employment, age discrimination, § 3.57

CITIZENS AND CITIZENSHIP
Food stamps, eligibility, § 18.7
Medicaid, eligibility, § 11.16
Medicare, voluntary payers, § 10.17
National origin,
    Consumer credit, discrimination, § 5.11
    Life expectancy, § 1.12
Supplemental security income, eligibility, § 17.13
    Deemed income, sponsors, § 17.33

CIVIL RIGHTS
Commitment proceedings, § 9.6
Discrimination, generally, this index
Guardianship, §§ 9.1, 9.20, 9.25
Medical treatment, right to refuse, living wills, § 8.31
Nursing homes, bill of rights, §§ 12.6, 12.7

CIVIL SERVICE RETIREMENT SYSTEM
Federal Employees Retirement, this index

CLASS ACTIONS
Age discrimination, labor and employment, § 3.47
Breach of warranty, federal law, § 6.26
Consumer credit, § 5.23
    Debt collection practices, § 5.79
Consumer protection, § 6.68
    Breach of warranty, federal law, § 6.26
    Truth in lending, § 5.38
    Unfair and deceptive trade practices, § 6.68
Debt collection practices, § 5.79
Labor and employment, age discrimination, § 3.47
Truth in lending, § 5.38
Unfair and deceptive trade practices, § 6.68

INDEX

INDEX

557

INDEX

INDEX

561

INDEX

INDEX

INDEX

DIVORCE
Alternatives, § 25.68
Child support, § 25.64
Financial effects,
    Both spouses, § 25.66
    Homemakers, § 25.67
Health insurance, § 25.67
Medicare, § 10.2
Pension benefits. Retirement and pensions, generally, post
Property division, § 25.62
Psychological effects, § 25.65
Railroad retirement, eligibility, § 20.36
Retirement and pensions,
    Qualified domestic relations order, § 23.15
    Retirement, §§ 23.15, 25.62
    Survivors, § 23.19
Social security retirement benefits, § 15.19
    Survivors, § 15.35 et seq.
Spousal support, § 25.63

DME
Durable medical equipment. Equipment and Machinery, generally, this index

DNR ORDERS
Do not resuscitate orders, § 13.25

DOCTORS
Physicians and Surgeons, generally, this index

DOCUMENTS
Comprehensive Planning, this index

DOMICILE AND RESIDENCE
Farmers home administration, loans and grants, repairs and improvements, § 22.21
Food stamps, eligibility, § 18.7
Medicaid, eligibility, § 11.16
Supplemental security income, eligibility, § 17.13

DONATIONS
Gifts, generally, this index

DOOR-TO-DOOR SALES
Consumer credit, cooling off period, § 5.51
Consumer fraud, home repair and improvement, §§ 7.31, 7.32
Warranty claims, federal law, § 6.25

DPA
Durable powers of attorney. Power of Attorney, this index

DRG
Diagnostic Research Groups, generally, this index

DRIVERS LICENSES
Anatomical gifts, § 14.13
Guardian and ward, risk management, § 9.34

DRUG ABUSE
Discrimination, §§ 4.12, 4.16
Guardian and Ward, generally, this index
Supplemental security income, § 17.18
Veterans, §§ 21.12, 21.16

DRUGS AND MEDICINE
Consumer fraud, §§ 7.11, 7.13

INDEX

INDEX

EMPLOYMENT
Labor and Employment, generally, this index

EMPLOYMENT AGENCIES
Age discrimination, § 3.41
Disability discrimination, § 4.62

END-STAGE RENAL (KIDNEY) DISEASE
Medicare, Part A, § 10.15
    Applications, § 10.19

ENERGY ASSISTANCE
    Generally, § 22.25
Income taxes, credits, § 24.12
Low income persons, homes, utilities expenses and weatherization, § 22.26

ENVIRONMENTAL PROTECTION
Guardian and ward, risk management, § 9.34

EOMB
Explanation of Medicare Benefits, generally, this index

EPILEPSY
Housing assistance, eligibility, § 19.12

EQUAL CREDIT OPPORTUNITY ACT
    Generally, § 5.11 et seq.
Coverage, § 5.11
Defenses, § 5.20
Disclosures, credit information, § 5.15
Enforcement, § 5.21 et seq.
    Administrative law and procedure, § 5.21
    Limitation of actions, § 5.24
    Private right of action, § 5.22
    Remedies, § 5.23
Factors in extending credit, § 5.12
Notice of adverse actions, § 5.14
Records, retention, § 5.16
Requirements, § 5.13
State statutes, § 5.25
Violations, § 5.17 et seq.
    Disparate impact, § 5.19
    Disparate treatment, § 5.18

EQUAL EMPLOYMENT OPPORTUNITY COMMISSION
Filing charge, limitation of actions, § 3.52 et seq.
Rehabilitation Act, enforcement, § 4.17

EQUIPMENT AND MACHINERY
Medical equipment,
    Medicare, Part B, § 10.62 et seq.
      Coinsurance and deductibles, § 10.62
      Coverage, §§ 10.63, 10.64
    Supplemental security income, assets, exemptions, § 17.24
    Veterans benefits, §§ 21.51, 21.52

EQUITY, HOME
Home Equity Conversion, generally, this index

ERISA
Employee Retirement Income Security Act of 1974, § 23.2

ERRORS AND MISTAKES
Debt collection, §§ 5.33, 5.35, 5.77

INDEX

INDEX

INDEX

FTC
Federal Trade Commission, generally, this index

FUNERAL DIRECTORS AND EMBALMERS
Anatomical gifts, services, § 14.33
Consumer fraud, §§ 7.81, 7.82
Social security, death benefits, § 15.31

FURNACES
Warranties, generally, this index

FURNITURE
Attorneys, offices, sensitivity to special needs, § 2.1
Supplemental security income, assets, exemptions, § 17.24

GAMBLING
Supplemental security income, income limits, § 17.28

GENDER DISCRIMINATION
Consumer credit, § 5.12
Social attitudes, § 1.2

GERONTOLOGY
Definitions, § 1.4

GIFTS
Anatomical Gifts, generally, this index
Expenditures, § 1.23
Food stamps, income limits, § 18.16
Housing, low income qualifications, § 19.14
Income taxes, nontaxable income, § 24.3
Power of attorney, § 8.17
Supplemental security income, assets, §§ 17.28, 17.29
Transfers, § 17.25

GLASSES
Eyeglasses, generally, this index

GRANDPARENTS
Adoption of Children, this index
Custody of Children, this index
Relationships with grandchildren, § 25.33
Rights, § 25.1 et seq.
Visitation of Children, this index

GUARANTY
Consumer credit, truth in lending, application of law, § 5.31
Nursing homes, financial responsibility, § 12.11
Pension benefit guarantee corporation, Employee Retirement Income Security Act of 1974, § 23.2
Warranties, generally, this index

GUARDIAN AND WARD
Generally, § 9.1 et seq.
Abuse, discovery and prevention, § 9.23
Accounts and accounting, §§ 9.5, 9.10
Commingling, § 9.30
Actions and proceedings, role of attorney, § 9.8 et seq.
Consideration of alternatives, § 9.8
Defending proceedings, powers and duties, § 9.13 et seq.
Identifying client, § 9.7
Preparing proceedings, §§ 9.8 et seq., 9.16, 9.17
Types of proceedings, requirements and effect, § 9.9

573

INDEX

INDEX

583

MENTAL DISABILITIES—Continued
Limited capacity, role of attorneys, § 2.3
Living Wills, generally, this index
Medicaid, applications, § 11.61
Medical care and treatment, decision-making, § 13.15 et seq.
    Advance directives, § 13.16
    Nursing homes, patients bill of rights, §§ 12.6, 12.7
    Procedural protections, § 13.22
    Standards, § 13.19 et seq.
        Best interest doctrine, § 13.20
        Hybrid standards, § 1er, § 10.95
        Substituted judgment doctrine, § 13.19
    Surrogates, § 13.17
Medicare, coverage,
    Outpatient mental health services, Part B, § 10.63
    Psychiatric hospitalization, Part A, § 10.35
Nursing homes,
    Patients bill of rights, §§ 12.6, 12.7
    Preadmission screening and annual resident review, § 12.22 et seq.
Planning, § 26.14
    Durable power of attorney, generally. Power of Attorney, this index
    Living Wills, generally, this index
Social Security Disability, generally, this index
Social security retirement benefits,
    Applications, § 15.82
    Representative payees, § 15.94
Veterans Benefits, generally, this index

MENTAL PAIN AND SUFFERING
Consumer credit, wrongful denial, § 5.23
Disability discrimination, intentional, § 4.20
Unfair and deceptive trade practices, state law, § 6.61

MERCY KILLINGS
Living Wills, generally, this index

MFS
Medicare Fee Schedule, generally, this index

MIGRATION
Domicile and residence, § 1.16

MILITARY FORCES
Veterans, generally, this index

MINIMUM MONTHLY MAINTENANCE NEEDS ALLOWANCE (42 USCA § 1396R)
Medicaid, spouses income available to institutionalized spouse, §§ 11.33, 11.34

MINORS
Children and Minors, generally, this index

MISREPRESENTATION
Fraud, generally, this index

MMMNA
Minimum Monthly Maintenance Needs Allowance (42 USCA § 1396r), generally, this index

MOBILE HOMES
Generally, § 22.15

MORTGAGES
Consumer credit, truth in lending, § 5.31 et seq.

INDEX

INDEX

PASARR
Nursing homes, preadmission screening and annual resident review, § 12.22 et seq.

PASSPORTS
Social security, filing for benefits, § 15.86

PAUPERS
Indigent Persons, generally, this index

PBGC
Pension benefit guarantee corporation, Employee Retirement Income Security Act of 1974, § 23.2

PEER REVIEW ORGANIZATIONS
Medicare, coverage, determination of medical necessity, § 10.38
    Authority, § 10.81
    Denial of claims, appeal and review, § 10.106
    Discharge, role of attorney, § 10.39

PENALTIES
Fines and Penalties, generally, this index

PENSION BENEFIT GUARANTEE CORPORATION
Employee Retirement Income Security Act of 1974, § 23.2

PENSIONS
Retirement and Pensions, generally, this index

PERMITS
Licenses and Permits, generally, this index

PERSONAL CARE SERVICES
    Generally, § 12.51
Area agencies on aging, § 1.34
Medicaid, §§ 11.85, 12.45

PERSONAL INJURIES
Damages, this index
Social Security Disability, generally, this index
Veterans Benefits, this index

PERSONAL REPRESENTATIVES
Executors and Administrators, generally, this index

PETS
Housing, federally assisted, § 4.31 et seq.

PHARMACISTS
Drugs and medicine, consumer fraud, §§ 7.11, 7.13

PHYSICAL EXAMINATIONS
Medicare,
    Exclusions from coverage, part A and part B, § 10.73
    Supplemental insurance, evaluating policies, § 10.63
Social security disability, § 16.27

PHYSICIANS AND SURGEONS
    See, also, Medical Care and Treatment, generally, this index
Anatomical gifts, eligible donees, § 14.31
Consumer fraud, § 7.11 et seq.
Guardian and ward, appointment, evidence, § 9.4
Medicare, this index
Nursing homes, patients bill of rights, §§ 12.6, 12.7
Social security disability, examination, § 16.27

INDEX

PNEUMOCOCCAL VACCINE
Coinsurance and deductibles, Medicare Part B, § 10.62

POOR PERSONS
Indigent Persons, generally, this index

POPULATION
Age divisions, § 1.3
Percentages, §§ 1.13, 1.14

POSTAL SERVICE
Disability discrimination, § 4.12 et seq.

POVERTY
Indigent Persons, generally, this index

POWER OF ATTORNEY
Conservators, alternatives, §§ 8.12, 9.2
Counseling client, §§ 8.1, 8.11
Durable powers of attorney, § 8.11 et seq.
   Conservators, alternatives, § 9.2
   Financial, generally, post
   Medical care and treatment, generally, post
   Statutes, § 13.33 et seq.
      Health care decisions, § 13.35
Financial, durable powers of attorney, § 8.12 et seq.
   Agent, § 8.13
   Custody of document, § 8.21
   Effective date, § 8.16
   Powers granted, §§ 8.14, 8.15
   Purposes, § 8.22
   Sample document, § 8.22
   Springing, § 8.16
Guardian and ward, alternatives, §§ 8.12, 9.2, 13.17
Medical care and treatment, durable powers of attorney, §§ 8.18, 13.16 et seq.
   Agent, §§ 8.19, 13.17
   Custody of document, § 8.21
   Effective date, § 8.21
   Powers granted, § 8.20
   Purpose, § 8.18
   Sample document, § 8.22
   Statutes, § 13.35

PPS
Prospective Payment System, generally, this index

PRACTICE
Attorneys, generally, this index

PREADMISSION SCREENING AND ANNUAL RESIDENT REVIEW
Nursing homes, § 12.22 et seq.

PREEMPTION
Americans with Disabilities Act, § 4.66
Employee Retirement Income Security Act of 1974, § 23.2
Equal Credit Opportunity Act, § 5.25
Federal Trade Commission Act, § 6.16
Magnuson-Moss Warranty Act, § 6.30
Reverse mortgages, § 22.48
Unfair and deceptive trade practices, § 6.48

PRESUMPTIONS
Consumer credit, discrimination, § 5.18

596

REAL ESTATE—Continued
Mortgages, generally, this index
Revocable living trusts, § 8.43
Vendor and Purchaser, generally, this index

REAL ESTATE SETTLEMENT PROCEDURES ACT
Consumer credit, §§ 5.61, 5.62

REASONABLE ACCOMMODATIONS
Disability discrimination, §§ 4.12, 4.43, 4.63

RECOUPMENT
Attorney Fees, generally, this index
Medicare, overpayments, §§ 10.93, 10.94
Social Security Retirement Benefits, this index

REHABILITATION ACT OF 1973
Disability Discrimination, this index

REINSTATEMENT
Labor and employment, age discrimination, § 3.69

RELATIVE VALUE UNITS
Medicare, Part B, physicians and surgeons, payments, § 10.86
    Omnibus Budget Reconciliation Act, § 10.90

RELATIVES
Family, generally, this index

RELIGIOUS ORGANIZATIONS
Fraudulent solicitation, § 7.111

REMAINDER INTEREST SALES
Generally, § 22.38 et seq.

RENTAL HOUSING
Landlord and Tenant, generally, this index

RENTS
Food stamps, income limits, § 18.15
Supplemental security income, income limits, § 17.29

REPAIRS AND MAINTENANCE
Homesteads, this index

REPORTS
Nursing homes, abusive practices, S

RESCISSION
Consumer credit,
    Door-to-door sales, § 5.51
    Home equity liens, truth in lending, § 5.39
Unfair and deceptive trade practices, § 6.66

RESEARCH
Gerontology, § 1.4

RESIDENCE
Domicile and Residence, generally, this index

RESOURCES
Local, § 27.11
National, § 27.13, Appendix B
State, § 27.12, Appendix A

INDEX

RESPIRATORS
Medicaid, § 11.93

RESPITE SERVICES
Generally, §§ 12.54, 27.6
Area agencies on aging, § 1.34
Medicaid, § 11.86

RESTITUTION
Unfair and deceptive trade practices, §§ 6.55, 6.59

RESTRAINTS
Nursing homes, patients bill of rights, §§ 12.6, 12.7

RETAINER AGREEMENTS
Generally, § 2.1

RETALIATION
Labor and employment, age discrimination, § 3.44

RETIREMENT AND PENSIONS
Generally, § 23.1
Age discrimination, §§ 3.59 et seq., 22.5
    Consumer credit, § 5.12
    Early retirement, § 3.31 et seq.
Annual report, § 23.11
Assignment, §§ 23.14, 23.15
Benefits,
    Accrual, § 23.6
    Claim procedure, § 23.13
Breaks in service, § 23.4
Changes in plan, vested rights, §§ 23.7, 23.8
Civil service retirement system, generally. Federal Employees Retirement, this index
Consumer credit, age discrimination, § 5.12
Discrimination. Age discrimination, generally, ante
Divorce, this index
Early retirement, age discrimination, § 3.31 et seq.
Federal Employees Retirement, generally, this index
Forced retirement, age discrimination, § 3.31 et seq.
Forfeitures, § 23.8
Information, § 23.9 et seq.
Interrupted employment, § 23.4
Mandatory retirement, § 3.31 et seq.
Participation, § 23.3
Plan description, § 23.10
Qualified domestic relations order, § 23.15
Railroad Retirement, generally, this index
Social Security Retirement Benefits, generally, this index
Statement of benefit rights, § 23.12
Survivors, § 23.16
    Divorced spouses, § 23.19
    Time of death, § 23.17
    Waiver, § 23.18
Termination of plan, § 23.20
Vested rights, § 23.7
Veterans Benefits, this index

RETIREMENT COMMUNITIES
Consumer fraud, land sales, § 7.61

REVERSE MORTGAGES
Home Equity Conversions, this index

INDEX

INDEX

INDEX

INDEX

INDEX

INDEX

INDEX

INDEX

†